The Trumpet Kings

The Trumpet Kings

The Players Who Shaped the Sound of Jazz Trumpet

by Scott Yanow

 Backbeat Books

San Francisco

Published by Backbeat Books
600 Harrison Street, San Francisco, CA 94107
An imprint of the Music Player Network
United Entertainment Media

Distributed to the book trade in the U.S and Canada by
Publishers Group West, 1700 Fourth Street, Berkeley, CA 94710

Distributed to the music trade in the U.S. and Canada by
Hal Leonard Publishing P.O. Box 13819, Milwaukee, WI 53213

Cover Composition by Rich Leeds
Text Design and Composition by Leigh McLellan
Front Cover Photo of Louis Armstrong: © Bettmann/CORBIS

Library of Congress Cataloging-in-Publication Data

Yanow, Scott
    The trumpet kings: the players who shaped the sound of jazz
trumpet / by Scott Yanow
        p. cm.
    Includes bibliographical reference (p.) and index
    ISBN 0-87930-640-8
    1. Trumpet players-Biography. 2. Jazz musicians-Biography.
I. Title
ML399.Y36 2001
788.9'2165'0922-dc21
[B]   2001025143

Printed in the United States of America

01 02 03 04 05   5 4 3 2 1

Contents

Introduction

nlike my other books (which include three in Backbeat Books' Third Ear series: *Swing,
Bebop,* and *Afro-Cuban Jazz*), *The Trumpet Kings* was a decade in the making. Well, maybe
that is not quite accurate, although I did think of the idea a decade ago! Back in 1990 (long
before I became involved with *The All Music Guide To Jazz*), I had planned to have *The Who's
Who of the Jazz Trumpet* as my first book. I envisioned this project as a different type of reference work. Many jazz reference books tend to be a bit dry, offering biographies that tell
who played with whom, when and where, but leaving out the human aspect of the individual stories and the "plot" behind the musicians' lives. I ambitiously saw my work as a series
of short stories, telling of the many colorful musicians who became important trumpeters,
with the emphasis on the purpose of their lives and how well they were able to survive the
jazz life.

The trumpet has been my favorite instrument ever since seeing the 1950s movie *The Five
Pennies,* in which Danny Kaye rather colorfully played the role of Red Nichols, a top early jazz
cornetist. Never mind that the Hollywood screenplay is mostly fiction (Nichols did not really
sing, nor did he record "Battle Hymn of the Republic" in the 1920s); this is a hugely entertaining film. To see Nichols/Kaye come out of the audience at a nightclub to "battle" with Louis
Armstrong on "Battle Hymn" is one of the great jazz moments on film.

After seeing that movie at age ten, I knew that I had to play trumpet. But years later, when
I finally had an opportunity to blow an instrument (coincidentally a cornet), I discovered that
I could hit only two notes. One sounded God-awful and the other was much worse! I found
the saxophone to be much easier, at least to get a variety of sounds out of, so my respect for
trumpeters rose. How could they play so many notes and develop so many individual styles
on such an impossible instrument?

In 1990 I started writing *The Who's Who of the Jazz Trumpet,* sending out questionnaires
to major trumpeters listed in the union books of Los Angeles and New York and putting together a few preliminary entries. However, the project did not get very far at that point, since
I had neither a publisher nor the large amount of time I knew it would take to do it properly.

Writing for eight different jazz magazines (none of which paid even minimum wage) and having a day job made writing a large jazz book an impossibility at that time.

Years passed. I became involved in *The All Music Guide to Jazz* and then in 1999 started writing a series of jazz books for Miller Freeman. Before I even began *Swing* (the first in the series), I had a contract to write the trumpet book. I immediately sent out more questionnaires to today's trumpeters but once again fell short on time due to the work needed to write the three books *Swing*, *Bebop*, and *Afro-Cuban Jazz* in a 13-month period. Finally, ten years after the original false start, it was the trumpet book's turn. Although I had always called it *The Who's Who of the Jazz Trumpet*, Matt Kelsey of Miller Freeman thought that might sound a bit clinical, and he suggested *The Trumpet Kings*. Since the great early New Orleans trumpeters were considered "kings" (including Buddy Bolden, Freddie Keppard, Joe "King" Oliver, and Louis Armstrong) and the Trumpet Kings name was used for a series of all-star dates by the Pablo label in the 1970s (featuring Dizzy Gillespie, Roy Eldridge, Harry "Sweets" Edison, Clark Terry, and Jon Faddis), Matt's suggestion was perfect.

Since the beginnings of jazz, the trumpet (and its predecessor the cornet) has often been the lead instrument, with the top players generally being leaders. Trumpeters have had a significant role in virtually every style of jazz, and the jazz trumpet is in a golden age these days, with several dozen major players currently active. There is no shortage of tragedies and triumphs in the lives of the most significant trumpeters (so many died young!), and through the stories of their individual lives, readers can experience virtually the entire history of jazz. Although I have done my best to make each of the 479 entries into short stories, the lack of information in some cases means that a few of the entries are of the "who played with whom" variety. But hopefully, by reading the entries it will be obvious why all of these trumpeters are significant and what the highlights were of their musical careers, along with the "plots" of their lives.

Many individuals have helped this project, in big and small ways, particularly in gaining the addresses of individual trumpeters for the questionnaires. Among the more notable people who deserve heartfelt thanks are (in alphabetical order) publicist-writer Lynda Bramble, pianist Al Cresswell, Arbors Records' Matthew Domber, jazz fan Vanessa Ellis, publicist-manager Tina Evans, pianist Allan Farnham, singer Banu Gibson, jazz and classical journalist Richard Ginell, jazz journalist Linda Gruno, publicist Terri Hinte, the late manager Helen Keane, the late great singer Susannah McCorkle, concert producer Dan McKenna, pianist Marian McPartland, publicist Marty Morgan, trombonist Jon Nelson, singer Joannie Pallatto, singer Suzanne Pittson, pianist Trish Ramstein, the late trumpeter-arranger Shorty Rogers, photographer-writer Susan Rosmarin, publicist Merrilee Trost, singer Brooke Vigoda, and writer-photographer Valerie Wilmer. Drummer Hal Smith was especially helpful in making sure that I included every significant modern-day trad trumpeter and cornetist.

And of course, without Matt Kelsey, Dorothy Cox, and the great staff at Backbeat Books, this project would not have been possible. I also wish to thank my wife, Kathy, and my daughter, Melody, for their love and support.

The History of the Jazz Trumpet

n the beginning there was Buddy Bolden, the first superstar of jazz, a cornetist who in 1895 formed his earliest band. Although the history of jazz before the first recordings in 1917 is quite cloudy, Bolden's fame and the testimony of other musicians demonstrate that even if Bolden was not the actual founder of jazz, he was its first real popularizer.

Prior to the mid-1920s, many of the brass players actually played cornet rather than trumpet. The two instruments are quite similar, having three valves, cylindrical tubing, a mouthpiece, and a bell from which the sound comes out. The cornet (which is slightly shorter) allegedly has a mellower tone, while the trumpet cuts through ensembles a bit more easily, although I have never been able to hear any real difference in their sounds! After the mid-1920s, most jazz cornetists (including Louis Armstrong) switched to trumpet, even though there would always be some prominent cornetists in jazz, including Bix Beiderbecke, Rex Stewart, Ruby Braff, Nat Adderley, and Don Cherry (who played the pocket cornet), to name five. The flugelhorn, which did not come to prominence in jazz until the 1950s, with Shorty Rogers, Miles Davis, and Clark Terry, has a distinctly different sound from the trumpet (being much softer) and is a slightly larger instrument. Since the 1960s, most trumpeters (particularly those playing in big bands) double on flugelhorn part of the time. Other related instruments, such as the bass trumpet (which is larger than the flugelhorn and sounds more like a trombone) and the slide trumpet, never really caught on.

The standard frontline of New Orleans jazz bands during the early part of the century was typically cornet, trombone, and clarinet. The cornetist's role was to state the melody and to play subtle variations, often adding a bluish element to the music. Buddy Bolden was the first cornet (or trumpet) "king." After his mental deterioration resulted in his permanent retirement in 1906, Bolden was succeeded by Freddie Keppard, who was considered the top cornetist in New Orleans until he moved up North in 1914. Keppard and his contemporaries had a direct link with military brass bands in their staccato phrases and simple but effective repetitions. Joe "King" Oliver was his successor. And when Oliver relocated to Chicago in 1918, Louis Armstrong was given the unofficial crown of "trumpet king." Other contenders included Manuel Perez, Chris Kelly, and Buddy Petit.

When the Original Dixieland Jazz Band made its first recordings in 1917, Nick LaRocca became the first jazz cornetist to record. LaRocca stuck almost exclusively to melody statements, and the ODJB did feature any real solos. Although jazz was ensemble-oriented on records until at least 1923, there were a few early cornet/trumpet solos by Phil Napoleon and Paul Mares (with the New Orleans Rhythm Kings). Johnny Dunn emerged as one of the first trumpet stars on record, due to his use of mutes to achieve wa-wa effects, devices also featured by Louis Panico with Isham Jones' orchestra. King Oliver's Creole Jazz Band in 1923 was the ultimate in classic New Orleans jazz, with both Oliver and Louis Armstrong heard on cornets, mostly playing ensembles other than brief harmonized breaks and a few rare choruses (including Armstrong on "Chimes Blues" and Oliver's classic three-chorus statement on "Dippermouth Blues").

The year 1924 was the breakthrough year for the jazz trumpet/cornet. Louis Armstrong joined Fletcher Henderson's orchestra and showed New York musicians how to swing, use silence to dramatic effect, and build up individual solos. A comparison of Henderson's recordings from 1923 and 1925 shows the huge effect that Satch had, both on his fellow trumpeters/cornetists and on jazz in general. And 1924 was also when Bix Beiderbecke debuted on records with the Wolverines, introducing an important new voice and founding a "cool" school that served as a contrast to Armstrong's "hot."

With the remarkable string of Hot Five and Hot Seven recordings by Armstrong during 1925–28, jazz trumpeters emerged as soloists rather than just as lead voices in ensembles. In fact, by 1929 there were three overlapping types of trumpeters in jazz: the hot, explosive playing of Armstrong, Jabbo Smith, and Red Allen, the more lyrical cooler stylists such as Beiderbecke, Joe Smith, Red Nichols, and Arthur Whetsol, and the specialists with mutes, best typified by Bubber Miley and his successor, Cootie Williams.

Early big bands usually had two or, later, three trumpeters; not including trumpeters at all would have been unthinkable! By the beginning of the swing era, the trumpet sections were divided in most orchestras into the lead (high-note) player, a section trumpeter, and a soloist, although some bands (particularly Duke Ellington's) might have each of the trumpeters solo at one time or another.

By the late 1920s, Louis Armstrong was the main influence on most jazz trumpet soloists, and he cast a wide shadow on jazz up until the mid-1940s. Such diverse swing-era trumpet soloists as Roy Eldridge, Bunny Berigan, Harry James, Muggsy Spanier, Buck Clayton, Hot Lips Page, and Charlie Shavers considered Satch to be their main influence. The swing era was also notable for being the period when the range of the trumpet really began to expand beyond that of Armstrong's, with such high-note specialists as Tommy Stevenson, Snooky Young, and Erskine Hawkins eventually being topped by Cat Anderson, Ernie Royal, Al Killian, and (in the late 1940s) Maynard Ferguson.

Roy Eldridge was the pacesetter among modern trumpeters in the early 1940s. By 1945, with the rise of the bebop era, Eldridge had been supplanted by Dizzy Gillespie (arguably the most complex of all trumpeters), Howard McGhee, and Fats Navarro. Just as Beiderbecke had offered a cooler alternative to Armstrong in the 1920s, Miles Davis' mellower (but no less modern) style was a contrast to that of his idol, Gillespie. Davis' cooler approach was an inspiration for such 1950s West Coast-style players as Shorty Rogers, Chet Baker, and Don Fagerquist.

The comeback of New Orleans jazz in the mid-1940s resulted in the resurrection of Bunk Johnson (who in some ways was a throwback to the days of Freddie Keppard) and a surge of interest in freewheeling Dixieland, including the styles featured by Eddie Condon's groups (which included such colorful voices as Wild Bill Davison, Bobby Hackett, and Max Kaminsky) and the San Francisco jazz movement of Lu Watters and Bob Scobey. Although often overlooked by the general jazz press, trad jazz has been artistically healthy much of the time since then, with Ruby Braff emerging as a major individualist in the 1950s and world-class players performing in the older styles ever since.

While Dizzy Gillespie was one of the key founders of bebop, Miles Davis and Fats Navarro were actually more direct influences on younger trumpeters after 1950. Navarro's bright sound and logical ideas became the basis for Clifford Brown's highly appealing style of the mid-1950s, and Brownie's playing was the inspiration for such important musicians as Lee Morgan, Freddie Hubbard, and Woody Shaw (among many others) in the 1960s and '70s. With the adoption of the LP in the early 1950s, trumpet solos became much longer (78s had limited playing time for a song to around three minutes) and jazz recordings in general became much more frequent. Lee Morgan, Kenny Dorham, Donald Byrd, and Blue Mitchell were only four of the trumpeters who were well featured on relatively lengthy hard bop records, while Booker Little was one of the few trumpeters from this period who seemed to be looking forward beyond bop.

Bebop dominated the mainstream of jazz during 1945–60 (cool jazz and hard bop were direct relatives of bop), but the arrival of the Ornette Coleman Quartet in New York in 1959 gave trumpeters a new alternative: avant-garde jazz. Rather than strictly following chord changes and emulating aspects of the styles of Dizzy, Fats/Brownie, or Miles, Don Cherry and such slightly later players as Bobby Bradford, Bill Dixon, Lester Bowie, and Leo Smith engaged in sonic explorations, stretching the potential of the trumpet and creating new types of sounds. But because of the intensity of such emotional saxophonists as John Coltrane, Archie Shepp, Pharoah Sanders, and Albert Ayler, trumpeters often took a backseat in the free jazz movement, offering a lyrical and more thoughtful approach that contrasted with the free-form tenors.

In the late 1960s Woody Shaw, Charles Tolliver, and Freddie Hubbard were symbolic of the young, adventurous trumpeters who could play both "outside" (very free) and "inside" (chordal-based bebop). However, the rise of fusion (a mixture of jazz improvisation with the sound and rhythms of rock) pushed the trumpet very much into the background. Ironically, though Miles Davis had helped to launch fusion, his experiments with electrifying his horn were not as influential as the playing of his sidemen (Eddie Henderson and, to a lesser extent, Randy Brecker were among the few trumpeters who tried to emulate Davis' fusion playing at the time). In fact, the 1970s can be thought of as a bit of a drought for the jazz trumpet. Freddie Hubbard (during the first part of the decade) and Woody Shaw did some of their finest work, but very few major new trumpeters emerged during that decade.

One of the few to arrive on the scene was cornetist Warren Vache, who, along with tenor saxophonist Scott Hamilton in the mid-1970s, showed that there was nothing wrong with younger players' choosing to play creatively in older styles. But while Vache explored mainstream swing, it was Wynton Marsalis (who joined Art Blakey's Jazz Messengers in 1980, when he was 19) who launched the "Young Lions" movement. Marsalis performed modern hard bop and the music of the mid-'60s Miles Davis Quintet. His articulate nature, obvious virtuosity, and insistence on swinging in acoustic jazz formats inspired a younger generation to start playing straightahead jazz on the trumpet. Following in his footsteps were such talents as Terence Blanchard, Wallace Roney, Roy Hargrove, and Nicholas Payton. By the late 1980s, the trumpet was having a major renaissance.

As with jazz itself, currently there is not one dominant force or direction among trumpeters; one can imagine any of a dozen trumpeters winning the Downbeat polls. The deaths of Dizzy Gillespie, Miles Davis, and Lee Morgan, along with the retirement of Freddie Hubbard, left unfillable holes. Despite that, the 21st century promises to be a golden age for the jazz trumpet. Just consider the talents of Marsalis, Blanchard, Hargrove, Payton, Arturo Sandoval, Claudio Roditi, Tom Harrell, Jon Faddis, Byron Stripling, Ingrid Jensen, Dave Douglas, Kenny Wheeler, Randy Sandke, Eddie Henderson, and Randy Brecker, to name just a few!

And at this point in time, it seems as if each month brings to light the work of another potentially great young trumpeter who will have to be included in any future edition of *The Trumpet Kings.*

Introduction to the Biographies

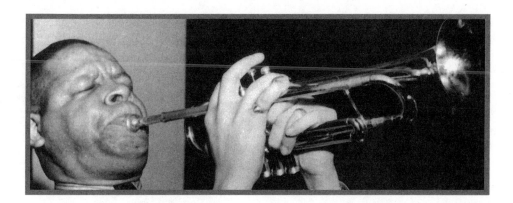

The goal of the following biographies is to give readers a good idea of the importance of each trumpeter and an idea of what his or her life was/is like. Around 100 trumpeters answered questionnaires, and all of the uncredited quotes are taken from their responses, some of which were from the early 1990s while others are much more recent. Many of the responses did not generate usable quotes but helped to confirm birth dates and places. The lists of recommended CDs and LPs are not meant to be complete but to serve as a guide to some of the artists' more valuable recordings.

Why did I decide to have 479 biographies in this book? Because that is how many I ended up with! All of these trumpeters had significant solo careers; most have been highly regarded soloists with a few being primarily important lead players. Not every trumpeter who ever recorded (or led a record date) is in this book, for otherwise the number would have been closer to 1,000. Among the ones who came close to making the cut but were reluctantly left out (often due to lack of information) are Tony Almerico, Edgar "Puddinghead" Battle (love that name!), Lyn Biviano, Arthur Briggs, Wendell Brunious, Pokey Carriere (who played with Jack Teagarden in the film *Birth of the Blues*), Norma Carson, Larry Cramer (closely associated with Jane Bunnett), Earl Cross, Johnny DeDroit, Don Ferrara, Max Goldberg, Dave Grover (who played with Lionel Hampton), Willie Hightower, Art Hoyle, Bobby Johnson, Chuck Mackey, Leo McConville, Clyde McCoy (famous for his cornball but influential hit recording of "Sugar Blues"), Hazy Osterwald, Randy Reinhardt, Leo "The Whistler" Shepherd, Alan Shorter and Art Troncozo. My apologies to any trumpeter who belonged in the book but is not included; if the book had 600 entries you would be here!

Profiles of the Trumpet Kings

AL AARONS

. . . .

b. Mar. 23, 1932, Pittsburgh, PA

Each city has its talented local trumpeters, players who are somewhat taken for granted but, when called upon, always give their best and usually excel. Albert Aarons fills that niche in Los Angeles.

A fine bop-based trumpeter with a mellow sound, Aarons remembers: "I started playing the trumpet at the age of eight because of the interest and generosity of an uncle who played in an American Legion band. My earliest and most important influence was my high school band and orchestra director, who was also my private teacher, Carl McVickers, whom I still think of often. My earliest heroes began with Harry James, followed by Dizzy Gillespie, Miles Davis, Fats Navarro, and, later, Clifford Brown, Freddie Hubbard, and Kenny Dorham. From the age of eight or nine, I never had a desire to do anything except play a musical instrument. The trumpet was decided upon by a coin flip!"

Aarons played locally in Pittsburgh, worked with Yusef Lateef (1956–57) and Barry Harris in Detroit, moved to New York, and was with Count Basie's orchestra during 1961–69, occasionally getting solos. In 1969, at the urging of producer Quincy Jones, he left Basie to settle in Los Angeles, where he was a part of a television show called *The Music Scene*. Aarons became a busy studio musician, often working with Jones and Henry Mancini, appearing on freelance recordings (including with Sarah Vaughan and Ella Fitzgerald), and playing at local clubs. He has since gigged with saxophonist Buddy Collette, the Juggernaut, and the Gerald Wilson Orchestra and has also been involved with the Los Angeles Jazz Society, an organization founded by his late wife, Terri Merrill-Aarons. Al Aarons modestly sums up his life: "I don't know if I have made any noteworthy contributions other than to do my best at all times, to be as good a musician as I could be, and to be serious about the legacy of jazz and the creative process."

Recommended CDs: *Al Aarons and the L.A. Jazz Caravan* (L.A. Jazz Society unnumbered), with the Juggernaut: *Juggernaut Strikes Again* (Concord Jazz 4183)

Videos to Get: *Count Basie-Whirlybird* (1965; Vintage Jazz Classics 2005)

AHMED ABDULLAH

. . . .

b. May 10, 1947, Harlem, NY

A powerful avant-garde trumpeter who deserves much greater recognition, Ahmed Abdullah has held his own on records with such major saxophonists as Charles Brackeen and David Ware. Born Leroy Bland, he remembers, "My older sister listened to music a great deal, so jazz was in the house while I was growing up. Another sister had a husband who played clarinet and had a huge jazz collection. Besides that, jazz was on the jukebox in the candy store on the street that I grew up on. I bought my first trumpet at a pawnshop in Harlem on 125th Street for $37 at age 13."

Abdullah attended Queens College (1965–67) and Kingsborough Community College (1979–81). He became a professional musician in 1968 and was always attracted to the more adventurous side of jazz. He named as his trumpet heroes Miles Davis, Booker Little, Lee Morgan, Kenny Dorham, Joe Gordon, and Don Cherry; a bit of their tones can be heard in his own highly original playing. During 1970–74 Abdullah worked with the Melodic Artet, a group that included Brackeen and bassist Ronnie Boykins. Abdullah was part of the now-legendary New York loft scene and played with many of the major players of the 1970s, including Arthur Blythe, Rashied Ali, Ed Blackwell, Hamiett Bluiett, the Sam Rivers big band, and a co-op called The Group (1986–87) that also included Marion Brown, Billy Bang, Sirone, and Andrew Cyrille. Of particular significance to Abdullah was his association with Sun Ra, which lasted on and off from 1975 until the early 1990s.

In 1972 the trumpeter formed a band called Abdullah, which along the way utilized such sidemen as Billy Bang, Chico Freeman, Oliver Lake, Arthur Blythe, David Murray, Frank Lowe, Jay Hoggard, and other avant-garde players. In 1987 he started leading the Solomonic Quartet, which, as it grew, became the Solomonic Quintet and finally the Solomonic Sextet. "Having grown up in Harlem in the '50s and early '60s, my music has a natural relation with urban African American life. The music I have been most influenced by has been the music of the '60s that challenged the status quo. The Solomonic dynasty is the oldest dynasty known, having started with Solomon and Sheba and ending with Haile Sellasie. When one understands that they are related to the oldest people on this planet, then it can be understood that there is no limit to the music that one may play."

Thus far this musically inquisitive trumpeter has led albums for Cadence, About Time, Silkheart, and CIMP in addition to recording with Ed Blackwell, Billy Bang, Arthur Blythe, Dennis Gonzalez, and Sun Ra. By coincidence, the first LPs put out by the Cadence and About Time labels, and the initial Silkheart CD, are all by Ahmed Abdullah.

Recommended CDs: *Ahmed Abdullah and the Solomonic Quintet* (Silkheart 100), *Liquid Magic* (Silkheart 104), *Dedication* (CIMP 152), *Actual Proof* (CIMP 192), with Arthur Blythe: *Metamorphosis/The Grip* (India Navigation 1029)

LPs to Search For: *Live at Ali's Alley* (Cadence 1000), *Life's Force* (About Time 1001)

NAT ADDERLEY

● ● ● ● ● ● ● ● ● ● ● ● ●

b. Nov. 25, 1931, Tampa, FL, d. Jan. 2, 2000, Lakeland, FL

Nat Adderley spent much of his career in the shadow of his older brother, altoist Cannonball Adderley, even after Cannonball's death in 1975. But at his best (particularly during the early 1960s), Nat was a powerful cornetist who, although touched by the style of Miles Davis, had his own sound in the hard bop tradition, along with a lot of fire. He was also an underrated composer who wrote "Work Song," "Jive Samba," "Sermonette," "Hummin'," and "The Old Country." In fact, so successful was "Work Song" that Adderley referred to it as his "Social Security song."

Nat began playing trumpet in 1946 and switched permanently to cornet in 1950. Adderley attended Florida University (majoring in sociology, with a minor in music), served in the military during 1951–53 (playing in an Army band part of the time), and worked with Lionel Hampton during part of 1954–55, including a European tour. However, he seemed destined to become a schoolteacher in Florida, as did his brother. But the Adderleys' lives changed when they visited New York during their summer vacation in 1955. Sitting in with Oscar Pettiford's group at the Café Bohemia, they caused a sensation. Soon they were making records, relocating to New York, and forming a quintet under Cannonball's leadership. Although the bebop-oriented band made some exciting records for Emarcy during 1956–57, it was unable to gain enough work to survive. After the Adderleys reluctantly broke up the group, Cannonball became a member of the Miles Davis Sextet with John Coltrane (where he recorded *Kind of Blue*) while Nat kept busy playing with J.J. Johnson and the Woody Herman sextet.

In October 1959 the new Cannonball Adderley Quintet debuted, and this time the band caught on, helped greatly by pianist Bobby Timmons' hit "This Here." Within a short time, the ensemble was one of the most popular groups in jazz, symbolizing soul jazz yet also playing high-quality hard bop. At its peak during the first half of the 1960s (particularly when in 1963 Yusef Lateef on tenor, flute, and oboe made the group a sextet), the band was a perfect outlet for both Nat and Cannonball.

Nat, who took many powerful solos during the first half of the 1960s, first began to fade a bit in the late 1960s. His range gradually shrank, and his trumpet chops lost a lot of their endurance. Still, he remained quite active, touring and recording with his brother's band. After Cannonball's sudden death in 1975, Nat formed a similar quintet that had Sonny Fortune and eventually Vincent Herring (who could emulate Cannonball) in the alto chair, recording and touring frequently. Adderley had first recorded as a leader back in 1955 for Savoy and had made occasional records (for Wing, Emarcy, Riverside, Jazzland, Atlantic, Milestone, A&M, Capitol, and Prestige) during his years as Cannonball's "brass section." In his post-Cannonball period, Adderley led many record dates, including for Steeplechase, Little David, Galaxy, Theresa, In & Out, Evidence, Landmark, Enja, Timeless, Challenge, and Chiaroscuro. In 1978 he acted, played trumpet, and sang a little in an off-Broadway play based on the life of Mahalia Jackson called *Mahalia*. The good-humored cornetist kept up a busy schedule in his later years, even though his chops were often a bit erratic.

Nat Adderley remained active until his health declined in the mid-1990s (due to diabetes), forcing his retirement in late-1997, a little over two years before his death at age 68.

Recommended CDs: *Introducing Nat Adderley* (Verve 314 543 828), *Branching Out* (Original Jazz Classics 255), *Work Song* (Original Jazz Classics 363), *That's Right* (Original Jazz Classics 791), *Autumn Leaves* (Evidence 22102), *Live at the 1994 Floating Jazz Festival* (Chiaroscuro 334), with Cannonball Adderley: *Sophisticated Swing* (Emarcy 314 528 408), *Cannonball Adderley Quintet in San Francisco* (Original Jazz Classics 035), *Dizzy's Business* (Milestone 47069), *Mercy, Mercy, Mercy* (Capitol 29915)

LPs to Search For: *Autobiography* (Atlantic 1493), *Sayin' Something* (Atlantic 1460), *A Little New York Midtown Music* (Galaxy 5120)

Film Appearances: Nat Adderley ghosts the trumpet solos for Sammy Davis Jr. in *A Man Called Adam* (1966).

Videos to Get: *Cannonball Adderley/Teddy Edwards: Jazz Scene USA* (1962; Shanachie 6310), *Paris Reunion Band* (1988; Proscenium Entertainment 10004)

SYLVESTER AHOLA
· · · · · · · · · · · · · · · · · ·

b. May 24, 1902, Gloucester, MA, d. 1995, Gloucester, MA

Although his name is forgotten today, Sylvester Ahola was the most important American musician in England during 1928–31. Due to his ability to play concise and melodic jazz solos, his solid section work, and his sight-reading ability, Ahola was in tremendous demand for both studio work and jazz dates. However, his prolific efficiency eventually resulted in his being sacrificed to soothe the British Musicians Union.

Early on Sylvester Ahola, whose family was from Finland, acquired the nickname of "Hooley," which is Finnish for "embouchure." He started playing drums when he was six, switching to cornet two years later. Ahola worked with Frank Ward's orchestra in New England during 1921–24 and played with other local groups. He moved to New York in mid-1925 to work with Paul Specht's orchestra, a stint that included a two-month trip to England in 1926. Brief periods followed with the California Ramblers, Bert Lown, and Peter Van Steeden. In August 1927, Ahola was recruited to play with Adrian Rollini's all-star (and now legendary) band, an ensemble that included Bix Beiderbecke and C-melody saxophonist Frankie Trumbauer. The group did not last long and unfortunately never recorded, but it gave Ahola (who was the only member not hired primarily as a soloist) an opportunity to sit next to Bix. Although very impressed by Beiderbecke, Hooley's playing was actually more strongly touched by that of Red Nichols.

After the band broke up (and Bix and Tram joined Paul Whiteman), Ahola was lured to England by a high-paying job with the Savoy Orpheans. Although he had recorded a bit during the 1924–27 period (ten selections with the California Ramblers and dates with Paul Specht plus a few freelance jobs), it did not come close to comparing to his work in England, where it must have seemed at times as if Ahola lived in the studios. He is estimated to have appeared on more than 3000 titles during 1927–31! He recorded extensively not only with the Savoy Orpheans and Bert Ambrose (whose orchestra he joined in October 1928) but also with an enormous number of dance bands and vocalists. In 1928 Ahola appeared on at least 115 recording sessions and in 1929 he was on over 190 dates. Most of those recordings are scarce today, although two LPs of music by Philip Lewis' Rhythm Maniacs with Ahola were issued by the British Retrieval label in the 1980s.

Because Ahola was getting most of the best jobs, a group of British trumpeters successfully circulated a petition in March 1930 that caused him, as a foreigner, to be banned from recording with any group other than the one run by his official boss, Ambrose. The effect was immediate, because, although he had already appeared on 47 dates by the end of March, Ahola was only on 11 sessions the remainder of the year.

Hooley's career after 1930 was anticlimactic. He remained in England until August 1931 (appearing on just 16 British sessions that year), when he returned to New York. He spent the Depression playing commercial music with Ray Noble, Peter Van Steeden, and the NBC staff orchestra. His only post-British recordings (not counting anonymous work on the radio) are three dates with Van Steeden in 1931–32 and one session apiece with the San Remo Dance Orchestra (1932), the A.R.C. Brunswick Band (1932), Al Bowlly (1935), and Lud Gluskin (1935), none of which made an impression. In 1940 Sylvester Ahola moved back to his hometown, Gloucester, where he played locally with the Cape Ann Civic Symphony into the 1980s. It is doubtful if many of his neighbors realized that the mild-mannered trumpeter was once a pawn in British politics!

LPs to Search For: Phillip Lewis Rhythm Maniacs Vols. 1–2 (Retrieval 410 and 412)

Recommended Reading: Sylvester Ahola-The Gloucester Gabriel by Dick Hill (Scarecrow Press, 1993)

ALVIN ALCORN

• • • • • • • • • • • •

b. Sept. 7, 1912, New Orleans, LA

As trumpeter with Kid Ory's Creole Jazz Band during 1954–56, Alvin Alcorn proved to be the perfect ensemble player. On the hotter records, Alcorn expertly led the New Orleans group through as many as four straight ensemble choruses, perfectly timing his climactic note in each chorus for maximum impact and turning up the heat ever so slowly until the song's conclusion. His distinctive sound, inventive use of dynamics, and logical middle-register melodic lead has made many listeners regret that Alcorn's pre-Ory period was buried in obscurity and that his later years offered little more than a gradual decline.

Alcorn was taught music theory by his brother, clarinetist Oliver Alcorn (who later worked with Lee Collins). He freelanced in New Orleans and Dallas, including with Armand J. Piron's Sunny South Syncopators (1930–31). Alcorn played and recorded with Don Albert's swing band (1932–37) but probably did not take any individual spots (Billy Douglas was Albert's trumpet soloist), also working with Paul Barbarin, Sidney Desvignes (on and off during 1941–50), Oscar Celestin (1951), George Lewis, and Octave Crosby (1951–54). Alcorn, who served in the Army during part of World War II, also had day jobs, including as decorator for a real estate company in 1947.

Even after all of this experience, when Alcorn moved to Los Angeles in 1954 to join Ory, he had been barely documented. But fortunately he appeared on four of the trombonist's best Good Time Jazz recordings, which allow today's New Orleans jazz fans to hear how effective a trumpeter he was in this setting. Alcorn also appeared briefly with Ory in the film *The Benny Goodman Story* and toured Europe.

After returning to New Orleans in 1956, Alcorn played locally into the 1980s, often with musicians not quite up to his level, although he did make a fine Verve album with George Lewis and gigged with the Eureka Brass Band and Paul Barbarin. Alcorn visited Europe a few times (including with Chris Barber in 1978) and Australia in 1973, but most of his later recordings (including with Sweet Emma Barrett, Capt. John Handy, the Eagle Brass Band, Paul Barnes, Louis Nelson, and Louis Cottrell) were for tiny labels and many are erratic.

Although Ira Gitler's *Biographical Encyclopedia of Jazz* shows Alvin Alcorn as passing away in New Orleans in 1981, he is reportedly still alive at this writing!

Recommended CDs: *Sounds Of New Orleans, Vol. 5* (Storyville 6012), with Kid Ory: *Kid Ory's Creole Jazz Band 1954* (Good Time Jazz 12004), *Kid Ory's Creole Jazz Band* (Good Time Jazz 12006), *The Legendary Kid* (Good Time Jazz 12016), *Favorites* (Good Time Jazz 60-009)

Recommended Reading: *The Jazz Crusade* by Big Bill Bissonnette (Special Request Books, 1992)

Film Appearances: *The Benny Goodman Story* as part of Kid Ory's band (1955), *Un Homme Qui Me Plait* (1969), and a small speaking role in *Live and Let Die* (1973)

RALPH ALESSI
. . . .

A top-notch avant-garde trumpeter who also sounds comfortable playing advanced hard bop, Ralph Alessi has been increasingly in demand for performances and recordings in recent years. His own debut as a leader, *Hissy Fit* (from 1999), is quite eccentric and a bit forbidding. Ralph Alessi has also been heard on recordings with (among many others) Michael Cain, Uri Caine, James Carney, Steve Coleman, Ravi Coltrane, Carola Grey, Andy Milne, Lonnie Plaxico, and the Sam Rivers big band.

Recommended CDs: *Hissy Fit* (Love Slave 102), with Michael Cain: *Circa* (ECM 1622), with James Carney: *Fables from the Aqueduct* (Jacaranda 71001), with Ravi Coltrane: *Moving Pictures* (RCA 55887), with Lonnie Plaxico: *With All Your Heart* (Muse 5525)

DANNY ALGUIRE
. . . .

b. Aug. 30, 1912, Chickasha, OK, d. July 8, 1992, Portland, OR

T he Firehouse Five Plus Two was the epitome of a part-time "purely for the fun of it" Dixieland band. When the group caught on, few were as surprised as its own members. Comprising mostly animators, writers, and regular employees of the Disney Studios, it began as an informal lunchtime jam session and grew to become one of the most popular trad jazz groups of the 1950s, even though its musicians never gave up their day jobs! The band gained its name when it made an early appearance at an antique car show, playing while riding in a 1914 fire truck. When its original trumpeter, Johnny Lucas, found it difficult to meet the band's busy schedule, his replacement was a 36-year-old veteran cornetist, Danny Alguire.

Born Reuben Dan Alguire, young Danny learned how to read music from his father, a professional drummer. He debuted with the Fort Worth Rotary Club Boys Band in 1921 on mellophone and, after moving to Kansas City in 1923, joined that city's Rotary Band. Taking up the trumpet, Alguire played with a dance band in his hometown of Chickasha (1928–30) and attended the University of Oklahoma (1930–33). He decided to become a professional trumpeter in 1933 "when I realized that it was the only thing I could do to stay alive in the Depression. The joints paid $2 a night plus tips." Alguire worked with Jimmie Thornhill's band (1934–35) in West Texas, freelanced in Los Angeles, switched permanently to cornet in 1937, and spent two years (1938–40) in Bakersfield gigging with a four-piece group led by pianist Bill Norris. In November 1941 (thanks to the recommendation of Benny Strickler) Alguire joined the 16-piece big band led by Western swing pioneer Bob Wills, recording 18 sides for Okeh during his year with the Texas Playboys and taking the vocal on "Home in San Antone." A similar association with T. Texas Tyler's Western swing band during 1946–48 resulted in a dozen titles for the 4-Star label. But Alguire was a relative unknown before hooking up with the Firehouse Five Plus Two.

"That was a perfect fun band; we really enjoyed ourselves and made good money," remembered Alguire, who eventually worked for Disney as an assistant director in their animation department during 1955–75. As the Firehouse's cornetist during 1949–74, Alguire contributed a solid lead and crisp melodic solos, leading a frontline that also featured trombonist Ward Kimball and clarinetist Clarke Mitchell (who was succeeded by George Probert on soprano and clarinet in 1954). Although the band's humor could sometimes border on corn (they were not shy about having a siren roar during their final chorus, as if the music were so hot that it had started a fire!), there was no doubt that the Firehouse Five Plus Two gave both themselves and their audiences a great time. Their dozen records for Good Time Jazz (most have been reissued in the Original Jazz Classics series) are all quite fun.

Danny Alguire, whose favorite trumpeters included Benny Strickler (who "influenced me greatly" when they played together with Bob Wills), Louis Armstrong, Red Nichols, Bix Beiderbecke, Don Finch, Harry James, and Manny Klein, proudly stated in 1991 (11 years after he had stopped playing) that "I have done everything I wanted to do in music." His autobiography (*Dust Bowl to Disney*) remains unpublished.

Recommended CDs: with the Firehouse Five Plus Two: *The Firehouse Five Plus Two Story* (Good Time Jazz 22055), *The Firehouse Five Plus Two Goes South* (Good Time Jazz 12018), *16 Dixieland Favorites* (Good Time Jazz 60-008)

Film Appearances with the Firehouse Five Plus Two: *Grounds for Marriage* (1950) and *Hit Parade of 1951* (1950)

JAN ALLAN

• • • • • • • • • •

b. Nov. 7, 1934, Falun, Sweden

A top Swedish trumpeter, Jan Allan has shown that he is quite capable of playing with top bop-oriented musicians, including famous Americans. Jan Allan's father was a bassist and violinist in the 1920s and '30s. Allan began on piano when he was six, switching to trumpet eight years later. In 1951 he moved to Stockholm, where he worked with George Riedel, the Modern Swedes (1954), the Lars Gullin-Rolf Billberg band (1954–55), and Carl-Henrik Norin (1955–57). Allan led his own groups during the 1960s, with his orchestra later in the decade expanding its repertoire and performing some pop and rock (á la Herb Alpert's Tijuana Brass and Blood, Sweat and Tears). Allan was a regular with the Swedish Radio Jazz group (1968–75) and a fixture at European jazz festivals, having opportunities to play with Thad Jones, John Lewis, Warne Marsh, and Bob Brookmeyer. Despite all this activity (which includes recordings with Thad Jones, Bobby Shew, and Lee Konitz plus his own dates for the Four Leaf Clover label), Jan Allan has at the same time been an elementary particle physicist at Stockholm University.

Recommended CDs: *Jan Allan '70* (Phono Suecia 130)

LPs to Search For: with Bobby Shew: *Dialogic* (Four Leaf Clover 5061)

ED ALLEN

• • • • • • • • • •

b. Dec. 15, 1897, Nashville, TN, d. Jan. 28, 1974, New York, NY

Ed Allen owes his place in jazz history to Clarence Williams. During 1927–37, Ed Allen (not to be confused with Henry "Red" Allen) was closely associated with Williams, recording at least 160 titles on sessions led by the pianist, not counting other dates that Williams organized. A fine journeyman cornetist, Allen was expert with mutes, could play both bluesy and melodic, and was a subtle lead voice who did not dominate the music. However, if he had not become a favorite of Williams, Allen would probably not have been even a footnote in jazz history.

Allen grew up in St. Louis, began working professionally when he was 16, spent a period playing in Seattle, and worked for two years with Charlie Creath on riverboats. Allen played in New Orleans with his own band in 1923. After moving to Chicago in late 1924, he played with Earl Hines for a couple of months, relocated to New York in July 1925 as a member of Joe Jordan's Sharps and Flats, and worked with Jordan in Ed Daily's Black and White Show for a year. While Allen performed with Allie Ross' group (which in 1930 became the Leroy Tibbs Orchestra) and with Earle Howard (1932–33), his recording career was much more significant than his night work. Thanks largely to Williams, Allen appeared on dates accompanying such singers as Anna Bell, Laura Bryant, Mary Dixon, Katherine Henderson, Bertha Idaho, Sara Martin, Clara Smith, Eva Taylor, and most memorably Bessie Smith (including a prominent role on her classic version of "Nobody Knows You When You're Down and Out"). In addition to his appearances on Clarence Williams' extensive series of hot combo sides, he also cut sides with the Barrelhouse Five, the Alabama Jug Band, the Blue Grass Foot Warmers, the Birmingham Serenaders, Dixie Washboard, the Gallon Jug Band, TeRoy Williams, Leroy Tibbs, Willie the Lion Smith, and Joe Jordan. Nearly all of these overlapping groups were run by Clarence Williams, who certainly kept his associates busy!

Williams became much less active after 1937, and Ed Allen (then only 40) virtually disappeared from records, never even leading a date of his own. He worked mostly as a cornetist with low-level dance hall bands (including Benton Heath's for 18 years starting in 1945) until his retirement in 1963. Other than four selections cut with Cliff Jackson on a Swingville session in 1961 (a rare date not organized by Clarence Williams!), Ed Allen spent his last 40 years in obscurity.

Recommended CDs: with Clarence Williams: *1927* (Classics 736), *1928–1929* (Classics 771), *1929* (Classics 791), *1933* (Classics 845)

EDDIE ALLEN
. . . .

b. Milwaukee, WI

An adventurous player with a mellow tone, Eddie Allen (also known as E. J. Allen) has long been a valuable and flexible trumpeter. He began playing the trumpet in junior high school, studying music at the Wisconsin Conservatory of Music and the University of Wisconsin in Green Bay. After playing locally, he moved to New York in 1981. Allen first recorded with Charli Persip's Superband in 1984 and since then has appeared on records with Muhal Richard Abrams, Cyrus Chestnut, Chico Freeman, Craig Harris, Louis Hayes, Bobby Previte, Vanessa Rubin, and Mongo Santamaria (with whom he played extensively), among others. Eddie Allen, who was the musical director (in addition to playing trumpet and contributing arrangements) for Lester Bowie's Brass Fantasy, has recorded as a leader for Enja and the Japanese Venus label.

Recommended CDs: *Another's Point of View* (Enja 8004), *R 'n' B* (Enja 9033), *Summer Days* (Enja 9388), with Cyrus Chestnut: *Earth Stories* (Atlantic 82876), with Louis Hayes: *Nightfall* (Steeplechase 31285), *Blue Lou* (Steeplechase 31340), with Rob Reddy: *Songs That You Can Trust* (Koch 7876)

HENRY "RED" ALLEN
. . . .

b. Jan. 7, 1908, Algiers, LA, d. Apr. 17, 1967, New York, NY

In 1965, when Henry "Red" Allen was 57 and near the end of his 11-year period at New York's Metropole, fellow trumpeter Don Ellis (who was from a much later generation), in a famous *Downbeat* article, called Allen

the most avant-garde trumpeter in New York today…. What other trumpet player plays such asymmetrical rhythms and manages to make them swing besides? What other trumpeter plays ideas that may begin as a whisper, rise to a brassy shout, and suddenly become a whisper again, with no discernible predictability? Who else has the amazing variety of tonal colors, bends, smears, half-valve effects, rips, glissandos, flutter-tonguing (a favorite on a high 'D'), all combined with iron chops and complete control of even the softest, most subtle tone production?

Henry "Red" Allen was the last of the great New Orleans trumpeters to emerge during the 1920s and the most advanced of all of them. Although he was most often heard with Dixieland or trad jazz bands throughout his career, Allen (like the eccentric clarinetist Pee Wee Russell) tended to be much more modern than the setting he was in and the repertoire in which he was featured. His speechlike solos often sounded quite conversational, with unpredictable phrasing sometimes only abstractly connected to the beat. Allen (an underrated vocalist) sang in the same manner and was a masterful showman.

Allen's father, Henry Allen Sr. (1877–1952), led one of the top brass bands in New Orleans. Red picked up early experience playing drums, ukulele, violin, and alto horn before switching to trumpet, and he was proud to march with his father's band whenever he had the opportunity. He co-led a kid's group with clarinetist John Casimir and in the early 1920s was advanced enough to play with most of the top musicians in New Orleans, including on riverboats with Fate Marable and with George Lewis, a lifelong friend. Unlike Lewis (who would stay in the South for another 15 years), Allen moved up North in 1927 to join King Oliver. He made his recording debut with Clarence Williams (Allen would not record with Oliver until 1930, when he guested on two sessions) and made a strong impression. However, the 19-year-old became homesick after a few months and returned to New Orleans. He spent time playing with Fate Marable again and then in 1929 was offered his choice between New York jobs with Luis Russell or with Duke Ellington. Allen chose Russell's band, because he had more friends in the group (Cootie Williams would soon take the Ellington job), and quickly became the star of the outfit. Although Bill Coleman was the other trumpeter, Red Allen was such a strong player that he was given virtually all of the solo space; "Jersey Lightning," "Saratoga Shout," and "Louisiana Swing" are three of the more outstanding recordings that Allen cut with Russell.

The success of Louis Armstrong with his records for Okeh led other labels to try to discover and document their own "trumpet kings." Allen was signed in 1929 by Victor and, unlike his competitors Jabbo Smith and Reuben "River" Reeves, Red's association with the label launched his career rather than just serving as its high point. He is quite outstanding on "It Should Be You" and "Biff'ly Blues." Allen also recorded with Victoria Spivey, Spike Hughes, Don Redman, Jelly Roll Morton, and Billy Banks' Rhythmakers (which in 1932 teamed him with Pee Wee Russell), among others during this period.

Allen starred with Luis Russell until 1932. After a few months with Charlie Johnson, he became a well-featured soloist with Fletcher Henderson's orchestra (1933–34). His playing on Coleman Hawkins' very advanced "Queer Notions" is downright radical, and his other solos with Henderson in general led Roy Eldridge years later to mistakenly claim that Allen had made "mistakes"; Red's ear was simply further advanced than Roy's. When Henderson's orchestra began to struggle, Allen departed and joined the Mills Blue Rhythm Band, where he was one of the key soloists for three years (1934–37); his frenzied showcase "Ride, Red, Ride" came from this period. In addition, Allen continued recording fairly often as a leader throughout the 1930s,

One of the great originals, Henry "Red" Allen was the most modern of the 1920s New Orleans trumpeters.

using many top sidemen, including J. C. Higginbotham, Dicky Wells, Tab Smith, Buster Bailey, and (on two occasions) Coleman Hawkins. However, many of those records feature inferior pop tunes, and Allen (unlike Fats Waller) tried to uplift the songs rather than satirize them, which in some cases was impossible!

Despite all this activity, Red Allen did not become one of the more famous names of the swing era. He never led his own big band and spent 1937–40 back with the Luis Russell Orchestra, which was then functioning as Louis Armstrong's backup band. Although Allen was well featured in the orchestra's opening set in concerts, the main star of course was Armstrong, and there was little interaction between the two.

In 1940, when the Russell band was laid off, Allen permanently went out on his own. It was perfect timing, because the New Orleans jazz revival was making it easier for players from the older styles to get work. Allen, who had recorded with Jelly Roll Morton in 1939 and would team up with Sidney Bechet on record in 1941, put together a rambunctious sextet that included trombonist Higginbotham, clarinetist Edmond Hall, and pianist Kenny Kersey. Allen worked with this group for a year at Café Society in New York and then spent four years at the Down Beat in Chicago; by then the great (if now forgotten) altoist Dan Stovall had taken Hall's place. At the Down Beat, Allen noticed that the female washroom attendant had a strong voice. Her name was Ruth Jones but Allen called her "Dinahmite" and had her sit in with his band. One night she sang for Lionel Hampton, and soon she was Hamp's new singer and being called Dinah Washington.

During this era, Red Allen really developed as a showman. He counted off tempos by growling "whamp, whamp," which could sound particularly hilarious when he was starting a ballad! He ended performances that he approved of with "Nice!" Largely ignoring bebop, Allen led a jump group that could get quite heated on blues and standards, falling between swing and rhythm and blues; their 1946 recording of "The Crawl" is a perfect example of how exciting the ensemble could be. Allen was able to keep working throughout the 1950s, heading the often-riotous house band at the Metropole during 1954–65. A 1957 album, *I Cover the Waterfront*, has one of Allen's great solos on the title cut, and he was one of the stars of the legendary *Sound of Jazz* television special, playing memorable versions of "Wild Man Blues" and "Rosetta." Red toured Europe with Kid Ory in 1959 and took a liking to England (and vice versa); he would make several additional trips in the 1960s. By then Allen usually led a quartet, a format that allowed him a great deal of freedom in his solos.

Unlike most of his contemporaries, Allen never did decline, and he continued to progress, even in his later years, without losing his musical personality. At the 1965 Monterey Jazz Festival, where he was teamed in a set with Clark Terry, Rex Stewart, and Dizzy Gillespie, Allen (the least known of the four) was widely reported as having stolen the show. He also defied stereotypes in other ways, for Allen did not smoke or use drugs, rarely drank, was always on time, and was happily married for 37 years. Up until late 1966, when he was diagnosed with cancer of the pancreas, Red Allen was at his prime. And even when his health was failing, he took a final (and triumphant) tour of England before passing away a few weeks after his return. Allen did not influence later musicians (unlike Roy Eldridge and Dizzy Gillespie), because his style (like Eric Dolphy's) was too unusual and unique. That fact has resulted in his sometimes being overlooked in jazz history books, but in reality Henry "Red" Allen ranks near the top of his field.

Recommended CDs: *1929–1933* (Classics 540), *1933–1935* (Classics 551), *1935–1936* (Classics 575), *1936–1937* (Classics 590), *1937–1941* (Classics 628), *World on a String* (Bluebird 2497), *Live 1965* (Storyville 8290), with Luis Russell: *1926–1929* (Classics 588), *1930–1934* (Classics 606)

Recommended Reading: *American Musicians II* by Whitney Balliett (Oxford University Press, 1996), *Jazz Masters of New Orleans* by Martin Williams (Macmillan Publishing Co., 1967), *Jazz Talking* by Max Jones (Da Capo Press, 1987)

Videos to Get: *The Sound of Jazz* (1957; Vintage Jazz Classics 2001), *Kid Ory/Red Allen in Europe* (1959; 30N-90W Video NWV02), *Chicago and All That Jazz* (1961; Vintage Jazz Classics 2002)

OVIE ALSTON

•••••••••••

b. 1906, Washington, DC

Ovie Alston had a style in the 1930s that was quite "cool" (as opposed to Louis Armstrong's "hot"), with behind-the-beat phrasing and subtle ideas performed in an unhurried way. He is chiefly remembered as the trumpet soloist and occasional singer with pianist Claude Hopkins' big band of 1931–36.

The mellow tone and inner excitement (which occasionally broke out) were the most striking qualities of Ovie Alston's playing. He started his career with Bill Brown's Brownies (1928–30), recording two selections, including taking a vocal on "Zonky." Alston co-led a band with Charlie Skeete that pianist Claude Hopkins took over in 1931; Hopkins was wise enough to retain the trumpeter as his star soloist for the next five years. Alston's playing on Jimmy Mundy's classic "Mush Mouth" is a standout, as is his spot on "King Porter Stomp." Alston also took occasional good-natured vocals and cowrote with Hopkins such songs as "Chasing All the Blues Away," "Swingin' and Jivin'," "Washington Squabble," and "Everybody Shuffle."

After leaving Hopkins in 1936, the trumpeter put together his own 11-piece band. Alston recorded eight selections during two record dates in 1938 (with Hopkins guesting as his pianist) but only recorded four additional titles in later years, in 1946 for the tiny Urab label. Alston was based at the Roseland Ballroom during 1939–47 (the team of Noble Sissle and Eubie Blake fronted his orchestra during 1941–42 for some USO tours) and the Baby Grand Café (1948–52). Ovie Alston, who could be thought of as one of the first cool jazz trumpeters, then faded into complete obscurity.

Recommended CDs: with Claude Hopkins: *1932–1934* (Classics 699), *1934–1935* (Classics 716), *1937–1940* (Classics 733)

CHICO ALVAREZ

•••••••••••

b. Feb. 3, 1920, Montreal, Canada, d. Aug. 12, 1992, Las Vegas, NV

Chico Alvarez was the first significant soloist in Stan Kenton's orchestra and an original member of the band in 1941. His trumpet playing was swing oriented while looking toward bebop, and he was well featured during his periods with Kenton.

Alvarez grew up in Inglewood, near Los Angeles, starting out on piano and violin. He played those instruments for nine years before switching to the trumpet. "I heard Bunny Berigan's recording of 'I Can't Get Started.' It inspired me to get an old, discarded cornet, tape it together, and learn the chromatic scale." Alvarez was with Kenton's band during 1941–43 (a period when the orchestra had its first successes along with some early struggles) and, after serving in the Army, he was back with Kenton during 1946–48 and 1950–51. Among the many numbers in which he is heard taking solos are "Machito" and "Harlem Holiday." During Kenton's one-year "vacation" in 1949, Alvarez freelanced, playing with Red Norvo, Benny Carter, and Charlie Barnet.

After spending a year with Kenton's radical Innovations Orchestra of 1950–51, Alvarez (who was still just 31) opened up a music store in Hermosa Beach, studied at the Los Angeles Conservatory of Music and Arts, and worked as a trumpeter and arranger for local Latin bands. Instead of having a major solo career, he relocated in 1958 to Las Vegas, where for the next 24 years he worked anonymously but steadily in show bands, playing jazz occasionally with his own band but never recording under his own name. Chico Alvarez spent his last years in semiretirement before passing away from cancer at the age of 72.

Limited Edition Box Set: *The Complete Capitol Studio Recordings of Stan Kenton 1943–47* (Mosaic 7-163)

FRANCO AMBROSETTI
. . . .

b. Dec. 10, 1941, Lugano, Switzerland

An excellent trumpeter and flugelhornist most influenced by Lee Morgan and Freddie Hubbard, Franco Ambrosetti actually has music as a second career. He has been an executive at his family's business for many years, supplying steel wheels to European auto manufacturers. However, there is no way, listening to his stirring solos, that listeners would know that Ambrosetti is essentially a part-time player!

The son of a notable saxophonist, Flavio Ambrosetti (b. 1919), Franco Ambrosetti studied classical piano during 1952–59 but was self-taught on the trumpet, which he began playing in 1959, when he was 17. Ambrosetti gained an economics degree from the University of Basel. But despite his "day job," he has been a professional musician since he turned 21. He played locally in Switzerland, was a member of his father's group (1963–70), recorded with pianist George Gruntz as early as 1964 and, first appeared in the United States in 1967. Ambrosetti was an original member of George Gruntz's Concert Jazz Band, and he has worked in Europe with many top American jazzmen, including Phil Woods, Dexter Gordon, Cannonball Adderley, Joe Henderson, Michael Brecker, John Scofield, and Kenny Barron, among others.

Franco Ambrosetti led his first record date in 1965 and recorded an impressive string of albums for Enja during 1978–90, topped off by the classic *Music for Symphony and Jazz Band*. Not bad for an auto executive!

Recommended CDs: *Movies* (Enja 5035), *Movies, Two* (Enja 5079), *Music for Symphony and Jazz Band* (Enja 6070)

CAT ANDERSON
. . . .

b. Sept. 12, 1916, Greenville, SC; d. Apr. 29, 1981, Norwalk, CA

Ever since the emergence of Louis Armstrong in the mid-1920s, the range of the trumpet has been gradually expanded as trumpeters continually try to top each other. Any list of exciting high-note men has to include Tommy Stevenson from the 1934 Jimmy Lunceford Orchestra, Al Killian, Maynard Ferguson, Jon Faddis, and Arturo Sandoval, but arguably the greatest of them all was Cat Anderson. On "Satin Doll," from the two-CD Blue Note set *Duke Ellington's 70th Birthday Concert,* Anderson begins his solo over three octaves above middle C and at one point hits G'''', only 2½ steps below the highest note on the piano! Even more remarkable is that all of his notes are in tune as he constructs a logical (and rather miraculous) chorus.

William Alonzo Anderson lost both of his parents at age four and grew up at the Jenkins Orphanage in South Carolina. Anderson started playing trombone when he was seven and soon added the baritone horn, drums, and mellophone. He earned his lifelong nickname when he won a schoolyard fight against a bully and a kid exclaimed, "Hey, you fight like a cat!" The Jenkins Orphanage raised money by sending out school orchestras on tour, and in 1929 Anderson had his first opportunity to go on the road. When the trumpeters in his band ran away, Cat volunteered to switch instruments, and soon he was the nominal leader of the orchestra, inspired to stick to trumpet after hearing Jabbo Smith and Peanuts Holland (both of whom had been at the orphanage earlier). In 1932 Cat Anderson was part of a contingent from the orphanage that was the nucleus of the Carolina Cotton Pickers, a territory band in which he spent five years and made his recording debut (six obscure titles cut during March 24–25, 1937). After leaving the band, Anderson played with guitarist Hartley Toots, Claude Hopkins' big band, Doc Wheeler's Sunset Orchestra (1938–42), with whom he recorded a few titles during 1941–42, and Lucky Millinder. He spent a brief period with the Erskine Hawkins Orchestra but was reportedly fired because he played higher notes than the leader! Two stints with Lionel Hampton (recording "Flying Home #2" in 1944) sandwiched a period in Boston with Sabby Lewis' orchestra.

Cat Anderson debuted with Duke Ellington on September 1, 1944. An exciting arrangement of "Blue Skies" normally ended with cornetist Rex Stewart playing a high-note solo. At a concert in Canton, Ohio, when Stewart failed to show up on time, Ellington gave the spot to his newest trumpet player. Anderson played the solo an octave higher than Stewart normally did, ending on a double C. Rex walked in the door as Cat was playing and, when Duke permanently gave the solo to Anderson, Stewart did not talk to the younger trumpeter for 15 years!

As Ellington's high-note wizard, Anderson was well utilized, simulating a train whistle on "Happy Go Lucky Local," climaxing the uptempo "Jam with Sam," and having such showcases as "El Gato" and "The Eighth Veil." After leaving Ellington in January 1947, Anderson headed his own unsuccessful big band for two years and briefly rejoined Sabby Lewis. But by 1950 he was back with Ellington, this time until 1959. Another two-year hiatus preceded a ten-year (1961–71) off-and-on association with Duke. To label Cat Anderson as merely a high-note master is to ignore his talents with the plunger mute (influenced by Cootie Williams and Ray Nance), his expertise with half-valve effects, and his ability to play creative solos in the lower register. Anderson's own occasional recordings as a leader (most of which have not yet been reissued on CD) usually emphasized those qualities. But, on the other hand, his stratospheric blasts are impossible to ignore!

After leaving Ellington for the last time in January 1971, Cat Anderson settled in the Los Angeles area, remaining active in the Hollywood studios, touring Europe, and gigging with local orchestras, including those led by Bill Berry and Louie Bellson. He died from a brain tumor at the age of 64, still the unchallenged high-note king. It is certainly a pity that Cat and Maynard Ferguson (who were well acquainted with each other) never traded off!

Recommended CDs: *Plays W. C. Handy* (Black & Blue 886), with Bill Berry: *Hello Rev* (Concord Jazz 4027); with Duke Ellington: *Sir Duke* (Drive Archive 41019), *The Duke Ellington Octet* (Moon 049), *Duke Ellington's 70th Birthday Concert* (Blue Note 32746)

LPs to Search For: *Cat Anderson and the Ellington All Stars in Paris* (Swing 8412), *Cat Speaks* (Classic Jazz 142)

Recommended Reading: *The World of Duke Ellington* by Stanley Dance (Charles Scribner's Sons, 1970)

Videos to Get: with Duke Ellington: *Jazz Festival Vol. 2* (1962; Storyville 6074)

RAY ANTHONY

. . . .

b. Jan. 20, 1922, Bentleyville, PA

It is the tragedy of Ray Anthony's life that he was not born ten years earlier. Throughout his career, this good-looking and energetic trumpeter always seemed like a throwback to the swing era, sounding quite natural playing dance music in front of a big band in a tone most influenced by Harry James. But because his prime period was during the 1950s and not the '40s, Anthony has generally been thought of as a commercial and overly nostalgic player rather than as a swing stylist. The irony is that the era that he epitomizes was over before he really had his start.

Ray Anthony was born Raymond Antonini and raised in Cleveland. His father started him on the trumpet when he was five, and he was soon playing in the Antonini Family Orchestra. From nearly the beginning, Anthony was a natural-born leader, fronting a high school band and joining Al Donahue's orchestra in 1938 when he was just 16. When he became part of Glenn Miller's big band in November 1940, it must have seemed as if he had been given his big break. But Anthony's cocky attitude (along with youthful immaturity) soon soured his relationship with Miller, and he lasted only until July 1941, getting no real opportunities to solo. An uneventful six-month stint with Jimmy Dorsey in 1942 preceded four years in the Navy, during which Anthony led a successful service show band in the Pacific.

When the recently discharged 24-year-old trumpeter started his own big band in 1946, the swing era was in the process of ending. Anthony fought against the trend, and, after some recordings for Sonora and Signature (including 1947's "Man with a Horn"), he signed with Capitol in 1949, a move that led to his commercial successes during the following decade. Mixing together swing standards, current pop tunes, and dance music, Anthony hit upon a formula that resulted in quite a few big-selling records, most notably "Harlem Nocturne," "Mr. Anthony's Boogie," "Slaughter on Tenth Avenue," "Dragnet," "Peter Gunn," and "Bunny Hop." He was in 15 movies (including *Daddy Long Legs,* with Fred Astaire, and portraying his former boss, Jimmy Dorsey, in *The Five Pennies*) and had steady television work (including five of his own television series).

A household name throughout the 1950s, Anthony kept his big band together until the early '60s. He has remained active during the years since, leading part-time orchestras (which always include a heavy dose of nostalgia), recording for Ranwood during 1968–76, and founding a successful big band mail-order catalog business and label called Aerospace. Having turned 79 in 2001, Ray Anthony still sounds strong on the trumpet, and he has enjoyed the comeback of swing during the past few years.

But, commercial successes aside, listeners can look only in vain at Ray Anthony's career for any signs of originality or innovation. Anthony's swing style has remained unchanged through the years, and he has seemingly been content to play the role of a second-generation Harry James, despite his technical skills, happy to represent an era in which he was too young to have actually played a major part.

Recommended CDs: *Young Man with a Horn* (Hindsight 412), *Swing Back to the '40s* (Aerospace 1035)

Film Appearances: *Daddy Long Legs* (1955), *The Girl Can't Help It* (1956), *This Could Be the Night* (1957), *Girls Town* (1959), *High School Confidential* (1959), *Night of the Quarter Moon* (1959), *The Beat Generation* (1959), *The Big Operator* (1959), *The Five Pennies* (1959)

ARMANDO "CHOCOLATE" ARMENTEROS

b. April 4, 1928, Ranchuelo, Santa Clara, Las Villas Province, Cuba

Thought of by some as the Louis Armstrong of Cuba (although he has been primarily a sideman), Chocolate Armenteros has been a fixture on the Cuban and Latin jazz scene for quite a few decades. Armenteros came from a musical family, took up the trumpet quite young, and was playing with a local orchestra at the age of 11. He moved to Havana and worked with Septeto Habanero, making his recording debut in 1949 with Rene Alvarez y Su Conjunto Los Astros, also recording with Arsenio Rodriguez.

While with Julio Gutierrez's group, Armenteros gained the lifelong nickname of "Chocolate" when a woman thought that he was the 1932 world featherweight boxing champion, Kid Chocolate. That would have been quite a trick, for Armenteros would have had to have been champion when he was four!

Armenteros spent the 1950s working in the studios of Cuba and freelancing with many groups, including those led by his cousin, singer Beny More, pianist Bebo Valdes, and arranger Chico O'Farrill. He moved to the United States later in the decade, working with (among many others) Machito, Mongo Santamaria, Johnny Pacheco, the Tico All-Stars, Charlie Palmieri, Ismael Rivera, Eddie Palmieri, and Cachao. It was not until 1974 (when he was 46) that Armenteros made his recording debut as a leader. Among his more notable later recordings are a rare set outside of Cuban music (*Eastern Rebellion 4*) and Paquito D'Rivera's *40 Years of Cuban Jam Sessions*. Although somewhat underrecognized in the American jazz world, Chocolate Armenteros remains a legendary name among fans of Afro-Cuban jazz.

Recommended CDs: with Cachao: *Master Sessions, Vol. 1* (Crescent Moon/Epic 64320), with Paquito D'Rivera: *40 Years of Cuban Jam Sessions* (Messidor 15826), with Machito: *1983*

Grammy Award Winner (MCA/Impulse 33106)

LPs to Search For: with Cedar Walton: *Eastern Rebellion 4* (Timeless 184)

LOUIS ARMSTRONG

• • • • • • • • • • • • • • • • • • • •

b. Aug. 4, 1901, New Orleans, LA, d. July 6, 1971, New York, NY

Of all of the trumpeters in jazz history, Louis "Satchmo" Armstrong is the most significant, for he permanently changed the music. When Armstrong first arrived upon the scene, jazz was primarily a dance music that emphasized ensembles. Most of the trumpet soloists that were around tended to play staccato phrases, were reluctant to move much beyond the melody, and thought that being "hot" meant playing loud and doubling the number of notes, usually by repeating the same phrases over and over. After Armstrong made his initial impact during 1923–25, jazz was permanently changed into a music that was powered by virtuosic soloists and adventurous improvisers.

Armstrong's main contributions were in three different areas. As a trumpeter his legato phrases greatly influenced the ideas not only of trumpeters but also of other horn players and pianists too, who adopted his ideas as their own. He knew how to use space dramatically and was brilliant at building up solos to climaxes rather than playing everything he knew in the first few seconds. Satch also had a beautiful sound that for a time defined the jazz trumpet, and he had the ability to infuse a blues feeling into any song.

As a vocalist, the gravelly voiced Armstrong often phrased like one of his horn solos (even when sticking to the words), and his phrasing influenced nearly all singers, including most notably Bing Crosby and Billie Holiday. Although he was not the first scat singer, he greatly helped to popularize scat singing, making up inventive nonsense syllables spontaneously. And as a goodwill ambassador, few could compete with Armstrong. His good-humored personality, natural comedic abilities, love of people, and joyful music made him the most accessible of all jazz performers. In fact, he was so beloved for his personality that in later years few listeners probably realized his enormous contributions as a trumpeter.

Louis Armstrong was born in New Orleans on August 4, 1901, although he believed throughout his life that his birthday was July 4, 1900 (which would have been perfect for an American hero). Armstrong's birth certificate was discovered years after his death. Judging from his very modest beginnings, the odds were certainly against Armstrong's name someday becoming a household word. He came from a very poor environment and was raised by his mother; his father abandoned the family when Louis was quite young. His earliest musical activity was singing in a vocal group on the streets for pennies. Armstrong also enjoyed hearing the many brass bands that played at parades and at social functions all over the city, and he got his first cornet when he was 11. On New Year's Eve of 1912, the unsupervised youth shot off a pistol in the air in celebration and was quickly arrested. As punishment, he was sent to live in a waifs' home, since his mother was deemed unable to take care of him properly.

Although it certainly did not look like it initially, this turned out to be Armstrong's biggest break. In the disciplined atmosphere of the waifs' home, he began seriously playing the cornet. By the time he was released after two years, he was a promising young musician. Armstrong worked at odd jobs as a teenager during the day in order to support himself and at night had many opportunities to play with the local bands. "Little Louis" idolized Joe "King" Oliver, who helped him out a bit. When Oliver left the city in 1918, he recommended Armstrong for his spot with Kid Ory's popular band. Armstrong also spent time playing on riverboats with Fate Marable's group. By then Satch was improving rapidly.

In 1922 King Oliver decided to expand his Creole Jazz Band (which was based at the Lincoln Gardens in Chicago) and he sent for his protégé. Armstrong was thrilled to get the offer, and it was obvious when he first played with the group that he fit right in. The octet, a classic New Orleans ensemble-oriented band, also featured clarinetist Johnny Dodds, trombonist Honore Dutrey, and Armstrong's future wife (his second of four), Lil Harden, on piano. Although at this early stage Armstrong was already a stronger player than Oliver, he went out of his way not to outshine his hero, happily playing second cornet. He made his earliest recordings with Oliver, having his most notable solo on "Chimes Blues."

In 1924 Lil Harden persuaded a reluctant Armstrong to leave Oliver and accept an offer to go to New York and join the Fletcher Henderson Orchestra. Henderson had the top big band of the period (along with Paul Whiteman), but in reality his group had not yet learned how to swing. Soloists such as tenor saxophonist Coleman Hawkins were great sight readers and played fancy lines, but their phrasing was square and their solos led nowhere. At Armstrong's first rehearsal with Henderson, the other musicians initially looked down on the cornetist due to his primitive clothes and rural manners. But as soon as he played, their opinions changed. Within a short period of time, arranger Don Redman was streamlining his charts for the orchestra and the other musicians were learning from Armstrong's phrasing and beginning to swing. Although Satch's playing remained a decade ahead of the other players, he had had a major impact and jazz would not be the same again.

Armstrong was with Henderson's orchestra from October 1924 until November 1925. During this time he began recording with blues singers (including Bessie Smith), playing backgrounds and short solos that uplifted many records. He also teamed up with soprano saxophonist Sidney Bechet (who had preceded him by a few months as the first major jazz soloist on records) with Clarence Williams' Blue Five, taking outstanding solos on several numbers, including a classic rendition of "Cake Walking Babies from Home."

Returning to Chicago, Armstrong (who switched permanently to trumpet in 1927) began to lead his own record dates, under the title of the Hot Five and (for a brief period in 1927) the Hot Seven. The impact was enormous, because although utilizing freewheeling New Orleans-style ensembles, these records also included many dramatic Armstrong solos. It is obvious that a soloist of this stature could not be confined to just a few short breaks or a chorus. If there is any doubt that he was the top soloist of the era, all listeners have to do is put on such masterpieces as "Cornet Chop Suey," "Wild Man Blues," "Potato Head Blues," and "Struttin' with Some Barbecue" for proof. The Hot Five match Armstrong with Kid Ory, clarinetist Johnny Dodds, his wife Lil on piano, and Johnny St. Cyr on banjo and guitar. Despite strong playing from his sidemen (particularly Dodds), it is the trumpeter who continually steals one's attention. In addition, Louis Armstrong the singer is heard for the first time on these recordings (he had only had one brief vocal before The Hot Five), and his scatting on "Heebies Jeebies" was unprecedented.

Ironically, the Hot Five (which became the Hot Seven when Pete Briggs on tuba and drummer Baby Dodds were added) did not exist outside of the recording studio, appearing in public only once. Armstrong's regular jobs were playing with Erskine Tate's Vendome Orchestra and Carroll Dickerson's big band. As the 1920s progressed, he became the biggest star in jazz, and the orchestras in which he appeared largely became a backdrop for his trumpet solos and singing.

One of the few musicians who was on Armstrong's level at the time was pianist Earl Hines, whose ability to suspend time and then jump back in without losing a beat (he had the trickiest left hand in jazz) remained exciting for decades. After the original Hot Five recordings ended, Armstrong began recording with his Savoy Ballroom Five in 1928, a sextet/septet that featured the trumpeter with Hines and drummer Zutty Singleton plus trombonist Fred Robinson, Jimmy Strong on clarinet and tenor, banjoist Mancy Cara, and sometimes Don Redman on alto. Armstrong was at his most advanced during this period, constantly challenging and being inspired by Hines. The magnificent "West End Blues" (with its stunning opening cadenza) remained Armstrong's personal favorite recording, and his duet with Hines on "Weatherbird" is quite thrilling.

In 1929, Louis Armstrong's career changed. He began fronting the Carroll Dickerson Orchestra (Armstrong would never again be a sideman) and he relocated to New York. He appeared in a featured role in the revue *Hot Chocolates* at the Hudson Theatre on Broadway, introducing Fats Waller's "Ain't Misbehavin'." His recordings during the next 18 years would mostly be with big bands, putting the emphasis almost entirely on the leader's trumpet and vocals. Armstrong began focusing on pop songs rather than New Orleans tunes, but that was not a bad change since many of the pop tunes tended to be superior and he turned everything into jazz anyway. Armstrong's mostly classic recordings of the early big band period followed a pattern, with his big band playing the melody and Louis taking a vocal and contributing a dramatic trumpet solo. He had already helped such songs as "Heebies Jeebies," "Muskrat Ramble," "Big Butter and Egg Man," "Struttin' with Some Barbecue," "Basin Street Blues," and "St. James Infirmary" become standards. During 1929–31, Armstrong helped introduce "Ain't Misbehavin'," "Black and Blue" (one of the first antiracism protest songs), "When You're Smiling," "Rockin' Chair," "I'm Confessin' That I Love You," "Body and Soul," "Lazy River," "Stardust," and his theme song, "Sleepy Time Down South."

Armstrong fronted Luis Russell's band for six months in 1930 and was in California for nine months during 1930–31, during which he led the Les Hite Orchestra. A marijuana bust resulted in a brief period in jail but did nothing to hurt his popularity; Armstrong happily smoked grass during his entire life. When he visited New Orleans in June 1931, he was given a hero's welcome. By the time he first visited Europe in July 1932, he was a major international star. Known originally as "Satchelmouth" (King Oliver had been "Dippermouth"), the nickname was shortened to "Satchmo" when a writer garbled Armstrong's name while he was visiting England.

Armstrong's 1932–33 recordings are generally not up to the level of his earlier work, due to using underrehearsed big bands and indifferent material, but his fame as an entertainer continued to grow. Having trouble with managers, Armstrong returned to Europe in 1933, staying overseas for 29 months, a period when he had only one recording session but did appear in his first performance film (playing classic versions of "I Cover the Waterfront" and "Dinah"). Trouble with his lips resulted in his mostly taking it easy during this period. By the time he returned to the United States and began recording for Decca on October 3, 1935, the swing era was under way and Benny Goodman was famous.

Although now identified with an earlier time, Satchmo remained a popular figure during the next decade, leading functional big bands (including for five years the former Luis Russell Orchestra) that mostly served as background for his playing and singing. He began appearing in movies (starting with 1936's *Pennies from Heaven*), toured constantly, and recorded a wide variety of material for Decca, some of it classic and some of it saved only by his trumpet solos. Although his fellow trumpeters still considered him their main inspiration, by the early 1940s Armstrong's music was in danger of slipping behind the times.

Starting with the January 1944 Esquire All-Stars concert, which featured him with an all-star combo that included Roy Eldridge, Coleman Hawkins, Jack Teagarden, and Art Tatum, and continuing through some V-disc recordings, the 1946 film *New Orleans,* and a Town Hall Concert in 1947, Satchmo was heard in small groups on an occasional basis. Reluctant to break up his big band (he hated to throw his sidemen out of work), he finally relented in 1947, forming the Louis Armstrong All-Stars. The sextet, which originally included trombonist Jack Teagarden, clarinetist Barney Bigard, pianist Dick Cary, bassist Arvell Shaw, and drummer Big Sid Catlett, was based in New Orleans Dixieland, mixing together older tunes with occasional new songs from the present. It proved to be the perfect outlet for Armstrong.

From mid-1947 until nearly the end of his life, Armstrong worked constantly with the All-Stars. While their studio recordings were generally quite rewarding (reaching high points in the mid-1950s with albums dedicated to the music of W. C. Handy and Fats Waller), their live performances became increasingly predictable through the years, with set solos and the same old jokes. However, Armstrong never lost his enthusiasm, and his trumpet playing was always full of beauty, even if many listeners knew what he was going to play beforehand. In 1948 Earl Hines joined the All-Stars for a few years. Hines eventually tired of the routines and was replaced by Billy Kyle. Teagarden was succeeded by the very reliable Trummy Young, while Bigard's departure had Edmond Hall taking his place. In reality it did not matter all that much who was in the band, because the leader was the main star and he got what he wanted from his players. Armstrong's records (some of which were with larger orchestras) always sold well, with his hits of the 1950s including "Blueberry Hill," "La Vie en Rose," "C'est Si Bon," and especially 1955's "Mack the Knife." He also collaborated on some delightful recordings with Ella Fitzgerald and appeared regularly in small roles in films, with his best spot of the era being his features in *The Five Pennies.*

Armstrong toured the world on a nearly nonstop basis and became known as the United States' goodwill ambassador. There were predictable complaints from civil rights advocates that Satchmo clowned around too much and was an "Uncle Tom," but those detractors did not fully appreciate the fact that Armstrong simply loved to perform and, even while making fun of himself and of life in general, he displayed genius any time he picked up his horn.

He also made a very public criticism of President Dwight Eisenhower in the late 1950s when Ike was slow in reacting to racist attacks against blacks in Little Rock, Arkansas.

Louis Armstrong never lost his popularity. In 1959 in Italy he had a heart attack but made a fast recovery and resumed his touring. As he aged in the 1960s, his range gradually shrank and he emphasized his singing even more than before. In 1964 he had his biggest hit in "Hello Dolly," a record that temporarily knocked the Beatles out of their number 1 slot on the best-selling charts. Armstrong appeared regularly on television, even after his health problems became worse in 1967. He had to stop playing trumpet altogether by 1969 but still appeared as a singer with his All-Stars. What was believed to have been his 70th birthday was celebrated in grand style at the Newport Jazz Festival in July 1970.

On July 6, 1971, at the age of 69, Louis Armstrong passed away. Even now, over 30 years after his death, he is still the most famous and influential of all jazz performers, an inspiration to trumpeters around the world.

Recommended CDs: *Vol. 5: Louis in New York* (Columbia/Legacy 46148), *Vol. 6: St. Louis Blues* (Columbia/Legacy 46996), *Vol. 7: You're Driving Me Crazy* (Columbia/Legacy 48828), *1934–1936* (Classics 509), *1936–1937* (Classics 512), *1937–1938* (Classics 515), *Satchmo at Symphony Hall* (GRP/Decca 661), *Louis Armstrong Plays W. C. Handy* (Columbia/Legacy 64925), *Louis Armstrong Plays Fats Waller* (Columbia/Legacy 64927), with King Oliver: *King Oliver's Creole Jazzband 1923–1924* (Retrieval 79007), with Fletcher Henderson: *1924–1925* (Classics), with Clarence Williams: *1924–1926* (Classics 695)

Box Sets: *Louis with Fletcher Henderson* (3 CDs; Forte 38001/2/3), *The Complete Hot Five and Hot Seven Recordings* (4 CDs; Columbia/Legacy 63527), which includes Vols. 1–4 of the Columbia/Legacy series, *Complete RCA Victor Recordings* (4 CDs; RCA 68682), *The California Concerts* (4 CDs; GRP/Decca 4-613)

LPs to Search For: *Hello Dolly!* (Kapp 573)

Recommended Reading: *An Extravagant Life* by Laureen Bergreen (Broadway Books, 1997), *The Best of Jazz* by Humphrey Lyttelton (Taplinger Publishing Co., 1982), *The Best of Jazz II* by Humphrey Lyttelton (Taplinger Publishing Co., 1982), *From Satchmo to Miles* by Leonard Feather (Da Capo Press, 1984), *In His Own Words* by Louis Armstrong, ed. by Thomas Brothey (Oxford University Press, 1999), *Jazz Masters of New Orleans* by Martin Williams (Macmillan Publishing Co., 1967), *Jazz Masters of the Twenties* by Richard Hadlock (Macmillan Publishing Co., 1965), *Jazz Masters of the Thirties* by Rex Stewart (Macmillan Publishing Co., 1972), *Louis Armstrong* by Hugues Panassie (Charles Scribner's Sons, 1971), *The Louis Armstrong Companion,* ed. by Joshua Berrett (Schirmer Books, 1999), *The Louis Armstrong Story 1900–1971* by Max Jones and John Chilton (Da Capo Press 1988), *My Life in New Orleans* by Louis Armstrong (Da Capo Press, 1954), *Satchmo* by Gary Giddins (Doubleday, 1988), *With Louis and the Duke* by Barney Bigard and Barry Martyn (Oxford University Press, 1988)

Film Appearances: *Pennies from Heaven* (1936), *Artists and Models* (1937), *Going Places* (1938), *Every Day's a Holiday* (1938), *Cabin in the Sky* (1942), *Jam Session* (1944), *Atlantic City* (1944), *Pillow to Post* (1945), *A Song Is Born* (1948), *Botte e Risposta* (1951), *Here Comes the Groom* (1951), *The Strip* (1951), *Glory Alley* (1952), *The Glenn Miller Story* (1953), *High Society* (1956), *Satchmo the Great* (1956), *Die Nacht vor Der Premiere* (1959), *The Beat Generation* (1959), *The*

Five Pennies (1959), *Kaerlighedens Melodi* (1959), *Auf Wiedersehn* (1961), *Paris Blues* (1961), *When the Boys Meet the Girls* (1965), *A Man Called Adam* (1966), *Hello Dolly!* (1969)

Videos to Get: *At the Jazz Band Ball* (1931 and 1934; Yazoo 514), *New Orleans* (1947; Kino Video), *Jazz on a Summer's Day* (1958; New Yorker Video 16590), *Jazz Festival Vol. 1* (1962; Storyville 6073)

FRANK ASSUNTO

• • • • • • • • • • • • • • •

b. Jan. 29, 1932, New Orleans, LA, d. Feb. 25, 1974, New Orleans, LA

F rank Assunto, one of the finest trad-style trumpeters of the 1950s and '60s, led the Dukes of Dixieland throughout most of his life. His father, Papa Jac Assunto (1905–85), played banjo and trombone, while his brother, Fred Assunto, (1929–66) was an excellent trombonist. In addition, two sisters grew up playing woodwinds.

In high school Frank led the Basin Street Four, Five, or Six (depending on how many musicians were needed), with Fred on trombone. In January 1949 the brothers formed the Dukes of Dixieland to play at a Horace Heidt talent show. After winning, the Dukes (under the temporary name of the Junior Dixie Band) toured with Heidt for a few weeks. They soon started working regularly in New Orleans, replacing Sharkey Bonano's band at the Famous Door for a very successful 44-month run that gave them their initial fame. The Dukes recorded for Band Wagon, Imperial, and Okeh during 1951–53. On a Vik album in 1955, the Assunto brothers were joined in the frontline by clarinetist Pete Fountain. Jac Assunto joined the band later that year on banjo and second trombone. The Dukes really caught on when they recorded 14 albums during 1956–59 for the Audio Fidelity label, including two in which they worked very well with Louis Armstrong (Assunto's idol). By then, they were one of the best-known Dixieland bands in the United States.

After clarinetist Jerry Fuller joined the Dukes in 1959, the group had its strongest lineup. They signed with Columbia in 1961 and started using fairly modern rhythm sections, which included pianist Gene Schroeder (formerly with Eddie Condon), Jim Hall or Herb Ellis on guitar, bassist Jim Atlas, and drummer Charlie Lodice. The Dukes' six records for Columbia during 1961–64 were the finest of their career. Assunto's solid lead, attractive sound, and exciting solos (along with his personable vocals) gave the band a lot of its personality and spirit.

Unfortunately Fred Assunto was stricken with cancer and had to drop out by 1965, passing away the following year at the age of 36. The Dukes' later records for Decca and Coral (1965–66), although not without interest, tend to be filled with overly brief (two- to three-minute) renditions of lightweight songs. There were no further recordings after 1966, but Frank Assunto kept the Dukes working for a time. However, by 1974 he too had cancer and passed away at the age of 42. Although the name of the Dukes of Dixieland is still used by a band of lesser interest, few recordings by the original Dukes have yet been reissued on CD, and Frank Assunto's joyful playing has not been heard much by today's listeners.

Recommended CDs: *The Dukes of Dixieland at Disneyland* (Columbia 11149)

HERMAN AUTREY

•••••••••••••••••

b. Dec. 4, 1904, Evergreen, AL, d. June 14, 1980, New York, NY

Herman Autrey is best known for his work as a key member of Fats Waller's Rhythm, taking short colorful solos on hundreds of recordings with the jovial pianist-singer.

Autrey's earliest musical experience, at age five, was playing his father's tuba whenever the elder Autrey was away from home! He studied alto horn when he was eight, switching permanently to trumpet when he was 13. After moving to Pittsburgh in 1923, Autrey spent the next decade played in theaters, for shows, and in territory bands, with long stops in Florida, Boston, Washington, D.C., and Philadelphia (including spending 1929–32 with Doc Hyder's band). In 1933 he joined Charlie Johnson's orchestra at Small's Paradise in New York and soon afterwards was discovered by Fats Waller.

As part of Waller's sextet and occasional big band during 1934–39 and 1941–42, Autrey recorded over 200 selections and worked steadily. His trumpet and usually Gene Sedric's clarinet and tenor served as props behind the exuberant Waller's vocals, acting as foils to Fats' interjections. Autrey was on nearly all of the pianist's important Victor records of the era, and his trumpet was a major part of the Rhythm's sound. He proved quite adept at coming up with something meaningful to say not only on superior Waller compositions but such potential dribble as "My Very Good Friend the Milkman," "Us on a Bus," "You Meet the Nicest People in Your Dreams," "Cash for Your Trash," and "The Girl I Left Behind Me"!

When Fats Waller was hired for solo tours or guested in films, Herman Autrey freelanced, including playing trumpet with Fletcher Henderson's commercially unsuccessful orchestra in 1935 and gigging with Luis Russell and Claude Hopkins (1938 and 1940). The trumpeter appears with Waller in a few Soundie shorts in the early 1940s. Autrey permanently left Waller in 1942 (a year before the pianist's death), playing regularly with violinist Stuff Smith, having a record date as a leader (four little-known titles for Sapphire) in 1946, leading his own band on the West Coast, and touring Canada in the late 1940s.

Most of Autrey's post-Waller years were spent playing at low-profile jobs. A serious car accident in 1954 put him out of action for much of a year, but he made a complete comeback. During 1965–69 Autrey was part of pianist Red Richards' group the Saints and Sinners, recording several albums with the band and touring Europe in 1968 and '69. As age took its toll in the 1970s, Autrey (who recorded a few titles as late as 1973 for French RCA) emphasized his singing; he retired altogether in the mid-1970s.

Even though he outlived Fats Waller by 37 years, Herman Autrey's name will always be linked with the immortal Waller.

Recommended CDs: with Fats Waller: *The Early Years, Part 1* (Bluebird 66618), *The Early Years, Part 2* (Bluebird 66640), *The Early Years, Part 3* (RCA 66747), *The Middle Years, Part 1* (Bluebird 66083), *The Middle Years, Part 2* (Bluebird 66552), *The Last Years* (Bluebird 9883)

DONALD AYLER

••••••••••••••

b. Oct. 5, 1942, Cleveland, OH

The younger brother of tenor saxophonist Albert Ayler, Donald Ayler was a major asset to his sibling's career during its prime. He attended the Cleveland Institute and gigged locally, including with saxophonist Charles Tyler. During 1965–68 he was part of his brother's group, often adding primitive marching-band style trumpet to the very free yet strangely melodic ensembles. The Aylers during this era managed to look back toward the beginnings of jazz (sounding at times like a spaced-out New Orleans band from 1905) even while they were creating startling new music that stretched the boundaries of jazz with sound explorations.

In 1968, the brothers split up and Donald moved back to Cleveland and slipped into obscurity. Since Albert's mysterious death in 1970 (he was discovered drowned in New York's East River), almost nothing has been heard from Donald Ayler other than his recording of three LPs for the Frame label in Italy in 1981 (the only sessions he ever led) and rumors that he had begun to play saxophone.

Recommended CDs: with Albert Ayler: *Spirits Rejoice* (ESP 1020), *At Slug's Saloon,* Vols. 1–2 (ESP 3031 and 3032), *Live at Lorrach: Paris, 1966* (Hat Musics 3500), *Live in Greenwich Village* (Impulse 2-273)

BENNY BAILEY

••••••••••••••

b. Aug. 13, 1925, Cleveland, OH

It is ironic that Benny Bailey's best-known solos are on the famous Eddie Harris/Les McCann *Swiss Movement* album, because he has since stated that he did not care for McCann's brand of funky jazz! Bailey's explosive spots on "Cold Duck Time" and "Compared to What" (which are now also available on video) will probably be what he is most remembered for, although he has been a fine trumpeter for over 50 years.

Born Ernest Harold Bailey, he studied piano and flute early on before switching to trumpet. After attending the Cleveland Conservatory of Music, Bailey worked in the 1940s with Bull Moose Jackson, Scatman Crothers, and Jay McShann. He played with Teddy Edwards and the Dizzy Gillespie big band (1947–48) and then gained some recognition as an important member of the Lionel Hampton Orchestra (1948–53). Bailey left Hampton during a European tour, becoming an expatriate.

Because he has spent so much time in Europe, Bailey has been overlooked in the United States, but he has been quite active during his many years overseas. He spent a long period in Sweden, worked with Harry Arnold's big band (1957–59), recorded with Stan Getz, and joined Quincy Jones (who composed and recorded "Meet Benny Bailey") during his European tour of 1959. In 1960 Bailey returned to the United States long enough to record a classic album for Candid, *Big Brass.* He then settled permanently in Amsterdam. Bailey recorded with Eric Dolphy (1961), was a soloist with the Kenny Clarke-Francy Boland Big Band, toured with George Gruntz's Concert Jazz Band, and in 1986 was a member of the Paris Reunion band. Through the years he has recorded as a leader for many European labels, including Sonet, Metronome, Saba, Freedom, Enja, Ego, Jazzcraft, Hot House, Gemini, and Mons, and has appeared as a sideman on many records. But despite all of these accomplishments, Benny Bailey's fiery trumpet solo on "Cold Duck Time" (from the 1968 Montreux Jazz Festival) remains his main claim to fame.

Recommended CDs: *Big Brass* (Candid 9011), *Grand Slam* (Storyville 8271), *The Satchmo Legacy* (Enja 9407), with Eric Dolphy: *Berlin Concerts* (Enja 3007), with Eddie Harris and Les McCann: *Swiss Movement* (Rhino 72452), with Phil Woods: *Right of Swing* (Candid 79016)

Videos to Get: with Les McCann and Eddie Harris: *Swiss Movement* (1968; Rhino Home Video 2258), *Gil Evans and His Orchestra* (1987; View Video)

CHET BAKER

. . . .

b. Dec. 23, 1929, Yale, OK, d. May 13, 1988, Amsterdam, Netherlands

Chet Baker has long been a major cult figure, a situation that did not start with his mysterious death but was actually true throughout much of his career. He was an example of a charismatic artist who had a potentially charmed life, threw it all away, and then succeeded on his own odd terms. Famous in the 1950s for his cool-toned trumpet solos, vulnerable vocals, and movie star looks, Baker by the 1980s looked quite decrepit and his vocal abilities had greatly declined. But, remarkably enough, his trumpet playing (which was largely intuitive) on his better days was stronger than ever.

Baker was born in Oklahoma (where his father, Chet Baker Sr., at one time had played guitar with country groups) and moved with his family to the Los Angeles area when he was ten. He sang in church choirs before ever playing music. His father hoped that he would play trombone. But, since his arms were too short for the instrument when he was 13, Baker took up the trumpet instead. He played in school bands, before dropping out of school at age 16 in 1946 to enlist in the Army, saying that he was 17. Baker had an opportunity to pick up musical experience playing in an Army band while stationed in Germany. After his discharge, he spent 1948–50 living in Los Angeles, occasionally sitting in at jam sessions. Baker returned to the Army in 1950 but after a year was transferred to the Arizona desert, grew frustrated with the slow lifestyle, and deserted. After much wrangling, he was able to get a general discharge and return home.

The trumpeter's musical career really began in 1952 when he appeared at local jam sessions and began to gain some notice. Baker won an audition to play with Charlie Parker, who was visiting Los Angeles, and his earliest recording is a live set with Bird. When baritonist Gerry Mulligan decided to form a quartet (which would end up being pianoless), he picked Baker as his trumpeter, and the combination was quite magical. Chet's soft sound, emphasis on the middle register of his horn, and lyrical style (which epitomized cool jazz) matched perfectly with Mulligan's light tone and ability to instantly harmonize. Within a short time, they were playing regularly at the Haig in Los Angeles and recording for Pacific Jazz, a label that was originally formed specifically to document the popular band. The Mulligan Quartet rendition of

Although his physical appearance would evolve from a movie star to a derelict, Chet Baker's trumpet playing was actually at its prime during his last years.

"My Funny Valentine" was a hit (becoming a trademark song for Baker) and the group seemed to have a limitless future.

Unfortunately Mulligan was busted for heroin possession in June 1953, and he served several months in jail. The group became history when, after Mulligan's release, Baker asked for more money than the baritonist thought he was worth. There would only be two brief reunions by the duo; otherwise their musical partnership was over. However, Baker, after a brief period using Stan Getz in Mulligan's place, put together his own quartet, which co-starred pianist Russ Freeman. During that group's two years, Baker began winning *Down-*

beat and *Metronome* polls as jazz's top trumpeter, awards that embarrassed him, since he felt they belonged to Dizzy Gillespie. He began to sing in his little-boy voice (which sometimes sounded eerily close to that of the deep-toned female vocalist Chris Connor), and the vulnerability of his interpretations added to his popularity and mystique. Baker went on an extensive tour of Europe during 1955–56, one that found his promising young pianist, Dick Twardzik, dying from a drug overdose. Despite the horrors encountered by Mulligan, Twardzik, and Charlie Parker (who had passed away in 1955), Baker began using drugs himself after he returned to the United States. He would be an unapologetic heroin addict throughout most of the rest of his life.

Considered for a major part in a Hollywood film, Baker lost that opportunity when he was busted for drugs. After two months in prison, the trumpeter decided to go back overseas. In the autumn of 1959 he moved to Italy, remaining in Europe until 1964, playing quite well at times but also spending time in an Italian prison (1961–62). Baker was also tossed out of Germany (1962) after he was busted again. When he returned to the United States in 1964, at first it was thought of as a comeback, but Baker had many difficult years ahead. He recorded five very good records (on flugelhorn) for Prestige during a three-day period in 1965, leading a quintet that included George Coleman and Kirk Lightsey. But after that, Baker made a series of remarkably commercial and wretched World Pacific albums in which he was often joined by the Mariachi Brass (a low-level imitation of the Tijuana Brass), playing instantly dated pop tunes. On July 25, 1966, Baker was beaten up by drug dealers and had his teeth knocked out. For the next couple of years he kept on making inferior record dates (*Albert's House,* from 1968, was the worst) before retiring altogether. His career seemed over even though he was still just 39.

However, Chet Baker made a near-miraculous comeback. After he was outfitted with dentures, it took him three years to get his trumpet chops to the level that he wanted. When Dizzy Gillespie heard that Baker was playing again in 1973, he arranged for him to play an engagement at the Half Note in New York. From that point on, Chet was back. He had a reunion with Mulligan for a recorded concert in 1974, and his playing improved year by year. Baker moved to Europe in 1975 but returned to the United States on an occasional basis during the next dozen years. He had an odd lifestyle, for Baker was essentially homeless, living the life of a nomad yet playing regularly and seeming to record nearly every week, particularly during the 1980s. When he was inspired, Baker was at the peak of his powers (instrumentally if not vocally). But because there are so many late-period records by the trumpeter, listeners have to be a bit careful before purchasing every bootleg Baker album!

Chet Baker's end was quite ironic for a musician who lived on the edge and never gave up drugs. After playing a particularly rewarding concert (which would be his last recordings) with the NDR Big Band and Hannover Radio Orchestra on April 28, 1988, Baker had a few other gigs in Europe. In the early hours of May 13, he fell out of the second-story window of his hotel room in Amsterdam. Was he pushed, or did he stumble? That mystery has never been solved.

Chet Baker has been far from forgotten since his demise. His truncated memoirs, *As Though I Had Wings* (which cuts off in the early 1960s), have been published, countless recordings have been released (including two Mosaic LP box sets documenting the quartet with Russ Freeman), and *Let's Get Lost* (a very erratic film that depicts him as a washed-up singer rather than as a top trumpeter) played for a time in movie theaters. A uniquely American antihero, Chet Baker succeeded in living out his strange life without any compromises, creating some special music along the way.

Recommended CDs: *The Chet Baker Quartet with Russ Freeman* (Pacific Jazz 93164), *Grey December* (Pacific Jazz 97160), *Chet in Paris, Vol. 1* (Emarcy 837 474), *Chet in Paris, Vol. 2* (Emarcy 837 475), *The Route* (Pacific Jazz 92931), *The Italian Sessions* (Bluebird 2001), *Lonely Star* (Prestige 24172), *Live at Nick's* (Criss Cross 1027), *Chet's Choice* (Criss Cross 1016), *The Last Great Concert* (Enja 79650), with Gerry Mulligan: *The Original Quartet with Chet Baker* (Pacific Jazz 94407)

Box Set: *The Pacific Jazz Years* (Pacific Jazz 89292)

Recommended Reading: *As Though I Had Wings* by Chet Baker (St. Martin's Press, 1997)

Film Appearances: *Hell's Horizon* (1955), *Stolen Hours* (1963)

CLINT BAKER

* * * * * * * * * * * * *

b. Jan. 27, 1971, Mountain View, CA

Clint Baker, who plays New Orleans classic and revivalist jazz, is skilled not only on cornet but on trombone, alto sax, guitar, banjo, bass, tuba, and drums! On cornet his style tends to be primitive, influenced to an extent by Bunk Johnson and Kid Thomas Valentine. Baker, who started on trombone and tuba, discovered trad jazz and swing while listening to radio station KMPX in San Francisco. With the assistance of his grandfather, he bought a cornet for $40 and was largely self-taught. Baker credits Jim Borkenhagen with teaching him how to play New Orleans style, and he was encouraged along the way by Leon Oakley and Percy Humphrey. Although he took some music courses at a community college, he soon dropped out to lead his own band. "I started playing in the Zenith Jazz Band at 17 and knew then that that's what I wanted to do with my life."

Baker, who has been leading bands on and off since he was 13, has played with Jim Cullum, Caparone's Elysian Fields Orchestra, the Boilermaker Jazz Band, the New Orleans Rascals, Tom Sharpesteen, John Gill, Rebecca Kilgore, and Hal Smith's Roadrunners, among others, on various instruments. He appeared with his band (playing trombone) at the 1999 Monterey Jazz Festival and has performed in Europe and Japan. Baker cites as his own favorite recorded trumpet solo his spot on "Black Snake Blues," included on 1998's *Going Huge*. Referring to himself modestly as "a craftsman of music," Clint Baker is proudest of his ability to teach students about traditional jazz.

HAROLD "SHORTY" BAKER

b. May 26, 1914, St. Louis, MO, d. Nov. 8, 1966, New York, NY

Shorty Baker's mellow sound and lyrical style made him a natural successor to Arthur Whetsol with Duke Ellington's orchestra, playing "Mr. Cool" to the hotter solos of Ray Nance and Clark Terry. He tended to say the most with the fewest notes, setting a dreamy atmosphere with his haunting sound.

Baker started out on drums, switching to trumpet as a teenager. He picked up important early experience on the riverboats with Fate Marable and with the big bands of Erskine Tate, Eddie Johnson's Crackerjacks (1932–33), and Don Redman (1936–38), getting some important solo space while with the orchestras of Teddy Wilson (1939–40) and Andy Kirk (1940–42). While with Kirk, Baker met and married pianist Mary Lou Williams; they briefly co-led a sextet in 1942.

Baker spent several productive periods with Duke Ellington's orchestra, starting with a few months in 1938 and more importantly the 1943–51 years (other then spending part of 1944–46 in the military). In addition to his many sessions with Ellington (where his cool tone was well utilized), he was featured on a record date with Erskine Butterfield in 1946. After leaving Duke, Baker freelanced during 1952–57, including spending periods playing regularly with Teddy Wilson, Ben Webster, and Johnny Hodges (1954–55). Baker was back with Ellington for a third time during 1957–59. After departing once again (he returned to record Duke's *All American in Jazz* in 1962), the mellow trumpeter recorded with Bud Freeman and Doc Cheatham; he also led an album for King (1958), along with three selections for Camden (1959). In his later years, Shorty Baker led a quartet at the Metropole and the Embers (following in the tradition of Jonah Jones), before bad health forced his permanent retirement in 1964.

Recommended CDs: with Doc Cheatham: *Shorty and Doc* (Original Jazz Classics 839), with Duke Ellington: *Cornell University Concert* (Music Masters 65114)

LPs to Search For: *Bud Freeman All-Stars* (Original Jazz Classics 183)

Recommended Reading: *The World of Duke Ellington* by Stanley Dance (Charles Scribner's Sons, 1970)

Videos to Get: with Duke Ellington: *Jazz Festival, Vol. 2* (1962; Storyville 6074)

KENNY BAKER

b. Mar. 1, 1921, Withernsea, E. Yorkshire, England, d. Dec. 7, 1999, London, England

One of England's top jazz trumpeters of the 1940s and '50s, Kenny Baker was probably best known for his work as both lead trumpeter and main soloist with Ted Heath's orchestra during the second half of the 1940s. His father played saxophone and clarinet. Baker started off on the piano (getting lessons from his mother at the age of 12) and for brief periods played violin, saxophone, accordion, and tenor horn before switching to cornet (later trumpet) when he was 14. "My mother was quite determined that I should go into the music profession. There were no music schools in my youth, but I learned a lot playing in local orchestras." Baker, who listed his trumpet heroes as Louis Armstrong, Bix Beiderbecke, Bunny Berigan, and (in later years) Harry James and Dizzy Gillespie, played in local brass bands (including the West Hull Silver Band), with Manley's orchestra, and drummer Les Watson, and went on two tours with comedian Sandy Powell. In 1939 he settled in London, where he worked with the orchestras of Lew Stone, Jack Hylton, Ambrose, and George Chisholm. In addition, he served in the Royal Air Force (where he was fortunate enough to be in a military band) during 1942–44. He also had opportunities to play with visiting Americans in jam sessions.

After being discharged from the RAF, Baker became one of the stars with Ted Heath's new orchestra (1944–49), leading the ensembles, taking hot solos, and contributing many arrangements; his most famous feature was "Bakerloo Non-Stop." After leaving Heath, Baker became a busy studio musician (working in radio, television, and films) in addition to heading his own jazz group. "The most important highlight in my career was the radio program called *Let's Settle for Music,* which ran for eight years." The trumpeter's band (Baker's Dozen) was featured regularly on that popular program from April 1952 to the end of 1958, which made his name a household word in England. He also led a smaller band titled Baker's Half Dozen!

After the radio series ended, Kenny Baker stayed busy in the studios and with jazz projects, including playing with the Jack Parnell band in the early 1960s, recording with Benny Goodman (1969), making records with trombonist George Chisholm (1971 and 1973), guesting with the Ted Heath ghost orchestra, and recreating Harry James' sound for a 1976 project. In the 1980s Baker played the cornet for a successful British TV series (*The Beiderbecke Affair*) and was involved in a 15-CD project in which he recreated the solos of Louis Armstrong. Throughout his career, Baker led occasional record dates, including for Oriole (1946), Parlophone (1951–54), Polygon (1955), Nixa (1955–58), Columbia (1959), Decca (1968), and 77 (1974); his personal favorite was *After Hours,* a 1955 set with pianist Dill Jones.

Kenny Baker led a revived Baker's Dozen during his last years and stayed active until the end of his life. Although his fame rarely spread beyond England, his recordings still sound fresh and lively today.

LPs to Search For: *After Hours* (Polygon JTL4), *The Kenny Baker Half Dozen* (Nixa 10), *Baker's Jam* ('77' 56)

Film Appearances: *The Small Back Room* (1948)

KENNY BALL
● ● ● ● ● ● ● ● ● ● ● ●

b. May 22, 1930, Ilford, Essex, England

Kenny Ball's 1961 hit recording of "Midnight in Moscow" put him permanently in the jazz history books, but he has actually had a long career leading a trad/Dixieland band in England. Ball started on trumpet when he was 15, was introduced to jazz through the Ilford Rhythm Club, and played with the groups of Charlie Galbraith (1949–53), Eric Delaney (1953–54), Sid Phillips (1954–57), and Terry Lightfoot (1957–58).

Ball led his first record date in October 1957, formed his band in November 1958, and rode to fame during England's trad craze. In 1961 he had hit records in "Samantha" and "Midnight in Moscow," following them up with 1962's "So Do I." With trombonist John Bennett, clarinetist Dave Jones, pianist Ron Weatherburn, banjoist-singer Paddy Lightfoot, bassist Vic Pitt, and drummer Ron Bowden, Ball (who was also a jubilant singer) had stable personnel during 1961–67, recording regularly for Pye. Even after the trad fad ended with the rise of the Beatles and rock music, Ball was able to work regularly. He is particularly proud of getting to play with a visiting Louis Armstrong in 1969 and leading the first English band to tour the Soviet Union in 1984, naming as his personal favorite album 1968's *Ball in Berlin* (released by Fontana).

Kenny Ball is still quite active and a popular name in England as he enters his seventies, playing the Dixieland-oriented music that he loves most.

Recommended CDs: *Kenny Ball Now* (Jazzology 305), *Kenny Ball Now 2* (Jazzology 325), *Kenny Ball Now 3* (Jazzology 335)

Recommended LPs: *Midnight in Moscow* (Kapp 3276), *Recorded Live* (Kapp 3285), *Recorded Live* (Kapp 3294), *More* (Kapp 3314), *In Concert in the U.S.A., Vols. 1–2* (Jazzology 65 and 66)

Film Appearances: *It's Trad Dad!* (1962), *Live It Up* (1963)

AIME BARELLI
. . . .

b. Mar. 1, 1917, Loda, France, d. July 13, 1995, Monaco

Considered by many at the time to be France's top jazz trumpeter of the 1940s and '50s, Aime Barelli is virtually unknown in the United States. Mostly self-taught, Barelli started working in Paris in 1940 with the bands of Raymond Legrand, Fred Adison, Raymond Wraskoff, Hubert Rostaing, Alix Combelle, Maceo Jefferson, and Andre Ekyan. Barelli led record dates for the Swing label during 1940–43 in what must have been arduous circumstances under the German occupation. He headed a nonet during 1943–46 that recorded for Pathe and consisted of his trumpet, four (and later five) saxophones, and a rhythm section. Unfortunately those intriguing swing-oriented sides have yet to be issued in the United States.

Barelli fared well in recorded jam sessions with Dizzy Gillespie (1948), Charlie Parker (1949), Sidney Bechet (1949), and Django Reinhardt (1952). He recorded steadily as a bandleader in Paris for the Pathe label through 1958 (sticking to swing and dance music) and worked as a bandleader in Monte Carlo for many years, starting in 1966. But a logical reissue of Aime Barelli's most significant recordings has not yet happened, and he remains a shadowy figure in jazz history.

GUY BARKER

• • • • • • • • • • • •

b. Dec. 26, 1957, London, England

One of the most versatile trumpeters around, Guy Barker can play anything from Bix Beiderbecke songs to free jazz with equal creativity, although he generally performs hard bop. Barker gained his early experience playing in school brass bands in his native England and with the National Youth Jazz Orchestra starting when he was 13. After studying at the Royal College of Music, he worked with many of the top British jazz musicians, including John Dankworth, Mike Westbrook, Chris Hunter, and Clark Tracey. In addition, when Gil Evans led a British band, Barker was part of it, and he was flexible enough to be part of Ornette Coleman's Skies of America tour, perform with Carla Bley, and play hot 1920s dance music with pianist Keith Nichols.

Guy Barker has worked frequently through the years with pianist Stan Tracey, backed many pop singers, done studio work, and often led his own ensembles. He has recorded as a leader for Miles Music (1989's Holly J), Verve, Portraits Plus, and Spotlite.

Recommended CD: *Isn't It* (Spotlite 545), with Tommy Smith: *Beasts of Scotland* (Honest 5054)

BOB BARNARD

• • • • • • • • • • • •

b. Nov. 24, 1933, Melbourne, Australia

One of the top Dixieland/mainstream trumpeters from Australia, Bob Barnard has been on many records through the years and is an important part of the rich Australian trad jazz tradition. "My mother and father had a dance band, so music was always played at home. The radio stations in those days (during the war) were playing the 'hits,' including many associated with jazz. At age 11 I had private lessons on the trumpet and joined the local brass band. A little after that, I joined the family dance band." Barnard, who considers his main influences to be Louis Armstrong, Jack Teagarden, and Bobby Hackett, played with the band of his older brother, drummer Len Barnard, during 1947–55. He made his recording debut with his brother in 1949 and recorded on and off with Len's groups into the 1970s.

Bob Barnard freelanced with some of Australian's best trad musicians and in 1962 moved to Sydney. He played with Graeme Bell (1962–67), worked as a studio musician (1967–77), recorded a lot with Don Burrows and John Sangster, and gigged with pianist Ralph Sutton, clarinetist Peanuts Hucko, and tenor saxophonist Bud Freeman, among others. Since forming his own band in 1974, Barnard has frequently toured North America, Europe, India, and Asia, appearing in the United States at many classic jazz festivals and jazz parties. Barnard, who first recorded as a leader in 1952 (a few titles for the Jazz Heritage label), has been documented fairly frequently since 1971, including for the Axis, Ata, Swaggie, Bix Lives, ABC, Calligraph, and Sackville labels. His favorite personal records through the years include *Music to Midnight* (a date with strings), *Partners in Crime* (with Ralph Sutton and Milt Hinton), *The Hobbit Suite*, *The International Set* (with pianist Dick Wellstood), and *The Lord of the Rings*.

"When I am not playing, I'm thinking of what I could be playing! I believe it is still possible to invent and play new phrases on the changes of a normal standard song. Because of this, I have never felt the desire to investigate modern or 'far out' music. Maybe one day I will."

Recommended CDs: *New York Notes* (Sackville 3061), *What's New* (Sackville 3064), with Ralph Sutton: *Partners in Crime* (Sackville 2023)

LPs to Search For: *Bob Barnard and Friends* (Swaggie 1374)

SCOTTY BARNHART
. . . .

b. Oct. 27, 1964, Atlanta, GA

William "Scotty" Barnhart is a powerful trumpeter who has been a fixture with the Count Basie Orchestra since 1993. "I started playing the trumpet at age nine. I originally wanted to play violin, just to be in the band like the rest of the kids. But when my mother went to the store to get the violin, the line was long with all of the other parents, so she went next door and brought a trumpet home for me instead. When I opened the case and saw a brand new shiny silver horn, I was hooked." Barnhart had a dental mishap at one point as a child and, when he could not play the trumpet for nine months, he learned a bit of piano and became more focused as a musician. He gained a degree in music education from Florida A&M and knew that he wanted to be a professional trumpeter by the time he was 16.

For Scotty Barnhart, the turning point was when he joined Marcus Roberts' band in 1989, an association that gave him some recognition. After freelancing, in 1993 he became a member of the Count Basie orchestra, where he gets occasional solos and travels the globe. "We play everywhere and are respected as the best big band in the world. To know that I have contributed to this fact is enormously gratifying." As of this writing, Scotty Barnhart was looking forward to completing his first solo album and to continuing his association with the Basie band, always "playing what the music tells me to play."

Recommended CDs: with Count Basie Orchestra: *Count Plays Duke* (MAMA 1024), *Swing Shift* (MAMA 1027), with Marcus Roberts: *Deep in the Shed* (Novus 3076), *As Serenity Approaches* (Novus 3130)

DARREN BARRETT
. . . .

b. June 19, 1967, Manchester, England

A fine trumpeter who began to emerge in the late 1990s, Darren Barrett has great potential for the future. Barrett, whose father played alto sax, grew up in Toronto, Canada. He studied at Berklee (graduating in 1990), Queens College (where one of his most important teachers was Donald Byrd), and the New England Conservatory. A strong hard bop-oriented trumpeter, Barrett was a key member of the Antonio Hart Quintet (1990–95). He has also played with Slide Hampton's Jazzmasters (1993), Roy Hargrove's 1995 big band, Greg Tardy,

Jackie McLean (1998), Robin Eubanks, Steve Turre, and Marcus Miller. Darren Barrett won first place in the 1997 Thelonious Monk trumpet competition and recorded his debut as a leader in 1999, *First One Up*.

Recommended CDs: *First One Up* (J Curve 1006), with Barbara Dennerlein: *Outhipped* (Verve 314 547 503), with Antonio Hart: *Don't You Know I Care* (Novus 63142), *For Cannonball and Woody* (Novus 63162), *It's All Good* (Novus 63183)

DUD BASCOMB
• • • • • • • • • • • • • •

b. May 16, 1916, Birmingham, AL, d. Dec. 25, 1972, New York, NY

Throughout much of his life, Wilbur "Dud" Bascomb was in the odd position of having his most famous trumpet solos attributed to someone else. Because Bascomb was a major part of Erskine Hawkins' popular orchestra, and the trumpet-playing leader was billed as "The 20th Century Gabriel," Dud's medium-register and occasionally muted statements (which contrasted well with Hawkins' high-note displays) were assumed by most listeners of the time as being by the bandleader. However, Dizzy Gillespie has cited Bascomb as an important early influence.

Dud was the youngest of ten children, including his brother Paul Bascomb, a tenor saxophonist; their father played drums and their mother was a pianist. Both brothers were part of the Alabama State Teachers College band (the 'Bama State Collegians) from an early age. Dud was still in high school in 1932 when he first joined the orchestra. The members of the group in 1934 quit school, and in time the band would be renamed the Erskine Hawkins Orchestra. Bascomb was a major part of the big band until 1944. His solo on "Tuxedo Junction" (Hawkins' version predated Glenn Miller's) was well known, although it was often thought of as being by the leader. Bascomb was on scores of records with the orchestra, including "Lucky Seven," "Midnight Stroll," "Bear Mash Blues," "Gin Mill Special," and many others that featured his short but effective statements.

In 1944 Dud Bascomb was persuaded by brother Paul to leave Hawkins and co-lead a sextet that in time grew into a moderately successful 15-piece big band. In 1947 the trumpeter was with Duke Ellington for a short time. He spent most of the next 15 years leading his own combos. In the 1960s Bascomb (whose son Dud Bascomb Jr. became a professional bassist) often worked in the studios, and he also toured with Sam "the Man" Taylor (with whom he visited Japan three times) and Buddy Tate. In addition, Bascomb worked in pit orchestras of Broadway shows and appeared on some soundtracks.

It seems only fitting that Dud Bascomb's last recording was an excellent reunion date with Erskine Hawkins in 1971, one in which the solo credits were not listed!

Recommended CDs: with Erskine Hawkins: *The Original Tuxedo Junction* (Bluebird 9682)

LPs to Search For: *Tuxedo Junction* (Savoy 1161), with Erskine Hawkins: *Live at Club Soul Sound* (Chess 9141)

Recommended Reading: *The World of Swing* by Stanley Dance (Charles Scribner's Sons, 1974)

GUIDO BASSO

• • • • • • • • • • • • •

b. Sept. 27, 1937, Montreal, Quebec, Canada

A fixture with Rob McConnell's Boss Brass since its beginning, Guido Basso is a cool-toned boppish trumpeter and flugelhornist with an appealing tone. He was originally considered a child prodigy on trumpet and studied early on at the Conservatoire de Musique de Montreal. Basso played in dance bands as a teenager, worked with Louie Bellson, and toured as part of Pearl Bailey's backup band during 1957–60. After moving to Toronto in 1960, he became a busy studio musician, which he still is. Guido Basso is on virtually all of the recordings by Rob McConnell's Boss Brass (usually taking one or two solos per disc), but he is heard at his best on his two CDs listed next.

Recommended CDs: *Guido Basso* (Innovation 0014), *Midnight Martini* (Justin Time 8471), with Rob McConnell: *Rob McConnell Tentet* (Justin Time 150)

MARIO BAUZA

• • • • • • • • • • • • •

b. Apr. 28, 1911, Havana, Cuba, d. July 11, 1993, New York, NY

Although never a major trumpet soloist, Mario Bauza was quite important to jazz history. On three different occasions he introduced people who would collaborate to make very significant music. A talented musician from an early age, Bauza began studying music when he was five and was already attending the Municipal Academy in Havana two years later, playing reeds. He played clarinet with the Havana Philharmonic when he was nine and became a regular member of the orchestra three years later on bass clarinet.

Bauza first discovered jazz when he visited New York in 1926 as part of pianist Antonio Maria Romeu's orchestra, making his recording debut with the band. Back in Havana, he graduated from the Municipal Conservatory in 1927 and played with Los Jovenes Rendencion, a group that also included Machito as a vocalist. In 1930 Bauza moved permanently to the United States. By chance he was on the same ship that carried Don Azpiazu's Havana Casino Orchestra (one of the first Cuban bands to play jazz), an ensemble that included singer Antonio Machin. When Machin left Azpiazu shortly after, he offered Bauza a job with his quartet if he would switch to trumpet. The 19-year-old Bauza was so inspired that he learned to play the instrument in just two weeks! He recorded quite frequently with Machin during the first half of the 1930s and worked with Cuban trumpeter Vicente Sigler, Noble Sissle (playing saxophone with the singer's big band during 1931–32), and Hi Clark's Missourians at the Savoy Ballroom. Bauza switched permanently to trumpet when he was hired to play lead with Chick Webb's orchestra (1933–38), where he had the distinction of introducing Webb to Ella Fitzgerald, convincing the drummer to give the inexperienced singer a chance. After leaving Webb, Bauza played with Don Redman's orchestra (1938–39) and with Cab Calloway (1939–40). While with Cab, one night Bauza pretended to be ill when Dizzy Gillespie was in the house so that Dizzy would be called on to substitute for him and Calloway could have the opportunity to hear the young trumpeter; Gillespie was promptly hired.

In January 1941 Mario Bauza joined Machito's Afro-Cubans as musical director, and he soon made the orchestra more jazz-oriented, transforming it into the very first Afro-Cuban jazz band. In fact, Bauza can be thought of as the unofficial founder of Afro-Cuban jazz. In 1943, when Machito was temporarily in the military, Bauza headed the Afro-Cubans for a few months, writing "Tanga," which is considered one of the first successful fusions of Cuban rhythms with jazz. A few years later his "Mambo Inn" became a standard. In 1947, when Dizzy Gillespie (who enjoyed Machito's music) mentioned to Bauza that he would like to add a percussionist, Bauza introduced Gillespie to conguero Chano Pozo, a very significant event in the history of Latin jazz.

Mario Bauza was Machito's musical director for 34 years, up until 1975. He rarely soloed (and gave up playing trumpet altogether in the 1970s), but his influence was felt throughout the band's history as he worked to integrate jazz soloists with Cuban rhythms and repertoire. A dispute over a proposed European tour led Bauza to leave Machito and go out on his own; they would have a reconciliation years later. Bauza freelanced as an arranger, led albums in 1977 and 1986, commissioned Chico O'Farrill to develop "Tanga" into the four-movement "Tanga Suite," and during his last years headed his own orchestra. Mario Bauza's Afro-Cuban Jazz Concert Orchestra recorded three excellent albums for Messidor, a final accomplishment for Bauza before his death from cancer at the age of 82.

Recommended CDs: *The Tanga Suite* (Messidor 15819), *My Time Is Now* (Messidor 15824), *944 Columbus* (Messidor 15828)

JEFF BEAL
• • • • • • • • • •

b. June 20, 1963, Hayward, CA

A cool-toned trumpeter and flugelhornist, Jeff Beal is also a very inventive arranger-composer and an underrated pianist. He began on trumpet when he was eight and was introduced to jazz by his grandmother, who gave him Miles Davis' *Sketches of Spain* album when he was ten. Beal earned a degree from the Eastman School of Music (1981–85), a period of time when he won 11 *Downbeat* awards (a record) for trumpet, jazz composition, and arranging.

Relocating to New York in 1985, Beal worked in Latin bands and recorded his own music (including the performances that resulted in the Antilles album *Liberation*) at a studio that he purchased. In 1992 Beal moved to Los Angeles, where he has worked on film scores. He excels both in acoustic formats and in utilizing electronics. In addition to his jazz compositions, Beal (whose wife, Joan Beal, is an operatically trained soprano) has written quite a few classical chamber works, including a lengthy piece featuring bassist John Patitucci (Concerto for Jazz Bass and Orchestra). His jazz originals have been recorded by several notables, including Patitucci, Wynton Marsalis, Bobby Shew, the Turtle Island String Quartet, Spyro Gyra, and vibraphonist Dave Samuels. Jeff Beal (who names Miles Davis, Kenny Wheeler, and Woody Shaw as his favorite trumpeters and Gil Evans, Thad Jones, and Bob Brookmeyer as the arrangers most influential on his writing) has recorded as a leader for Antilles, Triloka, and Unitone.

Recommended CDs: Three Graces (Triloka 7197), *Alternate Route* (Unitone 4801)

LPs to Search For: Perpetual Motion (Antilles 91237)

HARRY BECKETT

• • • • • • • • • • • • • •

b. May 30, 1935, St. Michael Parish, Barbados

Harry Beckett has been an important part of the British jazz scene since the mid-1950s. An adventurous player who has appeared in settings ranging from hard bop to the avant-garde, Beckett uplifts each session that he is on. He learned to play trumpet in his native Barbados before moving to England in 1954. Beckett was a member of Graham Collier's band from the early 1960s until 1977. He also appeared with Charles Mingus in the obscure 1961 film *All Night Long.*

Beckett has worked with Mike Westbrook's orchestra, Chris MacGregor's Brotherhood of Breath, John Surman, the New Jazz Orchestra, the Stan Tracey Octet, Mike Gibbs, Elton Dean, Ronnie Scott, John Dankworth, the London Jazz Composer's Orchestra, the Jazz Warriors, Pierre Dorge's New Jungle Orchestra (1986–91), and others through the years, in addition to leading a series of groups. Although barely known in the United States, in England Harry Beckett (who has recorded as a leader for Philips, RCA, Cadillac, Ogun, Paladin, ITM, and Spotlite) is very highly rated.

Recommended CDs: All Four One (Spotlite 547), with Pierre Dorge: *New Jungle Orchestra: Karawane* (Olufsen 5431), with Johnny Dyani: *Angolian Cry* (Steeplechase 31209), with David Murray: *Jazzpar Prize* (Enja 7031)

Film Appearances: All Night Long (1961)

BIX BEIDERBECKE

• • • • • • • • • • • • • •

b. Mar. 10, 1903, Davenport, IA, d. Aug. 6, 1931, Queens, NY

Bix Beiderbecke's life reads like a novel or a Hollywood movie. Born to a conservative family, Bix's love for jazz and his talents as a cornetist were disapproved of by his parents, who sent him to a military academy in hopes that he would learn discipline and find a "real" career. His eventual expulsion (due to skipping an excess of classes) was followed by an exciting but relatively brief period at the top of the music world during the roaring '20s. One of the few white jazz musicians of the decade who could hold his own with his black counterparts, Beiderbecke's rapid decline due to alcoholism and his death in 1931 right after the Depression had hit led to his later status as a martyr and jazz's first real cult figure.

All of this would be relatively unimportant except that Bix Beiderbecke was one of the greatest cornetists in jazz history. Possessor of a beautiful and haunting tone that defined "cool" yet was inwardly hot, Bix was a very advanced improviser, a true original who seemed to come out of nowhere before, like a shooting star, burning out before being truly appreciated.

Leon Bix Beiderbecke grew up in Davenport, Iowa. "Bix" was a family nickname that had also been applied to his father and grandfather. At age four, Beiderbecke began picking out songs on his family's piano, and within a short time it was obvious that he had a gift for music. His knack for reproducing tunes before he had had a single music lesson made the local newspapers in a story titled "Seven-Year-Old Boy Musical Wonder." Bix infuriated one of his early piano teachers by improvising "improvements" to classical works that he learned by ear rather than learning to read music properly. When he was 15, he heard one of his older brother's new records, "Tiger Rag" by the Original Dixieland Jazz Band. Soon afterward, inspired by Nick LaRocca's playing on the record, Bix astonished his parents by purchasing a cornet. He developed quickly while also playing piano in a local band.

In 1921, when Bix was 18, his worried parents, hoping to give him direction after his graduation from high school, sent him to Lake Forest Military Academy. But unknown to them, its location (just 35 miles north of Chicago) placed their son near the center of jazz! Soon Bix was spending most of his off-hours in local nightclubs, where he enjoyed the music of the New Orleans Rhythm Kings, occasionally getting to sit in with the pacesetting group. His late hours eventually took their toll, and he was expelled from the academy near the end of his first year. Bix was far from displeased by the turn of events, because now he was free to pursue music full time.

During 1922–23, Beiderbecke freelanced, although his inability to read music very well hindered him. He spent part of the time unemployed but was greatly impressed (and influenced) by the playing of the unrecorded Emmett Hardy and by hearing Louis Armstrong play on a riverboat. In October 1923, Beiderbecke joined a new band, the Wolverines, that was developing its own sound while using the New Orleans Rhythm Kings as a role model. On February 18, 1924, Bix (a month shy of being 21) made his recording debut. His thoughtful style and skill at melodic development signaled the birth of a new talent, and his playing did not go unnoticed. A few months later, Red Nichols copied Bix's initial solo ("Jazz Me Blues"), note for note, on George Olsen's recording of "You'll Never Get to Heaven with Those Eyes," one of the first "re-creations" in jazz history.

Beiderbecke developed quickly as an improviser throughout 1924 and was soon the leading soloist in the Wolverines. In September the group, having picked up a reputation due to their exciting records, traveled to New York. They made a strong impression, played some jobs, and cut their best recordings, including "Big Boy," which features Beiderbecke taking solos on both cornet and piano. Beiderbecke was offered a lucrative job with Jean Goldkette's large dance orchestra and he jumped at the chance, training Jimmy McPartland to take his place with the Wolverines.

Unfortunately, things did not go very well at this point for Bix. Because Goldkette had a jazz-influenced dance band rather than a spontaneous jazz group, Beiderbecke's weak sight-reading was a major liability, and in less than two months he was let go. Goldkette promised Bix that once his all-round abilities improved, he would be rehired. Beiderbecke, who was soon fired from Charlie Straight's band after four months for the same reason, had only one record date in 1925, a loose (and rather intoxicated) session with trombonist Tommy Dorsey in a quintet called the Rhythm Jugglers. That occasion was most notable for introducing Bix's

"Davenport Blues." Otherwise, he played jobs in the Midwest, enrolled briefly at the University of Iowa (but was expelled two weeks later for being in a drunken brawl), visited New York and Chicago, and spent the second half of the year in St. Louis, working in an orchestra led by C-melody saxophonist Frankie Trumbauer. Most importantly, Beiderbecke greatly improved his sight-reading.

Jean Goldkette kept his promise, and in March 1926 he rehired Bix. Beiderbecke would be with Goldkette's crew for over a year. Although the band quickly developed into one of the top orchestras in jazz (winning a "battle of the bands" contest over Fletcher Henderson in October 1926), due to difficulties with their label (Victor), most of the Jean Goldkette recordings are commercial dance band performances that do not show off the ensemble's jazz abilities except in brief spots. Bix was greatly underutilized on record with Goldkette, only recording one solo that is considered classic, "Clementine."

Bix Beiderbecke's peak year, 1927, was full of accomplishments and events for the 24-year-old cornetist. Beiderbecke started recording regularly with pickup groups headed by Frankie Trumbauer; Bix and Tram made for a classic team. "Singin' the Blues," from February 4, has Beiderbecke's most famous solo (Trumbauer's too) and it is considered one of the musical high points of the 1920s, a record where every note fit perfectly. "I'm Coming Virginia," from May 13, has Beiderbecke's longest-ever documented cornet solo, and it almost reaches the heights of "Singin' the Blues." In addition to the steady stream of adventurous Frankie Trumbauer recordings (which also include "Way Down Yonder in New Orleans," "Ostrich Walk," and a song by Bix's friend Hoagy Carmichael called "Riverboat Shuffle"), Beiderbecke began heading a series of Dixieland dates under the title of Bix and His Gang, which included his versions of such standards as "Jazz Me Blues," "Royal Garden Blues," and "At the Jazz Band Ball." Beiderbecke also composed four piano pieces, recording one ("In a Mist"), although the others ("Candlelights," "Flashes," and "In the Dark") would have to wait until after his death before they were documented. His piano style was influenced by classical composers Debussy and Ravel.

The year 1927 was also when the Jean Goldkette Orchestra broke up (ironically "Clementine" was their last recording). Bix and Tram played for a couple of months with the unrecorded Adrian Rollini Orchestra. After that legendary jazz band disbanded, they joined the Paul Whiteman Orchestra, becoming major parts of the huge ensemble headed by the "King of Jazz". Historical revisionists would partly blame Beiderbecke's early death on his frustration at playing the generally commercial music in Whiteman's repertoire, but the opposite was actually true. Whiteman had the most prestigious orchestra of 1920s America, and Beiderbecke was proud that he could now read well enough to be one of Whiteman's stars. In fact, of all of his records, he was proudest of playing the difficult cornet part in George Gershwin's *Concerto in F* flawlessly.

Because they were the most popular dance band in the country, Paul Whiteman and his orchestra were very busy during 1928, recording constantly, appearing on the radio, and performing at concerts. There are scores of records from Beiderbecke's period with Whiteman. Many feature the cornetist for just a short eight-bar solo but some have a more prominent role for him, including "There Ain't No Sweet Man That's Worth the Salt of My Tears," "San," "Dardanella," and "You Took Advantage of Me" (which has a famous tradeoff between Bix and

Bix Beiderbecke, photographed on August 30, 1921, would pack a great deal of living into his remaining ten years.

Tram). On "Sweet Sue," the arrangement for the Whiteman Orchestra is extremely pompous, using quite a few cliches from classical and pop music. Jack Fulton's vocal is horrendous, and the band sounds bored to death playing instantly dated concert music. And then, from out of nowhere, Bix gets a chorus and, propelled by Steve Brown's swinging bass, for a brief moment drastically changes the mood. The contrast is startling.

Unfortunately Beiderbecke's excessive drinking began to catch up with him later in 1928, and he spent time in the hospital with pneumonia. Whiteman's busy schedule could exhaust a sober musician, and the inferior quality of bootleg liquor during Prohibition started seriously affecting Bix. His playing became erratic, his tone became a little fuzzy, and in January 1929 he had a nervous breakdown. Whiteman, to compensate for Bix's absence, hired Andy Secrest as a sound-alike to fill in for Beiderbecke and kept him on after Bix returned, just in case. During the first half of 1929, Beiderbecke's decline on records can be heard; he really fumbles on "Futuristic Rhythm" from March 8. Beiderbecke was well aware of his decline, so the Bix and His Gang recordings came to a close and Beiderbecke suggested that Secrest take his place on Frankie Trumbauer's sessions; he knew that he was slipping. Bix struggled on gamely, but, after recording a short solo on the ironically titled "Waiting at the End of the Road" on September 13, he collapsed. Paul Whiteman sent Bix home to Davenport in hopes that he would recover, keeping him on his payroll.

But it was already too late. Beiderbecke checked into a hospital for a time, took occasional musical jobs, and tried to stop drinking, but he was not strong enough to beat his addiction. He made a few final record dates in 1930 (which show the deterioration of his tone), turned down an offer to rejoin Whiteman (knowing that he could no longer handle the job), tried out for the Casa Loma Orchestra (but by then was too weak), and on August 6, 1931, died at the age of 28 from pneumonia. Perhaps if there had been an Alcoholics Anonymous in the 1920s or if the quality of the liquor had been better, Bix might have recovered. It can only be surmised what this musical genius would have contributed to jazz and popular music during the swing era if he could have survived. Benny Goodman, when asked in the 1980s by Randy Sandke if he would have hired the cornetist for his famous band of the mid-1930s, replied that the question should be "Would Bix have hired me?"

Soon after his death, Bix Beiderbecke became one of jazz's most famous legends. Because it is possible to trace his rise and fall on records, every note he played is valuable, and record collectors for decades debated over which records he appeared on and which solos were actually taken by his admirers. Hoagy Carmichael said that his composition "Stardust" was inspired by Bix, and Bing Crosby considered Beiderbecke to be an influence on his phrasing. Many trad jazz cornetists and trumpeters tried to emulate Bix's tone at one time or another, from Jimmy McPartland and Bobby Hackett to Tom Pletcher (who comes the closest) and Dick Sudhalter. Sudhalter cowrote the definitive Bix Beiderbecke biography, *Bix—Man and Legend,* which gives practically a day-by-day account of the doomed cornetist's life. Bix's declining health robbed him of the chance of appearing in the Paul Whiteman film short *King of Jazz.* In the mid-1990s a newsreel was discovered of Whiteman's band performing part of "My Ohio Home" in 1928, with Beiderbecke leading the ensemble (although he does not solo). Thus far that is the only sound film ever found of Bix.

Nearly seven decades after his death, the legend of Bix Beiderbecke, the innocent who rose and fell during the 1920s before drinking himself to death, is a major part of jazz's early history. His name and his music are still magical.

Recommended CDs: *And the Chicago Cornets* (Milestone 47019), *Vol. 1: Singin' the Blues* (Columbia 45450), *Vol. 2: At the Jazz Band Ball* (Columbia 46175), *Bix Restored Volumes 1-2-3* (Sunbeam 1-3. 4-6 and 7-9)

Recommended Reading: *The Best of Jazz* by Humphrey Lyttelton (Taplinger Publishing Co., 1982), *Bix—Man and Legend* by Richard Sudhalter, Philip Evans, and William Dean Myatt (Schirmer Books, 1974), *Jazz Masters of the Twenties* by Richard Hadlock (Macmillan Publishing Co., 1965), *The Leon Bix Beiderbecke Story* by Philip and Linda Evans (Prelike Press, 1998), *Lost Chords* by Richard M. Sudhalter (Oxford University Press, 1999), *Voices of the Jazz Age* by Chip Deffaa (University of Illinois Press, 1990)

Videos to Get: *At the Jazz Band Ball* (which includes "My Ohio Home"; Yazoo 514), *Bix: An Interpretation of a Legend* (1990; Rhapsody Films), *Ain't None of Them Play Like Him Yet* (1994; Playboy Home Video)

MARCUS BELGRAVE

b. June 12, 1936, Chester, PA

A fine trumpeter sometimes associated with post-bop and the avant-garde but flexible enough to sound quite credible in a swing setting, Marcus Belgrave has long been an important figure (both as a trumpeter and as an educator) in the Detroit area. A cousin of baritonist Cecil Payne, and the son and brother of brass players, Belgrave began playing trumpet at a young age. He was encouraged when he was 17 by Clifford Brown and was playing professionally as a teenager. He spent 1954–59 touring with Ray Charles and also had opportunities to play with Max Roach and Charles Mingus. Belgrave moved to Detroit in 1963, cofounding the jazz studies program at Detroit Metro Arts Complex, teaching at the Oakland University Jazz Studies Program, and founding the Jazz Development Workshop. His students through the years have included saxophonists James Carter and Kenny Garrett, pianist Geri Allen, and bassist Robert Hurst.

Marcus Belgrave, who has led very few sessions in his career, fortunately has had opportunities to record as a sideman with quite a few notables, including Charles Mingus, Eric Dolphy, McCoy Tyner, Max Roach, David Newman, David Murray, Franz Jackson, Sammy Price, Kirk Lightsey, Cecil Payne, Art Hodes, and former students Geri Allen and Robert Hurst. He has also been featured occasionally with the Lincoln Center Jazz Orchestra and in his mid-sixties is beginning to gain the recognition he has long deserved.

Recommended CDs: with Geri Allen: *The Nurturer* (Blue Note 95139), with Regina Carter: *Motor City Moments* (Verve 314 543 927), with Al Grey: *Live at the Floating Jazz Festival* (Chiaroscuro 313), with Art Hodes: *Hot 'n' Cool Blues* (Parkwood 118), with Kirk Lightsey: *Kirk 'n' Marcus* (Criss Cross 1030)

LPs to Search For: *Gemini II* (Tribe 2228)

ROGER BELL

• • • • • • • • • • •

b. Jan. 4, 1919, Melbourne, Australia

A fine Dixieland-oriented trumpeter, Roger Bell is the younger brother of pianist Graeme Bell, one of the main leaders of the trad jazz movement in Australia. Roger Bell started out as a drummer, switching to cornet in 1938, and later settling on trumpet. He worked with his brother on and off through the decades (including most significantly 1947–52) and as late as 1962. Although he led isolated titles in 1943, 1949, and 1950, Roger Bell's first full album as a leader was with his "Pagan Pipers" in 1963 (a trad band similar to his brother's), and he recorded a series of fine sessions during 1968–74 for the Swaggie label, little of which has yet been reissued on CD.

LPs to Search For: *Roger Bell and his Pagan Pipers* (Swaggie 1244), with Graeme Bell: *Czechoslovak Journey 1947* (Swaggie 1394), *Paris 1948* (Swaggie 1395), *1948–49* (Swaggie 1396), *Melbourne 1949* (Swaggie 1268), *And His Australian Jazz Band* (Swaggie 1224)

BUNNY BERIGAN

• • • • • • • • • • • • • • • •

b. Nov. 2, 1908, Hilbert, WI, d. June 2, 1942, New York, NY

One of the most colorful trumpeters in jazz history, Bunny Berigan had a beautiful tone, loved to take death-defying chances in his solos, and possessed the technique to allow him to make most of what he attempted. The fact that he was a lovable alcoholic added to the drama of both his life and his music.

Rowland Bernard "Bunny" Berigan played the violin briefly as a child but soon switched to trumpet. He started his career playing with local bands, including the University of Wisconsin's jazz ensemble, although he never went to college! In 1928 Berigan tried out for Hal Kemp's band but was turned down due to his weak tone. Two years later, after a great deal of woodshedding, Berigan had improved dramatically. He now had complete control over his horn, a very appealing tone in all registers, and he had learned how to build up solos from listening to Louis Armstrong records. Kemp quickly hired him for his dance band. After touring Europe with Kemp and making a few recordings, Berigan became a very busy studio musician in New York.

During 1931–36 Berigan appeared on countless records, sometimes in a fairly anonymous role but often being featured on a hot trumpet chorus. He worked fairly regularly with Fred Rich's orchestra, spent an uneventful few months with Paul Whiteman during 1932–33 (unlike Bix Beiderbecke, Berigan found that association too confining), and was part of many dates alongside the top jazz-oriented studio players, including Benny Goodman and Tommy Dorsey. He is particularly prominent on sessions with the Dorsey Brothers and the Boswell Sisters.

When Benny Goodman formed his big band in late 1934, Bunny Berigan took notice. He was persuaded to leave the studios in June 1935 to work with the clarinetist and, although their association only lasted three months, it made history. Berigan took classic solos on Goodman's

Along with Louis Armstrong, Bunny Berigan was arguably the most exciting trumpeter of the 1930s.

first hit records ("King Porter Stomp" and "Sometimes I'm Happy") and he also traveled cross-country with Goodman's orchestra, an up-and-down trip that concluded with a dramatically successful engagement at the Palomar Ballroom in Los Angeles, which symbolically launched the swing era. However, Berigan had been making much more money in the studios than he did as Goodman's sideman, and he soon returned to New York. He appeared often during the next year on recordings and the radio, including the famous *Saturday Night Swing Club* series for CBS. Back with Fred Rich, in 1936 Berigan made his only film appearance, taking both a vocal and a trumpet solo on the brief but exciting "Until Today."

Berigan, who led some obscure commercial record dates in 1933, headed nine separate sessions during 1935–37 that mixed swing, Dixieland, and some erratic vocalists (including the overly enthusiastic Chick Bullock). Among the titles is an early version of "I Can't Get Started," from April 13, 1936, which features Berigan taking the vocal. He had first recorded the ballad ten days earlier as a sideman with singer Red McKenzie, but it was the third version that would become famous.

By 1937, with the proliferation of so many swing orchestras, Berigan began to think of putting together his own big band. But first he joined Tommy Dorsey's band for what would be a six-week stint. Lightning struck again as Berigan's solos on "Marie" and "Song of India" made those songs into two of Dorsey's biggest hits and Dorsey's orchestra into a major league outfit. So famous were Bunny's improvisations that in later years Dorsey had them orchestrated for the full trumpet section to play on a regular basis. It seemed logical that Bunny Berigan (having helped both BG and TD to become hugely successful) would leave Dorsey to start his own big band. Due to his growing fame, Berigan soon signed with the Victor label, and on August 7, 1937, he had a big hit of his own in his third version of "I Can't Get Started."

However it took more than just musical talent to lead a successful jazz orchestra during the swing era. Benny Goodman and Tommy Dorsey were taskmasters and strong businessmen (as were most of the other major bandleaders), while Berigan preferred to be one of the gang. For an orchestra to survive, it had to develop a unique musical personality, have a steady string of strong-selling records, and develop its own audience. Berigan's band had its leader's exciting trumpet and the young tenor saxophonist Georgie Auld as its main assets, and in September 1938 the phenomenal Buddy Rich joined on drums. But unfortunately the leader's excessive drinking led to many missed opportunities, there was never a follow-up to "I Can't Get Started," and, after its promising start, the Bunny Berigan Orchestra in 1938 was struggling. During an era when labels often dictated many of the songs that its orchestras had opportunities to record, Berigan's band was given consistently inferior material throughout the year (the better tunes were saved for the more commercially successful orchestras). Such songs as "An Old Straw Hat," "Never Felt Better, Never Had Less," "Moonshine Over Kentucky," "'Round the Old Deserted Farm," and "When a Prince of a Fella Meets a Cinderella" failed to help the band's reputation.

Although Bunny Berigan was arguably the top trumpeter in jazz during 1935–38 (other than Louis Armstrong), by 1939 both his band and his own playing were starting to decline. Ironically, in late 1938 his orchestra began to record better tunes (including Bix Beiderbecke's four piano pieces orchestrated for a nonet out of the big band), but there would only be two record dates in 1939. There were also plenty of mishaps along the way, including when the roof blew off of Barton's Ritz-Carlton Hotel (where Bunny's band had a prestigious gig) during a hurricane, and one occasion when Berigan and his musicians showed up for a Sunday night date in Bristol, Connecticut, but found Gene Krupa's band onstage; they were supposed to be at Bridgeport, Connecticut, instead! In early 1940 Berigan was forced to declare bankruptcy and break up his three-year-old orchestra.

From that point on it was a steady slide downhill. Berigan accepted an offer from his old boss, Tommy Dorsey, to rejoin the Dorsey band, taking a few recorded solos (including on "I'm Nobody's Baby" and "East of the Sun"), but by then his drinking was out of control. Berigan's drinking became legendary, and there are tales (possibly true) of his falling off a bandstand right when it was time for him to solo on the radio with Dorsey. After six months, Dorsey reluctantly gave up and fired the trumpeter. Berigan made two more attempts to lead his own big bands, recording eight vocal-dominated numbers during 1941–42. He was hired to ghost the trumpet solos in the film *Syncopation*, but Manny Klein had to fill in most of the time instead. In 1942 Berigan began to waste away, and on June 2,

1942, he died from pneumonia and a variety of drinking-related ailments. Bunny Berigan was just 33.

Recommended CDs: *The Pied Piper 1934–40* (Bluebird 66165), *Sing Sing Sing* (Jass 627), *Devil's Holiday* (Jass 638)

LPs to Search For: *The Great Soloists* (Biograph 10), *Down by the Old Mill Stream* (Jazz Archives 11)

Recommended Reading: *Elusive Legend of Jazz* by Robert Dupuis (Louisiana State University Press, 1993), *Lost Chords* by Richard M. Sudhalter (Oxford University Press, 1999)

Videos to Get: *Trumpet Kings* (which has Berigan playing "Until Today" with Fred Rich in 1936; Video Artists International 69076)

SONNY BERMAN
• • • • • • • • • • • • • •

b. Apr. 21, 1925, New Haven, CT, d. Jan. 16, 1947, New York, NY

Sonny Berman had a brief life and career, being one of the first casualties of the beboppers' "flirtation" with heroin. Unfortunately, his unexpected death did not lead others to reassess their own lifestyles; heroin would continue to plague much of the bebop generation for years.

Berman started his career working with Louis Prima's band in 1940 when he was 15 and followed it up by playing in the trumpet sections of the big bands of Sonny Dunham, Tommy Dorsey, Georgie Auld, Harry James, Boyd Raeburn, and Benny Goodman. Although Berman rarely soloed with those orchestras (other than Auld's, where he was heard on 1944's "Taps Miller"), he became an important star with Woody Herman's First Herd, which he joined in January 1945 at the age of 19, sharing the trumpet solos with Pete Candoli. Influenced by both Roy Eldridge and Dizzy Gillespie (and a fan of Louis Armstrong), Berman showed increasing originality as his period with Herman progressed.

Berman took some of his finest recorded solos on "Sidewalks of Cuba," a poignant "Let It Snow! Let It Snow! Let It Snow!" and the humorous "Your Father's Mustache." He is also heard with Woody Herman's Woodchoppers (a nonet drawn out of the big band), on radio broadcasts from the period, on four lengthy numbers for Dial that were issued under his name ("Nocturne" is particularly haunting), and on a live jam session later released by the Onyx label.

Sonny Berman was with Herman's Herd until its breakup in December 1946, but what he would have done next is not known. He died of a heart attack (caused by his drug use) while participating in an all-night jam session less than a month later. He was just 21.

Recommended CDs: with Woody Herman: *The Thundering Herds* (Columbia 44108), *At Carnegie Hall 1946* (Verve 314 559 837)

Recommended LPs: *Beautiful Jewish Music* (Onyx 211), *The Tempo Jazzmen/The Hermanites* (Spotlite 132)

BILL BERRY

• • • • • • • • • • •

b. Sept. 14, 1930, Benton Harbor, MI

Bill Berry is an excellent trumpeter who fits comfortably into both swing and bop settings, combos and big bands. He has named as his important trumpet influences Bunny Berigan, Charlie Shavers, Roy Eldridge, Harry "Sweets" Edison, Buck Clayton, Dizzy Gillespie, Miles Davis, and Clifford Brown, and bits of Clark Terry can be heard in his sound. Berry played piano from the time he was five. His parents were traveling musicians, and the youth often accompanied them on their tours. He first picked up the trumpet when he was 14 and began playing jazz professionally three years later, in 1947, working in territory bands in the Midwest. After a period in the Air Force (1951–55) and studying at the Cincinnati College of Music and Berklee, Berry picked up important experience playing with the orchestras of Woody Herman (1957–58 and 1960) and Maynard Ferguson (1961).

Most important to Berry was his period with Duke Ellington's orchestra (1961–63), an association that strongly affected both his playing and his musical outlook. After leaving Ellington (where he had been featured on occasional solos), Berry worked with the Thad Jones-Mel Lewis Orchestra (1965–67) and was a fixture in the New York studios (1964–71), playing with *The Merv Griffin Show* band during 1965–80. After leading a big band in New York, he moved permanently to Los Angeles in 1971 when Griffin relocated. He soon had organized the L.A. Big Band, an orchestra full of all-stars that often plays the music of Duke Ellington. Among the more notable musicians who have spent time in Berry's band were Cat Anderson, Blue Mitchell, Britt Woodman, Buster Cooper, Marshall Royal, and Richie Kamuca; the orchestra still plays occasionally. Berry, who for a time worked extensively in the studios, appears locally in combos, has guested with other big bands (including those of Louie Bellson and Benny Carter), and helps host an annual American-Japanese jazz party. He has also been quite active as an educator, most notably with the Monterey Jazz Festival education program. Bill Berry, who should be recorded much more often, has led dates for Parade (1962), Directional Sounds (1963), Beez (his own tiny label), Concord, and Drive Archives and has made records as a sideman with many musicians, including Herman, Ferguson, Ellington, Johnny Hodges, Thad Jones/Mel Lewis, Coleman Hawkins, Earl Hines, Jake Hanna, Scott Hamilton, and the Juggernaut.

Recommended CDs: *Hello Rev* (Concord Jazz 4027), *Shortcake* (Concord Jazz 4075), with Dave Pell: *The Dave Pell Octet Plays Again* (Fresh Sound 5009)

Film Appearances: *A Man Called Adam* (ghosting the trumpet solos for Frank Sinatra Jr., 1966)

Videos to Get: with Duke Ellington: *Jazz Festival, Vol. 2* (1962; Storyville 6074)

EMMETT BERRY

••••••••••••••••

b. July 23, 1915, Macon, GA

Emmett Berry is best remembered as a member of Count Basie's orchestra, although few fans could probably guess when he really was with Basie! A fine swing trumpeter, Berry came into his musical prime at a time when the rise of bebop had made his mainstream style already seem passé.

Berry grew up in Cleveland and first began playing music professionally with the Chicago Nightingales (a group actually based in Toledo, Ohio) in 1932. Moving to New York the following year, Berry freelanced for a time (particularly in Albany), gaining his first important recognition for his playing with Fletcher Henderson's orchestra (November 1936 through June 1939), where he replaced Roy Eldridge as the band's main trumpet soloist. After stints with the big bands of Horace Henderson and Earl Hines, Berry was with Teddy Wilson's sextet on two occasions (1941–42 and 1943–44), sandwiching a period (1942–43) with Raymond Scott's CBS Orchestra. He also played with Lionel Hampton, Don Redman, and Benny Carter. After leaving Wilson for the second time, Berry worked briefly with the John Kirby Sextet and Eddie Heywood (1945).

So when was Emmett Berry actually with Count Basie? He played regularly with Count during 1945–50, a period when Basie's band (although still strong musically) was struggling financially, breaking up altogether in early 1950. Berry was given a fair amount of solo space, sharing the trumpet spots with Harry "Sweets" Edison. But since it was the bebop era, the Basie Orchestra and Berry received much less attention than they would have gotten five years earlier.

After leaving Basie, Berry spent time in the groups of Jimmy Rushing, Johnny Hodges (1951–54), Earl Hines, Cootie Williams (1955), Sammy Price (touring Europe in 1955), and the Fletcher Henderson Reunion Band (1957). He recorded with most of these outfits plus with Jo Jones, Al Sears, and Coleman Hawkins among others. Berry toured Europe on a couple of occasions with Buck Clayton (1959 and 1961), appearing on a European television special with Clayton's group that is now available on video. Berry also was utilized for some Count Basie reunion sessions. In his career he led three four-song sessions, for Savoy in 1944 and Columbia in 1956 and 1959. In the 1960s the trumpeter was primarily in Los Angeles, where he was largely forgotten, although later in the decade he played in New York with Peanuts Hucko, Wilbur DeParis, Buddy Tate, and other swing survivors. In 1970 bad health persuaded Emmett Berry to retire, and he moved home to Cleveland, where he has rarely been heard from in the music world since, having had a substantial if underrated career.

Recommended CDs: with Count Basie: *Brand New Wagon* (Bluebird 2292), with Buck Clayton: *Copenhagen Concerts* (Steeplechase 36006/7), *Swiss Radio Days Jazz Series, Vol. 7* (TCB 02072), *Buck Clayton All-Stars 1961* (Storyville 8231), with Teddy Wilson: *Associated Transcriptions 1944* (Storyville 8236)

Film Appearances: with Teddy Wilson's sextet: *Boogie Woogie Dream* (1941)

JOHNNY BEST

• • • • • • • • • • •

b. Oct. 20, 1913, Shelby, NC

One of the last survivors of the Glenn Miller Orchestra and the swing era in general, Johnny Best was always a fine trumpeter whose style fell between swing and Dixieland, in a way similar to Billy Butterfield. He never became famous but was one of the main soloists with two of the most important swing-era big bands.

Best started out playing piano, switching to trumpet at 13. He was a member of the Duke Blue Devils in 1932, also playing with the University of North Carolina Dance Band, Hank Biagnini, and the early Les Brown Orchestra (1934–37). After a short stint with Charlie Barnet, Best became an occasional trumpet soloist with the Artie Shaw Orchestra of 1937–39, during a period when Shaw's ensemble became one of the most popular in the country. When Shaw dropped it all and fled to Mexico, Best joined Glenn Miller and was with Miller's orchestra during its glory years (1939–42), appearing on nearly all of its hit records and getting a fair amount of solo space without gaining any real fame or name recognition.

After Miller joined the Army, Best worked briefly with Bob Crosby and then entered the Navy himself, playing with the service bands of Artie Shaw (1942–43) and Sam Donahue (1944–45). After his discharge, Best worked with Benny Goodman (1945–46) before becoming a studio musician. Unlike many of his counterparts who became buried in the studios, Best (who never led his own record date) always did his best to stay active in jazz, playing with Bob Crosby, the Billy May Big Band (1953), and various pickup groups; he is also proud of the recording he made with the Ray Conniff Orchestra. In the 1970s he performed occasionally with the World's Greatest Jazz Band. Although a serious fall in 1982 forced him to be confined to a wheelchair, Johnny Best stayed active on a part-time basis throughout the early 1990s, often appearing with Glenn Miller reunion bands and Bob Crosby in addition to guesting at Dixieland festivals.

Recommended CDs: with World's Greatest Jazz Band: *Plays George Gershwin and Rodgers and Hart* (Jazzology 300), *Plays Cole Porter and Rodgers and Hart* (Jazzology 320)

JOE BISHOP

• • • • • • • • • •

b. Nov. 27, 1907, Monticello, AR, d. May 12, 1976, Houston, TX

Joe Bishop, a forgotten name today due to his brief career, was the first significant soloist on the flugelhorn in jazz history, 20 years before Clark Terry and Art Farmer.

Bishop played piano as a child before learning the trumpet and tuba. He played tuba with Al Katz's Kittens (with whom he recorded "Ace in the Hole" in 1926), switching to flugelhorn in time for his periods with Austin Wylie (1930) and the Isham Jones Orchestra (1931–36); why he chose the then-obscure flugelhorn instead of the trumpet is not known. After Isham Jones decided to break up his band, Bishop became a charter member of Woody Herman's orchestra, taking occasional solos on the flugelhorn. He also participated on blues sessions with Jimmie Gordon and Cow Cow Davenport (both in 1938). However, Bishop was most important as a composer and the chief arranger for Woody Herman's "Band That Plays the Blues." Among his compositions were "Woodchopper's Ball" (Herman's first hit), "Blues Upstairs," "Blues Downstairs," and the standard "Blue Prelude."

Bishop's playing career ended in September 1940 when he contracted tuberculosis. When he returned to music in 1942, it was strictly as an arranger. He remained active until illness forced his retirement from music in 1951. Bishop ended up running a store in Saranac Lake, New York, for many years. He may only be a footnote in jazz history, but when it comes to jazz flugelhornists, Joe Bishop was there before anyone else.

Recommended CDs: with Woody Herman: *Blues on Parade* (GRP/Decca 606)

ANDREW BLAKENEY

b. June 10, 1898, Quitman, MS, d. Feb. 12, 1992, Baldwin Park, CA

A top New Orleans jazz trumpeter who was still playing as he entered his nineties, Andrew Blakeney was never a major name, but he was an asset to many sessions through the years. After relocating to Chicago at 18, he played with local bands, including King Oliver (two weeks in 1925) and Doc Cook's Gingersnaps. In 1926 Blakeney moved to Los Angeles, where he often appeared on the soundtracks of movies and on radio. He recorded with Sonny Clay and Reb Spikes and worked with Paul Howard's Quality Serenaders, "Tin Can" Henry, Lee Herriford, Les Hite, and Lionel Hampton (1935). Blakeney spent most of the prime years of the swing era (1936–41) leading his own band in Hawaii. He had stints with Ceele Burke's orchestra (1942–46) and Horace Henderson before gaining some recognition for his work with Kid Ory (1947). From that point on, Blakeney mostly led Dixieland bands (even if he never led a record date of his own), usually in the Los Angeles area. Blakeney gained his greatest fame in the 1970s as a member of the Legends of Jazz, with whom he toured the United States and Europe. He still sounded quite strong at that point (far superior to most of the other ancient New Orleans trumpeters) and recorded with the Eagle Brass Band as late as 1984.

Andrew Blakeney was active till near the end, passing away at the age of 93 from kidney failure.

LPs to Search For: with the Legends of Jazz: *The Legends of Jazz* (Crescent Productions 1), with Kid Ory: *Storyville Nights* (Verve 8456)

Film Appearances: *Hotel* (1966), *The Great White Hope* (1970), *Mame* (1974)

ROB BLAKESLEE

b. Portland, OR

A technically skilled avant-garde trumpeter, Rob Blakeslee is perhaps best known for his association with Vinny Golia. He has worked primarily on the West Coast from 1970 on, other than during 1983–87, when he was a music teacher in Dallas, Texas. In 1987 he returned to Portland and became the Director of Jazz Ensembles at Oregon State University. Rob Blakeslee has since performed with many of the most adventurous local jazz players and has led CDs for Nine Winds and his new label, Louie.

Recommended CDs: *Lifeline* (Nine Winds 147), *Long Narrows* (Nine Winds 0167), *Waterloo Ice House* (Louie 012), *Last Minute Gifts* (Louie 019), with Vinny Golia: *Against the Grain* (Nine Winds 159), *Dante No Longer Repents* (Music & Arts 992), with Dennis Gonzalez: *Catechism* (Music & Arts 913)

TERENCE BLANCHARD

b. Mar. 13, 1962, New Orleans, LA

A superb trumpeter who continues to grow in power and range year by year, Terence Blanchard is also important as a composer of soundtracks, chiefly for Spike Lee films. He began playing piano in his native New Orleans when he was four and had extensive classical trumpet training, inspired to play jazz after hearing Alvin Alcorn play in 1970 for his third-grade class. Blanchard studied with Ellis Marsalis at the New Orleans Center for the Creative Arts (1978–80) and attended Rutgers University in 1980. He played early on with Lionel Hampton (1980–81) and gained his initial fame with Art Blakey's Jazz Messengers (1982–86), where he was Wynton Marsalis' successor.

Although often grouped with Wynton Marsalis and thought of as a major "Young Lion," Blanchard was not particularly influenced by Miles Davis (as were most of the other "Lions") and instead in his early days sometimes sounded a little like Freddie Hubbard. He co-led a group with altoist Donald Harrison (1984–89), a band that started recording for Concord even while they were still sidemen with Blakey. Blanchard had to break up the band and take a year off to redo his embouchure on the trumpet because he was playing incorrectly and was constantly cutting his lip. Since relearning how to play the trumpet during 1989–90, his playing has greatly improved and his range has become quite impressive.

Blanchard has led his own band since 1990, one that has consistently been one of the finest groups in jazz, performing advanced hard bop and recording regularly for Columbia and Sony. He began his association with Spike Lee in 1987 and has since written and/or performed for such films as *School Daze, Do the Right Thing, Mo' Better Blues* (in which he ghosted the trumpet for Denzel Washington), *Jungle Fever, Malcolm X* (in which he appears briefly), *Crooklyn,* and *Clockers.*

As the 21st century began, Terence Blanchard was one of the top trumpeters in jazz and one with seemingly unlimited potential.

As a trumpeter and a soundtrack composer, Terence Blanchard always sounds original.

Recommended CDs: *New York Second Line* (George Wein Collection 3002), *Nascence* (Columbia 40335), *Crystal Stair* (Columbia 40830), *Black Pearl* (Columbia 44216), *Terence Blanchard* (Columbia 47354), *Simply Stated* (Columbia 48903), *The Malcolm X Jazz Suite* (Columbia 53599), *Jazz in Film* (Sony 60671), with Art Blakey: *New York Scene* (Concord Jazz 4256), *Live at Kimball's* (Concord Jazz 4307)

Recommended Reading: *Jazz Profiles* by Reginald Carver and Lenny Bernstein (Billboard Books, 1998)

Videos to Get: *Art Blakey: The Jazz Messenger* (1987; Rhapsody Films)

PETER BOCAGE
. . . .

b. July 31, 1887, Algiers, LA, d. Dec. 3, 1967, New Orleans, LA

Peter Bocage was a Creole musician who was proud of his sight-reading abilities and who, like many Creoles of the early 1900s, felt that he was superior to the blues-oriented black musicians who were technically untrained. He was very much in his element in his recordings with Armand J. Piron's orchestra during 1923–25, displaying a soon-to-be-extinct ensemble style that was closer to ragtime than to the blues.

Part of a musical family, Bocage began his musical career as a violinist, working with Tom Albert, the Eagle Band, the Superior Orchestra, and the Peerless Orchestra during 1906–10. Bunk Johnson was an early musical friend. In exchange for his help in learning to read music, Bunk gave Bocage some cornet lessons. On his new ax, Bocage played with the Onward Brass Band, the Tuxedo Brass Band, the Excelsior Brass Band, Oscar Celestin, Fate Marable in 1918 (later recommending Louis Armstrong as his replacement), and, most importantly, Armand J. Piron's New Orleans Orchestra during 1919–28. With Piron's very musical society band, Bocage recorded 17 selections during two visits to New York, all of which were made available on a now-out-of-print Retrieval LP. Bocage's gentle sound, lightly swinging style, and melodic lead were perfect for Piron's group, which played primarily genteel upper-class dance music. Bocage also cowrote several songs with Piron, including "Mama's Gone Goodbye."

But unfortunately, Bocage never developed much beyond that early peak. In 1928, when Piron's orchestra broke up, Bocage became a member of the unrecorded Creole Serenaders for a decade, leaving music in 1939 (except for occasional gigs) in order to work days as an insurance salesman. In 1945, when Sidney Bechet tried to form a New Orleans jazz band in Boston and had given up on a frequently drunk Bunk Johnson, he sent to New Orleans for Bocage. Their brief collaboration, heard on *Bocage and Bechet* (Jazz Crusade 3042), did not work out, because the trumpeter's playing was not strong (or flexible) enough to deal with the faster tempos or with the fiery Bechet's often taking the lead in ensembles. However, in the 1950s and '60s Peter Bocage gradually became more active again, heading a new version of the Creole Serenaders, working with the Eureka Brass Band, leading three albums, including one for Riverside in 1961 (playing both trumpet and violin), and recording as a sideman with clarinetist Emile Barnes and the Eureka Brass Band. Frankly, Bocage often sounded a bit rusty, erratic, and over-the-hill, which, considering his advanced age (74 in 1961), was not too surprising.

For the "real" Peter Bocage, venture back to the mid-1920s and explore the music of Piron's orchestra.

Recommended LPs: *Piron's New Orleans Orchestra* (Retrieval 128)

BUDDY BOLDEN
• • • • • • • • • • • • • • •

b. Sept. 6, 1877, New Orleans, LA, d. Nov. 4, 1931, Jackson, LA

In some ways Buddy Bolden can be thought of as the George Washington of jazz, the first at doing nearly everything. He led the first important jazz band, was jazz's biggest name during its earliest days, and was jazz's first tragedy. Legend has overshadowed the true facts of his life. And although it has often been written (including in the recent *Biographical Encyclopedia of Jazz*), and Wynton Marsalis still says, that Bolden published a scandal sheet and ran a barbershop, neither of those statements is true. Donald Marquis, in his essential book *In Search of Buddy Bolden*, separates the facts from the legend, but Bolden still emerges as a vaguely mysterious figure.

The beginnings of jazz were unfortunately not documented. Although the Original Dixieland Jazz Band made the first jazz recordings in 1917, the music existed in an earlier form at least 20 years before. Because Buddy Bolden was jazz's earliest star and he formed his initial band in 1895, for convenience sake, the start of jazz can be dated to that day, even though chances are good that Bolden never used the word *jazz* to describe his music; the term did not come into general usage until 1916–17.

Charles Joseph "Buddy" Bolden was born and raised in New Orleans. Brass bands were a major part of New Orleans entertainment during his childhood years, and in 1894 (when he was 16 and four years after he had dropped out of school) Bolden decided that the cornet would be his instrument. He developed quickly and was soon playing with guitarist Charley Galloway's string band. By the following year, Bolden had formed a string band of his own, and starting around that time he occasionally also led a brass band. Bolden differed from his predecessors in that he "ragged" the popular and dance songs of the era, not being content just to play the same melody over and over again. And he was so in love with music that he reportedly never allowed anyone to touch his horn.

By the late 1890s Bolden's regular band consisted of valve trombone, clarinet, guitar, string bass, and drums, in addition to his cornet. As the 19th century ended, Bolden's innovative ideas made him the biggest name in musical New Orleans. He played at picnics, parties, dance halls, parks, and occasional parades all over the city, including in Storyville (although not in the brothels!). At one time, Bolden was so popular that he sent out six bands under his name, making brief appearances with each one throughout the night. He became particularly famous for his slow, emotional blues (few cornetists had previously bent notes with his facility), and in his repertoire were such songs as "Bucket's Got a Hole in It," "Make Me a Pallet on the Floor," and "Funky Butt" (which Jelly Roll Morton later immortalized as "Buddy Bolden's Blues," or "I Thought I Heard Buddy Bolden Say"). By 1903 he was frequently called King.

But in 1906 Bolden's world fell apart. He began to get bad headaches in March of that year, had major spells of depression, and started suffering periods of insanity. His playing and behavior became very erratic and his last gig, playing at a Labor Day parade, found him unable to finish the job. He was arrested for insanity a few days later. Although he was soon released, Bolden never recovered. His drinking increased, he became quite violent, and on March 13, 1907, he was arrested again. A month later he was committed to the East Louisiana State Hospital, where he spent his final 24 years. Although he rarely ever talked coherently again, Bolden did sit in with a patients' band during lunchtime for a while. Henry "Red" Allen reportedly went to visit Bolden in 1928, but Buddy never spoke or seemed to understand anything; his mind was completely gone. In 1931 he died of a heart ailment, 25 years after his mind had left him.

Although Buddy Bolden was rumored to have recorded a cylinder back in 1898, a copy has never been found, so it can only be guessed how the founder of jazz (and its first legend) really sounded.

Recommended Reading: *In Search of Buddy Bolden* by Donald Marquis (Louisiana State University Press, 1978), *Jazz Masters of New Orleans* by Martin Williams (Macmillan Publishing Co., 1967)

DUPREE BOLTON

· · · · · · · · · · · · · · · · ·

b. 1925, Oklahoma City, OK

Dupree Bolton is a mystery in jazz history. A talented bop-oriented trumpeter, Bolton's difficulties with drugs made his career very episodic and tragic, one in which his talent was mostly squandered.

Bolton left home when he was 14 but soon developed into a fine trumpeter. He worked with Buddy Johnson's orchestra in 1944–45 (taking a beboppish solo on "Walk 'Em") and was with Benny Carter's big band during part of 1945–46 before disappearing. Bolton did not re-emerge until 1959, when he recorded *The Fox* with tenor saxophonist Harold Land, sounding strong and healthy. But soon he was busted for drugs. Although Bolton played and recorded with altoist Curtis Amy in 1963 (*Katanga*) and was with vibraphonist Bobby Hutcherson's group for a period in 1967, he spent quite a few years in prison, even reportedly recording behind bars in 1980. After his release, he played a job with tenor saxophonist Dexter Gordon in 1982, moved to the West Coast, and has not been heard from since. It is not even known if the long-lost Dupree Bolton is alive as of this writing.

Recommended CDs: with Harold Land: *The Fox* (Original Jazz Classics 343)

LPs to Search For: with Curtis Amy: *Katanga* (Pacific Jazz 70)

SHARKEY BONANO

· · · · · · · · · · · · · · · · ·

b. Apr. 9, 1902, Milneburg, LA, d. Mar. 27, 1972, New Orleans, LA

Aforceful and brash trumpeter, Sharkey Bonano played New Orleans-style jazz throughout his career, gaining some popularity in the 1950s.

Born Joseph Gustaf Bonano and nicknamed after a boxer (Sailor Tom Sharkey), Bonano began working locally in the early 1920s in New Orleans, including with the bands of Chink Martin and Freddie Newman. The young trumpeter spent time in Chicago in 1924, playing with a group led by Jimmy Durante (who at the time was mostly a jazz-oriented pianist). After he unsuccessfully auditioned for the Wolverines as Bix Beiderbecke's successor (his style was considered too basic for the band), Bonano returned to New Orleans. He led a group and made his recording debut in 1925 with Brownlee's orchestra. Bonano returned to the North to play with Jean Goldkette's orchestra in 1927 (preceding Beiderbecke) before co-leading the Melody Masters with Leon Prima (Louis' older brother) during 1928–30 in New Orleans. Bonano, who recorded in 1928 with both Johnnie Miller and Monk Hazel, headed Dixieland combos during 1930–36. Moving to New York, he worked with Ben Pollack and led the Sharks of Rhythm, recording four Dixieland sessions during 1936–37 that mostly featured his vocals and trumpet. Bonano also appeared as a sideman on a 1938 session with a group, under the title of "The Original Dixieland Jazz Band," that included a few of the ODJB members.

After serving in the Army, Bonano returned permanently to New Orleans, where during the 1950s he was a strong tourist attraction, playing regularly in local clubs (sometimes collaborating with blues singer Lizzie Miles) and recording for Capitol, Riverside, Southland, GHB, Good Time Jazz, and Roulette during 1949–60. Sharkey Bonano remained a popular local figure in New Orleans until retiring in the late 1960s, sticking to the same hard-charging Dixieland style that he had played more than 40 years earlier.

Recommended CDs: *Sharkey Bonano* (Timeless 1–001), *Sounds of New Orleans, Vol. 4* (Storyville 6011), *Sounds of New Orleans, Vol. 8* (Storyville 6015)

LPs to Search For: *Sharkey and His Kings of Dixieland* (GHB 122)

STERLING BOSE

b. Feb. 23, 1906, Florence, AL, d. June 1958, St. Petersburg, FL

Sterling Bose was a fine second-level trumpeter who was most comfortable in freewheeling Dixielandish settings, although he was also a fine sight-reader. Despite engaging in a great deal of musical activity during the 1928–45 period, Bose is an obscure figure who never led his own record date and never seemed to have been interviewed. About all that is remembered about his personality is that he had a reputation for loving alcohol. It is rumored that he was once saved from drowning in the ocean when he attempted to play his trumpet for the fish!

Bose started working professionally in the early 1920s, moving to St. Louis in 1923. While in the city he worked with the Crescent City Jazzers and in 1925 recorded eight titles with the Arcadian Serenaders (a fine unit that was influenced by the New Orleans Rhythm Kings). Bose freelanced in the Midwest and was with the Jean Goldkette Orchestra during 1928–29. On a few Goldkette records (most notably "My Blackbirds Are Bluebirds Now"), Bose sounds pretty close to his predecessor, Bix Beiderbecke. After several years with Ben Pollack's orchestra (1930–33), Bose alternated between studio work and short stints with many orchestras. Among his more notable associations were those with the orchestras of Joe Haymes (1934–35), Tommy Dorsey (1935), Ray Noble (1936), Benny Goodman (two months in 1936, soloing on his records of "St. Louis Blues" and "Love Me or Leave Me"), Glenn Miller (the early unsuccessful band from 1937), Bob Crosby (1938–39), Bobby Hackett (1939), Bob Zurke (1939–40), Jack Teagarden (1940), Bud Freeman (his obscure big band in 1942), and Bobby Sherwood (1943). Bose had occasional solos with most of these outfits, faring best with Zurke, but never achieved much fame. Perhaps if he had stuck with one band long enough to be identified with it, he might have gained a name for himself.

It seems that Sterling Bose would have been a natural to flourish during the Dixieland revival period, but his lack of planning and foresight resulted in his being largely lost to history. He worked at Nick's on several occasions (including with Miff Mole and Art Hodes during 1943–44) but moved to Chicago in 1945, freelanced at low-profile jobs, permanently relocated to Florida in 1948, and had a regular gig at the Soreno Lounge in St. Petersburg during 1950–57. Seriously ill for a long period, he committed suicide in 1958. By then, even jazz aficionados had long forgotten the name of Sterling Bose, a solid trumpeter who never lived up to his potential.

LPs to Search For: with Jean Goldkette: *1924–1929* (The Old Masters 47), with Miff Mole: *And His World Jam Session Band-1944* (Jazzology 105), with Bob Zurke: *And His Delta Rhythm Band* (Meritt 16)

ALLAN BOTSCHINSKY

b. Mar. 29, 1940, Copenhagen, Denmark

Allan Botschinsky has a mellow tone and a lyrical style most influenced by Miles Davis. The son of a classical bassoonist, Botschinsky began playing trumpet when he was 11 and as a teenager studied at the Royal Danish Conservatorium. A professional by the time he was 16, the trumpeter played with the Ib Glindemann big band (1956–59), Bent Axen, Niels-Henning Orsted Pederson, and such Americans as Oscar Pettiford, Stan Getz, Dexter Gordon, Ben Webster, Lee Konitz, and Kenny Dorham. He spent a year in New York, attending the Manhattan School of Music (1963–64). Back in Denmark, Botschinsky became a longtime member of both the Danish Radio Jazz Group and the Danish Radio Big Band (1964–82) in addition to leading his own bands.

After moving to Hamburg, Germany, in 1985, the trumpeter worked with Peter Herbolzheimer's Rhythm Combination and Brass, the European Trumpet Summit, and his own combos. In 1987 he founded the M-A Music label, and since then, in addition to his performing and recording, he has been a busy jazz educator. During his career, Allan Botschinsky has recorded with many European groups, Oscar Pettiford, Sahib Shihab, Ben Webster, Kenny Dorham, Peter Herbolzheimer, Dexter Gordon, Lee Konitz, and George Gruntz's Concert Jazz Band, plus as a leader for Telefunken (1970), Stunt, Storyville, and M-A Music.

Recommended CDs: *Duologue* (M-A Music 2060), *The Night* (M-A Music 676), *Jazzpar 95* (Storyville 4207), with Kenny Dorham: *Short Story* (Steeplechase 36010)

CHRIS BOTTI

b. 1964, Portland, Oregon

Along with Rick Braun, Chris Botti emerged in the late 1990s to show that there is no reason that the trumpet (instead of the soprano sax) cannot be a lead instrument in instrumental pop settings. Botti is a fine player whose interest has always been much more in pop (making him a natural for the so-called "smooth jazz" scene) than in more adventurous music. He started playing trumpet when he was ten and within two years knew that he wanted to be a professional musician. In high school Botti played locally in Oregon, including with bassist David Friesen. He attended Indiana University (studying under David Baker) and later, in New York, had private lessons with tenor saxophonist George Coleman and Woody Shaw. However, the direction of his career went toward studio work and pop music. Botti became a first-call session player in New York (where he settled in 1985), working with many pop and rock acts, including Bob Dylan and Aretha Franklin, touring with Paul Simon on and off during 1990–95. After the latter association became part-time, Botti signed with Verve Forecast and recorded his first instrumental pop album (*First Wish*). He wrote the score for the film *Caught* in 1996 and has since recorded steady sellers in *Midnight Without You* (1997) and his GRP debut, *Slowing Down the World*. Chris Botti continues freelancing with pop acts when not involved in his own tours and thus far shows no inclination to alter his course toward pop stardom.

Recommended CDs: *First Wish* (Verve/Forecast 314 527 141), *Midnight Without You* (Verve/Forecast 314 537 132), *Slowing Down the World* (GRP 314 547 301)

LESTER BOWIE

● ● ● ● ● ● ● ● ● ● ● ● ● ●

b. Oct. 11, 1941, Frederick, MD, d. Nov. 8, 1999, New York, NY

One of the most inventive of all the avant-garde trumpeters, Lester Bowie (due to his sense of humor and his expertise at borrowing some of the more expressive qualities of earlier forms of jazz) was also one of the most accessible. Although he had a friendly and witty personality, Bowie had little patience for mere revivalists, copycats, or doomsayers. One of his early records found him saying "Is jazz, as we know it, dead? Well, it depends on what you know."

Bowie, who started playing trumpet when he was five, grew up in Arkansas and St. Louis, served in the Air Force (1958–60), and gained experience playing with blues and R&B bands (including Little Milton and Albert King). He was involved in helping set up the Black Artists Group in St. Louis, a loose unit that utilized the talents of many young avant-garde jazz artists. After moving to Chicago in 1965, he became the musical director for gospel singer Fontella Bass (who was his wife for a time). An early member of the Association for the Advancement of Creative Musicians (AACM), Bowie gravitated toward the most adventurous musicians in the city, including saxophonists Roscoe Mitchell and Joseph Jarman and bassist Malachi Favors. The four musicians (along with drummer Phillip Wilson) formed the Art Ensemble of Chicago. Wilson would soon depart, and his spot was permanently filled by Don Moye in 1970 during the band's two-year stay (1969–71) in France. Bowie was quoted as saying "From the time we were together about one month, we said to each other, 'Okay, we're gonna be together 30 years from now.'" He was remarkably accurate.

The Art Ensemble of Chicago was not a "free jazz," high-energy band that felt compelled always to fill the air with sound explorations. Bowie and the other musicians knew how to use silence dramatically, often augmenting their main axes with "little instruments" (exotic percussion and toys), and, although their music was often quite radical in the earlier years, they were not shy to hint strongly at aspects of the past now and then. Their slogan was "Great Black Music—Ancient to the Future." Dressed in a doctor's white lab coat, Bowie did "surgical operations" on music, often bending and distorting notes (he was a master at half-valve effects), punctuating his performances with surprising ideas and humor. The band's music (particularly in their early recordings for Delmark, Nessa, and Atlantic) was very advanced yet clearly a part of the jazz continuum.

In addition to his work with the Art Ensemble of Chicago, which continued on a part-time basis through the remainder of his life, Bowie recorded with such contemporaries as Cecil

Taylor, Archie Shepp, David Murray, Jimmy Lyons, Sunny Murray, and Kahil El'Zabar. He played in Jack DeJohnette's New Directions, teamed up with Arthur Blythe and Chico Freeman in The Leaders (a rare chance to hear him featured in a hard bop setting), and headed such bands as From the Root to the Source (which mixed gospel and rock with jazz), the New York Organ Ensemble, the Hip Hop Philharmonic Orchestra, and (starting in 1981) Brass Fantasy. This last band (all brass instruments plus drums) extended a humorous idea (turning current pop tunes into jazz) into a colorful if bewildering repertoire.

The brilliant and unpredictable trumpeter (whose younger brother, Joseph Bowie, is an adventurous trombonist) was at the peak of his powers and fame in 1999, before his unexpected death from kidney problems. Along the way he recorded as a leader for many labels (including MPS, Muse, Improvising Arts, Black Saint, ECM, and DIW) and with the Art Ensemble for such record companies as Nessa, Affinity, Freedom, Black Lion, JMY, Inner City, America, Prestige, Atlantic, Delmark, Paula, AECO, ECM, West Wind, BYG, Praxis, DIW, Columbia, and Birdology. Lester Bowie's humor can certainly be felt on such numbers as "F Troop Rides Again," "It's Howdy Doody Time," "Thirsty," and "Miles Davis Meets Donald Duck!" He is already sorely missed.

Recommended CDs: *The Great Pretender* (ECM 1209), *All the Magic* (ECM 1246/1247), *I Only Have Eyes for You* (ECM 1296), with the Art Ensemble of Chicago: *Live at Mandel Hall* (Delmark 432), *Fanfare for the Warriors* (Atlantic 90046), *Nice Guys* (ECM 1126), with The Leaders: *Out Here Like This* (Black Saint 120119)

LPs to Search For: *Fast Last* (Muse 5055), *Rope-a-Dope* (Muse 5081)

Film Appearances: *Les Stances à Sophie* (1970) with the Art Ensemble of Chicago

Videos to Get: *The Art Ensemble of Chicago: Live from the Jazz Showcase* (1981; Rhapsody Films)

BOBBY BRADFORD

• • • • • • • • • • • • • • • • • • •

b. July 19, 1934, Cleveland, MS

A contemporary of Don Cherry's, Bobby Bradford (who was actually born two years earlier) was one of the finest trumpeters to emerge from the early free jazz era. And because he has improved with age (while Cherry's trumpet chops declined as he worked in other areas and on other instruments), Bradford has largely fulfilled Cherry's potential, even though his decision to live in Los Angeles has resulted in his often being overlooked.

Bradford, who played piano from age eight, switched to cornet when he was 14. "My father liked jazz. We listened to jazz on the radio as children; it was always there." He grew up in Dallas, where he played in local groups, including with James Clay, David "Fathead" Newman, Cedar Walton, and Buster Smith. "My direct influences in jazz were Fats Navarro, Charlie Parker, Bud Powell, and, to a lesser degree, Dizzy and Miles." Shortly after moving to Los Angeles in 1952, Bradford met both Ornette Coleman (they were working in the stock room of the same department store!) and Eric Dolphy. Coleman and Dolphy both influenced him to open up his style. Bradford also played with the Gerald Wilson Orchestra and tenor saxophonist Wardell Gray ("He gave me personal encouragement and help."). A period spent in the Air Force (1954–58) kept Bradford from being recognized as one of free jazz's pioneers and, although he was Cherry's successor as a member of the Ornette Coleman Quartet (1961–63), this was a period when Coleman rarely worked and never recorded. Unfortunately, Bradford turned down a chance to record on Coleman's famous *Free Jazz* album in 1961 in order to stay in school; Freddie Hubbard got the gig.

After finally giving up on waiting for Coleman to become active again, in 1964 Bradford settled in Los Angeles, where he became a schoolteacher. He finally had an opportunity to record with Ornette Coleman in 1971 (when Ornette's Columbia albums featured most of his alumni). However, Bradford became best known for his work and occasional recordings with clarinetist John Carter, which began in 1966. The cornetist's mellow tone and thoughtful approach were a perfect contrast for Carter's often-screeching and rather abrasive flights. Their musical partnership lasted up until the clarinetist's death in 1991.

Bradford lived in London for a period in the early 1970s, playing with John Stevens and his Spontaneous Music Ensemble. Since then, he has often led a quintet called the Mo'Tet (as in "room for one mo'"), which features the multi-instrumentalist Vinny Golia on reeds. He has also teamed up with clarinetist and bass clarinetist Marty Ehrlich on a few occasions in addition to performing with John Stevens' Freebop, the David Murray Octet, and Charlie Haden's Liberation Music Orchestra. As a leader Bradford has recorded for Nessa, Soul Note, and Hat Art. In the early 1990s he named as his favorite examples of his own playing on record *One Night Stand,* John Stevens' *Love Dream,* John Carter's *Flight for Four* and *Self Determination,* and Ornette Coleman's *Science Fiction.*

In summary, Bobby Bradford (who is still quite active in the Los Angeles area) expressed happiness about his own life. "I hope that everyone can have the pleasure of a 'consuming passion' in his life similar to the one that I have experienced in music ever since I heard Charlie Parker when I was young."

Recommended CDs: *Comin' on* (Hat Art 6016), *One Night Stand* (Black Saint 121 168), with John Carter: *Seeking* (Hat Art 6085), *Dauwhe* (Black Saint 1053), with Ornette Coleman: *The Complete Science Fiction Sessions* (Columbia/ Legacy 63569), with Vinny Golia: *Lineage* (Nine Winds 0214)

LPs to Search For: *Lost in L.A.* (Soul Note 1068)

Videos to Get: *John Carter and Bobby Bradford: The New Music* (1980; Rhapsody Films)

RUBY BRAFF
• • • • • • • • • • • •

b. Mar. 16, 1927, Boston, MA

Ruby Braff deserves to be recognized as one of the all-time greats, but he was definitely born in the wrong decade. Ten years younger than Dizzy Gillespie and a contemporary of Miles Davis, Braff was part of a musical generation strongly influenced by the beboppers. However, he was always much more interested in the music of Louis Armstrong, Lester Young, and Billie Holiday and was very much out of place in his own time period. A very expressive cornetist who is instantly recognizable and has never played an unemotional note,

Ruby Braff has yet to play a passionless chorus, a directionless, solo or a note he didn't believe in.

Ruby Braff has carved his own musical path throughout his career, playing vintage standards in an idiom that falls between swing and trad jazz, usually with musicians either much older or much younger than himself. As with Thelonious Monk, Braff ignored musical trends and stuck to the music he loved most; eventually the jazz world accepted his unique brilliance.

"What is called jazz today was called popular music when I was young. You either played symphony or popular. The radio was full of great music, both live and recorded. I originally wanted a tenor sax but my parents saw a baritone and thought it was too big for me, so they got a trumpet. I switched to cornet a long time ago." Braff started playing when he was eight, was working in local bars when he was 11, and gained early experience gigging with veterans in Boston. He recorded with Edmond Hall (1949) and Pee Wee Russell (1951), and played with Bud Freeman and Sam Margolis. After he moved to New York in 1953, Braff was nearly the only world-class trumpeter/cornetist of his generation to be playing mainstream jazz rather than bebop. He recorded often in the 1950s, including with Vic Dickenson (1953–54), the Benny Goodman Sextet in 1955, and Buck Clayton (his jam session dates) and led some sessions for the Vanguard label, but worked much less frequently in public. In fact, during 1955–68, there were long stretches when Braff hardly played at all in public; his style was considered quite passé by those who think new jazz styles "replace" older ones.

Things began improving later in the 1960s as Braff gigged and recorded with George Wein's Newport All-Stars. The cornetist co-led a delightful quartet with guitarist George Barnes

(1973–75) that for a time was quite popular, and he also appeared with the New York Jazz Repertory Company. Almost always the youngest musician on his earlier gigs, by the late 1970s, when mainstream swing made its comeback, Braff was among the older swing stars. He has worked and recorded quite steadily during the past 20 years (the following recommended list is only a small sampling), teaming up on records with (among many others) Dick Hyman (their numerous duet dates are classics), Scott Hamilton, Howard Alden, and Ellis Larkins (with whom he first recorded in the mid-1950s). Ruby Braff, who in later years became a master at building up his solos to a low note (!), has never lost his passion for the music that he loves and still plays with great enthusiasm and sensitivity. "Those who were privileged to hear and fall in love with the beautiful American songbook will understand me very well!"

Recommended CDs: *Hustlin' and Bustlin'* (Black Lion 760908), *Best of Braff* (Bethlehem/Avenue Jazz 75822), *Hear Me Talkin'* (Black Lion 760161), *The Grand Reunion* (Chiaroscuro 117), *The Ruby Braff-George Barnes Quartet* (Chiaroscuro 126), *A First* (Concord Jazz 4274), *Music from "My Fair Lady"* (Concord Jazz 4393), *Music from "South Pacific"* (Concord Jazz 4445), *And His New England Songhounds, Vol. 1* (Concord Jazz 4478), *Controlled Nonchalance, Vol. 1* (Arbors 19134)

LPs to Search For: *Fireworks* (Inner City 1153),

Recommended Reading: *American Musicians II* by Whitney Balliett (Oxford University Press, 1996), *Jazz Spoken Here* by Wayne Enstice and Paul Rubin (Louisiana State University Press, 1992), *Jazz Talking* by Max Jones (Da Capo Press, 1987)

Videos to Get: *Ruby Braff Trio in Concert* (1995; Storyville 6054)

OSCAR BRASHEAR
• • • • • • • • • • • • • • • •

b. Aug. 18, 1944, Chicago, IL

A powerful hard bop trumpeter who surprisingly has never led a record date of his own, Oscar Brashear has been a strong player for over 30 years, influenced most by Freddie Hubbard but with his own sound. Brashear began piano lessons when he was seven (studying formally until he was 16), starting on the trumpet when he was ten. "My cousin gave me his old trumpet and I began playing in the Ebenezer Sunday School Church Band." Brashear studied under the legendary Captain Walter Dyett at DuSable High School and attended Wright College (1962–65) and Roosevelt University (1965–67).

Brashear, who joined the union when he was 16, toured with Woody Herman (1967) and Count Basie (1968–69). After spending a period as a member of the house band at Chicago's The Apartment (playing with visiting greats, including Sonny Stitt, Gene Ammons, Dexter Gordon, James Moody, and Eddie Harris), in 1970 he moved permanently to Los Angeles, where he became busy in the studios while also having a career in jazz. Among some of the trumpeter's most important jazz associations since then have been those with the Gerald Wilson Orchestra, Oliver Nelson, Horace Silver, Benny Carter, Teddy Edwards, and Billy Childs (with whom he has frequently performed duets), recording with Hampton Hawes, Bobby

Hutcherson, Joe Henderson, McCoy Tyner, and J.J. Johnson. In addition, Brashear has co-led a quintet with Harold Land and currently works with the Clayton-Hamilton Jazz Orchestra.

Although he listed as his future goal "to record my compositions on my CD," do not look in record stores for dates under Oscar Brashear's name, at least not yet! He remains one of the unsung greats.

Recommended CDs: with the Clayton-Hamilton Jazz Orchestra: *Groove Shop* (Capri 74021), with Joe Henderson: *Canyon Lady* (Original Jazz Classics 949), with J.J. Johnson: *Pinnacles* (Original Jazz Classics 1006)

LPs to Search For: with Harold Land: *Xocia's Dance* (Muse 5772)

RICK BRAUN
. . . .

b. Allentown, PA

Rick Braun was one of the first trumpeters to become famous in instrumental pop music of the 1990s, following Chuck Mangione by a decade and preceding the rise of Chris Botti. After a brief period on drums, he started playing trumpet in the third grade. Braun studied at the Eastman School of Music and became a member of Auracle, a fusion band that recorded two albums. In 1981 he recorded his first solo album, a vocal-oriented pop date for the Japanese label Teichiku Records. Braun was active as a pop songwriter for years in addition to playing trumpet with such acts as Rod Stewart, War, and Sade. In 1993 he recorded his first American pop/jazz date (*Intimate Secrets*) and since then has become an increasingly popular attraction on the "smooth jazz" crossover circuit. *Beat Street,* from 1995, and *Body and Soul,* from the following year, were big sellers. A mellow if somewhat lightweight player who is sometimes marketed as a poppish Chet Baker, Braun has insisted that his music is usually not jazz. However, Rick Braun's playing on tenor saxophonist Boney James' recent *Shake It Up* set shows that he could probably play creative jazz if he chose that path.

Recommended CDs: *Intimate Secrets* (Mesa 79047), *Night Walk* (Bluemoon (79193), *Beat Street* (Bluemoon 92559), *Body and Soul* (Bluemoon 92743), *Full Stride* (Atlantic 83141), with Boney James: *Shake It Up* (Warner Bros. 47557)

RANDY BRECKER
. . . .

b. Nov. 27, 1945, Philadelphia, PA

A very versatile trumpeter who has appeared on countless studio sessions, Randy Brecker is a bebopper at heart, sounding at his best when in a freewheeling straightahead session. Brecker was introduced to jazz through his father, whom he described as "a semipro jazz pianist and trumpet fanatic. In school when I was eight, they only offered trumpet or clarinet. I chose trumpet from hearing Diz, Miles, Clifford, and Chet Baker at home. My brother didn't want to play the same instrument as I did, so three years later he chose clarinet!" The older brother of tenor saxophonist Michael Brecker, Randy had classical trumpet lessons and attended Indiana University (1963–66) and New York University (1966–67). Brecker was a member of Blood, Sweat and Tears in 1967, the Horace Silver Quintet (1968–70 and 1971–72), and Art Blakey's Jazz Messengers (1972).

In the 1970s the trumpeter became very busy in the studios but also found time to play with the big bands of Clark Terry, Duke Pearson, Thad Jones/Mel Lewis, Joe Henderson, and Frank Foster, the fusion group Dreams (which included Michael Brecker), Larry Coryell's Eleventh House (1973–74), and Billy Cobham (1974–75). During 1975–80 he teamed up with his sibling to co-lead the Brecker Brothers, a band that mixed jazz solos with funk and R&B. The Brecker Brothers were a commercial success, and Randy Brecker is still most famous for that association.

In the 1980s Brecker co-led a short-term band with his wife, pianist Eliane Elias, and he was with Jaco Pastorius' Word of Mouth Orchestra during 1981–82. Since then he has mostly appeared in bop-oriented groups, in addition to working in the studios, guesting with the Mingus Big Band and special all-star groups, and occasionally participating in Brecker Brothers reunions. In the early 1990s he named as his favorite personal recordings two albums by the Brecker Brothers (*Brecker Brothers* and *Heavy Metal Bebop*), Jack Wilkins' *Merge,* and his own *In the Idiom* and *Live at Sweet Basil.*

"I grew up in the 'information age,' where media technology made many different styles of music available to my ears. This easy accessibility had a great influence on my development and continues today. I try to absorb all sounds and styles by osmosis and reorganize them into something personal." His many influences have given Randy Brecker a very flexible style, but he sounds particularly at home in boppish settings.

Recommended CDs: *Score* (Blue Note 82202), *In the Idiom* (Denon 33CY-1483), *Into the Sun* (Concord Vista 4761), with Jack Wilkins: *Merge* (Chiaroscuro 156)

Videos to Get: *Gil Evans and His Orchestra* (1987; View Video), *GRP All-Star Big Band* (1992; GRP 9672)

CECIL BRIDGEWATER

* * * * * * * * * * * * * * * * * * * *

b. Oct. 10, 1942, Urbana, IL

Cecil Bridgewater, a top-notch hard bop trumpeter, is most famous for his longtime membership in the Max Roach Quartet. Bridgewater, whose brother is tenor saxophonist Ron Bridgewater and who was married to singer Dee Dee Bridgewater in the 1970s, had a father, grandfather, and great-grandfather who were trumpeters. In addition, his mother played piano and sang, and his uncles on both sides of the family also played music. "The first concert I ever went to was to hear Louis Armstrong. The second one was to hear Duke Ellington. I was hooked! I started with piano, Mom taught me, and then I played alto sax before switching to trumpet. I also play drums. I think every musician should play drums in order to get a sense of time."

A solid soloist, Cecil Bridgewater has been a member of Max Roach's Quartet for nearly 30 years.

Although he was interested in becoming an athlete, music eventually took over. "Between my 15th and 16th years, during the summer I spent every waking moment practicing the trumpet and piano, teaching myself how to write music. In the fall I went out for the football team, totally out of shape. I got buried in a tackling drill. Music was it from then on!" After studying music at the University of Illinois (1960–64 and 1968–69), he played with his brother in the short-lived Bridgewater Brothers band in 1969 (which recorded *Lightning and Thunder* and *Generations Suite*), had a stint with Horace Silver's quintet, and worked with the Thad Jones/Mel Lewis Orchestra (1970–76).

Cecil Bridgewater has been a member of the Max Roach Quartet since 1971, and in 1992 finally recorded his debut as a leader. He has also worked with Art Blakey's Jazz Messengers (1972), Jimmy Heath (1974–76), Randy Weston, the Grover Mitchell Big Band, and the Count Basie Orchestra (1989), recording with Abdullah Ibrahim (1973), Charles McPherson, and Frank Foster, among others.

"I try to develop my ideas rather than just my technique. If someone hears only my technique, then I have failed. If I want to be like Louis Armstrong, Duke Ellington, Dizzy Gillespie, Max Roach, Thelonious Monk, John Coltrane, etc., then I have to be as original a thinker as they were, not just copy what they did."

Recommended CDs: *I Love Your Smile* (Bluemoon 79187), with Max Roach: *To the Max* (Bluemoon 79164)

RANDY BROOKS

• • • • • • • • • • • • • • •

b. Mar. 15, 1918, Sanford, ME, d. Mar. 21, 1967, Springvale, ME

Randy Brooks is an obscure name today due to a disastrous stroke that cut short his career. He seemed poised in the late 1940s to achieve the success that Ray Anthony would have, as an appealing swing-based trumpeter with a sweet tone.

Brooks began playing trumpet when he was six. Five years later he was discovered by Rudy Vallee, who for two years featured him as a soloist (as a novelty due to his age) with his Connecticut Yankees. Once Brooks had completed high school, his professional career really began, for he had stints with the big bands of Hal Kemp, Claude Thornhill, Bob Allen, Art Jarrett (who in 1941 led the Kemp ghost band), and, most importantly, Les Brown (1944–45).

The year 1945 was rather late for someone to start a swing orchestra, but Randy Brooks had surprising success for a couple of years. Utilizing the arrangements of John Benson Brooks (no relation), the trumpeter had hit records in "Tenderly" (which was a million seller), "Harlem Nocturne," and "The Man with the Horn." Brooks was a lyrical soloist who could play powerfully but was particularly strong on ballads, where his melancholy horn could be quite haunting. His orchestra also featured Shorty Allen on piano and vibes, altoist Eddie Kane, and for a short time in 1946, Stan Getz on tenor.

Randy Brooks married the glamorous bandleader Ina Ray Hutton, moved to the West Coast, and seemed set for what would at a minimum be a successful career in the studios. But a devastating stroke ended his career. After many years of being forgotten by the music world, he died in 1967 in a fire at his mother's home.

Recommended CDs: *Issued Recordings-1945–1947* (Jazz Band 2141), *Randy Brooks and His Orchestra 1945 and 1947* (Circle 35)

CLIFFORD BROWN

• • • • • • • • • • • • • • •

b. Oct. 30, 1930, Wilmington, DE, d. June 26, 1956, Bedford, PA

Of the many tragedies that have befallen jazz through the decades, it is difficult to come up with a more unfair one than Clifford Brown's death in a car accident. Sleeping in the back seat of a car that was also carrying pianist Richie Powell, Brownie was probably unaware of the fatal accident; Powell's wife (who was near-sighted) lost control of the car during a rainstorm. Brown, a clean liver who did not use drugs, did not smoke, and rarely drank, was only 25.

One of the finest trumpeters of all time, Brownie was also among the most influential. His style was based to a large extent on Fats Navarro's, although his tone was a bit more beautiful. After his death, such major players as Lee Morgan, Freddie Hubbard, and Woody Shaw (all of whom would become major influences themselves) used Brown's tone and style as a starting point for their own significant careers.

Even though he only recorded for four years, many jazz listeners consider Clifford Brown to be the greatest jazz trumpeter of them all.

Clifford Brown's father, an amateur musician, played trumpet, violin, and piano. Brownie began playing trumpet when he was 13, he gained experience with his high school band, and he managed to catch the tail end of the classic bebop era. Brown worked in clubs around Philadelphia as early as 1948 and was encouraged by Fats Navarro, Charlie Parker, and Dizzy Gillespie (getting a chance to sit in with Dizzy's big band), all of whom were quite impressed by him. He attended Delaware State College as a math major and was at Maryland State University for a short time, but this period was cut short by a serious car accident in June 1950 that kept him disabled for a year.

After his complete recovery, Brownie made his first recordings, in 1952 with Chris Powell's Blue Flames, a rhythm and blues band. In 1953 he really began to be noticed and was soon considered the most exciting new trumpeter in jazz. Brown worked and recorded with Tadd Dameron and toured Europe with Lionel Hampton's orchestra later in 1953. He did not make any studio recordings with Hampton, but while in Europe Brown headed sessions with a quartet (particularly excelling on ballads such as "It Might As Well Be Spring"), a sextet, and a big band.

In early 1954, Brown had a real opportunity to stretch out during a historic engagement at Birdland with a quintet also including Art Blakey (the leader), Lou Donaldson, Horace Silver, and Curly Russell, a group that directly preceded Blakey's Jazz Messengers; fortunately, quite a few selections were recorded. A few months later, the trumpeter traveled to Los Angeles to co-lead a new band with drummer Max Roach. Originally the quintet also included tenor saxophonist Teddy Edwards, pianist Carl Perkins, and bassist George Bledsoe. While in Los Angeles, Brownie starred on several exciting recorded jam sessions, made records with singers Dinah Washington, Helen Merrill, and Sarah Vaughan, and led a date with top West Coast jazz musicians, playing arrangements by Jack Montrose.

Within a couple of months, the Clifford Brown/Max Roach Quintet had its "permanent" personnel, with tenor saxophonist Harold Land on tenor, Richie Powell, and bassist George Morrow. A hard-swinging group that fell between bop and hard bop, the band recorded regularly for Emarcy and was a perfect vehicle for Brownie's playing. Brown, who was also a talented songwriter (among his compositions were "Joy Spring," "Daahoud," and "Sandu"), recorded with strings in 1955 and was considered one of the young giants of jazz. After Land had to return to Los Angeles due to family commitments, Sonny Rollins took his place, a change that made the Brown/Roach Quintet even stronger and very much into a supergroup.

On the night of June 25, 1956, Brownie appeared at a jam session in Philadelphia and his playing on "Walkin'," "A Night in Tunisia," and "Donna Lee" was stunning; the music was released on record a couple of decades later. But Clifford Brown would never get the chance to pick up his horn again. Just a few hours later his life ended in the tragic car accident. Benny Golson's emotional ballad "I Remember Clifford" best sums up the shock of Brownie's fellow musicians at this major loss.

Recommended CDs: *Clifford Brown Quartet in Paris* (Original Jazz Classics 357), *Clifford Brown and Max Roach* (Verve 314 543 306), *A Study in Brown* (Emarcy 814 646), *At Basin Street* (Emarcy 814 648), *The Beginning and the End* (Columbia/Legacy 66491)

Box Sets: *The Complete Blue Note and Pacific Jazz Recordings* (4 CDs; Pacific Jazz 34195), *The Complete Emarcy Recordings* (10 CDs; Emarcy 838 306)

Film Appearances: In the late 1990s a film clip from a long-lost 1955 Soupy Sales variety show was discovered, featuring Clifford Brown playing two songs; this is the only known footage of the great trumpeter.

MARSHALL BROWN

· · · · · · · · · · · · · · · · · ·

b. Dec. 21, 1920, Framingham, MA, d. Dec. 13, 1983, New York, NY

One of two musicians in this book who specialized on the bass trumpet (Cy Touff is the other), Marshall Brown also played valve trombone and was important as an educator. Born to a pair of performing parents (his mother played piano for silent movies, while his father was a magician in vaudeville), Brown taught himself the guitar when he was nine and began playing valve trombone at 16. He spent 1942–45 in the Army (where he had opportunities to play and arrange music), graduated from New York University in 1949, and earned a master's degree from Columbia University in 1953. Brown taught at Farmingdale High School during 1951–57, directing a student dance band that appeared at the 1957 Newport Jazz Festival. Producer George Wein liked what he heard, and soon Brown was appointed the head of the International Youth Band, organizing a group of teenagers from a variety of countries to play at the Brussels World Fair and the 1958 Newport Jazz Festival. In 1959 and 1960 he headed the Newport Youth Band at the Newport Jazz Festival. Among the musicians from these ensembles who became well known in later years are Jimmy Owens, Dusko Goykovich, Albert Mangelsdorff, Gabor Szabo, and Ronnie Cuber.

As a musician, Marshall Brown did his most significant work in the 1960s. He worked with Ruby Braff during 1960–61 and then collaborated with Pee Wee Russell during 1961–62 and 1965, persuading the unique clarinetist to perform and record advanced material (including songs by John Coltrane and Ornette Coleman) with his bass trumpet in a pianoless quartet. Eventually Russell (a very spontaneous player who was an alcoholic) rebelled at Brown's restrictive settings, but two fine recordings by this musical odd couple resulted before the group broke up. Brown also worked with Bobby Hackett in 1964, Eddie Condon (1966–67), Roy Eldridge (1968–70), and altoist Lee Konitz in various groups during 1971–74. Marshall Brown, who never led his own record date, stayed active as a teacher during the remainder of his life.

LPs to Search For: with Pee Wee Russell: *Ask Me Now* (Impulse 96)

TOM BROWNE

· · · · · · · · · · · · · · · ·

b. Oct. 30, 1954, Queens, NY

A technically skilled trumpeter with a tone that is a little reminiscent of Freddie Hubbard, Tom Browne has mostly pursued a career in commercial music despite his potential talents. Browne started on piano when he was 11, soon switching to trumpet. He attended New York's High School of Music and Art and was a physics major at Kingsborough University and Queens College. However, he recorded with altoist Sonny Fortune in 1976 and soon decided to switch his career to music.

After being signed to the GRP label in 1979, Browne recorded mostly funk-oriented jazz, with just an occasional straightahead selection included to show what he could do if given the chance. After four best-selling albums for GRP and two for Arista, Browne retired from music in 1988 to become a charter pilot. Six years later he returned, recording *Mo' Jamaica Funk* for Hip-Bop. In 1995 he cut *The Essence of Funk* CD with a fairly straightahead jazz group and followed it up with his strongest jazz date yet, *Another Shade of Browne*. However, Tom Browne has since largely dropped out of music again, a loss to jazz.

Recommended CDs: *The Essence of Funk* (Hip Bop 8007), *Another Shade of Browne* (Hip Bop 8011)

PHILLIPPE BRUN
• • • • • • • • • • • • • • •

b. Apr. 29, 1908, Paris, France, d. Jan. 14, 1994, Paris, France

Phillippe Brun was the top jazz trumpeter in France during the 1930s and one of the very first European soloists who could be compared favorably with his American counterparts. Brun, who studied violin at the Paris Conservatoire of Music, switched to trumpet in 1926 and was completely self-taught. During 1928–29 he worked with Gregor, gigged with visiting Americans Bud Freeman and Danny Polo, and recorded with Ray Ventura's Collegians. In late 1929 Brun moved to England, where he was a key soloist with Jack Hylton's orchestra through 1935, also working with Ambrose.

Returning to Paris in the mid-1930s, Brun worked with the Jazz du Poste Parisien, Bob Huber, and Ray Ventura (1936–40). He recorded with Django Reinhardt (whenever the guitarist expanded his group), Alix Combelle, Danny Polo (six titles on a date in 1939), and the Hot Club Swing Stars in addition to cutting 20 selections as a leader during 1937–40, most of which included Reinhardt. Brun spent the occupation years (1941–44) in Switzerland, where he played with Andre Ekyan, Teddy Stauffer, and Eddie Brunner, recording 26 titles for the Swiss Elite Special label. After the war years, Brun primarily led his own bands in France before retiring from music in the early 1960s. Ironically, in the postwar years he just led a single three-song Dixieland session in the mid-1950s.

It is a pity that Philippe Brun never visited the United States, for his swing-oriented playing uplifted quite a few records in Europe during the 1930s and early '40s and his fame could have spread to the United States in the '50s.

Recommended CDs: with Alix Combelle: *1935–1940* (Classics 714)

ABBIE BRUNIES
• • • • • • • • • • • • • • •

b. Jan. 19, 1900, New Orleans, LA, d. Oct. 2, 1978, Biloxi, MS

The Brunies family was one of the most musical in all of New Orleans. While the Marsalis family is rightfully renowned for having a father and four famous sons who have made their mark on music, the Brunies clan included father Henry (violin), mother Elizabeth (piano), daughter Ada (guitar), and six sons: bassist Rudy, cornetist Richie (the latter two played on just a part-time basis), trombonist Henry, the famous trombonist George Brunies, Merritt Brunies (who doubled on cornet and valve trombone), and cornetist Abbie Brunies. In addition, there was a nephew who played drums, Albert "Little Abbie" Brunies.

Abbie, the fifth of the six sons, obviously grew up around music. He started performing in public as early as 1910, led one of Jack "Papa" Laine's bands as a teenager, and in 1919 took a group into a roadhouse located just outside of New Orleans called The Halfway House. That unit stayed together for nine years, and fortunately 22 recordings were made during 1925–28. The first two selections (from January 22, 1925) had the legendary and ill-fated clarinetist Leon Rappolo in the frontline. Otherwise, the sextet features Brunies' mellow and often low-register cornet (filling in quite ably for the lack of a trombone), the reeds of the underrated Charlie Cordella (later replaced by Sidney Arodin on clarinet), altoist Joe Loyacano (by late 1927), and a four-piece rhythm section. The Halfway House Orchestra was one of the finest bands to be recorded in New Orleans, and their ensemble-oriented music set the standard for New Orleans jazz of the mid-1920s before Louis Armstrong's solo-oriented approach became influential.

Once the 1920s ended, Brunies remained in New Orleans, playing at a variety of jobs and spending periods working outside of music. In 1946 he moved to nearby Biloxi, Mississippi, and opened a café. In 1957 he teamed up with his brother Merritt Brunies for a superior recording for the American Music label that has been reissued on CD and shows that Abbie was still in fine form, playing in a largely unchanged style. Otherwise Abbie Brunies was content just to play locally and let brother George gain all the fame.

Recommended CDs: *Halfway House Orchestra* (Jazz Oracle 8001), *Brunies Brothers Dixieland Jazz Band* (American Music 077)

MERRITT BRUNIES
● ● ● ● ● ● ● ● ● ● ● ● ● ● ● ● ● ● ●

b. Dec. 25, 1895, New Orleans, LA, d. Feb. 5, 1973, Biloxi, MS

The fourth of six musical brothers (the best known of whom was trombonist George), Merritt Brunies was a fine cornetist in his early days and the bandleader of the family. He first played with the Brunies family band, and, growing up in New Orleans, there were plenty of opportunities to perform music. He led the Original New Orleans Jazz Band during 1916–18 (at one time or another it included his brothers George, Henry, and Albert), a group that he took to Chicago but that unfortunately never recorded. Merritt and Henry spent some time in Los Angeles playing with Angelo Schiro and in San Francisco with Chris Mann. Back in Chicago, when the influential New Orleans Rhythm Kings (which included George Brunies) left the Friars Inn in 1923, Merritt put together his own Friars Inn Orchestra and took its place.

Merritt Brunies' Friars Inn Orchestra played at the establishment for two years and lasted until 1926, recording 15 selections; all of the tunes plus two test pressings were issued in the 1980s on a Retrieval LP. In addition to Merritt (who had an enthusiastic style) and Henry (heard on trombone), the octet/nonet included clarinetist Volly DeFaut and three other horn players. Among the songs performed by the unit was the standard "Angry," which Merritt and Henry cowrote.

Brunies continued leading bands until the late 1920s, when he moved permanently to Biloxi, Mississippi. During his last four decades he became a policeman and played music only part-time. By the time he made his next (and final) recording (a 1957 American Music album with Abbie called *The Brunies Brothers Dixieland Jazz Band*), Merritt Brunies had switched to valve trombone. He continued working at occasional musical jobs in the old New Orleans jazz style up until his death in 1973.

Recommended CDs: *Brunies Brothers Dixieland Jazz Band* (American Music 077)

LPs to Search For: *Up Jumped the Devil* (Retrieval 124)

BOBBY BRYANT
• • • • • • • • • • • • • •

b. May 19, 1934, Hattiesburg, MS, d. June, 1998, Los Angeles, CA

A fine lead trumpeter and all-round player who occasionally soloed, Bobby Bryant was based in the Los Angeles area for many years. He started out playing both trumpet and tenor in school bands. Bryant studied classical music and trumpet at the Cosmopolitan School of Music in Chicago (1952–57), worked locally (including with the MJT + 3 and Red Saunders), spent part of 1960 in New York, and then moved permanently to Los Angeles in 1961. He spent much of his career working in the studios (appearing on many movie soundtracks and as part of countless horn sections) but also played with the big bands of Oliver Nelson and Gerald Wilson, appeared with Charles Mingus at the 1964 Monterey Jazz Festival, and was a member of both the Juggernaut and (late in his life) the Clayton-Hamilton Jazz Orchestra, in addition to his own part-time big band.

Bryant, who also worked as an educator, was a very valuable contributor to jazz behind the scenes. Bad health plagued him in the 1990s, but he was playing part-time almost to the end. As a leader, Bobby Bryant (who never recorded enough as a soloist) led big band dates for VeeJay (1961), two for Pacific Jazz in 1969, and one for Cadet (1971), in addition to a sextet set for Cadet in 1967; unfortunately, all are quite difficult to find.

Recommended CDs: with Clayton-Hamilton Jazz Orchestra: *Groove Shop* (Capri 74021)

CLORA BRYANT
• • • • • • • • • • • • • •

b. May 30, 1929, Denison, TX

One of the top female trumpeters of the 1950s and in the decades since, Clora Bryant has recorded surprisingly little through the years, but she was an excellent bop improviser. After starting on piano, she switched to trumpet so she could go to her high school football games as part of the marching band. Bryant attended Prairie View University in Texas, playing with the all-girl school orchestra. She also had brief stints with the Sweethearts of Rhythm (one week in 1946), the Four Vees, the Queens of Swing, Jack McVea's all-female orchestra, and the Sepia Tones (1951). In 1957 Bryant led a quartet album for Mode (her only recording as a leader), and afterward she spent much of her career playing with show bands or gigging in obscurity in Los Angeles. Bryant toured with Johnny Otis (1980–82) and was with Jimmy and Jeannie Cheatham's Sweet Baby Blues Band during 1986–89. In 1989 she wrote a letter to Mikhail Gorbachev and as a result played for ten days in the Soviet Union. An occasional vocalist and a flexible trumpeter who could also fare well on Dixieland gigs, Clora Bryant retired from active playing in the 1990s.

Recommended CDs: *Gal with a Horn* (V.S.O.P. 42), with the Cheathams: *Back to the Neighborhood* (Concord Jazz 4373)

Recommended Reading: *Central Avenue Sounds*, ed. Clora Bryant, et. al. (University of California Press, 1998)

TEDDY BUCKNER

. . . .

b. July 16, 1909, Sherman, TX, d. Sept. 22, 1994, Los Angeles, CA

A technically skilled Dixieland player, Teddy Buckner (no relation to the Jimmy Lunceford altoist Ted Buckner) was content to spend his entire career emulating his idol, Louis Armstrong (even using Satch's All-Stars on a 1958 recording), never developing a musical personality of his own.

Buckner worked mostly in Los Angeles in the 1930s, including with Speed Webb, Sonny Clay, Cee Pee Johnson, and Les Hite; he also played with Buck Clayton's orchestra in Shanghai, China, in 1934. Buckner was Louis Armstrong's stand-in for the 1936 film *Pennies from Heaven*. After working with Lionel Hampton at the Paradise Club in Los Angeles during part of 1936, Buckner took over leadership of the band for a few years when Hampton joined Benny Goodman. The trumpeter had a second stint with Cee Pee Johnson (1944–45) and played with Benny Carter's big band (on and off during 1945–48) and Lionel Hampton's orchestra (1947–48). During 1949–54 he made a particularly strong impression while with Kid Ory's Creole Jazz Band, where his powerful playing gave Ory's group a very different sound than it had had in other eras.

In 1955 Buckner formed his own Dixieland band, which he led for decades. While in France in 1958, he held his own with Sidney Bechet, refusing to play a support role behind the fiery soprano saxophonist; Louis Armstrong had had the same battle with Bechet 18 years earlier! During 1965–81 Buckner's group was a regular fixture at Disneyland, playing nightly for tourists and to a large extent emulating the Louis Armstrong All-Stars. Teddy Buckner, who recorded as a leader for GNP/Crescendo and its subsidiary Dixieland Jubilee in the 1950s plus for the Real Jazz label in 1978, retired from playing in 1985.

LPs to Search For: *A Salute to Louis Armstrong* (Dixieland Jubilee 505), *On the Sunset Strip* (Dixieland Jubilee 510)

Film Appearances: *King of Burlesque* with Fats Waller (1935), *The Wild Party* (1956), *St. Louis Blues* (1958), *King Creole* (1958), *4 for Texas* (1963)

BOB BURNET

•••••••••••

b. 1912, Chicago, IL, d. Aug. 3, 1984, Guadalajara, Mexico

A fine swing trumpeter, Bob Burnet recorded many solos with Charlie Barnet's orchestra but dropped out of music when he was 30 and has been forgotten ever since.

Burnet started out playing drums, piano, and banjo before switching permanently to trumpet. At Berkshire School (where at one point he traded a watch for a trumpet!), Burnet led the school orchestra. After playing with hotel bands in Bermuda and gigging with Eddie Neibauer's orchestra in Chicago, Burnet was with Charlie Barnet's big band during 1938–40. The main soloist in the group, next to the leader, Burnet displayed an attractive tone and an expertise with mutes, plus consistent swing and subtle wit in his playing that perfectly fit the Duke Ellington-influenced music that Barnet preferred. When Burnet originally left Barnet, he led a short-lived integrated sextet (which had five black musicians) at Café Society Uptown. A second stint with Barnet (1941–42) lasted until the trumpeter was drafted. After working as a radio engineer in the military during World War II, Burnet decided to stay in the electronics field rather than return to music after his discharge. Surprisingly, in 1957 he popped up on an obscure Dixieland record by Freddie Wacker's Windy City Seven, but that was his only postwar recording. Bob Burnet moved to Mexico in 1958 and was not heard from in the music world again other than occasionally playing flute with a local symphony orchestra.

Recommended CDs: with Charlie Barnet: *Clap Hands, Here Comes Charlie* (Bluebird 6273), *The Transcription Performances 1941* (Hep 53)

DAVE BURNS

•••••••••••

b. Mar. 5, 1924, Perth Amboy, NJ

An excellent early bebop trumpeter who was one of the first to be influenced by Dizzy Gillespie, Dave Burns never rose above the journeyman level, despite his talents.

Burns started playing trumpet when he was nine. Although Louis Armstrong was his first trumpet hero, hearing Dizzy Gillespie jamming at Minton's Playhouse stimulated Burns to modernize his style. He played with the Savoy Sultans during 1942–43 and, after leading an Army Air Force Band while in the military (1943–45), gained some recognition for his work with the first two Dizzy Gillespie big bands (1945 and 1946–49), even though he was in a support role behind the leader. Burns spent 1950–52 with Duke Ellington's orchestra (where he rarely had a chance to solo) but was a valuable member of James Moody's octet during 1952–57, where he did have solo space. Other associations included the Billy Mitchell-Al Grey band (1961–63), Willie Bobo (1963–65), and co-leading a group with drummer Bill English at Minton's Playhouse (1966–68). Primarily active as a jazz educator after 1970, Dave Burns in his career recorded with Gillespie, Ellington, Moody, the Bebop Boys, Eddie Jefferson, Milt Jackson, Johnny Griffin, Dexter Gordon, George Wallington, and Art Taylor, among others, plus he led two little-known albums for Vanguard during 1962–63.

Recommended CDs: with James Moody: *Moody's Mood for Blues* (Original Jazz Classics 1837), *Hi-Fi Party* (Original Jazz Classics 1780), *Wail, Moody, Wail* (Original Jazz Classics 1791), with Art Taylor: *A.T.'s Delight* (Blue Note 84047)

LPs to Search For: with Dexter Gordon: *Landslide* (Blue Note LT-1051)

Videos to Get: *Jivin' in Bebop* (1947) with Dizzy Gillespie's orchestra, *Sweet Love Bitter* (1967).

HENRY BUSSE

• • • • • • • • • • • • • •

b. May 19, 1894, Magdeburg, Germany, d. Apr. 23, 1955, Memphis, TN

Although Henry Busse's solos from the 1920s sound quite dated today and he rarely improvised, if a poll had been conducted in 1924 asking white America to name the top jazz cornetist, Busse would have won in a landslide! A part-time cornetist during World War I who played with various ensembles, Busse teamed up with Paul Whiteman in 1918 to form a dance orchestra. Legend has it that Whiteman became the sole leader because the cornetist had a thick German accent and was very shy to talk on stage. The Paul Whiteman Orchestra became the most popular dance band of the 1920s, with Whiteman being crowned by press agents "The King of Jazz." Although that title was inaccurate (unlike Benny Goodman in the mid-1930s being rightfully called "The King of Swing"), Whiteman did his best to integrate jazz into popular music of the era. During 1918–28, Henry Busse was his most famous sideman, taking muted solos on "Wang Wang Blues," "Hot Lips" (which was written specifically for Busse by Henry Lange and Lou Davis in 1922), and Whiteman's favorite song, "When Day Is Done." The latter best shows off Busse's role as "hot cornet" with the orchestra. The overarranged concert rendition is full of semi-classical effects, giving way for one chorus as Busse (backed by a swinging bass) beautifully plays the melody, a bit of musical relief before the ponderous effects return.

By 1928, Busse was making $350 a week with Whiteman, but he was increasingly dissatisfied with the amount of solo space given to the young upstart Bix Beiderbecke. "Mary" and "Love Nest" contrast Busse's increasingly dated sweet sound with that of Bix's, showing the progress that jazz had made since 1920. In April 1928, after an argument with Whiteman, Busse was fired and quickly replaced by the sound-alike Harry Goldfield (father of Don Goldie).

Busse quickly formed his own orchestra, with which he worked steadily up until 1955, mostly featuring commercial dance music with shuffle rhythms on the more uptempo material. Busse's exaggerated vibrato remained unchanged, and he never tired of playing "Hot Lips" and "When Day Is Done" in unchangeable note-for-note renditions.

Henry Busse met an unusual end, suffering a heart attack while playing at the National Undertakers Convention in Memphis, Tennessee. Whether members of the audience fought over his body is not known!

Recommended CDs: with Paul Whiteman: *Original 1927 Recordings* (Nostalgia Arts 3006)

LPs to Search For: *The Uncollected Henry Busse-1935* (Hindsight 122), *Paul Whiteman, Vol. 1* (RCA LPV 555)

BILLY BUTTERFIELD

. . . .

b. Jan. 14, 1917, Middletown, OH, d. Mar. 18, 1988, North Palm Beach, FL

Billy Butterfield was a very valuable trumpet player, having an appealing warm tone, being an expert sight-reader, and showing equal skill on ballads and hot jazz jams. Throughout his career he was one of the most consistent and reliable of all trumpeters. And whether in a big band or a studio orchestra, he had the ability to play any of the parts (from lead to soloist) and sound effortless.

Butterfield played violin, bass, and trombone before settling on trumpet. He attended high school in Wyoming and studied medicine at Transylvania College but was more interested in playing jazz. Early associations included stints with the bands of Dick Raymond, Andy Anderson, and Austin Wylie (1935). At the age of 20, Butterfield found his initial fame as a member of the Bob Crosby Orchestra and the Crosby Bobcats, where he was an important soloist during 1937–40, particularly after Yank Lawson departed in 1938 to join Tommy Dorsey. Most notable among his solos was his lyrical spot on Bob Haggart's "I'm Free," a song that would soon be retitled "What's New."

After leaving Crosby in 1940, Butterfield worked briefly with Bob Strong's orchestra and appeared in the Hollywood movie *Second Chorus* as part of Artie Shaw's orchestra. Butterfield soloed on "Concerto for Clarinet" and ghosted the trumpet part for actor Burgess Meredith. After the film was completed, he became a member of Shaw's new big band. The clarinetist recognized Butterfield's talents and gave him the opening chorus on his classic version of "Stardust." That solo alone would have ensured Butterfield's immortality. The trumpeter was also a featured member of Shaw's Gramercy Five. When Shaw broke up his orchestra, Butterfield had stints with the big bands of Benny Goodman (1941–42) and Les Brown before working in the studios for NBC and CBS and spending a period in the military (1944–45). After his discharge, Butterfield formed a big band, which unfortunately folded after two years despite making some excellent recordings (many of which were ballad oriented and featured arrangements by clarinetist Bill Stegmeyer) for Capitol.

That rare failure was just a temporary setback for Butterfield. He became a full-time studio musician while still remaining quite active in jazz. The trumpeter was often utilized on the mood music records of Jackie Gleason and Ray Conniff but more importantly popped up on many Dixieland dates with Eddie Condon, the Lawson-Haggart band, and Bob Crosby alumni. He also led many records of his own, including a 1959 tribute to Bix Beiderbecke. Butterfield recorded along the way with Lester Young, Benny Goodman, Jack Teagarden, Billie Holiday, and Mel Powell and on some of Buck Clayton's jam sessions. Although he left the studios in the mid-1960s to settle in Florida, the trumpeter was far from inactive and during 1968–72 toured the world with the World's Greatest Jazz Band. Reuniting with Yank Lawson and Bob Haggart in the WGJB, Butterfield's interplay with Lawson was always memorable and exciting.

Billy Butterfield remained a popular attraction on the Dixieland circuit up until his death, appearing often at classic jazz festivals, touring Europe, and recording as late as 1982 before cancer forced him to stop playing.

Recommended CDs: *Pandora's Box-1946* (Hep 49), with Bob Crosby: *South Rampart Street Parade* (GRP/Decca 615), with Artie Shaw: *Personal Best* (Bluebird 61099), *The Complete Gramercy Five Sessions* (Bluebird 7637), with the World's Greatest Jazz Band: *Live* (Atlantic 90982)

LPs to Search For: *Ted Easton's Jazzband* (Circle 37), *Watch What Happens* (Jazzology 93)

Recommended Reading: *Stomp Off, Let's Go* by John Chilton (Jazz Book Service, 1983)

Film Appearances: *Second Chorus* (1940) with Artie Shaw, also ghosts trumpet solos for Burgess Meredith

DONALD BYRD

•••••••••••••

b. Dec. 9, 1932, Detroit, MI

Donald Byrd has had a very episodic career. One of the most promising young trumpeters of the 1950s, he realized much of his potential in the 1960s, switched to a very commercial brand of R&B and funk in the '70s, was barely active on the trumpet during the '80s, and made a partial comeback in the '90s.

Born Donaldson Toussaint L'Ouverture II (it is obvious why he simplified his name!), the trumpeter attended Wayne State University (graduating in 1954) and later on the Manhattan School of Music. Byrd played with bands while in the Air Force (1951–53) and then became part of the Detroit jazz scene during 1954–55. After moving to New York in mid-1955, Byrd worked with George Wallington, Art Blakey's Jazz Messengers (for a few months in 1956), and Max Roach, co-leading the Jazz Lab with Gigi Gryce.

Starting in 1955, Byrd began to record quite regularly, often in jam session formats for the Prestige label with the likes of John Coltrane and Jackie McLean. Byrd co-led a quintet with baritonist Pepper Adams (1958–61) and also had opportunities along the way to work with Sonny Rollins, Coleman Hawkins, and Thelonious Monk. After leading dates for Transition, Savoy, Columbia, Riverside, RCA, and Jubilee, in 1958 he made his debut as a leader for Blue Note. He would remain with that label almost exclusively until 1976, recording quite a few gems during his prime years in the 1960s, including *Byrd in Flight, Free Form, A New Perspective* (which utilizes voices and is highlighted by "Cristo Redentor"), and *Fancy Free*.

During the same period, Byrd became an educator, studying composition in Europe (1962–63), earning a doctorate from Columbia Teachers College, attending Howard University Law School (earning his law degree in 1976), and teaching in New York City's public schools. He would later teach at Rutgers, New York University, Brooklyn College, North Carolina Central State University, the Hampton Institute, and Howard University. This led to his surprising turn toward commercial music in the 1970s as he used some of his students on his recordings. *Electric Byrd*, from 1970, was his last straightahead jazz album for some time. In the early 1970s, Byrd became involved in performing R&B-oriented funk music, and his later Blue Note albums (*Street Lady, Stepping Into Tomorrow, Black Byrd, Places and Spaces,* and *Caricatures*) have very little jazz content and less and less of his trumpet playing. The instantly dated pop music (which resulted in the trumpeter's being branded a "sellout" by many in the jazz community) sold quite well, and it featured some of Byrd's students from Howard University, the nucleus of whom soon became the Blackbyrds, which eventually had a musical life independent of the trumpeter. After a few rather wretched releases for Elektra (including an album called *Thank You for Funking Up My Life!*), Byrd for a few years largely retired from playing trumpet to concentrate on teaching.

In 1987 Byrd again surprised the jazz world, this time by recording a straightahead album for Landmark, using a quintet of top young players (including Kenny Garrett and Mulgrew Miller). Unfortunately, his trumpet chops were not at prime form (although his solos are quite listenable), and Byrd's two succeeding Landmark dates also show what he had lost by taking time off from his horn. Since that time, Donald Byrd has played on a part-time basis, continuing his teaching career and passing his knowledge down to such up-and-coming trumpeters as Darren Barrett.

Recommended CDs: Byrd in Paris, Vols. 1 & 2 (Polydor 833 394 and 833 395), *Byrd in Hand* (Blue Note 84019), *Donald Byrd at the Half Note Café, Vols. 1 & 2* (Blue Note 57187), *Free Form* (Blue Note 84118), *A New Perspective* (Blue Note 84124), *Fancy Free* (Blue Note 89796)

Box Set: The Complete Blue Note Donald Byrd/Pepper Adams Studio Sessions (4 CDs; Mosaic 4-194)

ERNIE CAGNOLATTI
. . . .

b. Apr. 2, 1911, Madisonville, LA, d. Apr. 7, 1983, New Orleans, LA

Ernie Cagnolatti was a solid New Orleans-style jazz player who lived in the South during his entire life. He had a longtime association with the obscure big band of Herbert Leary (1933–42) and gigged locally with many ensembles, including with Oscar Celestin, Alphonse Picou, and a brass band led by bass drummer George Williams. Cagnolatti gained greatest recognition for his work with drummer Paul Barbarin's group (1950–65), with whom he recorded several times. Ernie Cagnolatti (who never led his own record date) also played with Jim Robinson in the 1960s and was a fixture at Preservation Hall during 1974–80 before a stroke ended his career.

Recommended CDs: with Paul Barbarin: *Sounds of New Orleans, Vol. 1* (Storyville 6008)

ROY CAMPBELL
. . . .

b. 1952, Bronx, NY

Roy Campbell, although associated primarily with the avant-garde, is proud of his flexibility and his ability to play R&B, funk, and bebop too. He started on trumpet when he was 15 and studied in the Jazz Mobile program with Lee Morgan, Kenny Dorham, and Joe Newman. Campbell played in Manhattan Community College big bands in the late 1960s before discovering avant-garde jazz.

Since becoming an important part of the New York jazz scene, the fat-toned trumpeter has recorded and/or performed with Woody Shaw, Cecil Taylor, Jemeel Moondoc, Ellen Christi, Carlos Garnett, David Murray, Billy Bang, William Hooker, Matthew Shipp, William Parker, and other very advanced improvisers. He spent time in Holland in the early 1990s, touring with bass saxophonist Klaas Hekman's band and writing film scores, sometimes sitting in with Don Cherry's big band. After returning to the United States, Roy Campbell (who continues to free-lance with the top avant-garde players) led Other Dimensions in Music and the Pyramid Trio, a pianoless group with bassist William Parker and various drummers that he first formed in 1984.

Recommended CDs: *New Kingdom* (Delmark 456), *Other Dimensions in Music* (Silkheart 120), *Communion* (Silkheart 139), *La Tierra del Fuego* (Delmark 469), *Ancestral Homeland* (No More 7), with Matthew Shipp: *Pastoral Composure* (Thirsty Ear 57084)

CONTE CANDOLI

· · · · · · · · · · · · · · ·

b. July 12, 1927, Mishawaka, IN

There are very few trumpeters still active today who are survivors of the bebop era; even fewer of those are still playing in their prime. Conte Candoli, who has long been under-rated because he has spent most of his life living in Los Angeles, remains one of the bebop greats, performing swinging music year in and year out for decades.

The younger brother of Pete Candoli (with whom he studied trumpet in 1940), Conte (born Secondo Candoli) first played professionally as a young teenager in South Bend, Indiana. Pete was a member of Woody Herman's First Herd and helped make it possible for Conte to play with Woody Herman during his summer vacation in 1944. Conte was an official member of Herman's orchestra during January–September 1945, a period cut short by his induction in the Army. After his discharge, Candoli worked with the Chubby Jackson Sextet (touring Scandinavia in 1947–48), Stan Kenton's orchestra (1948), Charlie Ventura (1949), Herman again (1950), and Charlie Barnet (1951). His second period with Kenton (1951–53) found Candoli one of the orchestra's main stars and top soloists. After a short period in Chicago, he moved to Los Angeles in 1954. Charlie Parker was so impressed with Candoli's playing that he asked the trumpeter to be a member of the new group he was forming, but Bird died soon afterward.

Candoli became a busy studio musician as well as a regular member of Howard Rumsey's Lighthouse All-Stars, appearing on quite a few records with Rumsey for the Contemporary label. Candoli also worked with the Terry Gibbs Dream Band, Gerry Mulligan's Concert Jazz Band (in New York during 1960–61), the Shelly Manne Quintet, Pete in the Candoli Brothers, and Stan Kenton's Neophonic Orchestra for some special concerts.

Since the 1960s, Candoli has been quite active, appearing in countless settings, including as a member of Johnny Carson's *Tonight Show* orchestra for many years (starting in 1968), Supersax, Louie Bellson, the reunited Lighthouse All-Stars of the 1980s (led by Shorty Rogers), and his own small combos. Conte Candoli, influenced in the 1940s by Dizzy Gillespie and a decade later by Clifford Brown, has long had his own sound within the bebop tradition, where he remains one of its unheralded giants.

Recommended CDs: *Powerhouse Trumpet* (Bethlehem/Avenue Jazz 75826), *Conte Candoli 4* (V.S.O.P. 47), *Portrait of a Count* (Fresh Sound 5015), *Conte-Nutty* (Fresh Sound 5028), with Stan Kenton: *New Concepts of Artistry in Rhythm* (Capitol 92865), with Lighthouse All-Stars: *Volume 6* (Original Jazz Classics 386), *Music for Lighthousekeeping* (Original Jazz Classics 636), *In the Solo Spotlight* (Original Jazz Classics 451), *America the Beautiful* (Candid 79510), *Eight Brothers* (Candid 79521), with Shelly Manne: *At the Manne-Hole, Vols. 1–2* (Original Jazz Classics 714 and 715)

Film Appearances: *Bell, Book and Candle* (1958)

Videos to Get: *Shelly Manne/Shorty Rogers-Jazz Scene USA* (1962; Shanachie 6012)

PETE CANDOLI
• • • • • • • • • • • • •

b. June 28, 1923, Mishawaka, IN

The older brother of Conte Candoli, Pete Candoli could be a fine jazz player, but he spent most of his career as a first trumpeter in big bands and in the studios. He began his career in the swing era playing with such wartime orchestras as Sonny Dunham (1940–41), Will Bradley, Benny Goodman, Ray McKinley, Tommy Dorsey, Freddie Slack, and Charlie Barnet. Candoli's most important contributions to jazz history were made as a member of Woody Herman's Herd during 1944–46. Candoli not only played many of the high notes in the ensembles but shared the solo trumpet space with Sonny Berman. He also had a routine where on the hottest number (usually "Apple Honey"), he would appear at its climax in a Superman costume to hit screaming high notes!

After the Herman Herd broke up, Candoli worked with the big bands of Boyd Raeburn, Tex Beneke (1947–49), and Jerry Gray (1950–51) before moving to Los Angeles to became a busy studio musician. He took time off to work with the orchestras of Les Brown (1952) and Stan Kenton (1954–56) and co-led a popular local band with Conte (the Candoli Brothers) that made quite a few records during 1957–62. Pete Candoli, whose wives have included actress Betty Hutton and singer Edie Adams, has stayed active up to the present time (including in some Lionel Hampton all-star groups in the 1990s). Although his trumpet chops have declined a bit since the 1980s, his playing is still full of infectious spirit.

Recommended CDs: with Woody Herman: *The Thundering Herds* (Columbia 44108)

LPs to Search For: *The Brothers Candoli* (MCA/Impulse 29064), *Blues, When Your Lover Has Gone* (Somerset 17200)

Film Appearances: *Earl Carroll Vanities* (with the Woody Herman Orchestra 1945), *Bell, Book and Candle* (1958)

MARC CAPARONE

b. Nov. 19, 1973, San Luis Obispo, CA

An excellent preswing trumpeter who has studied early jazz closely (he listed 34 different names as his trumpet heroes!), Marc Caparone has strong potential for the future. His father, a trombonist, introduced his son to jazz. Caparone began playing trumpet when he was ten and knew early on that he wanted to be a jazz musician. He played his first gigs when he was 15, attended the University of California, Davis (studying history rather than music), and joined the Creole Syncopators in 1989. He has since played with Clint Baker (starting in 1991), Hal Smith, Chris Tyle, and other young musicians in the classic jazz field. Marc Caparone has also worked with his Elysian Fields Orchestra since 1994 and the Imperial Serenaders since 1999. "I try to play good music (not just good jazz) and avoid all the utter nonsense that surrounds old jazz today. I try to let good music and good scholarship stand alone."

Recommended CDs: with the Imperial Serenaders: *Music of the Bolden Era* (Stomp Off 1351), with Hal Smith: *Concentratin' on Fats* (Jazzology 299)

MUTT CAREY

b. 1891, Hahnville, LA, d. Sept. 3, 1948, Elsinore, CA

Mutt Carey's playing abilities are a little difficult to assess, since he only recorded under primitive circumstances in 1922 and at the end of his career. Thomas "Mutt" Carey was the youngest of 17 children! He played drums, guitar, and alto horn, not starting on the trumpet until he was already 22. He first joined Kid Ory's band in 1914 (after having played trumpet for only one year). Carey also worked in New Orleans with his brother Jack Carey's Crescent Brass Band, Frankie Dusen, King Oliver (an important early influence), Jimmy Brown, and Bebe Ridgeley. The trumpeter, who had the ability to play very softly and was strongly influenced by King Oliver, soon gained the nickname of "Blues King of New Orleans."

In 1917 Carey went on a vaudeville tour with a four-piece unit (which included Johnny Dodds) called Mack's Merrymakers. Carey left the band in Chicago to play with Lawrence Duhe's group, but the cold winter weather did not appeal to him and he soon returned home. In 1919 he moved to California to join Kid Ory's band, working steadily with the trombonist for the next six years. When King Oliver passed through California in 1921, audiences who had never heard him thought that he was a Mutt Carey imitator! With Ory's band (which was billed as Spikes' Seven Pods of Pepper Orchestra) in 1922, Carey recorded two instrumentals (considered the first recordings by a black New Orleans band) in addition to a few numbers backing singers Roberta Dudley and Ruth Lee. In 1925, when Ory left Los Angeles to join King Oliver in Chicago, Carey took over his small band, which he expanded and renamed the Liberty Syncopators and later the Jeffersonians. Carey's orchestra often worked in the silent film studios (providing atmospheric music for Hollywood film sets) during the next few years. However, with the rise of sound pictures and the onset of the Depression, Carey was mostly outside of music in the 1930s, having day jobs as a Pullman porter and a mailman.

He returned to full-time music in February 1944 when Kid Ory assembled a new band to play a featured song during each episode of Orson Welles' radio show. The surprise popularity of the group led them to record and perform independent of the program. Carey can be heard today on several records with Ory, including low-fidelity transcriptions of the Welles broadcasts released on Folklyric, half of an LP for Columbia, and a full album for Good Time Jazz. His style was virtually unchanged from the early days, sticking close to the melody and employing a wide vibrato, but his direct message and subtle power have a charm of their own, best displayed on "Weary Blues" and "Careless Love." Carey's lone session as a leader (ten selections last available on a Savoy double LP) is also enjoyable (particularly the fairly straight renditions of ragtime pieces), as is a 1946 session in which he backs singer-pianist Hociel Thomas. The latter has been reissued by American Music. It is almost as if King Oliver had been captured on record in the 1940s.

The trumpeter remained with Ory for 2 years, until the summer of 1947. At that point, Mutt Carey moved to Los Angeles and put together a new band. But he died of a heart attack while on vacation.

Recommended CDs: *Mutt Carey and Lee Collins* (American Music 72), with Kid Ory: *Kid Ory's Creole Jazz Band 1944/45* (Good Time Jazz 12022)

LPs to Search For: *Giants of Traditional Jazz* (Savoy 2251); with Kid Ory: *The Great New Orleans Trombonist* (Columbia 835)

Film Appearances: *Legion of the Condemned* (1928) and *The Road to Ruin* (1928), both silent films. Carey can also be seen briefly in *New Orleans* (1947).

IAN CARR
• • • • • • • • •

b. Apr. 21, 1933, Dumfries, Scotland

A versatile trumpeter who is also a fine writer on jazz, Ian Carr has made strong contributions in several areas. He grew up in England and had some piano lessons. His older brother, pianist Mike Carr, "bought me a secondhand trumpet-cornet when I was 17. Before that I was using a bugle mouthpiece and playing make-believe trumpet." Self-taught on his horn, Carr gained a degree in English literature from Durham University. After a period in the Army (1956–58), Carr spent a couple of years traveling (mostly on the European continent) before returning to Scotland in 1960 and making a firm decision to become a professional musician.

Carr worked with the Emcee Five (1960–62), with whom he recorded, co-led a quintet with Don Rendell (1962–69), had a quartet in 1965 that included guitarist John McLaughlin, and gigged with Neil Ardley, Joe Harriott, and Don Byas (touring Portugal in 1968). In 1969 he put together the fusion band Nucleus, which would be his main group during the 1970s and was still playing festivals as late as 1988. One of the first trumpeters to be influenced by Miles Davis' fusion recordings (along with Eddie Henderson), Carr became influential himself in Europe for a time. In addition, starting in 1975 he was a member of the United Jazz and Rock Ensemble, and he has since worked with the New Jazz Orchestra, Mike Gibbs, the

Hamburg Radio Orchestra, George Russell, and his own combos. In the early 1990s he called *Old Heartland* his personal favorite of the recordings he has made.

In addition to playing and teaching jazz (at the Guildhall School of Music and Drama), Ian Carr has written biographies on Miles Davis and Keith Jarrett and was one of the key contributors to *Jazz: The Essential Companion* (1987) and its successor, *Jazz: The Rough Guide* (1995). "The books I write are all part of the process of coming to grips with the making of music. Real writing is a process of discovery, and so these meditations on music are a way of growing, a way of enlarging and changing oneself."

LPs to Search For: *Social Plexus* (Vertigo 6360039), *In Flagranti Delicto* (Capitol 11171), *Out of the Long Dark* (Capitol 11916), *Awakening* (Mood 24400), *Old Heartland* (MMC 1016)

BAIKIDA CARROLL
• • • • • • • • • • • • •

b. Jan. 15, 1947, St. Louis, MO

A major utility player in avant-garde jazz who uplifts other people's sessions but is often overlooked himself, Baikida Carroll deserves to have his own music much more fully documented and exposed. Carroll attended Southern Illinois University and (while in the military) the Armed Forces School of Music. After his discharge, he directed the free jazz big band of the Black Artists Group (BAG) in St. Louis. Carroll has since recorded with Oliver Lake (1971 and 1980–81), Julius Hemphill, Michael Gregory Jackson, Muhal Richard Abrams (1980–83), Jack DeJohnette, David Murray, the Sam Rivers big band, and many others. Baikida Carroll, a highly expressive improviser, can be heard at his best on his dates as a leader for Soul Note.

Recommended CDs: *Shadows and Reflections* (Soul Note 1023), with Julius Hemphill: *Coon Bid'ness* (Black Lion 760127), with David Murray: *New Life* (Black Saint 100)

ERNIE CARSON
• • • • • • • • • • • • •

b. Dec. 4, 1937, Portland, OR

Although underpublicized, Ernie Carson is one of the great trad jazz cornetists of the past 40 years. He manages to bring back to life the emotional style of his hero, Wild Bill Davison, without resorting merely to copying. Carson started playing trumpet as a youth and was working in theater bands by the time he was a junior in high school. He was a member of the Castle Jazz Band (1954–56), served in the Marines for two years (1956–58), and then freelanced in the Los Angeles area with various local bands, including Ray Bauduc's. Since having a stint with Turk Murphy (1961–62), Carson has mostly led his own bands, including (since 1972) the Capitol City Jazz Band and (starting in 1992) a new version of the Castle Jazz Band.

Carson lived in Atlanta during 1972–95 and has since been based in Oregon, playing often at classic jazz festivals and recording for small labels. Carson's singing is humorous (in Eddie Condon's words, he "doesn't hurt anyone!") and he is a functional pianist who recorded behind Wild Bill Davison on a few 1970 sessions. But most significant is Ernie Carson's exciting cornet playing and his dedication to trad jazz; his recordings are well worth searching out.

Recommended CDs: *Southern Comfort* (GHB 162), *Every Man a King* (GHB 327), *Wher'm I Gonna Live* (Stomp Off 1277), *Old Bones* (Stomp Off 1283), with Rick Fay: *Oh Baby* (Arbors 19105)

LEE CASTLE

· · · · · · · · · ·

b. Feb. 28, 1915, New York, NY, d. Nov. 16, 1990, Hollywood, FL

The mellow-toned Lee Castle had a rather odd career, spending much of his life playing nostalgic swing. Born Aniello Castaldo, he started on drums but was inspired to start playing trumpet at 15 after his brother brought home a record of Louis Armstrong. Castaldo was initially influenced by Satch's early '30s records and was working professionally by the time he was 18. He played with a variety of small-time bands, including those of Paul Tremaine and Paul Martell. Castaldo joined Joe Haymes' orchestra in mid-1936, making his recording debut. He worked with quite a few of the key jazz orchestras of the swing era, including Artie Shaw's first big band (1936), where his trumpet was often backed by a string quartet, Red Norvo, Glenn Miller (briefly in 1939), Jack Teagarden (taking fine solos on "Beale Street Blues" and "Muddy River Blues"), a later version of the Artie Shaw Orchestra (1941), Will Bradley (1941), and Benny Goodman (1943).

Most important was Castaldo's association with Tommy Dorsey (initially off and on during 1937–41). So close was the trumpeter's relationship to the fiery bandleader that he was sent by Dorsey for a couple months to live with and take lessons from his father, a highly rated music teacher; he was soon thought of as the third Dorsey son. Castaldo, who recorded next to Lester Young in Glenn Hardman's Hammond Five in 1938, made three attempts to lead his own big band (starting in 1940), but each was a flop. The trumpeter, who was given the name of Lee Castle in the early 1940s by a booking agent so his name would fit on marquees, was just not well known enough to have a chance against the heavy competition in the swing band business. After working in the studios for a time and having a third association with Artie Shaw in 1950, in 1953 Lee Castle rejoined Tommy Dorsey.

Tommy and Jimmy Dorsey soon decided to pool their resources as the Dorsey Brothers Orchestra. Castle became their musical director, occasionally being featured on trumpet when Charlie Shavers was working elsewhere. After both of the Dorseys passed away during 1956–57, the big band was divided into two ghost orchestras, with Castle becoming the leader of the Jimmy Dorsey Orchestra (which had just recorded the hit "So Rare"). Although he was a fine soloist who enjoyed playing Dixieland (as he showed on his 1954 Jay-Dee LP, *Dixieland Heaven*, and a Miff Mole date in 1958), Lee Castle was content to de-emphasize his playing and lead the nostalgia ghost band for many years, playing predictable music associated with both of the Dorsey Brothers. By the early 1960s he owned all of the rights to the Jimmy Dorsey Orchestra, and ironically "the third Dorsey Brother" ended up being a bandleader longer than either Jimmy or Tommy Dorsey, 33 years!

DICK CATHCART

b. Nov. 6, 1924, Michigan City, IN., d. Nov. 8, 1993, Los Angeles, CA

A solid Dixieland player with a big tone, Dick Cathcart became best known for ghosting the trumpet for the various productions of *Pete Kelly's Blues.* The son of a cornetist, Cathcart started on clarinet when he was four, switching to trumpet at 13. He worked with Ray McKinley, Alvino Rey (1942), and (while in the military) the Army Air Force Radio Orchestra (1943–46). After his discharge, Cathcart was with Bob Crosby, whose group in 1946 was more of a swing orchestra than the earlier, famous Dixieland-oriented big band. Cathcart also worked in the MGM film studios (1946–49) and played Dixieland with Ben Pollack (1949–50). In 1952 he began playing the trumpet for the radio series *Pete Kelly's Blues,* which was soon succeeded by the Jack Webb movie of the same name (1955) and a television series in 1959 that had singer Connie Boswell as one of the actresses. Cathcart's own band, which recorded for RCA, Capitol, and Warner Bros., became known as Pete Kelly's Big Seven; among his sidemen at various times was Eddie Miller, Matty Matlock, Ray Sherman, Nick Fatool, and George Van Eps.

A fixture in West Coast Dixieland, in later years Cathcart played freewheeling jazz with pickup groups (sometimes using alumni from Pete Kelly's Big Seven), primarily in the Los Angeles area, often at traditional jazz festivals.

LPs to Search For: Bix MCMLIX (Warner Bros. 1275), Pete Kelly's Blues (Warner Bros. 1303)

Film Appearances: Dragnet (1954), Pete Kelly's Blues (1955), for which he dubbed Jack Webb's trumpet solos

OSCAR CELESTIN

b. Jan. 1, 1884, Napoleonville, LA, d. Dec. 15, 1954, New Orleans, LA

An important New Orleans jazz pioneer who was fortunate enough to record under favorable circumstances in the 1920s, Oscar "Papa" Celestin survived long enough to be celebrated as a living legend in the early 1950s.

After short stints early in life on guitar and mandolin, Celestin switched to trumpet. He moved to New Orleans in 1906 and played with the Indiana Brass Band, Henry Allen Sr.'s Excelsior Brass Band, the Algiers Brass Band, and the Olympia Band in addition to his own Tuxedo Band (1910–13). Celestin co-led the Original Tuxedo Orchestra with trombonist William Ridgley during 1917–25, renaming it the Tuxedo Jazz Orchestra after Ridgley dropped out; the group stayed together until the early 1930s. Not considered a major trumpeter himself (Richard Alexis split the trumpet solos with Celestin during his 1920s sessions), Celestin always led excellent ensembles, as can be heard on his five record dates of 1925–28, which include such numbers as "Original Tuxedo Rag," "Station Calls," and "It's Jam Up."

With the onset of the Depression in the 1930s, Celestin retired from music except on a part-time basis, working in a shipyard. However, by 1946 conditions had greatly improved, and he made a comeback with a new version of the Tuxedo Jazz Orchestra, one that was soon featuring veteran clarinetist Alphonse Picou (best known for his famous chorus on "High Society"). Still able to play effective melodic solos, Celestin concentrated as much on his spirited singing in his later years as his playing, and his band became a major tourist attraction in New Orleans. Oscar Celestin appeared with his group often on radio and television, made recordings during 1950–54, and even played a special concert at the White House for Dwight Eisenhower in 1953, a year before the trumpeter's death at age 70.

Recommended CDs: *Celestin's Original Tuxedo Jazz Orchestra/Sam Morgan's Jazz Band* (Jazz Oracle 8002), *The 1950s Radio Broadcasts* (Arhoolie 7024), *Marie Laveau* (GHB 106)

Film Appearances: *Cinerama Holiday* (1953)

BILL CHASE
• • • • • • • • • • •

b. 1935, Boston, MA, d. Aug. 9, 1974, Jackson, MN

A well-respected high-note trumpeter, Bill Chase seemed on the brink of fame beyond the jazz world when he was killed in a plane crash. Chase studied at Berklee and recorded with Herb Pomeroy's Berklee Big Band in 1957. His expertise at hitting high notes landed Chase jobs with the big bands of Maynard Ferguson (1958) and Stan Kenton (1959). Chase gained quite a bit of recognition during his period with Woody Herman's orchestra (1959–70), where he was not only the lead trumpeter but one of the Young Thundering Herd's key soloists (along with tenor saxophonist Sal Nistico and trombonist Phil Wilson).

In 1970 the trumpeter formed the nine-piece group Chase, a pop/rock band with four trumpets that was following in the brief tradition of Chicago and Blood, Sweat and Tears. The group's first recording (called simply *Chase*) was its most popular, although its jazz content was small. The band broke up a couple of years later after other albums failed to sell as well. In 1974 Chase reorganized for what was supposed to be a comeback tour. On August 9, 1974, a plane carrying Bill Chase and three of his musicians crashed; all of the passengers were killed.

Recommended CDs: with Woody Herman: *Jazz Masters 54* (Verve 314 529 903)

LPs to Search For: *Chase* (Epic 30472)

DOC CHEATHAM
• • • • • • • • • • • • • •

b. June 13, 1905, Nashville, TN, d. June 2, 1997, Washington D.C.

V irtually all trumpeters begin to decline once they hit their sixties and certainly their seventies. Their range starts shrinking, their tone wavers a bit, and their intonation slips— that is, all trumpeters but Doc Cheatham, who was a true phenomenon. Cheatham

The greatest 90-year-old trumpeter ever, Doc Cheatham was one of the last living links to the 1920s.

actually improved as a soloist while he was in his seventies, and he was still hitting solid high notes when he was 91! No trumpeter over the age of 80 in any style of music was ever on Cheatham's level.

Ironically, Adolphus "Doc" Cheatham was not known as a soloist until he was already in his mid-sixties. Self-taught, Cheatham began working as a professional musician in the early 1920s in the South as a member of the pit band of the Bijou Theatre, where he accompanied many top blues singers, including Bessie Smith. Cheatham moved to Chicago in 1925, worked with the Synco Jazzers, recorded with Ma Rainey (on soprano sax!), gigged with trombonist Albert Wynn, and performed with many different show bands. Cheatham spent time playing in Philadelphia with Wilbur DeParis (1927–28) and performed with Chick Webb in New York. Doc was a member of Sam Wooding's orchestra during 1928–30, touring Europe and playing jazz and dance music in many exotic lands. Back in the United States, Cheatham worked with Marion Hardy's Alabamians (1930–32) and McKinney's Cotton Pickers.

In 1932, Doc Cheatham joined Cab Calloway's orchestra as lead trumpeter. His tone and range were greatly admired, but he received almost no solo space during the next seven years (1932–39), instead leading the ensembles in an important but anonymous role. Whatever chance Cheatham had for fame during the swing era was largely lost by his being typecast as a section player. A brief illness led him to leave Calloway in 1939. Cheatham worked with the big bands of Teddy Wilson, Benny Carter (1940–41), Fletcher Henderson (1941), and Don Redman. He recorded with Billie Holiday and was a member of the original Eddie Heywood Sextet (1943–45), but played a subsidiary role to the pianist-leader.

With the end of the swing era, Cheatham (who was virtually unknown to the general public) made it through the next 20 years primarily by playing with Latin bands (including those of Marcelino Guerra, Perez Prado, Machito, and Herbie Mann) and Dixieland groups, most notably Wilbur DeParis' New New Orleans Jazz Band, where he played second trumpet to the ailing Sidney DeParis. He also worked with Vic Dickenson, Eddie Condon, and Sammy Price, with his own group (regularly at the International in New York during 1960–65), and with Benny Goodman (1966–67).

Age 62 by the time he left Goodman, Cheatham was at the crossroads of his career, and he knew that he was going to have to develop quickly as a soloist if he was going to continue getting jobs. By working on developing a style, Cheatham (who attributed his longevity to the fact that he did not drink) became a much stronger soloist at an age when most trumpeters are declining. By the early 1970s he was able to begin recording and performing as a leader in mainstream swing and Dixieland settings. Where earlier his solos could be a bit stiff, by the time he turned 70, Cheatham had developed a warm sound and was a living link to 1920s jazz. He used a mouthpiece given him by King Oliver, took charming vocals, reminisced happily about subbing for Louis Armstrong in the 1920s, and created dramatic and energetic solos, often wearing out his much-younger rhythm sections. I remember seeing him at Los Angeles' Jazz Bakery (around 1992, when he was 87) playing a 60-minute set as the main soloist with a quartet and, after a short break, following it up with 90 more minutes!

Cheatham's fame grew throughout the 1970s and '80s, and he was featured in countless settings, recording regularly and appearing every Sunday afternoon starting in 1980 at Sweet Basil in New York. Even in the 1990s, he remained in his musical prime. One of his final studio albums found the 91-year-old holding his own with 23-year-old trumpeter Nicholas Payton. In fact, in the ensembles of their Verve recording, Cheatham often played the high notes!

The remarkable Doc Cheatham, who never retired, worked at his final gig the night before suffering a stroke that resulted in his death two days later, ending his 75 years as a performer at the height of his fame.

Recommended CDs: *Duets and Solos* (Sackville 5002), *At the Bern Jazz Festival* (Sackville 3045), *The Fabulous Doc Cheatham* (Parkwood 104), *Live at Sweet Basil* (Jazzology 283), *The Eighty-Seven Years of Doc Cheatham* (Columbia 53215), *Swinging Down in New Orleans* (Jazzology 233), *Doc Cheatham and Nicholas Payton* (Verve 314 537 062)

Recommended Reading: *American Musicians II* by Whitney Balliett (Oxford University Press, 1996), *I Guess I'll Get the Papers and Go Home* by Doc Cheatham and Alyn Shipton (Casell, 1995), *In the Mainstream* by Chip Deffaa (Scarecrow Press, 1992), *Jazz Gentry* by Warren Vache Sr. (Scarecrow Press, 1999), *Talking Jazz* by Ben Sidran (Pomegranate Artbooks, 1992), *The World of Swing* by Stanley Dance (Charles Scribner's Sons, 1974)

Videos to Get: *The Sound of Jazz* (1957; Vintage Jazz Classics 2001), *Wilbur DeParis in Europe* (1960; 30N-90W Video NWV01)

DON CHERRY

. . . .

b. Nov. 18, 1936 Oklahoma City, OK, d. Oct. 19, 1995, Malaga, Spain

Don Cherry was a world traveler, both musically and geographically. Always very curious about other idioms of music, Cherry (who played a pocket cornet) was able not only to relate to Ornette Coleman's revolutionary music in the late 1950s but also to carve out his own unique niche. His life has inspired many other musicians to stretch themselves in search of their own individuality.

Cherry's father owned the Cherry Blossom Club in Oklahoma City, where guitarist Charlie Christian used to play. The Cherry family moved to Los Angeles in 1940. Don Cherry began playing trumpet while in junior high school and was actually expelled from Samuel Adams High School for cutting too many classes to play with the Jefferson High School band! Cherry started his career freelancing in Los Angeles, playing bebop with Dexter Gordon and Wardell Gray among others. He first met Ornette Coleman in 1953, finding Coleman's method of improvising without using chord changes quite intriguing, and soon they were practicing together regularly. In 1957 the pair turned pianist Paul Bley's trio into a quintet at the Hillcrest Club, where their playing mystified the audience. The expanded group received its notice fairly quickly, although a few live performances were documented and later issued on albums. Coleman and Cherry arranged an appointment with Lester Koenig of Contemporary Records in hopes of selling a few of Ornette's songs. Koenig surprised the musicians by offering to record their group instead; two albums resulted.

The somewhat radical recordings were heard and approved by pianist John Lewis and composer Gunther Schuller, and the new Coleman Quartet (with bassist Charlie Haden and drummer Billy Higgins) were invited to attend and perform at the Lenox School of Music in August 1959. Soon afterwards they were signed to the Atlantic label and in the fall were booked for a long stay at New York's Five Spot Café. Almost overnight, the Ornette Coleman Quartet was the talk of jazz as listeners and musicians debated and argued over the new music's merit.

While Coleman had an unusual tone on the alto, Cherry's sound was more accessible and his ties to bebop (even when he improvised quite freely) more obvious. Cherry recorded

Don Cherry always had a fertile imagination and a boundless musical curiosity.

quite a few influential albums with Coleman during 1959–61, including the almost totally improvised *Free Jazz*. He co-led an album (*The Avant-Garde*) with John Coltrane in 1960 and went out on his own the following year, although there would be many reunions with Coleman during the next three decades. Cherry had opportunities to play with Steve Lacy, Sonny Rollins (touring with the tenor in 1963), and the very adventurous saxophonist Albert Ayler. The trumpeter co-led the New York Contemporary Five during 1963–64 (which included the ferocious tenor of Archie Shepp and altoist John Tchicai), relocated to Europe, and often used Gato Barbieri as his tenor during 1964–66.

Though Don Cherry was never a virtuoso, his cornet chops were at their best in the late 1960s. However, they would gradually decline in future years as his interests spread elsewhere. Cherry taught at Dartmouth College in 1970, recorded with the Jazz Composer's Orchestra

(1973), became a world traveler, and moved his home base to Sweden. He became involved in exploring world music, often playing flute, percussion, and both ethnic and "little instruments," including the *doussn'gouni* (a hunter's guitar from Mali), often using his cornet almost as a contrast, rather than his main voice. Cherry, who studied both Turkish and Indian music, was a member of Codona (an unusual trio with sitarist Collin Walcott and percussionist Nana Vasconcelos) and of Old and New Dreams (an Ornette Coleman reunion group that included Dewey Redman, Charlie Haden, and Ed Blackwell but not Coleman). Some of his later years were spent in San Francisco playing with Peter Apfelbaum's Hieroglyphics, when he was not leading his own groups.

Don Cherry always added a cheerful and open-minded presence to any date he was on, never losing his quest for additional musical knowledge nor his enthusiasm.

Recommended CDs: *Complete Communion* (Blue Note 84226), *Symphony for Improvisers* (Blue Note 28976), *El Corazon* (ECM 1230), *Art Deco* (A&M 5258), *Dona Nostra* (ECM 1448), with Codona: *Codona* (ECM 1132), with Ornette Coleman: *Something Else* (Original Jazz Classics 163), *The Shape of Jazz to Come* (Atlantic 1317), *Change of the Century* (Atlantic 81341), *Free Jazz* (Rhino/Atlantic 75208), *The Complete Science Fiction Sessions* (Columbia/Legacy 63569), with Old and New Dreams: *Old and New Dreams* (Black Saint 1154), *One for Blackwell* (Black Saint 120 113)

Videos to Get: *Sarah Vaughan and Friends* (1986; A*Vision 50209), *Don Cherry's Multi-Kulti* (1995; View Video 1348)

BUDDY CHILDERS

. . . .

b. Feb. 12, 1926, St. Louis, MO

Buddy Childers, who has had a lengthy if underrated career, proved able to play both lead trumpet and very credible bop-oriented solos. The self-taught trumpeter had seven different stints with Stan Kenton's orchestra during 1942–54. Between those engagements, he played with other big bands, including those of Benny Carter (1944), Les Brown (1947), Woody Herman (his 1949 Second Herd), Tommy Dorsey (1951–52), and Charlie Barnet (1954). After he left Kenton the final time, Childers became a studio musician. He has appeared in countless settings in Los Angeles and Las Vegas through the years (including the Toshiko Akiyoshi-Lew Tabackin big band in 1981), balancing his studio work with nightclub work in both small group and big band settings.

Buddy Childers is one of the few Stan Kenton alumni from the early period still in prime musical form in the early years of the 21st century.

LPs to Search For: *Sam Songs* (Liberty 6009), *Just Buddy's* (Trend 539)

BUCK CLAYTON

• • • • • • • • • • • •

b. Nov. 12, 1911, Parsons, KS, d. Dec. 8, 1991, New York, NY

One of the great trumpeters to emerge during the swing era, Buck Clayton was a major player for 30 years. His timeless style was adaptable enough to fit into both bop and Dixieland settings without really being part of either movement. In fact, critic Stanley Dance coined the term *mainstream* in the mid-1950s to describe the small-group swing music that was typified by Clayton.

Wilbur "Buck" Clayton started playing piano when he was six, taught by his father, who played tuba (in addition to being a minister!). Since the church orchestra rehearsed regularly at the Clayton home and left their instruments there, young Buck had an opportunity to try out some of the horns. However, he gigged on piano with a kids' band from the time he was seven and did not switch to trumpet until he was 18; Louis Armstrong was his original inspiration. Other than once being shown by his father how to play scales , Buck was completely self-taught on trumpet. After graduating from high school in 1930, Clayton set out for California. At first he worked day jobs, but he soon proved to be a strong enough musician to be playing full time. Clayton worked with local bands led by the Irwing Brothers, Duke Ellighew, Lavern Floyd, Charlie Echols, and Earl Dancer, also contributing arrangements. Because Dancer had a lot of contacts in the film industry, his band appeared briefly in many movies and on several film soundtracks. But after Dancer began gambling with the band's money, he was tossed out and Clayton was elected leader.

Pianist Teddy Weatherford came to Los Angeles in 1934 with the goal of finding an orchestra to take to China; he picked Clayton's. During 1934–35, Clayton's big band played at the International Settlement in Shanghai, making very high salaries for the period. Only the war with Japan persuaded Clayton and his musicians to return home, and they left China just ten days before the Japanese invaded.

Shortly after arriving back in Los Angeles, Clayton received an offer to join Willie Bryant's orchestra in New York. On his way across the country he visited his mother in Kansas and dropped by Kansas City to check out the local music scene. While there he was persuaded to join Count Basie's orchestra (as the replacement for the recently departed Hot Lips Page). Buck's timing was perfect. After years of being in Kansas City, the Count Basie Orchestra would soon be heading East, and they quickly became one of jazz's most important orchestras. Clayton was their main trumpet soloist (even after Harry "Sweets" Edison joined) and a key star. Some of his best recorded solos with Basie were on "Swinging at the Daisy Chain," "Good Morning Blues," "Topsy," the original version of "Jumpin' at the Woodside," the first two renditions of "One O'Clock Jump," "Swinging the Blues," "Sent for You Yesterday," and his feature, "Fiesta in Blue." Most of the time Clayton (at Basie's request) utilized a cup mute that softened his sound. Years later many fans and fellow musicians were surprised to find out how wide a range Buck really had!

Clayton was a welcome guest on many Teddy Wilson and Billie Holiday records during 1937–39, where he was usually teamed with Lester Young. "This Year's Kisses," "I Must Have

That Man," "Mean to Me," "Without Your Love," and "Why Was I Born" have some of his more memorable statements with Lady Day. He also recorded with the Kansas City Five and Six in 1938 ("Way Down Yonder in New Orleans" and "I Want A Little Girl" were given classic treatments) and was part of Benny Goodman's 1938 Carnegie Hall Concert. As a writer, Clayton contributed occasional tunes to the Basie band, including "Red Bank Boogie," "Taps Miller," "Avenue C," "Love Jumped Out," and "Down for Double," plus he wrote some charts for Benny Goodman, Tommy Dorsey, and Duke Ellington.

In 1943 Clayton was drafted, and his period with Count Basie ended. His Army experience was useful because he was able to spend most of his three years playing music, including in bands headed by Sy Oliver and Mercer Ellington. Buck even made a record date in 1944 with Coleman Hawkins. After he was discharged in 1946, Clayton could have rejoined Basie, but instead he chose to play with small groups. He was part of Norman Granz's all-star Jazz at the Philharmonic for part of the next two years, often sharing the stage with both Lester Young and Coleman Hawkins. Although the swing style was being replaced by bebop, Clayton was able to work and record fairly regularly, visiting Europe on an occasional basis starting in 1949, including a tour with Mezz Mezzrow in 1953. He played with Jimmy Rushing's band in the early 1950s, appeared at the Embers with Joe Bushkin, and then spent time with New Orleans clarinetist Tony Parenti, where he familiarized himself with the Dixieland repertoire, which greatly increased his work opportunities.

While he often played Dixieland dates in clubs, starting in 1953 the trumpeter was featured at the head of a series of recorded Buck Clayton jam sessions for Columbia. These legendary all-star outings were consistently rewarding, giving veteran mainstream players an opportunity to really stretch out on LP; all of the sessions have been reissued as a limited Mosaic box set. Clayton also recorded many other dates as a leader during the 1950s and '60s (including for Vanguard), can be seen as part of the Benny Goodman Orchestra in the 1955 film *The Benny Goodman Story,* performed with Sidney Bechet at the 1958 World's Fair in Brussels, and worked and recorded with Eddie Condon on several occasions during 1959–64. Clayton's 1961 Count Basie reunion band appeared at concerts and on European television; two of the television shows from that tour have been released as a video by Shanachie. Clayton also played and recorded with Humphrey Lyttelton's band in England, and he managed to stay quite busy up until 1967, the year he appeared at John Hammond's 30th anniversary Spirituals to Swing concert.

A variety of serious health problems and difficulties with his teeth started to affect Clayton in 1967, and within two years he had to stop playing altogether; later attempts to come back as a trumpeter went nowhere. He was only 58. The 1970s were understandably a depressing period for Clayton. He worked in the musicians' union for a year, had a day job as a salesman, and supervised some newer Buck Clayton jam sessions for Chiaroscuro. He also taught at Hunter College for five years, but did not enjoy the work much. Fortunately, Clayton did have another special musical talent, that of a composer-arranger. Inspired by his close friend photographer Nancy Elliott, he began to write music again. In the 1980s, Clayton contributed arrangements for a Basie alumni band, Loren Schoenberg's orchestra, the Dick Melodonian-Sonny Igoe big band, Grover Mitchell, Humphrey Lyttelton, the Juggernaut, Panama Francis' Savoy Sultans, and a particularly rewarding album by the Dan Barrett-Howard Alden Quintet. In 1987 he completed his memoirs (*Buck Clayton's Jazz World*) and in 1988 formed a big band that during his last couple of years performed (and recorded) his music. At the time of his death (a month after his 80th birthday), Buck Clayton was once again an active jazz writer and was back where he belonged, on top.

Recommended CDs: *The Classic Swing of Buck Clayton* (Original Jazz Classics 1709), *Buck Clayton in Paris* (Vogue 68358), *The Essential Buck Clayton* (Vanguard 103/4), *Copenhagen Concert September 1959* (Steeplechase 36006/7), *Buck Clayton All Stars 1961* (Storyville 8231), *Baden, Switzerland 1966* (Sackville 2028)

Box Set: *The Complete CBS Buck Clayton Jam Sessions* (6 CDs; Mosaic 6-144), with Count Basie: *The Complete Decca Recordings* (3 CDs; GRP/Decca 611)

Recommended Reading: *Buck Clayton's Jazz World* by Buck Clayton and Nancy Miller Elliott (Oxford University Press, 1986), *Jazz Talking* by Max Jones (Da Capo Press, 1987), *Swing Legacy* by Chip Deffaa (Scarecrow Press, 1989), *The World of Count Basie* by Stanley Dance (Charles Scribner's Sons, 1980)

Film Appearances: *The Benny Goodman Story* (1955), with Count Basie: *Reveille with Beverly* (1943)

Videos to Get: *Trumpet Kings* (1958, playing "This Can't Be Love" with Charlie Shavers; Video Artists International 69076), *Vintage Collection, Vol. 2* (1959, with Ben Webster; A*Vision 50239), *Buck Clayton All-Stars* (1961; Shanachie 6303), *Born to Swing* (1973; Rhapsody Films)

SONNY COHN

. . . .

b. Mar. 14, 1925, Chicago, IL

One of Count Basie's most loyal sidemen, Sonny Cohn was a reliable bop-based soloist and an occasional soloist (if not quite a star) who played quite well in the ensembles and helped contribute to the Basie sound. Cohn started off his career working in Chicago with Richard Fox (1942), Walter Dyett's DuSable-ites (1943–45) and Red Saunders (off and on during 1945–60, including 11 years as the house band at the Club DeLisa). He was also part of the Regal Theatre's house band, playing with many visiting jazz greats. Cohn, who had short stints with Louie Bellson and Erskine Hawkins and recorded with Tab Smith and Jodie Christian, made his mark while with Basie during 1960–84, staying with the orchestra until Basie's death. Sonny Cohn, who never led his own record date, has since gone into semiretirement, but he can be heard taking all-too-brief statements on many of Basie's recordings.

Recommended Reading: *The World of Count Basie* by Stanley Dance (Charles Scribner's Sons, 1980)

KID SHEIK COLAR

. . . .

b. Sept. 15, 1908, New Orleans, LA, d. Nov. 7,1996, Detroit, MI

A spirited if erratic revival Dixieland trumpeter, George "Kid Sheik" Colar was a fixture in New Orleans for decades. Colar formed his first band in 1925, when he was 17, and played regularly in New Orleans (unfortunately without recording) until he joined the Army in 1943. Discharged two years later, Colar returned to New Orleans and worked with George Lewis (1949), the Eureka Brass Band, the Olympia Brass Band, and other local groups. In 1961 he recorded with both his Swingsters and his Storyville Ramblers. Colar toured England with Barry Martyin in 1963, often played with Captain John Handy in the 1960s, and in the 1970s and '80s was based at Preservation Hall, sometimes touring with the Preservation Hall Jazz Band. Kid Sheik Colar, who recorded fairly frequently during 1961–81, always had plenty of enthusiasm in his playing and was a real crowd pleaser.

Recommended CDs: *Kid Sheik–Jim Robinson New Orleans Stompers* (GHB 76), *Kid Sheik and Brother Cornbread in Copenhagen* (Jazz Crusade 3002)

LPs to Search For: *Kid Sheik's Swingsters* (Jazzology 31), *Kid Sheik in England* (GHB 187)

Recommended Reading: *The Jazz Crusade* by Big Bill Bissonnette (Special Request Books, 1992)

BILL COLEMAN

. . . .

b. Aug. 4, 1904, Centreville, KY, d. Aug. 24, 1981, Toulouse, France

O ne of jazz's first expatriates, Bill Coleman was a subtle but swinging trumpeter with a mellow tone. In danger of being lost in the shuffle while in the United States in the early to mid-1930s, his move to Paris in 1935 made him a large fish in a small pond. Although he returned to the United States during World War II, Coleman spent his last 33 years happily working in Europe, where his skills were better appreciated than in his native land.

Ironically Bill Coleman (who spent a lot of time in Paris, France) was born in a small town located near Paris, Kentucky. He grew up in Cincinnati, starting on clarinet before switching to trumpet when he was 12, inspired originally by Louis Armstrong's playing on "Money Blues" with Fletcher Henderson's orchestra. Coleman gigged locally (including with J. C. Higginbotham and Edgar Hayes) before moving to New York in 1927. His early gigs included associations with Cecil Scott, Lloyd Scott, and Luis Russell. While with Russell's all-star group in 1929, Coleman was frustrated because virtually all of the solos went to the more flamboyant Henry "Red" Allen.

After working with Cecil Scott's Bright Boys, Charlie Johnson, Russell again (1931–32), and Ralph Cooper's Kongo Knights (recording along the way with Russell, Scott, and Don Redman), in 1933 Coleman visited France for the first time, with Lucky Millinder. Back in the United States, Coleman played with Benny Carter and Teddy Hill (1934–35) and recorded with Fats Waller before getting an offer from Freddy "Snake Hips" Taylor to return to Europe. The trumpeter spent five rewarding years overseas, playing with Taylor, Willie Lewis, in Bombay with Leon Abbey, back with Lewis, and in Egypt with the Harlem Rhythm Makers (1938–40). Coleman's recordings as a leader in Paris (which sometimes included such sidemen as Django Reinhardt and Stephane Grappelli) and a session with trombonist Dicky Wells were quite notable from this period. He also recorded with Garnett Clark's Hot Club Four, Willie Lewis, Alix Combelle, Eddie Martin, and Eddie Brunner, among others. While Coleman was a minor name in the United States, he was very much a star in Europe.

During 1940–48 Bill Coleman spent his last long period in the United States. He had opportunities to record with Lester Young (the Kansas City Six), Billie Holiday, and Coleman Hawkins. Coleman also worked with many top swing players, including the Benny Carter Orchestra (1940), Fats Waller, Teddy Wilson, Andy Kirk's orchestra (1941–42), Ellis Larkins, Mary Lou Williams (several recordings in 1944), the John Kirby Sextet, Sy Oliver, and Billy Kyle, in addition to occasionally leading his own groups. Although Coleman never became famous domestically, he was well respected by the top jazz musicians.

In December 1948 Coleman returned to Paris, and he spent the remainder of his career in Europe (visiting the United States only briefly in 1954 and 1958), where he worked and recorded steadily, often appearing at jazz festivals. A mainstream swing player whose style was mostly untouched by bebop, Coleman (whose excellent autobiography, *Trumpet Story,* came out in 1981) also occasionally played Dixieland. In Europe, Bill Coleman had a much more secure career than he would probably have had had he chosen to stay in the United States, and he stayed quite active up to the time of his death.

Recommended CDs: *Bill Coleman 1936–1938* (Classics 764), *The Great Parisian Session* (Polydor 837235), *Bill Coleman Meets Guy Lafitte* (Black Lion 760182)

Recommended Reading: *Trumpet Story* by Bill Coleman (Northeastern University Press, 1991)

JOHNNY COLES
● ● ● ● ● ● ● ● ● ● ● ● ● ●

b. July 3, 1926, Trenton, NJ, d. Dec. 21, 1997, Philadelphia, PA

Johnny Coles, an advanced hard bop trumpeter, is perhaps best remembered for his association with the Charles Mingus Sextet during their European visit of 1964, even though he became ill halfway through the tour and had to drop out.

Coles was self-taught on the trumpet, played with a military band while in the service, and during 1945–48 was in a group called Slappy and his Swingsters. He picked up experience playing with the R&B-oriented bands of Eddie "Cleanhead" Vinson (1948–51, including the period when John Coltrane was in the group), Bull Moose Jackson (1952), and Earl Bostic (1955–56). Coles gained some recognition in the jazz world for his playing with James Moody (1956–58) and his recordings with the Gil Evans Orchestra (1958–64). In addition to his work with Mingus (being joined in the short-lived but well-documented sextet by multireedist Eric Dolphy, tenor saxophonist Clifford Jordan, pianist Jaki Byard, and drummer Danny Richmond), Coles recorded with pianist Duke Pearson and singer Astrud Gilberto plus as a leader. He was a member of the Herbie Hancock Sextet for a few months in 1968–69 (before being succeeded by Eddie Henderson) and toured with Ray Charles (1969–70), Duke Ellington

(1970–73), Art Blakey's Jazz Messengers (1976), and the Count Basie Orchestra (1985–86); Coles also worked with Dameronia and Mingus Dynasty.

Johnny Coles, who recorded as a leader for Epic (1961), Blue Note (1963), Mainstream (1971), and Criss Cross (1982), was always a distinctive if somewhat overlooked player, one of jazz's unsung trumpet heroes.

Recommended CDs: *The Warm Sound* (Koch 7804), *Little Johnny C* (Blue Note 32129), *New Morning* (Criss Cross 1005), with Charles Mingus: *Town Hall Concert* (Original Jazz Classics 042)

LPs to Search For: *The Great Concert of Charles Mingus* (Prestige 34001)

Videos to Get: *Charles Mingus Sextet* (1964; Shanachie 6307)

DICK COLLINS

• • • • • • • • • • • • •

b. July 19, 1924, Seattle, WA

Dick Collins always had an underground reputation in jazz, being much better known to his fellow musicians than he was to the general public. He always had a fluent style and a soft tone, playing with inner fire. Collins studied trumpet with Red Nichols' father during 1929–30 and in 1930 (when he was six years old) appeared on his own radio show in San Francisco, singing while backed by his sister's guitar. Collins gained additional early experience playing with Earl Gladman's orchestra (1938–40).

Dick Collins and his brother, trombonist Bob, were members of the innovative (if part-time) Dave Brubeck Octet (1946–50). Like Brubeck, Collins studied with composer Darius Milhaud. While in France in 1948, Collins had an opportunity to play with Hubert Fol's Be-Bop Minstrels and recorded with both Fol and drummer Kenny Clarke. Back in the United States, he worked with Charlie Barnet (1951), Charles Mingus, Alvino Rey (1952), and most importantly Woody Herman (1954–56), getting some solo space on Herman's records. Collins also recorded with Charlie Mariano, Nat Pierce, Paul Desmond, and Cal Tjader (1953–54) in addition to leading two of his own long out-of-print albums for Victor in 1954, including one called *King Richard the Swing Hearted*!

However, Collins never gained much fame. He settled in California, became a studio musician, toured with Les Brown on and off during 1958–66, worked with Nat Pierce's quintet in 1978, and was briefly with the Capp-Pierce Juggernaut in the 1990s. But Dick Collins mostly kept a low profile in his later years.

Recommended CDs: with Dave Brubeck: *The Dave Brubeck Octet* (Original Jazz Classics 101), with Paul Desmond: *Featuring Don Elliott* (Original Jazz Classics 712), *Nat Pierce/Dick Collins/Ralph Burns & The Herdsmen Play Paris* (Fantasy 24759), with Cal Tjader: *Tjader Plays Mambo* (Original Jazz Classics 274)

LEE COLLINS
• • • • • • • • • • • •

b. Oct. 17, 1901, New Orleans, LA, d. July 3, 1960, Chicago, IL

Probably the most interesting aspect to Lee Collins' life was nonmusical. Starting in 1943 and finishing shortly before his death, Collins wrote his autobiography. With the assistance of his wife, Mary Collins, and Frank Gillis and John Miner, *Oh Didn't He Ramble* was published posthumously by the University of Illinois Press in 1974. It is a colorful book that not only documents Collins' life (including his comments on what would be his final illness!) but gives his evaluations of many early New Orleans trumpeters, including several who never recorded.

Lee Collins was a fine New Orleans trumpeter who recorded far too little throughout his career. Born the same year as Louis Armstrong, he was forever in Satch's shadow, although Collins can be heard at his very best on the four hot numbers recorded in 1929 with the Jones-Collins Astoria Hot Eight. Born into a musical family (his father played trumpet and his uncle was a trombonist), Collins started on trumpet himself when he was 12; within three years he was gigging professionally. He organized the Young Eagles with Pops Foster and also worked with the Columbia Band, the Young Tuxedo Orchestra, Oscar Celestin, Zutty Singleton, and many other groups in New Orleans. After a stay in Florida, in 1924 Collins moved to Chicago to play with King Oliver as Louis Armstrong's replacement. He made his recording debut with Jelly Roll Morton (four primitively recorded numbers, including his own "Fish Tail Blues," which Morton later claimed and retitled "Sidewalk Blues"). But after six months he chose to return to New Orleans, where he was mostly based until 1930, being one of the best trumpeters in town. The Jones-Collins Astoria Hot Eight recordings (available as part of a Frog CD) show just how powerful a player he was.

In 1930 Collins joined Luis Russell's band in New York briefly (filling in for Red Allen when Russell's star trumpeter was on vacation) and then moved to Chicago, which, in retrospect, was clearly a mistake. The Chicago jazz scene was on a steep downslide, making Collins greatly underrated and largely forgotten outside of the city, despite his being quite active. Among the bands he worked with in the 1930s were those of Dave Peyton, W. McDonald (the Chicago Ramblers), Johnny Dodds, and Zutty Singleton. He also had opportunities to record with blues-oriented groups in 1936, including Blue Scott's Blue Boys, Richard M. Jones, Hannah May's State Street Four, Lil Johnson, and Victoria Spivey. From the late 1930s on, Collins mostly led his own bands in Chicago (having a longtime engagement at the Victory Club, starting in 1945), but his ensemble did not make any studio recordings; fortunately, live sets from 1951 and 1953 were released years later that find him still in fine form. Collins did make five excellent titles backing blues singer Chippie Hill in 1946 and four with Little Brother Montgomery in 1947, but strangely enough the New Orleans jazz revival largely passed him by. In 1948 Collins toured briefly with Kid Ory, he was with Art Hodes during 1950–51, and he toured Europe with Mezz Mezzrow in 1951 (recording three sessions with the clarinetist for Vogue) before illness forced him to return to Chicago. After recovering, he worked in San Francisco in 1953, visited New Orleans (where four numbers with Jack Delaney would comprise his final recordings), and in 1954 returned to Europe with Mezzrow. This time Collins became very ill. After returning home, he suffered a stroke and emphysema, which ended his playing career.

Lee Collins' life was largely affected by his bad judgments about where to be based. Had Lee Collins remained in Chicago in 1925 (where he would certainly have recorded with Jelly Roll Morton's Red Hot Peppers) and spent the 1930s in New York rather than Chicago, his story might have been much different. But at least he wrote his book!

Recommended CDs: *Sizzling the Blues* (Frog 5), *Mutt Carey and Lee Collins* (American Music 72), *Club Hangover Airshots, Vols. 1 & 2* (Jazz Crusade 3056 and 3057)

Recommended Reading: *Jazz Talking* by Max Jones (Da Capo Press, 1987), *Oh Didn't He Ramble* by Lee and Mary Collins (University of Illinois Press, 1989)

SHAD COLLINS
• • • • • • • • • • • • •

b. June 27, 1910, Elizabeth, NJ, d. June 6, 1978, New York, NY

Although Shad Collins spent only one year as a member of the Count Basie Orchestra, during which time he was overshadowed by fellow trumpeters Buck Clayton and Harry "Sweets" Edison, he is best remembered for his connection with Basie.

Collins actually played with many other groups during his career. He had stints with the big bands of Charlie Dixon (1928), Eddie White (1929–30), Chick Webb (1931), Benny Carter (1933), and Tiny Bradshaw (1934), among others. Collins was with Teddy Hill's orchestra during 1936–37, touring Europe, recording with Dickie Wells, and settling in Paris for a time. After returning to the United States, he played with Count Basie from December 1938 until January 1940; one of his better recordings is with a Basie small group on "You Can Depend on Me." A fine swing soloist with a tone of his own, Collins worked with Benny Carter, Lester Young's sextet in late 1940, and Buddy Johnson before becoming a longtime member of Cab Calloway's orchestra (1941–46), although Jonah Jones received virtually all of the trumpet solos.

Collins was actually in his prime in the 1950s but was little noticed, since he was not a modernist or a revivalist. He worked with Buster Harding, Al Sears, and Jimmy Rushing and recorded with Vic Dickenson in 1954 but also appeared somewhat anonymously on many low-profile jobs and recordings (including with R&B tenor Sam "The Man" Taylor). He can be heard playing at the peak of his powers on a pair of Basie reunion sessions with Paul Quinichette from 1957–58. But Shad Collins gave up altogether in the 1960s, retiring from music and becoming a taxicab driver.

Recommended CDs: with Vic Dickenson: *Nice Work* (Vanguard 79610), with Paul Quinichette: *For Basie* (Original Jazz Classics 978), *Basie Reunion* (Original Jazz Classics 1049)

LOU COLUMBO

. . . .

b. Aug. 22, 1927, Brockton, MA

Asolid and subtle swing-oriented trumpeter, Lou Columbo has performed pleasing music throughout his career, mostly in the Massachusetts area and Florida. He chose not to travel much during the 1960s and '70s, preferring to stay at home with his wife and five children. "At the age of ten I started playing a bugle that my father had brought home because he wanted me to play in the local drum-and-bugle corp. When I was 12 he bought me a cornet, and the next year I was playing in a three-piece band with my first trumpet. Roy Eldridge, Billy Butterfield, and Harry James were my first influences." Although Columbo knew by the time he was in high school that he wanted eventually to be a musician, he was a professional baseball player for seven years, until a broken ankle ended his sports career.

Among Columbo's most important musical associations have been Dick Johnson (with whom he has played off and on since they first met back in 1938), Dick McKenna (a friend since 1947), the Charlie Spivak Orchestra (in the early 1950s), and Dizzy Gillespie (with whom he played in the late 1980s). In 1956 he won on the *Arthur Godfrey's Talent Scouts* show and appeared on television several times. In 1964 Columbo had difficulty with the muscle on his upper lip and had to relearn to play the trumpet on the right side of his mouth, but he was able to in time.

Colombo has been underrecorded throughout his career, although in 1990 he finally had his recording debut as a leader, *I Remember Bobby,* which was dedicated to his friend Bobby Hackett."When I was younger I tended to overplay a little and play too loud. Bobby Hackett gave me some invaluable advice: 'Play a little softer, and don't play everything you know in the first chorus—save some for your last.' Another thing I've learned since then is that although I feel I've never been able to express myself verbally as well as I would like, I find that I'm able to express my feelings more wholly through my playing."

Recommended CDs: *I Remember Bobby* (Concord Jazz 435), with Meredith d'Ambrosio: *South to a Warmer Place* (Sunnyside 1039), with George Masso: *That Old Gang of Mine* (Arbors 19173), *C'est Magnifique* (Nagel-Heyer 60)

KEN COLYER

. . . .

b. Apr. 18, 1928, Great Yarmouth, Norfolk, England, d. Mar. 8, 1988, France

One of the leaders of Great Britain's trad jazz movement of the 1950s, Ken Colyer was one of the most important British musicians of the era. Colyer was self-taught on trumpet and guitar and started his career playing New Orleans-oriented music with the Crane River Jazz Band (1949–51) and the Christie Brothers Stompers (1951), recording with both bands. In late 1951 he joined the Merchant Marines specifically so he could ship out to New Orleans and jam with the local legends. Since the closest he was able to come was Mobile, Alabama, he went AWOL and stayed in the United States illegally into 1953. Colyer jammed with George Lewis in New Orleans, recorded with clarinetist Emile Barnes, and learned a great deal about classic jazz, becoming quite idealistic. Eventually the authorities caught up with him, and he was briefly jailed and deported back to England.

Back home in March 1953, Colyer now played in a much bluesier and more primitive style than he had previously, emulating Bunk Johnson to an extent, although with his own sound. He had a group that included trombonist Chris Barber and clarinetist Monty Sunshine. But due to musical differences, in 1954 he broke away to form Ken Colyer's Jazzmen. With trombonist Mac Duncan and clarinetist Ian Wheeler as regular members of his septet, Colyer's band played the type of melodic ensemble-oriented music that he most loved, recording frequently and working steadily. In a parallel career, Colyer was also a guitarist and vocalist whose performances of folk music (including some songs from Leadbelly's repertoire) helped pioneer skiffle music.

Personnel changes found Colyer utilizing trombonist Geoff Cole and clarinetist Sammy Rimington (later Tony Pyke) during the 1960s and other frontline partners in the 1970s but playing in an unchanged style. Despite erratic health, Colyer was active until a year before his death in 1988. Documented during his career by such companies as Storyville, Decca, KC Records, Columbia, "77," Joy, Black Lion, GHB, and Stomp Off, Ken Colyer's legacy has been kept alive since his death by a series of extensive reissues from the Lake and Upbeat labels.

Recommended CDs: *In the Beginning* (Lake 014), *The Decca Skiffle Sessions* (Lake 7), *The Decca Years* (Lake 1), *Serenading Annie* (Upbeat 111), *The Classic Years* (Uptown 149), *Up Jumped the Devil* (Uptown 114), *Ken Colyer's Jazzmen with Sammy Rimington* (GHB 152)

WILLIE COOK

• • • • • • • • • • •

b. Nov. 11, 1923, Tangipahoa, LA, d. Sept. 22, 2000, Stockholm, Sweden

A fine trumpeter who occasionally took solos while with Duke Ellington's orchestra, the reliable Willie Cook tended to be overshadowed by the other trumpeters. He grew up in East Chicago, Indiana, and first played professionally in 1940 with King Perry. Cook worked with Claude Trenier (1941), his own short-lived band, Jay McShann (1943), the Earl Hines Orchestra (1943–48), the Jimmy Lunceford ghost band (1948), and the big bands of Dizzy Gillespie (1948–50) and Gerald Wilson (1950–51). Most memorable was his ten-year period (off and on during 1951–61) with Duke Ellington, where he shared solo space with Clark Terry, Ray Nance, and Cat Anderson. Cook's style, which fell between bop and swing, led him to fill a role formerly held by Taft Jordan.

After leaving Duke, Cook freelanced in New York, gigged with Mercer Ellington, and returned to Ellington's band on several occasions during 1968–73. Moving to Houston, Cook retired from music for several years, but he came back in 1977 to play with Clark Terry and Count Basie's orchestra. In the late 1970s he settled in Sweden, where he was active during his final 20 years, often appearing in Duke Ellington reunion bands when not leading his own combo.

LPs to Search For: *Christl Mood* (Phontastic 7563), with Count Basie: *Kansas City 6* (Original Jazz Classics 449), with Paul Gonsalves: *Buenos Aires Session* (Catalyst 7913)

Recommended Reading: *The World of Duke Ellington* by Stanley Dance (Charles Scribner's Sons, 1970)

JACKIE COON

. . . .

b. June 21, 1929, Beatrice, NE

A soft-toned soloist who has specialized mostly on the flugelhorn since the 1960s, Jackie Coon is also a friendly vocalist who loves to sing "What A Wonderful World." He grew up in Southern California and remembers that when he was 11 "I started with Louis Armstrong. My older brother played his recording of 'West End Blues' for me and that's what convinced me to start learning trumpet." The main emphasis throughout Coon's career has been mainstream swing and Dixieland. After he graduated from school, he went on the road with Red Fox and his Musical Hounds. Coon played with Jack Teagarden's band for three months ("That was a high point in my life"); his tapes from this period with Mr. T. were finally released by Arbors in the 1990s. He also had unrecorded but valuable stints with Earl Hines, Louis Prima, and Charlie Barnet. Coon made his official recording debut with clarinetist Barney Bigard in 1957 and played a notable mellophone solo on Red Nichols' greatest recording of "Battle Hymn of the Republic" (1959).

Coon, who did studio work and played with Bob Crosby and Pete Fountain, worked regularly at Disneyland for nine years (1968–78). "I was too busy making a living and raising a family to chase after fame and take chances with my life." After the Disneyland period ended, he settled in Big Sur near Monterey, where he plays regularly when not appearing at trad jazz festivals. Jackie Coon has recorded enjoyable sets for Sea Breeze (1986) and Arbors (a few since 1991) that feature his very laid-back style and vocals.

Recommended CDs: *Back in His Own Backyard* (Arbors 19109), *Jazzin' with Jackie* (Arbors 19110), *Softly* (Arbors 19162), with Jack Teagarden: *The Club Hangover Broadcasts* (Arbors 19150-51)

LPs to Search For: *Jazzin' Around* (Sea Breeze 1009)

RAY COPELAND

. . . .

b. July 17, 1926, Norfolk, VA, d. May 18, 1984, New York, NY

A n obscure legend who was a solid bop soloist with an appealing tone and a wide range, Ray Copeland (whose son is drummer Keith Copeland) appeared in many settings throughout his career. Classically trained on trumpet, Copeland started his career working with Cecil Scott (1945), Chris Columbus, Mercer Ellington (1947–48), and the Savoy Sultans (1948–49). However, he only played music on a part-time basis during 1950–55 (including with Andy Kirk, Lucky Thompson, and Sy Oliver and recording with Thelonious Monk in 1954), a period when he had a day job working at a paper company.

Copeland returned to music full time in 1955 and worked with Lionel Hampton, Randy Weston (1957–58), Monk (making additional recordings in 1957), Tito Puente, Oscar Pettiford, Johnny Richards, Gigi Gryce (1958–59), and his own occasional big band. He can be heard throughout the soundtrack of the 1959 film *Kiss Her Goodbye* with the Johnny Richards Orchestra. Copeland toured with Louis Bellson and Pearl Bailey (1962–64), Ella Fitzgerald, Randy Weston (1966 and 1970, including a visit to Morocco), and the 1967 Thelonious Monk Nonet (with whom he visited Europe). His "Classical Jazz Suite in Six Movements" premiered at Lincoln Center in 1970, and in 1974 he toured Europe with the revue *The Musical Life of Charlie Parker*. In later years Ray Copeland (who never led his own record date) frequently played in the pit bands of Broadway shows and was active as an educator.

Recommended CDs: with Thelonious Monk: *Monk* (Original Jazz Classics 016), *Thelonious Monk with John Coltrane* (Original Jazz Classics 039), with Oscar Pettiford: *Deep Passion* (GRP/Impulse 143), with Randy Weston: *How High the Moon* (Biograph 147), *Monterey '66* (Antilles 314 519 698), *African Cookbook* (Koch 8517), *Tanjah* (Antilles 314 527 779), with Phil Woods: *Sugan* (Original Jazz Classics 1841)

SAL CRACCIOLO

S al Cracciolo is a reliable trumpeter who plays with spirit. His claim to fame thus far has been his longtime membership in Poncho Sanchez's Latin Jazz band. Cracciolo joined Sanchez in 1985, in time to appear on the conguero's fifth recording (and third for Concord Picante). The trumpeter has been on practically every Sanchez recording since then, and his solos have consistently been among the high points. Although he has not had a solo career (or a single record date of his own) thus far, Sal Cracciolo has proven to be a very valuable sideman, able to play Afro-Cuban jazz, bebop, and salsa with equal skill.

Recommended CDs: with Poncho Sanchez: *El Conguero* (Concord Picante 4286), *Papa Gato* (Concord Picante 4310), *La Familia* (Concord Picante 4369), *Para Todos* (Concord Picante 4600), *Freedom Sound* (Concord Picante 4778), *Afro-Cuban Fantasy* (Concord Picante 4847), *Latin Soul* (Concord Picante 4863)

Videos to Get: *Poncho Sanchez: A Night at Kimball's East* (1991; Concord Jazz Video)

CHARLIE CREATH

b. Dec. 30, 1890, Ironton, MO, d. Oct. 23, 1951, Chicago, IL

C harlie Creath was more significant as a bandleader than as a trumpeter. In fact, he was considered the most important orchestra leader in St. Louis during the 1920s, when his sidemen at various times included Ed Allen, Leonard Davis, Dewey Jackson, blues guitarist Lonnie Johnson, bassist Pops Foster, and Creath's brother-in-law, drummer Zutty Singleton.

Originally an alto saxophonist, Creath started playing trumpet seriously as a teenager, gaining experience working with circus bands and in theater shows. Creath first led his own band in Seattle. He moved to St. Louis in 1918 and by 1921 was heading a significant jazz-influenced ensemble that often played on riverboats and in St. Louis-area clubs. In late 1926 he began collaborating with the legendary Fate Marable. Unfortunately, illness knocked Creath out of action during 1928–30 (which might otherwise have been his peak years). When Creath finally returned to music, he was mostly playing alto sax and accordion. After a period working with Harvey Lankford's Synco High Hatters (1933) and co-leading a group with Marable in the mid-1930s, he moved to Chicago, ran a nightclub, and eventually worked outside of music.

Charlie Creath would have been completely forgotten except for the fact that he recorded a dozen selections (six in 1924, four in 1925, and two final ones in 1927) during three sessions with his "Jazz-O-Maniacs." On such numbers as "Pleasure Mad," "King Porter Stomp," and "Market Street Stomp," Creath and his ensemble showed that, even at that early stage, viable jazz was being created outside of New York and Chicago.

Recommended CDs: *Jazz in St. Louis* (Timeless 1036)

JIM CULLUM
• • • • • • • • • • •

b. Sept. 20, 1941, San Antonio, TX

Because of his series of very well-conceived programs for National Public Radio (the series is called *Live at the Landing*), Jim Cullum is known beyond the trad jazz world. These shows (which have been a regular fixture now for several years) pay tribute in informative and very musical fashion to various aspects of jazz's past styles.

Clarinetist Jim Cullum Sr. led the Happy Jazz Band in the 1960s and '70s until his death in 1973. Growing up around music, Cullum Jr. (inspired most by Louis Armstrong, Bobby Hackett, and the Bob Crosby Bobcats) began playing the trumpet at an early age, working at his first professional job in 1958, when he was 17. He attended San Antonio College and Trinity University and in 1962 joined his father's band, which played regularly at the Landing in San Antonio after it opened in 1963. The trumpeter recorded 15 albums with the Happy Jazz Band during 1963–73 for the Audiophile and Happy Jazz labels.

After his father's death, Jim Cullum (who developed into a powerful soloist) took over the group, which in time became known simply as the Jim Cullum Jazz Band. Since then the ensemble has been one of the top trad bands, featuring such sidemen through the years as clarinetists Allan Vache, Brian Oglivie, and Evan Christopher and pianist John Sheridan. Cullum and his ensembles have recorded for Audiophile, American Jazz, Jazzology, World Jazz, and Stomp Off, plus a perfectly realized set of themes from *Porgy and Bess* for CBS. The Jim Cullum Jazz Band still plays regularly at the Landing and at festivals, but it is its radio programs that have given the group its greatest fame.

Recommended CDs: *Jim Cullum's Happy Jazz Band* (Jazzology 252), *Live at the Memphis Jazz Festival* (Jazzology 132), *Porgy and Bess* (Columbia 42517), *Hooray for Hoagy* (Audiophile 251), *Shootin' the Agate* (Stomp Off 1254), *New Year's All Star Jam* (Riverwalk 1), *Battle of the Bands* (Riverwalk 4), *Fireworks! Red Hot and Blues* (Riverwalk 6)

LPs to Search For: *Look Over Here* (Audiophile 125), *'Tis the Season to Be Jammin'* (World Jazz 21), *Super Satch* (Stomp Off 1148)

Recommended Reading: *Jazz Gentry* by Warren Vache Sr. (Scarecrow Press, 1999)

TED CURSON

• • • • • • • • • • •

b. June 3, 1935, Philadelphia, PA

A distinctive trumpeter with a flexible style, Ted Curson has shown throughout his career that he can fit into many types of settings, ranging from bop to free jazz. "When I was five years old, a man selling newspapers came through my neighborhood playing a trumpet to attract attention. It looked so easy and it was silver." Five years later his father, who had hoped that Curson would play alto sax like Louis Jordan, relented and bought him his first trumpet for his birthday. Curson credits the Heath family (of Jimmy, Percy, and Tootie) for helping him get started in jazz. "I played with Tootie in school and I studied with Jimmy Heath. I used to go to their house. Very famous musicians were often there, and I used to ask them stupid questions!" He attended Mastbaum High School (a special music school), Granoff Musical Conservatory, and Costello Studios.

Curson worked with Charlie Ventura in 1953, moved to New York three years later (at the encouragement of Miles Davis), and played with Red Garland, Mal Waldron, and Philly Joe Jones. Curson's debut recording was with avant-garde pianist Cecil Taylor in 1959, and he sounded quite comfortable in the free-form setting. His most famous association was as a member of the Charles Mingus Quartet during 1959–60, along with multireedist Eric Dolphy and drummer Danny Richmond, recording an album with Mingus that included the classic "Folk Forms No. 1." Mingus' music, which looked both forward toward free jazz and back to bebop and New Orleans jazz, was a perfect setting for the open-minded trumpeter.

After leaving Mingus, Curson co-led a band with tenor saxophonist Bill Barron during 1962–66 and also worked with Max Roach and Archie Shepp. He moved to Denmark in the mid-1960s, playing regularly in Europe until he returned to New York in 1976. Curson has freelanced ever since, recording with Andrew Hill, Nick Brignola, Sal Nistico, Mingus Dynasty, Ran Blake, and others but mostly heading his own bands, including his Spirit of Life Ensemble. He is particularly proud of his work helping younger players. As a leader, Curson has recorded for Old Town, Prestige, Audio Fidelity, Fontana, Atlantic, Supraphon, Columbia, Four Leaf Clover, Marge, India Navigation, Inner City, Interplay, and Evidence, among other labels, naming as his favorite personal albums *Plenty of Horn, Pop Wine, Fire Down Below, Tears for Dolphy,* and *Traveling On.* Curson also took up the guitar in the 1970s (playing some theater jobs in Europe) and enjoys singing.

When asked to sum up his life, Ted Curson says: "Young man from South Philadelphia takes up trumpet at an early age because he wants to play with the giants, travel, and record. He lives to see all of his dreams come true, and still enjoys practicing and performing more than anything else in the world."

Recommended CDs: *Plenty of Horn* (Boplicity 018), *Fire Down Below* (Original Jazz Classics 1744), *Tears for Dolphy* (Black Lion 760190), *Pop Wine* (Futura 26), *Traveling On* (Evidence 22182), with Andrew Hill: *Spiral* (Freedom 741007), with Charles Mingus: *Mingus at Antibes* (Atlantic 90532), *Presents Charles Mingus* (Candid 79005), with Cecil Taylor: *Love for Sale* (Blue Note 94107)

LPs to Search For: *The Canadian Concert of Ted Curson* (Can-Am 1700)

PETE DAILY

b. May 5, 1911, Portland, IN, d. Aug. 23, 1986, Los Angeles, CA

Although hampered by bad health throughout too much of his life, Pete Daily was an excellent Dixieland player who contributed fiery solos to many dates during his prime. After briefly playing baritone horn, tuba, and bass sax, he switched permanently to cornet in high school. Daily was a major part of the Chicago jazz scene during 1930–42, although this was a period of time when Chicago was out of the spotlight. Among the musicians with whom he worked were Jack Davies' Kentuckians (making his recording debut in 1930), Frank Melrose, Art Van Damme, Bud Freeman, and Boyce Brown. Moving to California in 1942, Daily worked with Mike Riley and Ozzie Nelson before serving a year in the Merchant Marine.

After his discharge, Daily was back with Nelson in 1945 and then led the Pete Daily Chicagoans (based in Los Angeles) from the mid-1940s on. The postwar years were a good period for the cornetist. He worked steadily with his Dixieland band and recorded for several labels, including Jump and Capitol, up to 1954. Among his most notable sidemen were Rosy McHargue (on clarinet and C-melody sax) and pianist Marvin Ash. Bad health started to plague Daily in the 1960s. He began doubling on valve trombone, moved back to Indiana, and played with Smokey Stover's band. Daily's health really worsened during the 1970s, but he remained active on a part-time basis in the Los Angeles area until a stroke in 1979 ended his career. Pete Daily's hard-driving yet lyrical style still sounds lively on records today, although most of his own sessions have yet to be reissued on CD.

Recommended CDs: *Jazz Band Ball* (Good Time Jazz 12005)

LPs to Search For: *Pete Daily and His Chicagoans* (Jump 12-5), *Pete Daily's Dixieland Band* (Capitol 183), *Dixie by Daily* (Capitol 385)

Film Appearances: *Rhythm Inn* (1951)

OLU DARA

b. Jan. 12, 1941, Louisville, MS

Best known as a thoughtful avant-garde cornetist, Olu Dara surprised many of his fans in the late 1990s by exploring country blues on the guitar during his long overdue recording debut as a leader. Born Charles Jones III (he changed his name in 1969), Dara grew up in Natchez, Mississippi. He began playing trumpet when he was seven, but it would be some time before he really pursued music. Dara was briefly in college, served in the Navy starting in 1959, and moved to New York in 1963. Having played throughout his military service, he was burned out on music and worked in other fields until he was 30 in 1971. Upon his return to jazz, Dara worked briefly with Art Blakey's Jazz Messengers and then became part of the New York loft scene, performing avant-garde explorations with Oliver Lake, Hamiet Bluiett, Sam Rivers, Henry Threadgill, James Newton, Don Pullen, and most notably David Murray, among many others. Even in those settings, Dara's ability with plunger mutes and his knowledge of earlier styles allowed him to use aspects of the past in his playing.

In the 1980s Dara remained busy as a freelancer, working with such notables as Charles Brackeen, Cassandra Wilson, James Blood Ulmer, Threadgill, and Murray (both his big band and his octet). Also, early in the decade he formed both the seven-piece Okra Orchestra and the four-piece Natchezsippi Dance Band, mixing advanced jazz with West African music and R&B. Dara, who in 1996 appeared in the somewhat disastrous film *Kansas City,* has been involved in theater and modern dance, writing the music for theater productions, including his own musical melodrama, *From Natchez to New York.* Still, all of his diverse activity did not lessen the surprise of hearing Olu Dara's guitar playing and singing (plus some cornet work) on his intriguing 1998 CD *In the World: From Natchez to New York.*

Recommended CDs: *In the World: From Natchez to New York* (Atlantic 83077), with Greg Bandy: *Lightning in a Bottle* (Big On Productions 9701), with Charles Brackeen: *Attainment* (Silkheart 110), *Worshippers Come Nigh* (Silkheart 111), with Julius Hemphill: *Flat Out Jump Suite* (Black Saint 120040), with David Murray: *Flowers for Albert* (India Navigation 1026), *Ming* (Black Saint 120045), *Home* (Black Saint 120055), with James Newton: *African Flower* (Blue Note 85109), with Cassandra Wilson: *Blue Light 'til Dawn* (81357), *Traveling Miles* (Blue Note 54123)

LPs to Search For: with Hamiet Bluiett: *Endangered Species* (India Navigation 1025), with Craig Harris: *Tributes* (OTC 804), with Oliver Lake: *Heavy Spirits* (Freedom 1008), with Cecil McBee: *Flying Out* (India Navig. 1053)

WALLACE DAVENPORT
. . . .

b. June 30, 1925, New Orleans, LA

Because he was raised in New Orleans, Wallace Davenport is identified with trad jazz, but he has also played in more modern styles throughout his long career. In fact, with his strong technique and flexible style, if he had had the desire, Davenport could have broken away and found his voice in bebop or hard bop. He played early on with the Young Tuxedo Brass Band (1938) and Oscar Celestin (1940–41). After serving in the Navy, Davenport worked mostly in New Orleans when not touring with Lionel Hampton (on and off during 1953–76), visiting Paris with Mezz Mezzrow (mid-1950s), playing with Count Basie (1964–66), or gigging as a member of the Ray Charles Orchestra.

Wallace Davenport had his own My Jazz label during 1971–76 and also recorded with Arnett Cobb, Bob Wilber, George Wein, and Panama Francis. He remained active (generally in Dixieland settings) into the 1990s.

Recommended CDs: with Arnett Cobb: *Wild Man from Texas* (Black & Blue 892)

LPs to Search For: *Darkness on the Delta* (Fat Cat's Jazz 130), *French Festival* (Black & Blue 33172)

TRUMP DAVIDSON

. . . .

b. Nov. 26, 1908, Sudbury, Canada, d. May 2, 1978, Sudbury, Canada

Trump Davidson was considered Canada's leading trumpeter (actually cornetist) of the 1930s, '40s and '50s. Unfortunately, because Canada's recording industry was in its infancy and Davidson rarely came to the United States, he did not record until 1961, when he was already 52, a major loss to jazz history. Other than a version of "Darktown Strutters Ball" from a 1937 broadcast and perhaps a couple other brief radio appearances, Davidson's early prime years went completely undocumented.

Davidson formed the Melody Five in 1925, played with the orchestra of violinist Luigi Romanelli in Toronto (1929–36), and had his own big band during the swing era (1937–42), taking time off to tour England with Ray Noble during 1938–39. He worked for a time with pianist Horace Lapp's orchestra and then led a dance band (1944–62) that played regularly at the Palace Pier in Toronto. The big band played swing, with a combo from the orchestra also being featured on some Dixieland numbers. Davidson led mostly small groups after 1962, other than a big band that he sometimes used during 1974–78. He did lead five Dixieland albums for Canadian labels during 1961–69 (none made available in the United States or reissued on CD yet), but listeners can only guess how Trump Davidson must have sounded when he was young.

Recommended Reading: *Jazz in Canada: Fourteen Lives by Mark Miller* (Nightwood Editions, 1988)

GREGORY DAVIS

. . . .

b. Jan. 30, 1957, New Orleans, LA

A founding member of the Dirty Dozen Brass Band, Gregory Davis has helped the pacesetting band redefine and open up the possibilities for New Orleans brass bands. Davis remembers: "At age 13 I enrolled in a music class in school. My intention was to play drums, but there were 20 other students who also wanted to play drums. The teacher offered me two choices: French horn and cornet. The cornet case was smaller, so I chose the cornet!" Davis, who listed his trumpet heroes as Clark Terry, Dizzy Gillespie, and Louis Armstrong, attended Loyola University during 1975–79. "Although I started playing funk and soul gigs when I was 14, it wasn't until my association with the Dirty Dozen Brass Band that I realized that I had become a professional musician. The band started in April 1977 and the gigs really started pouring in to us by 1979."

Gregory Davis has been associated with the DDBB ever since, appearing on its recordings and playing countless jobs with the innovative band, which, in addition to playing some traditional tunes, showed that bebop, R&B, and funk could sound fresh and new when given parade rhythms and performed with the instrumentation of a brass band. "We changed the way brass bands are viewed. We made jazz fun again, made jazz interactive, and were able to combine music and entertainment. When all of the 'experts' said that the Dirty Dozen was a fluke and it wouldn't last, we proved them wrong. It has been 23 years, and counting."

Recommended CDs: with Dirty Dozen Brass Band: *My Feet Can't Fail Me Now* (Concord 43005), *Voodoo* (Columbia 45042), *The New Orleans Album* (Columbia 45414), *Jelly* (Columbia 53214)

LEONARD DAVIS

• • • • • • • • • • • • • • •

b. July 4, 1905, St. Louis, MO, d. 1957, New York, NY

Some trumpeters have recorded scores of exciting albums that feature their playing. In the case of Leonard "Ham" Davis, although he spent 15 years playing in the big leagues of jazz, the high point of his career was his playing on two selections recorded on a single day. On February 8, 1929, Davis took beautiful solos on "I'm Gonna Stomp Mr. Henry Lee" and particularly on the blues "That's a Serious Thing" during a date with Eddie Condon's Hot Shots. Both numbers (performed with an integrated unit also featuring trombonist-singer Jack Teagarden) are fortunately available in two versions apiece on a Teagarden double CD. Davis' memorable tone, wide range, and creative ideas that day put him near the top of his field, but there would be no real encore.

Leonard Davis grew up in St. Louis, where he played locally and worked with Charlie Creath (with whom he made his recording debut) during 1924–25. After moving to New York, he had stints with Charlie Skeets, Edgar Hayes (1927), Arthur Gibbs, and Charlie Johnson (1928–29). Because of his beautiful tone and range, qualities that made his playing during the one day with Eddie Condon so memorable, Davis was ironically employed mostly as a lead trumpeter rather than as a soloist throughout his career, a valuable but anonymous section player in orchestras. He worked with many groups, including Elmer Snowden (1930–31 and the 1933 short film *Smash Your Baggage*), Don Redman, Russell Wooding, Benny Carter (1933), Luis Russell (1934–35), with Russell as Louis Armstrong's backup band (1935–37), Edgar Hayes (1938), the Blackbirds Show (1938–39), with Sidney Bechet in a nonet (1940), George James (1943), and flutist Alberto Socarras. After the mid-1940s Davis was a part-time player. During the entire time he was active, other than that one day, amazingly enough no one took advantage of how great a soloist Leonard Davis could be.

Recommended CDs: *The Indispensable Jack Teagarden* (RCA Jazz Tribune 66606)

MILES DAVIS
....

b. May 25, 1926, Alton, IL, d. Sept. 28, 1991, Santa Monica, CA

Miles Davis was not only one of the most important jazz trumpeters of all time, he was one of the giants of 20th century music. Unlike most musicians who develop their sound and style in their twenties and then spend most of the rest of their careers perfecting their approach without making any major changes, Davis was about constant evolution and new innovations. He not only played bebop in his own way early in his career but was at least partly responsible for founding and popularizing cool jazz, hard bop, modal music, a unique type of avant-garde jazz, and fusion.

Although never a virtuoso on the level of Dizzy Gillespie, Davis developed a distinctive cool-toned sound, stripping the bebop vocabulary to its essentials and making every note and silence count. On ballads (where he often utilized a Harmon mute and played close to the microphone), his playing was often exquisite.

Like Fletcher Henderson and Art Blakey, Davis was also a masterful talent scout whose sidemen quite frequently became the giants of the next musical generation. He was able to recognize potential in its formative stage and bring out the best in his players. Among the many musicians who were somewhat unknown before they benefited from performing with Davis were Gerry Mulligan (who was in Miles' Birth of the Cool Nonet), Gil Evans, Sonny Rollins, John Coltrane, Red Garland, Paul Chambers, Philly Joe Jones, Cannonball Adderley, Bill Evans (the pianist), Jimmy Cobb, Wynton Kelly, George Coleman, Wayne Shorter, Herbie Hancock, Ron Carter, Tony Williams, Chick Corea, Jack DeJohnette, Dave Holland, John McLaughlin, Joe Zawinul, Keith Jarrett, Steve Grossman, Gary Bartz, Dave Liebman, Al Foster, Sonny Fortune, Mike Stern, John Scofield, Bill Evans (the saxophonist), Marcus Miller, and Kenny Garrett.

As a human being, Davis (sometimes called "The Prince of Darkness") was a major contrast to the cheerful personalities of Louis Armstrong, Dizzy Gillespie, and Clark Terry (three of his heroes). An introvert who combated his shyness by creating a forbidding image, Davis frequently appeared angry in public, not only generally ignoring his audience but acting as if he despised them. Perhaps it was his way of reacting to the discovery that, even though he came from a middle-class family, in the racist America of the 1940s he was valued less than the lowliest white derelict.

Miles Dewey Davis grew up in East St. Louis, Illinois, the son of a prominent dentist and landowner. He was given his first trumpet by his father for his 13th birthday. Among his early idols were Bobby Hackett (particularly because of the lyrical solo that Hackett took on a 1938 recording of "Embraceable You"), Harry James, and Clark Terry (a local star at the time). Davis played with his high school band, worked with Eddie Randall's Blue Devils during 1941–43, and had what he described as the greatest musical experience of his life when he had the opportunity to sit in with the Billy Eckstine Orchestra in 1944; among its stars were Dizzy Gillespie and Charlie Parker.

After graduating high school, Davis moved to New York in September 1944 to study at Juilliard—at least that was the original plan. At the time he had a small range, an eerie sound, and a strong interest in the emerging bebop music. Among the first things that Miles did in

New York was to find Charlie Parker. He ended up spending more time at 52nd Street clubs than he did in school, and he soon dropped out. For a time, he played nightly with Coleman Hawkins. Davis made his recording debut on April 24, 1945, on a set led by singer-dancer Rubberlegs Williams, but he sounded quite nervous and hesitant. He did better on his second record date, a Charlie Parker session a few months later that resulted in the original versions of "Now's the Time" and "Billie's Bounce." Gillespie did have to fill in for Davis on "Ko Ko" because the 19-year-old could not handle the rapid tempo yet.

During the bop years, Miles was to Dizzy what Bix Beiderbecke had been to Louis Armstrong in the 1920s, a "cool" alternative to the "hot" virtuoso. Initially frustrated that he could not play on Gillespie's level, Davis made his technical limitations an asset by developing a simpler (but no less effective) style, one that became hugely influential.

When Charlie Parker traveled with Gillespie to California later in 1945, Davis followed Bird by joining Benny Carter's orchestra, since Carter was heading for Los Angeles too. Once on the West Coast, Davis became an occasional member of Parker's quintet, recording with Parker (including classic versions of "Moose the Mooche," "Yardbird Suite," and "Ornithology") and sounding much more confident than he had earlier. When Parker was put into the mental institution at Camarillo (due in large part to his reluctant withdrawal from heroin addiction), Davis returned to the East Coast. Bird was released in early 1947, and back in New York he formed his most significant working band, a quintet with pianist Duke Jordan, bassist Tommy Potter, drummer Max Roach, and Davis. Some bebop fans at the time were surprised that Bird did not have Dizzy Gillespie or Fats Navarro as his trumpeter, but Gillespie was running his big band and Parker enjoyed contrasting his blazing solos with the more thoughtful improvisations of Miles.

Davis, who led a very obscure session with tenor saxophonist Gene Ammons on October 18, 1946, that found him backing two singers (the music was not released until the 1980s), had his first real date as a leader on October 14, 1947. Fronting the Charlie Parker Quintet (with Bird switching to tenor), Davis introduced his four compositions "Milestones" (which is different from the 1958 song of the same name), "Little Willie Leaps," "Half Nelson," and "Sippin' at Bells."

The trumpeter's first attempt to lead a band of his own took place in the fall of 1948, when he was still in Parker's group. He had met arranger Gil Evans (who became his lifelong best friend) and, together with Gerry Mulligan, they conceived of forming a group that had the tonal qualities of Claude Thornhill's orchestra (which utilized French horns and a tuba) along with the innovations of bebop. The resulting nonet consisted of Davis, Mulligan, altoist Lee Konitz, trombonist Mike Zwerin, pianist John Lewis, bassist Al McKibbon, Max Roach, French horn, and tuba, putting an emphasis on softer tones and the arrangements of Davis, Evans, Mulligan, Lewis, and Johnny Carisi. Amazingly, this innovative band had only one gig, two weeks in September 1948 playing at the Royal Roost as the intermission band for Count Basie's orchestra. Fortunately (with J.J. Johnson or Kai Winding on trombone) the group had three recording sessions for Capitol during 1949–50, and it was so influential that it has been credited with largely starting cool, or West Coast, jazz.

As was typical for Davis, by the time the records of his "Birth of the Cool Nonet" were having an impact, he had long since moved on. He left the Charlie Parker Quintet in De-

From 1948 to 91, Miles Davis continually kept listeners guessing and his fellow musicians paying close attention.

cember 1948 and the following year played surprisingly fiery bebop at the Paris Jazz Festival in a group with pianist Tadd Dameron and tenor saxophonist James Moody.

When he returned to the United States, it was not long before Davis became a heroin addict, even though he had ironically avoided drugs during his period with Bird. The 1950–53 years were a personal low point for him as he constantly scuffled for money to feed his addiction. But, although overlooked at the time, he created some important music during this so-called "off period." Davis made a final recording in 1953 with Charlie Parker (who played tenor for the occasion, opposite Sonny Rollins) and some of his records helped to introduce Rollins and altoist Jackie McLean. Davis' Blue Note recordings of 1952–54 were particularly significant, for they were among the first hard bop sessions (five years before hard bop really caught on), utilizing such important musicians as J.J. Johnson, tenor saxophonist Jimmy Heath, pianist Horace Silver, and drummer Art Blakey, a few years before Blakey and Silver launched their own influential bands.

In 1954, Miles Davis got his life together, permanently kicking heroin. He recorded a classic version of "Walkin'" that showed listeners that he had moved away from cool jazz into harder swinging, introduced the songs "Four" and "Solar," and in December had a memorable recorded session with Thelonious Monk and Milt Jackson. The following year, Davis really broke through. At the Newport Jazz Festival he played in peak form (including performing "'Round Midnight" with Monk) before an important group of critics, who finally realized that he was a giant. Before the year was out, he was leading his first "classic quintet," a group with the unknown tenor saxophonist John Coltrane, pianist Red Garland, bassist Paul Chambers, and drummer Philly Joe Jones. Miles Davis at 29 had finally arrived.

During 1955–56, the Miles Davis Quintet recorded four fine straightahead albums for Prestige (sounding similar to how they performed in clubs) and a gem (*Round About Midnight*) for Columbia; Davis signed with the latter company, where he would remain into the 1980s. His muted ballads in particular were quite popular, and the well-dressed trumpeter became a national celebrity, often making headlines. His voice by then had become quiet and raspy (due to his getting into a verbal argument when he should have been resting in preparation for throat surgery), and his angry persona (he occasionally played with his back to the audience) was looked upon as a measure of black pride, since he did not feel compelled to compromise himself in the white-dominated world. The fact that he treated most women rather poorly, had a violent temper, and loved to cuss up a storm (often to shock white fans) was often overlooked.

By 1957 the first quintet had broken up, due partly to Coltrane's and Philly Joe Jones' drug use; Trane kicked heroin later in the year. Davis led a few short-term bands and recorded the first of his full-length collaborations with Gil Evans, the brilliant *Miles Ahead*. He went to France, where he recorded the soundtrack for the French film *Lift to the Scaffold*. In 1958 he reformed the quintet, but this time with an addition, altoist Cannonball Adderley. Garland was soon succeeded by Bill Evans and eventually Wynton Kelly, with Jones departing in favor of Jimmy Cobb. With his super sextet (arguably his finest band), Davis created a pair of classic albums: *Milestones* and *Kind of Blue*. The latter introduced "So What" and "All Blues" along with a fresh way of improvising, off of scales rather than chord structures. Davis also had two other famous collaborations with Gil Evans (1958's *Porgy and Bess* and 1960's *Sketches of Spain*), mostly playing flugelhorn on these best-selling albums.

In 1960, Miles Davis was just 34. By then Adderley had departed and Coltrane was ready to lead his own group. The tenor spot was filled briefly by Sonny Stitt and for a year by Hank Mobley. Although Davis seemed to be resting during 1960–63, not advancing as quickly as during the previous five years, he performed some of his finest bebop trumpet playing during this era, particularly on the two albums *Friday* and *Saturday Night at the Blackhawk*; his chops were in peak form and his range was surprisingly wide. But when the Kelly-Chambers-Cobb rhythm section joined Wes Montgomery in 1962, Davis was without a regular band for the first time in seven years. It took him into 1963, but he eventually had a brilliant young rhythm section in pianist Herbie Hancock, bassist Ron Carter, and drummer Tony Williams. Moving beyond hard bop, Davis (with George Coleman on tenor) was still playing his older standards, but often at very fast tempos, really stretching himself. The rhythm section was open to the influences of Ornette Coleman and the avant-garde, and Williams in particular pushed Davis to continue to evolve. After Coleman departed in 1964, Sam Rivers filled the tenor spot for a couple months before Wayne Shorter joined the group, making it the second classic Miles Davis Quintet.

During 1965–68, Davis' band developed a freer type of jazz that was quite original. Shorter's compositions, Williams' drumming, the new role of the piano in the group, and Davis' constant musical curiosity led the band into many uncharted areas, sometimes seeming to suspend both time and chords, although they continued to hang onto both (if just barely at times). It would not be until the 1980s (when Wynton and Branford Marsalis emulated the group) that the often-overshadowed second Miles Davis Quintet really became influential.

In 1968, Davis persuaded Hancock to start using electric keyboards, Shorter began doubling on soprano, and the influence of both modern R&B and rock started to be felt, in small ways at first. By the following year, the second classic quintet was no more, as the rhythm section gradually became keyboardist Chick Corea, electric bassist Dave Holland, and drummer Jack DeJohnette. Getting away from jazz forms, Davis began to record lengthy rockish jam sessions in the studios. The atmospheric *In A Silent Way* and particularly the double-LP *Bitches Brew* signaled the beginnings of the fusion era, mixing rock and funk rhythms with jazz improvisations.

Because Miles Davis refused to stand still and his live shows tended to be a few years ahead of his most recently released records, he bewildered many of his older fans, first with the second quintet and particularly after 1968, when his music became more rock-oriented. He continued moving ahead during 1970–75, and *Bitches Brew* sounded tame compared to the dense music that he was performing live, often with two or three guitarists and several keyboardists. Steve Grossman replaced Shorter on soprano and was succeeded along the way by Dave Liebman and Sonny Fortune. Rhythmic vamps became the basis of many pieces, and Davis around 1971 began distorting the sound of his horn with electronics. It would not be until the late 1990s that other jazz musicians would start to fully explore Davis' ideas of this era; he was so far ahead of his time! Of his recordings of the period, *Live/Evil, Jack Johnson,* and *Pangaea* (from 1975) are quite exciting, while *On the Corner* (which has been both overpraised and damned) is one of his few duds, excerpts from jams that barely feature the trumpeter at all.

In 1975 Miles Davis did the unexpected and retired from music, not returning for six years. At 49, he was experiencing bad health and becoming very involved with recreational drugs, including cocaine. His next few years were a complete blur of personal excess while the jazz world speculated about whether he would ever return, and what would happen if he did play trumpet again. In 1981 Davis came back, disappointing some fans by not suddenly reverting to his 1955 self. The bands that he led during his final decade tended to be lighter and sparser than his 1970–75 groups, still using rock rhythms but also with pop elements. Instead of two or three guitarists, he used one, and Davis no longer electrified his horn, letting his famous melancholy tone be heard in the newer settings. His trumpet playing, a bit weak at first, became stronger as the years progressed, and even his personality gave the appearance of mellowing a little, although he was always capable of suddenly launching a furious verbal attack.

Davis kept up a busy schedule during the 1980s, touring the world and coasting a bit. Among his most interesting later sidemen were electric bassist Marcus Miller and altoist Kenny Garrett. There were times when Davis would look back briefly, playing over blues chord changes or hinting at his earlier ballad style. In fact *Siesta* (recorded with Miller's arrangements) could be thought of as an updated tribute to Gil Evans. During these later years Davis appeared in the film *Dingo* and (with Quincy Troupe) wrote his fascinating if expletive-filled autobiography, *Miles*.

In the summer of 1991, Davis surprised everyone by letting Quincy Jones talk him into performing vintage Gil Evans arrangements at the Montreux Jazz Festival. Although he shared the solo space with Wallace Roney and Kenny Garrett, he was in stronger-than-expected form. Perhaps Davis had given in to this request because he knew that his time was short. He also had reunions with some of his surviving sidemen of the past during the final European tour, while keeping his last group together. Two months after the Montreux concert, the remarkable career and life of Miles Davis came to an end, at the age of 65.

Recommended CDs: *The Complete Birth of the Cool* (Capitol 94550), *Volume One* (Blue Note 81501), *Volume Two* (Blue Note 81502), *Walkin'* (Original Jazz Classics 213), *Miles Davis and the Modern Jazz Giants* (Original Jazz Classics 347), *Miscellaneous Miles* (Jazz Unlimited 2050), *Cookin'* (Original Jazz Classics 128), *Workin'* (Original Jazz Classics 296), *Relaxin'* (Original Jazz Classics 190), *Steamin'* (Original Jazz Classics 391), *Round About Midnight* (Columbia 40610), *Miles Ahead* (Columbia/Legacy 65121), *Milestones* (Columbia/Legacy 40837), *Porgy and Bess* (Columbia/Legacy 65141), *Kind of Blue* (Columbia/Legacy 64935), *Sketches of Spain* (Columbia/Legacy 65142), *Friday Night at the Blackhawk* (Columbia/Legacy 44257), *Saturday Night at the Blackhawk* (Columbia/Legacy 44425), *Seven Steps to Heaven* (Columbia/Legacy 48827), *The Complete Concert: 1964* (Columbia/Legacy 48821), *E.S.P.* (Columbia/Legacy 65683), *Miles Smiles* (Columbia/Legacy 65682), *Nefertiti* (Columbia/Legacy 65681), *Filles de Kilimanjaro* (Columbia/Legacy 46116), *In a Silent Way* (Columbia/Legacy 40580), *Bitches Brew* (Columbia/Legacy 65774), *Live-Evil* (Columbia/Legacy 65135), *A Tribute to Jack Johnson* (Columbia/Legacy 47036), *Pangaea* (Columbia/Legacy 46115), *Amandla* (Warner Brothers 25873), *Live Around the World* (Warner Brothers 46032)

Box Sets: *Chronicle-The Complete Prestige Recordings 1951–56* (8 CDs; Prestige 012), *Miles Davis and John Coltrane-The Complete Columbia Recordings 1955–1961* (6 CDs; Columbia/Legacy 65833), *The Complete Miles Davis Quintet* (6 CDs; Columbia/Legacy 67398)

LPs to Search For: *The Paris Festival International* (Columbia 34804), *We Want Miles* (Columbia 38005), *Siesta* (Warner Bros. 25655)

Recommended Reading: *From Satchmo to Miles* by Leonard Feather (Da Capo Press, 1984), *The Jazz Life* by Nat Hentoff (Da Capo Press, 1975), *Jazz Masters of The '50s* by Joe Goldberg (Macmillan Publishing Co., 1965), *Kind of Blue* by Ashley Kahn (Da Capo Press, 2000), *The Man in the Green Shirt* by Richard Williams (Henry Holt and Co., 1993), *Miles* by Miles Davis and Quincy Troupe (Simon and Schuster, 1989), *Miles and Me* by Quincy Troupe (University of California Press, 2000), *Miles Davis* by Ian Carr (Quill, 1982), *A Miles Davis Companion* ed. by Gary Carner (Schirmer Books, 1996), *A Miles Davis Reader* ed. by Bill Kirchner (Smithsonian Institution Press, 1997), *Milestones* by Jack Chambers (Da Capo Press, 1998), *Talking Jazz* by Ben Sidran (Pomegranate Artbooks, 1992)

Film Appearances: (on soundtrack) *Jack Johnson* (1970)

Recommended Videos: *Vintage Collection, Vol. 2* (1959, with John Coltrane and Gil Evans; A*Vision 50239), *Live in Sweden* (1965; Sony Music), *Miles in Paris* (1990; Warner Reprise Video 38186), *Dingo* (1990; Greycat Home Video), *Live at Montreux* (1991; Warner/Reprise Video), and also Davis' trumpet is very prominent on the soundtrack of *Elevator to the Gallows* (1957; New Yorker Video 20792)

SPANKY DAVIS

• • • • • • • • • • • •

b. Mar. 6, 1943, Indianapolis, IN

An excellent soloist specializing in mainstream swing, Roland "Spanky" Davis has been a valuable utility player for years. He grew up in Ft. Wayne, Indiana, took piano lessons at age six, and switched to trumpet the next year. He started his career playing locally in Indiana with the Thunderbirds (1958–59), the Silhouettes (1959–61) and Jess Gaylor's orchestra (1961–62). During the next 15 years Davis worked with Don Glasser in Chicago (1963–65), the Howard McGhee big band, Tiny Hill (1966–68), Ralph Marterie (1970–74), Bill Reinhardt (1977), Jim Beebe's Chicago Jazz Band (1977–78), and his own Dixieland groups.

After moving to New York in 1978, Davis subbed regularly for Roy Eldridge at Jimmy Ryan's (taking over the position during 1980–83) and worked with (among many others) Charlie Palmieri (1979), Machito (1979–80), the Sam Jones big band (1979–81), Gerry Mulligan, the Benny Goodman Sextet (1981–82), Panama Francis' Savoy Sultans, Butch Miles, and the Buck Clayton Big Band (1988–91). Although his profile was raised slightly in the 1990s, Spanky Davis still ranks as one of the most underrated trumpeters in today's mainstream swing scene.

Recommended CDs: *Passing the Torch* (Challenge 70035), with Chuck Folds: *Remember Doc Cheatham* (Arbors 19208)

STANTON DAVIS

b. Nov. 10, 1945, New Orleans, LA

Although he has been a part of the modern jazz scene for over 25 years, Stanton Davis has been primarily a valuable sideman rather than a bandleader. Davis attended Berklee (1967–69) and the New England Conservatory (1969–73). A very versatile trumpeter who ranges between hard bop and the avant-garde, Davis has performed with top jazz musicians from a variety of styles. Some of his most notable associations include stints with George Russell, Lester Bowie's Brass Fantasy, Charlie Haden, George Gruntz, Jim Pepper, Bob Stewart, Muhal Richard Abrams, Sam Rivers, Jaki Byard, James Moody, Ray Anderson, and Steve Turre. A fine (if somewhat underutilized) soloist, Stanton Davis has also long been active as both a jazz educator and an ensemble player for television and Broadway shows.

Recommended CDs: *Manhattan Melody* (Enja 5089), with Muhal Richard Abrams: *View from Within* (Black Saint 120081), with Ray Anderson: *It Just So Happens* (Enja 5037)

LPs to Search For: with Bob Stewart: *First Line* (JMT 880014)

TINY DAVIS

b. 1907, Memphis, TN, d. Jan. 30, 1994, Chicago, IL

Ernestine "Tiny" Davis is best known for being one of the star soloists with the International Sweethearts of Rhythm (the top all-female big band of the 1940s) during 1942–46. Davis, who had worked earlier with the Harlem Playgirls, could play heated swing solos and took good-humored blues vocals. After leaving the Sweethearts in the late 1940s, she briefly had her own all-female orchestra and led a sextet called the Hell-Divers. Tiny Davis, who in 1949 as a leader recorded six songs for Decca (none of which have been reissued) but apparently nothing else during the remainder of her career, worked locally in Chicago for years and was still active into the 1980s. But the prejudice against female instrumentalists did not help, and she remained obscure for decades, despite her musical talents.

LPs to Search For: *International Sweethearts of Rhythm* (Rosetta 1312)

Recommended Reading: *The International Sweethearts of Rhythm* by D. Antoinette Handy (Scarecrow Press, 1998)

Videos to Get: *The International Sweethearts of Rhythm* (Jezebel Productions)

WILD BILL DAVISON

b. Jan. 5, 1906, Defiance, OH, d. Nov. 14, 1989, Santa Barbara, CA

Of all of the Dixieland cornetists and trumpeters, it would be difficult to find one who was more colorful (both onstage and off) then Wild Bill Davison. He was involved in countless escapades throughout his life (with an often-extreme amount of drinking and

There are few greater thrills in listening to jazz than hearing Wild Bill Davison drive a Dixieland ensemble.

carousing) yet died of old age. He once told writer Nat Hentoff that the secret to drinking was to consume a quart of milk beforehand, since that lines one's stomach. Davison had five marriages (his first marriage was so brief that he could never remember his first wife's name!) and countless affairs, yet his final marriage (to Anne Davison from 1954 on) lasted 35 years and was happy. As a musician, Davison was the perfect cornetist in Dixieland settings, because he had a distinctive tone, was highly expressive (with emotions ranging from sentimentality and warmth to complete sarcasm), knew the perfect spots to toss in screaming high notes, and could liven up any situation. He made most other Dixieland trumpeters sound bland in comparison.

Davison, who grew up in Defiance, Ohio, began playing professionally on banjo, mandolin, guitar, and mellophone before switching to cornet early on; he never had a music lesson. He quit high school after one year to play banjo with a dance band, but by the mid-1920s he was exclusively a cornetist. In the 1920s, Davison picked up experience playing with the Ohio Lucky Seven, James Jackson, Roland Potter's Peerless Players, the Chubb-Steinberg Orchestra (later renamed the Omer-Hicks Orchestra), the Seattle Harmony Kings (1927), and Benny Meroff, recording with Chubb-Steinberg and Meroff. Davison played in Chicago for several years and in 1931 formed a big band with clarinetist Frankie Teschemacher. However, before the orchestra was set to debut, Teschemacher was killed in an automobile accident. Davison was the driver and (due to his reputation) for years he was blamed by many other jazz musicians for being at fault, but in reality he was blindsided by a cab running a red light. Partly due to the anger of other musicians, Davison moved to Milwaukee, where he worked steadily but in obscurity during 1933–41.

Wild Bill's exile ended in the spring of 1941 when he moved to New York. His hard-charging style was fully formed by then. In 1942 he led his own band regularly at Nick's, participated in a recreation of the Original Dixieland Jazz Band, and became associated with Eddie Condon's all-star groups. In 1943 he recorded some classic Dixieland sides for Commodore (including the definitive version of "That's a-Plenty"). Although he was in the Army from late 1943 to 1945 (missing Condon's famous Town Hall radio series), Wild Bill's reputation was now secure. He began working immediately after his discharge and was a regular member of Eddie Condon's gang during 1945–57 and occasionally afterwards. His mixture of growls, screams, and roars, along with his desire to stick to Dixieland, made him a popular attraction. During this era, Davison also had an antique shop; antiques were one of his many hobbies, along with collecting German helmets from World War I, building train sets, and turning old horns into lamps.

Davison, who made some successful recordings with Sidney Bechet, was featured on a couple of best-selling Columbia albums with strings in the mid-1950s (*Pretty Wild* and *With Strings Attached*) that helped increase his appeal, contrasting his swaggering and boisterous style with his sentimental approach to ballads. After 1957, Davison mostly led his own bands, popping up in countless settings, including playing with Tommy Saunders' Surf Side Six starting in 1963 and touring England for a couple of months in 1964 with Freddie Randall's band. Although his own repertoire did not change much through the years, he never lost his enthusiasm or his joy for the hard-charging Chicago jazz that he loved. By 1965, Davison was becoming a world traveler, and during the next ten years he appeared with over 100 different bands, visiting Europe often. In 1967 a perforated ulcer caused internal bleeding, and Davison was on the critical list for a week but pulled through. In fact, a month later he was playing in England with Alex Welsh's group!

In 1968 Davison was featured with the Jazz Giants, an all-star group that included Barney Bigard and Claude Hopkins. During 1971–72 he toured college campuses with Art Hodes' Stars of Jazz. Davison spent a lot of time overseas (including living in Copenhagen during 1975–80) before settling in Santa Barbara in 1980. In Switzerland for his 75th birthday, Wild Bill's birthday was celebrated with a giant cake that had tiers comprising 75 bottles of whiskey! Try as he did, Davison did not get to drink too many of the bottles. When he was 78, he was told by a doctor that if he touched one more drop of whisky, he would not live ten days more. Wild Bill stopped drinking completely. But because he had not played sober in years, he had to relearn how to play cornet; it took several months!

Although his range gradually declined after he turned 70, Davison remained quite active up until the end and never lost his instantly recognizable sound. At 83 he had surgery for an aneurysm and fell into a coma. Tommy Saunders flew in from Detroit and played his cornet for Davison at the hospital, hoping that the music would penetrate his coma. It might have, but Davison died 15 days after the operation. Because he appeared on hundreds of albums during his career (with occasional "new" sessions still coming out), the exciting music of the legendary Wild Bill Davison can still be enjoyed today.

Recommended CDs: *Commodore Master Takes* (Commodore 405), *Showcase* (Jazzology 83), *Pretty Wild/With Strings Attached* (Arbors 19175), *With Freddy Randall and His Band* (Jazzology 160), *Jazz on a Saturday Afternoon, Vols. 1–2* (Jazzology 37 and 38), *With Papa Bue* (Storyville 5526), *With the Alex Welsh Band* (Jazzology 201), *Wild Bill in Denmark, Vols. 1–2* (Storyville 5523 and 5524), *Solo Flight* (Jazzology 114)

LPs to Search For: *Live at the Rainbow Room* (Chiaroscuro 124), *Surfside Jazz* (Jazzology 25), *Wild Bill in New Orleans* (Jazzology 170), *Together Again* (Storyville 4027)

Recommended Reading: *The Wildest One* by Hal Willard (Avondale Press, 1996)

Videos to Get: *Jazz Festival, Vol. 1* (1962, with Eddie Condon; Storyville 6073)

JOHNNY D'EARTH

• • • • • • • • • • • • • • •

b. Mar. 30, 1950, Framingham, MA

A forward-thinking hard bop improviser, Johnny D'Earth has an appealing sound and a flexible style. Somewhat typical of today's top jazz trumpeters, D'Earth is not closely associated with any one group or style, freelancing in many areas and adding vitality to each setting in which he appears. D'Earth originally started on drums (taught by his father), switching to trumpet when he was eight. He worked in Massachusetts with Ken Sawyer's Big Nine (1964–69), attended Harvard during 1968–71 (a period when he often performed with Bennie Wallace and Don Grolnick), and moved to New York in 1971. D'Earth was part of the New York loft scene for a year before joining Larry Elgart's commercial dance band (1972–76), a good example of his versatility!

D'Earth has since worked with many top musicians, including Bob Moses (1973–84), Gunter Hampel (1974), Deodato (1974–76), the Lee Konitz Nonet (1976–77), Buddy Rich (1977), Lionel Hampton (1977–78), Tito Puente (1979–80), the Thad Jones/Mel Lewis big band (1976–80), Harvie Swartz (1979–80), Jane Ira Bloom (1983), Emily Remler (1983–85), Dave Liebman, and George Gruntz's Concert Jazz Band (1991–95). He has also frequently led his own groups and during 1973–84 co-led Cosmology with his future wife, singer Dawn Thompson. He may not have won any jazz polls, but John D'Earth can always be counted on for a creative and stirring performance.

Recommended CDs: *One Bright Glance* (Enja 6040), with Emily Remler: *Transitions* (Concord Jazz 4326), *Catwalk* (Concord Jazz 4265)

RUSTY DEDRICK

• • • • • • • • • • • • • • •

b. July 12, 1918, Delaware, NY

R usty Dedrick has always been a little difficult to place stylistically. Although a product of the swing era, Dedrick fit quite well into bop, cool jazz, and mainstream settings. In fact, his 1957 tribute to Bunny Berigan is more West Coast Jazz than it is swing. Dedrick attended Fredonia State Teachers College but soon switched to full-time music.

He worked with the big bands of Dick Stabile (1938–39) and Red Norvo (1939–41) but became best known for his association with Claude Thornhill. He played and arranged for Thornhill during 1941–42 and, after spending 1942–45 in the Army and having a brief stint with Ray McKinley in 1946, was back with Thornhill during 1946–47. With the end of the big band era, Dedrick became a busy studio musician in New York as both trumpeter and arranger, writing for Don Elliott, Maxine Sullivan, and Lee Wiley, among others. He recorded two albums as a leader for Esoteric in the 1950s (including the Bunny Berigan tribute), led a series of nostalgia swing albums for Monmouth Evergreen in the 1960s, played with Urbie Green (1967) and Lionel Hampton (1970–71), and recorded with Maxine Sullivan and Lee Wiley in the 1970s. In 1971 Rusty Dedrick (who sounds at his best on the Wiley album) joined the faculty of the Manhattan School of Music, eventually becoming its director of jazz studies.

Recommended CDs: *A Salute to Bunny Berigan* (DCC 624), with Don Elliott: *Double Trumpet Doings* (Original Jazz Classics 1925), with Maxine Sullivan: *A Tribute to Andy Razaf* (DCC Compact Classics 610), with Claude Thornhill: *Snowfall* (Hep 1058), with Lee Wiley: *Back Home Again* (Audiophile 300)

SIDNEY DEPARIS

● ● ● ● ● ● ● ● ● ● ● ● ● ● ● ● ●

b. May 30, 1905, Crawfordsville, IN, d. Sep. 13, 1967, New York, NY

Sidney DeParis was a solid and occasionally exciting soloist who was able to play both swing and Dixieland quite effectively. His use of growls was distinctive, and he was very handy with mutes. The younger brother of trombonist Wilbur DeParis, Sidney studied music with his father, who led a carnival band that played in vaudeville. After a period with his father's group (touring throughout the South), DeParis worked with Sam Taylor in Washington, D.C. (1924), played in New York with Andrew Preer's Cotton Club Orchestra (with whom he made his recording debut), and then was a major soloist with Charlie Johnson's Paradise Ten. Other than a year spent with his brother's band in Philadelphia, DeParis was with Johnson throughout 1926–31, being featured on several classic records, including "The Boy with the Boat" and "Walk That Thing"; in addition, he recorded in 1929 with McKinney's Cotton Pickers.

Although primarily a small-group player, DeParis was at home in the big bands of Fletcher Henderson (briefly in 1931), Don Redman (1932–36), Willie Bryant, and Benny Carter (1940–41). He recorded with Mezz Mezzrow in 1938 (a stormy session with Tommy Ladnier), Jelly Roll Morton in 1939, and both Sidney Bechet (including "Old Man Blues") and Willie "the Lion" Smith the following year. DeParis worked mostly on 52nd Street in the early 1940s, including with Zutty Singleton and Art Hodes, although he was also part of the Roy Eldridge big band for a period in 1944.

Starting in 1943 and particularly from 1947 on, Sidney worked regularly with his brother's band (which was based for much of the time at Jimmy Ryan's during 1951–62), an ensemble that became known as Wilbur DeParis New New Orleans Jazz. The DeParis Brothers' music, although essentially New Orleans jazz and Dixieland, was full of surprises and sounded quite fresh, taking an occasional song at a ridiculously fast tempo and often exploring unusual material in a trad setting. Their string of recordings for Atlantic (which unfortunately have been scarce for quite a few years) have long been valued collectors' items.

Later in the 1950s, Sidney DeParis (who occasionally doubled on tuba) began to become ill, so Doc Cheatham was added to the band, on second trumpet. By 1964 illness had forced DeParis to stop playing music altogether, and he passed away when he was 62. In addition to his recordings with his brother, Sidney DeParis can be heard at his best on a pair of his Blue Note sessions recorded in 1944 and 1951 and a strangely successful date for Swingville in 1962 (reissued as half of a CD by the Swingville All-Stars) that finds him turning country and western songs into swinging jazz.

Recommended CDs: with Wilbur DeParis: *Dr. Jazz Series, Vol. 7* (Storyville 6047), *An Evening at Jimmy Ryan's* (Jazz Crusade 3005), *Live in Canada 1956* (Jazz Crusade 3032), with Charlie Johnson: *The Complete Charlie Johnson Sessions* (Sweet & Hot 5510S), with McKinney's Cotton Pickers: Various Artists: *Hot Jazz on Blue Note* (Blue Note 35811), with Swingville All-Stars: *At the Jazz Band Ball* (Good Time Jazz 10080)

Box Set: *The Complete Hall/Johnson/DeParis/Dickenson on Blue Note* (4 CDs; Mosaic 4-109)

LPs to Search For: with Wilbur DeParis: *Marchin' and Swingin'* (Atlantic 1233), *That's a-Plenty* (Atlantic 1318), *The Wild Jazz Age* (Atlantic 1336)

Videos to Get: *Wilbur DeParis in Europe* (1960; 30N-90W Video NWV01)

JIMMY DEUCHAR
. . . .

b. June 26, 1930, Dundee, Scotland, d. Sept. 9, 1993, Dundee, Scotland

One of Scotland's finest jazz trumpeters, Jimmy Deuchar was a talented bebop player who could hold his own with the best in the field. He started his career playing locally and first played in London's Club Eleven while he was in the Royal Air Force. Deuchar was a member of Johnny Dankworth's Seven (1950–51), worked with Jack Parnell (1952), Ronnie Scott (1953–54), and Tony Crombie (1955), played some jobs with Lionel Hampton in 1956, and toured the United States with Ronnie Scott (1957). In addition to recording with most of these notables, Deuchar also appeared on records with Victor Feldman and Zoot Sims.

Deuchar moved to Germany for a few years, working as one of the main soloists with the Kurt Edelhagen Orchestra (1957–59). His most significant associations in the 1960s were with Ronnie Scott (1960–62), Tubby Hayes (1962–64), and the Kenny Clarke-Francy Boland Orchestra (1963–71). In addition to his trumpet playing, Deuchar was a skilled arranger who wrote for Edelhagen and arranged for the BBC. Jimmy Deuchar, who was not really known in the United States despite his talents, moved back to Scotland in the early 1970s, made an album as a leader as late in 1979, and in 1986 toured the United States with Charlie Watts' all-star big band.

Recommended CDs: with Victor Feldman: *Suite Sixteen* (Original Jazz Classics 1768)

Box Set: *Bebop in Britain* (4 CDs; Esquire 100)

LPs to Search For: *Pub Crawling with Jimmy Deuchar* (Contemporary 3529)

R.Q. DICKERSON

• • • • • • • • • • • • • • •

b. 1898, Paducah, KY, d. Jan. 21, 1951, Glen Falls, NY

R.Q. (short for Roger Quincey) Dickerson is a bit of a mystery figure in jazz history due to his brief career, although collectors of 1920s jazz will recognize his name. He was a fixture with several versions of the Cotton Club Orchestra and an occasional soloist with a mellow sound.

Dickerson grew up in St. Louis, playing locally in theaters as early as 1918. Five years later he toured with Wilson Robinson's Bostonians, a group that, under the leadership of violinist Andrew Preer, became the house band of the Cotton Club. As the Cotton Club Orchestra, they recorded six songs in 1925, and Dickerson also appeared on two numbers recorded by Harry's Happy Four that same year. The Cotton Club band cut only one title under Preer's name (1927's "I've Found A New Baby") before the violinist's unexpected death. Renamed the Missourians, the group performed 14 exciting selections during three sessions in 1929–30. Dickerson's lyrical trumpet solos contrast with the more fiery statements by Lammar Wright, and these are his most significant recordings.

Despite their joyful ensemble sound, the Missourians were in dire straits financially when an up-and-coming singer, Cab Calloway, took them over. Renamed the Cab Calloway Orchestra, the ensemble continued working at the Cotton Club and soon flourished (although in a more anonymous role), particularly after Cab recorded "Minnie the Moocher" on March 3, 1931. R. Q. Dickerson, however, departed shortly after Calloway's ninth recording session, leaving music altogether at the age of 33 and working for many years as a cab driver before passing away from a throat ailment.

Recommended CDs: *Cab Calloway and the Missourians 1929–30* (JSP 328)

BILL DILLARD

• • • • • • • • • • • •

b. July 20, 1911, Philadelphia, PA, d. Feb. 12, 1995, Elmhurst, NY

Although never a major soloist, Bill Dillard had a playing career that spanned more than 60 years. John Chilton has reported that in the early 1920s, Dillard was given a bugle by a musician who was playing on a tour by politician Marcus Garvey and that the youth learned to play the bugle without a mouthpiece! When he was 12, Dillard was given a cornet by his father (which did have a mouthpiece) and he developed quickly. After moving to New York in 1929, Dillard toured and recorded with Jelly Roll Morton, appeared on records with King Oliver, and had stints with Bingie Madison (1930) and the Luis Russell Orchestra (1931–32). He recorded in 1933 (as a nonsoloing first trumpeter) with Spike Hughes and Benny Carter. Dillard visited Europe with Lucky Millinder, spent 1934–38 with Teddy Hill's orchestra (often doubling as a so-so ballad singer), and recorded with Dicky Wells in Europe in 1937.

After leaving Hill, Dillard worked with the big bands of Coleman Hawkins (1939), Louis Armstrong (1940), and Red Norvo (1942–43). He then had a surprising career change in 1943, appearing on the stage as a singing actor (and occasional trumpeter), acting in such Broadway shows as *Carmen Jones, Anna Lucasta, Memphis Bound,* and *Beggars' Holiday.* Dillard toured France in 1949 with Leadbelly, continued working on Broadway (including the shows *Regina, Lost in the Stars, Green Pastures,* and *My Darling Aida*), was a regular on the radio soap opera *Love of Life,* and appeared on some television shows. Most of his later jobs were lower-profile gigs, but Bill Dillard recorded with Earle Warren in 1974 and in the 1980s often starred (singing and playing trumpet) in the musical revue *One Mo' Time.*

Recommended Reading: *In the Mainstream* by Chip Deffaa (Scarecrow Press, 1992)

BILL DIXON

* * * * * * * * * * *

b. Oct. 5, 1925, Nantucket, MA

Bill Dixon is one of the most original trumpet soloists to emerge from the free jazz movement of the mid-1960s. His music tends to be dark and thoughtful rather than extroverted, emphasizing low notes and space. Although he has listed such influences from the jazz world as Rex Stewart and the writing of Duke Ellington, Gil Fuller, George Russell, and Charles Mingus, Dixon sounds unlike anyone else.

In 1934 Dixon moved with his family to New York, where he had the chance to hear Louis Armstrong in person. "I consciously wanted a trumpet from the time that I first heard Armstrong. I briefly attempted the clarinet in high school but that fizzled." Dixon studied painting at Boston University, served in the Army, and in 1946 (when he was already 21) finally began studying the trumpet. He would later also play cello and a bit of piano.

Dixon studied at the Hartnette Conservatory of Music during 1946–51. "I originally started to study because of intense interest in and affection for music. I wanted to know how it was done. Later on, becoming professionally involved sort of 'snuck' up on me. But that is not strange since there was so much musical activity in New York at that time that it was almost impossible not to want to join in the fray." Dixon met Cecil Taylor as early as 1951, and he freelanced musically in New York. But he also had day jobs until the early 1960s, including working at the United Nations during 1956–62.

Dixon first recorded with a group that he co-led with tenor saxophonist Archie Shepp for Savoy. He was a member of the New York Contemporary Five in 1963 and in late 1964 organized and produced the six "October Revolution" concerts at New York's Cellar Café that featured 20 avant-garde jazz groups that had rarely had opportunities to play in New York clubs, including Sun Ra, Roswell Rudd, Paul Bley, and himself. "The work that I was involved in at the Cellar Club in New York (the 'October Revolution' music series) and the formation of the Jazz Composers' Guild during 1964–65 was stimulating musically but nerve-shattering and disillusioning, relating to the collective inability of the musicians to really and literally seize the time. But it was a frightfully moving time for the music."

In 1964 Dixon helped establish the short-lived Jazz Composers' Guild, along with Sun Ra, Cecil Taylor, Archie Shepp, George Russell, Paul and Carla Bley, and others, hoping that creative musicians would be able to take control of their own careers. Unfortunately that venture broke down due to infighting and differences of opinions over its direction. Dixon recorded *Intents and Purposes* as a leader for RCA during 1966–67 (unfortunately, it is long out of print) and was in Cecil Taylor's band for 1967's *Conquistador*. Since that burst of activity, Bill Dixon has not recorded all that often (private tapes from the 1970s released by Cadence, a couple of Italian releases on the Fore label, and five albums of material from 1980–85 put out by Soul Note). For decades, however, he has been quite active as a skilled painter, as one of the first musicians to produce concerts that mixed together free jazz and dance (often working with dancer Judith Dunn during 1965–75), and as a music educator. Bill Dixon has taught at Ohio State University (1966), Columbia University (1967–70), Yale (1990), and most notably Bennington College (1968 to the present).

Recommended CDs: *In Italy, Vols. 1–2* (Soul Note 1008 and 1011), *November 1981* (Soul Note 1037/38), *Thoughts* (Soul Note 1111), *Son of Sisyphus* (Soul Note 121138)

LPs to Search For: *Intents and Purposes* (RCA 3844), with Cecil Taylor: *Conquistador* (Blue Note 84260)

Recommended Reading: *Dixonia* by Ben Young (Greenwood Press, 1998)

NATTY DOMINIQUE

* * * * * * * * * * * * * * * * * * * *

b. Aug. 2, 1896, New Orleans, LA, d. Aug. 30, 1982, Chicago, IL

Whatever can be said about Natty Dominique's limited skills, he certainly had his own sound. For a rather minor figure of the 1920s, Dominique is quite legendary, especially among traditional jazz musicians, as much for his miscues as for his better solos. A very streaky player, Natty compensated for his lack of technical ability with enthusiasm and a brash tone, yet he was always proudest of his sight-reading abilities.

Raised in New Orleans, Natty (a nickname that was easier to spell than his original name of Anatie) was the cousin of clarinetist Barney Bigard and the uncle of Don Albert. Originally a drummer, he studied cornet with Manuel Perez, worked with Perez's Imperial Band, and played at many parades. In June 1913 Dominique left for Chicago, where he worked as a cigar maker during the day and played music at night. By the 1920s he was playing music full time. Among Dominique's most important associations during that decade were Carroll Dickerson's orchestra (where for a time he played second trumpet behind Louis Armstrong), Al Simeon's Hot Six, Jimmie Noone, and Johnny Dodds, working regularly with Dodds from 1928 on.

In the 1920s, Dominique recorded with Jelly Roll Morton (a couple of obscure band sides in 1923), Jimmy Bertrand (1926), Jimmy Blythe, and singer Sippie Wallace ("I'm a Mighty Tight Woman"). However, his best-known records were made with Dodds, sometimes under the band names of the Chicago Footwarmers, the Dixieland Thumpers, and the State Street Ramblers. On such numbers as "Brush Stomp," "Oriental Man," and "Lady Love," Dominique was in fine form, providing a spirited lead, brass-band phrasing, and colorful outbursts reminiscent of Freddie Keppard. However, on more complicated pieces, Dominique's shaky intonation and erratic technique could cause trouble. During "Tack It Down," made on one of the State Street Ramblers sessions without Dodds, the trumpeter stubbornly stuck to playing an original melody during his solo, despite the fact that it did not come close to relating to the chord changes!

Natty Dominique continued working with Johnny Dodds and Baby Dodds in Chicago on and off through the 1930s, but his playing gradually declined, although he was just in his thirties. In fact, Dominique's out-of-tune cornet hurt separate sessions in 1940 led by Dodds and Noone, the final studio sides by both of the classic clarinetists. Shortly after, heart trouble forced Dominique to put down the cornet altogether. He worked as a porter at a Chicago airport for years, returning to part-time playing by the late 1940s. Dominique recorded two selections as a leader in 1953 (expanded to nine for an American Music CD) and four songs during 1954, but these are far from impressive. Natty Dominique continued gigging on an occasional basis into the 1970s, a historic legend who is now remembered as much for his worst spots on potentially classic records as he is for his inspired moments.

Recommended CDs: with Johnny Dodds: *1927* (Classics 603), *1927–1928* (Classics 617), *1928–1940* (Classics 635), with the State Street Ramblers: *Vol. 1* (RST 1512)

BARBARA DONALD

• • • • • • • • • • • • • • • •

b. Feb. 9, 1942, Minneapolis, MN

A musician who spent her prime years playing avant-garde jazz, Barbara Donald was one of the most powerful trumpeters in free jazz. She grew up in Southern California, started her career playing R&B in New York, and worked in Los Angeles with Dexter Gordon and pianist Stanley Cowell. Starting in 1963, she was closely associated with altoist Sonny Simmons (whom she married in 1964), playing free jazz that showed off her intensity, range, and creative ideas. In fact, even with Don Cherry, Lester Bowie, and Bobby Bradford on the scene, Donald ranked near the top of all the avant-garde trumpeters of the late 1960s.

In addition to her work with Simmons, Donald also gigged with bassist Richard Davis, flutist Prince Lasha, and Rahsaan Roland Kirk during the era. After taking time off from music, she broke up with Simmons, moved to Washington State, and recorded two albums for Cadence during 1981–82. Unfortunately not much has been heard from Barbara Donald since that time, but her recordings still sound exciting today.

Recommended CDs: with Sonny Simmons: *Staying on the Watch* (ESP 1030), *Music from the Spheres* (ESP 1043)

LPs to Search For: *Olympia Live* (Cadence 1011), *The Past and Tomorrows* (Cadence 1017), with Sonny Simmons: *Manhattan Egos* (Arhoolie 8003), *Rumasuma* (Contemporary 7623)

KENNY DORHAM

• • • • • • • • • • • • • •

b. Aug. 30, 1924, Fairfield, TX, d. Dec. 5, 1972, New York, NY

Though Kenny Dorham was a talented bebop trumpeter, it was his fate never to rank higher than number three or four on the jazz scene at any given time, resulting in his being continuously underrated. He was overshadowed throughout his career by such players as Dizzy Gillespie, Fats Navarro, Miles Davis, Clifford Brown, and, later on, Lee Morgan and Freddie

Hubbard. But the fact that he was never number 1 should not result in his consistently satisfying recordings and inventive compositions being overlooked.

Dorham began studying piano when he was seven, not taking up the trumpet until he was already in high school. While attending pharmacy school, he picked up experience playing in the dance band at Wiley College. After serving in the Army during 1942–43, he worked with Russell Jacquet and then moved to New York. Dorham took quickly to the new music of bebop and was greatly in demand for sessions, including two recording dates with the all-star Bebop Boys in 1946; on one of the sets he played opposite Fats Navarro. He worked with Dizzy Gillespie's first short-lived big band in 1945, was with the Billy Eckstine Orchestra (1946), and had stints with Lionel Hampton (1947) and Mercer Ellington (1948). In December 1948, Dorham became Miles Davis' replacement with the Charlie Parker Quintet, staying for almost a year.

Dorham remained quite busy in the 1950s, freelancing, leading his first record dates, becoming an original member of the Jazz Messengers (1954), leading the Jazz Prophets in 1955, joining the Max Roach Quintet (1956–58) after Clifford Brown's tragic death, and recording as a sideman with the who's who of hard bop. From 1958 on, Dorham was primarily a bandleader, recording quite frequently as a leader for Riverside during the next six years (including a 1958 date that featured his personable singing), New Jazz, Time, and most notably Blue Note. He helped to discover tenor saxophonist Joe Henderson, making him co-leader of his band during 1962–63. Dorham, who wrote such songs as the standard "Blue Bossa," "Minor Holiday," "Lotus Blossom," "Prince Albert," and "Una Mas," was at his peak during the first half of the 1960s but surprisingly did not record as a leader after 1964.

Dorham's health became shaky later in the 1960s, so he de-emphasized his playing, worked in the post office, became a jazz educator, and also wrote witty if often-scathing reviews for *Downbeat*, clearly enjoying cutting down the free jazz players. Kenny Dorham died in 1972, at age 48, from kidney disease, underrated to the end.

Recommended CDs: *Kenny Dorham Quintet* (Original Jazz Classics 113), *Afro-Cuban* (Blue Note 46815), *Jazz Contrasts* (Original Jazz Classics 028), *Blue Spring* (Original Jazz Classics 134), *Showboat* (Bainbridge 1034), *Whistle Stop* (Blue Note 29978), *Matador/Inta Somethin'* (Blue Note 84460), *Una Mas* (Blue Note 46515)

DAVE DOUGLAS
• • • • • • • • • • • • • •

b. Mar. 24, 1963, Montclair, NJ

As the 20th century ended, Dave Douglas suddenly became a poll winner and a bit of a celebrity in the jazz world, seemingly discovered overnight even though he had been playing adventurous music in many bands since the late 1980s.

The son of an amateur pianist, Douglas started playing piano at five, trombone at seven, and finally trumpet at nine. He began performing improvised music while spending a year living in Barcelona in a high school exchange program; European folk music would soon be one of his many musical interests. Douglas studied at Berklee (1981–82) and the New England Conservatory (1982–83). After moving to New York City in 1984, he played on the streets with a variety of bands and studied at New York University, making the acquaintance of many up-

and-coming avant-garde musicians. Douglas played with Horace Silver during a three-month tour in 1987 but otherwise has been based primarily in New York, performing with a bewildering assortment of bands.

A list of some of Douglas' most important work as a sideman includes the Mosaic Sextet (1988–91), New and Used (starting in 1989), Don Byron's klezmer band (1990–94), John Zorn's Masada (performing abstract and spirited renditions of Jewish folk melodies and klezmer), Myra Melford, Mark Dresser, Kenny Werner, Uri Caine, and Anthony Braxton, plus many short-term projects. As far as his own groups go, a partial list includes the Tiny Bell Trio (formed in 1993 and consisting of Douglas, guitarist Brad Schoeppach, and drummer Jim Black) which explores Balkan folk music, a sextet with trombonist Josh Roseman and tenor saxophonist Chris Speed, an acoustic free bop quartet with saxophonist Chris Potter, the chamber group Charms of the Night Sky, his electric ensemble Sanctuary, the string group Parallel Woods (with violinist Mark Feldman, cellist Erik Friedlander, and bassist Mark Dresser), and an Indian jazz ensemble called Satya; all are at least partly active as of this writing!

While Dave Douglas considers Woody Shaw an important influence on his playing, his interest in East European music, modern classical music, and other idioms sets him apart.

Every Dave Douglas project (and there are many) is intriguing, very musical, and full of surprises.

He has recorded tributes (in his own way) to Booker Little (*In Our Lifetime*), Wayne Shorter (*Stargazer*), and Mary Lou Williams (*Soul on Soul*), leading sessions for such labels as Arabesque, Avant, Hat Art, Knitting Factory Works, Konnex, New World, Songlines, Soul Note, Winter & Winter, and most recently RCA.

Now that the technically skilled and very musically curious trumpeter has been winning jazz polls, Dave Douglas stands as proof (as did Thelonious Monk four decades earlier) that it is possible to gain recognition eventually by sticking to one's own individual path, although in his case he has blazed quite a few paths at the same time!

Recommended CDs: *In Our Lifetime* (New World/Countercurrents 80471), *Five* (Soul Note 121276), *Convergence* (Soul Note 121316), *Leap of Faith* (Arabesque 145), *Magic Triangle* (Arabesque 139), *Wandering Souls* (Winter & Winter 910 042), *Soul on Soul* (RCA 63603), *A Thousand Evenings* (RCA 63698), with Anthony Braxton: *Seven Standards* (Knitting Factory Works 108), with Myra Melford: *Same River, Twice* (Gramavision 79513)

JESSE DRAKES

b. Oct. 22, 1926, New York, NY

A decent journeyman bop trumpeter, Jesse Drakes is best known for his association with Lester Young. He began playing professionally in 1945 and worked with Al Cooper's Savoy Sultans, J.C. Heard, Sid Catlett, and Eddie Heywood's Sextet, recording with Sarah Vaughan in 1947. Off and on during 1948–56, Drakes was a regular member of Lester Young's band, not only playing with the great tenor saxophonist but at various times taking care of the depressed veteran. Drakes made some records and many live appearances with Young, playing in a boppish style that often worked well with Pres.

During time off, the trumpeter also worked a bit with the Gene Ammons-Sonny Stitt band (1953), Louie Bellson (1955), and Duke Ellington (1956). After his period with Young ended, Drakes eventually left jazz, touring with King Curtis and becoming involved in soul music, often working with Motown singers in the 1960s. As a jazz trumpeter, Jesse Drakes (who never led his own record date) did not fulfill his potential, but he did make life easier for a time for the troubled Lester Young.

Box Set: *The Complete Lester Young Studio Sessions on Verve* (8 CDs; Verve 314 547 087)

GLENN DREWES

b. Apr. 24, 1949, Brooklyn, NY

An excellent trumpeter associated mostly with big bands, Glenn Drewes not only plays ensemble parts well but is a very capable straightahead soloist. The brother of saxophonist Billy Drewes (who plays with the Vanguard Jazz Orchestra), he remembers, "Some of my earliest recollections are that of my Dad lullabying my brother, Billy, and myself to sleep playing Duke Ellington tunes on the piano!" Drewes started playing piano when he was eight, switching to trumpet in the sixth grade. He continued playing piano for a time, including gigging at a local strip joint and playing organ and piano with Lionel Hampton for three months during 1971–72, before switching his focus exclusively to trumpet.

Drewes attended the Crane School of Music and Potsdam University (1967–71). "As a young player I never really zeroed in on a musical career. I was busy gigging and learning and having a ball, but never thought I was good enough to make it. However, as I gained more and more knowledge and experience, more doors opened for me." Drewes played in a quintet led by Pete Procopio in Syracuse, New York, during 1971–75 and then worked with the big bands of Hampton (1975–76), Woody Herman (1977–79), Buddy Rich (1981–82), Gerry Mulligan (1981–85), Toshiko Akiyoshi/Lew Tabackin (1983–84), Dizzy Gillespie (1987), and Gene Harris. Most important has been his association with the Vanguard Jazz Orchestra (starting in September 1985, when it was the Mel Lewis Big Band). "That band has all of the ingredients: swinging charts, hot soloists, great ensemble concept, a tradition, and, most of all, a steady gig. I can't wait for Mondays!"

Recommended CDs: with the Mel Lewis Jazz Orchestra: *Soft Lights and Hot Music* (Music Masters 60172)

SONNY DUNHAM
. . . .

b. Nov. 16, 1914, Brockton, MA, d. June 18, 1990, Florida

Sonny Dunham is best remembered for his impressive high-note solo on the Casa Loma Orchestra's recording of "Memories of You" in 1937. Although he played for quite a few years, that would serve as the height of his career and earn him the title of "The Man from Mars" (due to his "out of this world" range).

Born Elmer Dunham, he learned both trumpet and trombone early on; in fact his first major job was playing trombone with Ben Bernie in the late 1920s. Dunham worked on both instruments with Paul Tremaine for two years and briefly led a band called Sonny Lee and his New York Yankees. Dunham was the Casa Loma's main trumpet soloist during 1932–40, other than for a brief period trying to head his own orchestra during 1937, a 14-piece band that included ten musicians who could double on trumpet! He appeared on many records with the Casa Loma Orchestra in addition to "Memories of You," including "Old Man River," "No Name Jive," and "Nagasaki," and his range impressed many fans.

After leaving the popular orchestra in 1940, Dunham put together his own big band. Although the outfit lasted until 1949, it had no hits and was never much of a commercial success, not gaining an identity of its own beyond the leader's trumpet. Dunham was with Tommy Dorsey for a period in 1951 but mostly led smaller swing bands until he retired to Florida in the 1960s. As a leader, Sonny Dunham recorded six intriguing numbers in 1940 that featured him on trumpet and trombone backed by a rhythm section. Otherwise, his big band cut 20 titles for Bluebird during 1941–42, its broadcasts of 1942–46 have been issued by many collector's labels, and "The Man from Mars" recorded an additional four-song studio session in both 1946 and 1949.

LPs to Search For: Sonny Dunham and His Orchestra (Golden Era 15044), *Half-Past Jumpin' Time* (Golden Era 15008), with the Casa Loma Orchestra: *Greatest Hits* (Decca 75016)

Film Appearances: Off the Beaten Track (1942), Behind the Eight Ball (1942)

JOHNNY DUNN

• • • • • • • • • • • • • • • •

b. Feb. 19, 1897, Memphis, TN, d. Aug. 20, 1937, Paris, France

Johnny Dunn is an example of how quickly styles changed in jazz during its formative years. He was considered the top cornetist in New York during 1917–24, known for his double-time runs and expertise at creating wa-wa effects with his plunger. Yet by 1926, Dunn's staccato style was considered completely out of date.

Dunn attended Fisk University in Nashville and had a solo act in Memphis before being discovered by W. C. Handy. He joined Handy's band in 1917 and during the next three years became well known for his feature on "Sergeant Dunn's Bugle Call Blues" (which later became the basis for the standard "Bugle Call Rag"). Dunn pioneered the use of the plunger mute, and his growls often caused a sensation during the era. He also gained recognition for his torrid if repetitive double-time breaks, which, because of their inflexible jerky rhythms, had a direct link to military bands.

Although it is uncertain whether he was on Mamie Smith's famous 1920 "Crazy Blues" (the first blues record), Dunn was an integral part of the blues singer's Jazz Hounds during much of 1920–21, and he appeared on many of her other recordings (including "Don't Care Blues" and "Lovin' Sam from Alabam"). Significantly, when Dunn left to lead his own Original Jazz Hounds, his replacement was Bubber Miley, who, after being initially influenced by Dunn, would far surpass him with his mastery of mutes.

In 1921 Dunn's band accompanied Edith Wilson in the show *Put and Take*. During 1921–23 he recorded 18 selections with Wilson and 14 instrumentals of his own; all are included on his pair of RST CDs along with his later sessions. Dunn joined Will Vodery's Plantation Orchestra in February 1922, visiting Europe for the first time with the revue *Dover to Dixie* the following year. However, his time as a pacesetter was running out, for the Chicago-based jazz musicians (many of whom were originally from New Orleans) had advanced far ahead of the better-publicized New Yorkers. Visiting Chicago, Dunn saw Louis Armstrong perform with a show at Dreamland and was determined to show him up. He reportedly went on the bandstand, asked for Armstrong's horn, and tried to sit in during what he thought was a simple piece, not realizing until it was too late (and to his grief) that the song was in seven sharps!

By the time Dunn sailed to Europe with the *Blackbirds of 1926* show, he was thought of as a has-been, even though he was only 29 at the time. He recorded four selections with the Plantation Orchestra in London. Back in the United States in 1927, Dunn briefly led his own big band, and then the following year he made what would be both his finest and his final recordings. On March 13, 1928, Dunn utilized a group that featured both Jelly Roll Morton's piano and frameworks for four numbers, highlighted by "You Need Some Lovin'" and the definitive version of the cornetist's original hit, "Sergeant Dunn's Bugle Call Blues." Thirteen days later he cut a pair of sides (the rollicking "What's the Use of Being Alone" and "Original Bugle Blues") in which his simple but effective playing was greatly assisted by creative arrangements and the twin pianos of James P. Johnson and Fats Waller.

Soon afterward, Johnny Dunn rejoined Lew Leslie's Blackbird Company and returned to Europe. He played with Noble Sissle in Paris and then worked with his own group (the New Yorkers), mostly in Holland, for the remaining years of his life. Strangely enough, he made no further visits to the recording studios despite playing regularly, so it can only be speculated whether he ever updated his style. Johnny Dunn moved to Paris in 1937 shortly before his death at age 40, a totally forgotten former "King of Jazz."

Recommended CDs: *Johnny Dunn and Edith Wilson, Vol. 1* (RST 1522), *Johnny Dunn, Vol. 2* (RST 1523)

JON EARDLEY

* * * * * * * * * * * *

b. Sept. 30, 1928, Altoona, PA, d. Apr. 2, 1991, Cologne, Germany

Jon Eardley, considered one of the top "cool jazz" trumpeters of the 1950s (although he was overshadowed by Chet Baker), had his career slightly revitalized when he moved later in life to Europe. The son of a trumpeter who had played with Paul Whiteman, Eardley began to play trumpet himself when he was 11. He picked up early experience performing with bands at circuses and fairs during summer vacation from school, starting when he was 15. Eardley spent 1946–49 in the Air Force, playing in a military band while stationed in Washington, D.C. After his discharge, he worked with Buddy Rich (1949) and Gene Williams' orchestra (1949–50) before returning home to Altoona, where he played locally for three years. Eardley returned to New York in 1953, worked with Phil Woods in 1954, and gained recognition for his playing with the Gerry Mulligan Quartet and Sextet during 1954–57. He also led two albums during 1954–56, using such sidemen as Pete Jolly, J.R. Monterose, Phil Woods, and Zoot Sims.

But then, when he should have built on his connection with Mulligan to start his own solo career, Eardley dropped out of music and returned to Altoona. Not much was heard from him until 1963, when he moved to Brussels, where he played with the Belgian radio and television orchestra. In 1969 Eardley joined the WDR Radio Big Band in Cologne, Germany, a job that he kept for the remainder of his life. In addition to obscure albums for the Dutch Niagram and Munich labels during 1969–70, Jon Eardley made his final recordings as a leader on a trio of releases for Spotlite in 1977, showing that he was still a cool-toned and swinging soloist with a timeless style.

Recommended CDs: *From Hollywood to New York* (Original Jazz Classics 1746), *The Jon Eardley Seven* (Original Jazz Classics 123), *Namely Me* (Spotlite 17), *Stablemates* (Spotlite 11), with Gerry Mulligan: *California Concerts, Vols. 1 and 2* (Pacific Jazz 46860 and 46864)

PETER ECKLUND

• • • • • • • • • • • •

b. Sept. 27, 1945, San Diego, CA

Peter Ecklund has long been one of the top cornetists in prebop mainstream jazz. His crisp tone and melodic solos have sparked many ensembles, most notably the Orphan News-boys. He started playing trumpet when he was 12 (primarily classical music), discovering jazz through the father of a high school friend who had played with the Yale Collegians in the early 1930s. Ecklund graduated from Yale in 1969 with a master's degree but decided in 1972 that his career was going to be in music. He worked with a variety of rock, blues, and pop bands during the era, including those of David Bromberg, Gregg Allman, Maria Mul-daur, Leon Redbone, and Paul Butterfield. But Ecklund's most significant work has always been in classic jazz, starting off with leading the Galvanized Jazz Band and touring with singer Paula Lockheart. During the 1980s he began his long-time association with rhythm guitarist Marty Grosz in the Orphan Newsboys (formed in 1988) and other small-group settings. Since then Peter Ecklund (who has led CDs for Arbors) has become a fixture at jazz parties and festivals, where his superior ensemble playing and colorful solos have become quite popular.

Recommended CDs: *Strings Attached* (Arbors 19149), *Ecklund in Elkhart* (Jazzology 246), with Marty Grosz: *Swing It* (Jazzology 180), *Extra* (Jazzology 190), *Keep a Song in Your Soul* (Jazzology 250), *Rhythm for Sale* (Jazzology 280)

LPs to Search For: *And the Melody Makers* (Stomp Off 1175)

Recommended Reading: *Traditionalists and Revivalists in Jazz* by Chip Deffaa (Scarecrow Press, 1997)

JOHN ECKERT

• • • • • • • • • • • •

b. Mar. 13, 1939, New York, NY

A solid bop-oriented soloist often heard with big bands, John Eckert has been an asset to many different orchestras through the years. He began playing trumpet while in grammar school and was introduced to jazz through his older sister's boyfriend of the time. Eckert studied at the Eastman School of Music (1957–61) and North Texas State University (1961–63). Since that time he has played with the big bands of Stan Kenton (1963), Si Zentner, Maynard Ferguson (1965–68), Gerry Mulligan, Toshiko Akiyoshi, Benny Goodman (1988–89), Woody Herman, Sam Rivers, Joe Henderson, Buck Clayton, Grover Mitchell, Muhal Richard Abrams, Louie Bellson, and Loren Schoenberg, among others. Probably his most significant small-group association was with the Lee Konitz Nonet (1971–79).

John Eckert, who has recorded with Konitz, Akiyoshi, Goodman, Schoenberg, Jaki Byard, Benny Carter, and Ken Peplowski (but has yet to lead his own record date), in recent times toured with Bobby Short, when the singer was accompanied by the Loren Schoenberg Orchestra.

Recommended CDs: with Jaki Byard: *Phantasies, Vol. 1* (Soul Note 121175), with Lee Konitz: *Lee Konitz Nonet* (Chiaroscuro 186), *Yes, Yes, Nonet* (Steeplechase 31119)

HARRY "SWEETS" EDISON

b. Oct. 10, 1915, Columbus, OH, d. July 25, 1999, Columbus, OH

Harry "Sweets" Edison had the rare talent of being able to say a great deal with a minimum of notes; a jazz minimalist as was his former boss Count Basie. He was immediately recognizable after a note or two and, although he often played very simply (using repetition and bent notes), Edison was also capable of throwing in a Dizzy Gillespie phrase when he felt that it fit.

Edison began playing trumpet when he was 12, being completely self-taught except for an uncle who showed him a few scales. While in high school he played with Earl Hood's band and Morrison's Grenadiers. After graduating, he worked with several of the major territory bands, including Alphonso Trent's, Eddie Johnson's Crackerjacks, and the Jeter-Pillars Orchestra (1933–35). Moving to New York in 1937, Edison spent six months with the Mills Blue Rhythm Band (with whom he made his recording debut) and then in June 1938 joined the Count Basie Orchestra.

Edison's 11-year stay with Basie (which lasted until February 1950) found him developing into a highly original voice. He gained the lifelong nickname of "Sweets" from Lester Young due to his tone, and in time (sharing the trumpet solos with Buck Clayton until Buck

Harry "Sweets" Edison, a Count Basie–style minimalist who made every sound count, knew the value of a well-placed note.

was drafted in 1943) became one of the Basie band's main stars. Whether with the full orchestra or on small-group dates, Edison (who is prominent in the 1944 Lester Young short *Jammin' the Blues*) was a major asset. Even after the Basie Orchestra broke up at the end of 1949, Edison remained with Count for a few months, playing with the first version of Basie's octet. He would be reunited with Basie on quite a few occasions in later periods.

After the Basie years ended, Edison worked with Jimmy Rushing, appeared at Jazz at the Philharmonic concerts, played with Buddy Rich (1951–53), and led combos. Settling in Los Angeles, Sweets was greatly in demand for studio work, including playing background solos on many Frank Sinatra/Nelson Riddle records (starting in 1954). He also appeared on countless mainstream sessions and recordings. Jazz styles may have been changing in the 1960s, '70s, and '80s, but Edison's brand of joyful and melodic swing always seemed to be in vogue. In 1961 he was Joe Williams' musical director, and in the '60s he started teaming up now and then with tenor saxophonist Eddie "Lockjaw" Davis, a partnership that became more frequent during the next two decades. Sweets did not record as a leader during 1966–74. But with the rise of Norman Granz's Pablo label in the mid-1970s, he once again took his place as one of the "Trumpet Kings," recording in many freewheeling settings. As his range shrunk year by year and he reached his eighties, Harry "Sweets" Edison continually simplified and pared down his message, showing that he could still make a poignant statement with one or two well-placed notes.

Recommended CDs: *Jawbreakers* (Original Jazz Classics 487), *Just Friends* (Black & Blue 59106), *Edison's Lights* (Original Jazz Classics 804), *Simply Sweets* (Original Jazz Classics 903), with Lester Young: *Pres and Sweets* (Verve 849 391)

Box Set: with Count Basie: *The Complete Decca Recordings* (3 CDs; GRP/Decca 3-611)

Recommended Reading: *Jazz Talking* by Max Jones (Da Capo Press, 1987), *The World of Count Basie* by Stanley Dance (Charles Scribner's Sons, 1980)

Film Appearances: *Jammin' the Blues* (1944)

Videos to Get: *L.A. All Stars* (early 1970s; Rhapsody Films), three songs on *Ken Peplowski Quartet* (1994; Concord 8002)

THORE EHRLING

b. Dec. 29, 1912, Stockholm, Sweden

One of Sweden's top swing bandleaders, Thore Ehrling made an impact locally if not internationally. Ehrling started his career playing with tenor saxophonist Frank Vernon (1930–34) while attending the Royal Swedish Musical Academy (1931–35). He worked with Hakan von Eichwald (1935–38), recording with the visiting Benny Carter in 1936. In 1938 Ehrling formed a septet, which soon grew and by the early 1940s was a big band, one of neutral Sweden's most popular swing orchestras of the World War II years. Ehrling, who was most influenced by Harry James, also enjoyed playing Dixieland and contributed many of his band's arrangements. During the second half of the '40s he often de-emphasized his own excellent playing in favor of Gosta Torner. After the early 1950s, Thore Ehrling gave up the trumpet altogether. But his big band lasted until 1958, and he led a nostalgia swing album as late as 1972.

Recommended CDs: *Jazz Highlights 1939–55* (Dragon 236), *1945–47* (Ancha 9503), *Flash* (Phontastic 9318)

ROY ELDRIDGE
● ● ● ● ● ● ● ● ● ● ● ● ●

b. Jan. 30, 1911, Pittsburgh, PA, d. Feb. 26, 1989, Valley Stream, NY

Roy Eldridge was such a fiery and combative trumpeter that he could be thought of as a jazz warrior, one who went into battle each time he went on stage. It did not matter if he did not have any other trumpeters or horn players to trade off with because Eldridge still gave 110% to each chorus, pushing himself and taking wild chances. He would rather stumble than play it safe, and his emotional solos were always full of excitement.

David "Roy" Eldridge was known throughout his career as "Little Jazz" (a title given him by altoist Otto Hardwicke). After playing drums when he was six, he took up the trumpet. He was a professional in Pittsburgh by 1927, when he was leading a group called Roy Elliott and His Palais Royal Orchestra. Eldridge picked up experience playing with Horace Henderson's Dixie Stompers, Zach Whyte, and Speed Webb (1929–30). His early inspirations were tenor saxophonist Coleman Hawkins (memorizing Hawk's solo on "Stampede") and the exciting if sometimes reckless Jabbo Smith. Eldridge also began to appreciate Louis Armstrong in the early 1930s when he saw him in a performance hit dozens of high notes before climaxing his solo by reaching for an even higher one.

Eldridge moved to New York in November 1930 and worked with Cecil Scott, Elmer Snowden, Charlie Johnson, Teddy Hill, and the declining McKinney's Cotton Pickers. In 1935 he began to get noticed, rejoining Hill (with whom he recorded) and appearing on records with Teddy Wilson and Billie Holiday. He would in time become one of the most influential trumpeters of the swing era, particularly affecting the young Dizzy Gillespie and the bebop movement in general. In 1936 Eldridge was with Fletcher Henderson's orchestra (his trumpet solo helped make "Christopher Columbus" into a hit), recorded on a heated date with Gene Krupa and Benny Goodman, and led a small band that included older brother Joe Eldridge on alto. He led groups through 1941 (including a big band by 1938) and impressed many listeners with his crackling solos. By 1939, Eldridge was arguably the most advanced trumpeter in jazz, as can be heard in his solo on Mildred Bailey's recording of "I'm Nobody's Baby."

During 1941–43, Eldridge was one of the main stars of Gene Krupa's orchestra. He was showcased on Krupa's recordings of "After You've Gone" and "Rockin' Chair" and assisted Anita O'Day on "Let Me Off Uptown" and "Thanks for the Boogie Ride." Being a black trumpeter with a white big band in those segregated days was extremely difficult, but Eldridge stayed with Krupa until the band's breakup and during 1944–45 repeated the role with Artie Shaw's orchestra. With Shaw, Eldridge was featured on "Little Jazz" and "Lady Day," also recording with the clarinetist's Gramercy Five.

Eldridge spent the second half of the 1940s leading groups (including a short-lived big band in 1946), playing with Jazz at the Philharmonic, and in 1949 rejoining Krupa for a few months. But he also had an identity crisis during this time because, having long been the

A jazz warrior, Roy Eldridge was always ready to battle other competitors—and his own limitations.

most modern of trumpeters, now he was faced with the bebop revolution and a competitor (Dizzy Gillespie) who could usually defeat him in trumpet battles. While touring Europe with Benny Goodman in April 1950, the trumpeter decided to stay overseas for a while. A few months later he realized that being considered the most modern trumpeter was not as important as simply being himself and doing his best at all times. No one played like Roy Eldridge as well as Little Jazz himself, and there was no reason for him to completely change his style whenever jazz moved in a new direction. When he returned to New York in April 1951, Eldridge's confidence was back.

The 1950s would be a busy decade for the swing veteran, recording regularly for Norman Granz's labels (including Verve), touring with JATP, and often co-leading a quintet with Coleman Hawkins (including making an exciting recording at the 1957 Newport Jazz Festival). To increase his commercial potential, Eldridge also learned Dixieland standards so he could work in trad settings too.

The 1960s were a bit slower, and Eldridge's stints with Ella Fitzgerald (1963–65) and Count Basie (1966) did not work out; he was not needed at all by the former and was underutilized by the latter. But the 1970s were more productive as Eldridge worked nightly at Jimmy Ryan's and was recorded extensively again by Norman Granz, this time for his Pablo label. His playing at the 1977 Montreux Jazz Festival with the Oscar Peterson Trio bordered on miraculous.

Unfortunately Eldridge's life would be much quieter in the 1980s. His weak heart led a doctor in 1980 to tell him that he either had to restrain himself when he played trumpet or give up the horn altogether. Eldridge knew that he could not possibly take it easy, so he gave up playing. Other than a few appearances as a vocalist, Roy Eldridge watched music from the sidelines during his last nine years, a frustrating ending to the career of an exciting jazz warrior.

Recommended CDs: Little Jazz (Columbia 45275), *After You've Gone* (GRP/Decca 605), *Roy Eldridge in Paris* (Vogue 68209), *Just You, Just Me* (Stash 531), *Happy Time* (Original Jazz Classics 628), *Montreux 1977* (Original Jazz Classics 373), with Gene Krupa: *Uptown* (Columbia 65448), with Artie Shaw: *Blues in the Night* (Bluebird 2432)

LPs to Search For: At the Three Deuces Club 1937 (Jazz Archives 24), *Arcadia Shuffle* (Jazz Archives 14),

Recommended Reading: American Musicians II by Whitney Balliett (Oxford University Press, 1996), *The Best of Jazz II* by Humphrey Lyttelton (Taplinger Publishing Co., 1982), *The World of Swing* by Stanley Dance (Charles Scribner's Sons, 1974)

Film Appearances: Ball of Fire (1941) with the Gene Krupa Orchestra

Videos to Get: The Sound of Jazz (1957; Vintage Jazz Classics 2001), *After Hours* (1961; Rhapsody Films)

DON ELLIOTT

* * * * * * * * * * * *

b. Oct. 21, 1926, Somerville, NJ, d. July 5, 1984, Weston, CT

Don Elliott had so many talents that his trumpet playing has sometimes been overlooked. In addition to trumpet, he played vibes, mellophone, and bongos, plus he became known for his multivoice overdubs.

Elliott started on piano when he was six, began accordion at eight, and shortly afterward took up baritone horn, mellophone, and trumpet. He played trumpet in his high school band and often jammed with the young pianist Bill Evans. Elliot studied at Juilliard (1944–45) and, while in the military, played trumpet in an Army band. At the University of Miami in 1947 he studied arranging and started playing vibes. Elliott worked with the Jan Raye Trio in 1948 and was vocalist with Hi, Lo, Jack and the Dame (1948–49). Moving to New York, Elliott was a member of the George Shearing Quintet (on vibes) during 1950–51. Basically a swing player who could fit into cool jazz settings, Elliott worked with Teddy Wilson, Benny Goodman (1952), Terry Gibbs (1952–53), Buddy Rich (1953), and his own quartet (1954–60). Although he certainly had the least competition on mellophone, Elliott was also an excellent trumpeter, as he shows on *Double Trumpet Doings,* an album in which he holds his own with Rusty Dedrick.

Elliott, who also led now-obscure sessions for Savoy, Victor, Bethlehem, Vanguard, and ABC-Paramount (all of which are long overdue to be reissued on CD), had a novelty hit record in 1960 with Sascha Burland as *The Nutty Squirrels.* That album features songs that refer to birds in their titles (such as "Yardbird Suite," "Bye Bye Blackbird," "Skylark," and even "That's Owl, Brother"). Don Elliott worked mostly as a composer and producer for commercials, television, and film scores during his last two decades, not recording any jazz after 1961, although he occasionally played his instruments in later years.

Recommended CDs: *Double Trumpet Doings* (Original Jazz Classics 1925)

LPs to Search For: *A Musical Offering* (ABC Paramount 106), with Paul Desmond: *Paul Desmond Quartet Featuring Don Elliott* (Original Jazz Classics 712)

DON ELLIS
. . . .

b. July 25, 1934, Los Angeles, CA, d. Dec. 17, 1978, Los Angeles, CA

One of the most colorful and original big band leaders of the late 1960s, Don Ellis became famous for utilizing difficult and sometimes bizarre time signatures in his music. Rather than playing music in 4/4 time, his orchestra made 7/8 and 9/8 seem easy, particularly compared to 31/4 and 11/12, which they also played! In addition, Ellis had his own distinctive sound on trumpet, was interested in both quarter-tone and Indian music, and was a pioneer in utilizing electronics on horns.

Ellis began playing trumpet and leading ensembles quite early in his life. He led his own dance band as early as junior high school. After graduating from Boston University in 1956, he worked briefly with Ray McKinley, served in the Army (playing in jazz bands in Germany during 1957–58), and, after his discharge, worked with Charlie Barnet. Ellis spent much of 1959 as a member of the Maynard Ferguson big band, sharing the solo space with Ferguson and fellow trumpeter Rick Kiefer on "Three More Foxes." He led a trio and recorded four small-group albums as a leader during 1960–62 (for Candid, New Jazz, and Pacific Jazz). As a member of the George Russell Sextet during 1961–62, Ellis made a few recordings, including one in which he shared the frontline with multireedist Eric Dolphy and trombonist Dave Baker. In addition, during this period, Ellis was involved in experimental "jazz happenings" (avant-garde explorations) and third-stream projects, including being trumpet soloist with the New York Philharmonic on Larry Austin's *Improvisations* (1963) and on Gunther Schuller's *Journey into Jazz* with the National Symphony Orchestra in Washington, D.C.

All of that activity was just a prelude. In 1964 Ellis moved to Los Angeles, studied at UCLA, and formed the Hindustani Jazz Sextet, an early jazz/world music fusion band that unfortunately did not record. In 1965 he put together a 20-piece big band that, in addition to the usual five trumpets, three trombones, five reeds, and piano, included three bassists, two drummers, and between one and three percussionists. The hit of the 1966 Monterey Jazz Festival, the Don Ellis big band performed such numbers as "Barnum's Revenge" (a nutty version of "Bill Bailey" in 7/4 time), "33 222 1 222" (which was in 19/4), and Ellis' showcase on "Concerto for Trumpet." Signed by Columbia in 1967, the orchestra experienced a golden age from 1967–71, resulting in the classic albums *Electric Bath, Autumn, Live at Fillmore,* and *Tears of Joy;* only *Electric Bath* has thus far been reissued on CD.

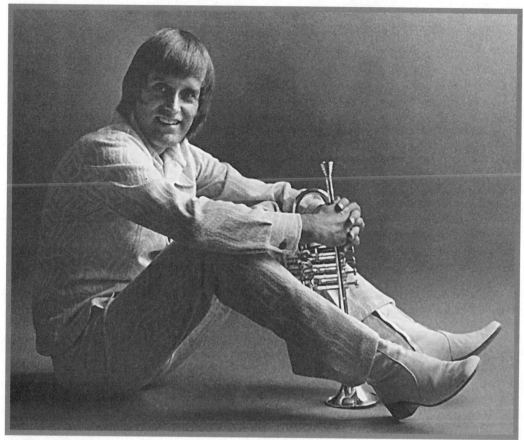

Don Ellis' big bands were among the most adventurous, rambunctious, and craziest in jazz.

With trombonist Glenn Ferris and tenor saxophonist John Klemmer joining Ellis as the band's top soloists (pianist Milcho Leviev would become a key player in 1971), the horn players using all types of electrical devices (including the echoplex, quarter-tone four-valve trumpets, ring modulators, and phasers), and the expansion of the drum section (even the constantly moving Ellis began doubling on drums), this was certainly a unique band! Knowledgeable audience members would request the band's greatest hit, "Pussy Wiggle Stomp," by clapping in 7/4 (accenting beats 2, 4, 6, and 7); "Indian Lady" was also a popular number. In 1971 Ellis wrote an award-winning film score for *The French Connection.* For the fascinating *Tears of Joy* album, Ellis utilized eight brass, a woodwind quartet, a string quartet, and a five-piece rhythm section with two drummers. By 1974, Ellis had added a vocal quartet to his big band (although that version of the orchestra never recorded).

In 1975 the energetic 41-year-old trumpeter had a serious heart attack that greatly slowed him down. For a time he played a "superbone," a valve/slide trombone designed by Maynard Ferguson. By 1977 Ellis had a new big band, becoming the first to record the *Star Wars* theme (although Maynard Ferguson would soon have the hit version) and recording with his 23-piece orchestra at the Montreux Jazz Festival. But once again Don Ellis pushed himself too hard, and a second heart attack in late 1978 ended his colorful life.

Recommended CDs: *How Time Passes* (Candid 9004), *Out of Nowhere* (Candid 9032), *New Ideas* (Original Jazz Classics 431), *Live at Monterey* (Pacific Jazz 94768), *Live in* $3\frac{2}{3}$ *Time* (Pacific Jazz 23996), *Electric Bath* (Columbia/Legacy 65522)

LPs to Search For: *Autumn* (Columbia 63503), *Don Ellis at Fillmore* (Columbia 66261), *Tears of Joy* (Columbia 67216)

Recommended Reading: *From Satchmo to Miles* by Leonard Feather (Da Capo Press, 1984)

ZIGGY ELMAN

. . . .

b. May 26, 1914, Philadelphia, PA, d. June 26, 1968, Van Nuys, CA

Ziggy Elman should have been a major star. He was the main trumpet soloist with Benny Goodman's orchestra in 1936, and three years later he had a big hit with "And the Angels Sing." But unlike Harry James, Elman never became well known as a bandleader, had a second hit, or developed musically beyond his early days.

Born Harry Finkelman, he grew up in Atlantic City and learned to play both brass and reed instruments, settling on the trumpet. In the early 1930s the renamed Ziggy Elman worked with Alex Bartha's group, with whom he made his recording debut in 1932 (on trombone). The biggest break of his career occurred in September 1936, when Benny Goodman picked Elman to join his band, replacing Sterling Bose. For a short time Elman was the King of Swing's main soloist among his sidemen, and his fiery solos would seem to have ensured stardom. However, the following year Goodman hired another young up-and-comer, Harry James. Elman and James actually had very similar styles at the time, making it difficult for listeners to know who was soloing on what record. However, James had the extra ingredient of charisma and was soon generating most of the attention.

Ziggy did star on Goodman's record of "Bei Mir Bist Du Schon," where his explosive solo was quite distinctive. Elman led a series of dates during 1938–39 while still with Goodman (using the clarinetist's sidemen), and his "Fralich in Swing" gained some attention. In 1939, when Goodman recorded "Fralich" under the new title of "And the Angels Sing" (with Martha Tilton on the vocal and new lyrics by Johnny Mercer), Elman played a classic solo, and he now had his trademark song.

Logically Elman should have left Goodman's orchestra at that time and formed his own big band. But instead he stuck with Goodman until the clarinetist temporarily broke up his band in August 1940, and then he accepted an offer to become a member of Tommy Dorsey's orchestra. Dorsey featured Elman generously (he had a famous trumpet battle with Chuck Peterson on "Well, Git It"), and Ziggy appeared in a few films with Dorsey (including *The Fabulous Dorseys,* in which he was part of a jam session with Art Tatum), but Elman's fame began to fade. After serving in the military and then rejoining Dorsey, Ziggy finally formed his own orchestra in 1947. But by then the big band era was over. Since Elman was not a bebopper, his orchestra was mostly reduced to playing nostalgia music and lasted only two years. Ziggy worked in the studios in the early 1950s, but his health started to give him trouble. He appeared in *The Benny Goodman Story* briefly. But when he stood up to perform his famous chorus on "And the Angels Sing," his part was actually played by Manny Klein.

Ziggy Elman, who made one of his last recordings on an album led by pianist Jess Stacy, was mostly retired by 1956, running a music store and only playing on an occasional basis in later years.

Recommended CDs: *1938–1939* (Classics 900), *The Issued Recordings 1947–1949* (Jazz Band 2154), with Tommy Dorsey: *Yes, Indeed* (Bluebird 9987)

Film Appearances: with the Tommy Dorsey Orchestra in *Du Barry Was a Lady* (1943), in a jam session scene with Art Tatum in *The Fabulous Dorseys* (1947), *The Benny Goodman Story* (1955)

ROLF ERICSON
. . . .

b. Aug. 29, 1922, Stockholm, Sweden, d. June 16, 1997, Stockholm, Sweden

A reliable bop-oriented trumpeter from Sweden, Rolf Ericson never had any difficulty keeping up with his American counterparts. He began playing trumpet when he was eight, and in 1933 he had a chance to see Louis Armstrong at a concert in Stockholm. Ericson became a professional musician in 1938, working in Sweden during the war years. He first moved to New York in 1947 and freelanced with various top-notch big bands, most notably Charlie Barnet's Bebop Orchestra of 1949 and Woody Herman's Third Herd (1950), in addition to Benny Goodman, Charlie Ventura, Benny Carter, and Elliot Lawrence. Ericson returned to Sweden in 1950, just in time to work with Charlie Parker during Bird's European tour. Ericson recorded as a leader in Sweden during 1950–52, playing music that fell between swing and bop. During 1953–56 in the United States, he worked with Charlie Spivak, Harry James, the Dorsey Brothers, Les Brown, and the Lighthouse All-Stars. Ericson toured Europe with singer Ernestine Anderson and baritonist Lars Gullin during 1956. Back in the United States, he worked with the who's who of jazz during the next 15 years, including Dexter Gordon, Harold Land, Stan Kenton, Woody Herman, Maynard Ferguson's orchestra (1960–61), Buddy Rich, Charles Mingus (1962–63), Benny Goodman, Gerry Mulligan, and Duke Ellington (off and on during 1963–71).

Ericson remained on the move during his final 25 years. He spent part of the 1970s in Germany as a studio musician and appeared in the United States with Count Basie, the Juggernaut, the Clayton-Hamilton Orchestra, and Louis Bellson. He was active up until the end of his life, remaining a boppish soloist with a warm tone. Although usually overlooked when the top European jazz musicians are mentioned, few Europeans (or even Americans) could match Rolf Ericson's resume!

Recommended CDs: *Rolf Ericson and His American Stars 1956* (Dragon 255), *Stockholm Sweetnin'* (Dragon 78), *Ellington and Strayhorn* (Sittle 9223)

PEE WEE ERWIN

• • • • • • • • • • • • • •

b. May 30, 1913, Falls City, NE, d. June 20, 1981, Teaneck, NJ

The word *journeyman* could have been invented to describe Pee Wee Erwin. Although a talented swing trumpeter, Erwin spent many of his most important years as a fill-in for someone else. His reliability and consistency were admired, but Erwin never came close to becoming a famous name, despite his abilities.

George "Pee Wee" Erwin began playing trumpet when he was four, and he performed on the radio with the Coon-Sanders Nighthawks just four years later. Erwin, who grew up in Kansas City, worked with a variety of territory bands before playing with the big bands of Joe Haymes (1931–33) and Isham Jones (1933–34). Settling in New York, Erwin was often used on studio dates, where his appealing tone and sight-reading abilities were appreciated. Pee Wee worked with Benny Goodman on the *Let's Dance* programs during 1934–35 but left before Goodman made it big. He played with Ray Noble's American Orchestra in 1935–36 and indirectly played an important part in musical history. Glenn Miller was Noble's main arranger at the time, and he wrote Pee Wee's trumpet part (at Erwin's urging) quite high, voicing it with the saxophonists. When Erwin's successor could not play the parts, Miller gave them to the clarinetist; thus the birth of the Glenn Miller sound!

Erwin replaced Bunny Berigan (whom he could closely emulate) in both the Goodman (February–September 1936) and Tommy Dorsey (1937–39) orchestras. He never really carved out a niche for himself with either band, remaining in Berigan's shadow. After leaving Dorsey, Erwin returned to the studios, where he worked steadily throughout the 1940s and '50s. Erwin also led a short-lived big band in 1940–42 (built out of the remains of the Bunny Berigan Orchestra) and starting in 1949, he had a Dixieland band that played regularly at Nick's in New York for almost a decade. During the 1960s Erwin ran a trumpet school with Chris Griffin; one of his star pupils was Warren Vache. In the '70s he worked with the Tommy Dorsey Ghost Orchestra (under the direction of Warren Covington), the New Jazz Repertory Company, and his own band, the Kings of Jazz.

Pee Wee Erwin, who had earlier recorded eight titles for King as a leader (1950) and cut albums for Urania, Cadence, and United Artists (plus two posthumous sets that later came out on Broadway Intermission), was surprisingly quite active during his final 18 months. During that period he recorded three albums for Qualtro, a set for a private label, one for Jazzology, and a final record for the Dutch Jazz Crooner label that was cut just three weeks before his death; his playing never declined!

LPs to Search For: *And His Dixieland Band* (Broadway Intermission 155), *Oh Play That Thing!* (United Artists 5010), *Swingin' That Music* (Jazzology 80)

Recommended Reading: *Jazz Gentry* by Warren Vache Sr. (Scarecrow Press, 1999)

DUANE EUBANKS

b. 1970, Philadelphia, PA

The younger brother of both guitarist Kevin Eubanks and trombonist Robin Eubanks and a nephew of pianist Ray Bryant, Duane Eubanks (whose mother, Vera, plays gospel piano) certainly seems to have impeccable musical genes! He first played trumpet while in the sixth grade. Eubanks studied for a business degree at the University of Maryland. But after playing with the university's jazz band, he permanently changed direction. Eubanks became a jazz major at Temple University and took two years of private lessons from Johnny Coles. In 1996 he moved to New York, and he has become known as one of the top up-and-coming trumpeters around. During the past few years he has played with many top musicians, including the Illinois Jacquet Big Band, the Next Legacy Orchestra, the Oliver Lake Big Band, Benny Golson, Jimmy Heath, James Moody, Donald Byrd, Terell Stafford, Lionel Hampton, Antonio Hart, Bobby Watson, and Robin Eubanks. In 1995 Duane Eubanks recorded with brother Robin, and a few years later he had his debut as a leader, TCB's *My Shining Hour*.

Recommended CDs: *My Shining Hour* (TCB 99202), with Robin Eubanks: *4 JJ/Slide/Curtis & Al* (TCB 97802), with Amos Hoffman: *The Dreamer* (Fresh Sound 060)

DOC EVANS

b. June 20, 1907, Spring Valley, MN, d. Jan. 10, 1977, Minneapolis, MN

A solid Dixieland player who hated bebop (and was not shy to be quoted about it!), Paul "Doc" Evans managed to gain a reputation in the jazz world despite spending much of his life working in his native Minnesota. He started on violin, piano, drums, and sax before switching to cornet. Evans played with amateur bands in the Minneapolis area during the 1930s while also teaching school for a year and raising champion cocker spaniels. In 1939, when he worked in a trad group with Red Dougherty, he finally became a full-time player and soon was leading his own no-nonsense Dixieland bands.

Evans played in Chicago and New York in the early 1940s, including with Joe Sullivan (1940–41), Eddie Condon, and Tony Parenti. He eventually returned to Minneapolis but did work with Bunk Johnson (1947), trombonist Miff Mole (1949), and in Chicago with Jazz Ltd. Based in Minneapolis, his band was quite popular throughout the 1950s. Evans, who had a chance to record with Turk Murphy, led many albums during 1947–59 (for Folkways, Paramount, Jazzology, Soma, and particularly Audiophile), along with six later sessions, including a final live concert from 1975. Doc Evans saw no reason to modernize his style, and he remained a high-quality Dixielander throughout his entire career.

Recommended CDs: *Down in Jungle Town* (Jazzology 19)

LPs to Search For: *Doc Evans and His Dixieland Jazz Band* (Folkways 2855), *Muskrat Ramble* (Audiophile 56), *At the Gas Light* (Audiophile 95)

Recommended Videos: *Art Hodes' Jazz Alley Vol. 1* (1968; Storyville 60640)

MILES EVANS

• • • • • • • • • • •

b. July 5, 1965, New York, NY

The son of arranger Gil Evans, Miles Evans (named after you-know-who) has developed into a fine trumpeter. He started out on drums, switched to trumpet (first sitting in with the Gil Evans big band in 1974, when he was just nine), studied at New York's Music and Art High School, and took lessons from Lew Soloff and Jon Faddis. He played with an all-British version of the Gil Evans Orchestra in 1982 and became a regular member of his father's band the following year. After Gil Evans died in 1988, Miles Evans became the leader of the orchestra, with whom he has continued working on a regular basis.

Recommended CDs: with Gil Evans Orchestra: *Farewell* (King/Intersound 680), *Tribute to Gil* (Soul Note 121209)

JON FADDIS

• • • • • • • • • • •

b. July 24, 1953, Oakland, CA

Dizzy Gillespie's style was so complex in 1945 that, after futile attempts by other players to emulate him, the younger beboppers eventually turned to Fats Navarro and Miles Davis for their musical role models. Thirty years later there was finally a young trumpeter who could not only copy Gillespie's impossible runs but had a wider range and could build his own voice from Dizzy's innovations.

Jon Faddis had Gillespie's style mastered by the time he was 19. He started playing trumpet when he was eight, and as a teenager his range developed quickly to an astounding level. When he was 15, Faddis met Dizzy at the Monterey Jazz Festival, getting Gillespie to sign a huge batch of LPs and befriending him. A short time later he had the opportunity to sit in with Dizzy at the Jazz Workshop in San Francisco. In 1971 Faddis toured with Lionel Hampton and appeared with Charles Mingus (filling in on the complex feature "Little Royal Suite" for an ailing Roy Eldridge) at a 1972 concert that was recorded. The young phenomenon led two albums for Pablo while in his early twenties (including a duet date with Oscar Peterson) and sometimes played with Dizzy Gillespie, although unfortunately their most exciting encounters do not seem to have been recorded. But then he seemed to get cold feet and disappeared from the jazz scene.

Actually Faddis never stopped playing, but during 1977–84 he worked primarily as a studio musician. He was rarely heard in a solo role during this period (other than an album for Stash and a few rare guest spots) and many wondered if he would be able to fulfill his great potential. However, Faddis re-emerged in 1985 (making *Legacy* for Concord, one of his greatest recordings), and he has been quite active in jazz ever since. Faddis, who has since recorded as a leader for Epic and Chesky, was musical director of Dizzy Gillespie's big band (1987–88) and since 1993 has led the Carnegie Hall Jazz Orchestra. Although he can still sound just like Dizzy Gillespie (even when he plays an octave higher), Jon Faddis can also emulate Roy Eldridge and Louis Armstrong and has proven to be a brilliant all-round trum-

The first trumpeter to really capture the essence of Dizzy Gillespie, while often playing an octave higher, Jon Faddis always puts on colorful shows.

peter. He has also kept the bebop flame alive by appearing with Slide Hampton's Jazz Masters and Lalo Schifrin, and heading a variety of Dizzy Gillespie tribute bands.

Recommended CDs: *Legacy* (Concord 4291), *Hornucopia* (Epic 46958), with Oscar Peterson: *Oscar Peterson and Jon Faddis* (Original Jazz Classics 1036)

LPs to Search For: *Youngblood* (Pablo 2310-765)

DON FAGERQUIST
● ● ● ● ● ● ● ● ● ● ● ● ● ● ● ● ● ● ●

b. Feb. 6, 1927, Worcester, MA, d. Jan. 24, 1974, Los Angeles, CA

Don Fagerquist had a fluent style and a quiet sound that fit into both bebop and cool. Fagerquist started off as a teenager playing with Mal Hallett's orchestra in 1943. He was a key soloist with three big bands led by swing bandleaders in the postwar years: Gene

Krupa (1944–45 and 1948), Artie Shaw (his short-lived bebop orchestra and Gramercy Five of 1949–50), and Woody Herman's Third Herd (1951–52). While a member of Les Brown's orchestra in 1953, Fagerquist began teaming up with tenor saxophonist Dave Pell in Pell's octet, a combo that soon had a musical life independent of Brown. Fagerquist was one of the main voices with the Dave Pell Octet during 1953–59, when it was one of the major cool jazz combos.

Fagerquist, who led an album for Mode in 1957 (reissued by V.S.O.P.) and three selections for Capitol in 1955, also recorded with Pete Rugolo, Mel Torme, Shelly Manne, and Art Pepper. He became a studio musician in 1956 (joining the staff of Paramount Films) and unfortunately played very little jazz after the Dave Pell Octet broke up in 1959. Don Fagerquist died prematurely from kidney disease when he was two weeks shy of turning 47.

Recommended CDs: *Eight By Eight* (V.S.O.P. 4), with Artie Shaw: *1949* (Music Masters 234)

AL FAIRWEATHER

* * * * * * * * * * * * * * * * *

b. June 12, 1927, Edinburgh, Scotland, d. June 21, 1993, Edinburgh, Scotland

A top mainstream trumpeter from Scotland who could play both swing and Dixieland quite effectively, Al Fairweather (whose original inspiration was Louis Armstrong) was mostly self-taught. He was associated with Scottish clarinetist Sandy Brown for many years, playing regularly with Brown during 1948–53 and 1954–57. Fairweather also worked with Cy Laurie in London (1953–54) and had a sextet from 1958 on. He led record dates (mostly for Columbia) during 1955–62, often using Brown on clarinet. Fairweather worked for the popular clarinetist Acker Bilk (1966–68) and then became a full-time teacher, performing music on just a part-time basis. In later years he played and arranged for Stan Greig's London Jazz Band, had reunions with Sandy Brown, and worked with Groove Juice Special. A heart attack in 1983 slowed him down, but Al Fairweather played locally in his native Edinburgh until his death at age 66.

DIGBY FAIRWEATHER

* * * * * * * * * * * * * * * * * * * *

b. Apr. 25, 1946, Rochford, Essex, England

Digby Fairweather (unrelated to Al Fairweather) also explores mainstream swing, although he plays cornet. Fairweather started off on drums and later on learned a bit of euphonium, violin, and clarinet before making cornet his main ax around 1960. "I taught myself to play—using Jazz records—and finally took lessons from Bert Collier (lead trumpet with Joe Loss) in 1965. Later on I took odd lessons from Harry Beckett, Colin Smith, and Tommy McQuater. But to begin with, it was a 'work it out for yourself' system. For a long time I played by ear alone, until around 1984–85." Fairweather worked locally in Essex starting in 1970, leading Dig's Half Dozen and first recording in 1975 with Alex Welsh while keeping a day job as a librarian. "I had worked my way up to working with all my British idols (Dave Shepherd, Roy Williams, Lennie Hastings, Brian Lemon) and they all seemed to be reasonably happy with what I did. So I resigned from Southend Library and 'went pro' on January 1, 1977. Then the waters got rougher!"

Since then, Fairweather has worked with Keith Nichols' Midnight Follies Orchestra, the quartet Velvet, the Pizza Express All-Stars (1980–83), the Alex Welsh Reunion Band (1983–87), the Great British Jazz Band (1994), his Jazz Super Kings, pianist Stan Baker, and various British trad bands. In addition to playing, teaching, and hosting jazz radio shows, Digby Fairweather is one of the authors of *Jazz: The Essential Companion* (1987) and its successor, *Jazz: The Rough Guide* (1995). "I consider myself blessed in that every day now for over 30 years my thoughts, actions, and life patterns have been controlled by the inspirations of Jazz."

Recommended CDs: *With Nat in Mind* (Jazzology 247), *Something to Remember Us By* (Jazzology 288/289), *A Portrait of Digby Fairweather* (Black Lion 76505), with Susannah McCorkle: *The Songs of Johnny Mercer* (Jazz Alliance 10031)

MAFFY FALAY
· · · · · · · · · · · ·

b. Aug. 30, 1930, Izmir, Turkey

Maffy Falay (who was born Ahmed Muvaffak Falay) first played jazz while attending the Ankara Conservatory in the early 1950s. Skilled not just on trumpet but on piano and the Indian flute, Falay has long been interested in combining the folk music of Turkey with jazz. He lived and played in Germany during 1956–59 before moving to Sweden. In 1960 he recorded with Harry Arnold's big band, Boris Lindquist, and Arne Domnerus, recording with Quincy Jones the following year. Falay worked with Francy Boland (1963), Kurt Edelgarden (1964), Bernt Rosengren (1969–73), George Russell, Don Cherry (1971), and other advanced jazz players. He led the group Sveda, which recorded three albums during 1972–73 that fused Turkish music with bop. In 1986 Maffy Falay made a stimulating (if more conventional) bop-oriented album for Phontastic, showing that he deserves much more recognition as one of the very few significant jazz trumpeters born in Turkey.

Recommended CDs: *We Six* (Phontastic 7675)

CHARLIE FARDELLA
· · · · · · · · · · · · · · ·

An exciting cornetist whose chance-taking solos sometimes recall Bunny Berigan, Charlie Fardella was a regular with singer Banu Gibson's New Orleans Hot Jazz throughout much of the 1980s, recording with Banu during 1983–90. When he departed, his replacement was Duke Heitger. Charlie Fardella still plays in the New Orleans area, although he is long overdue to have his own record date.

Recommended CDs: with Banu Gibson: *Vintage Banu* (Swing Out 109), *Spreading Rhythm Around* (Swing Out 102), *Let Yourself Go* (Swing Out 103), *You Don't Know My Mind Blues* (Swing Out 104)

EVERETT FAREY

· · · · · · · · · · · · ·

b. 1930, San Francisco, CA

Everett "Ev" Farey was one of the many cornetists active in the 1950s who were inspired by Lu Watters and the Yerba Buena Jazz Band. Farey began playing jazz when he was 14, and in 1953 he was briefly with Turk Murphy's band. Along with trombonist Sanford Newbauer, Farey cofounded and led the Bay City Jazz Band, a San Francisco-style trad octet that recorded spirited albums for Good Time Jazz during 1956–57. Farey, who also recorded with clarinetist Bob Helm, kept the Bay City Jazz Band going through 1975, leading the Bay City Five and the Bay City Six in the early '70s, succeeding Bill Allred as leader of the Golden State Jazz Band around 1977. Everett Farey is currently with the Port City Jazz Band and recently played with the Grand Dominion Jazz Band. His cornet playing remains solidly in the classic jazz ensemble-oriented tradition.

Recommended CDs: with the Bay City Jazz Band: *The Bay City Jazz Band* (Good Time Jazz 12017), *Golden Days!* (Good Time Jazz 10053)

ART FARMER

· · · · · · · · · · · ·

b. Aug. 21, 1928, Council Bluffs, IA, d. Oct. 4, 1999, New York, NY

A very reliable musician who never garnered many headlines, Art Farmer may not have been the most flamboyant brassman but he was, year-in year-out, one of the most consistently satisfying. The twin brother of bassist Addison Farmer (who died on February 20, 1963), Art was raised in Phoenix. He started with piano when he was six, spent short periods playing violin and tuba, and finally settled on trumpet when he was 14. Moving to Los Angeles, Art and Addison Farmer were part of the Central Avenue jazz scene starting in 1945. Art worked with Horace Henderson, Floyd Ray, Johnny Otis, Benny Carter, Gerald Wilson, Jay McShann, and the Roy Porter big band, appearing at many jam sessions. From the time of his earliest records, Farmer was able to adapt the innovations of Dizzy Gillespie to his own mellower tone, sounding relaxed even when playing at blistering tempos.

Farmer worked with tenor saxophonist Wardell Gray during 1951–52, including recording his "Farmer's Market," an original soon turned into vocalese by singer Annie Ross. He was in one important group after another for years. Farmer played with the Lionel Hampton big band (1952–53), sitting next to Clifford Brown in the trumpet section (they shared the solo space) and visiting Europe. He co-led a quintet with Gigi Gryce (1954–56), was a member of the Horace Silver Quintet (1957–58), and was in the Gerry Mulligan Quartet during 1958–59. Farmer was in constant demand for record dates, including Gene Ammons jam sessions and adventurous recordings led by Teddy Charles, Teo Macero, and George Russell. Farmer's calm style and appealing tone made the potentially forbidding music seem accessible, and he had the musicianship to make complex arrangements sound logical.

In 1959, Farmer and tenor saxophonist Benny Golson formed and co-led the Jazztet. Although it was one of the definitive hard bop bands and their first record (which had Curtis

Fuller and McCoy Tyner in the sextet) introduced Golson's "Killer Joe," the Jazztet was never a financial success. Its initial gig found the group booked opposite the Ornette Coleman Quartet at the Five Spot, which symbolically demonstrated how quickly the evolution of jazz was advancing during the era, and the band did not receive the publicity it deserved. In 1962, Farmer and Golson reluctantly broke up the Jazztet when it failed to generate enough work.

Around that time, Farmer switched to the flugelhorn, which proved to be a perfect vehicle for his quiet sound. He had a quartet with guitarist Jim Hall (1962–64), in 1965 led a quartet that included pianist Steve Kuhn, and spent some time in Europe during 1965–66. Back in the United States, Farmer often teamed up with tenor saxophonist Jimmy Heath (1966–68).

Due to the worsening economic situation for jazz musicians in the United States and the expanding opportunities abroad, Farmer moved to Vienna, Austria, in 1968. Soon he had become a member of the Austrian Radio Orchestra and was also working with the Kenny Clarke-Francy Boland big band and the Peter Herbolzheimer Orchestra. Farmer returned to the United States on an occasional basis starting in 1975 and more frequently in the 1980s and '90s. He sometimes had a quintet with tenorman Clifford Jordan, and in 1982 he participated in the first of several reunions with Benny Golson and Curtis Fuller in a new version of the Jazztet. He also toured with Gerry Mulligan's Rebirth of the Cool Nonet.

In 1991 Farmer began playing the flumpet, a horn designed for him by David Monette that has aspects of both the trumpet and the flugelhorn. The mellow-toned stylist stayed quite active and in strong demand until ill health greatly slowed him down during his final year. Fortunately Art Farmer made many records as a leader starting in 1953 (for such labels as Prestige, Vogue, ABC-Paramount, Contemporary, United Artists, Argo, Mercury, Atlantic, Columbia,

Consistent, reliable and swinging, Art Farmer was one of the unsung greats.

MPS, Mainstream, Sonet, East Wind, CTI, Soul Note, Optimism, Concord, Enja, and Sweet Basil).

Recommended CDs: *The Art Farmer Septet* (Original Jazz Classics 054), *Early Art* (Original Jazz Classics 880), *Portrait of Art Farmer* (Original Jazz Classics 166), *Modern Art* (Blue Note 84459), *Meet the Jazztet* (MCA/Chess 91550), *On the Road* (Original Jazz Classics 478), *A Work of Art* (Concord Jazz 4179), *Warm Valley* (Concord Jazz 4212), *Back to the City* (Original Jazz Classics 842), *Something to Live For* (Contemporary 14029), *Blame It on My Youth* (Contemporary 14042)

Recommended Reading: *American Musicians II* by Whitney Balliett (Oxford University Press, 1996), *Central Avenue Sounds,* edited by Clora Bryant, et. al. (University of California Press, 1998)

Film Appearances: briefly with Gerry Mulligan in *I Want to Live* (1958)

Videos to Get: *Ron Carter and Art Farmer Live at Sweet Basil* (1992; View Video 1330)

MAYNARD FERGUSON
• •

b. May 4, 1928, Montreal, Quebec, Canada

A phenomenon who could pop out stratospheric high notes with little effort during his prime years, Maynard Ferguson became a model for college trumpeters by the 1970s, a macho performer who could easily play faster, louder, and higher than his competitors. But although he would not be called the epitome of good taste (listen to his "Rocky II Disco Theme" from 1977!), Ferguson is actually a well-rounded musician quite capable of playing heated bebop in the normal register of his horn too.

Maynard Ferguson told me in 1979:

> My parents were both school principals and music lovers. My mother had a slight prejudice towards classical music, so she was a bit disappointed when my father agreed to buy me a trumpet and my brother a saxophone, since both of us, from the age of four, were piano and violin students. My father had been a great contributor in starting the instrumental music education in the Quebec school system at that time. For that reason, sometimes during the vacation months, we would have something like 147 instruments in our basement. Our house looked like a music store, and my brother and I grew up treating instruments like toys! I'm self-taught on hitting high notes. Years later, when I met people into yoga, I discovered that I almost breathe perfectly, which very few people do. I was playing in the upper register when I was very young. By the time I was 16, I think I'd already nailed the lid on my classical career!

Ferguson, who started playing trumpet when he was nine, won a scholarship to the French Conservatory of Music in Montreal and at 13 soloed with the Canadian Broadcasting Company Orchestra. He led the warm-up band in Canada for the top orchestras passing though Montreal and in his late teens was starting to get offers from American bands. Ferguson came to the United States in late 1948 to join Stan Kenton but arrived just as Kenton was taking a year's sabbatical. Ferguson instead worked with the big bands of Boyd Raeburn, Jimmy Dorsey, and Charlie Barnet. While with Barnet (whose group was quite boppish at the time), Ferguson was challenged in the upper register by Doc Severinsen and Ray Wetzel. When Kenton formed his Innovations Orchestra (the huge ensemble with strings) in 1950, Ferguson became one of its stars. At that point in time he could play higher notes than anyone else in jazz other than Cat Anderson. "The air power is so important, the velocity of your air stream. I like to swim 100 laps in the pool each morning when I'm home, so I'll have the air power. If you're breathing and standing correctly, you won't hurt yourself by trying for high notes."

In 1953 Ferguson moved to Los Angeles and became a studio musician. In addition to the movie soundtracks, Ferguson had opportunities to record jazz for Emarcy, including jam session dates, highlighted by one Dinah Washington album in which he was teamed with Clifford Brown and Clark Terry. In 1956 he formed The Birdland Dream Band, a six-week venture that included an extended engagement at Birdland plus some recordings. "After that stint was over, several agents tried to get hold of me when I got back home in California. Joe Glaser got to me first and asked, 'Why don't you form a band?' When I did the All-Star thing at Birdland, they made a deal with me that if I signed with their record company (Roulette), I could do 16 weeks of the year at Birdland. That's a great base to work out of." The Maynard Ferguson Orchestra of 1956–64 was his finest band, a bop-oriented ensemble that at various times included in its personnel Don Ellis, Bill Berry, trombonist-arrangers Slide Hampton and Don Sebesky, altoist Lanny Morgan, Don Menza and Joe Farrell on tenors, and pianists Jaki Byard, John Bunch,

Maynard Ferguson stretched the range of the trumpet by a couple octaves, somehow making stratospheric notes look easy to play.

and Joe Zawinul. Ferguson (who doubled on valve trombone) fulfilled his early potential with this big band, whose complete works were in recent times reissued on a limited-edition Mosaic box set.

By the mid-1960s, Ferguson was becoming a bit restless. "It seemed like I was playing the same places year after year after year to an audience who would demand that I'd play the same things year after year after year. I was becoming very bored." By 1966 the Maynard Ferguson Big Band was history. After a couple of years of freelancing, Ferguson toured Europe with an Anglo-American band, briefly led an all-British ensemble, and spent time in India studying music and spirituality. In 1970 he was ready to return, and he put together a new big band in London. Ferguson immediately had a hit in "MacArthur Park" (from the *M. F. Horn* album), and in general his English orchestra had a commercial repertoire filled with pop tunes. In 1973 Ferguson moved back to the United States and continued balancing recent pop numbers with some jazz, all played in somewhat bombastic fashion. *M. F. Horn, Vols. 4 and 5* (from 1973) is the best jazz album from this era, but much more popular were his recordings of the *Rocky* theme ("Gonna Fly Now") and the "Theme from *Star Wars*."

Ferguson kept the big band going until early 1986, led a mediocre funk group called High Voltage (1986–88), and in 1988 returned to his roots by forming his Big Bop Nouveau Band. The small big band (which has a full trumpet section) has been Ferguson's main group ever since. Even though his range has shrunk a bit in recent years, Maynard Ferguson at 73 is still amazing.

Recommended CDs: *The Birdland Dream Band* (Bluebird 6455), *A Message from Newport* (Roulette 93272), *Maynard '61* (Roulette 93900), *Orchestra 1967* (Just A Memory 9504), *These Cats Can Swing!* (Concord Jazz 4669), *One More Trip to Birdland* (Concord Jazz 4729), with Stan Kenton: *The Innovations Orchestra* (Capitol 59965)

Box Set: *The Complete Roulette Recordings of the Maynard Ferguson Orchestra* (10 CDs; Mosaic 10-156)

LPs to Search For: *M. F. Vols. 4 and 5* (Columbia 32732)

Videos to Get: *Sarah Vaughan and Friends* (1986; A*Vision 50209)

MONGEZI FEZA

. . . .

b. 1945, Queenstown, South Africa, d. Dec. 14, 1975, London, England

Mongezi Feza is most famous for his association with pianist Chris McGregor. He started playing trumpet when he was eight and worked as a teenager in South Africa, including with Ronnie Beer's Swinging City Six. In 1962, when he was 16, Feza joined Chris McGregor's Blue Notes, an important and adventurous jazz band in South Africa that was interracial at a time when it was becoming increasingly dangerous. After the group performed at the Antibes Jazz Festival in 1964, they became expatriates and settled in England. However, the band (exploring free jazz in a manner parallel to the Ornette Coleman Quartet) never really caught on and worked only on an occasional basis; it was too far ahead of its time. A little later, when McGregor formed his big band Brotherhood of Breath, Feza became the orchestra's main trumpet soloist. He also worked in England with altoist Dudu Pukwana and pianist Keith Tippett.

In 1972 Feza moved to Denmark, where he played with South African bassist Johnny Dyani and again with Pukwana. That unit recorded for Sonet in Sweden. But Mongezi Feza did not take good care of his health, and he passed away when he was 30. He led just one album in his life, the obscure *Assagai* for the Vertigo label in 1970.

Recommended CDs: with the Brotherhood of Breath: *Live at Wellisau* (Ogun 001)

LPs to Search For: *Assagai* (Vertigo 6360.630)

Recommended Reading: *Chris McGregor and the Brotherhood of Breath* by Maxine McGregor (Bamberger Books, 1995)

REBECCA COUPE FRANKS

b. Nov. 27, 1961, San Jose, CA

A fine trumpeter who made a strong impression in the early 1990s, Rebecca Franks grew up in Santa Cruz, California. She started playing trumpet when she was ten and became a professional at 15. "I grew up hearing my brother (who became an entertainer) practice trumpet, and my grandfather, great uncle, and mother had played it too!" She picked up experience in a wide variety of settings, from circus bands to classical music. After moving to New York in 1987 (where for two years she attended The New School of Social Research), Franks recorded with Virginia Mayhew for the Philogy label (they also appeared at the Monterey Jazz Festival), guested on a CD led by comedian Bill Cosby, recorded with guitarist Herb Ellis, and led CDs of her own for Justice.

"I have to admit that there have been a few times when I thought of not continuing my music due to other people's preconceived ideas of what a woman trumpet player is suppose to sound like. But I love to play and I just want to play me and not prove anything to anybody." Rebecca Franks, who has a potentially significant future, considers her main influences to be Clifford Brown and Miles Davis.

Recommended CDs: *Suit of Armor* (Justice 901), *All of a Sudden* (Justice 902), with Herb Ellis: *Roll Call* (Justice 1001)

GUY FRICANO

b. 1943

Considered a legend in Chicago, the virtuoso trumpeter Guy Fricano has years of show band and studio experience behind him. Unfortunately he has not made many jazz records in his life, even though he has appeared in Chicago-area clubs (both with big bands and combos) on a fairly regular basis. His *Jazz Inside Out* (from 1984) features his trumpet mostly with a big band, while *The New York Sessions* finds Guy Fricano holding his own with Cedar Walton and Ron Carter in a sextet; neither have appeared on CD yet.

LPs to Search For: *Jazz Inside Out* (Forever Jazz 0013), *The New York Sessions* (AFP 81242)

TONY FRUSCELLA

b. Feb. 14, 1927, Orangeburg, NJ, d. Aug. 14, 1969, New York, NY

Tony Fruscella was a solid, cool-toned bop player whose career and life were ruined by drug abuse. Fruscella lived in an orphanage until he was 14. He started playing trumpet the following year. After a stint in the Army, he worked with altoist Chick Maures (1948), Lester Young (1950 and 1954), Don Joseph, Brew Moore (1953), Gerry Mulligan (1954), and Stan Getz (1955). Fruscella recorded his one studio album as a leader for Atlantic in 1955 and also recorded with Getz. But by 1957 he was just semiactive in jazz and unsuccessfully battling drug addiction. Tony Fruscella, who recently had all of his recordings reissued on the four-CD *Complete Works*, died in obscurity at the age of 42.

Recommended CDs: *Tony's Blues* (Cool N' Blue 107)

Box Set: *Complete Works* (4 CDs; Jazz Factory 22808)

LPs to Search For: *Fru 'n Brew* (Spotlite 151), *Tony Fruscella* (Atlantic 1220)

WALT FOWLER

b. Mar. 2, 1955, Salt Lake City, UT

There is no shortage of music-playing Fowlers in Los Angeles! Walt Fowler is the son of educator William Fowler and brother of trombonist Bruce, bassist-keyboardist Ed, flutist-altoist Steve, and bassist-violinist Tom. "I actually started on piano, but I liked trumpet when I heard Woody Herman's band (with Bill Chase on lead). My Dad got a used one from one of my neighbors when I was eight. I knew that I wanted to be a musician within a couple of days."

Walt Fowler started his career in 1974, traveling with Frank Zappa (with whom he would also play during 1987–88). He worked with the Fowler Brothers band, Billy Cobham, Johnny "Guitar" Watson, the Buddy Rich big band, and Ray Charles. He has played with altoist Brandon Fields on and off since 1980, been in guitarist George Benson's backup band (1985–87), worked with pianist Billy Childs, and freelanced in many settings through the years. Walt Fowler is a fine, open-minded soloist with a strong sense of humor and lots of potential, although his solo talents have often been underutilized (too often doing section work in the background), and he has yet to lead his own record date.

Recommended CDs: with Billy Childs: *His April Touch* (Windham Hill Jazz 131), with Brandon Fields: *Brandon Fields* (Positive 77812), *Other Places* (Nova 9025), with The Fowler Brothers: *Breakfast for Dinosaurs* (Fossil 1002), with Bruce Fowler: *Ants Can Count* (Terra Nova 9002), with Andy Summers: *Green Chimneys* (RCA 63472)

    THE TRUMPET KINGS

WALTER FULLER

b. Feb. 15, 1910, Dyersburg, TN

Walter Fuller is best remembered for his association in the 1930s with the Earl Hines Orchestra, where he was the main trumpet soloist and an occasional vocalist. His singing in 1934 on the earliest version of Hines' "Rosetta" earned him the nickname of "Rosetta." When he was 12 Fuller started playing professionally with Dr. Stoll's Medicine Show, touring with that outfit during three summers. In 1925 he moved to Chicago and played with Emma Smith's band for a year. After a period with Sammy Stewart (1927–30) and a short time with Irene Edie's group, Fuller joined Earl Hines' big band in 1931, when he was 21. Except for a stint during 1937–38 with Horace Henderson, Fuller would be with the pianist's orchestra for over nine years.

Influenced during his later years with Hines by Roy Eldridge and always considering Louis Armstrong to be his idol, Fuller was one of Earl Hines' main stars of the 1930s. In addition to "Rosetta," he helped "After All I've Been to You" and "You Can Depend on Me" to become minor hits in 1939–40. In 1941 Fuller went out on his own, forming a big band that included some of the Earl Hines alumni and a young singer named Dinah Washington. However, the orchestra never really caught on and soon broke up. After leading a small group in Los Angeles that included Omer Simeon, Fuller moved to San Diego in 1946. Walter Fuller continued playing with a combo into the 1990s (including 12 years at the Club Royal and eight years at the Moonglow). But, although continually active, his later years have been spent in obscurity and are almost completely undocumented on record, with just two songs in 1948 for the Miltone label and four in 1954 for the equally obscure Kicks company.

Recommended CDs: with Earl Hines: *1932–1934* (Classics 514), *1934–1937* (Classics 528), *1939–1940* (Classics 567)

Recommended Reading: *The World of Earl Hines* by Stanley Dance (Charles Scribner's Sons, 1977)

JOHN FUMO

b. June 5, 1957, Kenosha, WI

John Fumo is one of the major players in the Los Angeles-based avant-garde scene that is led by saxophonist Vinny Golia and documented by the Nine Winds label. His ability to improvise under any setting (from bop to free form) has long been a valuable asset. He started playing free jazz literally at the very beginning, for, as he recalls, "Dad bought me a cornet at age seven or so. I would play improvised duets with him every night (with him on drums)." Fumo attended the New England Conservatory of Music (1976–78) and in 1978 settled in Los Angeles. He soon met Golia and became an important part of the local scene. Since then, John Fumo has worked in many settings, including session work with commercial groups, Tito Puente, Charlie Haden, Japan's Inner Galaxy Orchestra, Golia, and his own bands, recording as a leader for Nine Winds.

LPs to Search For: After the Fact (Nine Winds 116), with Vinny Golia: *Goin' Ahead* (Nine Winds 117), *Pilgrimage to Obscurity* (Nine Winds 130), *Decennium Dans Axlan* (Nine Winds 140), *Commemoration* (Nine Winds 150/160)

EDDIE GALE

b. Aug. 15, 1941, Brooklyn, NY

An adventurous avant-garde trumpeter, Eddie Gale has been associated with Cecil Taylor and Sun Ra. Born Edward Gale Stevens Jr., he started playing bugle with his local Boy Scouts marching band before taking private lessons on the trumpet. Early on Gale had opportunities to sit in with Jackie McLean, Illinois Jacquet, Booker Ervin, and John Coltrane, eventually gravitating toward freer forms of jazz. Gale recorded *Unit Structures* with pianist Cecil Taylor in 1966, also appeared on records with organist Larry Young, and during 1968–69 cut two albums of his own (*Ghetto Music* and *Black Rhythm Happening*) for Blue Note. Since then he has worked and recorded with Sun Ra and led further sessions for the tiny Roof Top label and (most recently) Mapleshade (1992).

Recommended CDs: *A Minute with Miles* (Mapleshade 1132), with Sun Ra: *Lanquidity* (Evidence 22220)

LPs to Search For: with Cecil Taylor: *Unit Structures* (Blue Note 84237)

WARREN GALE

Warren Gale, who has long been based in the San Francisco Bay area, is best known for his playing and recordings with Mel Martin's Bebop and Beyond. He toured with Stan Kenton in 1970, recorded with Mark Murphy, James Zitro, and Mike Vax's Trpts., and has been a member of Bebop and Beyond ever since its formation in the early 1980s. Warren Gale (who has never led his own record date) is a top-notch hard bop player whose solos are swinging yet unpredictable.

Recommended CDs: with Bebop and Beyond: *Plays Thelonious Monk* (Bluemoon 79154), *Plays Dizzy Gillespie* (Bluemoon 79170)

LPs to Search For: with Bebop and Beyond: *Beautiful Friendship* (Concord Jazz 244), with Trpts.: *Transforming Traditions* (Black-Hawk 51701)

LUIS GASCA

b. Mar. 3, 1940, Houston, TX, d. Feb. 1997, Hawaii

A top-notch Latin jazz trumpeter, Luis Gasca had a strong presence for a relatively brief time before slipping into complete obscurity. Gasca started on trumpet when he was 13. After attending Berklee (1959–60), he worked with Perez Prado (1960) and was one of

THE TRUMPET KINGS

the mellophonium players with Stan Kenton's orchestra in 1962. Gasca kept busy during the next 13 years, working with Maynard Ferguson, Lionel Hampton (1963–64), Woody Herman (1967), Mongo Santamaria (1967–69), Janis Joplin, Carlos Santana, Count Basie, Cal Tjader, and his own groups. He recorded with Santamaria, Tjader, George Duke (1971), and Joe Henderson (1973), leading record dates for Atlantic (1968–69) Blue Thumb (1971) and Fantasy (two during 1974–75). But after the mid-1970s, an erratic lifestyle and personal problems resulted in Luis Gasca's completely disappearing from the jazz scene; he was found murdered in Hawaii in 1997.

LPs to Search For: *Born to Love You* (Fantasy 9461), with Joe Henderson: *Canyon Lady* (Original Jazz Classics 949), with Cal Tjader: *Descarga* (Fantasy 24737)

KARL GEORGE

b. Apr. 26, 1913, St. Louis, MO

Karl George was a fine swing trumpeter who managed to make the transition to bebop without changing his style very much. George began his career playing with McKinney's Cotton Pickers (1933) and the Jeter-Pillars Orchestra. He gained some recognition for his work with the Teddy Wilson big band (1939–40) and Lionel Hampton (1941–42). After serving in the Army (1942–43), George became one of the few black players ever to be a member of the Stan Kenton Orchestra (1943). His prime period was the mid-1940s, when he worked with Benny Carter (1944), Count Basie (1945), and Happy Johnson (1946). During this era George also led a combo and appeared on many records in the Los Angeles area, including with Charles Mingus, Slim Gaillard, Oscar Pettiford, and Lucky Thompson. He also led three sessions (resulting in a dozen titles) during 1945–46, using such sidemen as J.J. Johnson, Buddy Tate, and Lucky Thompson; Xanadu and IAJC reissued nine of the numbers. Unfortunately, bad health soon forced his retirement, and Karl George was not heard from again in the jazz world after the late 1940s.

Recommended CDs: with Lucky Thompson: *The Beginning Years* (IAJRC 1001)

DIZZY GILLESPIE

b. Oct. 21, 1917, Cheraw, SC, d. Jan. 6, 1993, Englewood, NJ

One of the most remarkable trumpeters of all time (he was arguably the most complex improviser), Dizzy Gillespie was a true giant in several areas. Although he was originally influenced on trumpet by Roy Eldridge, Gillespie's playing was so radical by 1945 that it sounded like a completely new language altogether. He had the ability to play notes that seemed completely wrong, hold on to them, and somehow make them fit, similar to fitting a square inside a triangle (though there was nothing square about Dizzy!). While he had a distinctive sound and impressive technique, Gillespie's extensive knowledge of chord structures really set him apart, making him both influential and very difficult to copy. It would not be until Jon Faddis rose to prominence in the 1970s that anyone really captured the Gillespie style.

In addition, as a bandleader, Gillespie led a classic bop-oriented orchestra during 1946–49 and an important globetrotting big band in 1956–57. And, as if helping to found bebop were not enough, Gillespie was a very significant pioneer in Afro-Cuban jazz.

Born the last of nine children to a poor family, John Birks Gillespie (nicknamed Dizzy early in life due to his wit and sly brilliance) first played trombone, switching to trumpet at 12. One of his earliest opportunities to play in public resulted in an odd historical fact: In 1933 (when he was 16) Gillespie sat in with the King Oliver Orchestra! He won a scholarship to an agriculture school (the Laurinburg Institute in North Carolina), where he had an opportunity to study music. However, his desire to play professionally led him to drop out of school in 1935 to try to make it as a musician.

Gillespie, inspired by the dramatic playing of Roy Eldridge, closely emulated his idol for a few years. He played with Frankie Fairfax's orchestra in Philadelphia and was in Eldridge's old spot with Teddy Hill's big band in 1937. Gillespie had his recording debut with Hill, soloing on "King Porter Stomp," sounding a lot like Little Jazz. However, he was soon stretching himself as he tried to form his own style, and was being criticized by his fellow sidemen for not playing it safe.

Gillespie visited Europe with Hill and, after his return to the United States, he freelanced for a year. With the help of Mario Bauza, he joined Cab Calloway's orchestra in 1939. Although Calloway soon called Dizzy's solos "Chinese music," Gillespie actually took short solos on a lot of the singer's records during a two-year period; his most famous recording of the era was "Pickin' the Cabbage." Calloway's criticism of his young trumpeter was actually quite reasonable, for Gillespie was improvising over more complex chords than the rhythm section was playing, and many of his recorded solos do seem to contain some "wrong" notes.

In 1941 someone threw spitballs at Calloway while he was singing on stage, and he accused Gillespie. A fight broke out and Dizzy was fired; decades later it would be revealed that Jonah Jones (who was with Calloway for another decade) was the culprit! During 1941–42, Gillespie spent brief periods with many swing-era big bands, including those of Ella Fitzgerald (the Chick Webb ghost orchestra), Coleman Hawkins, Benny Carter, Charlie Barnet, Fess Williams, Les Hite, Claude Hopkins, Lucky Millinder, Calvin Jackson, and Duke Ellington (with whom he subbed for four weeks). His solos on records with Hite ("Jersey Bounce") and Millinder ("Little John Special") show that his style was quickly progressing.

Gillespie first met altoist Charlie Parker (whom he later called "my heartbeat") in 1940, and they jammed together as often as possible. Dizzy also took part in spontaneous sessions at Monroe's Uptown House (where he was captured on a few private recordings) and Minton's Playhouse. During this period, he wrote some advanced arrangements for the big bands of Woody Herman ("Down Under" and "Woody 'n You"), Benny Carter, and Jimmy Dorsey. Herman was so impressed with Gillespie's writing that he suggested he quit playing trumpet and stick to arranging!

In late 1942, Gillespie became a member of the Earl Hines big band (the first bebop orchestra), a band that also included Charlie Parker (on tenor), Sarah Vaughan, and Billy Eckstine. Unfortunately the group never recorded, due to the Musicians' Union recording strike. During his year with Hines, Gillespie wrote his most famous composition, "A Night in Tunisia." After leaving Hines, Dizzy co-led (with bassist Oscar Pettiford) the first bebop combo to be

The most advanced trumpeter in jazz, Dizzy Gillespie was ironically also one of the most accessible, friendly and humorous personalities.

heard on 52nd Street. In early 1944, Billy Eckstine formed a boppish big band, hiring Bird (on alto) and Diz. By the time the recording strike ended, Parker had already departed, but Gillespie was still there, and he can be heard soloing on "Opus X" and "Blowing the Blues Away." Dizzy was also part of the first full-fledged bop recording dates (Coleman Hawkins sessions that have Gillespie soloing on "Woody 'n You" and "Disorder at the Border") and can be heard on a rare radio broadcast, sounding positively radical as a member of the John Kirby Sextet. In December 1944, Gillespie helped out on a Sarah Vaughan record date that included Vaughan's vocal version of "A Night in Tunisia" (renamed "Interlude"); the song had already been recorded by the Boyd Raeburn Orchestra and heard on a broadcast by the Glenn Miller All-Stars.

1945 is when Dizzy Gillespie became famous and bebop seemed to explode. In a world much more accustomed to Glenn Miller and Harry James, Gillespie recorded a series of classic bebop records with Charlie Parker, including "Hot House," "Salt Peanuts," "Dizzy Atmosphere," "'Shaw Nuff," and "Groovin' High" (all Dizzy originals except "Hot House"). He also composed "Blue 'n Boogie," "Tour de Force," "Bebop," and, in later years, "Con Alma." His complex reharmonization of "I Can't Get Started" (which Bunny Berigan had made famous just eight years before) is a masterpiece, and throughout the year Gillespie's playing sounded quite futuristic. However, because his music was so new, there was opposition. Dizzy's first big band did not last long, dying during a tour of the South, where audiences complained that the music was not danceable. He visited Los Angeles later in the year with Charlie Parker, but their stint at Billy Berg's Club in Hollywood failed to attract much of an audience; the West Coast had never heard sounds like these before. After playing a few concerts with Jazz at the Philharmonic and making a few recordings, Gillespie returned to New York.

In 1946 Gillespie formed his second big band, one that lasted for most of four years. Bebop had been thought of (even by its fans) as a small-group music, so Dizzy's ensemble was quite innovative. Among his sidemen were James Moody, Jimmy Heath, Cecil Payne, John Lewis, Milt Jackson, Ray Brown, Kenny Clarke, J.J. Johnson, Yusef Lateef, and (in 1949) John Coltrane; Gil Fuller and Dizzy himself contributed many of the arrangements. "Things to Come" acted as a radical statement for the orchestra. Even when playing familiar pop tunes, the harmonies were quite advanced. During 1947–48, Chano Pozo played conga with the orchestra, and the fusion of his rhythms and chants with the other musicians on such numbers as "Manteca," "Tin Tin Deo," and George Russell's "Cubana Be/Cubana Bop" did a great deal to popularize Latin jazz.

Gillespie, with his glasses, beret, and goatee, became symbolic of the entire bebop movement, though no one could imitate the way his cheeks puffed out when he played. His famous bent trumpet originated in 1953 when a dancer tripped over his horn. In trying out his damaged trumpet, Gillespie discovered that he could hear what he played a split-second sooner with his trumpet shaped at that eccentric angle.

Although his trumpet playing was quite complex, Gillespie did a great deal to make bop seem accessible. A natural showman, he loved to make wisecracks to his audiences, perform comedy vocals, and scat. He was also an important unofficial jazz educator, always eager to explain and demonstrate to other musicians what it was he was doing. Gillespie insisted that other musicians learn to play chords on the piano so that they would understand how to improvise better. He did a great deal to make bop a major part of jazz's mainstream and the foundation for future styles.

In addition to the work with his big band (which included visits to Europe), Gillespie reunited with Charlie Parker on a few memorable occasions, including a 1947 Carnegie Hall concert, a 1951 radio broadcast, and the 1953 Massey Hall concert. Bird's death in 1955 was a major blow to the trumpeter. Another loss was in late 1949, when he had to reluctantly break up his struggling orchestra. Gillespie led small groups during the next six years, including a sextet that originally included Milt Jackson and John Coltrane. He cofounded the short-lived Dee Gee label, used Joe "Bebop" Carroll as his vocalist for a few years (although Dizzy was actually a better singer), and recorded some commercial but entertaining material that included R&B and humorous vocals. He also went on tours with Jazz at the Philharmonic, engaging in nightly trumpet battles with Roy Eldridge in 1954. Recording regularly for Norman Granz's labels (including Verve), Gillespie was heard at the peak of his powers throughout the decade, including on memorable recordings with Stan Getz, Sonny Stitt, and Sonny Rollins.

In 1956 Gillespie was contacted by the U.S. State Department to put together a new big band to tour the world, acting as a goodwill ambassador. Dizzy jumped at the chance, and during the next two years he and his hard-swinging unit performed in Europe, the Near East, and South America. Some of his more notable sidemen were Lee Morgan, Joe Gordon, Melba Liston, Al Grey, Billy Mitchell, Benny Golson, Ernie Henry, Phil Woods, Wynton Kelly, and Quincy Jones. The orchestra can be heard at its best on its recording from the 1957 Newport Jazz Festival.

The spirited big band broke up in 1958, and from then on Gillespie usually led quintets, except on special occasions. Pianist Junior Mance and altoist-flutist Leo Wright were with him in the late 1950s, being succeeded eventually by James Moody (on tenor, alto, and flute) and pianists Lalo Schifrin and Kenny Barron. Dizzy debuted Schifrin's "Gillespiana" with a big band at Carnegie Hall in 1961, was a regular at jazz festivals, had a humorous write-in campaign running for President in 1964, and toured Europe with a reunion big band in 1968. By the late 1960s Gillespie's recordings were becoming erratic (most record labels did not want pure bebop during the time), and his music was sometimes funk oriented. But in the 1970s, Norman Granz returned to the record business, started the Pablo label, and was quick to sign up Gillespie and record him under favorable conditions again.

Dizzy, who still sounded in fine form with the Giants of Jazz (an all-star sextet with Sonny Stitt and Thelonious Monk) during 1971–72, began to fade as a trumpeter from the mid-1970s on, losing his range and his once-impressive intonation. He had a steady musical decline during his final 20 years, but remained quite popular, in generally good spirits, and in prime form as a virtuoso scat-singer and humorist. Always a beloved figure and an inspiration, Gillespie worked steadily; during 1988–92 he led the United Nation Orchestra, an exciting Latin jazz band that included Arturo Sandoval, Claudio Roditi, altoist Paquito D'Rivera, and pianist Danilo Perez.

After an early month-long celebration of his 75th year in January 1992, the trumpeter became quite ill. Dizzy Gillespie was inactive during his final year before passing away. His accomplishments, like those of Louis Armstrong and Miles Davis, are impossible to overstate.

Recommended CDs: *Shaw Nuff* (Musicraft 53), *The Complete RCA Victor Recordings* (Bluebird 66528), *Dizzy Gillespie and His Big Band* (GNP Crescendo 23), *Dee Gee Days* (Savoy 4426), *Dizzy Gillespie in Paris, Vol. 2* (Vogue 68361), *Dizzy Gillespie in Paris, Vol. 1* (Vogue 68360), *Jazz at Massey Hall* (Original Jazz Classics 044), *Diz and Getz* (Verve 883 559), *Dizzy Gillespie with Roy Eldridge* (Verve 314 521 647), *Birk's Works: The Verve Big Band Sessions* (Verve 314 527 900), *At Newport* (Verve 314 513 754), *Sonny Side Up* (Verve 825 674), *Gillespiana/Carnegie Hall Concert* (Verve 314 519 809), *An Electrifying Evening* (Verve 314 557

544), *Dizzy Gillespie's Big Four* (Original Jazz Classics 443), *To a Finland Station* (Original Jazz Classics 733), *Live at Royal Festival Hall* (Enja 79658)

LPs to Search For: *Reunion Big Band* (MPS 821 622), *Giants of Jazz* (Atlantic 2-905)

Recommended Reading: *American Musicians II* by Whitney Balliett (Oxford University Press, 1996), *From Satchmo to Miles* by Leonard Feather (Da Capo Press, 1984), *Groovin' High* by Alyn Shipton (Oxford University Press, 1999), *Jazz Masters of the Forties* by Ira Gitler (Macmillan Publishing Co., 1966), *Jazz Spoken Here* by Wayne Enstice and Paul Rubin (Louisiana State University Press, 1992), *Talking Jazz* by Ben Sidran (Pomegranate Artbooks, 1992), *To Be or Not to Bop* by Dizzy Gillespie and Al Fraser (Doubleday & Co., 1979)

Recommended Videos: *Things to Come* (1947; Vintage Jazz Classics 2006), *Sarah Vaughan and Friends* (1986; A*Vision 50209), *A Night in Chicago* (1993; View Video 1334)

GEORGE GIRARD

b. Oct. 7, 1930, New Orleans, LA, d. Jan. 18, 1957, New Orleans, LA

George Girard was one of the most popular trumpeters in New Orleans during the first half of the 1950s; only an early death kept him from receiving the fame that would later be given Al Hirt.

A likable trumpeter and a fine singer, Girard started working in local clubs in 1946. He played with Johnny Archer's orchestra and Phil Zito, recording with the latter. In 1950 Girard organized the Basin Street Six, a group that included the young clarinetist Pete Fountain. A couple of years later it was succeeded by Girard's own band, which played regularly at the Famous Door in New Orleans' French Quarter. But in 1955 the trumpeter contracted cancer. He had surgery in January 1956, came back for four months in the spring and summer, and then was forced to stop playing, passing away at the age of 26. George Girard's death was a major loss to New Orleans jazz, although fortunately he was captured on some fine records (for Southland, Imperial, Good Time Jazz, and Storyville plus two full albums for Vik) during the brief time he had.

Recommended CDs: *Sounds of New Orleans, Vol. 6* (Storyville 6013), with the Basin Street Six: *Basin Street Six* (GHB 103)

LPs to Search For: *Stompin' at the Famous Door* (Vik 1058)

GREG GISBERT

b. Feb. 2, 1966, Mobile, AL

An excellent hard bop trumpeter, Greg Gisbert is both consistent and underrated. His parents were quite musical (Gisbert's father played piano and saxophones, while his mother played trumpet) and he started out as a drummer, gigging with his father when he was ten. As a teenager, Gisbert switched to trumpet. Since attending Berklee (1984–85), Gisbert has worked with many top bands and musicians, including Buddy Rich, Woody Herman's orchestra (1987–89), Gary Burton, the Toshiko Akiyoshi-Lew Tabackin big band (starting in 1989), Mingus Epitaph, Frank Wess, Clark Terry, the Buck Clayton Big Band (1991), Danny D'Imperio's sextet, and the Maria Schneider Orchestra. As a leader, Greg Gisbert has recorded a trio of fine straightahead sessions for Criss Cross.

Recommended CDs: *Harcology* (Criss Cross 1084), *On Second Thought* (Criss Cross), *Court Jester* (Criss Cross), with Danny D'Imperio: *Blues for Philly Joe* (VSOP 81), *Glass Enclosure* (VSOP 96), with Scott Hamilton: *Blues, Bop and Ballads* (Concord Jazz 4866)

DON GOLDIE
• • • • • • • • • • • •

b. Feb. 5, 1930, Newark, NJ, d. Nov. 19, 1995, Miami, FL

A very impressive trumpeter with superior technique, Don Goldie emphasized Dixieland and swing throughout his career. His father, Harry "Goldie" Goldfield, played trumpet with Paul Whiteman (assuming the role of Henry Busse) for over 15 years, while his mother was a concert pianist who also played jazz at night. After studying violin and piano (starting at age three), Goldie settled on the trumpet when he was ten and worked with his father's orchestra when he was 14. After serving in the Army (1951–54), Goldie played with Joe Mooney (1955–59), Neal Hefti, Buddy Rich, and Gene Krupa.

Goldie's most important association was as a regular member of Jack Teagarden's last band (1959–63), working and recording with the great trombonist. After Teagarden's death in early 1964, Goldie became a studio musician (including being featured on some of Jackie Gleason's mood music records) and eventually settled in Miami. He worked steadily at hotels and clubs, recorded for his Jazz Forum label (cutting at least 11 albums during the 1970s and showing off both his virtuosity and his love for prebop jazz). Unfortunately Don Goldie was quite depressed during his later years, and he ended up committing suicide when he was 65.

Recommended CDs: *And the Dangerous Jazz Band* (Jazzology 135)

LPs to Search For: *Brilliant!* (Argo 4010), *Trumpet Caliente* (Argo 708), *Don Goldie's Jazz Express* (Jazzology 135)

NAT GONELLA
• • • • • • • • • • • •

b. Mar. 7, 1908, London, England, d. Aug. 6, 1998, Gosport, Hampshire, England

I n the 1930s Nat Gonella was thought of as the "Louis Armstrong of England." An excellent soloist who was most influenced by Satch, Gonella also sang in a jivey manner more reminiscent of Wingy Manone and, to a lesser extent, Louis Prima. He began playing trumpet when he was nine and early on played theaters with Archie Pitt's Busby Boys for four years. He tripled on trumpet, clarinet, and violin with Bob Dryden's Louisville Band (1928–29), and then, after a stint with Archie Alexander in 1929, Gonella hit the big time as a featured soloist with Billy Cotton, playing trumpet from that point on exclusively. Gonella was in great demand with British dance bands and jazz groups throughout the '30s and was considered one of Europe's finest jazz musicians. Among the many ensembles that he played with were the orchestras of Cotton (1929–33), Roy Fox (1931–32), Ray Noble (on and off during 1931–34), and Lew Stone (1932–35). Because his rendition of "Georgia on My Mind" was quite popular, Gonella's own bands (which started as a combo out of the Stone orchestra) were called the Georgians.

Nat Gonella was at the height of his popularity during 1934–39, when he was a major star in England, recording frequently and appearing regularly on the radio. Gonella visited the United States in 1939 (recording with John Kirby's Sextet) but opted to return to England; his life might have turned out quite different had he stayed in the United States. He joined the Army in August 1941 and played in service bands up until the summer of 1945. After World War II, Gonella worked less frequently and largely stopped recording, not leading any dates during 1947–57. Stints leading a big band and trying to play bebop did not work out well, so he became a solo act in variety shows. In 1959 Gonella formed the New Georgia Jazz Band, and he was active on a part-time basis in the 1960s and '70s, regaining some of his former popularity during the early '60s trad boom.

After a final outburst of activity (including cutting three final albums in 1975), Gonella stopped playing trumpet due to his health. He still occasionally sang in public, including on his 90th birthday in 1998. A biography on Nat Gonella (*Georgia on My Mind* by Ron Brown and Cyril Brown) was published in 1985. Unfortunately, his recordings have yet to be made available on CD in the United States, but Nat Gonella was one of the jazz giants of the 1930s.

LPs to Search For: *Mister Rhythm Man* (EMI 26 0188), *Crazy Valves* (ASV 5055), *Yeah Man* (Harlequin 3019), *How'm I Doin'?* (Old Bean 011)

Film Appearances: *Sing As You Swing* (1937)

DENNIS GONZALEZ

● ● ● ● ● ● ● ● ● ● ● ● ● ● ●

b. 1954, Abilene, TX

Dallas, Texas, may not be known as one of the main centers of avant-garde jazz, but Dennis Gonzalez has done his best to document the surprisingly viable local scene. After having some early piano lessons, Gonzalez started playing trumpet in sixth grade. A short time after discovering jazz, he was attracted to the avant-garde. Moving to Dallas in 1977, Gonzalez started his Daagnim label (short for Dallas Association for Avant-Garde and Neo-Impressionist Music), and between 1978 and 1987 he recorded frequently, playing not only trumpet but bass clarinet, soprano, alto, flute, bass sax, melodica, bass, drums, musette, tabla, and zither! Dennis Gonzalez has also recorded as a leader for Silkheart, Music & Arts, and the European label Konnex.

Recommended CDs: *Stefan* (Silkheart 101), *Namesake* (Silkheart 106), *Catechism* (Music & Arts 913), *Debenge-Debenge* (Silkheart 112), *The Earth and the Heart* (Music & Arts 960)

LPs to Search For: with Charles Brackeen: *Bannar* (Silkheart 105), *Worshippers Come Nigh* (Silkheart 111)

JERRY GONZALEZ

••••••••••••••••••

b. June 5, 1949, Bronx, NY

Jerry Gonzalez, with his Fort Apache Band, has been an innovative force in moving Afro-Cuban jazz beyond bebop to a more advanced but no less stirring style. Gonzalez's father sang in Latin bands, his uncle played guitar, and his younger brother, Andy Gonzalez, is a superior bassist who has often played in his groups.

Gonzalez began on trumpet when he was 12, and from nearly the start he doubled on conga, being inspired by Mongo Santamaria. Throughout his career he has alternated between straightahead and Latin-oriented jazz. Gonzalez co-led the Latin Jazz Quintet in 1964 with brother Andy, studied at New York City's Music and Art High School (1964–67), and attended the New York College of Music, where he learned from and befriended Kenny Dorham. Among his early gigs was working with Pupi Legarreta, Monguito Santamaria (Mongo's son), the Beach Boys, and Dizzy Gillespie, recording the *Portrait of Jenny* album (on conga) with the great trumpeter in 1970.

In the 1970s, Gonzalez came into his own, working with Eddie Palmieri for four years, was a founding member of Manny Oquendo's Conjunto Libre, and freelanced, playing with Clifford Thornton's Grupo Experimental, Machito, Ray Barretto, Tito Puente, Paquito D'Rivera, Tony Williams, Archie Shepp, Joe Chambers, Woody Shaw, and Kirk Lightsey, among others.

Gonzalez (whose trumpet style is influenced by Miles Davis and Dizzy Gillespie) began leading his own group in 1980, and within two years it was known as the Fort Apache Band, a pacesetting ensemble that updates the Cubop tradition by mixing Latin rhythms with post-bebop jazz solos. Sidemen through the years have included Andy Gonzales, trombonist Steve Turre, saxophonists Sonny Fortune, Carter Jefferson, John Stubblefield, and Joe Ford, and pianists Larry Willis and Kenny Kirkland. In addition, the versatile and always exciting Jerry Gonzalez has appeared in many other settings, including with Tito Puente, Chico O'Farrill, McCoy Tyner, Franco Ambrosetti, Bob Belden, Don Byron, and James Williams, being a major asset in both jazz and Latin settings.

Recommended CDs: *Rumba Para Monk* (Sunnyside 1036), *Obtala* (Enja 5095), *Earthdance* (Sunnyside 1050), *Pensativo* (Milestone 9242), *Fire Dance* (Milestone 9258)

Film Appearances: *Calle 54* (2000)

HENRY GOODWIN

••••••••••••••••••

b. Jan. 2, 1910, Columbia, SC, d. July 2, 1979, New York, NY

Henry Goodwin was a fine journeyman trumpeter and a subtle player who, although never becoming famous, was considered quite reliable in trad and swing settings. Goodwin played drums and tuba early on before settling on trumpet. When he was only 15, he traveled to Europe with the Claude Hopkins Orchestra (which was accompanying Josephine Baker), becoming good friends with Sidney Bechet. He also visited Argentina with a group led by Paul Wyer. Back in New York, Goodwin in the late 1920s worked regularly, including with Elmer Snowden and Cliff Jackson's Krazy Kats (with whom he recorded in 1930). He returned to Europe with Lucky Millinder in 1933 and in the United States played with the big bands of Willie Bryant, Charlie Johnson, Cab Calloway (1936), and Edgar Hayes 1937–40).

Switching to smaller groups for the remainder of his career, Goodwin was heard with Sidney Bechet in 1940–41 (including recording a version of Duke Ellington's "The Mooche" that Duke called his favorite), Cecil Scott, Art Hodes, Mezz Mezzrow (with whom he visited Paris in 1948), Bob Wilber (1948–49), Jimmy Archey (1950–52), and (in San Francisco) Earl Hines (1956). Henry Goodwin (who never had the opportunity to lead his own record date) stayed active into the 1960s, playing in Dixieland bands in the New York area.

Recommended CDs: with Jimmy Archey: *Dr. Jazz Series, Vol. 4* (Storyville 6044), *Dr. Jazz Series, Vol. 13* (Storyville 6058), with Sidney Bechet: *1940–1941* (Classics 638), with Alberta Hunter: *Songs We Taught Your Mother* (Original Blues Classics 520)

JIM GOODWIN
• • • • • • • • • • • •

b. Mar. 16, 1944, Portland, OR

An excellent trad/Dixieland cornetist who also occasionally plays piano, Jim Goodwin started his professional career playing in Portland with Monte Ballou's Castle Jazz Band. In 1969 he moved to San Francisco, where he worked regularly for a few years at the New Orleans room of the Fairmont Hotel, often with pianist Ray Skjelbred. In 1974 Goodwin toured Europe with Max Collie's Rhythm Aces. Since then he has visited and played in Holland, Belgium, and throughout Europe on a nearly yearly basis. In 1985 Jim Goodwin moved back to Portland, where he plays locally, often visiting California to perform at classic jazz festivals. Although his recordings are few and far between, they are of consistently high quality, usually featuring his cornet on standards from the 1930s.

Recommended CDs: with Dave Frishberg: *Double Play* (Arbors 19118)

LPs to Search For: *Jim Goodwin and Friends* (Berkeley Rhythm 4), *Taking a Chance* (Rhythm Masters 101)

JOE GORDON
• • • • • • • • • • • •

b. May 15, 1928, Boston, MA, d. Nov. 4, 1963, Santa Monica, CA

A talented bop soloist whose life was cut short, Joe Gordon realized some of his great potential during his 35 years. He studied at the New England Conservatory and worked in Boston in 1947 with the Sabby Lewis band. During 1952–55 Gordon played with Georgie Auld, Lionel Hampton, and Art Blakey (a pre-Jazz Messengers group in 1954) and with Charlie Parker whenever Bird visited Boston.

Gordon was part of the Dizzy Gillespie big band in 1956, getting the opening solo on "A Night in Tunisia" (which would be Lee Morgan's spot the following year). The trumpeter gigged with Horace Silver and in Boston with Herb Pomeroy's big band (1957–58). After moving to Los Angeles, Gordon worked with many of the top players in town, including Harold Land, Dexter Gordon, Benny Carter, Barney Kessel, and Shelly Manne's Quintet (1958–60). He recorded with those musicians plus Thelonious Monk, Helen Humes, and Charlie Mariano, leading sessions for Emarcy (1954) and Contemporary (1961). But tragically it all came to an end in 1963 when Joe Gordon died in a fire.

Recommended CDs: *Looking Good* (Original Jazz Classics 1934), with Shelly Manne: *At the Blackhawk, Vols. 1–5* (Original Jazz Classics 656, 657, 658, 659 and 660)

LPs to Search For: *Introducing Joe Gordon* (Emarcy 36025)

DUSKO GOYKOVICH
• • • • • • • • • • • • • • • • •

b. Oct. 14, 1931, Jajce, Yugoslavia

One of the finest jazz trumpeters to emerge from Eastern Europe, Dusko Goykovich (who was born Dusan Gojkovic) is a fluent hard bop soloist. Goykovich studied at the Academy of Music in Belgrade (1948–53), worked with the Radio Belgrade Big Band (1951–55) and played in Germany with the Max Greger big band and Kurt Edelhagen's radio orchestra (1957–60). He visited the United States for the first time when he was chosen as a member of Marshall Brown's International Youth Band, appearing at the 1958 Newport Jazz Festival. Goykovich moved to the United States to attend Berklee (1961–63) and toured with the big bands of Maynard Ferguson (1963–64) and Woody Herman (1964–66), getting some solo space with Herman.

In 1966 Goykovich returned to Germany, where he has since worked with Sal Nistico (co-leading the International Jazz Quintet), Mal Waldron, Philly Joe Jones, the Kenny Clarke-Francy Boland big band (1968–73), Slide Hampton, and his own combos. Dusko Goykovich, an excellent straightahead soloist, also shows the influence of Yugoslavian folk music in some of his music.

Recommended CDs: *Soul Connection* (Enja 8044), *Bebop City* (Enja 9015)

LPs to Search For: *After Hours* (Enja 2020), *Celebration* (Hot House 1003), with Woody Herman: *Woody's Whistle* (Columbia 2436)

CONRAD GOZZO
• • • • • • • • • • • • • •

b. Feb. 6, 1922, New Britain, CT, d. Oct. 8, 1964, Burbank, CA

One of the top lead trumpeters and a legendary studio musician, the highly rated Conrad Gozzo soloed only on an occasional basis, although he came through whenever he had an opportunity. Gozzo originally studied with his father, a trumpet teacher. During 1938–42 he played with the big bands of Isham Jones (1938), Tommy Reynolds, Red Norvo, Johnny "Scat" Davis, Bob Chester, Claude Thornhill (1941–42), and Benny Goodman. During 1942–45, Gozzo was in the Navy, where he had an opportunity to play with Artie Shaw's service band.

After a second short period with Goodman, Gozzo was a member of Woody Herman's First Herd during 1945–46 (his solo on "Stars Fell on Alabama" was notable), and he had stints with the orchestras of Boyd Raeburn and Tex Beneke. In each of these bands, Gozzo took few solos, but his warm sound, impressive range, and impeccable sight-reading abilities were considered major assets. Just 25 in 1947, Gozzo settled in Los Angeles and became a very busy studio musician. He played on Bob Crosby's radio series (1947–51), on many records during the next 17 years (including with Woody Herman and Shorty Rogers), and for television and film soundtracks. Conrad Gozzo's death from a heart attack at the age of 42 was a major shock. The now-legendary trumpeter led only one record album during his career, a hard-to-find LP for Victor that features him with a big band, a sextet, and with strings.

Recommended CDs: with Cy Touff: *His Octet and Quintet* (Pacific Jazz 93162)

LPs to Search For: *Gozz the Great* (Victor 1124)

JOE GRANSDEN
• • • • • • • • • • • • • •

b. 1971, Yonkers, NY

On his debut CD as a leader, Joe Gransden purposely pays tribute to Chet Baker, both in his trumpet solos and especially in his sound-alike vocals. Gransden grew up in Buffalo and graduated from Georgia State with a degree in jazz performance. He toured with the Tommy Dorsey and Glenn Miller ghost orchestras, worked with a variety of pop acts, spent two years living in New York, and played in Atlanta with the Tempest Little Big Band. He began singing in 1996, and Joe Gransden (whose trumpet style, although in the Baker tradition, shows traces of originality) consistently displays strong potential as a jazz performer.

Recommended CDs: *I Waited for You* (Brass Menagerie 002)

CHRIS GRIFFIN
• • • • • • • • • • • • • •

b. Oct. 31, 1915, Binghamton, NY

Chris Griffin gained his greatest fame as the "other" trumpeter with Benny Goodman's 1937–38 big band, playing in an unbeatable trumpet section with Harry James and Ziggy Elman. A solid soloist and an excellent section player, Griffin was rarely featured with Goodman, but he would always be associated with the King of Swing.

Griffin began playing trumpet when he was 12, and within three years he was working locally with a dance hall band. His early years included a stint with Scott Fisher, playing and recording with Charlie Barnet (off and on during 1933–35), a summer with Rudy Vallee's band, gigging with Joe Haymes, and a short period in the studios with CBS. On John Hammond's recommendation, Griffin became a member of Benny Goodman's orchestra in May 1936, staying until August 1939. On January 12, 1938, he appeared with the pacesetting orchestra at their famous Carnegie Hall Concert (where he took a solo on "Blue Room"). Griffin was a valuable part of the trumpet section, which was praised by Duke Ellington as the best he had ever heard.

The reason Chris Griffin did not become better known (like Harry James and Ziggy Elman) is that, after leaving Goodman in 1939, he became a member of the CBS staff and played in the studios for over 30 years. Other than being briefly with Jimmy Dorsey in 1940 and once in a while joining Goodman in his occasional big bands, Griffin spent most of his career playing in anonymous settings. During 1966–70 he ran a trumpet school with Pee Wee Erwin, and in the 1970s and '80s he gigged locally with small jazz groups.

As a leader, Chris Griffin's only dates resulted in four selections that were released as V-Discs in 1947. In addition to his sessions with Goodman, he recorded in the 1930s with Barnet, Mildred Bailey (1935), the Little Ramblers (1935), Teddy Wilson (1936), Miff Mole (1937), and the Raymond Scott Big Band (1939). But, although making a good living and gaining the respect of his peers, Chris Griffin never really lived up to his potential in jazz.

Recommended Reading: *Jazz Gentry* by Warren Vache Sr. (Scarecrow Press, 1999), *Swing Legacy* by Chip Deffaa (Scarecrow Press, 1989)

FRANK GUARENTE

• • • • • • • • • • • • • • • • •

b. Oct. 5, 1893, Montelmilleto, Italy, d. July 21, 1942, New York, NY

Frank Guarente was a very significant jazz trumpeter during the first half of the 1920s but slipped into obscurity after that period. As the leader of the Georgians, a sextet/septet taken out of Paul Specht's larger dance orchestra, Guarente recorded 42 recordings during 1922–24 that rank with the top jazz of the period, even though the Georgians have been largely left out of the jazz history books. Their music swings, and the arranged ensembles of Guarente and pianist Arthur Schutt set up the solos quite well, unlike on most other recordings of the era, which either have jammed ensembles or very wooden writing.

Guarente began playing trumpet while in his native Italy. He moved to the United States in 1910 to join his brother in Allentown, Pennsylvania. After playing locally, he moved in 1914 to New Orleans, where he traded lessons with King Oliver, teaching Oliver classical technique while King gave Guarente pointers on hot jazz playing. In 1916 he played in Texas and with the Alabama Five before serving in the Army during World War I. After additional time spent in Texas in 1919 and with Charlie Kerr's band in Philadelphia, Guarente joined Paul Specht's orchestra in 1921. During the next three years he directed the Georgians and recorded regularly. On the evidence of the records, Frank Guarente was one of the finest jazz trumpeters of the period (both in short solos and in leading ensembles) along with being a talented arranger.

Guarente, who had already visited Europe twice (including with Specht for three months in 1923), spent most of the four years after May 1924 playing overseas. He led the New Georgians (which for a time was a big success), headed a record date in Zurich in 1926, was with Carroll Gibbon's Savoy Orpheans, and freelanced. But when Guarente returned to the United States in 1928 and rejoined Specht for two years, his playing was considered out of date, since jazz's evolution had sped up during his absence. Guarente was no longer a pacesetter. And although he worked steadily due to his technical skills (leading a final commercial date in 1928), it was as an anonymous studio player. Guarente remained active (working with Victor Young's orchestra during 1930–36) on radio as a section trumpeter, until illness forced him to give up playing altogether in 1941.

Few of his contemporaries were probably at all aware of Frank Guarente's importance as one of jazz's first great trumpeters on record.

Recommended CD: *The Georgians 1922–23* (Retrieval 79003)

ROGER GUERIN

b. Jan. 9, 1926, Saarebrucken, France

A bop trumpeter also comfortable in swing settings, Roger Guerin was one of France's top trumpeters for many years, and he has shared the stage with many major American jazz musicians. Guerin originally played violin for eight years before studying trumpet at the Conservatoire de Paris. Guerin worked with Aime Barelli (1947–48), Rex Stewart (1948), Kenny Clarke (1949), Charlie Parker (1950), Don Byas, James Moody (1951), Django Reinhardt (1951–53), Bobby Jaspar (starting in 1953), Peanuts Holland (1955), Claude Bolling, and Michel Legrand (1956–57), among his most important associations. He played with Martial Solal off and on starting in 1956 and into the 1980s, and also appeared on dates led by Andre Hodeir. Guerin was in the International Youth Band in 1958 (although he was already 32), co-led a record date with Benny Golson in 1958, and was a member of Quincy Jones' touring orchestra in 1960.

Guerin has also appeared as a sideman in France with the likes of Duke Ellington (1960), Dizzy Gillespie (1962), Woody Shaw, the Kenny Clarke-Francy Boland big band, Slide Hampton (1969–70), John Lewis, Gunther Schuller, and Bill Coleman (1980), among many others. Roger Guerin, who led his own big band in the 1970s, led only one full album in his career, but he has been highly rated for decades, as one can tell from his stellar list of associations!

Recommended CDs: *Des Chansons de Gershwin* (Oreili 889)

LPs to Search For: with Claude Bolling: *Nuance* (DRG 5201), with Benny Golson: *Benny Golson in Paris* (Swing 8418), with Django Reinhardt: *Brussels and Paris* (DRG 8473)

RUSSELL GUNN

b. Oct. 20, 1971, Chicago, IL

R ussell Gunn is a very unusual jazz trumpeter, in that his first love was actually rap and he has occasionally played in hip-hop settings. Gunn grew up in East St. Louis, Illinois, taking up the trumpet when he was ten. He made a deal with himself at that time that if he could not make it as a rapper by the time he was 16, he would pursue jazz. Although he performed at talent shows, Gunn ended up making the switch. In 1989 he appeared with his award-winning high school jazz band at the Montreux and North Sea Jazz festivals, and after graduation he studied at Jackson State University in Mississippi.

Gunn moved to New York in 1994 at the urging of altoist Oliver Lake, playing with Wynton Marsalis and the Lincoln Center Jazz Orchestra on their Blood on the Fields tour. Gunn, who became a regular member of the LCJO, has also worked with the Jimmy Heath big band, Branford Marsalis' Buckshot LaFonque (1995–96), Marcus Roberts, Roy Hargrove, James Moody, John Hicks, and Oliver Lake, plus some R&B bands—quite a bit of variety! Russell Gunn's future activity should be well worth following closely.

Recommended CDs: *Gunn Fu* (High Note 7003), *Love Requiem* (High Note 7020), *Ethnomusicology, Vol. 1* (Atlantic 83165), *Smokin' Gunn* (High Note 7056), with Gregory Tardy: *Serendipity* (Impulse 256)

JOE GUY

· · · · · · · · ·

b. Sept. 20, 1920, Birmingham, AL, d. ca. 1962, New York, NY, or Birmingham, AL

Joe Guy had potential that he never realized due to drug abuse. He grew up in New York and started his career by playing for a short time with the big bands of Fats Waller and Teddy Hill in the late 1930s. As a member of the Coleman Hawkins Orchestra (1939–40), Guy had occasional solos that showed off the influence of Roy Eldridge while being forward thinking. Guy was with Charlie Barnet briefly in 1941 and then became a regular at Minton's Playhouse, working as a member of the after-hours house band that also included Thelonious Monk, bassist Nick Fenton, and Kenny Clarke.

Guy appears on many of the live recordings captured by Jerry Newman during 1941–42 (including dates with Charlie Christian, Hot Lips Page, Don Byas, and Roy Eldridge), sounding enthusiastic but erratic, constantly overextending himself. Clearly, by that time Guy had heard Dizzy Gillespie at similar sessions and was doing his best to incorporate Dizzy's ideas into his own emerging style. Unfortunately, though, he never got beyond the awkward stage.

Guy's best moment on record was his solo on the Cootie Williams Orchestra's recording of Thelonious Monk's "Epistrophy" in 1942, one of the first bebop records. Guy became Billie Holiday's boyfriend, but they were very bad for each other, becoming heroin addicts during this period. Guy played with Jazz at the Philharmonic on a few occasions during 1945–46 (including on a very good Lady Day session) but in 1947 was busted for possession of heroin. After a short jail sentence, Guy freelanced in low-profile jobs and in 1950 permanently dropped out of music. By the time Joe Guy died in 1962, he was long forgotten.

Recommended CDs: with Billie Holiday: *Jazz at the Philharmonic* (Verve 314 521 642), with Cootie Williams: *1941–1944* (Classics)

LPs to Search For: with Charlie Christian: *Charlie Christian* (Everest 219), with Coleman Hawkins: *1940* (Alamac 2417)

BOBBY HACKETT

. . . .

b. Jan. 31, 1915, Providence, RI, d. June 7, 1976, Chatham, MA

Bobby Hackett was a lyrical cornetist with a soft sound and a melodic swing style who was also a subtle improviser. He rarely attempted to hit a high note and, like pianist Teddy Wilson, never seemed to hit a wrong one either. Although often heard in Dixieland settings, his cool approach was an early inspiration for Miles Davis, particularly his famous solo on a 1938 version of "Embraceable You."

Hackett originally played cornet, guitar, and violin. He dropped the violin by the time he hit 20 but stayed on rhythm guitar until near the end of the swing era. At 14 he dropped out of school to play music, mostly guitar, banjo, and violin at that point. Hackett led a band in Boston by 1936 and, after moving to New York, he worked with society orchestras and the freewheeling combos of Joe Marsala and Red McKenzie. For a time Hackett was called "the new Bix" due to the similarity in his tone at that early stage to Bix Beiderbecke's, but actually his main trumpet hero was always Louis Armstrong. He guested at Benny Goodman's Carnegie Hall concert in 1938, playing Bix's solo to "I'm Comin' Virginia." His playing on several Eddie Condon recording dates (including one resulting in "Embraceable You") gained him plenty of notice, and he had two recording dates of his own in 1938. In 1939 Hackett led a big band, but it soon failed. To get out of debt he played with the sweet orchestra of Horace Heidt during 1939–40. After a second Bobby Hackett big band quickly flopped, he became a member of the Glenn Miller Orchestra (July 1941–September 1942), often playing rhythm guitar but taking a famous cornet chorus on "A String of Pearls." Hackett was also with the Casa Loma Orchestra from October 1944 to September 1946.

Bobby Hackett spent most of the rest of his career playing in Dixieland bands, usually leading his own combo. He also did studio work and had notable sideman engagements, including with Louis Armstrong (Satch's famous 1947 Town Hall Concert), Eddie Condon, Jack Teagarden, Benny Goodman (1962–63), and the Newport All-Stars. Hackett appeared on many background-music albums of the 1950s and '60s (including some led by Jackie Gleason), due to the mellow sound of his horn. Hackett's 1956–57 band with the reeds of Bob Wilber and pianist-arranger Dick Cary was an intriguing venture that sought to create a more modern variety of trad jazz. Less interesting were an album of Hawaiian music (with steel guitar) and a pair of mood records that utilized two pipe organs! Hackett's best group of his later years was a quintet that he co-led with trombonist Vic Dickenson during 1968–70; at least nine records were eventually released (by Project 3, Phontastic, Fat Cat, Storyville, and especially Chiaroscuro).

Up until his death in 1976, Bobby Hackett retained a timeless style and a distinctive sound that appealed to a wide audience that reached beyond Dixieland and even the jazz world.

Recommended CDs: *1938–1940* (Classics 890), *Featuring Vic Dickenson at the Roosevelt Grill, Vols. 1–3* (Chiaroscuro 105, 138 and 161), with Eddie Condon: *Jammin' at Commodore* (Commodore 7007)

LPs to Search For: *Coast Concert* (Capitol 11795), *Creole Cookin'* (Verve 6698), *Strike Up the Band* (Flying Dutchman 0829)

Recommended Reading: *American Musicians II* by Whitney Balliett (Oxford University Press, 1996), *Jazz Talking* by Max Jones (Da Capo Press, 1987), *Lost Chords* by Richard M. Sudhalter (Oxford University Press, 1999)

Film Appearances: Hackett ghosts the trumpet solos for Fred Astaire in *Second Chorus* (1940),

Videos to Get: *Jazz Festival Vol. 1* (1962; Storyville 6073), *Jazz Festival Vol. 2* (1962; Storyville 6074)

TIM HAGANS

• • • • • • • • • • • •

b. Aug. 19, 1954, Dayton, OH

Although typically thought of as a hard bop player in the style of Freddie Hubbard and Lee Morgan, Tim Hagans has gone out of his way to stretch himself, exploring more adventurous styles of jazz in his recent projects. After attending Bowling Green State University

Although essentially a hard bop player, Tim Hagans is always willing to stretch himself into other musical areas.

(1972–74), Hagans was a member of Stan Kenton's orchestra (1974–77). Six weeks with Woody Herman in 1977 preceded time spent living in Sweden (1977–81), during which he played with Thad Jones, Ernie Wilkins, Sahib Shihab, Dexter Gordon, Kenny Drew, Horace Parlan, and radio bands (including the Danish Radio Orchestra). Upon his return to the United States, Hagans at first moved to Cincinnati, playing with the Blue Wisp big band, making his recording debut as a leader in 1983, and teaching at the University of Cincinnati. The trumpeter then spent 1984–87 in Boston, where he worked with Jimmy Mosher, Bert Seager, and Orange Then Blue, in addition to teaching at Berklee.

Since moving to New York in 1987, Hagans has been associated with the Mel Lewis Orchestra, Joe Lovano, Fred Hersch, George Russell, Bob Belden, Bob Mintzer, Gil Evans, Maria Schneider, the Yellowjackets, Steps Ahead, and seemingly countless other musicians in addition to his own groups. Tim Hagans has recorded several excellent sets for Blue Note, including a 1998 tribute to Freddie Hubbard with fellow trumpeter Marcus Printup.

Recommended CDs: *No Words* (Blue Note 89680), *Audible Architechture* (Blue Note 31808), *Hubsongs* (Blue Note 59509), *Future North* (Doubletime 140), *Cutting Edge* (Doubletime 141), with Bob Belden: *Treasure Island* (Sunnyside 1041), *Tapestry* (Blue Note 57891), with Joe Lovano: *Universal Language* (Blue Note 99830)

LP to Search For: *From the Neck Down* (Mopro 105)

PAT HALCOX

• • • • • • • • • • •

b. Mar. 18, 1930, London, England

Baritonist Harry Carney was famous for being with Duke Ellington's orchestra for a seemingly endless period of time: 49 years. Trumpeter Pat Halcox at this writing has been with Chris Barber's band for 47 years and counting!

Halcox is a solid trad trumpeter, flexible enough to play Barber's eclectic mixture of Dixieland, mainstream swing, and Chicago blues. He started piano lessons when he was three, at 17 switched to trombone, and, while serving in the Royal Air Force three years later, switched to cornet (later trumpet). As a part-time player, Halcox was a member of the Brent Valley Jazz Band and the Albermarle Jazz Band during 1950–54. "I decided in 1954 to try to make a living playing music; I'm still trying!"

In 1954 Halcox replaced Ken Colyer with trombonist Chris Barber's group, an association that continues to this day. While with Barber, Halcox has shared the bandstand with the likes of Muddy Waters, Edmond Hall, Louis Jordan, Trummy Young, Russell Procope, and other guests. Halcox has also had the opportunity to record with pianists Don Ewell and Art Hodes, although his only chances to record as a leader resulted in just a few titles for Columbia in 1960, a Plan Life album in 1980, and a Jazzology CD in 1989. Throughout his entire career, Pat Halcox has been able to play the music he most enjoys, no minor accomplishment!

Recommended CDs: *There's Yes! Yes! Yes! In Your Eyes* (Jazzology 186), with Chris Barber: *Original Copenhagen Concert* (Storyville 5527), *In Budapest* (Storyville 408), *Live in East Berlin* (Black Lion 760502), *Copulatin' Jazz* (Great Southern 11025)

BARRY LEE HALL

Barry (also frequently spelled Barrie) Lee Hall was the last in a prestigious line of plunger mute specialists featured with Duke Ellington's orchestra. Following in the footsteps of Bubber Miley, Cootie Williams, and Ray Nance, Hall joined Ellington in 1973, just in time for Duke's final year, which included a tour of Europe and the Third Sacred Concert. After Ellington's death, Hall stayed on in the part-time Mercer Ellington band, keeping the plunger mute tradition alive into the late 1980s. Since then he has recorded with Sebastian Whittaker's small group and with the Louie Bellson big band. Still, if Barry Lee Hall (who was almost too late) had been born a decade earlier, chances are that he would have gained much more fame.

Recommended CDs: with Louie Bellson: *Black, Brown & Beige* (Music Masters 65096), with Duke Ellington: *In Sweden 1973* (Caprice 21599), with Mercer Ellington: *Hot and Bothered* (Doctor Jazz 5006), *Digital Duke* (GRP 9548), with Sebastian Whittaker: *Searchin' for the Truth* (Justice 202), *One for Bu!! (Justice 203)*

LPs to Search For: with Duke Ellington: *Eastbourne Performance* (RCA 1023), with Mercer Ellington: *Continuum* (Fantasy 5991)

JOHN "BUGS" HAMILTON

b. Mar. 8, 1911, St. Louis, MO, d. Aug. 15, 1947, St. Louis, MO

John Hamilton was a fine swing trumpeter most notable for his association with Fats Waller. Herman Autrey was Waller's regular trumpeter, but Hamilton sat next to Autrey in Waller's occasional big band in 1938, and, when Autrey departed in mid-1939, Hamilton was his replacement. A solid player, Hamilton had picked up experience early on with the bands of trombonist Billy Kato (1930–31), Chick Webb, and Kaiser Marshall, in addition to other lesser-name orchestras. He remained with Waller through 1942, although Autrey sometimes filled in. Hamilton appeared on many records with Waller, which ranged from classics such as "Your Feet's Too Big" and "Jitterbug Waltz" to such throwaways as "Oh Frenchy," "Little Curly Hair in a High Chair," "You're a Square from Delaware," "My Mommie Sent Me to the Store," "Hey, Stop Kissin' My Sister," "I'm Gonna Salt Away Some Sugar," "Abercrombie Had a Zombie," and "Come Down to Earth, My Angel!"

John Hamilton, who appeared on a 1940 session with Waller's protégé Una Mae Carlisle, played with violinist Eddie South in the summer of 1943 and then faded from the scene. He died at the age of 36 from tuberculosis.

Recommended CDs: with Fats Waller: *The Last Years 1940–43* (Bluebird 9883)

WILBUR HARDEN

b. 1925, Birmingham, AL, d. 1960s?

A mystery figure who disappeared from jazz altogether after 1960, Wilbur Harden was on some important recordings in the late 1950s, including several that featured John Coltrane. He began his career playing with the blues ensembles of Roy Brown (1950) and Ivory Joe Hunter. After serving in the Navy (where he had an opportunity to play in a band), Harden moved to Detroit, playing and recording with Yusef Lateef in 1957. Harden recorded frequently with John Coltrane in 1958 (for Savoy and Prestige) and was one of jazz's first flugelhornists, a mellow hard bop soloist who was a fine player.

However, illness (possibly mental) forced his retirement in 1959. Harden recorded a lone selection with trombonist Curtis Fuller in 1960 but became ill and was replaced on the record by Lee Morgan. An introvert who rarely played in clubs, Harden dropped completely out of sight at that point. Although producer Orrin Keepnews turned up a letter that Harden wrote in 1966, no further trace has ever been found of him. It seems likely that Wilbur Harden passed away sometime in the late 1960s.

Recommended CDs: *The Complete Savoy Sessions with John Coltrane* (Savoy Jazz 92858), with John Coltrane: *Standard Coltrane* (Original Jazz Classics 246), with Tommy Flanagan: *Plays the Music of Rodgers and Hammerstein* (Savoy 4429), with Yusef Lateef: *Other Sounds* (Original Jazz Classics 399), *The Sounds of Yusef* (Original Jazz Classics 917)

BILL HARDMAN

b. Apr. 6, 1933, Cleveland, OH, d. Dec. 6, 1990, Paris, France

An excellent hard bop trumpeter who never gained much attention, Bill Hardman had a quiet, lyrical style but was able to play with fire when inspired, always holding his own with better-known players.

Hardman played with pianist-arranger Tadd Dameron while still in high school and picked up experience with Tiny Bradshaw's R&B band (1953–55). He worked with altoist Jackie McLean (who presented him on a record that was titled *Jackie's Pal*) and Charles Mingus (1955–56 and later during 1969–72). The reliable Hardman became best known for his work with Art Blakey's Jazz Messengers, which took place during several periods, sometimes also filling in when the group was between trumpeters. He first worked with Blakey during 1956–58, was with the Horace Silver Quintet for a short time in 1958, and often played with altoist Lou Donaldson during 1959–66. Hardman returned to the Jazz Messengers during 1966–69, 1970, and 1975–76. He also had his own combos on an occasional basis, including a quintet that he co-led with tenor saxophonist Junior Cook from the late 1970s into the mid-'80s. The underrated but valuable Bill Hardman moved to Paris in 1988, two years before he passed away.

Recommended CDs: *What's Up* (Steeplechase 31254), with Art Blakey: *Reflections of Buhaina/ Featuring Bill Hardman* (Savoy 9879), with Jackie McLean: *Jackie's Pal* (Original Jazz Classics 1714)

LPs to Search For: *Home* (Muse 5152), *Politely* (Muse 5184), *Focus* (Muse 5259)

EMMETT HARDY

· · · · · · · · · · · · · · · ·

b. June 12, 1903, Gretna, New Orleans, LA, d. June 16, 1926, New Orleans, LA

Because he made no recordings and died so young, Emmett Hardy's entire reputation rests with the fact that he was considered an early influence on Bix Beiderbecke, although he was actually Bix's junior by a few months.

Hardy first played piano and guitar, switching to the cornet when he was 12. In 1917 he started gigging with Papa Laine's Band, and in the early 1920s he was a member of Brownlee's orchestra. Hardy left New Orleans in January 1921 as part of singer Bee Palmer's backup group, a unit that also included clarinetist Leon Roppolo. The band played in the Midwest, including Davenport, Iowa (Bix's hometown), and Peoria, Illinois, before breaking up. Hardy and Roppolo returned to Davenport, where they worked regularly as part of Carlisle Evans' group from February 13 to May 30. Beiderbecke heard Hardy often during this period, was very impressed by his soft, mellow tone, and often practiced with him at a time when Hardy was much more advanced than the slightly older Bix.

After a few out-of-town engagements in June 1921, Hardy left Evans' band and returned to New Orleans. Back home, Hardy led a group, freelanced, and then moved up to Chicago in late 1923 or early 1924 in order to join the New Orleans Rhythm Kings, which was hoping to expand to two cornets and three reeds. Unfortunately a dispute with the local Musicians' Union led him to return to New Orleans. Hardy soon contracted pulmonary tuberculosis, developed an infection from an appendectomy, and was inactive for a year before succumbing at age 23. Reportedly he played his cornet for the last time at a party on his 23rd birthday, four days before his death. Drummer Monk Hazel years later remembered that Beiderbecke wrote Emmett Hardy's mother a letter that said, "Emmett was the greatest musician I have ever heard. If ever I can come near your son's greatness, I'll die happy."

Recommended Reading: *Lost Chords* by Richard M. Sudhalter (Oxford University Press, 1999)

ROY HARGROVE

· · · · · · · · · · · · · · · ·

b. Oct. 16, 1969, Waco, TX

One of the finest trumpeters to emerge in the 1990s, Roy Hargrove may not have a huge range, but he makes the most of what he has and puts on exciting shows, revitalizing modern hard bop. Hargrove grew up in Dallas, Texas, where his early idols were Freddie Hubbard, Clifford Brown, and Lee Morgan. At Arts Magnet High School, he studied trumpet and met the older Wynton Marsalis, who helped him out quite a bit, letting him sit in with his band at the Caravan of Dreams Arts Center when he was 17, helping point the way. Hargrove played in Europe with altoist Frank Morgan during the summer of 1987 (when he was a senior in high school) and worked with Jack McDuff, Clifford Jordan, Art Blakey's big band, and Johnny Griffin after graduating in 1988. He went to Berklee during 1988–89 and attended the New School in 1990.

Hargrove, who was closely identified with the Young Lions movement when he rose to prominence (he has since grown beyond that tag), has led his own quintet since 1990. He began recording as a leader for RCA/Novus in 1989 (altoist Antonio Hart was in his early group), toured with Jazz Futures, recorded with Sonny Rollins, and had a short-lived big band in 1995. In 1996 he and his ensemble were invited by pianist Chucho Valdes to play at the Havana Jazz Festival. His 11 days in Havana resulted during 1996–97 in Hargrove's putting together and touring with Cristol, an Afro-Cuban ensemble that included such notables as Valdes, Gary Bartz, David Sanchez, and Frank Lacy among others.

Roy Hargrove, who also recorded with such top musicians as Jackie McLean, Steve Coleman, Helen Merrill, Ralph Moore, Ricky Ford, Sonny Rollins and T.S. Monk among others, leads one of the finest groups in jazz, a quintet with altoist Sherman Irby (who departed in early 2001), pianist Larry Willis, bassist Gerald Cannon, and drummer Willie Jones III.

Recommended CDs: *Diamond in the Rough* (Novus 3082), *Public Eye* (Novus 3113), *The Tokyo Sessions* (Novus 3164), *The Vibe* (Novus 3132), *Of Kindred Souls* (Novus 3154), *With the Tenors of Our Time* (Verve 314 523 019), *Family* (Verve 314 526 730), *Parker's Mood* (Verve 314 527 907), *Habana* (Verve 314 537 563)

Recommended Reading: *Jazz Profiles* by Reginald Carver and Lenny Bernstein (Billboard Books, 1998)

PHILIP HARPER
. . . .

b. May 10, 1965, Baltimore, MD

For a time it looked as if Philip Harper, one of the Harper Brothers (along with drummer Winard Harper, who is three years older), would be content to spend his career trying to fill the shoes of the late Lee Morgan, an impossible task. However, since the breakup of the Harper Brothers Band, he has continued to grow as an improviser, developing a more individual voice. Harper picked up early experience playing with Jimmy McGriff, Little Jimmy Scott, Jackie McLean (1983), and Art Blakey's Jazz Messengers (1987). He also recorded with Cecil Brooks III, Joe Chambers, and Errol Parker. The Harper Brothers lasted from 1988 to 1993 and symbolized the Young Lions movement, receiving a great deal of publicity but not really breaking any new ground musically.

Since then, Philip Harper has worked with the Mingus Big Band, led his own record dates, freelanced, and maintained a lower profile overall, developing into a more original player out of the tradition than he had been previously.

Recommended CDs: *Soulful Sin* (Muse 5505), *The Thirteenth Moon* (Muse 5520), with the Harper Brothers: *Harper Brothers* (Verve 314 837 033), *Remembrance* (Verve 314 841 723), *Artistry* (Verve 314 847 956), *You Can Hide Inside the Music* (Verve 314 518 820)

TOM HARRELL

* * * * * * * * * * * *

b. June 16, 1946, Urbana, IL

Throughout his career, Tom Harrell (one of the top trumpeters of the past 20 years) has bravely fought the illness of schizophrenia with heavy medication that allows him to play music but gives him the appearance of being largely dead on stage when his horn is not on his lips. So focused is Harrell on music while performing that he seems unaware of anything else.

Harrell began playing trumpet when he was eight and was performing with local groups in the San Francisco Bay area by the time he was 13. After graduating from Stanford University in 1969 with a degree in music composition, he played with Stan Kenton's orchestra (1969), Woody Herman's big band (1970–71), Azteca (1972), and the last important version of the Horace Silver Quintet (1973–77). In each situation, the musicians were both sympathetic toward Harrell's physical plight and impressed by his creativity.

A period of freelancing followed that included stints with the Sam Jones Big Band, the Lee Konitz Nonet (1979–81), George Russell, and the Mel Lewis Orchestra (1981) plus recordings with Konitz, Bill Evans (1979), Bob Brookmeyer, Lionel Hampton, and others. During 1983–89 Harrell was an important member of the Phil Woods Quintet, touring the world and making many recordings. Harrell recorded with altoist George Robert in 1987 and with Charlie Haden's Liberation Orchestra (with whom he also toured) the following year.

Since 1989, Harrell has led his own groups, including an occasional big band, for which he contributes most of the arrangements. Harrell has developed both as a cool-toned modern hard bop trumpet soloist and as a highly original arranger-composer. Tom Harrell's productivity (which includes leading record dates for Pinnacle, Blackhawk, Criss Cross, SteepleChase, Contemporary, Chesky, and RCA) would be very impressive even without his illness. Considering what he has to overcome on a daily basis, his career has been rather miraculous.

Recommended CDs: *Moon Alley* (Criss Cross 1018), *Stories* (Contemporary 14043), *Visions* (Contemporary 14063), *Sail Away* (Contemporary 14054), *Upswing* (Chesky 103), *Time's Mirror* (RCA 63524), *Labyrinth* (RCA 68512), *Art of Rhythm* (RCA 68924), with Phil Woods: *Bop Stew* (Concord Jazz 345), *Evolution* (Concord Jazz 361)

BENNY HARRIS

* * * * * * * * * * * * *

b. Apr. 23, 1919, New York, NY, d. Feb. 11, 1975, San Francisco, CA

Benny Harris, an open-minded trumpeter who made the transition from swing to bebop, had a rather brief playing career. Harris first played French horn, switching to trumpet at 18. He played with the Tiny Bradshaw Orchestra (1939) and was with the Earl Hines Orchestra twice: in 1941 and with the legendary unrecorded unit of 1943. Harris' prime period was 1944–45. He worked on New York's 52nd Street with quite a few small groups, including Benny Carter, Pete Brown, the John Kirby Sextet, Herbie Fields, Coleman Hawkins, Don Byas, and Thelonious Monk. Bailey recorded with Clyde Hart (December 1944) and Byas (1945), and was with Boyd Raeburn's orchestra during part of that period too.

However, after 1945 Harris (who never led his own record date) played much less often. He was a member of the 1949 Dizzy Gillespie big band and appeared on a record date with Charlie Parker in 1952. But after moving to California during the latter year, Benny Harris retired altogether from music. He is most notable overall for having composed "Ornithology" (building the "How High the Moon"-based tune off of a lick that he heard Charlie Parker play with Jay McShann's big band), "Crazeology," "Reets and I," and "Wahoo" (based on "Perdido").

Recommended CDs: with Don Byas: *Savoy Jam Party* (Savoy 2213)

DICKIE HAWDON

* * * * * * * * * * * * *

b. Aug. 27, 1927, Leeds, Yorkshire, England

Richard "Dickie" Hawdon was a flexible British trumpeter who along the way played with the top jazz musicians of his native land, whether their style was trad or hard bop. He started playing trumpet when he was 17 but not seriously until he had served in the Army and was already 21. Hawdon led the Yorkshire Jazz Band (1948–50), moved to London in 1951, and worked with Chris Barber (1951–52), the Christie Brothers' Stompers (1952–54), the Don Rendell 6 (1954–55), Tubby Hayes (1955–57), and John Dankworth (1957–62). Hawdon performed with Terry Lightfoot during much of the 1960s, began doubling on bass, and freelanced, including once again with Dankworth. Active into the 1980s, by then Dickie Hawdon was busy as a jazz educator. "I consider myself extremely fortunate that I was able to bridge the generation gap between New Orleans and bebop. Only people of a specific era can do that."

Recommended CDs: *Christie Brothers' Stompers* (Cadillac 2011), with John Dankworth: *Tribute to Chauncey* (Roulette 96556)

LPs to Search For: with Tubby Hayes: *After Lights Out* (Tempo 6)

ERSKINE HAWKINS

* * * * * * * * * * * *

b. July 26, 1914, Birmingham, AL, d. Nov. 11, 1993, Willingboro, NJ

Leader of one of the most exciting big bands of the swing era, Erskine Hawkins was billed as "the 20th century Gabriel" due to his impressive technique and wide range. Although criticized by some writers for his flamboyant and often bombastic solos, Hawkins was a fine jazz player, and he went out of his way to feature his sidemen.

Hawkins began playing drums when he was seven, switched to trombone after a few years, and then finally settled on the trumpet when he was 13. After high school, he played with the band at the State Teachers' College (known as the 'Bama Street Collegians) in Montgomery, Alabama, and was soon appointed its leader. In 1934 the musicians became pros and split permanently from the college. By 1938 the ensemble had become known as the Erskine Hawkins Orchestra.

The band featured such key soloists as its leader, trumpeter Dud Bascomb (who took many of the famous if uncredited middle-register solos on their records), Paul Bascomb and/ or Julian Dash on tenors, pianist Avery Parrish (who made "After Hours" famous), and baritonist Haywood Henry; altoist Bobby Smith became a major asset by the mid-1940s. The band's use of dynamics, danceable tempos, and fairly basic arrangements, along with its skill at playing blues and driving swing, made the Hawkins Orchestra very popular during the swing era, leading to a nearly three-year stint at the Savoy Ballroom. Hawkins' hits included "After Hours" (during which its leader played subtle drums), the original version of "Tuxedo Junction" (predating the Glenn Miller version), and "Tippin' In" (1945).

Hawkins was able to keep his big band together into the early 1950s, sometimes leaning a bit towards R&B and showing the influence of bebop but retaining his distinctive group's sound. He finally cut down to a combo in the mid-'50s, and his own playing did not advance much beyond the 1930s, but Hawkins continued working as often as he wanted into the 1970s, having a very successful recorded reunion (documented by the Stang label) with his alumni in 1971. Erskine Hawkins recorded frequently during his prime years for Vocalion (1936–38), Bluebird (1938–42), Victor (1945–50), Coral (1950–51), and King (1951–53) plus later albums for Decca (1960), Imperial (1962), and Stang. The swing-era recordings of Erskine Hawkins (which still sound fresh and swinging today) are being reissued complete and in chronological order by the European Classics label.

Recommended CDs: *1936–1938* (Classics 653), *1938–1939* (Classics 667), *1939–1940* (Classics 678), *1940–1941* (Classics 701), *1941–1945* (Classics 868), *1946–1947* (Classics 1008)

LPs to Search For: *Live at Club Soul Sound* (Chess 9141)

Recommended Reading: *In the Mainstream* by Chip Deffaa (Scarecrow Press, 1992)

Film Appearances: *Deviled Hams* (1937), a film short

GRAHAM HAYNES
● ● ● ● ● ● ● ● ● ● ● ● ● ● ●

b. Sept. 16, 1960, Brooklyn, NY

The son of the great drummer Roy Haynes, Graham Haynes has carved out his own musical personality during his career. He started playing trumpet when he was 12, later switching to cornet. Haynes studied at Queens College (1979–81) and first worked professionally with Jaki Byard's Apollo Stompers (1978–83). Very open to the modern R&B music of his era, Haynes played with a variety of local funk bands, Michael Carvin (1981–82), and Steve Coleman's groups (1980–88), including the Five Elements. Haynes first recorded with Coleman in 1985 and became closely identified with the M-Base free funk idiom. The trumpeter freelanced in New York in the 1980s, performing with many of the top avant-garde and M-Base players, including the David Murray Big Band, Cassandra Wilson, Abbey Lincoln, Ralph Peterson, and George Russell. He also led No Image, a funky septet that recorded one album for Muse before breaking up in 1991.

Graham Haynes spent the 1991–93 period living in Paris, exploring world music. He has since returned to the United States, recorded as a leader for Muse, Antilles, Verve, and Knitting Factory Works, and participated on recordings with Rodney Kendrick, Arcana, Ed Blackwell, Uri Caine, Lonnie Plaxico, Bobby Previte, and his father, among many others.

Recommended CDs: *Griot's Footsteps* (Antilles 314 523 262), *Tones for the 21st Century* (Verve 314 537 692), *BPM* (Knitting Factory Works 270), with Ralph Peterson: *Art* (Blue Note 27645)

LPs to Search For: *What Time It Be* (Muse 5402)

DUKE HEITGER

• • • • • • • • • • • •

b. May 10, 1968, Toledo, OH

A hot cornetist and trumpeter influenced by Bunny Berigan, Raymond "Duke" Heitger has been a fixture with Banu Gibson's New Orleans band and made a major contribution to Retro swing with the Squirrel Nut Zippers.

Duke's father, Ray Heitger (who plays clarinet and soprano) founded the Cakewalkin' Jass Band in 1968, the year of his son's birth. Duke played a bit of drums, piano, and clarinet before settling on the cornet when he was eight. "An important influence was a good friend of mine, Jon-Erik Kellso, whom I heard when he was 16 and I was 12. That single evening changed my view of jazz, and from then on I wanted to play it seriously." Heitger earned a master's degree in geology from the University of New Orleans ("for the fun of it") and studied music at the University of Toledo. He worked on and off with the Cakewalkin' Jass Band during 1980–91 (starting when he was 12), but his career really got going when he moved to New Orleans in 1991.

Since then, Heitger has played with Jacques Gauthe's Creole Rice Jazz Band (1991–93), John Gill's Dixie Syncopators (1994–98), Chris Tyle's Silver Leaf Jazz Band (starting in 1993), Hal Smith's Creole Sunshine (1997–99), pianist Butch Thompson, and singer Banu Gibson (on and off during the past seven years), also appearing with Jim Cullum, James Dapogny, Dan Barrett, Doc Cheatham, Jay McShann, Kenny Davern, and other members of the who's who of trad jazz. Heitger gained his greatest exposure for his trumpet playing on the Squirrel Nut Zipper's eccentric but very popular 1997 CD *Hot,* a set that sold over a million copies.

In recent times Duke Heitger has led the Steamboat Stompers (which since 1998 has played regularly on the Steamer Natchez) and released a swing record on the Fantasy label. "I'm actually proud of being a part of a 'pop' hit with the Squirrel Nut Zippers that was considered a boundary jumper. But mostly I am proud of being called to work with some of the most fantastic musicians and to have made a decent living in a business that's not so easy."

Recommended CDs: *Steamboat Stompers* (GHB 399), *Rhythm Is Our Business* (Fantasy 9684), with Scott Black: *Scott Black's Hot Horns* (Good Time Jazz 15033), with Banu Gibson: *Zat You, Santa Claus?* (Swing Out 106), *Love Is Good for Anything That Ails You* (Swing Out 107), with Silver Leaf Jazz Band: *Great Composers of New Orleans* (Good Time Jazz 15005), with Hal Smith: *Sweet Little Papa* (GHB 403), with Squirrel Nut Zippers: *Hot* (Mammoth 354 980 137)

EDDIE HENDERSON

. . . .

b. Oct. 26, 1940, New York, NY

Although Eddie Henderson made his initial impression in the early 1970s, it was not until the 1990s that he really entered his prime as a jazz improviser. Henderson began on trumpet when he was nine, getting a few informal lessons from Louis Armstrong. He moved to San Francisco with his family when he was 14, studied at the San Francisco Conservatory of Music (1954–56), and served in the Air Force (1958–61). Always more than just a musician, Henderson gained a degree in zoology in 1964 from Berkeley and an MD from Howard University in 1968. He became a full-time psychiatrist by 1975.

Henderson began gigging in 1964 with John Handy, and he also worked in the San Francisco area with Philly Joe Jones, Joe Henderson, and his own groups. The technically skilled trumpeter was a member of the Herbie Hancock Sextet during 1970–73, and he became known as one of the first trumpeters to be influenced by Miles Davis' electronic period, often experimenting with electric wa-wa devices. Henderson led dates for Capricorn, Blue Note, and Capitol during 1973–79 that were electronic oriented and sound quite dated today. In addition to leading groups, Henderson worked with Art Blakey's Jazz Messengers (briefly in 1973), Pharoah Sanders, Norman Connors, and Azteca but seemed to be wasting his musical potential.

While pursuing his medical career, Henderson played more creative music with Elvin Jones (1978–80), George Coleman, Johnny Griffin, Slide Hampton, Benny Golson, Billy Harper, and Kenny Barron. His "comeback" got started in 1988, when he joined McCoy Tyner's band, and continued the following year, when he began recording straightahead dates for the Steeplechase label. Since then, Eddie Henderson has produced some of the finest work of his career (which can be heard on his Milestone CDs of the '90s), emerging as one of the top hard bop trumpeters of recent times. Not bad for a psychiatrist!

Recommended CDs: *Phantoms* (Steeplechase 31250), *Think of Me* (Steeplechase 31264), *Flight of Mind* (Steeplechase 31284), *Inspiration* (Milestone 9240), *Dark Shadows* (Milestone 9254), with Herbie Hancock: *Mwandishi: The Complete Warner Bros. Recordings* (Warner Archives 45732)

FREDDY HILL

. . . .

b. Apr. 18, 1932, Jacksonville, FL

After a promising start to his career, Freddy Hill (a solid hard bop player) faded from the jazz scene in the late 1960s. Hill studied at Florida A&M, served in the Army, and was a schoolteacher in Florida (1955–57). In the decade after moving to Los Angeles in 1957, Hill was quite busy. Among his many musical associates were Earl Bostic, the Gerald Wilson big band, Teddy Edwards, Leroy Vinnegar, Oliver Nelson, and Louie Bellson. Freddy Hill, who also appeared on pop records and worked as an arranger (but never led an album of his own), slipped into obscurity by 1970 and has been little heard from in the jazz world since.

Recommended CDs: with Leroy Vinnegar: *Leroy Walks Again* (Original Jazz Classics 454)

Videos to Get: *Cannonball Adderley/Teddy Edwards-Jazz Scene USA* (1962; Shanachie 6310)

LONNIE HILLYER

b. Mar. 25, 1940, Monroe, GA, d. July 1, 1985, New York, NY

During his prime in the 1960s, Lonnie Hillyer often displayed the influence of Dizzy Gillespie, particularly when heard in Charles Mingus' groups. Hillyer grew up in Detroit and began playing trumpet at 11; one of his teachers was pianist Barry Harris. He was part of the very viable Detroit jazz scene during the second half of the 1950s, often playing as a teenager at jam sessions held at the World Stage during 1955–57. Hillyer first visited New York in 1959. He recorded with Yusef Lateef, taught trumpet back in Detroit, and then in the summer of 1960 moved permanently to New York, where he worked with Slide Hampton.

Hillyer and altoist Charles McPherson joined Mingus' quartet later in 1960 when Ted Curson and Eric Dolphy departed. The trumpeter was part of Mingus' bands during three different periods (1960–61, 1964–65, and 1971–73), and he could always be counted on to add a strong bebop flavor to the group's sound. Hillyer (along with McPherson) was with Barry Harris' quintet during 1961–63, and he co-led a group with the altoist in 1966. After his third period with Mingus ended, Lonnie Hillyer largely retired from active playing (though he was just 33), becoming a music teacher for the final decade of his life.

Recommended CDs: with Yusef Lateef: *Cry!/Tender* (Original Jazz Classics 482), with Charles McPherson: *Live at the Five Spot* (Prestige 24135), with Charles Mingus: *Mingus Mingus!* (Candid 79021)

TERUMASA HINO

b. Oct. 25, 1942, Tokyo, Japan

Terumasa Hino has long been considered Japan's finest jazz trumpeter. He began on trumpet at nine, first playing professionally when he was 12, in 1955. Hino performed jazz at U.S. Army base camps during 1957–60, worked locally, was a member of the Hideo Shiraki Quintet (1962–65), and by 1965 (when he started leading combos) was highly rated.

Hino has since played at numerous jazz festivals throughout Europe and Japan. In 1975 he moved to New York, where he has worked with many top-notch musicians, including Jackie McLean, David Liebman, John Scofield, Elvin Jones, the Gil Evans Orchestra, and Larry Coryell's Eleventh House among others. A versatile musician, Hino has played hard bop (his main influences are Lee Morgan, Freddie Hubbard, and Miles Davis), post-bop, free jazz, and creative fusion. Terumasa Hino, who first recorded as a leader in 1967, received his greatest exposure in the United States though his Blue Note recordings of the 1990s.

Recommended CDs: *Bluestruck* (Blue Note 93671), *From the Heart* (Blue Note 96688), *Blue Smiles* (Blue Note 81191), *Unforgettable* (Blue Note 81191), *Spark* (Blue Note 83045)

AL HIRT

● ● ● ● ● ● ●

b. Nov. 7, 1922, New Orleans, LA, d. Apr. 27, 1999, New Orleans, LA

Amasterful virtuoso who probably should have played classical music, Al Hirt often seemed way overqualified for the Dixieland and pop music that he performed. Hirt began playing trumpet when he was six, studied at the Cincinnati Conservatory (1940–43), and served in the Army during 1943–46. Catching the very end of the swing era, he toured briefly with the big bands of Jimmy Dorsey, Tommy Dorsey, Ray McKinley, and Horace Heidt and then spent eight years as a staff musician at a New Orleans radio station.

In 1955, Hirt made his recording debut, a Dixieland date for Southland. In 1957 he left the studios, co-leading a short-lived but exciting combo with clarinetist Pete Fountain; Hirt and Fountain would have many reunions through the years. During 1958–59 Hirt recorded four heated Dixieland albums for Audio Fidelity and he really started making a name for himself.

Signed to RCA, for whom he recorded during 1960–65, Hirt had several popish hits (including "Java" and "Cotton Candy") and became so famous that he was a household name. In fact, next to Louis Armstrong and Harry James, Hirt was just about the best-known trumpeter in the United States in the 1960s, appearing regularly on television. After this period (climaxed by recording an album at Carnegie Hall in 1965 with Gerald Wilson's orchestra), Hirt returned to New Orleans, where he was happy to play Dixieland for the rest of his career, running his own club on Bourbon Street. Although with his tremendous technique Al Hirt could have gone much further artistically (it is strange that he never recorded a more modern jazz album), he seemed quite happy with his life and remained a popular New Orleans attraction.

Recommended CDs: *That's a-Plenty* (Pro Arte 659)

LPs to Search For: *New Orleans All Stars* (Southland 211), *The Very Best of Al Hirt and Pete Fountain* (MGM 4216), *Swingin' Dixie, Vols. 1–4* (Audio Fidelity 1877, 1878, 1926, and 1927), *Our Man in New Orleans* (Victor 2607), *Live at Carnegie Hall* (Victor 3416)

Film Appearances: a very humorous scene in *Rome Adventure* (1962)

Videos to Get: *Sarah Vaughan and Friends* (1986; A*Vision 50209)

PEANUTS HOLLAND

● ● ● ● ● ● ● ● ● ● ● ● ● ● ● ●

b. Feb. 9, 1910, Norfolk, VA, d. Feb. 7, 1979, Stockholm, Sweden

Herbert "Peanuts" Holland gained some recognition for his trumpet solos and occasional good-time vocals with Charlie Barnet's orchestra. But because he spent much of his life in Europe, his talents have tended to be overlooked. Holland was one of many youngsters who received musical training at the legendary Jenkins' Orphanage. He started off playing with one of the top territory bands of the era, Alphonse Trent's orchestra (1928–33), and spent brief periods with Al Sears (1932), the Jeter-Pillars Orchestra, Willie Bryant, Jimmie Lunceford, and Lil Armstrong's Big Band (1935–36). Holland led a group for a period in Buffalo, moved to

New York City in 1939, and was with both Coleman Hawkins' big band (1940) and one of Fletcher Henderson's last orchestras (1941).

Although he was featured on records with Trent and Henderson, Holland's best-known work was during 1942–46 with Charlie Barnet's orchestra, where he was well showcased, even on dates that included guest trumpeter Roy Eldridge. After leaving Barnet, Holland visited Europe with Don Redman's big band in 1946. As with some of the other musicians in the orchestra (including tenor saxophonist Don Byas), the trumpeter decided to make his home overseas. Holland spent his last 32 years in Europe, usually in Paris and Scandinavia. He led recording sessions in Europe during 1946–48,1950–52, 1954, 1957, and 1959–60, resulting in 46 titles in all, none of which have ever been made widely available in the United States. Peanuts Holland retained his good-natured mainstream swing style until he stopped playing in the early 1970s.

Recommended CDs: with Charlie Barnet: *Drop Me Off in Harlem* (GRP/Decca 612), with Don Byas: *1947* (Classics 1073), with Don Redman: *Geneva* 1946 (TCB 2112)

RON HORTON
. . . .

b. 1960, Bethesda, MD

An inventive post-bop trumpeter, Ron Horton has his own sound and in terms of style falls between hard bop and the avant-garde. Horton attended Berklee (1978–80) and, after playing locally in Boston, moved to New York in 1982. Since then he has performed with many top improvisers, including Andrew Hill, Jane Ira Bloom, Phillip Johnston, Ted Nash, Andy Laster, Matt Wilson, and Peggy Stern, among others. A member of the Jazz Composers Collective since 1992, Ron Horton (who also plays with the Herbie Nichols Project) recorded his impressive debut as a leader in 1999.

Recommended CDs: Genius Envy (Omnitone 11902), with the Herbie Nichols Project: *Love Is Proximity* (Soul Note 121313)

AVERY "KID" HOWARD
. . . .

b. Apr. 22, 1908, New Orleans, LA, d. Mar. 28, 1966, New Orleans, LA

When he recorded with George Lewis in 1943, Kid Howard was a fine New Orleans ensemble player who could take a hot solo when called upon. Unfortunately alcohol soon caused his decline, and his playing became quite erratic by the 1950s.

A professional drummer as a teenager, Howard worked with Andrew Morgan and Chris Kelly. He enjoyed Kelly's playing so much that he soon switched to cornet and would always consider Kelly to be his main influence. Howard played in many brass bands in New Orleans, including the Eureka Brass Band, the Tuxedo Brass Band, and the one led by Henry Allen Sr. He worked in New Orleans throughout the 1930s and was part of the pit band at the Palace Theater (1938–43). When Bunk Johnson was unavailable for a recording session on May 16,

1943, George Lewis suggested that Howard would be an able replacement; the results would be the creative high point of Kid's career.

Kid Howard also recorded in 1946 as the leader of the Original Zenith Brass Band. After freelancing in New Orleans, in 1952 he became a regular member of Lewis' band. Howard toured the world with the clarinetist, but his playing (and singing) was far from dependable, due to his alcoholism, sometimes inspiring the other musicians but at other times weighing down the band; it all depended on what day it was! Howard was with the popular group off and on until 1959 (recording with Lewis as late as 1963), survived a serious illness in 1961, and spent his last years playing in New Orleans, often at Preservation Hall. Kid Howard, who can be heard at his best on the George Lewis recordings listed next, also led record dates of his own during 1961–65 for Icon, Jazzology, San Jacinto, Nobility, and the Japanese Dan label.

Recommended CDs: with George Lewis: *The Beverly Caverns Sessions* (Good Time Jazz 12058), *Dr. Jazz* (Good Time Jazz 12062)

Box Set: *The Complete Blue Note Recordings of George Lewis* (5 CDs; Mosaic 5-132)

Recommended Reading: *Jazz Talking* by Max Jones (Da Capo Press, 1987)

FREDDIE HUBBARD
. . . .

b. Apr. 7, 1938, Indianapolis, IN

One of the greatest jazz trumpeters of all time, Freddie Hubbard for a variety of reasons had to stop playing altogether by the mid-1990s, interrupting a brilliant career. Hubbard started out playing the mellophone, trombone, tuba, and French horn before settling on the trumpet in high school. He grew up in a poor family and played locally in Indianapolis, including with the Montgomery Brothers, making his recording debut with Wes Montgomery in December 1957, sounding a little nervous but showing plenty of potential. Hubbard was offered a French horn scholarship to Indiana Central College but decided instead to concentrate on trumpet at Butler University. However, because he wanted to play jazz rather than classical music, he did not last long in school. In 1958 Hubbard moved to New York.

The young trumpeter formed his sound out of the Clifford Brown/Lee Morgan tradition but gradually developed a style of his own. Although basically a hard bop trumpeter, he was flexible enough to play more advanced music too. Hubbard befriended John Coltrane in 1959 (they would occasionally jam together) and roomed with Eric Dolphy. His first opportunity to play at Birdland was with Philly Joe Jones' group. Miles Davis was in the audience, which did not do much for Hubbard's nerves. However, Miles liked what he heard and called Alfred Lion of Blue Note, telling him to sign the young trumpeter as soon as possible. Hubbard debuted on Blue Note in 1960 and would be with the label for five years. He worked with Slide Hampton, J.J. Johnson, Quincy Jones, and for eight months with Sonny Rollins.

Hubbard became famous in the jazz world during the period when he was a member of Art Blakey's Jazz Messengers (1961–64), where he replaced Lee Morgan. He appeared on many important albums during the first half of the 1960s, including Eric Dolphy's *Outward Bound*, Ornette Coleman's *Free Jazz*, John Coltrane's *Ole*, Herbie Hancock's *Takin' Off*, Oliver Nelson's

Freddie Hubbard's explosive and fiery style was one of the most exciting in jazz.

Blues And The Abstract Truth, Dolphy's *Out to Lunch,* Herbie Hancock's *Maiden Voyage,* Coltrane's *Ascension,* and Sonny Rollins' *East Broadway Run Down,* not to mention his own sessions and those of the Jazz Messengers. The only musician to be on both *Free Jazz* and *Ascension,* Hubbard was also on the original version of "Watermelon Man" and the second (and most famous) rendition of "Stolen Moments." He also wrote two standards: "Up Jumped Spring" and the uptempo blues "Birdlike" (also often spelled "Byrdlike"). And along the way, Hubbard found time to record as a sideman with Paul Chambers, McCoy Tyner, Bobby Hutcherson, Andrew Hill, Dexter Gordon, Sam Rivers, Wayne Shorter, and (in the 1970s) Joe Farrell and George Cables.

Hubbard had a quintet during 1964–65, worked with Max Roach (1965–66) and Sonny Rollins, and from 1966 on was a leader. His 1966–69 group featured James Spaulding on alto and flute and was primarily advanced hard bop. In the 1970s Hubbard was arguably the top trumpeter in jazz, particularly after Lee Morgan's death. His work for CTI (particularly *Red Clay, Straight Life,* and *First Light*) was the height of his career, balancing producer Creed Taylor's commercial elements with lots of fiery and exciting playing. Hubbard was also on the original version of Stanley Turrentine's "Sugar." However, even though he was at the peak of his powers, Hubbard's recordings for Columbia (1974–79) ranged from decent (*High Energy* and *Super Blue*) to erratic (*Liquid Love, Bundle of Joy,* and *The Love Connection*) to pure garbage (*Windjammer*), leaving listeners wondering why the trumpeter was wasting his talent in fruitless searches for greater commercial success.

Hubbard returned to acoustic jazz by working with Herbie Hancock's VSOP (a reunion of the mid-1960s Miles Davis quintet, with Freddie taking Miles' spot) off and on during 1977–79. In the 1980s Hubbard (who was being overshadowed by Wynton Marsalis) had a rather aimless career. He had some great moments along the way and played quite well in general, but his recordings often either revisited past glories, were loose jam sessions, or were duds (avoid *Splash, Ride Like the Wind,* and *Times Are Changing!*). Even on a couple of recordings that matched him with Woody Shaw, Hubbard did not sound like he had grown much beyond the level he had been at in the early 1970s.

Starting around 1989, Hubbard's playing began to decline. A growth on his lip that had to be surgically removed, a disturbing unreliability (not showing up for his own gigs), "personal problems," and what sounded like a lack of practicing (often sounding rusty) made him increasingly erratic. His once-pretty tone on flugelhorn became very fuzzy and on trumpet he was constantly missing notes. Instead of being at his prime in the 1990s, Hubbard quickly declined and had to stop playing altogether by the middle of the decade when he should have been reaping the rewards of a very productive career. Although he has occasionally tried to come back since, the "real" Freddie Hubbard (who can be heard on recordings he led for Blue Note, Impulse, Atlantic, MPS, CTI, Columbia, Pablo, Real Time, Enja, Elektra/Musician, and Fantasy) has been absent from jazz since at least 1992, a major loss.

Recommended CDs: *Open Sesame* (Blue Note 84040), *Ready for Freddie* (Blue Note 32094), *Hub-Tones* (Blue Note 84115), *Breaking Point* (Blue Note 84172), *Backlash* (Koch 8535), *Red Clay* (CTI/CBS 40809), *Straight Life* (CTI/CBS 65125), *First Light* (CTI/CBS 40687), *Outpost* (Enja 3095), *Face to Face* (Original Jazz Classics 937), *Life Flight* (Blue Note 46895), with Art Blakey: *Mosaic* (Blue Note 46523), *Ugetsu* (Original Jazz Classics 090), with Oliver Nelson: *Blues and the Abstract Truth* (GRP/Impulse154)

LPs to Search For: *Backlash* (Atlantic 1477), *The Hub of Hubbard* (MPS 726)

Film Appearances: *'Round Midnight* (1985)

STEVE HUFFSTETER
• • • • • • • • • • • • • • • •

b. Feb. 7, 1936, Monroe, MI

A greatly in-demand trumpeter in the Los Angeles area, Steve Huffsteter plays with many big bands (due to his solo abilities, sight-reading skills, and attractive sound) but is also a very capable small-group improviser.

"I found my uncle's old high school cornet in the attic when I was eight or nine. There was an after-school band for grade-schoolers at the local high school. I enrolled and challenged my way up to first chair by the year's end." Huffsteter grew up in Phoenix, Arizona, briefly attended Arizona State, played lead trumpet at Koko's in Phoenix (backing acts from Las Vegas) during 1957–59, and then moved to Los Angeles. He has worked with many big bands through the years, including Stan Kenton (1960–61), Sy Zentner (1962), Ray Charles

(1966), Louie Bellson, Toshiko Akiyoshi-Lew Tabackin (mid-'70s to mid-'80s), Tom Talbert, and Bob Florence (from the mid-1960s up to the present). In addition, Huffsteter has played in countless small groups (including with Willie Bobo, Clare Fischer, and Poncho Sanchez), most recently with pianist Cecilia Coleman's quintet. Of this last association, he says, "How often does one get to grow after 50? This is where I finally learned to play."

Considering how busy he has been, it is surprising that Huffsteter has led only one record date in his career, the obscure *Circles* in 1982 for the Japanese Eastworld label. In recent times he has been leading a new orchestra. "I'm very excited over my big band. I've always thought of myself as a writer even more than as a trumpet player. As I slip into old age, I will be more and more a writer and less a player. But not yet; I'm enjoying playing too much!"

Recommended CDs: with Cecilia Coleman: *Home* (Resurgent 103), *Young and Foolish* (Resurgent 109), with Bob Florence: *Treasure Chest* (USA 680), *Earth* (MAMA 1016), *Serendipity 28* (MAMA 1025), with Bill Perkins: *The Bill Perkins-Steve Huffsteter Quintet* (Woofy 63)

PERCY HUMPHREY
. . . .

b. Jan. 13, 1905, New Orleans, LA, d. Aug. 22, 1995, New Orleans, LA

Part of a very musical family that included his brothers clarinetist Willie Humphrey and trombonist Earl Humphrey, Percy was a limited trumpeter who nevertheless appeared on many important New Orleans revival dates through the years. He started on drums but took trumpet lessons from his grandfather and eventually switched instruments. In 1925 Humphrey led his first band, and he worked with the Eureka Brass Band and other local groups. He visited Chicago with Kid Howard in 1929 but spent much of the 1930s and the first half of the 1940s outside of music. In 1946 Humphrey (who did not record at all in his early years) began playing music again, and he was soon leading the revived Eureka Brass Band, recording with them in 1951. He was a member of George Lewis' band (1951–53) but did not want to quit his day job in order to travel with the group, which in retrospect was a bad move, leading to more years of obscurity.

However, Humphrey worked locally on a part-time basis in the 1950s, and his profile rose during the following decade. In 1961 he recorded for Riverside with his Crescent City Joymakers and with pianist Sweet Emma Barrett in what was an early version of the Preservation Hall Jazz Band. Along with brother Willie, Percy eventually became a longtime member of the Preservation Hall Jazz Band, traveling around the world spreading the joy of New Orleans Jazz. When hearing this group, I always wished that the Humphrey Brothers were better musicians, for they certainly had the spirit, but their playing was erratic and gradually worsened as old age took its toll. Still, Percy Humphrey (who recorded albums of his own on an occasional basis during 1953–87) never tired of playing the warhorses for appreciative audiences, staying active until he died at age 90.

Recommended CDs: with Sweet Emma Barrett: *New Orleans—The Living Legends* (Original Jazz Classics 1832)

LPs to Search For: *Climax Rag* (Pearl 3)

CLYDE HURLEY

• • • • • • • • • • • •

b. Sept. 3, 1916, Fort Worth, TX, d. Sept. 1963, TX

Although largely forgotten today, one of Clyde Hurley's trumpet solos is one of the most familiar in jazz history, the hot chorus on the original Glenn Miller recording of "In the Mood!" As a youth, Hurley taught himself the trumpet by playing along with Louis Armstrong records. After gaining experience working locally, Hurley was heard by bandleader Ben Pollack when the drummer was passing through Texas. Hurley joined Pollack in 1938 (taking a solo on his record "So Unexpectedly"). However, he left the band when it toured Los Angeles the following year so he could become a studio musician, one of many notable Pollock "discoveries" who eventually deserted him for more lucrative work; other Pollack alumni include Benny Goodman, Jack Teagarden, Harry James, and Glenn Miller.

Hurley was soon hired by Glenn Miller and was with Miller's orchestra when it made it big. However, he quickly became bored with the music, did not get along all that well with the leader, and left within a year despite being featured on several of his records. Hurley played with the big bands of Tommy Dorsey (1940–41) and Artie Shaw (1941). The trumpeter then went back to the studios for much of his career, working regularly for MGM (1944–49) and NBC (1950–55). A talented Dixieland soloist, Hurley occasionally played with Matty Matlock's Rampart Street Paraders, and he can be heard in exciting form with pianist Ralph Sutton during some broadcasts from San Francisco's Club Hangover in 1954, matching his wit and power with clarinetist Edmond Hall. As a leader, Hurley cut only four sides for Keynote in 1946 and five Dixieland-oriented numbers for Crown in 1950. He eventually returned to his native Texas before passing away at the age of 47.

Although the name of Clyde Hurley would generate blank stares from most swing fans, they have certainly all heard at least one of his solos!

Recommended CDs: with Edmond Hall: *With the Ralph Sutton Group* (Storyville 6052)

LPs to Search For: with Rampart Street Paraders: *Dixieland, My Dixieland* (Columbia 785), *Texas! USA* (Columbia 1061)

JIVER HUTCHINSON

• • • • • • • • • • • • • • • •

b. 1907, Jamaica, British West Indies, d. Nov. 22, 1959, Weeting, England

Leslie "Jiver" Hutchinson was a talented swing trumpeter not known at all in the United States. He worked with Bertie King's band in the British West Indies (1934) before moving to England. Hutchinson was a member of Happy Blake's Cuba Club Band, Leslie Thompson's Emperors of Jazz, and most notably Geraldo's dance orchestra (late 1930s to early '40s).He led groups during 1944–50, touring Europe and India. Hutchinson returned to Geraldo's group in 1950, worked with Mary Lou Williams in 1952, and was touring as a leader with his band in England when he died in a car accident. Jiver Hutchinson led a lone recording session in 1947, six swing standards cut with a nonet while on tour in Czechoslovakia.

MARK ISHAM

· · · · · · · · · · ·

b. 1951, New York, NY

Mark Isham has long had a dual career as a Miles Davis-influenced trumpeter and as a composer of atmospheric soundtracks for films. His mother was a concert violinist and his father a music and art professor. Isham started on the piano and was well trained as a classical trumpeter. However, during high school he discovered Miles Davis, Wayne Shorter, and Weather Report and became interested in improvised music. Moving to San Francisco in the early 1970s, Isham played with the Oakland Symphony, the San Francisco Symphony, and the San Francisco Opera while also gigging locally with rock and jazz groups, including those of Charles Lloyd, Horace Silver, Pharoah Sanders, and Dave Liebman. He also explored electronic music during this period, becoming a synthesizer programmer.

Isham recorded two albums with Art Lande's Rubisa Patrol for ECM in 1976 and 1978. He played with Group 87 (which recorded for CBS in 1980 and 1984) and recorded albums as a leader for Windham Hill, Virgin, and Columbia, becoming known for a time as a new age artist due to his impressionistic music. Isham was with Van Morrison for six years (doubling on synthesizer) and began writing quite successfully for films in addition to being a session player and leading an acoustic jazz group.

In recent times Mark Isham has recorded and performed some very interesting music with The Silent Way Project, his effective tribute to electric Miles Davis, and been quite active as a player in jazz settings in addition to his soundtrack work.

Recommended CDs: *Blue Sun* (Columbia 67227), *Afterglow* (Columbia 67529), *Miles Remembered: The Silent Way Project* (Sony 69901)

DEWEY JACKSON

· · · · · · · · · · · · · · · · ·

b. June 21, 1900, St. Louis, MO, d. 1994, St. Louis, MO

Because only a few cities in the 1920s and '30s had recording facilities, some major players practically slipped through the cracks. Dewey Jackson, who preferred to stay at home, was considered St. Louis' top jazz trumpeter throughout the 1920s and '30s (Clark Terry and Miles Davis were both very much aware of him), yet he barely made it on to records despite a long career and a legendary reputation.

Jackson began playing professionally with Tommy Evans' group in St. Louis (1916–17). After a year with George Reynolds' Keystone Band, he joined Charlie Creath's unit for the first time (May 1919), playing on a riverboat. Jackson led the Golden Melody Band during 1920–23, played on the S.S. Capitol with Fate Marable in 1924, and then formed the St. Louis Peacock Charleston Orchestra. Jackson mostly led bands from then on, other than playing with violinist Andrew Preer's orchestra at the Cotton Club during a rare (and undocumented) four-month period in New York (August-November 1926); he also had several short stints with Marable and Creath as late as 1936.

Dewey Jackson spent virtually his entire career playing in the St. Louis area or on river-boats. In the early 1940s he started working at a day job in a hotel, but he became more active musically again in 1950, playing with Singleton Palmer, Don Ewell (1951), and with his Dixieland-oriented bands into the 1960s. Despite his longevity, Jackson does not ever seem to have been interviewed, and even his death date is obscure.

Dewey Jackson appeared on records a maximum of six times. For three of the sessions his participation is not definite: backing singers Missouri Anderson (1926), Luella Miller (1927), and Bert Hatton (1927). Otherwise, Jackson recorded only eight titles in his entire career: four songs as a leader on June 21, 1926 (including "She's Crying For Me" and "Going To Town"), two fine selections with Charlie Creath's Jazz-O-Maniacs on May 2, 1927 ("Butter-Finger Blues" and "Crazy Quilt"), and a pair of Dixieland standards in a sextet led by tuba player Singleton Palmer (September 30, 1950) that were put out by the obscure Disco label on a 78 record and have never been reissued ("Washington and Lee Swing" and "Tailgate Ramble"). The selections that he made as a leader and with Creath hint strongly at Dewey Jackson's talents and power, making it regrettable that the jazz world outside of St. Louis missed him completely.

Recommended CD: *Jazz in Saint Louis* (Timeless 1036).

HARRY JAMES

. . . .

b. Mar. 15, 1916, Albany, GA, d. July 5, 1983, Las Vegas, NV

Harry James was the most famous trumpeter of the swing era and the leader of the most popular swing orchestra in the world during 1943–46. This success followed him the rest of his career, with good and bad results. He was always able to work as often as he wanted and to keep his big band together at least on a part-time basis. The bad part was that by not being able (or willing) to escape his past, James would always be associated with World War II nostalgia.

Harry James began playing drums when he was seven and the following year started taking trumpet lessons from his father, who conducted bands for traveling circuses. By the time he was 12, Harry was leading one of the ensembles for the Christy Brothers Circus. During 1931–35, James played with a series of territory bands based in Texas. Even at this early age, his talent was obvious. In 1935 James was discovered by drummer Ben Pollack, who quickly signed him up. The following year the 20-year-old made his recording debut with Pollack on such numbers as "Jimtown Blues," his own "Peckin'," and "Zoom Zoom Zoom" (on which he took a rare vocal).

In January 1937, Harry James joined the Benny Goodman Orchestra, which was at the height of its fame. James became part of a trumpet section that included Ziggy Elman and Chris Griffin and that was so strong the three trumpeters took turns playing lead. Although Elman had previously been Goodman's main soloist, James (who at times had a similar sound) was soon getting most of the glory with his technically brilliant and enthusiastic outbursts. He can really be heard lifting the bandstand on Goodman's live version of "St. Louis Blues," which was spontaneously extended due to James' playing. He also contributed occasional tunes, such as "Peckin'" and "Life Goes to a Party." James spent nearly two years with Goodman, was one of the stars of Goodman's 1938 Carnegie Hall concert (where he was heard to mutter, "I feel like a whore in church"), and became a major name despite being a sideman.

When James left Goodman, it seemed only a matter of time before he would be a major success, although it did take longer than expected. James, who had gotten very tired of playing "Sing Sing Sing" with Goodman, put together his own big band, which took a couple of years to develop its own musical personality. In fact, although Frank Sinatra was his vocalist in 1939, James was unable to hold onto the singer when Tommy Dorsey gave Sinatra a more lucrative offer.

James had started recording his own sessions while still with Goodman (using members of the Count Basie Orchestra for some of his dates), and his first recording after becoming a bandleader resulted in four quartet titles that he cut, with Pete Johnson or Albert Ammons providing boogie-woogie piano. James' big band recordings of the 1939–40 era were fine (alternating swinging jazz instrumentals with ballad vocals and trumpet displays such as "Concerto for Trumpet" and "Flight of the Bumble Bee") and included his theme song "Ciribiribin" and "Two O'Clock Jump" (which was really just a renamed version of Count Basie's "One O'-Clock Jump"). But it was not until 1941 that James had his breakthrough, with an instrumental rendition of the old Al Jolson hit "You Made Me Love You," which he recorded because he loved Judy Garland's version. By that time, he had added a small string section to his big band and was beginning to emphasize ballads. This gamble paid off big, with such major hits as Dick Haymes singing "I'll Get By," Helen Forrest on "I Don't Want to Talk About You," "I Cried for You," and "I Had the Craziest Dream," and the instrumental "Cherry."

Formerly married to singer Louise Tobin, Harry James married Betty Grable (the actress with the million-dollar legs) and made appearances (usually playing a couple of songs) in many films of the era, including *Private Buckaroo, Bathing Beauty, If I'm Lucky, Springtime in the Rockies,* and *Best Foot Forward.* When Glenn Miller broke up his civilian orchestra in 1942 to join the Army, James' ensemble had no real competition at the top of the dance band business.

Because of Harry James' commercial success, years later his playing would often be downgraded by jazz fans, but in reality he was one of the finest of all swing trumpeters. He could be schmaltzy in some of his showcases (sporting a wide vibrato), but he could also swing up a storm with the best musicians. Unfortunately, the Columbia label has mostly chosen to endlessly repackage James' hits. Luckily, the European Classics company has been gradually reissuing all of his 1940s recordings, and there are many lesser-known instrumental gems to be discovered. A particular highlight is his version of "Sleepy Time Gal," played with just the rhythm section from his orchestra.

Although the recording strike of 1942–44 kept him off commercial records for two years, James' fame grew during the war years, helped by his movie appearances and constant work on radio. Back on records by November 1944, his version of Duke Ellington's "I'm Beginning to See the Light" was quite popular, and "It's Been a Long Long Time" from July 1945 (with Kitty Kallen as the singer) was the perfect song to close off World War II. Tenor saxophonist Corky Corcoran had been a key soloist with James' band since late 1941, and in 1945 altoist Willie Smith (who had left Jimmy Lunceford's orchestra) became James' longtime star, starting off with his feature on "Who's Sorry Now?"

The most popular trumpeter of the 1940s, Harry James was both a household name and an underrated jazz player.

Due to the changing of musical tastes and the passage of time, Harry James' string of hits stopped altogether in 1946. Struggling with the cost of his oversized orchestra, in December James temporarily broke up the band, although he was back a few months later. Despite being closely identified with the swing era, James did have open ears and he liked bebop. A two-part version of "Tuxedo Junction" from November 3, 1947, with an octet from the big band (re-issued on a Columbia sampler) finds him taking a very boppish solo that in terms of notes was worthy of Fats Navarro. James dropped his string section in 1948, and his orchestra played quite a few modern charts the following year. However, by 1950 the trumpeter reverted permanently back to swing, and his most creative years were over.

Despite "The Great James Robbery," which found James in early 1951 losing the services of altoist Smith, valve trombonist Juan Tizol, and his new drummer, Louis Bellson, to Duke Ellington (all three would return to James in time), the trumpeter continued on. He led his big band on a part-time basis, with Las Vegas as his home base. Always a great lover of Count Basie's sound, James modeled his band starting from the early 1950s after Basie's, using arrangements by Ernie Wilkins and Neal Hefti. James interacted with Doris Day's voice in the movie *Young Man with a Horn* (where he ghosted the music that Kirk Douglas allegedly played), appeared briefly in *The Benny Goodman Story*, recorded a set with Rosemary Clooney, often had Buddy Rich as his drummer, and incorporated more recent pop tunes in his repertoire along with remakes of his hits and his favorite swing standards. Although he was friends with Dizzy Gillespie and Miles Davis (all three trumpeters thought highly of one another), creatively Harry James was in a rut yet never seemed motivated enough to develop any further. Nothing much changed for him in the 1960s and '70s other than the eventual loss of Smith, Corcoran, and Rich, his divorce from Betty Grable, and the gradual shrinking of his range. The trumpeter refused to change or grow, content merely to repeat his earlier hits endlessly.

Harry James, who could have gone much farther but whose real accomplishments should not be overlooked, would remain a major name up until his death, both a celebrity and an underrated jazz trumpet player.

Recommended CDs: *1937–1939* (Classics 903), *Bandstand Memories* (Hindsight 503), *1939* (Classics 936), *1939–1940* (Classics 970), *1940* (Classics 936), *1940–1941* (Classics 1014), *1941* (Classics 1052), *1941, Vol. 2* (Classics 1092), *1941–1942* (Classics 1132), *Snooty Fruity* (Columbia 45447), with Benny Goodman: *The Harry James Years, Vol. 1* (Bluebird 66155), *Wrappin' It Up* (Bluebird 66549)

Recommended Reading: *Trumpet Blues* by Peter J. Levinson (Oxford University Press, 1999)

Film Appearances: *Hollywood Hotel* (1937, with Benny Goodman's orchestra), *Syncopation* (1942), *Private Buckaroo* (1942), *Springtime in the Rockies* (1942), *Best Foot Forward* (1943), *Bathing Beauty* (1944), *Two Girls and a Sailor* (1944), *Do You Love Me?* (1946), *If I'm Lucky* (1946), *Carnegie Hall* (1947), *A Miracle Can Happen* (1948), *I'll Get By* (1950), *The Benny Goodman Story* (1955), *The Opposite Sex* (1956), *The Big Beat* (1957), and *The Ladies' Man* (1961). In addition, in *Young Man with a Horn* (1949) James ghosted the many trumpet solos of Kirk Douglas.

THOMAS JEFFERSON
. . . .

b. June 20, 1920, Chicago, IL, d. Dec. 13, 1986, New Orleans, LA

One of the best New Orleans jazz trumpeters of the 1950s and '60s and a fine singer, Thomas Jefferson did not record all that much during his life, but he made every recording count. After playing drums and French horn early on, he switched to trumpet. Jefferson was in the Jones' Home Band and took trumpet lessons from Peter Davis, Louis Armstrong's early teacher. Satch would be a strong influence on Jefferson's playing and singing throughout his career.

Jefferson worked with many local groups in New Orleans, including those of Oscar Celestin (1936), Sidney Desvigne, Jimmy Davis, Jump Jackson, and John Casimir. He recorded with George Lewis, Santo Pecora, Raymond Burke, and Johnny St. Cyr, but can be heard at his very best on his five spirited albums as a leader, dates cut between 1960 and 1974 for Southland, Maison Bourbon, Storyville, and Nola. Thomas Jefferson may not have been an innovator or all that original, but his fluent trumpet solos and cheerful vocals resulted in some classic New Orleans jazz and some highly enjoyable music.

LPs to Search For: *Thomas Jefferson from New Orleans* (Storyville 131), *Thomas Jefferson's International New Orleans Jazz Band* (Storyville 254)

Recommended Reading: *Jazz Talking* by Max Jones (Da Capo Press, 1987)

Film Appearances: *Hard Times* (1975)

CLAY JENKINS

b. Oct. 4, 1954, Lubbody, TX

Clay Jenkins (born Delbert Clayton Jenkins) is a fine hard bop-oriented trumpeter who has long been a fixture in the Los Angeles area. His father and brother both played trumpet, so Jenkins began when he was 11. He attended North Texas State University and picked up important experience playing in the big bands of Stan Kenton (1977–78), Buddy Rich (1979), and Count Basie (1984–85).

Clay Jenkins settled in Los Angeles, has been a member of the Clayton-Hamilton Jazz Orchestra since its formation in 1987, and appears regularly with combos in local clubs, playing primarily modern straightahead jazz.

Recommended CDs: *Rings* (K2B2 2669), *Give and Gather* (Kazu 77704), *Yellow Flowers After* (Chase 8051), with the Clayton-Hamilton Jazz Orchestra: *Groove Shop* (Capri 74021), *Heart and Soul* (Capri 74028), with Bill Cunliffe: *Rare Connection* (Discovery 77007)

FREDDIE JENKINS

b. Oct. 10, 1906, NY, d. July 12, 1978, Tarrant County, TX

It is ironic that Freddie Jenkins (who was nicknamed "Posey") was one of the last surviving members of the early Duke Ellington bands, because he was actually forced to retire permanently from playing music due to bad health, 40 years before his death! Jenkins was a colorful trumpet soloist influenced by the bravado of the young Louis Armstrong, and his hot playing was an effective contrast in Duke's band with the plunger work of Bubber Miley and Cootie Williams and the lyricism of Arthur Whetsol.

Jenkins, who played left-handed, worked early on with the 369th Regiment Cadet Band. He attended Wilberforce University, had a brief stint with Edgar Hayes' Blue Grass Buddies, and then spent four years with Horace Henderson's Collegians (1924–28). When he joined Duke Ellington in 1928, Jenkins' playing worked well with the different styles of Miley and Whetsol and he had many short solos.

Jenkins worked steadily with Ellington before a serious lung ailment forced him to retire in April 1934, when he was 27. He began to play again in 1935, spent part of 1936 with the Luis Russell Band, was part owner of the Brittwood Club, and in March 1937 was back with Ellington. In May 1938 when he left Duke, it was to co-lead a band with bassist Hayes Alvis. But unfortunately before the year ended, Jenkins' lung ailment returned, he spent several months in the hospital, and he had to permanently give up playing trumpet. Jenkins held a variety of jobs during the remainder of his life, including as a songwriter, a press agent, and a disc jockey in addition to working in real estate and insurance, eventually settling in Fort Worth, Texas.

Jenkins recorded regularly with Duke Ellington during his six years with him, taking a famous solo on the two-part 1929 version of "Tiger Rag" and playing a solid melodic lead (à la Louis Armstrong) on "When You're Smiling." He also appeared on sessions led by Clara Smith (1928), the Musical Stevedores (1929), and Rex Stewart (1937), in addition to leading his lone record date in 1935 (which resulted in six titles, including hot versions of "Toledo Shuffle" and "I Can't Dance"). Freddie Jenkins' showmanship is very much in evidence on "Old Man Blues" in the 1930 Amos and Andy film *Check and Double Check.*

Recommended CDs: with Duke Ellington: *The Okeh Ellington* (Col. 46177)

Box Set: with Duke Ellington: *Early Ellington* (3 CDs; GRP/Decca 640)

Film Appearances: *Check and Double Check* (1930) with Duke Ellington's orchestra

PAT JENKINS

* * * * * * * * * * * *

b. Dec. 25, 1914, Norfolk, VA

Pat Jenkins is remembered primarily for being one of the regular trumpeters with Al Cooper's Savoy Sultans. A swing-based player with the ability to quickly come up with spontaneous catchy riffs, Jenkins fit in perfectly with the popular combo. After moving to New York in 1934, he was with the Savoy Sultans during virtually its entire existence, 1937–44. Jenkins reluctantly departed the Sultans to serve in the Army, was with Tab Smith's jump band (1947–50), and worked extensively with Buddy Tate's Celebrity Club Orchestra on and off during 1951–73.

Recommended CDs: with the Savoy Sultans: *1938–1941* (Classics 728), with Buddy Tate: *Groovin' with Tate* (Prestige 24152)

LPs to Search For: with Jimmy Rushing: *Going to Chicago* (Vanguard 8011)

INGRID JENSEN

* * * * * * * * * * * *

b. 1967, Vancouver, British Columbia

A major hard bop trumpeter who grows in power with each year, Ingrid Jensen has a great deal of potential. Inspired most by Lee Morgan and Woody Shaw, Jensen grew up in Canada. She attended Berklee, toured Europe with the Vienna Art Orchestra (in a production

Extending the innovations of Woody Shaw, Ingrid Jensen has broken away from all-female bands to become one of today's top jazz trumpeters.

of *Fe and Males*), and spent time abroad, becoming a professor at Austria's Bruckner Conservatory when she was 25.

After touring with Lionel Hampton, Jensen returned to the United States in 1994 and joined the all-female big band Diva, with whom she toured the United States. Since then, Ingrid Jensen has recorded several albums for Enja and often worked with altoist Virginia Mayhew in New York.

Recommended CDs: *Vernal Fields* (Enja 9013), *Here on Earth* (Enja 9313), *Higher Grounds* (Enja 9353), with Virginia Mayhew: *Nini Green* (Chiaroscuro 351), *No Walls* (Foxhaven 10010)

BUNK JOHNSON

* * * * * * * * * * * * *

b. Dec. 27, 1889, New Orleans, LA, d. July 7, 1949, New Iberia, LA

Bunk Johnson is one of the most colorful figures in jazz history. Considered by his more partisan fans to be a genius and by some detractors to be a complete fraud, Bunk Johnson was somewhere in between. Always a controversial figure because of his boasts (such as that he was one of Louis Armstrong's teachers, which Satch denied), even Bunk's birth date is in dispute, for he used to claim that he was born in 1879 and had played in the 1890s with

Buddy Bolden. More likely, he was born a decade later and at best might have seen Bolden perform. Johnson also claimed to have visited Mexico in 1900, New York in 1903, San Francisco in 1905, and also England, Australia, and Asia during the era, allegedly introducing jazz everywhere! Yet it is highly doubtful that Bunk (who sometimes lived up to his name) visited New York or any Northern city at all until 1942.

However, as with pianist Jelly Roll Morton (who claimed to have invented jazz when in fact he was merely one of its first important voices), Johnson's bragging should never overshadow his actual contributions to the music. What is known is that Bunk played in New Orleans from 1910 on (including with Billy Marrero's Superior Orchestra and Frankie Dusen's Eagle Band) and that he was known for having a pretty tone in his early days. In 1914 Bunk began freelancing throughout the South, and he worked in Texas, Kansas City (with Sammy Price around 1930), and many rural areas. Lack of work and problems with his teeth resulted in Johnson's no longer playing by 1934. He worked as a field laborer and a truck driver and appeared to be lost forever to jazz.

But a semimiracle happened. In 1937 Bunk was rediscovered by Bill Russell and Fred Ramsey, writers who used him as a source of information for their book *Jazzmen*. When that important work was published in 1939, it generated a great deal of interest in the long-lost pioneer. Money was raised to buy Bunk a set of teeth and a new trumpet. He worked as a music teacher during 1940–41 and began seriously playing again in 1941.

Johnson's first recordings were in June 1942, and they show him to be a struggling player but one whose style was a throwback to the pre-1920 period. Getting stronger as a musician during the next year, Johnson spent time in San Francisco in 1943, including recording one of his finest sets with the wartime version of the Yerba Buena Jazz Band. After returning to Louisiana (where he made further recordings, including with the band that would later be the nucleus of George Lewis' group in the 1950s), in March 1945 he arrived in New York. Soprano saxophonist Sidney Bechet persuaded Bunk to join his group in Boston, an ensemble that Bechet hoped would become a strong New Orleans band. However, Johnson was unable to adjust himself to Bechet's often playing lead, and he was drinking excessively during the period. The group did not last long.

Bunk recorded frequently during 1944–47 and was both hailed and damned by listeners. Some of his recordings (particularly his final set and the session with the Yerba Buena Jazz Band) show him as a vital link to early jazz, while others (especially ones made when he was drunk) have Bunk sounding quite incompetent and amateurish. Strangely enough, Johnson did not completely satisfy the more purist New Orleans fans, because his playing was not unaffected by the style of Louis Armstrong and other later players, and he often preferred to play current pop songs and jazzed versions of rags rather than the blues and early standards favored by some of his supporters.

After the Bechet fiasco, Bunk organized a new band and played at the Stuyvesant Casino in New York from September 1945 to January 1946 and again during April-May 1946. His appearance on the scene at the same time as Dizzy Gillespie and the other modern players made for quite a contrast, fueling the bebop vs. moldy fig "jazz wars" that raged on in the jazz press. Johnson spent time in Chicago in 1947, played some gigs in New York, and made his final recordings in December 1947. Shortly after returning to home in New Iberia, he became ill, passing away in mid-1949. Although thought of as ancient by some, he was not even 60 at his death.

Bunk Johnson's unlikely and rather unique life would make for a colorful (if slightly unbelievable) Hollywood movie!

Recommended CDs: *Bunk and Lu* (Good Time Jazz 12024), *1944* (American Music 3), *1944 2nd Masters* (American Music 8), *King of the Blues* (American Music 1), *Plays Popular Songs* (American Music 15), *Last Testament* (Delmark 225)

Recommended Reading: *Jazz Masters of New Orleans* by Martin Williams (Macmillan Publishing Co., 1967), *Jazzmen* edited by Frederic Ramsey Jr. and Charles Edward Smith (Harcourt Brace Jovanovich, 1939)

FRANK JOHNSON
. . . .

b. May 22, 1927, Melbourne, Australia, d. Oct. 16, 2000, Noosa Heads, Queensland, Australia

One of the giants of the Australian trad jazz movement, Frank Johnson was a bandleader throughout his career. He learned to play trumpet while in grade school and, after hearing Graeme Bell's group in 1945, was inspired to form his own band, the Fabulous Dixielanders. Surviving a serious bout with pleurisy in 1947 that knocked him out of action for eight months, Johnson led his band steadily up to 1956. During this period, the Fabulous Dixielanders recorded often, appearing at trad festivals and broadcasting regularly over the radio, becoming an influential force in Australia. A car accident in 1955 that killed trombonist Warwick Dyer, along with the dropping popularity of trad jazz in Australia, led the band to break up.

Frank Johnson led other, similar groups into the late 1970s, and although recordings were very few and his later bands did not reach the heights of his prime group, he remained a force in Australia's Dixieland scene for many years. Ironically, he died in a car accident too, 45 years after the one that had ended the Fabulous Dixielanders.

Recommended CDs: *Frank Johnson's Famous Dixielanders* (GHB 376)

LPs to Search For: *Frank Johnson's Fabulous Dixielanders 1949–1950* (Swaggie 1414), *Dixieland Jazz 1954–56* (Swaggie 1325)

MONEY JOHNSON
. . . .

b. Feb. 23, 1918, Tyler, TX, d. Mar. 28, 1978, New York, NY

A spirited swing player who had loads of musical experiences but very little fame, Harold "Money" Johnson could always be relied upon. He started playing trumpet when he was 15. Johnson worked early on with Eddie and Sugar Lou, in Dallas with Red Calhoun, and in Oklahoma City with Skinny Thompson. Johnson spent a long period (1937–42) associated with Nat Towles' territory band, staying with the ensemble when it was taken over by pianist-arranger Horace Henderson (1942–44). Johnson was briefly with Count Basie in 1944, played with Bob Dorsey in Rochester (1944–46), and had stints during the next three decades with

Cootie Williams, Lucky Millinder, Louis Jordan, Lucky Thompson, Buddy Johnson, Cozy Cole, Herbie Fields, Panama Francis, Reuben Phillips' band at the Apollo, and Earl Hines (1966–68) in addition to working in the studios.

Johnson gained his greatest recognition as a member of Duke Ellington's last orchestra (1969–74), taking occasional trumpet solos and good-humored vocals (sometimes imitating Louis Armstrong), helping to give spirit to Duke's big band in its final period. After Ellington's death, Money Johnson (who never led his own record date) freelanced, participating in one of Buck Clayton's recorded jam sessions. He remained active up until the night before his death from a heart attack.

Recommended CDs: *A Buck Clayton Jam Session-1975* (Chiaroscuro 143)

LPs to Search For: with Duke Ellington: *Eastbourne Performance* (RCA 1023)

CARMELL JONES
· · · · · · · · · · · · · · · ·

b. July 19, 1936, Kansas City, KS, d. Nov. 7, 1996, Kansas City, KS

Carmell Jones was a reliable bop soloist who spent many of his key years playing in Europe. Jones began on trumpet when he was 11. He served in the military (1956–58), studied at Kansas University (1958–60), and moved to Los Angeles in 1960. Jones' most significant jazz work took place during the first half of the 1960s. He was associated with the Gerald Wilson Orchestra (1961–63) and worked with Harold Land, Bud Shank, and the Horace Silver Quintet (1964–65), recording *Song for My Father* with Silver. Jones also recorded with Wilson, Land, Shank, Curtis Amy, Joe Henderson, Booker Ervin, and Charles McPherson, plus as a leader for Pacific Jazz and Prestige.

Jones moved to Europe in mid-1965, working with radio orchestras, on television in Berlin, and at European jazz festivals. Since he led only one album during his 15 years overseas, Jones became largely forgotten in the United States. In 1980 Jones moved back to Kansas City, where he worked as an educator and gigged in clubs till near the end of his life. But unlike Dexter Gordon, who gained a great deal of publicity when he had returned to the United States a few years earlier, no one seemed to notice that Carmell Jones was back.

Recommended CDs: *Jay Hawk Talk* (Original Jazz Classics 1938), with Charles McPherson: *Bebop Revisited* (Original Jazz Classics 710), with Horace Silver: *Song for My Father* (Blue Note 84185)

LPs to Search For: *The Remarkable Carmell Jones* (Pacific Jazz 29), *Carmell Jones in Europe* (Prestige 7669), with Horace Silver: *Live 1964* (Emerald 1001)

CONNIE JONES
· · · · · · · · · · · · · · · ·

A veteran trad cornetist long based in New Orleans, Conrad "Connie" Jones has played in many freewheeling settings through the years. In the early 1950s he joined an unrecorded version of the Basin Street Six, replacing George Girard. He had a short stint with Jack

Teagarden, played with Billy Maxted, and, after Frank Assunto's passing in 1974, was his first replacement with the Dukes of Dixieland.

Connie Jones, who has also recorded as a guest sideman, has led his own Crescent City Jazz Band in New Orleans for some time, heading dates for Jazzology, Maison Bourbon, Crescent City, and Challenge.

Recommended CDs: *Sweet, Hot and Blue* (Jazzology 306), *Get Out and Get Under the Moon* (Challenge 70054), with Jim Beebe: *Sultry Serenade* (Delmark 230), with Judi K: *It's Been a Long Long Time* (Jazzology 215), with Tim Laughlin: *Blue Orleans* (Good Time Jazz 15004)

LPs to Search For: *Connie Jones' Crescent City Jazz Band* (Jazzology 49)

JONAH JONES

· · · · · · · · · · · · ·

b. Dec. 31, 1908, Louisville, KY, d. Apr. 30, 2000, New York, NY

Jonah Jones was an exciting swing-era trumpeter who, by latching onto a formula that he discovered by accident, became an unlikely best-selling artist in the late 1950s.

Jones had a long and episodic career. He was born Robert Elliott Jones (the name Jonah came from a stuttering band director who had trouble saying Jones!) and was originally inspired to play music after seeing a large parade band. Jones started out on alto horn before switching to trumpet. He played locally with the groups of Artie Jones and Othello Tinsley as a teenager, turning pro to work with a series of mostly obscure territory bands (including Horace Henderson during 1928–29). In 1931 Jones was with Jimmie Lunceford's orchestra for a few months and then hooked up with Stuff Smith, one of the hardest-swinging jazz violinists ever. They played together regularly during 1932–34 (mostly in upstate New York) without really catching on. In 1935 Jones temporarily left Smith to work with Lil Armstrong's big band (he was billed by the pianist as "King Louis the Second," after her former husband) and with a later version of McKinley's Cotton Pickers.

When Jones rejoined Stuff Smith in 1936, this time everything clicked and they had a long and very successful engagement at the Onyx Club. Recordings resulted (including the novelty hit "I'se a Muggin'"), and the combination of violin and trumpet (with the two principles both being extroverted and exciting soloists) was classic, as can be heard on their recordings of "After You've Gone" and "Here Comes the Man with the Jive."

The band lasted until 1940. Jones (who had had some opportunities to record as a freelancer, including with Billie Holiday, Teddy Wilson, Lionel Hampton, Adrian Rollini, Georgia White, and Peetie Wheetstraw) had stints with the big bands of Benny Carter and Fletcher Henderson, turning down an offer to join Tommy Dorsey. In February 1941 he became part of Cab Calloway's orchestra and stayed with the colorful singer-personality for 11 years, until 1952. Jones was Cab's key soloist during those years (being featured early on during a song called "Jonah Joins the Cab"), and he remained with Calloway even when the singer was forced to cut back to a small group.

After Cab broke up his band altogether to concentrate on acting and work as a single, Jonah Jones kept busy. He worked with Joe Bushkin, played Dixieland with Earl Hines, appeared in the orchestra used for the Broadway production of *Porgy and Bess*, toured Europe (recording some exciting encounters with soprano saxophonist Sidney Bechet), and worked with society orchestras. But with the passing of the swing era, the 46-year-old Jones' period in the spotlight would seem to be over. However, the future would turn out to be more exciting than expected.

Jonah Jones was booked with a quartet to play the Embers in New York in 1955. Encouraged to use mutes and often playing over a shuffle beat, the result was a very catchy sound. The Groove label (later acquired by Victor) recorded a live album by Jones in early 1956 that included "It's All Right with Me" and some Dixieland and swing standards. The following year Jones was signed by Capitol, and a long series of quartet records resulted; his renditions of "On the Street Where You Live" and "Baubles, Bangles and Beads" were major hits that were known far beyond the jazz world and kept Jones working for years. His stint at the Embers lasted nine years!

Jones had modified his style only slightly and was playing primarily standards (along with some current pop tunes), but the happiness felt in his horn solos and his enthusiastic vocals, along with the shuffle rhythms, made him a big-selling artist for Capitol through 1963. He later recorded in the trumpet-with-rhythm format for the Decca and Motown (!) labels. Jones was less active in the 1970s and '80s, making a final record in 1986 and largely retiring around the time that he turned 80. Jonah Jones had the distinction of being one of the very few swing veterans who was actually much more popular 15 years after the big band era ended than he had been when swing was at its peak.

Recommended CDs: *1936–1945* (Classics 972), *Jumpin' with Jonah* (Capitol 24554), *Back on the Street* (Chiaroscuro 118), with Cab Calloway: *1940–1941* (Classics 629), *1941–1942* (Classics 682), *1942–1947* (Classics 996), with Stuff Smith: *1936–1939* (Classics 706)

LPs to Search For: *Paris 1954/Volume One* (Swing 8408), *Jonah's Wail* (Inner City 7021), *At the Embers* (Groove 1001), *Muted Jazz* (Capital 839), *Swingin' on Broadway* (Capitol 963), *Jumpin' with Jonah* (Capitol 1039)

Recommended Reading: *Jazz Talking* by Max Jones (Da Capo Press, 1987), *The World Of Swing* by Stanley Dance (Charles Scribner's Sons, 1974)

LEROY JONES
• • • • • • • • • • • •

b. Feb. 20, 1958, New Orleans, LA

A good-time trumpeter who has been a major attraction in New Orleans since the 1980s, Leroy Jones always enjoys himself while performing, and his enthusiasm is catchy. Jones started playing in Danny Barker's Fairview Baptist Church Christian Marching Band when he was 13, performing at the New Orleans Jazz and Heritage Festival that year (1971). He led the Hurricane Brass Band (1974–76) as a teenager, worked with Leroy Bates Hot Corp. Inc. and Hollis Carmouche, played in Southeast Asia for three years, appeared in the show *One Mo' Time*, and led a quintet modestly called New Orleans' Finest (1980–83). He also worked with the Louisiana Repertory Jazz Ensemble, the Young Tuxedo Brass Band, and other bands.

Leroy Jones made an impression working with Harry Connick Jr.'s big band (1990–94), and since then has led a quintet, working steadily in New Orleans, where his basic but effective trumpet playing (which features distinctive phrasing) and happy vocalizing are quite popular.

Recommended CDs: *Mo' Cream from the Crop* (Columbia 66628), *Props for Pops* (Columbia 67643)

THAD JONES

• • • • • • • • • • •

b. Mar. 28, 1923, Pontiac, MI, d. Aug. 20, 1986, Copenhagen, Denmark

Thad Jones was one of the finest trumpeters to emerge during the 1950s and a major arranger and bandleader. His decision to leave the United States jazz scene in 1978, abandoning the big band that he co-led with Mel Lewis to move to Denmark, was a major surprise and is still considered a mystery.

The younger brother of pianist Hank Jones and the older brother of drummer Elvin Jones, Thad was self-taught on the trumpet (starting when he was 13), playing with his brothers locally in the late 1930s. After serving in the Army during 1943–46, Jones worked for a time in Oklahoma City, was a regular member of Billy Mitchell's quintet in Detroit (1950–53), and became an important part of the viable Detroit jazz scene.

Jones became famous while with Count Basie's orchestra (1954–63), sharing the trumpet features with Joe Newman and taking a much-imitated solo on Basie's hit record of "April in Paris." Jones also made a strong impression working with Charles Mingus for some recordings in 1954 (his harmonically advanced solos and crisp sound perfectly fit Mingus' adventurous music). Developing quickly as a writer, he contributed charts to the big bands of Basie and Harry James.

After leaving Basie, Jones worked with Gerry Mulligan and George Russell, was part of the Thelonious Monk big band at its December 1963 Lincoln Center concert (he had previously recorded with Monk in the late 1950s), and co-led a quintet with Pepper Adams in 1965. In December 1965 Jones formed a big band with Mel Lewis featuring some of New York's top musicians, playing at the Village Vanguard nearly every Monday night from February 1966 on. Although always a part-time venture, the Thad Jones/Mel Lewis Orchestra was soon recognized as one of jazz's greatest big bands. Jones wrote most of the arrangements and became acclaimed for his inventive writing (which often featured a soprano sax in the lead). Among his compositions, the best-known are the standard "A Child Is Born," "Central Park North," "Tiptoe," "Mean What You Say," "Little Pixie," and "Fingers." He was also a highly individual soloist (often playing flugelhorn), although he was never featured enough with the band.

Jones left the orchestra and the United States suddenly in 1978, a move that has never really been explained. He formed the Thad Jones Eclipse in Denmark, which he led during 1979–84, often playing valve trombone when his lip had problems. Thad Jones returned to the United States to lead the Count Basie Orchestra in 1985, but bad health forced him to give up that job in February 1986, six months before he passed away at the age of 63.

Recommended CDs: *The Fabulous Thad Jones* (Original Jazz Classics 625), *The Magnificent Thad Jones* (Blue Note 46814), *Mean What You Say* (Original Jazz Classics 464), *Basle, 1969* (TCB 02042), *Thad Jones and the Mel Lewis Quartet* (A&M 0830), *Three and One* (Steeple-Chase 31197)

Box Sets: *The Complete Blue Note/UA/Roulette Recordings of Thad Jones* (3 CDs; Mosaic 3-172), *The Complete Solid State Recordings of the Thad Jones/Mel Lewis Orchestra* (5 CDs; Mosaic 5-151)

LPs to Search For: *Consummation* (Blue Note 84346)

Recommended Reading: *Swing Legacy* by Chip Deffaa (Scarecrow Press, 1989)

VIRGIL JONES

. . . .

b. Aug. 26, 1939, Indianapolis, IN

A talented utility trumpeter able to play effectively both in the background and during short hard bop-oriented solos, Virgil Jones deserves much greater recognition. He studied trumpet in high school and in the 1960s worked with Lionel Hampton (1960–63), Johnny "Hammond" Smith (1964), and Ray Charles (1967–68). A longtime New York studio musician, Jones performed on Monday nights with the Thad Jones-Mel Lewis Orchestra, made many record dates as a sideman for Prestige (often with funky organ groups), and has played with the who's who of straightahead jazz.

A partial list of Jones' associations through the years include the American Jazz Orchestra, the Smithsonian Masterworks Orchestra, Jimmy Heath, Frank Foster, Barry Harris, McCoy Tyner's big band, the Dizzy Gillespie big band (1987), Milt Jackson, Benny Carter, Dameronia, Rahsaan Roland Kirk, Sonny Stitt, Joey DeFrancesco, Joe Henderson, Teddy Edwards, T.S. Monk, and Clark Terry. The list could easily be three times longer, yet ironically Virgil Jones has never led a record date of his own!

Recommended CDs: with Rusty Bryant: *Legends of Acid Jazz* (Prestige 24168), with Dameronia: *Live at the Theatre Boulogne* (Soul Note 121202), with Charles Earland: *Black Talk* (Original Jazz Classics 335), with Teddy Edwards: *Midnight Creeper* (High Note 7011), with Frank Foster: *Fearless Frank Foster* (Original Jazz Classics 923), *Soul Outing!* (Original Jazz Classics 984), with Harold Mabern: *Wailin'* (Prestige 24134)

LPs to Search For: with Dameronia: *Look, Stop and Listen* (Uptown 27.15)

HERBERT JOOS

. . . .

b. Mar. 21, 1940, Karlsruhe, Germany

A mellow-toned flugelhornist with an adventurous and versatile style, Herbert Joos is best known for his playing with the Vienna Art Orchestra. He studied music at Karlsruhe University and played a variety of music in the 1960s with the Karlsruhe Modern Jazz Quintet. In the 1970s he had his own groups, leading albums (starting in 1973) for the Japo,

FMP, Plane, Sesam, Extraplatte Jazz, Free Flow, and ECM labels, plus a set of Billie Holiday songs in 1994 for Emarcy. Herbert Joos, who played with the Mike Gibbs Orchestra and recorded with Hans Koller, in 1979 became a member of the Vienna Art Orchestra, where he has been an important contributor ever since.

Recommended CDs: *Daybreak* (Polygram 841479), *Ballade Noire* (Free Flow 0392), *Herbert Joos Plays Billie Holiday Songs* (Emarcy 522634), with the Vienna Art Orchestra: *A Notion in Perpetual Motion* (Hat Art 6096), *The Original Charts* (Verve 521 998)

MARLON JORDAN

b. Aug. 21, 1970, New Orleans, LA

Part of the Young Lions movement of the late 1980s, Marlon Jordan has gradually developed into a fine trumpeter who has plenty of potential. His father, Kidd Jordan, is an avant-garde saxophonist, while his older brother, Kent Jordan, is a top flutist. Marlon Jordan played saxophone, violin, and drums before switching to trumpet in fourth grade. He was inspired by Wynton Marsalis and Terence Blanchard, both of whom he knew while still a youth. Jordan studied music extensively and was a featured soloist with the New Orleans Symphony during 1986–87.

Jordan made his recording debut with his brother in 1987, cut an album with Dennis Gonzalez for Silkheart, and recorded three records as a leader for Columbia (starting in 1988 when he was 18) that were quite influenced by Marsalis and did not show much individuality. After that initial outburst, Jordan toured with the Jazz Futures (where he played alongside Roy Hargrove), maintained a low profile for a few years, and then became more active again, starting in 1997 when he recorded as a leader for Arabesque. Perhaps overrated early in his career, Marlon Jordan is ironically underrated today, although he is a much more original player now than he was as an 18-year-old; he is capable of great things in the future.

Recommended CDs: *For You Only* (Columbia 45200), *Marlon's Mode* (Arabesque 127), with Donald Harrison: *For Art's Sake* (Candid 79501), with the Jazz Futures: *Live in Concert* (Novus 63158)

TAFT JORDAN

b. Feb. 15, 1915, Florence, SC, d. Dec. 1, 1981, New York, NY

An excellent swing soloist, Taft Jordan was always a valuable sideman but was rarely ever a leader. Jordan grew up in Norfolk, Virginia, studied music in Philadelphia, started on baritone horn, and switched to trumpet in 1929. He first appeared on records in the early 1930s with the Washboard Rhythm Kings. During 1933–41 Jordan was one of the Chick Webb big band's main soloists and an occasional vocalist, staying with the orchestra after Webb's death, when it was fronted by Ella Fitzgerald. In 1933 Jordan recorded a version of "On the Sunny Side of the Street" that was based on Louis Armstrong's concert routine. When Satch got around to recording it a year later, some people thought that he was copying Jordan!

After Ella broke up the Webb ghost band, Jordan led an octet at the Savoy Ballroom (1942–43). He landed a featured spot with Duke Ellington's orchestra (in the "hot trumpet" chair that was formerly occupied by Freddy Jenkins), being well showcased during 1943–47, including at Duke's classic Carnegie Hall concerts. Jordan's remaining 34 years after leaving Ellington were a bit anticlimactic but reasonably productive. He freelanced in New York, worked with the Lucille Dixon Orchestra (1949–53), gigged with Don Redman (1953) and Benny Goodman (1958), and co-led a group with trumpeter Dick Vance. Jordan also worked in the studios, played in the pit orchestras of Broadway shows, and was active into the late 1970s. Despite all of this activity, other than four numbers in 1935, Taft Jordan led just three albums in his career, one apiece for Mercury (1958), Aamco (the late 1950s), and Moodsville (a 1961 gem that has been reissued by Original Jazz Classics).

Recommended CDs: *Mood Indigo* (Original Jazz Classics 24230), with Duke Ellington: *1944–1945* (Classics 881), *Chicago Concerts* (Music Masters 65166), with Chick Webb: *1929–1934* (Classics 502), *1935–1938* (Classics 517)

Recommended Reading: *The World of Swing* by Stanley Dance (Charles Scribner's Sons, 1974)

DON JOSEPH
• • • • • • • • • • •

b. 1923, Staten Island, NY

The prime period of Don Joseph, a cool-toned trumpeter reminiscent of Chet Baker and Jon Eardley but much more obscure, was the 1950s. He began his career in the mid-1940s, playing in the big bands of Buddy Rich, Alvino Rey, and Lucky Millinder. Joseph freelanced in the New York area for years, jamming on a few occasions with Charlie Parker. In 1957 he worked with Gerry Mulligan (recording a big band album with Jeru), and he was featured on guitarist Chuck Wayne's *String Fever* record. But soon afterward, Joseph dropped out of the jazz scene. Frustrated with the music business and battling some health problems, Joseph spent many years as a music teacher, occasionally playing low-profile gigs. In 1984 he emerged out of nowhere to lead his first and only record date (*One of a Kind* for the Uptown label), but Don Joseph soon slipped back into obscurity, becoming a legendary historical footnote.

LPs to Search For: *One of a Kind* (Uptown 27.23)

MAX KAMINSKY
• • • • • • • • • • • •

b. Sept. 7, 1908, Brockton, MA, d. Sept. 6, 1994, Castle Point, NY

A solid Dixieland soloist who was part of the trad scene for quite a few decades, Max Kaminsky stuck to the music he loved throughout his long career. Kaminsky led a band in Boston when he was 12 (the Six Novelty Syncopators), and he started his professional career early, working with Art Karle's group as a teenager. After moving to Chicago in 1927, Kaminsky was an integral part of the local scene for the next two years, becoming associated with Eddie Condon, Bud Freeman, Frank Teschemacher, Jess Stacy, and the other top hot jazz players of the time.

In 1929 the trumpeter played in New England with Red Nichols. He stayed busy during the Depression by working with Leo Reisman's society orchestra during 1931–33, recording in New York with Benny Carter, Eddie Condon, and Mezz Mezzrow. Kaminsky worked with Joe Venuti (1934), Teddy Roy (1935), and the Tommy Dorsey big band and Clambake Seven during 1935–36. Although not thought of as a big band musician, Kaminsky was associated with quite a few orchestras during the swing era, including those of Jack Jenney, Benny Goodman (briefly in 1937), and Artie Shaw (1938). His work with Eddie Condon, Lee Wiley, and Bud Freeman's Summa Cum Laude Band (1939–40) gave him a strong reputation in Dixieland circles. Kaminsky also played with the big bands of Tony Pastor (1940–41), Artie Shaw (1941–42), Alvino Rey, and Joe Marsala, performing in the Pacific war zone with Shaw's military band during 1943–44.

After his discharge, Kaminsky was one of the stars of Eddie Condon's legendary Town Hall concerts (1944–45), and he recorded as a leader for Commodore in 1944. From 1945 on, Kaminsky was often associated with Eddie Condon and occasionally pianist Art Hodes when not leading his own Dixieland combos. He stayed busy during the 1950s, toured Europe with Jack Teagarden and Earl Hines (1957), visited the Far East with Teagarden in 1958–59, and was a regular at Jimmy Ryan's in the 1960s and '70s. Max Kaminsky, who led albums for MGM (1953), Victor (1954), Jazztone (1954), MK (1955), Westminster (1960), United Artists (1963), Fat Cat's Jazz (1974–75) and finally Chiaroscuro (1977), wrote one of the best of all musician autobiographies in 1963, *Jazz Band: My Life in Jazz*.

Recommended CDs: *Copley Terrace 1945* (Jazzology 15), with Eddie Condon: *Dixieland All-Stars* (GRP/Decca 637), with Tommy Dorsey: *Featuring the Clambake Seven* (Jazz Archives 3801262)

LPs to Search For: *Two for Tea* (Fat Cat Jazz 206), *When Summer Is Gone* (Chiaroscuro 176)

Recommended Reading: *Jazz Band: My Life in Jazz* by Max Kaminsky (Da Capo Press, 1963), *Jazz Talking* by Max Jones (Da Capo Press, 1987)

LEE KATZMAN
• • • • • • • • • • • •

b. May 17, 1928, Chicago, IL

A fine cool jazz trumpeter, Lee Katzman was a top-notch sideman in the 1950s and '60s with many major names, although he never became one himself. Katzman began playing trumpet when he was 13. He worked with the big bands of Sam Donahue (1947), Buddy Rich (1948), Claude Thornhill, and Jimmy Dorsey, also recording with Herbie Fields. Katzman moved to California in the mid-1950s, toured with Stan Kenton (1956), and was an important part of the local scene. Among his associations were the big bands of Les Brown (1958) and Terry Gibbs, plus Med Flory, Pepper Adams, the Bill Holman-Mel Lewis quintet, Anita O'Day, Jimmie Rowles, Sonny Stitt, June Christy, Shelly Manne (1965), and Les McCann. Lee Katzman had his only session as a leader in 1980, a real obscurity. But despite his lack of fame, he was a fine trumpeter in the Chet Baker mellow bop tradition.

Recommended CDs: with Bill Holman: *Jive for Five* (V.S.O.P. 19), with Jimmie Rowles: *Weather in a Jazz Vane* (V.S.O.P. 48)

LPs to Search For: *Naptown Reunion* (25th Century Ensemble 0626)

SHAKE KEANE

• • • • • • • • • • • •

b. May 30, 1927, St. Vincent, British West Indies, d. Nov. 10, 1997, Oslo, Norway

An important free jazz pioneer in England, Ellsworth "Shake" Keane was also versatile enough to play with big bands. He began learning the trumpet when he was five, performing in public for the first time the following year and leading a band when he was 14. Keane actually started out as a schoolteacher, was a published poet, and (after moving to London in 1952) studied English literature at London University in the early 1950s. Around this time he earned the nickname of "Shake," which is short for Shakespeare.

Keane began playing music seriously in the mid-1950s, influenced by Caribbean and African music. He recorded calypso music with Lord Kitchener, worked with the Harlem All-Stars, and led groups off and on during 1954–68. With saxophonist Joe Harriott during much of 1959–65, he co-led one of the earliest jazz bands to feature free improvisation in England. Keane also recorded in Germany with Kurt Edelhagen and was a member of the Francy Boland-Kenny Clarke Big Band (1967–68).

In 1972 Keane was appointed Minister of Culture of St. Vincent, and he became semi-retired from active playing. He spent time as the principal of Bishop's College in Georgetown, lived in Brooklyn during the 1980s, and occasionally wrote arrangements, but mostly he maintained a low profile during the remainder of his life. Ironically, most of Shake Keane's dates as a leader (including albums for Decca and Ace of Clubs) find him playing dance music with larger ensembles, but his adventurous (but sadly out-of-print) recordings with Harriott are his most important contributions to jazz.

LPs to Search For: with Joe Harriott: *Free Form* (Jazzland 49), *Indo-Jazz Suite* (Columbia 1465), *Abstract* (Columbia 1477), *High Spirits* (Columbia 1692)

JON-ERIK KELLSO

• • • • • • • • • • • • • •

b. May 8, 1964, Dearborn, MI

One of the major mainstream and trad cornetists to emerge during the 1990s, Jon-Erik Kellso has appeared on a large variety of enjoyable CDs, particularly for the Arbors label.

At age ten I discovered my parent's 78s, which included such artists as Harry James, Benny Goodman, and Tommy Dorsey. My father, who had played some trumpet in the late '30s and early '40s, encouraged me and introduced me to records by Bunny Berigan and Louis Armstrong. Around that time I asked if I could play trumpet in the school band, before I knew that my Dad had played. He was delighted. He dug out his old horn and gave me my first lessons. I played my first gig in seventh grade and starting working in Detroit when I was 15; Marcus Belgrave and Tom Saunders are great Detroit players who encouraged me to get up on stage with them.

Kellso started playing in the International Youth Symphony at 13 (1977–79), was in the Michigan Youth Symphony (1980–82), and attended Wayne Street University (1982–88). He played with the New McKinney's Cotton Pickers, J.C. Heard's orchestra (1987–89), and James Dapogny's Chicago Jazz Band before moving to New York in 1989 to work with Vince Giordano's Nighthawks. Since that time, Kellso has been featured in many mainstream, swing, and Dixieland settings, including continuing with Dapogny (recording four albums with his band) and working and recording with Dan Barrett, Dick Hyman, Kenny Davern, Howard Alden, Rick Fay, Bob Haggart, Harry Allen, Ralph Sutton, Marty Grosz, Ruby Braff, Bob Wilbur, the Flying Neutrinos, and singer Peggy Cone, among many others.

Jon-Erik Kellso started recording for Arbors in 1992, making his debut as a leader in 1993 and impressing many listeners with his hot playing at jazz festivals ever since. "I want to find ways of bringing a younger audience to mainstream jazz. I have strived to keep the ensemble tradition of small-group jazz alive by playing an economic swinging strong lead, leaving room for the other horns, à la Max Kaminsky and Yank Lawson."

Recommended CDs: *Chapter 1* (Arbors 19125), *The Plot Thickens* (Arbors 19160), with James Dapogny: *Laughing at Life* (Discovery 74006), *Original Jelly Roll Blues* (Discovery 74008), *Hot Club Stomp* (Discovery 74009), *On the Road* (Schoolkids 1555), with Marty Grosz: *Ring dem Bells* (Nagel-Heyer 022), with the Magnificent Seven: *Newport Beach Session* (Arbors 19129), with Ralph Sutton: *Echoes of Swing* (Nagel-Heyer 038)

Videos to Get: *Rick Fay and Friends: Live at the State Theatre* (1992; Arbors ARVHS-1), *Bob Wilber's Big Band: Bufadora Blow Up* (1997; Arbors ARVHS-3)

CHRIS KELLY
• • • • • • • • • • •

b. Oct. 18, 1885 or 1890, Plaquemine Parish, LA, d. Aug. 19, 1929, New Orleans, LA

Chris Kelly is one of the lost New Orleans legends, a highly rated cornetist who never recorded, died young, and left behind barely a trace (not even a photograph), other than some memories from his contemporaries.

Kelly studied cornet with Jim Humphrey (a trumpeter and the grandfather of trumpeter Percy and clarinetist Willie Humphrey) and in 1915, when he was 25, he moved to New Orleans to play in a society band led by the older Humphrey. Within a short time, Kelly was considered one of the city's top cornetists. In 1919 he joined clarinetist Johnny Brown's group, a band he soon took over. Kelly worked throughout the 1920s at dance halls, cabarets, and dances, often winning highly competitive cutting contests over his fellow players. He became known for his highly expressive version of "Careless Love" and for his expertise with the plunger mute.

An alcoholic whose drinking habits became progressively worse during the 1920s, Chris Kelly died suddenly from a heart attack in 1929. The large crowd at his funeral attested to his great popularity.

FREDDIE KEPPARD

• • • • • • • • • • • • • • • •

b. Feb. 27, 1890, New Orleans, LA, d. July 15, 1933, Chicago, IL

Of all the early jazz trumpeters/cornetists who made it to records, Freddie Keppard went back as far historically as anyone did, for he was considered the top New Orleans cornetist of the 1910–20 period. In Keppard's recordings, listeners can hear a musician whose training was in brass bands, whose sound had to be powerful enough to be heard during the pre-microphone era, and who provided a direct link to (and an extension of) the shadowy music of Buddy Bolden. It is the closest that we can come today to hearing what jazz must have sounded like in its earliest days.

Keppard played music from an early age, starting on mandolin, violin, and accordion (his older brother, Louis Keppard, was a guitarist) before settling on cornet. He played with John Brown's band when he was 12, and at 16, in 1906, he formed and led the Olympia Orchestra, also working with Frankie Dusen's Eagle Band. With Bolden's rapid decline into dementia at the time, Keppard was soon considered New Orleans' new cornet/trumpet king, an unofficial position that he held until leaving the city in 1914 to join Bill Johnson and the Original Creole Orchestra in Los Angeles. Johnson's band introduced the as-yet-unnamed jazz music to quite a few cities (including Chicago in 1914 and New York in 1915) through its performances at theaters on the Orpheum Circuit.

Freddie Keppard often covered his right hand with a handkerchief when he played, to keep other cornetists from stealing his ideas. A similar fear may have kept him from being the first jazzman to record. In 1916, the Victor label supposedly offered Keppard an opportunity to make records, but apparently he turned them down because he did not want other people copying his ideas (although an unissued and long-lost test pressing by the Original Creole Orchestra might have been made in 1918). That bad decision kept Keppard from ever gaining the fame he deserved as a pioneer jazzman.

In 1918 Keppard settled in Chicago. He worked mostly as a sideman during the next decade, including with Doc Cook's Gingersnaps, Erskine Tate, Ollie Powers, and Jimmie Noone. The cornetist first recorded in 1923, cutting two songs with Tate and a few with Cook the following year; both dates were very primitively recorded. Otherwise all of his recordings were made between June 1926 and January 1927, six sessions led by either Cook, Jimmy Blythe, Jaspar Taylor, or (in one case) Keppard himself. While virtually every jazz reference book that mentions Keppard is quick to note that he was past his prime at the time, in reality the cornetist sounds pretty strong on some of these selections, particularly "Stock Yards Strut" (his greatest recording), "Salty Dog," "Here Comes the Hot Tamale Man," and "Messin' Around." His playing offers early jazz fans a glimpse of what jazz might have sounded like when Louis Armstrong was just a child.

Unfortunately, Keppard was quite an alcoholic by that time (drinking a half-gallon to three quarts of liquor a day), and he declined quickly. He led a band into 1928 and worked with Charlie Elgar at Chicago's Savoy Ballroom but spent his last few years suffering from tuberculosis, which eventually caused his death at age 43. By then he had been forgotten by the jazz world for several years, since he was two generations before Louis Armstrong and had been inactive during his final period. Still, it is worth wondering what he might have done during the swing era (he would have been only 45 in 1935) or even in the bebop years (a decade later) had he quit drinking in the early 1920s.

All 25 of Freddie Keppard's recordings are currently available on one CD, a must for fans of early jazz.

Recommended CD: *The Complete Freddie Keppard 1923/27* (King Jazz 111)

AL KILLIAN

. . . .

b. Oct. 15, 1916, Birmingham, AL, d. Sept. 5, 1950, Los Angeles, CA

Prior to the rise of Maynard Ferguson, Al Killian was Cat Anderson's main competition as jazz's top high-note trumpeter. Killian picked up experience early in his career working with Charlie Turner's Arcadians (mid-1930s) and the big bands of Baron Lee, Teddy Hill, Don Redman, Claude Hopkins, and Count Basie (1940–42). Killian was a major asset with Charlie Barnet's band (off and on during 1943–46), also spending a second short period with Basie and touring with Lionel Hampton for a few months in 1945.

Killian had a band late in 1946, toured with Jazz at the Philharmonic (usually taking the climactic solo), and was briefly with the orchestras of Billy Eckstine, Earle Spencer, and Boyd Raeburn. He toured with Duke Ellington during 1948–50 and led a four-song record date while in Stockholm, also recording with Lester Young and at several jam sessions. But after leaving Ellington and settling in Los Angeles, Al Killian was tragically murdered by a psychopathic landlord, cutting short a potentially significant career before he reached the age of 34.

Recommended CDs: with Jazz at the Philharmonic: *Bird and Pres—The '46 Concerts* (Verve 0898)

DON KINCH

. . . .

b. May 14, 1917, Kelso, WA

In his career, Don Kinch was a major part of three important Dixieland bands: the Castle Jazz Band, Turk Murphy, and the Firehouse Five Plus Two. Kinch grew up in Southern California and, after graduating from high school in San Diego, worked with a variety of dance bands. Kinch often worked outside of music (including in a shipyard, at a steel mill, and as a carpenter), since music was rarely ever a full-time job for him. Musically, he worked with the Castle Jazz Band during 1947–50 (when they made some obscure records for their own Castle label) and played with Turk Murphy's group in San Francisco (1950–53).

After leaving Murphy and settling in Los Angeles, Kinch worked as a studio musician, doubling on bass. He reunited with the Castle Jazz Band to participate in their two Good Time Jazz albums of 1957 and 1959. Since he frequently worked at the Disney studios, in 1958 Kinch took up the tuba so he could join the Firehouse Five Plus Two (most of whose members were Disney employees). He was with that popular group until its final recording

FRANZ KOGLMANN

. . . .

b. 1947, Modling, Austria

A top avant-garde trumpeter and an impressive composer, Franz Koglmann has an atmospheric sound and the ability to play on an equal level with the most advanced improvisers around. Koglmann studied jazz at Vienna's State Conservatory (1969–72). Early on he led a group called Masters of Unorthodox Jazz. Koglmann started the Pipe record label in 1973, and he recorded using Steve Lacy and Bill Dixon. A thoughtful but occasionally fiery player, Koglmann performed with the Improvising Music Orchestra (from around 1975–85), the Reform Art Unit, and in the 1980s with guitarist Eugene Chadbourne, pianist Georg Grawe, and his own groups (the Pipetet, KoKoKo, and the Pipe Trio).

Franz Koglmann recorded regularly for the Hat Art label during 1986–98, using such sidemen as Paul Bley, Lee Konitz, Tony Coe, and Misha Mengelberg. In 1999 the trumpeter founded the Between the Lines label, and he has continued recording consistently unpredictable and colorful sessions.

Recommended CDs: *The Use of Memory* (Hat Art 6078), *L'Heure Bleu* (Hat Art 6093), *We Thought About Duke* (Hat Art 6163), *Make Believe* (Between the Lines 10171), with Paul Bley: *12 + 6 in a Row* (Hat Art 6081), with Steve Lacy: *Itinerary* (Hat Art 6079)

LPs to Search For: *Flaps* (Pipe 151), *Opium for Fraz* (Pipe 152)

TOMMY LADNIER

. . . .

b. May 28, 1900, Florenceville, LA, d. June 4, 1939, New York, NY

T ommy Ladnier was a classic jazz trumpeter who hated to compromise. At his best on blues and uptempo stomps, Ladnier worked steadily in the 1920s but was somewhat lost during the early Depression days, when commercial music was dominant, and he did not fit into the swing era. Unfortunately, just when the New Orleans revival was beginning, he died prematurely, missing his chance for fame.

Ladnier grew up near New Orleans, where at one point he had trumpet lessons with Bunk Johnson. He moved to Chicago around 1917, working in a band led by drummer John H. Wickcliffe. Among his other early jobs were playing with Charlie Creath in St. Louis around 1921, gigging with violinist Milton Vassar the following year, and performing with Ollie Powers in 1923. Ladnier began appearing on records in 1923, and during the 1923–24 period he recorded in bands backing singers Ida Cox, Monette Moore, Alberta Hunter, Edmonia Henderson, Ma Rainey, Ethel Waters, Edna Hicks, Julia Davis, and the team of Ford and Ford. Instrumentally he was on no less than five takes of "Play That Thing" with Ollie Powers and may have appeared on two very primitively recorded early numbers by Jelly Roll Morton. Most significant are seven selections cut with Lovie Austin's Blues Serenaders during 1924–25, which find him matching well in a trio/quartet with clarinetist Jimmy O'Bryant, taking solos that fit stylistically between King Oliver and Louis Armstrong.

Ladnier had brief stints with Fate Marable and King Oliver before sailing to Europe with Sam Wooding's Chocolate Kiddies in June 1925. He played all over the continent with Wooding (recording a date in Berlin), leaving in June 1926 to work in Poland with Louis Douglas' revue. Returning to New York by August, he gigged with Billy Fowler's orchestra before joining Fletcher Henderson's big band. The latter would be Ladnier's most high-profile association of the 1920s, for during the next 17 months he was Henderson's main trumpet soloist, being featured on many records, including "The Chant" (which had Fats Waller guesting on piano), "Clarinet Marmalade," "Snag It" (where Ladnier had a chance to top King Oliver's famous version), "Tozo," "I'm Coming Virginia," "St. Louis Blues," and several versions of "St. Louis Shuffle." He also uplifted record dates led by Clarence Williams, Eva Taylor, Bessie Smith, and the obscure Clara Herring.

At the height of his fame, in 1928, Ladnier returned to Sam Wooding's orchestra for another yearlong stint in Europe, recording ten titles in a marathon session in Barcelona, Spain, in July 1929. After departing from Wooding, Ladnier stayed in Europe, working with Benny Peyton, Harry Flemming's Blue Birds, Louis Douglas, and his own band in France (spring 1930). Ladnier was with Noble Sissle's Sizzling Syncopators when they returned to the United States in 1931.

All of the overseas activity led Tommy Ladnier to be largely forgotten back in his homeland. Louis Armstrong was now the trumpet king, New Orleans jazz was considered passé, and Ladnier's brand of hot trumpet playing had been replaced by a more tightly arranged form of dance music. Ladnier and his good friend Sidney Bechet (who had also played with Sissle) decided to try to buck the trend and formed the New Orleans Feetwarmers. The Feetwarmers played at the Saratoga Club in Harlem and the Savoy, recording one session in 1932. Their six exuberant performances are extremely exciting examples of New Orleans jazz, particularly the blazing versions of "Shag" and "Maple Leaf Rag." During the same period, Ladnier and Bechet ran the Southern Tailor Shop, but they spent more time playing jam sessions in the back room than pressing clothes! Both the Feetwarmers and the Tailor Shop came to an end in 1933, when Bechet gave up and rejoined Sissle.

At that point Ladnier seemed to disappear, and he was not heard of in New York City for five years. In 1938, French jazz critic Hugues Panassie arrived in the United States with the main goal of recording some small New Orleans-style bands, feeling that Tommy Ladnier would be the ideal trumpeter. It took a long search before Ladnier was discovered working in Newburgh, New York. He had gigged for a time with his own group in New Jersey, taught music, and then settled in upstate New York. By the time Panassie found him, Ladnier was a heavy drinker, but his trumpet chops were still in excellent form. He was at first teamed with the erratic but well-intentioned clarinetist Mezz Mezzrow, but the November 21, 1938, session was a fiasco, because Ladnier did not care for Sidney DeParis' swing-based trumpet playing and became very drunk. However, a date under Ladnier's name a week later found him working well with both Sidney Bechet and Mezzrow; their "Really the Blues" is a classic. He also appeared successfully on another Mezz date on December 19 and four days later teamed up with Bechet as the co-leader of the revived New Orleans Feetwarmers at John Hammond's "Spirituals to Swing" concert at Carnegie Hall. In addition, Ladnier appeared on a couple of songs from a session on February 1, 1939, backing blues singer Rosetta Crawford.

It all came to an end when Tommy Ladnier, while staying with Mezzrow, suffered a fatal heart attack a week after his 39th birthday. Four days later the Port of Harlem Jazzmen, an all-star group that included Sidney Bechet, recorded "Blues for Tommy" to remember the fallen trumpeter.

Recommended CDs: with Lovie Austin: *1924–1926* (Classics 756), with Fletcher Henderson: *1926–1927* (Classics 597), *1927* (Classics 580)

Box Set: with Sidney Bechet: *Master Takes 1932–43* (3 CDs; Bluebird 2402)

STEVE LANE

b. Nov. 7, 1921, London, England

A fine trad player, Steve Lane has led bands for a half-century in England. Lane actually started out as a guitarist. After serving in the military during World War II and playing guitar with the Ragtime Trio, he switched to cornet while in his twenties. Always most interested in trad jazz, Lane formed the Southern Stompers, which debuted in November 1950.

He has led the Southern Stompers ever since, although they changed their name to the Red Hot Peppers in the mid-1980s. In addition to his playing, Lane has written for jazz magazines and produced many classic reissues of early jazz records for the VJM label. Steve Lane and his band recorded quite frequently during the 1960s, '70s and '80s, including for the VJM, Stomp, 77, Stomp Off, and Azure labels, helping to keep revivalist Dixieland alive in Great Britain long after the trad boom of the early '60s ended.

Recommended CDs: *Easy Come-Easy Go* (Azure 14)

LPs to Search For: *Just Gone* (Major Minor 202), *Snake Rag* (Stomp Off 1040)

NICK LAROCCA

b. Apr. 11, 1889, New Orleans, LA, d. Feb. 22, 1961, New Orleans, LA

Nick LaRocca was the founder and leader of the Original Dixieland Jazz Band, the first jazz group ever to record. However, his prickly personality was partly to blame for the ODJB's breaking up, and his later claims about his group's role as the "founder of jazz" definitely hurt his cause.

LaRocca's accomplishments as a jazz pioneer were significant enough that his absurd claims were not needed. The son of an amateur cornetist, LaRocca grew up around music in New Orleans and began playing cornet as a child. He formed his first band in 1908, freelanced with many groups, and during 1912–16 was with Papa Jack Laine's Reliance Bands. In 1915 LaRocca had begun working with drummer Johnny Stein, and on March 1, 1916, he left New Orleans with Stein to accept a job in Chicago. With Alcide "Yellow" Nunez on clarinet, pianist Henry Ragas, and trombonist Eddie Edwards, Stein's Dixie Jass Band became a hit at Schiller's Café, staying for most of three months. A dispute over salary (LaRocca and the other sidemen wanted to break the contract and accept a higher-paying job) resulted in the cornetist's becoming the leader of the new Original Dixieland Jazz Band. Tony Sbarbaro replaced Stein on drums and, at the end of October, when Yellow Nunez was fired due to unreliability, Larry Shields took over as clarinetist. The lineup was set.

Relocating to New York in 1917, the ODJB became a sensation playing at Reisenweber's, helping to launch the jazz age. They made their first recordings for Columbia ("Darktown Strutters Ball" and "Indiana") on January 30, 1917. However, the label chickened out and shelved the recordings, considering them too barbaric and freewheeling. LaRocca soon brought the group to Columbia's main rival, Victor, and on February 26 the quintet recorded "Livery Stable Blues" (which found the three horn players imitating the sounds of animals) and the hyper "Dixie Jazz Band One-Step." Victor quickly released the music, "Livery Stable Blues" became a giant hit, and the ODJB became nationally famous. Columbia found their two ODJB recordings and soon released them too.

The playing of Nick LaRocca with the ODJB was pretty basic. The group stuck exclusively to ensembles, and LaRocca's role was primarily to play the melody, chorus after chorus, with little change. The little bit of improvising that LaRocca indulged in took place mostly in two-bar breaks and in his phrasing. However, compared to the other music that was recorded during 1912–17, the ODJB was quite revolutionary and influential (not to mention noisy!). But it was only an early first step, and within five years the band would seem quite prehistoric.

During 1917–18, the Original Dixieland Jazz Band introduced such future Dixieland standards (in addition to those already mentioned) as "Tiger Rag," "At the Jazz Band Ball," "Fidgety Feet, "Sensation," and "Clarinet Marmalade." By 1918 there were several early jazz groups on record doing their best to imitate the ODJB. During 1919–20 the ODJB became the first jazz band to visit Europe, working regularly in England (where it recorded) and duplicating their American success. Emile Christian was the band's trombonist overseas (Edwards had been drafted), while J. Russell Robinson was its pianist (Henry Ragas had died during the 1918–19 flu epidemic). Returning to the United States, the ODJB was reasonably successful during 1920–22, although an altoist (Benny Krueger) was often added for recording dates (including a hit version of "Margie") to make the group conform a bit to the later dance music trends. But, although the band struggled on into January 1925, it recorded only four titles during its final three years, turnover lessened the band's uniqueness (Shields, Edwards, and Robinson all departed), and the group failed to evolve with the times. Nick LaRocca had a mental breakdown in January 1925, was advised to give up music, and returned home to New Orleans.

Eleven years passed as LaRocca ran a contracting business. In 1936 he was approached about getting the ODJB back together to appear in the movie *The Big Broadcast of 1937*. Although LaRocca turned down the offer (knowing that the group could not be reorganized so quickly, particularly since Sbarbaro was the only member still actively playing music), he began to toy with the idea of bringing back the band. After months of practice, the Original Dixieland Jazz Band (LaRocca, Edwards, Shields, Robinson, and Sbarbaro) came back together to play on an Ed Wynn radio show. Their rendition of "Tiger Rag" generated a great deal of fan mail, and their comeback was on. In addition to getting together the ODJB, LaRocca organized a 14-piece big band. During three recording sessions in September and November 1936, the larger group (which included LaRocca, Shields, Robinson, and Sbarbaro) performed okay versions of nine songs, while the ODJB remade six of their earlier classics in exciting fashion.

LaRocca's ensemble trumpet style had not changed much at all through the years, other than perhaps becoming a bit smoother, but the quintet sides in particular were successful, reminding the swing audiences where their music had come from.

The comeback did not last long. The group was filmed briefly for *The March of Time* (they had previously appeared in a Charlie Chaplin silent movie in 1917, *The Good-for-Nothing*), but personality conflicts resulted in the disbanding of the ODJB on February 1, 1938, and La-Rocca's permanent retirement from music.

During his last 23 years, Nick LaRocca did not participate in any of the occasional ODJB reunions, and the bitterness that he had felt since the 1930s when the ODJB was in danger of being completely forgotten was expressed in a series of angry and sometimes racist letters. Richard Sudhalter's book *Lost Chords* reprinted these comments from a 1936 *Metronome* article (when the ODJB comeback was on), and they are a sad commentary on LaRocca's state of mind: "Our music is strictly a white man's music. We patterned our earlier efforts after military marches, which we heard at park concerts in New Orleans in our youth. Many writers have attributed this rhythm that we introduced as something coming from the African jungles, and crediting the Negro race with it. My contention is that the Negroes learned to play this rhythm and music from the whites."

Unlike Jelly Roll Morton, who was overly ridiculed for bragging that he was the inventor of jazz when he was actually one of jazz's first innovators, there is little truth in Nick La-Rocca's comments, and they make him look very small. However, as an early bandleader and propagandist for jazz, he was quite significant before later developments overtook him.

Recommended CDs: with the Original Dixieland Jazz Band: *75th Anniversary* (Bluebird 61908), *In England* (EMI Pathe 252716)

Recommended Reading: *The Best of Jazz* by Humphrey Lyttelton (Taplinger Publishing Co., 1982), *Jazz Masters of New Orleans* by Martin Williams (Macmillan Publishing Co., 1967), *Lost Chords* by Richard M. Sudhalter (Oxford University Press, 1999), *The Story of the Original Dixieland Jazz Band* by H. O. Brunn (Louisiana State University Press, 1960)

Film Appearances: with the Original Dixieland Jazz Band: *The Good-for-Nothing* (1917)

SASKIA LAROO

· · · · · · · · · · · · · ·

b. July 31, 1959, Amsterdam, Netherlands

A European trumpeter who took a while to dedicate herself to jazz, Saskia Laroo has the potential to develop into a fine jazz player.

As a child, at home we had several instruments that we used to jam on: me, my sisters, and the village kids. When I was seven I started to take musical lessons on the recorder, and a year after that I joined the local brass band on trumpet. I also had cello lessons for three years and played classical guitar for a year when I was 15. I heard jazz for the first time when I was 16, joining a local big band. A friend gave me a tape of trumpeters, and when I came to Miles Davis' 'Someday My Prince Will Come,' I played it over and over.

The influence of Miles Davis can still be heard in Laroo's playing, particularly on ballads.

After studying mathematics in Amsterdam during 1978–79, Laroo (who also plays alto sax and bass) switched permanently to music, attending music schools during 1979–85 (graduating from the Hilversum Conservatory) and working locally with her own groups. She has since played with the Pim Jacobs trio, Denise Jannah, Madeline Bell, Toots Thielemans, Ronnie Cuber, and tenor-saxophonist Teddy Edwards plus been involved in her own projects. The trumpeter has thus far recorded four CDs for her own Laroo label. The first two discs (1994's *It's Like Jazz* and *Bodymusic*) include poetry, rap, electronic rhythms, and hip hop. However, *Jazzkia*, from 1999, is straightahead jazz and *Sunset Eyes* teams her with Teddy Edwards.

> I used to be very scared and nervous for many years, and I had reason to be because I had to learn so much and was not easily accepted by some musicians. I was moving freely in between different styles while other musicians stay in one scene, but it has helped me to be a well-rounded musician. Now my future goal is to get the most out of my talents and career in an artistically balanced way.

Recommended CDs: *It's Like Jazz* (Laroo 9401), *Jazzkia* (Laroo 9901), *Sunset Eyes* (Laroo 9902)

YANK LAWSON
• • • • • • • • • • • • • •

b. May 3, 1911, Trenton, MS, d. Feb. 18, 1995, Indianapolis, IN

A powerful Dixieland player with a wide range and an attractive sound, Yank Lawson formed his style early on and kept it viable for 60 years. Born John Lawson but always known as Yank, Lawson started out playing saxophones and piano before switching to trumpet as a teenager. He played music at the University of Missouri and freelanced down South (including with Slatz Randall, with whom he made his recording debut in 1932) before joining Ben Pollack's orchestra in 1933. Pollack's band had a great deal of potential, but the leader's desire to excessively feature his conservatively talented girlfriend on vocals and to try to turn her into a Hollywood movie actress (both ventures failed) led to the orchestra's breakup in late 1934. Lawson worked for a short time with Will Osborne, did some studio work, and recorded with the Mound City Blue Blowers before becoming a member of the group that emerged from Pollack's band, the Bob Crosby Orchestra.

Lawson was with Crosby during 1935–38, being a featured soloist with both the big band (including "South Rampart Street Parade," "Dogtown Blues," and "Five Point Blues") and the small Dixieland band drawn from the larger unit, Bob Crosby's Bobcats. It was during this time that he became close with Crosby's bassist, Bob Haggart, forming a lifelong friendship.

Lawson left Crosby in August 1938 to become part of Tommy Dorsey's orchestra, where he received a lot of solo space (including on "Milenberg Joys" and "Hawaiian War Chant") and was also featured with Dorsey's Clambake Seven ("You Must Have Been a Beautiful Baby" and "Rancho Grande," among many other recordings). Considering that it was the height of the swing era, Lawson was quite fortunate to have played for two bandleaders so open to the sound of Dixieland that they featured it with their small groups.

Tiring of the road, Lawson left Dorsey in November 1939 and had stints with Abe Lyman, Richard Himber, and theater orchestras, returning to Crosby for a year (1941–42). After playing for a short time with Benny Goodman in late 1942, Lawson became a studio musician. However, unlike some other trumpeters who disappeared into the comfortable but anonymous life, Lawson always played jazz on a freelance basis. During the early 1950s he recorded frequently as co-leader of the Lawson-Haggart band. He worked now and then with Eddie Condon, was honored to play the musical role of King Oliver in *Louis Armstrong's Musical Autobiography* (a recorded series of mid-1950s remakes of Satch's gems from the 1920s and '30s) and was usually available for reunions of the Bob Crosby Bobcats. During 1966–68 Lawson worked regularly at Eddie Condon's club. In 1968 he helped form and co-lead the World's Greatest Jazz Band with Haggart. The WGJB (which lasted until 1978) nearly lived up to its name and for a decade ranked at the top of Dixieland-oriented groups. Lawson's trumpet was joined in the group's early years by the complementary Billy Butterfield to create exciting ensembles.

Yank Lawson spent his last period making many freelance recordings (often with Haggart) and appearing at classic jazz festivals and jazz parties. Although his stamina and range declined a bit during his final years, he never lost his sound or his enthusiasm for hard-charging Dixieland.

Recommended CDs: *That's a-Plenty* (Dr. Jazz 40064), *Jazz at Its Best* (Jazzology 183), *Singin' the Blues* (Jazzology 193), with Bob Crosby: *1937–1938* (ABC 838 477), *South Rampart Street Parade* (GRP/Decca 615), with Tommy Dorsey: *The Music Goes Round and Round* (Bluebird 3140), with the World's Greatest Jazz Band: *Live* (Atlantic 90982), *Plays George Gershwin and Rodgers and Hart* (Jazzology 300), *Plays Cole Porter and Rodgers and Hart* (Jazzology 320)

LPs to Search For: with the Lawson Haggart Band: *Plays Jelly Roll's Jazz* (Decca 5368), *Plays King Oliver's Jazz* (Decca 5437)

Recommended Reading: *Stomp Off, Let's Go* by John Chilton (Jazz Book Service, 1983)

MICHAEL LEONHART
· · · · · · · · · · · · · · · · · ·

b. Apr. 21, 1974, New York, NY

A lyrical trumpet with lots of promise, Michael Leonhart is the son of bassist-songwriter Jay Leonhart and brother of singer Carolyn Leonhart. He started originally on violin, studied classical trumpet, and then switched to jazz. Leonhart developed quickly, wrote a "Suite for Jazz Trumpet" that was premiered (and featured Clark Terry) in 1991, and won over 20 international music awards while still in high school. Since then, Michael Leonhart has played with the Mel Lewis Orchestra, Phil Woods, James Moody, Jon Faddis, Stanley Turrentine, and Milt Hinton, recording as a leader for Sunnyside and with his father.

Recommended CDs: *Aardvark Poses* (Sunnyside 1070), *Glub Glub* (Sunnyside 1070), with Meredith d'Ambrosio: *Out of Nowhere* (Sunnyside 1085)

JOHNNY LETMAN

. . . .

b. Sep. 6, 1917, McCormick, SC, d. July 17, 1992, New York, NY

A fluent swing trumpeter, Johnny Letman never rose above the level of a journeyman despite his ability. He grew up in Chicago and played with the young, unknown pianist Nat Cole during 1934–35. Letman spent years out of the spotlight, making contributions to the Midwest bands of Gerald Valentine (Illinois), Scat Man Carruthers (Columbus, Ohio), Jimmy Raschelle, Delbert Bright (Chicago), Bob Tinsley, Johnny Long, his own group (1940–41), Horace Henderson, Red Saunders, and Ted Buckner (Detroit). It was not until 1944 that Letman moved to New York, which was unfortunately quite late, because he had managed to miss the glory years of the swing era. Letman's associations with Phil Moore (1945–46), Cab Calloway (1947–50), Milt Buckner, Lucky Millinder, Count Basie (1951), and Sammy Benkin did little to gain him any fame.

In the 1950s, '60s, and '70s Letman alternated between leading combos and playing as a sideman with others (including Eddie Condon, Sam "The Man" Taylor, Wilbur De Paris, Claude Hopkins, Panama Francis, and Tiny Grimes). He also worked in the studios and in the orchestras of Broadway shows. Letman recorded as a leader (half an album for Columbia in 1959, a Bethlehem quintet set in 1960, and an outing for Black & Blue in 1968) and as a sideman with Joe Thomas (1958), Stuff Smith, Chubby Jackson, Panama Francis, Lionel Hampton, Cozy Cole, and Earl Hines, playing in Paris in 1968 with Milt Buckner. But it was only in the 1980s while touring Europe with the New Orleans Blues Serenaders, appearing at festivals, and playing with Lars Edegran's orchestra that Letman began to be noticed by the classic jazz community; he had finally become old enough to be a legend!

Recommended CDs: with the Buck Clayton Orchestra: *Swingin' Dream* (Stash 281)

LPs to Search For: *Many Angles of John Letman* (Bethlehem 6053), *A Funky Day in Paris* (Black & Blue 33015)

BOBBY LEWIS

. . . .

b. Jan. 23, 1936, Oshkosh, WI

A constant on the Chicago jazz scene since the 1960s, Bobby Lewis has in recent times finally been gaining exposure beyond the city limits through his recordings for Southport. Lewis' father and uncle were musicians. He first played cornet in school when he was nine. "At an early age I listened to records and, having a good ear, tried to play what I heard. I was never restricted to just reading notes." By the time he was 16, Lewis had his own band and was playing professionally. He graduated from the University of Wisconsin at Madison in 1958 with an education degree and a master's degree in music. Lewis moved to Chicago in 1961, played with Jack Teagarden on and off during 1962–63, and in 1964 became a busy studio musician. Lewis played and toured regularly with Peggy Lee during 1967–85. Among the jazz groups that he has led in the Chicago area have been Ears (which played every Tuesday night during 1975–92 at Orphan's Pub), Muggles (a trad band), the Rhythmakers (performing each Friday night at Andy's during 1978–92), and the Forefront (a contemporary trumpet ensemble). A thoughtful player with a cool tone who takes occasional vocals, Bobby Lewis began recording for Southport in 1993.

"I feel fortunate to have lived and played in the last half of the 20th century with many of the stars who are no longer alive and to have played over 7,000 recording sessions (radio and TV commercials, records, and films) during that time. I'm 65 now—I hope to keep playing trumpet for 30 more years!"

Recommended CDs: *Inside This Song* (Southport 0016), *Passion Flower* (Southport 0022), *Flugel Gourmet* (Southport 0045), *Just Havin' Some Fun* (Southport 0063), *In the Forefront* (Southport 0079)

CAPPY LEWIS

. . . .

b. May 18, 1917, Brillion, WI, d. Early 1990s

Carroll "Cappy" Lewis is best known for being a key trumpeter with Woody Herman's orchestra during its days as "The Band That Plays the Blues." "I started playing trumpet at the age of ten; it was always my favorite instrument. I occasionally played harmonica and flugelhorn later on in my career, taking a harmonica solo on 'True Love' with Frank DeVol's orchestra." Lewis considered Bunny Berigan and Louis Armstrong to be his main influences, with Bix Beiderbecke also being a favorite. He was with Woody Herman's orchestra during 1939–44, except for six months with Tommy Dorsey in 1943. "It's My Turn Now" and "Blues on Parade" are among his favorite solos from that period. After serving in the military, Lewis returned to Herman's big band for part of 1946, playing with the First Herd. He then gradually became a studio musician.

"Some of my musical high points were when I was working in Hollywood in all the major studios, playing trumpet (occasionally harmonica) for features and television. I played with Nelson Riddle on many records." Lewis was proud of having played lead trumpet with Benny Goodman on several occasions, working on the films *Hello Dolly* and *The Jungle Book*, and taking solos (mostly uncredited) on a few Frank Sinatra records. In 1959 he recorded his one album as a leader, *Get Happy with Cappy*, which has not been reissued on CD. The father of trumpeter Mark Lewis (who also played with Woody Herman), Cappy Lewis was active until a stroke in 1978 put him permanently out of action.

Recommended CDs: with Helen Carr: *The Complete Bethlehem Collection* (Avenue Jam/Bethlehem 76682); with Woody Herman: *Blues on Parade* (GRP/Decca 606)

LPs to Search For: *Get Happy with Cappy* (Hi Fi 611).

ED LEWIS

. . . .

b. June 22, 1909, Eagle City, OK, d. Sep. 18, 1985, Blooming Grove, NY

Ed Lewis' career can easily be divided into two parts. He was the lead trumpeter with Count Basie's orchestra for many years, always in the background and never getting any features. Few who heard the Basie band during that long period even knew Ed Lewis' name, and even fewer probably realized that he was a major soloist with Bennie Moten's orchestra (the direct predecessor of Basie's group) in the 1920s.

Lewis grew up in Kansas City, Missouri. His first instrument was the baritone horn, which he played in Shelly Bradford's Brass Band and with Jerry Westbrook's group. In 1925 he switched to trumpet. After brief stints with Paul Bank and Laura Rucker, he became a key member of Bennie Moten's Orchestra during 1926–32. On Moten's many Victor recordings, Lewis often had solo space (which he split with Lammar Wright in the early days and later with Booker Washington). He was one of the first black trumpeters to be influenced by such white players as Red Nichols and Bix Beiderbecke.

After leaving Moten in February 1932, Lewis became recognized for his sight-reading abilities and strong chops, which worked against his achieving any fame in the long run. He played with Thamon Hayes' Kansas City Skyrockets, Pete Johnson, Jay McShann, Harlan Leonard, and other leaders in the Kansas City area during the next few years. Lewis was with the Count Basie Orchestra from February 1937 until September 1948, appearing on virtually all of the Basie big band records but always as an ensemble player, playing a supporting role while fellow trumpeters Buck Clayton and Harry "Sweets" Edison gained the acclaim. He did write one Basie standard, "It's Sand, Man," but otherwise was an anonymous part of Count's success.

After the Basie years ended, Lewis worked outside of music as a cabdriver and as a motorman on the New York subways. He returned to part-time playing in 1954, leading a 12-piece band and touring Europe with the Countsmen as late as 1984. Although he can be heard on many famous Count Basie records, Ed Lewis' main contributions to jazz can be heard in the short but colorful spots that he had in the 1920s with Bennie Moten.

Recommended CDs: with Bennie Moten: *South* (Bluebird 3139)

RAY LINN

. . . .

b. Oct. 20, 1920, Chicago, IL, d. Nov. 1996, Columbus, OH

A versatile trumpeter, Ray Linn seemed to work his way backwards chronologically throughout his career. After gaining experience in a few local society bands, Linn was a member of Tommy Dorsey's band during 1940–41. He worked on and off with the big bands of Woody Herman (1941–42 and also 1945 and 1947), Jimmy Dorsey (1942–45), Benny Goodman (1943 and 1947), and Artie Shaw (1944–46) as a swing soloist and led two swing-oriented recording dates of his own in 1945. But Linn also played advanced bop with Boyd Raeburn's eccentric outfit in 1946 and sounded quite comfortable in that setting.

Linn became a studio musician by 1946 but in the 1950s had opportunities to work with Bob Crosby (1950–51), Shorty Rogers, Maynard Ferguson, Buddy DeFranco, Barney Kessel, Les Brown, and for a fourth time with Woody Herman (1955–59). He was busy in the studios for decades, working primarily in television during the 1960s. Surprisingly, when he formed a jazz band in 1973, it played Dixieland. Ray Linn's only chances to really stretch out on records were with the latter group, which made a couple of fine recordings (in 1978 and 1980) for the Discovery label, playing music older in style than what the trumpeter had been performing in 1940!

LPs to Search For: Chicago Jazz (Trend 515), *Empty Suit Blues* (Discovery 823)

STEVE LIPKINS

• • • • • • • • • • • • • •

Steve Lipkins was the star soloist with Will Bradley's orchestra during 1939–41, soloing on the hit "Beat Me Daddy, Eight to the Bar" and on most of Bradley's jazz records. Otherwise, very little is known about his life, even whether he is still living (though the odds are against it). Before joining Bradley, Lipkins had short stints with the big bands of Bunny Berigan (1937), Larry Clinton, Tommy Dorsey, Glenn Miller, Artie Shaw, and Red Norvo. After the swing era ended, he became a studio musician. Steve Lipkins' only date as a leader resulted in a single for Atco in 1958 ("TD's Boogie Woogie" and "Ja-Da Cha Cha") that is as obscure as the trumpeter's life.

Recommended CDs: with Will Bradley: *Best of the Big Bands* (Columbia 46151), *Hallelujah* (Hep 1061)

BOOKER LITTLE

• • • • • • • • • • • • • •

b. Apr. 2, 1938, Memphis, TN, d. Oct. 5, 1961, New York, NY

The first major original voice on the trumpet to emerge after Clifford Brown's death in 1956, Booker Little also died tragically young, during his most productive year. Little started out on clarinet when he was 12 but a few months later switched to trumpet. He was part of a very viable Memphis jazz scene while growing up, playing with Charles Lloyd, Phineas Newborn, and Harold Mabern. Little moved to Chicago, where he attended the Chicago Conservatory while gigging at night, including with Johnny Griffin and the MJT + 3.

The 20-year-old joined the Max Roach Quintet in June 1958, staying until February 1959, making his first recordings with Roach and as a leader for United Artists; he would lead other albums for Time/Bainbridge (1960), Candid, and Bethlehem (the latter two in 1961). Little's melancholy tone was distinctive from the start and placed him ahead of his contemporaries, who at the time were more closely emulating Clifford Brown. After moving to New York in 1959, he played with Mal Waldron, John Coltrane (with whom he recorded Africa/Brass), and back with Roach (rejoining the drummer in February 1960). In the summer of 1961, Little appeared with Eric Dolphy at the Five Spot in New York for two weeks; three albums resulted.

Although he could play very effective hard bop, while with Dolphy Little he was moving beyond bop into freer improvising.

Unfortunately he never had a chance to fully realize his potential, for Booker Little soon died from uremia (a kidney disease) at the age of 23. But in his brief career, he made his mark on jazz; Dave Douglas considers him an influence.

Recommended CDs: *Booker Little 4 and Max Roach* (Blue Note 84457), *Booker Little* (Bainbridge 1041), *Out Front* (Candid 79027), *Booker Little and Friends* (Avenue Jazz/Bethlehem 79855); with Eric Dolphy: *At the Five Spot, Vols. 1–3* (Original Jazz Classics 133, 247, and 353), with Abbey Lincoln: *Straight Ahead* (Candid 79015)

Box Set: with Max Roach: *The Complete Max Roach Plus Four Sessions* (7 CDs; Mosaic 7-201)

HENRY LOWTHER
· · · · · · · · · · · · · ·

b. July 11, 1941, Leicester, England

Avaluable trumpeter able to stretch from hard bop to the avant-garde, Henry Lowther has been involved in many interesting projects throughout his career. Son of a cornetist in a Salvation Army band, Lowther studied cornet with his father (eventually switching to trumpet) and had violin lessons (studying at the Royal Academy of Music) but taught himself jazz. In the 1960s, in addition to his own groups, he played with Mike Westbrook, Graham Collier, the New Jazz Orchestra, and John Mayall, among others. Since then, Henry Lowther has worked with most of the who's who of British jazz, including John Dankworth (1967–77), Mike Gibbs, the Kenny Wheeler Big Band, Barbara Thompson, John Taylor, Kurt Edelhagen, Stan Tracey, Gordon Beck, John Surman's Brass Project, Pete King, the Charlie Watts Big Band, the Berlin Contemporary Jazz Orchestra, the London Jazz Orchestra (1988–92), and his own group, Still Waters. He has thus far only recorded one album as a leader.

Recommended CDs: with John Surman: *Brass Project* (ECM 1478)

LPs to Search For: *Child Song* (Deram 1070)

TONY LUJAN
· · · · · · · · · · ·

b. 1957, Albuquerque, NM

Afine trumpeter and flugelhornist who works regularly in the Los Angeles area, Tony Lujan (whose main influences are Lee Morgan and Freddie Hubbard) sounds equally comfortable in Latin jazz and boppish settings. He studied at New Mexico State University and the University of Las Vegas and cut two hard bop-oriented albums for the Capri label in 1990 and 1992. Among the many jazz artists with whom he has worked and/or recorded have been Clark Terry, Bill Holman, Ray Charles, Henry Franklin, Gerald Wilson, Luis Bonilla, William Cepeda, the Garcia Brothers, the H.M.A. Salsa/Jazz Orchestra, Eddie Palmieri, and Tito Puente.

Recommended CDs: *Magic Circle* (Capri 74023), *Zulu* (Capri 74041), with Tito Puente: *Royal "T"* (Concord Picante 4553)

BRIAN LYNCH

• • • • • • • • • • • •

b. Sept. 12, 1956, Urbana, IL

An exciting hard bop trumpeter with a very wide range and a warm sound who is still improving year by year, Brian Lynch was the last in a long line of major trumpeters who played with Art Blakey's Jazz Messengers. Lynch remembers that his parents played Louis Armstrong records in his home while he was growing up. He started playing trumpet when he was nine and knew that he wanted to be a musician when he was 15 and had heard Miles Davis and John Coltrane. Lynch played locally in Milwaukee and studied at the Wisconsin Conservatory (1974–80). After working with Buddy Montgomery (1975–80) and with Charles McPherson in San Diego during 1981, he moved to New York.

Lynch has played with Brazilian, Puerto Rican, and Cuban bands plus some notable straightahead jazz groups. Among his key associations have been the George Russell big band, Junior Cook (1982), Horace Silver (1982–85), Toshiko Akiyoshi's big band (1982–88), Jim Snidero, Jack McDuff (1986–87), Eddie Palmieri (since 1987), and the Jazz Messengers (from December 1988 until Art Blakey's death in October 1990). Brian Lynch has been a member of the Phil Woods Quintet since 1992, appeared with Benny Golson in a Jazz Messengers reunion band, and led combos, recording sessions for Criss Cross, Ken, and Sharp Nine.

The last graduate of Art Blakey's Jazz Messengers, Brian Lynch is an exciting straightahead trumpeter.

"For the future, I hope to continue playing better and expand my writing to become a successful large-ensemble writer. I see myself as a continuation of the jazz trumpet tradition exemplified by the Blakey/Silver lineage, and also as part of the movement to forge jazz for the 21st century through the mix of jazz and Latin rhythms. I love music more now at 44 than I ever have. The best is yet to come!"

Recommended CDs: *Peer Pressure* (Criss Cross 1029), *Back Room Blues* (Criss Cross 1042), *In Process* (Ken Music 011), *At the Main Event* (Criss Cross 1070), *Keep Your Circle Small* (Sharp Nine 1001), *Spheres of Influence* (Sharp Nine 1007), *Tribute to the Trumpet Masters* (Sharp Nine 1017), with Art Blakey's Jazz Messengers: *One for All* (A&M 75021 5329), with Phil Woods: *Souvenirs* (Evidence 22177)

HUMPHREY LYTTELTON

* * * * * * * * * * * * * * *

b. Mar. 23, 1921, Eton, England

One of the all-time greats of British jazz and a major force both in the New Orleans revival movement and in mainstream swing, Humphrey Lyttelton is also a top jazz journalist. "I first heard jazz through listening to London dance bands on the radio in the early to mid-'30s, then via Nat Gonella's Georgians and Louis Armstrong's Decca recordings." Lyttelton first played harmonica in a quartet from his school, switching to trumpet in 1936 when he was 15, and he was completely self-taught except for one lesson. He names as his main influences Gonella, Armstrong, Jimmy McPartland, Muggsy Spanier, Henry "Red" Allen, Buck Clayton, Al Fairweather, and Dave Wilkins.

Lyttelton served in the military, played with George Webb's Dixielanders in 1947, and formed his influential band the following year. He recorded with Sidney Bechet in 1949 and usually featured clarinetist Wally Fawkes during the Dixieland days. During 1954–55 Lyttelton switched his band's emphasis to mainstream swing, which was considered a very controversial move by trad fans. From then on, Lyttelton often featured two or three saxophonists in his group (including Bruce Turner, Tony Coe, and Joe Temperley), although he sometimes recorded again in a trad setting. "In the autumn of 1956, after I had worked as a semipro for about ten years, my band was being booked with American musicians, including Louis Armstrong, Sidney Bechet, and Eddie Condon. That is when I realized that a 'day job' as cartoonist on the *Daily Mail* could no longer be sustained and I finally become a full-time musician."

Lyttelton's group worked with Jimmy Rushing during 1958–59 and with Buck Clayton on a few occasions and recordings in the 1960s. Humphrey Lyttelton, who started doubling on clarinet in the 1960s (playing in a New Orleans style), has recorded frequently throughout his life; in the 1980s he founded the Calligraph label to further document his music. In addition to his playing, he has written several very good jazz books (his 1954 autobiography, *I Play As I Please*, *The Best of Jazz 1: Basin Street to Harlem*, and *The Best of Jazz 2: Enter the Giants, 1931–1944*), appeared often on television and radio, and written many articles about jazz. "I believe that the most important things are, in this order, 'Get there, do it, pick up the money, and go home.' Leave abstractions such as 'art,' 'self-expression,' 'purpose,' etc. to your subconscious. For the future my main goal is to stay upright as long as possible!"

Recommended CDs: *Jazz at Royal Festival Hall* (Dormouse 22), *Best of British Jazz from the BBC Jazz Club, Vol. 2* (Upbeat Jazz 119), *Rent Party* (Stomp Off 1238)

LPs to Search For: *Delving Back and Forth with Humph* (Stomp Off 1160), *Duke Ellington Classics* (Black Lion 12108), *In Canada* (Sackville 3033), *Scatterbrains* (Stomp Off 1111)

Recommended Reading: *I Play As I Please* by Humphrey Lyttelton (Mac Gibbs and Kie Ltd., 1954)

Film Appearances: *The Tommy Steele Story* (1957)

KID SHOTS MADISON

b. Feb. 19, 1899, New Orleans, LA, d. Sept. 1948, New Orleans, LA

Though Louis "Kid Shots" Madison was a performer in New Orleans throughout his life, his premature death made it impossible for him to take advantage of the revival of interest in New Orleans jazz. Madison was in the same Waifs' Home Band as Louis Armstrong and Kid Rena in 1915, although he played drums at the time. After studying cornet, Madison permanently switched instruments. He worked with the Eagle Band and during 1923–26 was with Oscar Celestin's Original Tuxedo Orchestra, recording three songs with Celestin in 1925.

During his career, Madison worked with many local ensembles, including those of Frankie Dusen, Big Eye Louis Nelson, and Alphonse Picou. In the 1930s he was with a WPA brass band and in the '40s played with the Eureka Brass Band and George Lewis. Kid Shots Madison had opportunities to record with Lewis and with Bunk Johnson's Brass Band. But a stroke in January 1948 ended his career and, eight months later, his life, at the age of 49.

Recommended CDs: *George Lewis with Kid Shots Madison* (American Music 2)

JOE MAGNARELLI

b. Jan. 19, 1960, Syracuse, NY

A valuable hard bop trumpeter better known at this point to his fellow musicians than to the jazz public, Joe Magnarelli has played in countless straightahead settings in the New York area. Magnarelli started his career working in Syracuse. He graduated from Fredonia State University in 1982, toured with show bands (including those accompanying *Ain't Misbehavin'* and *A Chorus Line*), and had associations with Lionel Hampton (1987–89) and Jack McDuff (1989–94). In recent times Magnarelli has performed with the Toshiko Akiyoshi big band, the Vanguard Orchestra, Maria Schneider, the New York Hardbop Quintet, and the Buddy Rich reunion orchestra.

Joe Magnarelli has uplifted quite a few recordings, including a date that he co-led with John Swana for Criss Cross and sessions with the New York Hardbop Quintet, Hampton, McDuff, Akiyoshi, Dado Moroni, and Walt Weiskopf, among others. He can always be relied upon to add excitement to a jazz session.

Recommended CDs: *Why Not* (Criss Cross 1104), *Always There* (Criss Cross 1141), with The New York Hardbop Quintet: *The Clincher* (TCB 95202), *Rokermotion* (TCB 96352), with John Swana: *Philly: New York Junction* (Criss Cross 1150), with Walt Weiskopf: *Song for My Mother* (Criss Cross 1127)

RAPHE MALIK

An important if underrated avant-garde trumpeter, Raphe Malik was a member of the Cecil Taylor Unit during the second half of the 1970s, playing alongside altoist Jimmy Lyons and (part of the time) tenor saxophonist David Ware. Just as Bobby Bradford tended to sound melodic in his pairings with clarinetist John Carter (who was much more dissonant), Malik added a lyricism to Taylor's forbidding group. Raphe Malik also played with Jimmy Lyons in his projects away from Taylor in the early 1980s, participated in Rova's revisit to John Coltrane's Ascension, and led sessions in the 1990s for Eremite, Boxholder, Tautology, and FMP.

Recommended CDs: *The Short Form* (Eremite 5), *Consequences* (Eremite 13), with Jimmy Lyons: *New Sneezawee* (Black Saint 120067), with ROVA: *John Coltrane's Ascension* (Black Saint 126180), with Cecil Taylor: *Dark unto Themselves* (Enja 79638), *One Too Many Salty Swifty and Not* (Hat Art 6090)

CHUCK MANGIONE

b. Nov. 29, 1940, Rochester, NY

Chuck Mangione became one of the most famous jazz trumpeters (actually flugelhornists) in the world by simplifying and watering down his music, emphasizing catchy melodies and his appealing tone. He had a strong jazz background before gaining pop success, and occasionally Mangione's roots in bebop can still be heard.

Mangione started on piano (an instrument that his older brother Gap played) when he was eight. Because his father was a big jazz fan, young Chuck got to meet notable musicians who were invited over to the house, including Dizzy Gillespie (a family friend who gave Mangione a trumpet in the early 1950s), Horace Silver, and Art Blakey. When he was 18, Mangione organized and led the Jazz Brothers with Gap, a bebop group that included tenor saxophonist Sal Nistico, bassist Steve Davis, and drummer Roy McCurdy at the beginning of their careers. The Jazz Brothers lasted until 1961 and recorded three albums for Riverside. Mangione studied at the Eastman School (graduating in 1963) during this period and in 1962 had his first solo record date, *Recuerdo*.

After a period teaching music locally, in 1965 Mangione moved to New York, where he worked briefly with the Woody Herman Orchestra, Kai Winding, and Maynard Ferguson. He spent an important two years with Art Blakey's Jazz Messengers (1965–67), replacing Lee Morgan; Keith Jarrett was the band's pianist during this period.

Back in Rochester, Mangione began to move away from his Dizzy Gillespie-inspired bebop style. He formed a quartet with altoist Gerry Niewood in 1968 and switched to flugelhorn, doubling on electric piano. Mangione wrote compositions for larger ensembles, and he had two concerts of orchestral music presented at Eastman during 1969–70. He guest conducted the Rochester Philharmonic in 1970 on a PBS broadcast that featured his flugelhorn solos and original music. "Hill Where the Lord Hides" from the broadcast (and released on the Mercury LP *Friends and Love*) was a hit, and very quickly Mangione became famous. He toured with his quartet (a fine jazz group) and performed with orchestras, often featuring the vocals of Esther Satterfield. The music from the latter projects was melodic and often a bit insipid, but very popular, including "Land of Make Believe," "Legend of the One-Eyed Sailor," "Chase the Clouds Away," and "Bellavia." Mangione hit the commercial height of his career in 1977 with the recording of "Feels So Good" (featuring guitarist Grant Geissman) which made it to number 2 on the pop charts.

It would take a few years to realize it, but Mangione had no further hits ahead of him. In 1980 he did record the two-LP set *Tarantella* that, on a few bebop numbers (including "Things to Come," "'Round Midnight," and "Manteca") featured Dizzy Gillespie as a guest. But Mangione's career soon became aimless (his Columbia recordings are a low point and did not even sell well), and, after a reunion tour of the Jazz Brothers in 1986 and a couple of recordings for his short-lived Feels So Good label, he was rarely heard from for a decade.

In 1997 Chuck Mangione began to perform again, putting together a new "Feels So Good" band that included old friends Gerry Neiwood and Grant Geissman. Whether the flugelhornist develops any further or will decide to rest on his laurels is not known yet, but his playing ability is still potentially in prime form as he enters his sixties.

Recommended CDs: *The Jazz Brothers* (Original Jazz Classics 997), *Hey Baby* (Original Jazz Classics 668), *Spring Fever* (Original Jazz Classics 767), *Recuerdo* (Original Jazz Classics 495), *Feels So Good* (A&M 3219)

LPs to Search For: *Chuck Mangione Quartet* (Mercury 1-631), *Alive* (Mercury 1-650), *Tarantella* (A&M 6513)

Recommended Videos: Mangione plays "Ichana" on *Monterey Jazz Festival '75* (1995; Storyville 6021), *Sarah Vaughan and Friends* (1986; A*Vision 50209)

WINGY MANONE

. . . .

b. Feb. 13, 1904, New Orleans, LA, d. July 9, 1982, Las Vegas, NV

A Dixieland trumpeter influenced by Louis Armstrong and a jivey good-humored singer, Joseph "Wingy" Manone recorded many joyful gems in the 1930s. He earned the lifelong name of "Wingy" when he lost his right arm in a streetcar accident when he was ten. Shortly after, Manone started playing trumpet (the one major instrument that can be played one-handed!) and developed quickly, becoming a professional by the time he was 17. Manone performed on riverboats, worked in Chicago and New York, was a member of the Crescent City Jazzers in Mobile in 1924, and recorded with the same group in St. Louis when they were called the Arcadian Serenaders. Wingy was constantly on the road during the next few years, performing with many territory bands, including one led by the legendary pianist Peck Kelley in Texas. He first recorded as a leader in 1927, and his 1930 piece "Tar Paper Stomp" used a riff that would later be the basis for Glenn Miller's hit "In the Mood."

Manone worked with Ray Miller, Charlie Straight, and Speed Webb, freelanced, and in 1934 started recording quite prolifically in New York. He made many records during 1934–41 with freewheeling combos that were much different than the big bands that were so popular during the era. Some of his records (which varied in quality but were always full of spirit) used obscure players, but others included such greats as tenors Eddie Miller, Bud Freeman, and Chu Berry, clarinetists Matty Matlock, Joe Marsala, and Buster Bailey, and trombonists George Brunies, Santo Pecora, and Jack Teagarden. Wingy's 1935 recording of "The Isle of Capri" was his biggest hit.

In 1940 Manone settled in Los Angeles, where he appeared on the radio regularly with Bing Crosby (and in Bing's movie *Rhythm on the River*), coauthored his memoirs, *Trumpet on the Wing* in 1948, and played his brand of Dixieland in clubs. Wingy Manone moved to Las Vegas in 1954, recorded regularly until 1960 (there would also be an album in 1966 and two final numbers in 1975), visited Europe a few times in the 1960s, and was active until the mid-1970s, always performing freewheeling and cheerful jazz.

Recommended CDs: *The Wingy Manone Collection, Vols. 1–4* (Collector's Classics 3, 4, 5, and 20), *1936* (Classics 849), *1936–1937* (Classics 887), *1937–1938* (Classics 952), *1940–1944* (Classics 1091)

LPs to Search For: *With Papa Bue's Viking Jazzband* (Storyville 4066)

Recommended Reading: *Jazz Talking* by Max Jones (Da Capo Press, 1987)

Film Appearances: *Rhythm on the River* (1940), *Beat Me Daddy Eight to the Bar* (1940), *Juke Box Jenny* (1942), *Hi'ya Sailor* (1943), *Tocadero* (1944), *Sarge Goes to College* (1947), *Rhythm Inn* (1951)

MICHAEL MANTLER

. . . .

b. Aug. 10, 1943, Vienna, Austria

A trumpeter with a dry wistful sound and an adventurous style that makes liberal use of space, Michael Mantler is probably more significant for his activities behind the scenes than he is for being an improviser. Mantler started on trumpet when he was 12, attended the Akademie in Vienna, and moved to the United States in 1962, studying at Berklee. By 1964 he was living in New York and performing with pianists Lowell Davidson and Cecil Taylor. Part of the avant-garde jazz movement, Mantler married pianist Carla Bley (their daughter is organist Karen Mantler) and worked with her, co-leading the Jazz Composer's Orchestra (which began in 1965). Mantler and Bley also played in Europe with Steve Lacy in a quintet called Jazz Realities.

The next decade would be full of accomplishments for Mantler. He was part of Charlie Haden's Liberation Music Orchestra, played on Gary Burton's *A Genuine Tong Funeral* in 1967, and helped his wife start the JCOA record label. Mantler recorded with the Jazz Composers Orchestra, assisted Bley on her ambitious *Escalator Over the Hill* project (1970–71), and formed the New Music Distribution Service in 1972 to distribute records from independent labels. In 1973 Mantler and Bley began the Watt Works label to document their work. Mantler was in Bley's big band during 1977–85 and, although they have since divorced, they have worked together on an occasional basis since.

Michael Mantler's playing and compositions are very difficult to classify, often crossing over into contemporary classical music, but his recordings tend to grow in interest with each listen.

Recommended CDs: *Cerco Un Paese Innocente* (ECM 1556), with Carla Bley: *Dinner Music* (ECM 825 815), *European Tour* 1977 (ECM 831 830), *Social Studies* (ECM 831 831), *Musique Mechanique* (ECM 839 313)

LPs to Search For: *Movies* (Watt 7), *More Movies* (Watt 10)

PAUL MARES

. . . .

b. June 15, 1900, New Orleans, LA, d. Aug. 18, 1949, Chicago, IL

Unlike his counterpart Nick LaRocca of the Original Dixieland Jazz Band, cornetist Paul Mares was modest about his own playing, freely admitting the influence of King Oliver. Because his band, the New Orleans Rhythm Kings, also included the brilliant if ill-fated martyr Leon Roppolo on clarinet and a major Dixielander in trombonist George Brunies, Mares' contributions as a mellow and lightly swinging player tend to be overlooked.

Paul Mares' father played cornet, but the youth was self-taught and never learned to read music. At 16, Mares gigged with Roppolo and with Tom Brown on the riverboat Capitol. In late 1919, when Abbie Brunies turned down an offer to join drummer Ragbaby Stevens in Chicago, he sent Mares in his place. George Brunies also left New Orleans around this time, and the pair joined up briefly with Roppolo in Davenport, Iowa.

In August 1921, Paul Mares was hired to put together a band to back singer Bee Palmer's show at the Friar's Inn in Chicago. He picked Brunies as his trombonist and sent for Roppolo (who had returned to New Orleans). After a few weeks, Palmer departed and Mares became leader of the Friar's Society Orchestra, a residency that lasted 18 months. After a change in managers, Mares renamed the band the New Orleans Rhythm Kings. Mares was an important figure in de-emphasizing the military roots of the cornet, playing smooth legato phrases rather than choppy staccato runs. His solid yet often sparse lead gave the other horns opportunities to weave creative lines around him, and his lyrical style was Chicago's answer to New York's Phil Napoleon. In addition, Mares' use of mutes was inspired by King Oliver, and his playing in general would be a strong inspiration for many younger musicians, including Jimmy McPartland and Bix Beiderbecke (who had an opportunity to jam with the NORK).

During 1922–23, the New Orleans Rhythm Kings recorded three separate times, as a well-integrated octet (with Jack Pettis on C-melody sax), as a basic quintet, and on the first integrated jazz date (with Jelly Roll Morton sitting in on piano). Unlike Nick LaRocca, who tended just to state the melody, chorus after chorus, Mares was inventive within the limitations of the era, taking brief solos and adding punch to the ensembles. Under his guidance, the NORK was the best band on records in 1922, and they introduced such future Dixieland standards as "Farewell Blues," "Bugle Call Blues" (later renamed "Bugle Call Rag"), "Panama," "That's a-Plenty," "Weary Blues," "Tin Roof Blues," and Morton's "Milenberg Joys."

The NORK's stay at the Friar's Inn ended in the spring of 1923 and they soon disbanded. Mares and Roppolo joined Al Siegal's band in New York, returned to the Midwest for the session with Morton, and then went back to New Orleans. Mares in late 1924 was offered the opportunity to succeed Bix Beiderbecke with the Wolverines (which would have been a historical irony) but chose to stay home. In 1925 he attempted to reorganize the NORK and had two final recording sessions, but Roppolo's fragile mental health sank that effort. Just 25, Mares retired from full-time music and chose to enter his family's fur business.

Nine years later Mares returned to Chicago, where he opened a barbecue restaurant. He soon had the itch to play music again and he formed a new band. On January 26, 1935, Mares recorded four titles with his Friar's Society Orchestra. Although his sound was largely unchanged, Mares' style was flexible enough to fit comfortably into the Dixieland/swing format, at times hinting at Bunny Berigan.

But rather than serving as a new beginning, this lone recording date would be Paul Mares' last. He operated his barbecue restaurant for a few more years, did defense work during World War II, and was musically active near the end of his life, planning a new group shortly before his death at age 49. Paul Mares remains an unsung early jazz great.

Recommended CDs: *New Orleans Rhythm Kings and Jelly Roll Morton* (Milestone 47020)

Recommended Reading: *Jazz Masters of New Orleans* by Martin Williams (Macmillan Co., 1967), *Lost Chords* by Richard M. Sudhalter (Oxford University Press, 1999)

MARKY MARKOWITZ

* * * * * * * * * * * * * * * * * *

b. Dec. 11, 1923, Washington, DC, d. Nov. 11, 1986, New York, NY

I rving "Marky" Markowitz was a fine if somewhat underutilized bop player. Markowitz started out at the tail end of the swing era, playing with the big bands of Charlie Spivak (1942–43), Jimmy Dorsey (1943–44), Boyd Raeburn (1944–45), and most notably the Woody Herman First and Second Herds (1946 and 1948–49), along with Buddy Rich's short-lived bebop big band (1946–47). He had occasional solos with most of these groups but never emerged as a star.

From the 1950s on, Markowitz freelanced in a variety of settings in New York and Washington, D.C., including in orchestras for shows. An excellent soloist with a wide range, Markowitz played with (among many others) Dizzy Gillespie, Gene Krupa, Art Farmer, George Russell, Al Cohn, Herbie Mann, Bill Evans, and Gato Barbieri. He led his only album for Famous Door in 1976 and can also be heard in good form on a 1946 jam session with Sonny Berman.

LPs to Search For: *Marky's Vibes* (Famous Door 111), with Sonny Berman: *Beautiful Jewish Music* (Onyx 211)

SAL MARQUEZ

. . . .

b. Dec. 21, 1943, El Paso, TX

Most influenced by 1950s Miles Davis, Sal Marquez has a mellow tone and a lightly swinging style. Marquez studied at Texas A&M and North Texas State University, working with the big bands of Woody Herman (1968), Buddy Rich (1969), Gerald Wilson (1970), Louie Bellson (1971), and Dee Barton. In addition he did a great deal of anonymous background work, including with the bands of the Beach Boys, Frank Zappa, and Gregg Allman. Marquez has played with Dave Grusin (including on some movie soundtracks) and for a period was a member of the *Tonight Show* band. Sal Marquez, a regular in Los Angeles area clubs, led one CD for GRP.

Recommended CDs: One for Dewey (GRP 9678)

Recommended Videos: GRP All-Star Big Band (1992; GRP 9672)

MARTY MARSALA

. . . .

b. Apr. 2, 1909, Chicago, IL, d. Apr. 27, 1975, Chicago, IL

A fine swing/Dixieland trumpeter, Marty Marsala was the younger brother of clarinetist Joe Marsala. Marty started out playing drums in Chicago in bands led by Red Feilen and Joe Bananas (!) before switching to trumpet in the late 1920s. After freelancing in Chicago, he played and recorded as a member of Joe Marsala's band (an ensemble that featured harpist Adele Girard) during 1936–41. Marsala also recorded with Tempo King (1936–37) and Bob Howard, worked for a short time with the Will Hudson Orchestra, led a band at Nick's, and was with Chico Marx's group (which was actually run by Ben Pollack) during 1942–43.

After serving in the Army (1944–45), Marsala was heard in a variety of freewheeling Dixieland settings, including with his brother, Miff Mole, Tony Parenti, and others. Marsala moved to San Francisco in 1955, where he worked with Earl Hines and Kid Ory (recording some of his best work with the latter) and led groups. In the early 1960s he became less active due to erratic health, retiring altogether in 1965. Marty Marsala, who never led his own record date, can fortunately be heard in excellent form as a sideman on a variety of heated sessions.

Recommended CDs: with Earl Hines: At Club Hangover 1955 (Storyville 6036), with Joe Marsala: *1936–1942* (Classics 763), with Tempo King: *Tempo King* (Timeless 1-002)

Box Set: The Complete Kid Ory Verve Sessions (8 CDs - Mosaic 8-189)

WYNTON MARSALIS

. . . .

b. Oct. 18, 1961, New Orleans, LA

One of the major trumpeters in jazz since 1980 but also a lightning rod for controversy due to his selective views on jazz history, Wynton Marsalis has been a household name during the past two decades. His father is pianist-educator Ellis Marsalis, his older brother is

The leader of the Young Lions who developed into a controversial spokesman for jazz, Wynton Marsalis has also evolved into a great trumpeter who found his own sound by going back in time.

tenor and soprano saxophonist Branford, and his younger brothers are trombonist Delfeayo and drummer Jason, truly the first family of jazz!

Named after pianist Wynton Kelly, Marsalis was given his first trumpet when he was six by Al Hirt (Ellis Marsalis' employer at the time). He was well trained in both classical music (starting when he was 12) and jazz. Marsalis played with Danny Barker's Fairview Baptist Church Band when he was eight and performed the Haydn Trumpet Concerto with the New Orleans Philharmonic when he was just 14, becoming the lead trumpeter with the New Orleans Civic Orchestra. Marsalis also played locally as a teenager with R&B and funk bands (including the Creators, Killer Force, and the Crispy Critters!), music he would later write off.

A brilliant technician as a teenager, Marsalis attended the New Orleans Center for the Performing Arts, the Berkshire Music Center at Tanglewood, and Juilliard (1979–81). As a 17-year-old, Marsalis played with the Art Blakey big band in 1979 (making his recording debut) and then gained his initial fame with Blakey's Jazz Messengers (1980–81 and 1982). Marsalis went on tours with Herbie Hancock's V.S.O.P. (a quartet that also included Ron Carter and Tony Williams) in 1981 and 1983, not having any difficulty keeping up with the very fast company. He was signed to the Columbia label in 1981 and by 1983 was touring the world with his quintet (which also included Branford Marsalis, pianist Kenny Kirkland, drummer Jeff "Tain" Watts, and a few different bassists, including Charles Fambrough).

Marsalis was destined for fame. His ability to play both jazz and classical music (he would soon be acclaimed as one of the finest classical trumpeters of all time) on such a high level was quite noteworthy. In the early '80s it garnered headlines that a young and very talented black musician would choose to make a living playing acoustic jazz rather than fusion, funk, or R&B. His success started the "Young Lions" movement, with major labels (most of whom had neglected jazz during the past decade) rushing to sign and promote young hard bop-oriented players. Also, it might be a coincidence, but there had been a major shortage of new trumpeters since 1970. That drought ended with Marsalis' rise to fame, inspiring a golden age for the trumpet that continues to this day.

Despite all of the acclaim that greeted Marsalis during 1982–85, the truth is that he had not found his own voice yet. When he first joined the Jazz Messengers, Marsalis sometimes sounded a bit like Freddie Hubbard. Within a short time he took to closely emulating Miles Davis, not so much in the choice of notes (Wynton had much more technique than Miles) but in his sound. The first real criticism that he received (a backlash caused by his getting so famous so fast) was that he was a Miles Davis imitator. However that was a premature judgment, since Marsalis has continued improving as a player year by year since that time. Also, it was obvious to many that the quintet that he had with brother Branford was an extension of the mid-'60s Miles Davis Quintet, 15 years later. Their music (heard at its best on the 1985 record *Black Codes from the Underground*) was often quite exciting but still slightly derivative, although it did lead many other Young Lions to explore that style.

In 1985 Marsalis received a shock when Branford Marsalis and Kenny Kirkland left his group to join pop singer Sting. A rift quickly developed between Wynton and Branford (who eventually returned to creative jazz with his own groups) that fortunately healed after a little while. Marsalis next led a quartet that featured his new discovery, pianist Marcus Roberts, along with bassist Bob Hurst and drummer Watts. During 1988–89 his group expanded to a septet with the addition of trombonist Wycliffe Gordon, altoist Wes Anderson, and tenor saxophonist Todd Williams; Roberts was joined in the rhythm section by bassist Reginald Veal and drummer Herlin Riley.

During this time, Marsalis found himself musically. He studied jazz history extensively, in 1987 became the cofounder of Jazz at Lincoln Center, and by 1989, with the release of the soundtrack for *Tune In Tomorrow*, he no longer sounded like Miles Davis. By exploring earlier styles of jazz (including the roots of New Orleans music), mastering the plunger mute (à la Cootie Williams), and studying Duke Ellington, Marsalis at 28 found his own sound. He also developed as a writer while leading the septet, with his arranging very influenced by Duke Ellington (although as a composer, he has yet to write a standard).

Marsalis kept his septet together through 1995 (with Eric Reed succeeding Marcus Roberts), touring the world and recording frequently. But his activities were increasingly taken up by composing lengthy and very ambitious works (including "Blood on the Fields," which in 1997 became the first jazz composition ever to win a Pulitzer Prize) and leading the Lincoln Center Jazz Orchestra. Because (under the influence of writer Stanley Crouch) Marsalis tends to think little of post-1965 avant-garde jazz and fusion, he was involved in many wasteful verbal battles with more adventurous jazz musicians and critics that cast a shadow over some of the activities of the Lincoln Center Jazz Orchestra. Perhaps because of Marsalis' prominence and brilliant trumpet playing, it is expected that he always be very open minded and extremely knowledgeable about all styles of jazz, and in those areas he often falls short, insisting that all jazz has to swing.

However, the LCJO (a colorful if erratic all-star repertory big band) has done a lot of good in introducing younger listeners to older styles. Marsalis has inspired many youngsters to play acoustic jazz by becoming very involved in jazz education, directly helping many up-and-coming players (such as Roy Hargrove), and his championing of the music of Louis Armstrong and Duke Ellington (although sometimes stating the obvious) is a good thing.

With the passing of so many jazz figures in the late 1990s, Wynton Marsalis' importance (as a trumpeter, leader, writer, and spokesman for jazz) continues to grow. He may never become an innovator, but he is certainly a major force in jazz of the 21st century. Wynton Marsalis can be heard at his very best with his septet on the highly recommended seven-CD set *Live from the Village Vanguard*.

Recommended CDs: *Wynton Marsalis* (Columbia 37574), *Think of One* (Columbia 38641), *Black Codes from the Underground* (Columbia 40009), *Live at Blues Alley* (Columbia 40675), *Original Soundtrack From Tune in Tomorrow* (Columbia 47044), *Blue Interlude* (Columbia 48729), *In This House, On This Morning* (Columbia 53320), *Citi Movement* (Columbia 53324), with Art Blakey: *Keystone 3* (Concord Jazz 4196)

Box Set: *Live from the Village Vanguard* (7 CDs; Columbia 69876)

Recommended Reading: *Jazz Profiles* by Reginald Carver and Lenny Bernstein (Billboard Books, 1998), *Skain's Domain* by Leslie Gourse (Schirmer Books, 1999), *Sweet Swing Blues on the Road* by Wynton Marsalis and Frank Stewart (W. W. Norton & Co., 1994), *Talking Jazz* by Ben Sidran (Pomegranate Artbooks, 1992)

BOBBY MARTIN

. . . .

b. May 15, 1903, Long Brach, NJ

Bobby Martin was an excellent swing trumpeter who spent most of his playing years overseas. He was an important part of Sam Wooding's orchestra during 1925–31, touring Europe and Russia and helping to spread the message of jazz around the world. When Wooding returned home in 1931, Martin opted to stay in Europe, where he worked with Willie Lewis (1932–36), one of the top big bands in Europe during the era. Martin was well featured with the ensemble, making quite a few recordings. In 1936 he left Lewis, spent a little time in the United States, gathered together musicians, and then played throughout Europe during 1937–39 with his own band. Unfortunately only two selections were cut by the Bobby Martin Orchestra, which included Bill Coleman and pianist Ram Ramirez.

With the outbreak of World War II, Martin relocated permanently to the United States, freelanced in New York, and permanently retired from music in 1944 to run a family business. Logic says that he is no longer living, but there has been no verification yet of Bobby Martin's passing.

Recommended CD: with Willie Lewis: *1932–1936* (Classics 822)

HUGH MASEKELA

. . . .

b. Apr. 4, 1939, Witbanks, South Africa

Probably the biggest internal debate I had over who to include in this book dealt with Hugh Masekela. He is known primarily for playing African-oriented pop music, but since he was involved with jazz early in his career and that background has had an influence on some of his music since then, he made the cut!

At 13 Masekela saw the Kirk Douglas film *Young Man with a Horn* and was so impressed that he began playing the trumpet the following year. His early musical experiences in South Africa included working with the Huddleston Jazz Band, the Merry Makers of Springs (which he cofounded), and Alfred Herbert's Jazz Revues in addition to playing in orchestras behind singers. Masekela's most notable work in his native country was with the Jazz Epistles, a group that included Dollar Brand (who later changed his name to Abdullah Ibrahim) on piano.

Due to the worsening racial situation in South Africa, Masekela and his future wife, folk singer Miriam Makeba, emigrated in 1961 to England, where he studied at the Guildhall School of Music, eventually moving to the United States (attending the Manhattan School of Music). After his music by the mid-1960s shifted toward instrumental pop rather than creative jazz, the trumpeter-vocalist soon had a commercially successful solo career, recording for MGM and his label, Chisa. In 1968 he had a major pop hit in "Grazing in the Grass," which sold 4 million copies. Since that time, Hugh Masekela has been a household name, playing his brand of African pop music in large stadiums, visiting Africa many times to reaffirm his heritage, touring with pop singer-composer Paul Simon, and staying active performing his unusual blend of styles.

Recommended CDs: *Lasting Impressions of Ooga Booga* (Polygram 531 630), *Beaten Aroun' De Bush* (Novus 63136), *Hope* (Worldly Triloka 7203)

LPs to Search For: *Home Is Where the Music Is* (Blue Thumb 6003)

ROD MASON

. . . .

b. Sept. 28, 1940, Plymouth, England

Rod Mason is a top-notch trad jazz trumpeter influenced by Louis Armstrong but having a sound of his own. His father, Frank "Pop" Mason, was a drummer who worked with the Savannah Orchestra in England during 1928–31. The younger Mason has performed Dixieland throughout his career, first playing professionally in 1959 with Cy Laurie. Since then he has worked with Monty Sunshine (1962–66), Acker Bilk (1970–71), and the Dutch Swing College Band (early to mid-1980s), but his main significance is as a bandleader.

Rod Mason has led a sextet called the Hot Five since the early 1970s, along with a revived Savannah Orchestra. The trumpeter has recorded quite a few excellent albums starting in 1974 (for the WAM, Black Lion, Jeton, and Timeless labels) and has worked extensively in Holland and Germany in addition to England.

LPs to Search For: *Good Companions* (Black Lion 12145), *After Hours* (Black Lion 12194), *Rod Mason Hot Five* (Timeless 538), *Rod Mason's Hot Music* (Timeless 550)

DMITRI MATHENY

b. Dec. 25, 1965, Nashville, TN

Dmitri Matheny is a mellow-toned flugelhornist who particularly excels on ballads, a fine composer, and an unlikely but successful record company executive. Matheny, who grew up in Tucson, Arizona, started paying trumpet when he was nine. He led his first group at 16 and was such an impressive player as a teenager that the Tucson Jazz Society financed his music studies at the local university. In 1983 Matheny attended the Interlochen Arts Academy in Michigan, playing locally with Ramsey Lewis. He studied at Berklee (1984–89) and led the hard bop-oriented New Voice Jazz Sextet in Boston during 1984–90.

In the late 1980s, Matheny began concentrating on playing flugelhorn, and along the way he had lessons from Art Farmer. In the early '90s he moved to San Francisco and unexpectedly landed a major position with the brand new Monarch label, supervising their recordings. Since then, Dmitri Matheny has recorded three CDs of his own, featuring his subtle but emotional playing on a variety of strong melodies.

Recommended CDs: *Red Reflections* (Monarch 1009), *Penumbra—The Moon Sessions* (Monarch 1014), *Starlight Café* (Monarch 1018), with the Crown Project: *Gershwin on Monarch* (Monarch 1017)

JIMMY MAXWELL

b. Jan. 9, 1917, Stockton, CA, d. 1997

Jimmy Maxwell always had a beautiful tone and was a strong swing soloist, even if he was never featured enough. He began playing at age four, and one of his teachers in the 1930s was the former Sousa cornetist Herbert L. Clarke. A pro by the time he was 15, Maxwell worked as a teenager with arranger-pianist Gil Evans in California during 1932–36. Maxwell also played with Maxine Sullivan and the big bands of Jimmy Dorsey (1936–37) and Skinny Ennis (1938–39). He became best known for his association with Benny Goodman, working with the King of Swing off and on during 1939–43 and occasionally afterward, including Goodman's 1962 tour of the Soviet Union.

Maxwell became a studio musician in 1943, playing anonymously behind the scenes, where his tone and musicianship were greatly appreciated, including for *The Perry Como Show* (1945–63) and Johnny Carson's *Tonight Show* (1963–73). He also played swing-oriented jazz now and then with such big bands as Woody Herman (1958), Quincy Jones, Oliver Nelson, Gerry Mulligan, Count Basie, and Duke Ellington (three weeks as a sub in 1961 and a couple of months in 1973). In later years Maxwell (who recorded his only set as a leader in 1977) appeared with the New York Jazz Repertory Company's tribute to Louis Armstrong,

Chuck Israels' National Jazz Ensemble, Dick Sudhalter's New California Ramblers, and other swing recreation bands. Little known is the fact that Jimmy Maxwell took up bagpipes as a hobby and marched during 1958–64 in New York's St. Patrick's Day parade and also played bagpipes on a John Lennon record!

LPs to Search For: *Let's Fall in Love* (Circle 50), with Bob Wilber: *I'm in the Mood for Swing* (Phontastic 7526)

IRVIN MAYFIELD

b. Sept. 7, 1977, New Orleans, LA

One of the most recent in a long line of New Orleans trumpeters to make an impact, Irvin Mayfield clearly has a great future ahead of him. He started playing trumpet at a young age and picked up important experience working with local brass bands. Mayfield attended the New Orleans Center for Creative Arts, has recorded as a leader for Basin Street and (on his 21st birthday) Half Note, and performs regularly with the intriguing Latin jazz/New Orleans R&B band Hombres Calientes. A fiery player, Irvin Mayfield is inspired by Wynton Marsalis, Terence Blanchard, and Nicholas Payton but already is far along in developing a voice of his own.

Recommended CDs: *Irvin Mayfield* (Basin Street 0401), *Live at the Blue Note* (Half Note 4905), with Wessell Anderson: *Live at the Village Vanguard* (Leaning Hour 008), with Hombres Calientes: *Hombres Calientes* (Basin Street 0201), *Hombres Calientes, Vol. 2* (Basin Street 0202)

SHORTY MCCONNELL

Maurice "Shorty" McConnell is one of those trumpeters that made an impression for a short period of time, along with a few recordings, and then disappeared completely from the jazz scene. What is known about him is that he was a solid swing soloist who played with the Earl Hines Orchestra during 1942–43, taking solos on "Second Balcony Jump" and "Stormy Monday Blues." McConnell remained with the band during the unrecorded period when Charlie Parker (on tenor) and Dizzy Gillespie were in the personnel. Along with Bird and Diz, McConnell joined the Billy Eckstine Orchestra when the singer broke away from Hines. McConnell was with Eckstine during 1944–46, and he modernized his style to bebop. He was part of Lester Young's quintet in 1947, recording a couple of sessions with the great tenor saxophonist. And then shortly after that, Shorty McConnell dropped out of the jazz world, not to be heard from again.

Recommended CDs: with Lester Young: *Complete Aladdin Sessions* (Blue Note 32787), with Earl Hines: *1942–1945* (Classics 876)

HOWARD MCGHEE

· · · · · · · · · · · · · · · · ·

b. Mar. 6, 1918, Tulsa, OK, d. July 17, 1987, New York, NY

Howard McGhee was one of the key "missing links" in the evolution of the jazz trumpet. Influenced by Roy Eldridge and Dizzy Gillespie, McGhee was an early influence on Fats Navarro (whom he sat next to in Andy Kirk's orchestra). Navarro's style became the

"The missing link," Howard McGhee ranked with Dizzy Gillespie and Fats Navarro among bebop trumpeters of the 1945–49 period.

basis of Clifford Brown's, and Brownie in turn influenced practically every trumpeter that came up after the mid-1950s, including Lee Morgan, Freddie Hubbard, and Woody Shaw. And yet McGhee is largely forgotten.

He originally played clarinet and tenor, not starting on the trumpet until he was already 17. McGhee picked up experience working in territory bands in the Midwest and gigged with Lionel Hampton in 1941. While with Andy Kirk's orchestra (1941–42), he gained his earliest recognition for playing on his feature "McGhee Special." During this era McGhee (whose clipped sound was already quite individual) often performed at the after-hours jam sessions at Minton's Playhouse and Monroe's Uptown House that helped result in bebop.

"Maggie" played with the big bands of Charlie Barnet (1942–43), Andy Kirk (it was during this second stint that Fats Navarro was also in the trumpet section), Georgie Auld, and Count Basie. By 1945, McGhee ranked near the top of modern jazz trumpeters, with only Dizzy Gillespie ahead of him among beboppers. He was a member of Coleman Hawkins' quintet that year, recording with the great tenor and traveling to Los Angeles with Hawk. McGhee decided to stay in Los Angeles for a couple of years, helping to introduce bebop to the West Coast. He performed with Jazz at the Philharmonic, gigged and recorded with Charlie Parker (including the infamous "Lover Man" date), and worked on Central Avenue. After returning to New York in 1947, McGhee was on an exciting recording session with Navarro and worked steadily. He traveled to Europe to appear at the Paris Jazz Festival in 1948 and also guested with Machito's orchestra.

In 1949 McGhee was at the peak of his powers, and he could have grown to become a truly major force in jazz. But unfortunately heroin (a plague for the bebop generation) soon made his career erratic and resulted in his slipping into obscurity. He toured the Far East on a USO tour during the Korean War (1951–52) and made a few records during the decade for Bethlehem, but otherwise the 1950s (particularly after 1952) were largely a waste. Eventually McGhee was able to break free of drugs, and he made a comeback during 1960–62 (recording some gems) but was barely on records again (other than a 1966 big band album) until 1976. He had a final burst of activity during 1976–79, but by then Miles Davis, Clifford Brown, Lee Morgan, Freddie Hubbard, and others had long overshadowed him. When the name of Howard McGhee was mentioned to jazz fans who had actually heard of him in the 1980s, it seemed always to be accompanied by the question "Is he still alive?"

Recommended CDs: *1945–1946* (Classics 1125), *Trumpet at Tempo* (Jazz Classics 6009), *1948* (Classics 1058), *Maggie: The Savoy Sessions* (Savoy 2219), *Maggie's Back in Town* (Original Jazz Classics 693), *Sharp Edge* (Black Lion 60110), with Coleman Hawkins: *Hollywood Stampede* (Capitol 92596)

Film Appearances: One exciting number with Coleman Hawkins in *The Crimson Canary* (1945)

JOHN MCNEIL

. . . .

b. Mar. 23, 1948, Yreka, CA

An excellent hard bop and post-bop player who can hold his own with the best (as he has shown on albums in which he used Joanne Brackeen, Dave Leibman, and Tom Harrell as sidemen), John McNeil deserves to be much better known. McNeil started playing trumpet when he was eight and was self-taught. A professional while in high school, McNeil gigged after his graduation in Louisville, Kentucky, moving to New York in 1975. He played with Horace Silver and the Thad Jones-Mel Lewis Orchestra in the 1970s. John McNeil, who became a jazz educator, has worked steadily during the past 25 years, playing in a modern style a bit reminiscent of Freddie Hubbard. He has recorded as a leader for Steeplechase and Brownstone.

Recommended CDs: Hip Deep (Brownstone 9612)

LPs to Search For: Embarkation (Steeplechase 1099), Faun (Steeplechase 1117), Look to the Sky (Steeplechase 1128), The Glass Room (Steeplechase 1133), Clean Sweep (Steeplechase 1154), I've Got the World on a String (Steeplechase 1183)

JIMMY MCPARTLAND

. . . .

b. Mar. 15, 1907, Chicago, IL, d. Mar. 13, 1991, Port Washington, NY

Inspired originally by Bix Beiderbecke, Jimmy McPartland was a Dixielander with his own sound. McPartland started off on violin when he was five but switched to cornet at 15. One of the Austin High Gang, McPartland and his friends (including tenor saxophonist Bud Freeman, clarinetist Frankie Teschemacher, drummer Dave Tough, and guitarist Eddie Condon) learned from the records of the New Orleans Rhythm Kings and the Original Dixieland Jazz Band, gaining an enthusiasm for freewheeling jazz that never left them.

McPartland worked with Al Haid (1923), Frisco Haase, Charles "Murph" Podolsky, and the Maroon Five before, in late 1924 (when he was 17), becoming Bix Beiderbecke's replacement with the Wolverines, making his recording debut on the group's final session and staying with the band for over a year. He worked with Art Kassel (1926), appeared on the classic McKenzie-Condon Chicagoans session that helped to define Chicago jazz in 1927, and moved to New York later that year. As a member of Ben Pollack's orchestra (1927–29), McPartland was one of the group's key soloists, along with Benny Goodman and Glenn Miller (who was later succeeded by Jack Teagarden). McPartland made it through the Depression years by working in Broadway pit bands, backing singer Russ Columbo, and being a sideman with the commercial orchestras of Horace Heidt, Smith Ballew, and Harry Reser (1933–35), although he always played jazz on the side. Back in Chicago by the mid-1930s, the musical climate had improved and McPartland led combos; clarinetist Rosy McHargue and altoist Boyce Brown were among his sidemen, plus his older brother, guitarist Dick McPartland (1905–57).

After a brief stint with Jack Teagarden's big band, McPartland was in the Army during 1942–45, becoming one of the soldiers who landed on Normandy Beach on D-Day. He did have some opportunities to play music and met Marian Turner at a USO show in Belgium; they soon married, and Marian McPartland became his pianist. After his discharge, Jimmy McPartland was part of the Dixieland scene in Chicago and New York for the next 30 years, sometimes reuniting with Eddie Condon but usually leading his own bands. While his wife developed into a more modern stylist, the cornetist stuck to the Chicago style that he loved best, happily playing the old standards and taking occasional cheerful vocals. The McPartlands were divorced in 1970 but remained close friends and remarried two weeks before Jimmy's death.

Jimmy McPartland, who recorded during his career as a leader for Decca, Harmony, Prestige, MGM, Brunswick, Grand Award, Jazztone, Epic, Mercury, Camden, Design, Jazzology, Halcyon (Marian's label), and Riff, worked less often in the 1980s due to ill health but played at a concert 15 months before his death.

Recommended CDs: with Marian McPartland: *A Sentimental Journey* (Jazz Alliance 10025), with Ben Pollack: *Vols. 1–3* (Jazz Oracle 8015, 8016, 8107)

LPs to Search For: *Shades of Bix* (Brunswick 2-4410), *Jimmy McPartland's Dixieland* (Epic 3371), *The Music Man Goes Dixieland* (Epic 3371), *Meet Me in Chicago* (Mercury 60143)

Recommended Reading: *Jazz Talking* by Max Jones (Da Capo Press, 1987), *Voices of the Jazz Age* by Chip Deffaa (University of Illinois Press, 1990)

Recommended Videos: *Jazz Dance* (1954; Rhapsody Films), with Eddie Condon in *Chicago and All That Jazz* (1961; Vintage Jazz Classics 2002), *Art Hodes' Jazz Alley, Vol. 1* (1968; Storyville 6064), *Jazz at the Top* (1976; Rochester Area Educational)

JOE MCPHEE
. . . .

b. Nov. 3, 1939, Miami, FL

An adventurous trumpeter who also plays saxophones and (on rare occasions) trombone, Joe McPhee has followed his own singular path throughout his career. The trumpet, which he started on when he was eight, was his first instrument. McPhee played in an Army band in Germany (1964–65) and, after his discharge, made his recording debut in 1967 with Clifford Thornton. He played with the Matt Jordan Orchestra in the late 1960s and around that time was self-taught on saxophone. McPhee worked with Thornton, Don Cherry, and the Jazz Composers Orchestra in the early 1970s, was in Europe during 1975–77, and since the early 1980s has played in an expressive avant-garde style that he calls "Po Music." Joe McPhee has frequently played in Europe through the years and made quite a few recordings for Hat Hut/Hat Art (including the label's first releases), Cadence, and CIMP in addition to dates for Atavistic, Boxholder, Deep Listening, and Okka, among others. He is always a stimulating improviser.

Recommended CDs: *Oleo and a Future Retrospective* (Hat Art 6097), *Visitation* (Sackville 3036), *Legend Street One* (CIMP 115), *Inside Out* (CIMP 120), *Legend Street Two* (CIMP 132)

LPs to Search For: *Underground Railroad* (Cadence Jazz Records 1), *Rotation* (Hat Hut D), *Graphics* (Hat Hut I/J)

TOMMY MCQUATER

. . . .

b. Sept. 4, 1914, Maybole, Scotland

A top British swing trumpeter, Tommy McQuater was largely self-taught. McQuater played cornet at age 11 with the Maybole Brass Band. He started playing professionally with Louis Freeman's group on transatlantic liners and worked with the orchestras of Jack Payne (1934–35), Lew Stone (1935–36), Bert Ambrose (1936–38, 1939), and the Heralds of Swing (1939), helping to found the last group. McQuater appeared on many small-group dates during the era, including with such visiting Americans as Benny Carter and clarinetist Danny Polo.

McQuater played with the Squadronaires both before and after World War II. He spent the 1950s working in pit bands and on radio and television (including playing with Kenny Baker's Dozen), often teaming up in jazz settings with trombonist George Chisholm (a friend since the mid-1930s). Tommy McQuater (who never led his own record date) worked as a freelance musician into the 1990s. As a teacher, his students have included Digby Fairweather and Ian Carr.

Recommended CDs: with Benny Carter: *1933–1936* (Classics 530), with George Chisholm: *Swinging Britain-The Thirties* (Decca 5013/14)

LOUIS METCALF

. . . .

b. Feb. 28, 1905, Webster Groves, MO, d. Oct. 27, 1981, New York, NY

L ouis Metcalf, best known for his short stint with Duke Ellington's orchestra in the 1920s, was largely forgotten for decades and then surprisingly appeared on a record in 1966, playing advanced swing that was touched by bop.

Metcalf originally started on drums before switching to cornet. He gigged with Charlie Creath's band in St. Louis off and on for several years, arriving in New York in 1923 to perform with Jimmie Cooper's Black & White Revue. A good sight-reader and an exciting soloist who was modern for the mid-1920s, Metcalf was in great demand for both club appearances and recordings. During 1924–26 he worked with Willie "the Lion" Smith, Andrew Preer's Cotton Club Syncopators, Elmer Snowden, Sam Wooding, and Charlie Johnson. The association with the greatest potential was when he was hired by Duke Ellington to join Bubber Miley in his trumpet section. But, although he was with Ellington during the period when Duke first rose to prominence (late 1926–June 1928), Metcalf's role with the band was never really determined. Sometimes he seemed to be trying to imitate Miley (as on "New Orleans Lowdown" and "Black Beauty"), but he used the plunger mute with much less warmth and humor. On other occasions (as on "Yellow Dog Blues"), he sounded like a bloodless version of the lyrical Arthur Whetsol. Most of the time he was simply passed over, as when Ellington hired Jabbo Smith on one record to fill in for an absent Miley. Metcalf was most effective on "Harlem River Quiver" and "Bugle Call Rag," and it would have made sense to have him fill the role that Freddie Jenkins would soon initiate (which was continued later on by Taft Jordan, Willie Cook, and Clark

Terry), that of a hot modern soloist. But in mid-1928, when Whetsol rejoined Duke, Louis Metcalf became one of the first ex-Ellingtonians.

However, Metcalf did not lack for work. He joined Jelly Roll Morton for a period in 1928, and his recording career, which had really gotten going in 1924, continued to flourish. Among Metcalf's many freelance records during the 1924–29 period were dates backing singers Butterbeans and Susie, Martha Copeland, Mary Dixon, Helen Gross, Rosa Henderson, Maggie Jones, Sara Martin, Viola McCoy, Hazel Meyers, Josie Miles, Lizzie Miles, and Mamie Smith, plus combo dates with the Cotton Club Orchestra, Clarence Williams, James P. Johnson, the Musical Stevedores, the Jungle Town Stompers, Jasper Davis' Orchestra, the Gulf Coast Seven, Harry's Happy Four, the Kansas City Five, the Original Jazz Hounds, the Wabash Trio, and King Oliver (filling in for the ailing leader on five numbers). In most situations Metcalf contributed a short but colorful solo full of fire.

During the first half of 1929, Louis Metcalf was the regular trumpeter with Luis Russell's up-and-coming orchestra, recording one session with the pianist. But a falling out in the summer resulted in his return to freelancing; Henry "Red" Allen took his place. After the Depression hit and Metcalf's recording career ground to a halt, he worked with the Connie's Inn Revue and Vernon Andrade's orchestra before moving to Montreal for three years, where he performed mostly in vaudeville as a singer, dancer, and emcee. Later in the decade he was briefly with Fletcher Henderson's orchestra (March 1935), made his only recording of the '30s (two songs with Richard M. Jones' big band), played on riverboats near St. Louis, spent time in Chicago, and eventually returned to New York. Metcalf led a band at the Heatwave Club for a few years, returned to Montreal in 1944, and organized the International Band, a versatile group whose repertoire stretched from Dixieland to bebop. He came back to New York in 1951 and led small groups at various clubs in the city for the next two decades.

Metcalf's later activities were barely documented. He recorded a few long-out-of-print selections for the Franwill (1954), Stereocraft (1958), and Pickwick (1963) labels, but these are quite obscure. In 1966 Victoria Spivey gave him the opportunity to record a full album for her Spivey company, and his playing at that point was a bit reminiscent of Jonah Jones. But there were no encore sessions. And when he died in 1981, Louis Metcalf was still best known for his work with his employer of 53 years earlier, Duke Ellington.

Recommended CDs: with Duke Ellington: *The Okeh Ellington* (Columbia 46177)

Box Set: with Duke Ellington: *Early Ellington* (3 CDs; GRP/Decca 3-640)

LPs to Search For: *I've Got the Peace Brother Blues* (Spivey 1008)

MIKE METHENY

* * * * * * * * * * * * *

b. 1949, Lee's Summit, MI

Originally a classical trumpeter, Mike Metheny (the older brother of guitarist Pat Metheny) successfully made the transition to becoming a jazz flugelhornist. Mike's father and one of his grandfathers also played trumpet. He was classically trained on trumpet and earned a degree in music education from the University of Missouri (1971). After three years in the Army, Metheny taught at North Missouri State University and began listening to jazz, urged on by brother Pat. At 25, Metheny found that his biggest problem in switching genres was losing his worry about making mistakes, since in classical music errors are simply not permitted!

Metheny became a member of Berklee's faculty (1976–83), switched his focus to flugelhorn, and recorded *Blue Jay Sessions* for Headfirst in 1982. He followed it up with *Day In—Night Out, Kaleidoscope* (both for MCA), and more recently *Street of Dreams* (for Altenburgh). Metheny often doubles on an E.V.I. (electronic valve instrument), a trumpet synthesizer that has as much as a seven-octave range. He has a light, mellow sound (heard at its best on atmospheric sessions), a melodic style influenced by both jazz and pop music, and a very healthy attitude about being the older brother of a famous jazz musician. Mike Metheny is also a freelance music journalist who edits the magazine *JAM* in Kansas City.

Recommended CDs: *Street of Dreams* (Altenburgh 20)

LPs to Search For: *Blue Jay Sessions* (Headfirst 9712), *Day In—Night Out* (Impulse 5755)

DOUG METTOME
. . . .

b. Mar. 19, 1925, Salt Lake City, UT, d. Feb. 17, 1964, Salt Lake City, UT

A talented bebop trumpeter, Doug Mettome was significant for a relatively brief period of time. He led a band in his native Salt Lake City, spent three years in the military, and played with the Billy Eckstine Orchestra during 1946–47. Influenced initially by Roy Eldridge, Mettome was also touched by the playing of Dizzy Gillespie and Fats Navarro. During 1947–50 he freelanced in New York, playing with Herbie Fields, recording with Allen Eager, and being the bebop trumpet soloist with Benny Goodman's orchestra and sextet in 1949, including on the notable record "Undercurrent Blues."

When Goodman broke up his band and switched back to swing, it ended Mettome's prime period. He had stints with Woody Herman's Third Herd (1951–52) and the orchestras of Tommy Dorsey, Pete Rugolo, and Johnny Richards, also recording with Sam Most and Urbie Green. However, fame eluded Doug Mettome (who never led his own record date). He had a swing quartet in the early 1960s, moved back home to Salt Lake City, and passed away a month before his 39th birthday.

Recommended CDs: with Benny Goodman: *Undercurrent Blues* (Capitol 32086)

PALLE MIKKELBORG
. . . .

b. Mar. 6, 1941, Copenhagen, Denmark

P alle Mikkelborg has proven to be equally important as a trumpeter and as a composer, being influenced in the former by Miles Davis and in the latter by Gil Evans. Other than studying conducting at the Royal Music Conservatory in Copenhagen, Mikkelborg is completely self-taught. He started playing trumpet in 1956 and was a professional four years later. Mikkelborg joined the Danish Radio Jazz Group in 1964, leading the ensemble during 1966–72. He also worked with the Danish Radio Big Band (1965–71), co-led a quintet with Alex Riel, and was with the Peter Herbolzheimer big band starting in 1970.

Mikkelborg led Entrance during 1975–85, had a trio with pianist Thomas Clausen and bassist Niels Pedersen (1983–85), and has written quite a bit for films and television. He has worked with such Europeans and South Africans as Joachim Kuhn, Eje Thelin, Jan Garbarek, Terje Rypdal, Abdullah Ibrahim, Philip Catherine, Johnny Dyani, Karin Krog, and George Gruntz, among others. But as is often the case for Europeans, Mikkelborg is best known in the United States for his work with Americans, including such visitors to Denmark as George Russell, Dexter Gordon (writing for the tenor's album *Strings And Things*), Charlie Mariano, Maynard Ferguson, Don Cherry, Ben Webster, Yusef Lateef, and the Gil Evans Orchestra. Palle Mikkelborg, who led albums for Debut (1967), Metronome, and Storyville, gained his greatest recognition for his writing for Miles Davis' *Aura* (1984).

Recommended CDs: *Imagine* (Storyville 5012), with Miles Davis: *Aura* (Columbia 45332)

LPs to Search For: *Entrance* (Metronome 15826), *Heart to Heart* (Storyville 4114)

RON MILES

• • • • • • • • • •

b. May 9, 1963, Indianapolis, IN

A thoughtful and modest (but quite talented) trumpeter based in Colorado, Ron Miles' post-bop style is open to the influences of the avant-garde and hip-hop rhythms. He moved with his family to Denver from Indiana at the age of 11, shortly after he had started playing trumpet. "I really got into playing jazz through my junior high jazz band director, Dale Hamilton, who turned me on to Miles Davis, Dizzy, and Maynard, who was my first hero, even though it's not really apparent in my playing." He considers a turning point in his musical development to have taken place in 1983 when he heard Roscoe Mitchell's classic free jazz album *Sound*. Miles studied at the University of Denver (1981–85), the Manhattan School of Music (1985–86), and the University of Colorado (1986–91), becoming Assistant Professor of Music at Denver's Metropolitan State College. He played in Denver with the Boulder Creative Music Ensemble during 1984–88 (recording three local albums with the group), the Jazz Worms (1985–88), Kim Stone (1987–88), and the Bruce Odland Big Band. Miles was in the Duke Ellington Orchestra for part of 1993, when it was directed by Mercer Ellington.

Although continuing to work as an educator, Ron Miles has also performed with Bill Frisell on and off since 1994. He has recorded as a leader for Gramavision and Capri plus with Bill Frisell, displaying a great deal of potential, along with a strong musical curiosity.

Recommended CDs: *Witness* (Capri 74014), *Ron Miles Trio* (Capri 74049), *My Cruel Heart* (Gramavision 79510), *Woman's Day* (Gramavision 79516)

BUBBER MILEY

· · · · · · · · · · · · ·

b. Jan. 19, 1903, Aiken, SC, d. May 24, 1932, New York, NY

The legacy of Duke Ellington largely began with Bubber Miley. One of the finest trumpeters of 1926–30, Miley was largely responsible for Duke Ellington's adopting the colorful "jungle sound" that gave his orchestra such a distinctive personality by 1927. More than any other trumpeter up to that time, Miley was a master at using the plunger mute, often in conjunction with a straight mute in order to achieve a wide variety of otherworldly and speech like sounds.

Miley moved with his family to New York when he was six. His father played guitar on an amateur basis, and his three sisters all later sang professionally as the South Carolina Trio. Bubber began playing the trombone as a child before switching to cornet and eventually trumpet. He was in the Navy as a teenager during 1918–19 and then picked up musical experience working with the Carolina Five, Willie Gant's Band, and, most importantly, Mamie Smith's Jazz Hounds (1921–22), with whom he made his recording debut. During that time, Miley heard King Oliver's band at the Dreamland in Chicago, and he was very impressed by Oliver's playing, particularly his use of a plunger mute to achieve different tones. Miley, already a strong technical player, was soon experimenting with distorting his sound. He was also inspired by Johnny Dunn, his predecessor with Mamie Smith.

After leaving Smith, Miley freelanced for a couple of years. He appeared with Thomas Morris' Past Jazz Masters in 1923 and on many record dates in 1924, including with Perry Bradford (sitting next to Johnny Dunn on two songs), the Kansas City Five, and the Six Black Diamonds, also backing singers Helen Gross, Margaret Johnson, Louella Jones, Hazel Meyers, Julia Moody, and Monette Moore. In addition, Miley recorded three versions apiece of two songs in odd duets with the reed organ of Arthur Ray. He may have actually been on many more sessions during this era but was not yet distinctive enough to be definitively identified. That would change quite soon.

Bubber Miley worked with the Washingtonians for a short time in September 1923, when Elmer Snowden was the leader and Ellington just the band pianist. Even that early, his work with the plunger mute impressed Duke. A year later, when Ellington had taken over the ensemble, Duke went out of his way to hire Miley for his struggling band, quickly altering the group's repertoire from a sweet-sounding dance band to one that was infused with the blues and tonal distortions. On November 1924, the Duke Ellington Orchestra recorded their first two songs ("Choo Choo" and "Rainy Nights"), and the young trumpeter (sounding like himself for the first time) was the obvious star.

Miley would continue with Ellington (with occasional periods off) into January 1929. There would be some freelance recordings during the period (including appearances with Perry Bradford's Georgia Strutters, singers Sara Martin, Alberta Hunter, and Martha Copeland, and, best of all, four titles with Clarence Williams in 1926, including "I've Found a New Baby" and "Jackass Blues"). From June 1926 on, Miley and his musical partner Tricky Sam Nanton (who was his musical equivalent on trombone) starred on dozens of Duke Ellington recordings, and they helped make Duke a major success at the Cotton Club, the band's home base starting in late 1927. In addition to being the orchestra's best soloist, Miley co-wrote some of the band's most atmospheric pieces, including "Black and Tan Fantasy," "Creole Love Call," "Doin' the Voom Voom," and Ellington's original theme song, the haunting "East St. Louis Toodle-oo." Other notable solos by Miley during his Ellington years can be heard on "Jubilee Stomp," "The Mooche," "Hot and Bothered," the bizarre "Bandanna Babies," "Diga Diga Do," and "Tiger Rag."

Although Duke Ellington would become known later on for never firing any of his musicians, he made a reluctant early exception with Bubber Miley due to the trumpeter's excessive drinking and increasing unreliability. Miley had simply made the plunger chair too important in Duke's band for him to be constantly absent, and by early 1929 his alcoholism was so serious that he could no longer be counted upon. His successor, Cootie Williams, built upon his innovations, and the "plunger chair" would later be filled by Ray Nance and (in the 1970s) Barry Lee Hall.

Miley's post-Ellington years were anticlimactic and brief but not without interest. He visited France with Noble Sissle's orchestra in May 1929, gigged in New York with Zutty Singleton and Allie Ross, and in 1930 worked with Leo Reisman's white orchestra, usually appearing with the band during those segregated times hidden behind a screen. His haunting solo on their recording of "What Is This Thing Called Love" is quite memorable and a major contrast to the straight playing of the orchestra. Miley also appeared on a variety of very interesting recordings in 1930: four titles with Jelly Roll Morton, including "Fussy Mabel," guesting with King Oliver on "St. James Infirmary" in a trumpet section that also included Henry "Red" Allen, sitting next to Bix Beiderbecke on a Hoagy Carmichael session (they both solo on "Rockin' Chair"), and having his only dates as a leader, resulting in six songs, including "I Lost My Gal from Memphis" and "Black Maria."

The following year the trumpeter backed dancer Roger Pryor Dodge in the *Sweet and Low* revue for several months and then formed a band backed by Irving Mills. Unfortunately his alcoholism weakened his system so, when he was struck with tuberculosis in February 1932, it only took three months before Bubber Miley passed away. He was just 29.

Recommended CDs: *Thumpin' and Bumpin'* (Frog 11), with Duke Ellington: *Early Ellington* (Bluebird 6852), *The Okeh Ellington* (Columbia 46177)

Box Set: with Duke Ellington: *Early Ellington* (3 CDs; GRP/Decca 3-640)

PUNCH MILLER

· · · · · · · · · · · · · · ·

b. June 10, 1894, Raceland, LA, d. Dec. 2, 1971, New Orleans, LA

A fine trumpeter who was underrecorded during his prime years, Ernest "Punch" Miller always had a strong reputation among fans of New Orleans jazz. He gained his nickname because his twin sister (Ernestine Miller) had the middle name of Judy! After playing bass drum, baritone horn, and trombone, Miller switched to cornet. He worked locally, was in the service during World War I (luckily playing in Army bands), and returned to New Orleans after his discharge. Miller was a major part of the New Orleans jazz scene during the first half of the 1920s, playing with Kid Ory, Jack Carey, Fate Marable, and his own band.

After working in Dallas with Mack's Merrymakers, Miller moved to Chicago in 1926. He worked (and in most cases recorded) with Kid Ory, Albert Wynn, Freddie Keppard, Chippie Hill, Tiny Parham, Omer Simeon, Jimmy Bertrand, Jelly Roll Morton, Erskine Tate, Frankie Franko's Louisianians (on and off during 1929–35), Zilner Randolph's W.P.A. Band, and Walter Barnes, plus his own groups at local clubs. In the 1930s Miller (who stayed in Chicago rather than relocating to New York) could be heard on records with a variety of blues performers, including Big Bill Broonzy and Tampa Red. In 1947 he made a rare visit to New York, where he recorded 13 selections for Savoy, but mostly Miller freelanced in Chicago, including playing in a rock and roll revue at a circus during 1954–56!

In 1956 Miller returned to New Orleans, where he played on a part-time basis. It was ironic that, now past his prime, Miller had many opportunities to record, leading sets for Icon, Imperial, Southland, Atlantic, GHB, and Jazz Crusade during 1960–67. Punch Miller mostly spent his last years in New Orleans, other than touring Japan with George Lewis in 1963–64. His death at age 77 (just a short time after he appeared at the New Orleans Jazz Festival) was documented in the 1971 documentary film '*Til the Butcher Cuts Him Down.*

Recommended CDs: *Punch Miller 1925–1930* (RST 1517), *And Louis Gaillaud* (American Music 68)

LPs to Search For: *Punch and Handy's California Crusaders, Volumes One, Two, and Three* (GHB 191, 192, and 193)

Recommended Reading: *The Jazz Crusade* by Big Bill Bissonnette (Special Request Books, 1992)

Recommended Videos: '*Til the Butcher Cuts Him Down* (1971; Rhapsody Films)

PETE MINGER

. . . .

b. Jan. 22, 1943, Orangeburg, SC, d. Apr. 14, 2000, Pompano Beach, FL

Pete Minger should have been famous. His playing on *Straight from the Source* (originally an LP for Spinnster that was reissued years later by Jazz Alliance as *Minger Paintings*) finds him really excelling as a bop soloist in a quartet setting. But unfortunately that set was not heard by many, and instead he spent much of his career teaching and playing in big bands.

Minger started on the saxophone but soon switched to trumpet, where he was self-taught. He played with an Army band during 1967–69, attended Berklee (1969–70), and then gained some recognition for his work with Count Basie's orchestra (1970–80), often being the main trumpet soloist. Minger also gigged with Al Grey and Curtis Fuller. However, he decided to become a jazz educator, studying at the University of Miami (1981–85) and working as a teacher in Florida from 1985 on. Pete Minger, who also recorded with Hilton Ruiz, Melton Mustafa, and Turk Mauro, and worked with the Frank Wess big band in 1990, led small combos and recorded an album for Concord before losing a battle with cancer at the age of 57.

Recommended CDs: *Minger Paintings* (Jazz Alliance 10005), *Look to the Sky* (Concord Jazz 4555)

BLUE MITCHELL

. . . .

b. Mar. 13, 1930, Miami, FL, d. May 21, 1979, Los Angeles, CA

Richard "Blue" Mitchell, who had an immediately recognizable soulful sound, was a flexible hard bop soloist who uplifted every session that he was on. His early gigs included R&B dates with Paul "Hucklebuck" Williams (1951–52) and Earl Bostic (1952–55). After freelancing back in his native Miami, he was discovered by Cannonball Adderley, who persuaded Orrin Keepnews to record the young trumpeter for Riverside. Mitchell soon became famous for his work with the Horace Silver Quintet (1958–64), playing opposite tenor saxophonist Junior Cook, bassist Gene Taylor, and drummer Roy Brooks. Mitchell also recorded a string of impressive albums as a leader for Riverside, switching to Blue Note in 1963 and appearing on records as a sideman with such players as Dexter Gordon, Jimmy Smith, Lou Donaldson, and Stanley Turrentine.

In March 1964, after Silver broke up his quintet, Mitchell formed a similar group, using Cook, Taylor, drummer Al Foster, and several pianists, including most notably Chick Corea; Blue's "Fungii Mama" (included on his album *The Thing to Do*) became a standard. His quintet (with some changes in personnel) recorded three fine albums for Blue Note but only lasted a few years. Mitchell toured with Ray Charles (1969–71) and raised some eyebrows when he was featured with blues star John Mayall (1971–73) in a very effective mix of blues and bop. In 1974 Mitchell moved to Los Angeles, where he worked with Louie Bellson, Bill Berry's big band, and Richie Kamuca, co-leading a quintet with Harold Land in addition to recording as a leader for Mainstream, RCA, Jam, and Impulse. Even on his more commercial later dates, the trumpeter's playing is consistently stimulating and joyous. But in 1979 the beloved and clean-living Blue Mitchell died from cancer at the age of 49.

Recommended CDs: *Big 6* (Original Jazz Classics 138), *Out of the Blue* (Original Jazz Classics 667), *Blue Soul* (Original Jazz Classics 765), *Cup Bearers* (Original Jazz Classics 797), *Live* (Just Jazz 1007), with Horace Silver: *Finger Poppin'* (Blue Note 84008), *Blowin' the Blues Away* (Blue Note 46526), *Doin' the Thing* (Blue Note 84076)

LPs to Search For: *The Thing to Do* (Blue Note 4178)

GEORGE MITCHELL

. . . .

b. Mar. 8, 1899, Louisville, KY, d. May 22, 1972, Chicago, IL

George Mitchell was only a member of Jelly Roll Morton's Hot Peppers for five recording sessions during 1926–27, but his lyrical sound, impressive musicianship, and ability to fit perfectly into Morton's music made him immortal.

Mitchell actually played music on a full-time basis for only around 15 years, despite living to be 73. He started on trumpet when he was 12, and his early jobs in the South included work with the Louisville Musical Club Brass Band, the Rabbit's Foot Minstrel Show in Mississippi, A. G. Allen's Minstrels, and the L.M.C. Band. In late 1919 Mitchell moved to Chicago, and he had many short-term associations during the next few years, playing with Irving Miller's Brown Skin Models, Arthur Sims, Tony Jackson (in 1920), Clarence Miller, Doc Holly's Band, John Wickliffe, Carroll Dickerson (1923–24), and Doc Cook (1924–25).

All of that activity was a prelude to George Mitchell's most important work. In 1926 he recorded two songs with Luis Russell, backed singer Ada Brown on one session, and played with Lil Armstrong's band. The last association led the trumpeter to cut four titles apiece with the New Orleans Wanderers and the New Orleans Bootblacks; both of those combos were actually the Louis Armstrong Hot Five, with Mitchell in Armstrong's place and an altoist added. Jelly Roll Morton noticed Mitchell's solid playing and beautiful tone, and he was happy to use him on his five Victor recording sessions of 1926–27. On such classics as "Black Bottom Stomp," "The Chant," "Sidewalk Blues," "Doctor Jazz," and "The Pearls," it is difficult to know where Mitchell is reading Morton's charts and where he is improvising, so perfectly does he interpret the music.

Although it was not obvious at the time, Mitchell's recordings with Morton would be the high point of his career. He did record with Johnny Dodds in 1927 (including "Come on and Stomp, Stomp, Stomp"), Doc Cook, Jimmie Noone (several times during 1928–29), and the Dixie Rhythm Kings in addition to working with Dave Peyton. However, after being a member of Earl Hines' first big band during 1929–31 and gigging with banjoist Jack Ellis in the summer of 1931, Mitchell dropped out of music. Other than appearing on a Frankie "Half Pint" Jaxon recording in 1933 and occasionally playing with Elgar's Federal Concert Orchestra later in the decade, Mitchell concentrated on his day job as a bank messenger, a position he would hold into the 1960s. But due to his Morton recordings, George Mitchell remains a magical name to vintage jazz collectors.

Recommended CDs: with Jelly Roll Morton: *1924–1926* (Classics 599), 1926–1928 (Classics 612)

BILL MOBLEY
• • • • • • • • • • • •

b. Apr. 7, 1953, Memphis, TN

A fine hard bop trumpeter, Bill Mobley is one of many top players (including pianists James Williams, Mulgrew Miller, and Donald Brown) to emerge from the fertile Memphis jazz scene. Mobley began on cornet when he was five and was mostly self-taught. He played locally in Memphis, was inspired by Marvin Stamm, and attended North Texas State for a year, but returned to Memphis and earned a biology degree at Southwestern College while playing at local jam sessions (including with James Williams) at night.

Mobley worked with the Greg Hopkins-Wayne Naus big band in Boston during 1981–82, attended Berklee during 1982–86, and often played with Bill Pierce (1981–85). Since then Bill Mobley has worked with Donald Brown (1985–88), Geoff Keezer (1988–94), Marvin "Smitty" Smith, the Clifford Jordan big band, and his own groups.

Recommended CD: *Triple Bill* (Evidence 22163), with Donald Brown: *Early Bird* (Sunnyside 1025), with Bill Easley: *First Call* (Milestone 9186) with Geoff Keezer: *Waiting in the Wings* (Sunnyside 1035), *Other Spheres* (DIW 871), with Bill Pierce: *One for Chuck* (Sunnyside 1053)

AL MOLINA

. . . .

b. Dec. 18, 1935, San Francisco, CA

Al Molina has been a fixture in the San Francisco jazz scene since the 1960s. "My father, Al Molina Sr., was a professional musician and my first trumpet teacher. I was brought up listening to big bands and R&B." Molina, who studied piano for a year when he was eight, started on trumpet at 12, and his first influence was Harry James, though he was soon listening to the bop and hard bop players. He began playing in clubs when he was 16. Molina attended San Mateo Jr. College during 1960–62 and since then has performed regularly in the San Francisco area. He recorded with Pat Britt (1966) and the Sir Douglas Quintet in 1968, did studio work, and has been a longtime jazz educator. Al Molina has played with George Cables, Jessica Williams, Eddie Marshall, Eddie Moore, Eddie Henderson, Tom Harrell, Pete Escovedo, Johnny Griffin, Red Holloway, and Bill Watrous among others, leading two albums for his Jazzer label.

Recommended CDs: *The Gift* (Jazzer 1002), *Straight from the Heart* (Jazzer 1003)

BILL MOORE

. . . .

b. 1901, Brooklyn, NY, d. June 17, 1964, New York, NY

Bill Moore is an unusual figure in jazz history because he was a light-skinned black who spent most of his life "passing" and appearing in white bands. Some musicians knew that his parents had a mixed marriage, but apparently studio contractors and the general public never suspected that he was breaking down racial boundaries. In fact, on the occasions where there might have been some doubt about his origins, he billed himself as "The Hot Hawaiian"; never mind that he was actually from Brooklyn!

Moore (who was no relation to swing-era arranger Billy Moore) popped up on many records in the 1920s, taking countless short solos on a wide variety of dance-oriented recordings. He was with the California Ramblers (and their recording offshoots the Five Birmingham Babies, the Goofus Five, and the Lumberjacks), Ben Bernie (on and off during 1925–29), Don Voorhees, Bert Lown, and Lester Lanin. In addition, he recorded with Jack Pettis, Irving Mills' Hotsy Totsy Gang, the Whoopee Makers, the Mississippi Maulers, the New Orleans Blackbirds, the Vagabonds, the Varsity Eight, Bailey's Dixie Dudes, the Broadway Broadcasters, Al Goering's Collegians, the Kentucky Blowers, the Little Ramblers, Fred Rich, and the Dorsey Brothers (1930–31).

But after 1930, Bill Moore was permanently lost to jazz, being primarily a busy studio musician and virtually the only black to appear on countless sessions, even if few people ever realized it!

Recommended CDs: with Irving Mills: *The Hotsy Totsy Gang, Vols. 1–2* (Retrieval 122 and 123), with Jack Pettis: *1924–1929* (Kings Cross 005/006)

BOBBY MOORE

• • • • • • • • • • • • •

b. 1919, New York, NY

Bobby Moore is a long-lost trumpeter who at one time showed strong promise. Moore made his debut as a 16-year-old at an amateur talent contest at the Apollo in the summer of 1935, accompanied by Willie Bryant's band. He freelanced in New York and was a member of the Count Basie Orchestra from March to October 1937, recording some sessions with Basie and taking a few short solos. Moore was also with the Hot Lips Page big band in 1938 and briefly with the orchestras of Jimmy Mundy (with whom he recorded one obscure session) and Benny Carter in 1939. But in early 1940 he suffered a complete nervous breakdown, spent time in Bellevue Hospital, and was committed to the Matteawan Institution. Bobby Moore has not been heard from since.

Box Set: with Count Basie: *The Complete Decca Recordings* (3 CDs; GRP/Decca 611)

DANNY MOORE

• • • • • • • • • • • • •

b. Jan. 6, 1941, Waycross, GA

Danny Moore is an excellent hard bop soloist who has been underutilized on records. He attended Florida Agricultural and Mechanical University but soon became very interested in jazz and dropped out. In the early 1960s, Moore played with Ruth Brown, Quincy Jones, the house band at the Apollo Theatre, and Paul Williams (1962). His first important jazz gig was working with Art Blakey's Jazz Messengers during 1964 (although that version of the group did not record), and Moore also played with Count Basie's big band (1966) and in the 1970s with Aretha Franklin. Probably his greatest exposure was when he was a member of the Thad Jones-Mel Lewis Orchestra during 1968–72, taking a few notable solos.

Since then, Moore has worked with George Coleman's Octet (1972 into the 1980s), the 1975 Dizzy Gillespie big band, and his own groups, becoming involved in studio work. Danny Moore, who led his lone CD for the tiny Top Talent label, has also recorded with the Jones/Lewis Orchestra, Coleman, Freddy Cole, Pharoah Sanders, Charles Earland, Hank Crawford, and Al Grey.

Recommended CDs: with Freddie Cole: *A Circle of Love* (Fantasy 9674), with George Coleman: *Junior Cook/George Coleman* (Affinity 766)

LPs to Search For: with Hank Crawford: *Indigo Blue* (Milestone 9119)

HERB MORAND

• • • • • • • • • • • • •

b. 1905, New Orleans, LA, d. Feb. 23, 1952, New Orleans

Best known for his association with the Harlem Hamfats, Herb Morand was a New Orleans trumpeter with an eccentric style that was full of spirit. Morand started playing trumpet when he was 13. He worked with Nat Towles throughout the South in 1923, with his stepsister (blues singer Lizzie Miles) in New York, with Cliff Jackson's Krazy Cats (1925), and back in New Orleans with Chris Kelly. In the late 1920s Morand moved to Chicago, recording with the Beale Street Washboard Band (a small group with Johnny and Baby Dodds) and working with J. Frank Terry's Chicago Nightingales along with various local groups.

Morand played with the Harlem Hamfats during the second half of the 1930s, making many recordings during 1936–39. The unusual group usually featured Morand, the primitive clarinetist Odell Rand, a three-piece rhythm section plus Joe McCoy on guitar and vocals, and Charlie McCoy on mandolin. Its music fell between jazz and traditional country, with a healthy dose of jive vocals and emphasizing good-time lyrics and rhythms. Among its songs were "Let's Get Drunk and Truck," "You Done Tore Your Playhouse Down," "The Garbage Man," "Weed Smoker's Dream," "That's Going to Ruin Your Beauty Spot," "Take Me in Your Alley," and the like, all played with plenty of enthusiasm.

Morand also worked with Meade Lux Lewis and Jimmy Bertrand (1941). He returned to New Orleans in 1941 when jobs for the Hamfats dried up, playing locally with his group. As a member of George Lewis' band during 1948–50, Morand had an opportunity to record, and he also cut eight numbers as a leader during 1949–50. However, by then he was extremely overweight (over 300 pounds) and suffering from bad health. So, instead of getting to be part of George Lewis' success during the next few years, Herb Moran was forced to retire, passing away in 1952 at the age of 47.

Recommended CDs: New Orleans to Harlem (Jazz Crusade 3015), *Herb Morand 1949* (American Music 9)

LEE MORGAN

● ● ● ● ● ● ● ● ● ● ● ●

b. July 10, 1938, Philadelphia, PA, d. Feb. 19, 1972, New York, NY

One of the major trumpeters of the 1960s, Lee Morgan's career both started early and ended prematurely, with plenty of highlights along the way. Freddie Hubbard told me in 1979: "The critics call me fiery, but I think Lee played with more fire and he always had a bigger sound. We played some gigs together and he was always late, but he'd blow me out. I was playing slicker-than-hip lines, but he would blare me out. Crazy and cocky, he was a natural."

Morgan developed remarkably fast as a player. He was given a trumpet by his older sister for his 14th birthday. Within a year (1953), he was playing professionally in his hometown of Philadelphia. Early on, he developed a strong hard bop style influenced by Clifford Brown but with his own soul on display in his sound. In 1956, the 18-year-old Morgan became a member of the globetrotting Dizzy Gillespie big band, getting the first trumpet solo on "A Night in Tunisia" and (after Brownie's death) being touted in the jazz press as "the new Clifford Brown." Morgan was part of Gillespie's orchestra until its breakup in January 1958, at the same time recording six albums as a leader for Blue Note (including the first version of Benny Golson's "I Remember Clifford" and classic albums in *The Cooker* and, his quartet masterpiece, *Candy*).

Lee Morgan defined the adventure and brashness of 1960s hard bop.

Morgan joined Art Blakey's Jazz Messengers when he was barely 20, staying for three important years (1958–61). During that time he shared the frontline with tenors Benny Golson, Hank Mobley, and Wayne Shorter, appearing on such famous records as *Moanin', The Big Beat, Like Someone in Love,* and *The Freedom Rider.* He also recorded as a leader for Blue Note and Vee Jay and appeared often as a sideman (including on John Coltrane's *Blue Train* in 1957 and with Jimmy Smith and Hank Mobley).

When he left the Jazz Messengers (Freddie Hubbard, who was inspired by Lee, took his place), Morgan had a serious drug problem. He moved back to Philadelphia for a couple of years, playing locally (including with Jimmy Heath) but maintaining a lower profile. Late in 1963, Morgan was ready to make a comeback, and his first record as a leader (*The Sidewinder*) was a surprise hit, the biggest of his career. Suddenly he was back, in a big way, leading six more albums for Blue Note during 1964–65, including *Search for the New Land, The Rumproller, The Gigolo* (which introduced his blues "Speedball"), and *Cornbread* (highlighted by his beautiful ballad "Ceora"). After a second period with Blakey (1964–65), which was less significant than his first, Morgan led quintets.

During the second half of the 1960s, Lee Morgan evolved from a hard bop trumpeter to one who, while still swinging, was open to the influences of the avant-garde, modal music, and even some pop elements. He recorded frequently as a sideman and was constantly stretching himself. His last regular band was a forward-looking unit with either Bennie Maupin (doubling on bass clarinet) or Billy Harper on tenor. In the fall of 1971 he completed his 25th and final Blue Note album as a leader, a set with commercial elements that introduced flutist Bobbi Humphrey.

On February 19, 1972, at Slug's, Lee Morgan was shot and killed by his long-time girlfriend (who was 14 years older than he and had helped him finally kick drugs), whom he had recently spurned in favor of a younger woman. He was still just 33. Listeners can only guess what the trumpeter (whose death left a large hole in jazz) would have accomplished in the 1970s, '80s, and '90s.

Recommended CDs: *Candy* (Blue Note 46508), *The Sidewinder* (Blue Note 84157), *Search for the New Land* (Blue Note 84169), *The Gigolo* (Blue Note 84212), *Cornbread* (Blue Note 84222), with Art Blakey: *Moanin'* (Blue Note 46516), *The Big Beat* (Blue Note 46400), *Like Someone in Love* (Blue Note 84245)

Box Set: *The Complete Blue Note Lee Morgan Fifties Sessions* (4 CDs; Mosaic 4-162), *Live at the Lighthouse* (3 CDs; Blue Note 35228)

MARK MORGANELLI

b. May 15, 1955, Chincoteague, VA

An excellent hard bop soloist, Mark Morganelli has been important both as a trumpeter and as a producer of concerts, festivals, and recordings. "I was able to choose an instrument at the start of fourth grade. After one day with the violin, my father suggested I switch it for a trumpet!" Morganelli, who also played piano, led a group ("The Moonlighters") while in high school and studied at Bucknell University in Pennsylvania during 1973–77. He worked in Pennsylvania and Florida (leading the Bucknell Jazz and Rock Ensemble) before moving to New York in 1978.

During 1979–83, Morganelli had a musician's loft called the Jazz Forum, which allowed him to associate and play with many top musicians. In 1985 he started the nonprofit arts organization Jazz Forum Arts, presenting jazz at the Riverside Park Arts Festival for 13 years. Morganelli was also the music coordinator at Birdland during 1988–93 and has produced a wide variety of concerts, including Dizzy Gillespie's 75th birthday concert at Carnegie Hall. In addition, he has produced many CDs for the Candid label since 1989.

As a trumpeter, Morganelli has played with David Amram, Tiny Grimes (1989), David "Fathead" Newman, Paquito D'Rivera (1991), Vic Juris, Harold Ousley, Donald Harrison, Gary Bartz, Bobby Watson, John Hicks, and other top names. He recorded with Paquito D'Rivera and led dates for Jazz Forum and Candid. "I think that my mission has been to turn people on to music and the arts, specifically to jazz. I want to further the tradition of swing and bebop while trying to embrace Latin, Brazilian, and the more creative aspects of so-called fusion music."

Recommended CDs: *Five Is Bliss* (Jazz Forum 002), *Speak Low* (Candid 79054), with Paquito D'Rivera: *Who's Smoking?!* (Candid 79523), with Bill Heid: *Dark Secrets* (Savant 2033)

LPs to Search For: *Live on Broadway* (Jazz Forum 001)

FABIO MORGERA

* * * * * * * * * * * * *

b. Apr. 24, 1963, Naples, Italy

An excellent post-bop trumpeter with a flexible style, Fabio Morgera has been gaining more recognition lately due to his versatility. Morgera began his career playing in his native Italy, including with the Eurojazz Orchestra during 1982–85 and Giorgia Gaslini. He moved to the United States in 1986 and attended Berklee (1989–90). Fabio Morgera played with Igor Butman (1988), was a member of Groove Collective in the mid-1990s, and has since led his own groups, recording as a leader for Red and Ken Music.

Recommended CDs: *The Pursuit* (Ken Music 014), with Groove Collective: *Groove Collective* (Reprise 45541)

BUTCH MORRIS

* * * * * * * * * * * * *

b. 1940, Los Angeles, CA

Lawrence "Butch" Morris, a subtle yet adventurous cornetist with a mellow tone, will probably always be most famous for his "conductions." As an improvising conductor, Morris uses hand motions and gestures to direct freely improvising ensembles (essentially playing the orchestra and leading it in different directions), a logical innovation that was apparently not thought of before!

The brother of bassist Wilber Morris, he performed in California in the early 1970s with Horace Tapscott, Bobby Bradford, and Frank Lowe. Morris moved to New York in 1975 and lived in Paris during 1976–77, playing with Steve Lacy and Frank Wright. Since his return to New York, he has worked with Charles Tyler, Hamiet Bluiett, and especially David Murray, conducting his big band and performing in his octet. Butch Morris has led sessions for Kharma, Sound Aspects, and New World, including a ten-CD set of his "Conductions."

Recommended CDs: *Dust to Dust* (New World 80408), with David Murray: *Home* (Black Saint 120055), *Murray's Steps* (Black Saint 120065)

LPs to Search For: *In Touch … But Out of Reach* (Kharma 9)

JOE MORRIS

* * * * * * * * * * * * *

b. 1922, Montgomery, AL, d. Nov. 21, 1958, Phoenix, AZ

Joe Morris led an impressive band that straddled the boundaries between swing, bop, and R&B in the late 1940s. He had worked with Lionel Hampton's orchestra during 1942–46 (contributing the song "Tempo's Birthday") and spent a short period in Buddy Rich's bebop band. When he formed his group in 1947, Morris hired Johnny Griffin, who had been playing tenor with Hampton. "Little" Johnny Griffin was featured extensively, and the jump band also included at various times Elmo Hope, Percy Heath, and Philly Joe Jones. Morris' unit started out as a swing/bop group but by 1949 was more R&B oriented. Morris' trumpet fit well into both settings.

In 1950 Morris had a hit with "Anytime, Anyplace, Anywhere," a vocal feature for Laurie Tate. By then Griffin had departed, but Morris kept his band (sometimes known as "The Blues Cavalcade") going into 1953. Along the way Morris (who died prematurely at the age of 36) also recorded in backup bands with singers Wynonie Harris, Big Joe Turner, and Dinah Washington. It is a pity that in his later years, Joe Morris (who had strong potential) was not recorded extensively in jazz-oriented settings.

LPs to Search For: with Johnny Griffin: *Fly, Mister, Fly* (Saxophonograph 504)

THOMAS MORRIS
• • • • • • • • • • • • • • • • • •

b. 1898, New York, d. 1940s

A primitive cornetist whose playing was fine for 1923 but sounded out of date just four years later, Thomas Morris (like Johnny Dunn) was an excellent example of how New York brass players sounded before the rise of Louis Armstrong.

Not all that much is known about the mysterious cornetist outside of his playing and recording career. The uncle of pianist Marlowe Morris (a fine swing player of the 1940s), the elder Morris was associated with pianist-bandleader Clarence Williams and recorded with Williams and Sidney Bechet in 1923. During his prime years, he accompanied such blues/ vaudevillian singers on record as Fannie Mae Goosby, Helen Gross, Rosa Henderson, Jane Howard, Mike Jackson, Margaret Johnson, Mandy Lee, Sara Martin, Evelyn Preer, Mabel Richardson, Elizabeth Smith, Laura Smith, Mamie Smith (including "Goin' Crazy with the Blues"), Eva Taylor, Sippie Wallace, Edna Winston, and possibly others, where he has not been positively identified. Morris also appeared on instrumental recordings by many pickup groups with overlapping personnel, including Buddy Christian's Jazz Rippers, the Dixie Jazzers Washboard Band, the Five Musical Blackbirds, the Get-Happy Band, George McClennon's Jazz Devils, the Nashville Jazzers, the New Orleans Blue Five, and several groups headed by Clarence Williams.

Most significant were his own dates with his Seven Hot Babies, which resulted in eight songs in 1923 and ten in 1926. The latter sessions (his best recordings) at various times also featured Rex Stewart, Jabbo Smith, and trombonists Geechie Fields, Charlie Irvis, and Tricky Sam Nanton. But by 1927, when Morris was greatly outshone by Jabbo Smith on three numbers with Charlie Johnson's Original Paradise Ten, it must have been clear even to him that his time had passed. Morris' final records were made with Fats Waller on December 1, 1927. He eventually drifted out of music, becoming a redcap at Grand Central Station in New York. The strangest aspect to Thomas Morris' life occurred during his last few years, when he joined Father Divine's religious cult and changed his name to Brother Pierre!

Recommended CDs: *1923–1927* (Classics 822), *Thomas Morris 1926* (Frog 1)

JAMES MORRISON

• • • • • • • • • • • • • • • • • • •

b. Nov. 11, 1962, Boorowa, Australia

James Morrison is a remarkable multi-instrumentalist who not only plays trumpet, trombone, and all of the saxophones but also performs in styles ranging from Dixieland to hard bop. His father was a clarinetist and his mother played saxophone and taught dance. Morrison began on the cornet when he was seven. A year later he was already playing trombone, tuba, and euphonium, and a few years after that he had added the alto sax. Morrison led a Dixieland group when he was just nine and at 13 was playing in clubs four nights a week.

Morrison first visited the United States in 1979, performing at the Monterey Jazz Festival. After graduating from the NSW Conservatorium of Music in 1980 (where he was a lecturer in Jazz Studies when he was 20), he joined Don Burrows' Quintet (1980–82). In 1983 he formed the Morrison Brothers Big Bad Band with his brother John, a drummer; they recorded for ABC in 1984. Morrison first gained some recognition in the United States when he was with Red Rodney's quintet for five months in 1987. Since then he has been considered one of Australia's strongest jazz players. Morrison toured the world with Gene Harris' Philip Morris Superband in 1989–90, usually playing trombone. On his 1990 recording *Snappy Doo*, Morrison not only wrote all of the arrangements for a big band but played all of the horns himself via overdubbing (trumpets, trombones, euphonium, saxophones) in addition to piano!

James Morrison, who is quite witty, has the rare ability to play trumpet with one hand and slide trombone with the other (which looks impossible), trading off with himself. In addition, he does stunt flying, climbs mountains, and drives a racing car, which is almost as dangerous as playing a trombone one-handed!

LPs to Search For: *Swiss Encounter* (East West 91243), *Postcards from Down Under* (Atlantic 81972), *Snappy Doo* (Atlantic 82175)

MIKE MOSSMAN

• • • • • • • • • • • • • • • •

b. Oct. 12, 1959, Philadelphia, PA

A versatile trumpeter able to play both straightahead jazz and Afro-Cuban jazz, Mike Mossman is also a fluent trombonist. "I started trumpet in the third grade, when I was eight, but promptly quit lessons because they were boring. I played in the school bands by ear until age 15, when Marvin Stamm convinced me to learn to read music." As a teenager Mossman toured Europe with Anthony Braxton (1978). Although he also played in a group with Roscoe Mitchell and Leo Smith (Mitchell's Sound Ensemble during 1983–84), Mossman is generally more of a hard bop player.

After studying at the Oberlin Conservatory (1977–81), Mossman moved to Chicago in 1982, playing with the Jazz Members big band (1982–83), Bill Russo, and Mitchell. In 1984 he moved to New York. "The biggest turning point for me was coming to Rutgers from Chicago and changing my trumpet embouchure. It was a five-year process that took place during

1983–88. It led me through an extraordinarily difficult gauntlet of introspection and occasional terror."

Since his arrival in New York, Michael Mossman has worked with many of the top names in jazz and Latin music. Among his more notable associations are Machito (1984–85), Out of the Blue (which he led during 1985–90), Art Blakey's Jazz Messengers (on a few short occasions during 1984–89), Lionel Hampton, Horace Silver's Quintet (1989–91), Michel Camilo, the Count Basie Orchestra, Gerry Mulligan (1985–86 and his Rebirth of the Cool band in 1992), the Toshiko Akiyoshi big band, Eddie Palmieri, Tito Puente, the McCoy Tyner big band, Mario Bauza, Dizzy Gillespie's United Nation Orchestra, Jack McDuff, George Gruntz (1989–91), the Gil Evans Orchestra, Slide Hampton's Jazz Masters, the Carnegie Hall Jazz Band, Chico O'Farrill's orchestra, the Mingus Big Band, Michel Camilo, Benny Carter, Ray Barretto, and the Bob Mintzer big band; this is only a partial list!

A strong lead trumpeter and a talented soloist, Michael Mossman (who has led sessions for Red, Claves, and TCB) has also performed classical music.

Recommended CDs: *Spring Dance* (Claves Jazz 50-1094), *Mama Soho* (TCB 98102), with Ray Barretto: *My Summertime* (Owl 35830), *Contact!* (Blue Note 56974), with Out of the Blue: *Out of the Blue* (Blue Note 85118), *Inside Track* (Blue Note 85128), *Live at Mt. Fuji* (Blue Note 85141), *Spiral Staircase* (Blue Note 93006)

MICK MULLIGAN

. . . .

b. Jan. 24, 1928, Harrow, England

Peter "Mick" Mulligan was a busy trumpeter in the British trad scene in the 1950s. He was self-taught on trumpet, served in the military and (after his discharge) formed the Magnolia Jazz Band in 1948. The group was quite popular, recorded in 1950 and 1956–59 (for Tempo, Saga, Parlophone, and Pye), and played primarily Dixieland, eventually becoming known simply as Mick Mulligan's Jazz Band. It featured George Melly on vocals and, after the mid-1950s, clarinetist Ian Christie. The ensemble broke up in 1962, and the following year Mulligan went into semiretirement. Mick Mulligan, who considered his main influence to be Louis Armstrong, made guest appearances with several bands up until the early 1970s and then permanently retired from music.

Recommended CDs: *BBC Jazz Club, Vol. 4* (Upbeat Jazz 122)

MELTON MUSTAFA

. . . .

b. Nov. 23, 1947, Miami, FL

A talented trumpeter and leader of his own big band, Melton Mustafa has been a significant part of the jazz scene in Florida. Mustafa originally wanted to play saxophone. But when he got to junior high school, there were none available, so he was given an E-flat alto horn, switching to trumpet the following year. He played in the school band and as a teenager had a five-piece group that included his brother Jesse Jones on saxophones, performing calypsos and R&B. Mustafa attended Berklee, Mississippi Valley State University, and Florida A&M University, working early on with such R&B bands as Frank Williams' Rocketeers, the Uptown Funk All-Stars (Jaco Pastorius was a fellow sideman), and Chuck Jackson and the Marvelettes. However, his main love was jazz, and he was happy to be hired by Ira Sullivan to play in his group.

In the 1980s, Mustafa worked with Lionel Hampton (1980), Jaco Pastorius' Word of Mouth (1983), Bobby Watson's Horizon (on and off during 1983–90), Jon Hendricks, Frank Foster, the Duke Ellington Orchestra (when it was led by Mercer Ellington in 1985), James Williams, John Hicks, and Count Basie (1985–92). Melton Mustafa, an important jazz educator in Florida (heading the music department at the African Heritage Cultural Arts Center), has developed into a strong arranger (he considers Thad Jones and Frank Foster to be important influences) and has led a 17-piece big band since 1994, recording two albums for Contemporary.

Recommended CDs: *Boiling Point* (Contemporary 14075), *St. Louis Blues* (Contemporary 14085), with Eric Allison: *Mean Streets Beat* (Contemporary 14080), with Bobby Watson: *Gumbo* (Evidence 22078), *Inventor* (Blue Note 91915), *Tailor Made* (Columbia 53416)

RAY NANCE

. . . .

b. Dec. 10, 1913, Chicago, IL, d. Jan. 28, 1976, New York, NY

Ray Nance was the successor to Cootie Williams in the Duke Ellington Orchestra, where he displayed the ability to sound quite personal using the plunger mute, in addition to hinting at New Orleans jazz when he took his solos open. Nance was also a colorful performer who was one of jazz's top violinists and a swinging singer.

Nance's career before and after his Ellington years are interesting but relatively minor. He took piano lessons when he was six and studied the violin for seven years before he even started to play trumpet, being self-taught on the latter. Nance started out working with the Rhythm Rascals, the band at Lane College. He led a sextet in Chicago for a few years (1932–36) and worked with the big bands of Earl Hines (1937–38) and Horace Henderson (1939–40), recording with both.

In November 1940, after Cootie Williams surprised the swing world by leaving Ellington to join Benny Goodman's band, Nance was hired as his replacement Duke's orchestra. His very first gig with Ellington, a performance at Fargo, North Dakota, was recorded privately and released decades later. Other than a few short absences (including part of 1944–45), Nance was a regular member of the Duke Ellington Orchestra for 23 years. His most famous solo was on the original version of "Take the 'A' Train." Throughout his Ellington days, Nance was featured regularly as a plunger mute specialist, his violin added an important color to Duke's music, and he was Ellington's best-ever male vocalist.

When Cootie Williams ended his 21-year "vacation" and returned to the Ellington band in 1961, it put Nance in an uncomfortable position since Cootie reclaimed a few of his older features that Nance had long ago taken over. For two years they were both in Duke's band, but surprisingly there were no Ellington works that had them trading off or interacting, a lost opportunity. By 1963, Nance's drinking had become troublesome and Ellington let him go.

Nance mostly freelanced with small groups during his last dozen years, popping up in a few surprisingly modern settings (including with drummer Chico Hamilton and on a jam session record with Dizzy Gillespie and Chick Corea). He had a few minor reunions with Ellington and worked with clarinetist Sol Yaged, pianists Andre Chaix and Brooks Kerr, and trombonist Chris Barber (with whom he toured Europe in 1974). Ray Nance hardly recorded at all as a leader in his career (four selections in London in 1948 and an album apiece for Solid State in 1969 and MPS in 1972), but fortunately he was well featured with Duke Ellington for over two decades.

Recommended CDs: with Duke Ellington: *Duke Ellington Meets Coleman Hawkins* (Impulse 162), *Studio Sessions-New York 1963, Vol. 4* (Atlantic 83003)

Box Sets: with Duke Ellington: *Blanton/Webster Band* (3 CDs; Bluebird 5659), *Black, Brown and Beige* (3 CDs; Bluebird 86641)

Recommended Reading: *The World of Duke Ellington* by Stanley Dance (Charles Scribner's Sons, 1970)

Videos to Get: *Jazz Festival, Vol. 2* (1962, with Duke Ellington Orchestra; Storyville 6074)

PHIL NAPOLEON

. . . .

b. Sept. 2, 1901, Brooklyn, NY, d. Sep. 30, 1990, Miami, FL

A major candidate for most underrated trumpeter of the 1920s, Phil Napoleon's importance to jazz has been completely overlooked for many decades. He is generally grouped with revival Dixieland musicians because he led a trad band in the 1950s, but his early contributions to the music were very significant.

Phil Napoleon was the top trumpeter on records during 1921–22 and was arguably the first trumpeter based in New York to swing. During a period of time when most so-called "hot" brassmen (other than the New Orleans transplants who were in Chicago) were indulging in novelty effects (laughing or crying through their horn) or fumbling their way through repetitive double-time runs, Napoleon knew how to properly swing a song in tasteful fashion. Never a high-note virtuoso, he uplifted melodies, was expert at placing notes in the best spots, and improvised in a subtle and relaxed fashion. He was also on a remarkable number of recordings.

Phil Napoleon, who was born Filippo Napoli, first played trumpet in public when he was five. His brothers George and Joe were saxophonists, Matthew was a guitarist, and Ted Napoleon (who recorded with Phil) was a drummer. In addition, Phil's nephews Teddy Napoleon and Marty Napoleon would become notable swing pianists by the 1940s. When he was 12, Napoleon ran away from home and actually made it all the way to New Orleans (where he was enjoying the music) before he was caught. He made his first recordings in 1916, when he was 15 (one year before the Original Dixieland Jazz Band) as a classical cornetist, but the rapidly emerging jazz music was his true love. Inspired by the ODJB (whom he saw fairly often in New York and sat in with in the early 1920s), Napoleon formed the first version of his Original Memphis Five in late 1917, naming the band in tribute to W.C. Handy's "Memphis Blues."

After several years of freelancing (his strong technical skills and sight-reading ability made him in demand from the start for studio work), in 1921 Phil Napoleon began to record in jazz settings. After cutting "Memphis Blues" and "The St. Louis Blues" in July 1921 as Lanin's Southern Serenaders, Napoleon and his group followed up with hit versions of "Shake It and Break It" and "Aunt Hagar's Children's Blues" the following month. Then the flood began. As the Original Memphis Five, Phil Napoleon, trombonist Miff Mole (later replaced by Charles Panelli), clarinetist Jimmy Lytell, pianist Frank Signorelli, and drummer Jack Roth (with occasional additions and substitutes) recorded 111 titles during 1922–23 alone, and that does not include their many recordings under the names of the Ambassadors, Bailey's Lucky Seven, the Broadway Syncopators, the Cotton Pickers, Jazzbo's Carolina Serenaders, Ladd's Black Aces, Sam Lanin, the Savannah Six, the Southland Six, and the Tennessee Ten! Often playing current pop tunes rather than just copying the ODJB, Phil Napoleon and his many overlapping bands helped make jazz a major part of the mainstream pop music of the era.

Phil Napoleon remained quite busy throughout the 1920s, particularly in the recording studios. The Original Memphis Five recorded 43 more titles in 1924, 22 in 1925, and 13 in 1926. Napoleon was also on recordings backing singers Alberta Hunter, Leona Williams, and Leon Wilson. In December 1926 he had his first record date under his name, and the following year Napoleon officially formed his own group; the Original Memphis Five name was used for just 12 more songs during 1927–31. Napoleon's band did not go anywhere, but he was kept busy on many freelance jazz dates, including backup work with singers Irene Beasley, Lew Bray, Seger Ellis, Annette Hanshaw, Irving Kaufman, Lee Morse, and Carson Robison. He was also on instrumental-oriented sessions by the California Ramblers, the Charleston Chasers, the Dorsey Brothers, the Emperors, the Hot Air Men, the Hotsy Totsy Gang, Miff Mole's Little Molers, the New Orleans Black Birds, Boyd Senter, and Milt Shaw, all in the late 1920s.

For such a prolific musician, it is ironic that Phil Napoleon never became a major name. In the 1930s he primarily played anonymously with radio orchestras (particularly for RCA), and his short-lived big band of 1938 quickly flopped; he recorded only five songs as a leader during the 1930–44 period. Napoleon worked in the musical instrument business for a time and was only semiactive in music in the early 1940s (other than a short stint with Jimmy Dorsey's orchestra in 1943). However, by 1946 he was back, recording 16 Dixieland selections with a septet that included ODJB drummer Tony Spargo. In 1949 he put together a reformed Memphis Five that played regularly at Nick's in New York for seven years. Twelve titles for Decca and Columbia and some air-checks survive from this period.

In 1956 Napoleon moved to Florida, where he remained active until near the end, opening up his Phil Napoleon's Retreat club in 1966 and playing Dixieland into the mid-1980s. He recorded three Capitol records during 1959–60 heading a sextet that included clarinetist Kenny Davern and pianist Johnny Varro but did not appear on records again after he turned 60. Although some jazz historians knew of his importance, Phil Napoleon was never really interviewed at length, and he ended up being an unheralded pioneer of 1920s jazz.

Recommended CDs: *The Original Memphis Five, Vol. 1* (Collector's Classics 16), *Live at Nick's NYC* (Jazzology 39)

LPs to Search For: *Featuring the Original Memphis Five* (IAJRC 26), *1929–1931* (The Old Masters 24), *Phil Napoleon and the Memphis Five* (Capitol 1344)

Recommended Reading: *Lost Chords* by Richard M. Sudhalter (Oxford University Press, 1999)

VAUGHN NARK

b. 1956, Mt. Carmel, PA

Despite being a remarkable trumpet virtuoso who can play "Donna Lee" at a blinding speed and hit notes almost as high as can Arturo Sandoval, Vaughn Nark is a relative unknown. Nark developed very quickly as a youngster. He started on the trumpet when he was six, and the following year, while in second grade, he joined the Mt. Carmel High School Band! At eight he was a bandleader and playing professionally. The following year he was playing first trumpet in the high school band. In 1978 Nark joined the United States Air Force Jazz Ensemble (known as the Airmen of Note), and he has been based in the Washington, D.C., area ever since.

Because the Airmen of Note do not record commercially, Nark remained pretty anonymous during his nearly 20 years with the orchestra, despite being well featured. He did record two albums as a leader (not introverted affairs!) during that long period, worked with the Bill Potts big band, played with combos locally, and did some session and studio work. Since becoming a civilian in recent times, Vaughan Nark has recorded two CDs for Summit but has not yet found the fame he deserves, or the self-restraint that will make him a much more listenable player in the long run.

Recommended CDs: *Something Special* (Summit 225), *Flying High* (Summit 240)

LPs to Search For: *Cutting Through* (Lavenham 8103), *El Tigre* (Progressive 7073)

FATS NAVARRO

b. Sept. 24, 1923, Key West, FL, d. July 7, 1950, New York, NY

One of the great jazz trumpeters of all time, Theodore "Fats" Navarro was one of the leaders of bebop and a major influence on Clifford Brown. During 1946–49, Navarro was second to Dizzy Gillespie among modern jazz trumpeters, but his premature death was a major loss.

Navarro played piano and tenor sax before taking up the trumpet when he was 13. Five years later he joined Snookum Russell's territory band (1941–42). When he was with the Andy Kirk Orchestra (1943–44), Navarro sat next to Howard McGhee in the trumpet section. McGhee, Roy Eldridge, and Dizzy Gillespie would be Fats' major influences.

When Dizzy Gillespie left Billy Eckstine's big band, he recommended Navarro as his replacement. After that stint (1945–46) was finished, Fats spent the remainder of his career playing mostly with small groups. His beautiful tone and logical ideas were a little easier to emulate than Gillespie's, and he became a musical role model for some of his fellow trumpeters before the rise of Miles Davis. Navarro appeared on many important bop recording sessions during the second half of the 1940s, including with the Bebop Boys, Coleman Hawkins, Eddie "Lockjaw" Davis, Don Lanphere, Illinois Jacquet (he toured in his band during part of 1947–48), Bud Powell (a classic set that helped to introduce the young Sonny Rollins), and the 1949 Metronome All-Stars in addition to his own dates for Savoy and Blue Note. Navarro spent a couple of periods working with Tadd Dameron (helping to introduce some of the pianist-arranger's best songs) and in 1948 was a member of both the Lionel Hampton big band (a radio air-check exists of the otherwise unrecorded band) and Benny Goodman's small group (recording a boppish version of "Stealin' Apples").

Although a Birdland session with Charlie Parker that was documented is listed as being from 1950, because Navarro is heard in very strong form, the date would seem to be inaccurate. By then, Fats was suffering from tuberculosis that was exasperated by his longtime heroin use, and the once-overweight trumpeter was wasting away. His death at age 26 left a giant hole that was only temporarily filled by the equally ill-fated Clifford Brown. One can only speculate as to what Fats Navarro would have accomplished if he had lived to a normal age and been active in the 1950s, '60s, and '70s; he would be only 77 today!

Recommended CDs: *Goin' to Minton's* (Savoy 92861), *The Complete Blue Note and Capitol Recordings of Fats Navarro and Tadd Dameron* (Blue Note 33373), *With the Tadd Dameron Band* (Milestone 47041)

DAVE NELSON
• • • • • • • • • • • • •

b. 1905, Donaldsonville, LA, d. Apr. 7, 1946, New York, NY

The nephew of King Oliver, Dave Nelson was also considered his protégé. Nelson's career was both helped by Oliver and hurt by his association with the legendary cornetist, for he never really escaped from his shadow.

Early on, Nelson played violin and piano before settling on the trumpet. At one point in the 1920s he also studied arranging with Richard M. Jones. After moving to Chicago in the mid-'20s, Nelson worked with the Marie Lucas Orchestra, Ma Rainey (recording three titles with her in 1926), Jelly Roll Morton, Edgar Hayes' Eight Black Pirates (1927), Jimmie Noone, Leroy Pickett, and Luis Russell (1929) in addition to occasionally leading his own band. Nelson joined King Oliver's orchestra in the autumn of 1929 and stayed through early 1931. He not only played in the trumpet section but also contributed many of the arrangements for Oliver's 1929–31 recording dates. Because his uncle's playing ability was declining due to his bad teeth, Nelson took quite a few solos on King Oliver's records of the period in a similar style, leading years later to record collectors debating over whether certain solos were by Oliver or by Nelson. Generally Nelson sounded quite awkward when using mutes, but on open horn he was stronger and had a wider range than Oliver did at that point.

Nelson left King Oliver in 1931 but used his band on seven songs cut as a leader for two record dates under the title of either The King's Men or Dave's Harlem Highlights; Nelson sings on all of those numbers. From then on he mostly led his low-profile bands in New York and New Jersey, often doubling on piano. Other than an appearance on a Willie "the Lion" Smith date in 1937 and a completely unreleased session as a leader in 1942 (trombonist Clyde Bernhardt remembered that they cut a dozen songs), Nelson never recorded again. He spent his last four years as a staff arranger for the Lewis Publishing Co. before dying from a heart attack at the age of 41. Why Dave Nelson accomplished so little after his days with King Oliver is not known, for he certainly showed a lot of potential during 1929–31. But instead of gaining recognition as a fine player, he is today thought of as King Oliver's Andy Secrest, a substitute for the real thing.

Recommended CDs: with King Oliver: *The New York Sessions 1929–1930* (Bluebird 9903)

JOHN NESBITT
• • • • • • • • • • • •

b. 1900, Norfolk, VA, d. 1935, Boston, MA

John Nesbitt was the main trumpet soloist with McKinney's Cotton Pickers and was one of the first whose style crossed racial lines and mixed together aspects of both Louis Armstrong and Bix Beiderbecke. However, if he had lived longer, he probably would have been best known as a top swing-era arranger rather than as a trumpeter.

Nesbitt started out playing with Lillian Jones' Jazz Hounds and Amanda Randolph before joining William McKinney's Synco Septette in 1925. The band soon grew into McKinney's Cotton Pickers, an outfit in which Nesbitt would be an important part until he left in the summer of 1930. He recorded with the band during 1928–30 and, in addition to taking many short solos, Nesbitt contributed such arrangements as "Plain Dirt," "Travelin' All Alone," "Crying and Sighing," "Will You, Won't You Be My Babe?" and "Zonky." His chart of "Chinatown, My Chinatown" was recorded by Fletcher Henderson in 1930.

In his post-Cotton Pickers years, John Nesbitt wrote for Luis Russell and played with Zach Whyte's Chocolate Beau Brummels, Speed Webb, and Earle Warren. But a serious stomach ailment forced him to retire and resulted in his early death, cutting short what might have been a pretty significant career.

Recommended CDs: with McKinney's Cotton Pickers: *1928–1930* (Bluebird 2275)

JOE NEWMAN
• • • • • • • • • • • •

b. Sept. 7, 1922, New Orleans, LA, d. July 4, 1992, New York, NY

Joe Newman was an excellent swing trumpeter with a sound of his own that was influenced slightly by Harry "Sweets" Edison, though he always considered Louis Armstrong to be his main inspiration. He was (along with rhythm guitarist Freddie Green) the only significant sideman to be a longtime member of the two Count Basie Orchestras (the 1940s version and the post-1951 band).

Newman came from a musical family in New Orleans. His first big job was with Lionel Hampton's big band (1941–42). While with Basie the initial time (1943–46), he shared the trumpet solos with Edison. Newman left Basie to tour with Illinois Jacquet's very popular jump band during 1946–50. After a period of freelancing, Newman became a major part of the second Basie band during 1952–61, this time sharing the trumpet solos with Thad Jones. Newman also led quite a few sessions of his own for a variety of labels; his RCA recordings are classics.

After leaving Basie for the last time, the trumpeter toured the USSR with Benny Goodman in 1962, worked on jazz education (founding Jazz Interactions, Inc.), and freelanced as a soloist. Among Joe Newman's later activities were recording at the jam sessions of the 1972 Newport in New York Festival, performing with the New York Jazz Repertory Company, working in the pit bands of Broadway shows, participating in reunions of Basie alumni, touring with Benny Carter, and co-leading an album with Joe Wilder in 1984.

Recommended CDs: *The Complete Joe Newman* (RCA 88810), *I Feel Like a Newman* (Black Lion 760905), *Hangin' Out* (Concord Jazz 4262)

Recommended Reading: *The World of Count Basie* by Stanley Dance (Charles Scribner's Sons, 1980)

Videos to Get: *The Sound of Jazz* (1957 Vintage Jazz Classics 2001)

FRANKIE NEWTON
. . . .

b. Jan. 4, 1906, Emory, VA, d. Mar. 11, 1954, New York, NY

A lyrical trumpeter who was overshadowed by his contemporaries, Frankie Newton had a fairly brief career. Newton picked up early experience playing with Lloyd and Cecil Scott's band in 1927 (recording with Cecil Scott in 1929), Elmer Snowden, Eugene Kennedy, Chick Webb, Charlie Johnson, and Sam Wooding. Newton was on Bessie Smith's final recording session (1933), worked with Charlie Johnson's band (1933–35), and was Roy Eldridge's replacement with Teddy Hill (1936–37). He spent part of 1937 as a member of John Kirby's new sextet, but a personality conflict with the bassist led to his being replaced by Charlie Shavers. The chances are that Newton's career would have turned out completely different if he had been a part of Kirby's successful group.

Instead, Newton played with Mezz Mezzrow's Disciples of Swing and Lucky Millinder (1937–38) before leading small groups (which usually included altoist Pete Brown) through 1944, often based at Cafe Society and Kelly's Stable in New York. Newton is heard at his best on the record dates he led between 1937–39, including his personal favorite recording, "The Blues My Baby Gave to Me."

But after working with James P. Johnson during 1944–45, the trumpeter was completely out of the spotlight, content to occasionally play locally in Boston. By then Frankie Newton seemed to be more interested in painting and leftist politics than music, and he was largely forgotten by the time he died at age 48 in 1954.

Recommended CDs: *1937–1939* (Classics 643)

WOODEN JOE NICHOLAS

b. Sept. 23, 1883, New Orleans, LA, d. Nov. 17, 1957, New Orleans, LA

One of the most primitive of all jazz trumpeters, Wooden Joe Nicholas (who spent virtually his entire life in New Orleans) was best known for his loud volume and iron chops rather than for his tone or musicianship. The uncle of clarinetist Albert Nicholas, he actually began as a clarinetist and did not switch full time to cornet until 1915 (when he was already 32), inspired by the memories of Buddy Bolden. Nicholas played many street parades and led the Camellia Band from 1918 until the early 1930s. He was less active during the Depression years but came back in the 1940s, recording as a leader in 1945 (making his recording debut when he was 62) and 1949, plus as a sideman with Raymond Burke, Johnny St. Cyr, Big Eye Louis Nelson, and Baby Dodds. There is no mistaking the tone of Wooden Joe Nicholas for that of anyone else!

Recommended CDs: *Wooden Joe Nicholas* (American Music 5)

BOBBY NICHOLS

b. Sept. 15, 1924, Boston, MA

Bobby Nichols, an advanced swing player, was one of the most exciting solo stars of Glenn Miller's Army Air Force Band in 1944, so it is surprising that he did not have a more prominent career.

Nichols started playing trumpet when he was eight, and later on he attended the New England Conservatory. Due to the wartime shortage of musicians, Nichols started very early, becoming a member of Vaughan Monroe's orchestra when he was just 15 (1940–43). Nichols joined the Army in 1943 and was part of Glenn Miller's Army Air Force Band during its two years of existence (1943–45), taking the majority of the trumpet solos (starting when he was 19), as can be heard on many radio transcriptions, broadcasts, and live performances by this mighty orchestra.

After his discharge, Nichols worked with Tex Beneke (1946–47), Ray McKinley (1948), and his own short-lived group. Nichols was with Tommy Dorsey's orchestra in 1951 and then landed a long-term job with the Sauter-Finegan Orchestra (1952–61), getting some solo space but never becoming well known or getting the opportunity to lead his own record date. After the Sauter-Finegan band broke up, Bobby Nichols worked as a studio musician and drifted into obscurity. He is totally forgotten today, except by collectors of the Glenn Miller Army Air Force Band recordings.

Recommended CDs: *Major Glenn Miller and the Army Air Force Band* (Bluebird 6360)

RED NICHOLS

• • • • • • • • • • • • •

b. May 8, 1905, Ogden, UT, d. June 28, 1965, Las Vegas, NV

Both overrated and underrated during his long episodic career, Ernest Loring "Red" Nichols was one of the finest cornetists to emerge during the 1920s. He studied cornet with his father (a college music teacher) from the age of five and played with his father's brass band when he was 12. Nichols worked locally in Utah; was in the Culver Military Academy for part of 1920 before being kicked out, performed with pit orchestras, and in 1922 recorded with the Syncopating Five. He took over the band (renamed the Royal Palms Orchestra), playing in Atlantic City and Indiana.

By then, Nichols was a fan of the Original Dixieland Jazz Band, Bix Beiderbecke (who was an influence on his style, although Red had an emotionally cooler approach), and Phil Napoleon. He joined Sam Lanin in New York in late 1924 and soon was one of the busiest musicians in the world. Nichols had impressive technical skills, was a talented (if usually uncredited) arranger and a fine improviser who could read anything. In addition to Lanin, he worked with Harry Reser, Benny Krueger, Ross Gorman, Henry Halsted, Vincent Lopez, Don Voorhees, the California Ramblers, and many studio orchestras. Nichols spent a few months with Paul Whiteman's orchestra in 1927, and was always quite proud that his replacement was Bix Beiderbecke.

In 1926, Red Nichols started recording as a leader with his Five Pennies and the following year had a surprise hit in "Ida, Sweet As Apple Cider." The original group featured trombonist Miff Mole, pianist Arthur Schutt, guitarist Eddie Lang, and drummer Vic Berton (doubling on tympani), although the Five Pennies' recordings usually featured a group with more than five members. Other key players included Dudley Fosdick on mellophone, Jimmy Dorsey on clarinet and alto, and, later on, clarinetists Pee Wee Russell and Benny Goodman, trumpeter Leo McConville, drummer Gene Krupa, and trombonists Jack Teagarden and Glenn Miller. Nichols was a pioneer in using whole-tone runs in his arrangements, and the Nichols/Mole team (often jumping between unusual intervals), though not particularly influential, featured many original phrases and ideas. During the 1926–32 period, Nichols recorded a very impressive number of recordings under a variety of names in addition to the Five Pennies, including the Charleston Chasers, the Arkansas Travelers, the Red Heads, the Louisiana Rhythm Kings, and Red and Miff's Stompers. In addition, he headed larger ensembles on some recordings, took some dates as a sideman, and led the orchestra for the shows *Strike Up the Band* and *Girl Crazy.*

Because Nichols was a disciplinarian who demanded a lot from his hard-drinking sidemen, and because he was not a martyr like Beiderbecke or a primitive blues player, he was not all that popular among many of the jazz musicians of his time (although Louis Armstrong thought highly of him). Ironically Nichols was overrated for a time in Europe in the early 1930s, when his recordings became widely available before Armstrong's. But with the rise of the swing era, he was largely forgotten for a time.

Nichols worked extensively in the studios in the 1930s, led a so-so orchestra during the big band era, and took time off during 1942–44 to take care of his daughter (who had polio).

After working in the shipyards for a couple of years, he gradually made a comeback. Nichols was featured with the Casa Loma Orchestra for a few months in 1944, and later in the year he formed a new version of the Five Pennies, a sextet that was based in Los Angeles. The group, particularly after bass saxophonist Joe Rushton became a regular member, was one of the best Dixieland bands of the 1950s, recording for Jump, Jazzology, and Capitol and helping to popularize "Battle Hymn of the Republic" as a Dixieland tune.

After appearing as a subject of an episode of the television show *This Is Your Life* in October 1956, there was interest in filming Nichols' life story. The result was the 1959 movie *The Five Pennies,* which, although mostly fiction, was quite entertaining (starring Danny Kaye and Louis Armstrong), with Nichols ghosting the cornet solos for Kaye; it is one of the most watchable of all the jazz movies. The success of that film helped make Red Nichols famous, and he was quite active until his unexpected death from a heart attack at age 60 in 1965.

Recommended CDs: *Red Nichols and Miff Mole* (Retrieval 79010), *And His Five Pennies* (Jazzology 90), *And His Five Pennies, Vol. 2* (Jazzology 290)

LPs to Search For: *Red Nichols and His Five Pennies, Vols. 1–5* (Swaggie 836, 837, 838, 839, 840), *Red Nichols and His Five Pennies* (Jump 12-1), *Syncopated Chamber Music* (Audiophile 2), *All-Time Hits* (Pausa 9022)

Recommended Reading: *After Intermission 1942–1965* by Philip Evans, Stanley Hester, Stephen Hester, and Linda Evans (Scarecrow Press, 1997), *Jazzmen* edited by Frederic Ramsey Jr. and Charles Edward Smith (Harcourt Brace Jovanovich, 1939), *Lost Chords* by Richard M. Sudhalter (Oxford University Press, 1999), *Red Head* by Stephen Straff (Scarecrow Press, 1996)

Film Appearances: *Wabash Avenue* (1950), *Disc Jockey* (1951), *Quicksand* (1951), *The Gene Krupa Story* (1959), and playing Danny Kaye's solos in *The Five Pennies* (1959)

SAM NOTO
· · · · · · · · · ·

b. Apr. 17, 1930, Buffalo, NY

A fine bebop trumpeter, Sam Noto is often thought of as a Canadian, since he has spent so many years north of the border. Noto, who is actually from Buffalo, became a professional musician when he was 17. After working locally in upstate New York, he toured and recorded with the big bands of Stan Kenton (1953–58), Louis Bellson (1959), Kenton again (1960), and Count Basie (two periods during 1964–67). Despite that exposure, he was relatively unknown, and even more so after he settled into the anonymity of playing in Las Vegas show bands (1969–75). However, he befriended Red Rodney (who was also in Las Vegas during that time), and they recorded together on Rodney's *Superbop* album. That led to Noto's discovery as a Dizzy Gillespie and Fats Navarro-inspired bebopper. During 1975–78 he recorded frequently for the Xanadu label, both as a sideman and on four occasions as a leader, doing some of the finest work of his career.

Sam Noto moved to Toronto in 1975, where he has been based ever since. A member of Rob McConnell's Boss Brass for a time, he has often worked in the studios and occasionally appears on a bop recording or in concert with tenor saxophonist Don Menza.

LPs to Search For: Entrance (Xanadu 103), *Act One* (Xanadu 127), *Notes to You* (Xanadu 144), *Noto-Riety* (Xanadu 168), *2-4-5* (Unisson 1007), with Red Rodney: *Superbop* (Muse 5046)

Videos to Get: Don Menza: Live in New Orleans (1991; Leisure Video)

JIMMY NOTTINGHAM

. . . .

b. Dec. 15, 1925, Brooklyn, NY, d. Nov. 16, 1978, New York, NY

A lead trumpeter who could also take effective solos utilizing a plunger mute, Jimmy Nottingham was a valuable sideman throughout his career. He played with baritonist Cecil Payne in 1943 and, while in the military, was with Willie Smith's Navy band (1944–45). After his discharge, Nottingham worked with the big bands of Lionel Hampton (1945–47), Charlie Barnet, Lucky Millinder (1947), and Count Basie (1948–50), mostly as a lead trumpeter. He performed with Latin bands in New York during 1951–53 and in 1954 became a member of the staff of CBS, his main employment for the next 20 years.

Nottingham occasionally played jazz during his final 25 years, including co-leading a short-lived group with tenor saxophonist Budd Johnson in 1962 and working with Dizzy Gillespie, Oliver Nelson, Benny Goodman, the Thad Jones-Mel Lewis Orchestra (1966–70), and Clark Terry's big band (1974–75). Jimmy Nottingham was active until his death at age 52. His only date as a leader was in 1957, resulting in four songs (half an album) for the Seeco label.

Recommended CDs: with Lionel Hampton: *Midnight Sun* (GRP/Decca 625), with Clark Terry: *Big B-A-D Band Live!* (Vanguard 79756)

DICK OAKLEY

. . . .

b. Mar. 5, 1940, Carbondale, PA

D ick Oakley is a hard-driving cornetist and trumpeter who has played San Francisco-style trad jazz throughout his career. He grew up near Binghamton, New York, and began playing trumpet in grade school when he was nine, soon discovering Louis Armstrong's Hot Five and Seven recordings. Oakley co-led the Penn-Can Jazz Band with trombonist Jack Hockenberry during the late 1950s and picked up experience playing with Spiegle Willcox, the Muskrat Ramblers, the Dixie Racing & Clambake Society, and Chuck Slate. Sitting in with Turk Murphy's band in 1967 was a major turning point in Oakley's life.

In September 1968 Oakley officially joined Turk Murphy (moving to San Francisco), and he was an integral part of the trombonist's group for 11 years. After he left Murphy, he became a member of the South Frisco Jazz Band for 18 years (June 1980–November 1998), being one of the two cornetists (usually with Dan Comins) in the Lu Watters-styled group. The South Frisco Jazz Band worked often, appearing at many classic jazz festivals and making quite a few records.

Dick Oakley remains active up to the present time, sometimes playing with Lavay Smith's Red Hot Skillet Lickers, guesting with Jim Cullum's band on their famed radio broadcasts, and working with Chris Tyle's Silver Leaf Jazz Band, Ted des Plantes, and Bob Helm.

Recommended CDs: with Bob Helm: *Hotter Than That* (Stomp Off 1310), with Turk Murphy: *The Earthquake McGoon Recordings* (Merry Makers 9), with the South Frisco Jazz Band: *Got Everything* (Stomp Off 1240), *Big Bear Stomp* (Stomp Off 1307), *Emperor Norton's Hunch* (Stomp Off 1342)

LPs to Search For: *Leon Oakley and His Flaming Deuces* (GHB 153), *New Orleans Joys* (Stomp Off 1013), with Turk Murphy: *Turk Murphy's Frisco Jazz Band Live!* (MPS 22097), *The Many Faces of Ragtime* (Atlantic 1613), with the South Frisco Jazz Band: *Hot Tamale Man* (Vault 9008), *Live From Earthquake McGoon's* (Stomp Off 1027), *Broken Promises* (Stomp Off 1180)

BETTY O'HARA
. . . .

b. May 24, 1925, Morris, IL, d. Apr. 18, 2000, Los Angeles, CA

A very talented and versatile musician, Betty O'Hara played trumpet, valve trombone, and double-belled euphonium in addition to being a heartfelt singer. Although she often performed mainstream swing and a bit of Dixieland, she was also quite credible playing in more modern settings, with her cool tones on her instruments fitting very well in West Coast jazz groups.

O'Hara spent much of her career as a studio player based in Los Angeles. She toured with Billy Vaughn's orchestra in the 1970s and performed with Ann Patterson's all-female big band Maiden Voyage, the Jazz Birds, Dick Cathcart, and George Van Eps, often appearing at classic jazz festivals. O'Hara rehearsed regularly with Dick Cary's Tuesday Night Band (recording with the ensemble after Cary's death), cut a CD with saxophonist Rick Fay, and led two albums of her own. Betty O'Hara was a popular figure in the Los Angeles area, playing jazz regularly until a stroke two years before her death ended her career.

Recommended CDs: *Horns a-Plenty* (Delmark 482), *Woman's Intuition* (Sea Breeze 3025), with Dick Cary's Tuesday Night Friends: *Catching Up* (Klavier 77024), with Rick Fay: *Rick Fay's Endangered Species* (Arbors 19120)

SHUNZO OHNO
. . . .

b. Mar. 22, 1949, Gifu, Japan

A top-notch post-bop player, Shunzo Ohno is perhaps best known for playing with the Gil Evans Orchestra. Self-taught on the trumpet, Ohno (who is sometimes listed mistakenly as Ono) started working as a professional in 1968. He played with Keiichiro Ebihara's Lobsters and George Otsuka during 1970–73. Ohno, who moved to New York in 1973, became the first Japanese player to be a member of Art Blakey's Jazz Messengers (1973–74), although that version of the group unfortunately did not record. Some of his other important associations include Roy Haynes' Hip Ensemble (1975), Norman Connors, Machito (1981–83), Buster Williams, and the Gil Evans Orchestra (1983–88). Shunzo Ohno has led sessions for East Wind, Inner City, and King/Pro Arte, although his recordings are pretty scarce in the United States.

Recommended CDs: with Gil Evans: *Bud and Bird* (Projazz 671), *Farewell* (Projazz 680)

LPs to Search For: *Quarter Moon* (Inner City 1108)

TIGER OKOSHI
• • • • • • • • • • •

b. Mar. 21, 1950, Ashiya, Japan

Another top Japanese trumpeter (who ranks, along with Terumasa Hino, as the most famous one), Toru "Tiger" Okoshi has had a diverse career. He started playing when he was 11 and was greatly inspired when he saw a Louis Armstrong concert. Okoshi studied with altoist Sadao Watanabe, who suggested that he check out Berklee in Boston. The trumpeter took his advice and first came to the United States in 1972 during his honeymoon, driving cross-country with his bride. He attended Berklee during 1972–75 and taught there for a time. Okoshi worked with Buddy Rich, John Scofield, Bob Moses, David Sanborn, Pat Metheny, and, most notably, Gary Burton, with whom he gained his first real recognition.

Since then, Okoshi has mostly led his group, Tiger's Baku; "Baku" is a mythical creature that eats bad dreams. Tiger Okoshi, who has also worked with George Russell's Living Time Orchestra and recorded with Dave Grusin, Cercie Miller, and Jerry Bergonzi, has led several sessions for JVC. He is most influenced by fusion, even though he recorded an unusual tribute to his first trumpet hero, Louis Armstrong.

Recommended CDs: *Two Sides to Every Story* (JVC 239), with Gary Burton: *Times Square* (ECM 1111)

KING OLIVER
• • • • • • • • • • •

b. May 11, 1885, Abend, LA, d. Apr. 8, 1938, Savannah, GA

Joe "King" Oliver had a colorful career full of glory days and eventual tragedy. Although most famous today as Louis Armstrong's main inspiration (Satch never tired of giving Oliver credit for his success), there was a time (1915–23) when he was considered the best cornetist in jazz, succeeding Freddie Keppard. Oliver was a more flexible cornetist than most players from his generation, making the transition from playing jazz as an ensemble-oriented music to one featuring solos and arrangements. As a cornetist, Oliver was masterful at bending notes and was one of the first to be expert at using plunger mutes to get a variety of wa-wa sounds, inspiring Bubber Miley, Tommy Ladnier, and Muggsy Spanier among others. But his teeth failed him, and, unlike Bunk Johnson, he did not survive long enough to be part of the New Orleans jazz revival.

Raised in New Orleans, Oliver started out on trombone, switching to cornet as a young teenager. He worked early on with Walter Kinchin and the Melrose Band, playing with the major brass bands starting around 1907, a period of time when his day job was as a butler. Oliver became one of the busiest musicians in New Orleans during the 1910s, working with the Melrose Brass Band, the Olympia Band, the Onward Brass Band, the Magnolia Band, the Eagle

Band, the Original Superior Band, Allen's Brass Band, Richard M. Jones' Four Hot Hounds, and Kid Ory, among many others. He became known as "King" after defeating both Freddie Keppard and Manuel Perez in cornet battles.

In March 1919 Oliver moved to Chicago, and soon he was a member of two different groups, separate ensembles led by clarinetist Lawrence Duhe and bassist Bill Johnson. In 1920 when he had an offer to play at the Dreamland Café, he formed his Creole Jazz Band, a group that included clarinetist Johnny Dodds, trombonist Honore Dutrey, and pianist Lil Harden. Oliver took his band to San Francisco for a few months in 1921, and they appeared for a brief period in Los Angeles. When Oliver returned to Chicago in 1922, his Creole Jazz Band started playing regularly at Lincoln Gardens. Oliver soon sent for his protégé, Louis Armstrong (whom he had informally tutored a few years earlier), to join his group.

With the two cornets leading the ensembles in exciting fashion (often spontaneously harmonizing their breaks), King Oliver now had the most important band in jazz. The classic New Orleans jazz group was mostly ensemble oriented, although Oliver developed a famous three-chorus solo on his own "Dippermouth Blues." In 1923 the Creole Jazz Band made a highly influential series of recordings for Gennett, Okeh, Columbia, and Paramount that were closely studied by their contemporaries. Although jazz itself would be changing rapidly throughout

King Oliver's famous Creole Jazz Band, the best group on records in 1923: drummer Baby Dodds, trombonist Honore Dutrey, Oliver, Louis Armstrong, bassist Bill Johnson, clarinetist Johnny Dodds, and pianist Lil Hardin Armstrong.

THE TRUMPET KINGS

the decade, the Creole Jazz Band performances would always be considered among the most important records from the first half of the 1920s.

Louis Armstrong reluctantly departed in 1924; he had surpassed Oliver and was long overdue to be featured as a solo star. Oliver, who recorded a couple of duets with pianist Jelly Roll Morton that year (including "King Porter Stomp") and backed the vaudeville team Butterbeans and Susie on one record, led the Creole Jazz Band for a time with Bob Shoffner and later Tommy Ladnier on second cornet. By the fall of 1924, business had tailed off at the Lincoln Gardens and Oliver was given his notice; his band soon broke up. He spent a few months as featured soloist with Peyton's Symphonic Syncopators. In February 1925 he formed the Dixie Syncopators to play at the Plantation Café in Chicago. Its excellent records from 1926 show that Oliver was adapting well to the times. His group was larger than the Creole Jazz Band had been (including such notables as trombonist Kid Ory, clarinetist Albert Nicholas, and Barney Bigard on tenor) and utilized colorful arrangements. Oliver's break on "Snag It" became famous, his version of "Sugar Foot Stomp" (a remake of "Dippermouth Blues") was popular, and he introduced his original "Doctor Jazz," which, along with his "Canal Street Blues" and "West End Blues," would become a Dixieland standard.

After touring the Midwest in 1927, Oliver's band played at the Savoy Ballroom in New York. Offered a long-term contract with the Cotton Club, the cornetist made a fatal mistake and turned it down, feeling that the money was not enough. A little while later Duke Ellington got the job! Soon after closing at the Savoy, the Dixie Syncopators disbanded. Thanks to his friend Clarence Williams, Oliver made guest appearances on quite a few records during the second half of 1928, including with Texas Alexander, Katherine Henderson, Elizabeth Johnson, Sara Martin, Lizzie Miles, Hazel Smith, Victoria Spivey, Eva Taylor, and Williams himself. Among the 21 selections that he cut with Williams, Oliver sounds particularly strong on "Bozo" and "Bimbo."

Starting in early 1929 and continuing into 1931, King Oliver recorded regularly as a leader for Victor. Although his orchestra (which was 10–11 pieces) was modern for the period and featured first-class players (some of whom in 1929 became the nucleus of the Luis Russell Orchestra), Oliver's neglect of his teeth (he had loved "sugar sandwiches" as a youth) started to cause him serious problems. It began to hurt him to play, and his solos became briefer and riskier. On some records that were listed as being played by King Oliver's orchestra, the leader is not heard on a single note. A heroic example of Oliver's temporarily overcoming his physical problems can be heard on 1929's "Too Late," one of the most exciting records of his career. Unfortunately the situation worsened, and by 1930 Oliver's nephew Dave Nelson was taking many of the trumpet solos on his records. After April 1931, the recordings stopped altogether.

The 1930s would prove to be a steep and steady decline for the once-mighty cornetist. He left New York and formed a band that toured throughout the South and Midwest for seven years, with many misfortunes. Oliver was not well known outside of New York, and on several occasions his band was stranded without any money. Buses broke down, the Depression was in full swing, and the music world had passed him by. Worst of all, Oliver, once the king of New Orleans cornetists, could not even play without a great deal of pain. He struggled on with bands through 1937 and then ended up his last months (before his death at age 52) as a poolroom attendant in Savannah, Georgia, too proud to take charity from Louis Armstrong and his earlier friends. Swing might have been king by then, but King Oliver himself was largely forgotten, for the moment.

Ironically the music of Oliver's Creole Jazz Band would serve as the main inspiration for Lu Watters' Yerba Buena Jazz Band, a group that in the early 1940s helped to launch the New Orleans jazz revival. King Oliver once again became famous in the jazz world, but it was too late for him.

Recommended CDs: *King Oliver's Creole Jazzband 1923–1924* (Retrieval 79007), *Sugar Foot Stomp* (GRP/Decca 616), *King Oliver and His Orchestra* (RCA Tribune 66538)

Recommended Reading: *American Musicians II* by Whitney Balliett (Oxford University Press, 1996), *The Best of Jazz* by Humphrey Lyttelton (Taplinger Publishing Co., 1982), *I Remember* by Clyde Bernhardt (University of Pennsylvania Press, 1986), *Jazz Masters of New Orleans* by Martin Williams (Macmillan Publishing Co., 1967), *Jazzmen* edited by Frederic Ramsey Jr. and Charles Edward Smith (Harcourt Brace Jovanovich, 1939)

SY OLIVER

· · · · · · · · · ·

b. Dec. 17, 1910, Battle Creek, MI, d. May 28, 1988, New York, NY

Although ultimately much more significant as an arranger and composer, Melvin "Sy" Oliver was a fine trumpeter in the 1930s, particularly when he took muted solos with Jimmie Lunceford's orchestra. Raised in Zanesville, Ohio, Oliver originally wanted to be an attorney; his nickname of "Sy" was short for "psychology," attesting to his strong intelligence. However, Oliver, who studied trumpet under his father, chose music and began his career playing with Cliff Barnett's Club Royal Serenaders (1924–27) while still a teenager in high school. Oliver played with Zack Whyte's Chocolate Beau Brummels (with whom he made his recording debut) during 1927–30 and freelanced in Ohio, including performing with Alphonso Trent's legendary territory band.

Oliver joined Lunceford's orchestra in 1933 after submitting a few arrangements. He really made a major impact with his lightly swinging and often-witty charts. Some of the best Oliver arrangements for Lunceford include "Dream of You," "My Blue Heaven," "Ain't She Sweet," "Four or Five Times," "Swanee River," "Organ Grinder's Swing," "For Dancers Only," "'Tain't Whatcha Do," and "Cheatin' on Me." Oliver also took good-natured vocals, and his many concise trumpet solos showed that he was an excellent player, both with the trumpet open and particularly when using mutes.

In October 1939 a lucrative deal persuaded Oliver to join Tommy Dorsey's orchestra, put down his trumpet, and stick to arranging while taking an occasional vocal. He would not play trumpet again on a semiregular basis until the 1970s, when he mostly played ensembles with his big band of the period. Oliver's writing career was quite successful. For Tommy Dorsey he composed and arranged "Opus One," "Well Git It," "Easy Does It," and "Yes Indeed," arranging a hit version of "Sunny Side of the Street." Oliver was in the Army during 1943–45, led a service band, and, after his discharge, primarily wrote for the studios and record dates (including some sessions featuring Ella Fitzgerald and Louis Armstrong). Sy Oliver stuck to the swing style throughout his career, leading a big band at the Rainbow Room in New York during 1975–80. It is a pity though that his fine trumpet playing was neglected for so many decades and that he was not recorded as a player in his later years.

Recommended CDs: with Jimmie Lunceford: *Stomp It Off* (GRP/Decca 608), *For Dancers Only* (GRP/Decca 645), *1937–1939* (Classics 520)

Recommended Reading: *Jazz Talking* by Max Jones (Da Capo Press, 1987), *The World of Swing* by Stanley Dance (Charles Scribner's Sons, 1974)

JIMMY OWENS
• • • • • • • • • • • • • • •

b. Dec. 9, 1943, New York, NY

For decades, Jimmy Owens was thought of as a future great. Although he has not become one of the most influential trumpeters in jazz, he has been pretty productive throughout his career. Owens studied trumpet with Donald Byrd when he was a teenager and considers Miles Davis and Clifford Brown to be his most important early influences.

Owens played with Marshall Brown's Newport Youth Band during 1959–60. After graduating from the High School of Music and Art, he became a professional and soon seemed to be playing everywhere. Owens worked with Slide Hampton (1962–63), Lionel Hampton (1963–64), the big bands of Maynard Ferguson and Gerry Mulligan, Hank Crawford, Charles Mingus (1964–65), the original version of the Thad Jones/Mel Lewis Orchestra, Herbie Mann (1965–66), Max Roach, the Clark Terry big band, Duke Ellington (1968), the Dizzy Gillespie Orchestra, Count Basie, Billy Taylor's Quintet, the New York Jazz Sextet, and Billy Cobham (1973), among many others, plus he has frequently led hard bop-oriented combos.

In addition to his somewhat obscure albums as a leader for Atlantic, Polydor, and A&M Horizon, Owens has recorded as a sideman in many settings, including with Jaki Byard, the Gerald Wilson Orchestra (taking the majestic solo on the original version of Wilson's "Carlos" in 1966), Norman Simmons, the Jazzmobile All-Stars, Mike Longo, Joe Henderson, Kenny Burrell, Booker Ervin, Mingus Dynasty, Billy Cobham, and Erroll Parker. He has been particularly active behind the scenes as an educator (including teaching at Jazzmobile), serving on committees, and helping jazz. In 1990 he said, "I have a deep interest in doing more teaching under the concepts of jazz education I have developed over the last 25 years. I enjoy sharing my wide range of knowledge in performing jazz, composing and arranging, the business aspects of the performing arts, and trumpet practice techniques." However, as a trumpeter, Jimmy Owens has yet to carve out a legacy of his own.

Recommended CDs: with Gary Bartz: *Libra/Another Earth* (Milestone 47077), with Jaki Byard: *On the Spot* (Original Jazz Classics 1031), with Billy Taylor: *Jazzmobile All Stars* (Taylor-Made 1003)

LPs to Search For: *You Had Better Listen* (Atlantic 1491), *Young Men on the Move* (Horizon 712), *Headin' Home* (Horizon 729), with Gerald Wilson: *The Golden Sword* (Pacific Jazz 20111)

Although he never broke through to major commercial success, Hot Lips Page was a popular attraction for 20 years and a major asset at jam sessions.

HOT LIPS PAGE

· · · · · · · · · · · · ·

b. Jan. 27, 1908, Dallas, TX, d. Nov. 5, 1954, New York, NY

A great blues player flexible enough to excel both in swing-oriented big bands and free-wheeling jam sessions, Hot Lips Page was a beloved figure throughout his career. Page, who was also a very effective blues singer, should have been a big star during the swing era, but instead he remained a bit of an underground legend.

Oran "Hot Lips" Page started playing trumpet in his native Dallas when he was 12. He gained experience as a teenager working with groups behind blues singers, including Ma Rainey, Bessie Smith, and Ida Cox. Page performed with Troy Floyd's band in San Antonio and traveled throughout Texas with Sugar Lou and Eddie's Hotel Tyler Band. In 1928 he arrived in Kansas City, where he soon joined Walter Page's Blue Devils, one of the best bands in that jumping city. During his three years with the unrelated Page, Hot Lips developed his exciting style. As a member of Bennie Moten's big band (1931–35), Page appeared on several recording dates, including a classic outing in 1932 in which the Moten Orchestra hinted strongly at the Count Basie band to come.

After Moten's unexpected death in 1935, Page led a quintet for a short time before joining Count Basie's new orchestra in 1936. Although he was becoming the star of the band,

Page signed with manager Joe Glaser after a few months and moved to New York. If he had stayed with Basie a little longer, he would have been part of Count's success (his place was taken by Buck Clayton) and would have had a footing on which to start his own big band. Instead, the Hot Lips Page Orchestra lasted for only a little while during 1937–38 because the trumpeter was just not well known enough for it to be a success.

Page jammed with small groups from late 1938 until mid-1940. He was a sideman with the short-lived Bud Freeman big band and with Joe Marsala before making a strong impression as a featured soloist and singer with Artie Shaw (1941–42). When Shaw broke up the orchestra in order to enlist in the military during World War II, Page had a brief attempt at leading another big band and then spent the rest of his career heading combos. He was quite popular at jam sessions and on 52nd Street, worked steadily during the bebop era without changing his joyful style at all, and recorded a hit version of "Baby It's Cold Outside" with Pearl Bailey in 1949. Still, Hot Lips Page (who toured Europe a few times) never really broke through to the stardom his talents deserved. He died in 1954 from a heart attack when he was just 46.

Recommended CDs: *1938–1940* (Classics 561), *1940–1944* (Classics 809), *1944–1946* (Classics 950), *Dr. Jazz Series, Vol. 6* (Storyville 6046), with Bennie Moten: *Basie Beginnings* (Bluebird 3139), with Artie Shaw: *Blues in the Night* (Bluebird 2432)

LOUIS PANICO

• • • • • • • • • • • • •

b. 1903, d. 1940s?

Louis Panico gained a bit of fame with his playing on the novelty hit recording of "Wabash Blues" with Isham Jones' Orchestra in 1921, during which he laughed and cried through his horn. However Panico was actually one of the most interesting trumpeters on record during the era, displaying a lot of potential that he never really fulfilled.

Not much is known about Panico's life. He was Isham Jones' star soloist during 1921–24, an expert with mutes (reportedly carrying a dozen mutes in his oversized trumpet case), and quite capable of making a strong melodic solo statement during an era when there were few soloists on records. Panico was influenced by King Oliver and in turn was one of Bix Beiderbecke's early inspirations. When he left Jones in 1924, it was to lead his own medium-size group in Chicago with whom he recorded two titles in 1930 and four in 1934. Nothing much is known of Louis Panico' activities after the late 1930s.

Recommended CDs: with Isham Jones: *1922–1926* (Timeless 067)

NICHOLAS PAYTON

• • • • • • • • • • • • • • • • •

b. Sept. 26, 1973, New Orleans, LA

Still only 27 at this writing, Nicholas Payton has accomplished a great deal in his career thus far. A brilliant trumpeter, Payton has the ability to play both credible New Orleans jazz and hard bop à la Freddie Hubbard. His father, Walter Payton, is a top New Orleans bassist,

A major hard bop trumpeter, Nicholas Payton is never shy to pay tribute to his New Orleans roots.

while his mother, Maria Payton, is a classical pianist. When he was four, Payton requested a trumpet as a Christmas present. At eight, he was good enough to accompany his father on gigs with the Young Tuxedo Brass Band, and four years later he was playing with local bands. It was about this time that Wynton Marsalis called up Nicholas' father and young Nicholas spontaneously played his trumpet over the phone, impressing Marsalis. They would stay in touch and Wynton would be an inspiration and a guiding force for Payton in future years.

By the time he was in high school, Payton was playing regularly at parades and functions around New Orleans. He studied at the New Orleans Center for Creative Arts, attended the University of New Orleans (where he studied with Ellis Marsalis), and had some lessons from Wynton Marsalis. Payton played on cruise ships in 1990 with Clark Terry, worked with Art Blakey's Jazz Messengers and Carl Allen, and in 1992 toured with both Marcus Roberts and Jazz Futures; in the last group the 18-year-old played next to Roy Hargrove. Marsalis recommended him to Elvin Jones, and Payton was a member (and the musical director) of the drummer's Jazz Machine during 1992–94. He also worked with Joe Henderson and Jimmy Smith and was used by Marsalis for some of the Jazz at Lincoln Center concerts.

Payton avoided recording as a leader too early (as some of the other Young Lions had), finally signing with Verve in 1994. During that year he began leading his own group, which by 1996 had become a longtime quintet including Tim Warfield on tenor and soprano, pianist Anthony Wonsey, bassist Reuben Rogers, and drummer Adonis Rose. His finest moments as a trad trumpeter were on his delightful recording with the ancient Doc Cheatham in 1997, but in general Payton (whose tone at times recalls Freddie Hubbard's) explores original hard bop tunes, hinting at his New Orleans heritage fondly without feeling restricted to older styles. During 2000–2001 Nicholas Payton (who still has nearly unlimited potential) has been leading an intriguing if rather eccentric Louis Armstrong Tribute Band.

Recommended CDs: *New Orleans Collective* (Evidence 22105), *From The Moment* (Verve 314 527 073), *Gumbo Nouveau* (Verve 314 531 199), *Payton's Place* (Verve 314 557 327), *Nick at Night* (Verve 314 547 598), *Trumpet Legacy* (Milestone 9286), with Doc Cheatham: *Doc Cheatham and Nicholas Payton* (Verve 314 537 062)

Recommended Reading: *Jazz Profiles* by Reginald Carver and Lenny Bernstein (Billboard Books, 1998)

MANUEL PEREZ

• • • • • • • • • • • • •

b. Dec. 28, 1871, New Orleans, LA, d. 1946 New Orleans, LA

Manuel (or Emanuel) Perez, a contemporary of Buddy Bolden's, was a "legit" player who successfully made the transition to jazz. As early as 1895, he was playing cornet in John Robechaux's orchestra, and his most important early associations were with the Imperial Orchestra (which he organized and led during 1901–08) and the Onward Brass Band (which he also headed during 1903–30). In addition to his extensive parade work, Perez played in the Storyville district and with most of the top early New Orleans jazz players. His sidemen through the years included King Oliver, Peter Bocage, clarinetist Lorenzo Tio Jr., and a young Sidney Bechet.

Perez is remembered as an excellent reading musician with a wide range who was a popular music teacher, and his bands featured a large repertoire, including ragtime, folk songs, pop tunes, and some blues. But, although Perez's sound was renowned, he was shy and not much of a showman, being easily overshadowed by the flashier personalities of Buddy Bolden, Freddie Keppard, and King Oliver during his prime years. Perez visited Chicago in 1915 (playing with the Arthur Sims band), 1919, and in the summer of 1927, when he performed in the Windy City with Charles Elgar's orchestra. Unfortunately Perez joined Elgar's orchestra nearly a year after the band made its only recordings, the closest he ever came to being documented as a musician. He did speak a few words on a "talking record" with Sidney Bechet in the early 1940s, but those really do not count!

After the summer season of 1927 ended, Perez returned to New Orleans for his usual jobs of playing parades and dances. By 1930, Perez felt frustrated with his career, and he gradually chose to retire from music, becoming a full-time cigar maker. When Bunk Johnson made his improbable comeback in the early 1940s, there was talk of Perez also being rehabilitated. However, a series of strokes left him largely incapacitated before he died in 1946, and the comeback never started. Both Lee Collins and Punch Miller claimed Manuel Perez as a major influence. But without recordings, it is not known how this early pioneer really sounded.

BENT PERSSON

b. Sept. 6, 1947, Blekinge, Sweden

When it comes to emulating Louis Armstrong from the 1925–28 period, no cornetist gets closer than Bent Persson. He can recreate any of Satch's solos, but he is also creative within the boundary of the style, sounding as if the Armstrong of the period were still playing today. This talent comes in particularly handy when Persson performs Armstrong solos that were never recorded, most specifically Satch's legendary "Fifty Hot Choruses," music that was transcribed and recorded by Armstrong on long-lost cylinders in 1927. Persson made those 52 solos and 119 breaks really come alive on four LPs recorded during 1975–82; they have since been reissued on CD.

Persson has spent virtually his entire career in Sweden. Since becoming a professional in the late 1960s, he has played and recorded with many trad jazz groups, including Maggie's Blue Five, Kustbandet, the Weatherbird Jazzband, and Bent's Blue Rhythm Band, in addition to recording with Maxine Sullivan (in the 1980s), Kenny Davern and Bob Wilber. It is surprising, though, that classic jazz festivals in the United States have not thought to fly Bent Persson in and feature this major if largely unknown cornetist.

Recommended CDs: *Louis Armstrong's 50 Choruses for Cornet, Vols. 1–2* (Kenneth 3411), *Louis Armstrong's 50 Choruses for Cornet, Vols. 3–4* (Kenneth 3413)

LPs to Search For: with Kenny Davern: *El Rado Shuffle* (Kenneth 2050)

HANNIBAL MARVIN PETERSON

b. Nov. 11, 1948, Smithville, TX

"Hannibal" Marvin Peterson (who in recent times has changed his name to Hannibal Lokumbe) is an adventurous trumpeter who can play bop but also loves playing free and is never afraid to take chances. Peterson led his group the Soul Masters as early as 1961. He gained early experience playing blues with T-Bone Walker (1965–67) and Lightning Hopkins. Peterson studied at North Texas State University (1967–69) but was frustrated by the music that was being featured and dropped out, moving to New York. Hannibal was soon working in a wide variety of settings, including with Rahsaan Roland Kirk (1970), the Thad Jones/Mel Lewis Orchestra, the Gil Evans Orchestra (throughout the 1970s), Pharoah Sanders, Roy Haynes, Elvin Jones, and Archie Shepp, among others. He also led bands, including the Sunrise Orchestra in 1974.

Although sometimes maintaining a lower profile in the 1980s and '90s (moving back to Texas in 1993), Hannibal (who describes himself as a "musical archeologist") has remained quite active up to the present time. He recorded five albums as a leader in Europe (two apiece for MPS and Enja plus one for Mole) and two in Japan before finally getting a chance to cut *Visions of a New World* for Atlantic in 1989. Greatly interested in African history and in the concept of combining jazz with classical music, his compositions have been performed by the Kronos Quartet and many symphony orchestras. In addition, Hannibal is a published poet who wrote a book of poems, *The Ripest of My Fruit*.

Recommended CDs: *The Angels of Atlanta* (Enja 3085), *Visions of a New World* (Atlantic 891973), *African Portraits* (Teldec 98802), with George Adams: *Old Feeling* (Blue Note 96689), with Gil Evans: *There Comes a Time* (Bluebird 5783), *Plays the Music of Jimi Hendrix* (Bluebird 8401)

BUDDY PETIT
. . . .

b. 1897, White Castle, LA, d. July 4, 1931, New Orleans, LA

Considered one of the top New Orleans trumpeters of the 1920s, Buddy Petit's early death and his complete lack of documentation (none of the Southern field trips by record labels led to his being recorded) makes him both legendary and quite obscure

Born Joseph Crawford, he took the last name of his stepfather, the pioneering valve trombonist Joseph Petit (who ironically did have an opportunity to record in 1945 at the age of 72). Since the older Petit had founded the Olympia Brass Band, Buddy (whose early role model was Bunk Johnson) followed his example and formed the Young Olympia Band with his close friend Sidney Bechet around 1915. In 1916 Petit co-led a band with Jimmie Noone and the following year accepted an offer to play in Los Angeles with Jelly Roll Morton. However, Petit and the other New Orleans musicians were ridiculed by Morton for their out-of-date clothes and such country habits as cooking in the dressing room and eating on the bandstand. This association ended when Petit became fed up and quit, threatening to kill Morton if he ever returned to New Orleans!

The fiasco was doubly unfortunate, for in 1918 when bassist Bill Johnson sent for Petit to join his band in Chicago, Buddy refused to leave the South. Johnson then sent for King Oliver as his second choice, and Oliver became famous introducing New Orleans jazz to the Midwest. In contrast, Petit remained unknown outside of his hometown.

Once King Oliver and Louis Armstrong left to go North, Buddy Petit had few close rivals among cornetists in New Orleans, just the equally obscure Chris Kelly and some younger up-and-coming players such as Henry "Red" Allen. Petit was in such demand in the early 1920s that he frequently took four or five jobs a night, hurting his reputation a bit by sending out other bands under his own name.

Although he made a short visit to California as a member of Frankie Dusen's band in 1922 and sometimes played on riverboats, Buddy Petit rarely left the South after 1917. A hard drinker, Buddy Petit (who was later cited as an important influence by Punch Miller, Herb Morand, and Wingy Manone) became erratic during the last half of the 1920s but was active up until the very day of his death, when he passed away at the age of 34 from the combination of overeating and excessive drinking at an Independence Day picnic!

DE DE PIERCE

• • • • • • • • • • •

b. Feb. 18, 1904, New Orleans, LA, d. Nov. 23, 1973, New Orleans, LA

De De Pierce and Billie Pierce were one of the great married couples in jazz history, staying together and making music for over 30 years. De De (who was mostly self-taught) played trumpet with Arnold Dupas' Olympia Band and other groups in New Orleans starting in 1924 while having a day job as a bricklayer. De De met pianist-singer Billie (who had previously played with Bessie Smith, Ma Rainey, and Buddy Petit) in the early 1930s, and they were married in 1935. The Pierces worked together (sometimes as a duet and occasionally with additional musicians) for decades, making their first recordings in 1953.

In the mid-1950s both Pierces were hospitalized due to a serious illness. Billie recovered but De De was left permanently blind. After a period of being depressed, De De was persuaded by his wife to continue his career and they resumed working together. The Pierces recorded for Folklyric, Riverside (1961), Jazzology, and American Music, making a record with George Lewis in 1962. De De (a basic but quite effective melodic trumpeter) and Billie Pierce (a fine blues singer) spent their later years working and touring (including visiting Europe) with the Preservation Hall Jazz Band.

Recommended CDs: *New Orleans: The Living Legends* (Original Blues Classics 534), *Blues and Tonks from the Delta* (Original Jazz Classics 1847), *With Chris Barber's Band* (GHB 43)

LPs to Search For: *Billie and De De Piece at Luthjen's* (Center 15)

WARD PINKETT

• • • • • • • • • • • •

b. Apr. 29, 1906, Newport News, VA, d. Mar. 15, 1937, New York, NY

Ward Pinkett, who died before his 31st birthday, recorded only 62 selections (not counting alternate takes) during his brief life, yet these include quite a few significant sessions. Pinkett's distinctive tone, solid lead, and inventive ideas put him in great demand (particularly during 1929–31) before alcoholism ruined his life.

Pinkett's father played cornet as a hobby and started his son on the instrument when he was ten. After playing in the school band at Hampton Institute and attending the New Haven Conservatory of Music, Pinkett joined the White Brothers Orchestra in Washington, D.C., coming to New York with a traveling show. In 1926 he worked briefly with Charlie Johnson at Small's Paradise, and his associations during the next eight years included Willie Gant's orchestra, Billy Fowler, Joe Steele, Charlie Skeete, Chick Webb (1929), Bingie Madison, Rex Stewart (1933), and Teddy Hill (1934) in addition to being part of the house band at James Hogan's Joyland.

But much more important were the records. Pinkett made his recording debut with Jelly Roll Morton in 1928, taking excellent solos on "Georgia Swing," "Kansas City Stomps," and "Shoe Shiner's Drag" during the pianist's first (and arguably best) New York date. In 1929 Pinkett and Louis Metcalf took turns doing their impressions of the absent King Oliver on Oliver's February 1 session. He cut two sides with Joe Steele's orchestra and took short solos on the two numbers recorded by the Chick Webb's Jungle Band plus an enthusiastic scat vocal on Webb's "Dog Bottom." Pinkett also appeared on all of Jelly Roll Morton's recordings of 1930, and, although those sessions were often streaky, the output from July 14 resulted in two classics that contain some of the trumpeter's best playing: "Low Gravy" and especially "Strokin' Away." Other dates from 1930–31 include background work with Bubber Miley's Mileage Makers, a few sides with Clarence Williams, possible participation in Mamie Smith's last recordings, assisting an ailing King Oliver on his final dates, and three selections with James P. Johnson (soloing and scatting on "Just a Crazy Song").

After 1931, Ward Pinkett's activities slowed a bit, due to the Depression and his frequent overindulgence with alcohol. In 1935 Pinkett worked with Albert Nicholas at Adrian Rollini's Tap Room, and his recordings with Freddy Jenkins' Harlem Seven and the Little Ramblers found him adjusting quite well to 52nd Street-styled small-group swing. But after playing briefly with Louis Metcalf's short-lived orchestra and Albert Nicholas, Pinkett became ill. Danny Barker, in his memoirs, remembers the trumpeter as a hopeless alcoholic who could still play well near the end when he was sober. But Ward Pinkett refused to stop drinking. He developed a distaste for food of any sort, and he quickly wasted away, dying from pneumonia at the age of just 30.

Recommended CDs: with Jelly Roll Morton: *1926–1928* (Classics 612), *1929–1930* (Classics 642), *1930–1939* (Classics 654)

TOM PLETCHER
• • • • • • • • • • • • •

b. May 29, 1936, New Haven, CT

Although he describes himself as "a working amateur," Tom Pletcher has kept the Bix Beiderbecke sound and style alive in his playing through the years. He is the son of trumpeter Stew Pletcher (1907–78), who was best known for his playing with Red Norvo's orchestra in the 1930s. The younger Pletcher had piano lessons for four years starting when he was seven, but he hated them. Pletcher remembers: "I heard my first recording of Bix with Frankie Trumbauer ('Baltimore') and that was it! I was 16. My father discouraged me from taking up cornet, pleading with me to play piano or guitar." He attended City College in Los Angeles for three years as a business major and had no formal musical training and very few lessons. "I learned by listening and playing along with records." However, he did have the opportunity (through his father) to meet and hang out with Louis Armstrong, Jack Teagarden, and other associates.

Pletcher has never been a full-time musician, running his grandfather's metal business in Michigan during 1962–87, which he sold at age 51 when he retired. However, he played regularly with the Sons of Bix for 17 years, freelanced in New York, performed at jazz conventions in Australia, and recorded in Sweden with Bent Persson's Jazz Kings. For the future, Tom Pletcher says that he wants to "perpetuate the music of Bix and to inspire younger generation players to do the same."

Recommended CDs: *I'm Glad* (Stomp Off 1353), *Friends and Heroes* (Teaspoon 1Y2K), with Bill Challis: *The Goldkette Project* (Circle 118)

LPs to Search For: with the Sons of Bix: *The Sons of Bix's* (Fairmont 110), *With Guests* (Fat Cat's Jazz 202), *Ostrich Walk* (Jazzology 59), *Copenhagen* (Jazzology 99)

Film Appearances: ghosting the Bix Beiderbecke solos for the film *Bix: An Interpretation of a Legend* (1990; Rhapsody Films)

ED POLCER

· · · · · · · · · ·

b. Feb. 10, 1937, Paterson, NJ

A straightforward Dixieland player, Ed Polcer has a forceful and driving no-nonsense style. Polcer, who took xylophone lessons when he was six, began on trumpet when he was 10 or 11. Within two years he was playing solo trumpet in a couple of concert bands; he would switch to cornet later on. His uncle, trombonist Mickey Polcer, had played with Ben Bernie in the 1920s, and at one point he gave his collection of 78 records to Polcer, which excited the teenager's interest in classic jazz. Polcer, whose favorite cornetist is Wild Bill Davison and who considers Louis Armstrong his main influence, played with Stan Rubin's Tigertown Five during 1956–60, including performing at Grace Kelly's wedding. He graduated from Princeton in 1958 with a degree in mechanical engineering and served in the Air Force during 1960–62.

Polcer worked outside of music for a few years but gradually gravitated back to music while in his thirties. He played with Mezz Mezzrow during a tour of Europe in 1963, worked with Red Balaban on and off during 1969–85, and toured with Benny Goodman in 1973. Polcer was the manager and co-owner of the third and final Eddie Condon Club during 1975–85, leading the house band and gaining some recognition for his playing. Ed Polcer has been quite active at jazz parties and classic jazz festivals up to the present time and has recorded as a leader for Jazzology, BlewZ Manor, and Nagel-Heyer, helping to keep freewheeling classic jazz alive.

Recommended CDs: *In the Condon Tradition* (Jazzology 150), *The Magic of Swing Street* (BlewZ Manor), *Coast to Coast Swingin' Jazz* (Jazzology 198), *Some Sunny Day* (Jazzology 208), *Jammin' à la Condon* (Jazzology 238), with Terry Blaine: *Whose Honey Are You* (Jukebox Jazz 9201), *With Thee I Swing* (Jukebox Jazz 9904)

Recommended Reading: *Traditionalists and Revivalists in Jazz* by Chip Deffaa (Scarecrow Press, 1997)

HERB POMEROY

• • • • • • • • • • • • • •

b. Apr. 15, 1930, Gloucester, MA

Herb Pomeroy is most significant for his many years as an important jazz educator at Berklee, but he is also a fine bop trumpeter whose playing career took a backseat to his teaching. Pomeroy originally studied dentistry at Harvard but switched to music, studying at Schillinger House (which a few years later would be renamed Berklee). He freelanced in the Boston area for a few years, gigging with Charlie Mariano and Serge Chaloff, playing with Charlie Parker whenever Bird was booked locally, and touring with Lionel Hampton (1953–54). Pomeroy led a local big band, recorded a quintet date for Transition, and toured with Stan Kenton for a few months.

Pomeroy joined the faculty of Berklee in 1955 and, although he led a student big band that recorded fairly regularly (among his sidemen through the years were Joe Gordon, Bill Berry, and Dusko Goykovich), his main activity for the next 40 years was teaching. Pomeroy was a fixture at Berklee and also doubled at the Lenox School of Music for a couple of years in the early 1960s. His own playing activities were restricted, although he was part of John Lewis' Orchestra USA during 1962–63. Since retiring from Berklee in 1995, Herb Pomeroy has been more active again as a player, recording for Arbors and Daring and with singer Donna Byrne.

Recommended CDs: *This Is Always* (Daring 3021), *Walking on Air* (Arbors 19176)

LPs to Search For: with Charlie Parker: *Charlie Parker at Storyville* (Blue Note 85108)

VALERY PONOMAREV

• • • • • • • • • • • • • • • • • • • •

b. Jan. 20, 1943, Moscow, Russia

The first great jazz trumpeter to emerge from the Soviet Union, Valery Ponomarev is an exciting hard bop player with a wide range and a powerful sound. He started out with piano lessons, played drums from the age of ten, and switched to trumpet when he was 14. Ponomarev was introduced to jazz through Voice of America, and he was particularly inspired by Clifford Brown (deciding to become a professional musician after hearing Brownie's recording of "Blues Walk"), Lee Morgan, and, later on, Freddie Hubbard.

Ponomarev, who played music in the Soviet Union in a variety of settings, defected to Italy in 1971. After two years of freelancing in Italy, he moved to the United States in 1973. Following a period of struggle, he became a member of the Jazz Messengers in December 1976, recording nine albums with Art Blakey. He was with the Jazz Messengers until 1981. Since then, Valery Ponomarev (who is currently playing at the peak of his powers) has led Universal Language and recorded regularly for Reservoir. But it is surprising that he is not getting greater exposure and winning jazz polls, for there are few hard bop stylists on his level today.

Recommended CDs: *Trip to Moscow* (Reservoir 107), *Profile* (Reservoir 119), *A Star for You* (Reservoir 150), with Art Blakey: *In This Korner* (Concord Jazz 4068)

LPs to Search For: *Means of Identification* (Reservoir 101), with Art Blakey: *In My Prime, Vol. 1* (Timeless 114)

AL PORCINO

b. May 14, 1925, New York, NY

Although he was always capable of soloing, Al Porcino has spent much of his career as a high-note first trumpeter with jazz orchestras. He started his career as an 18-year-old with the Louis Prima big band in 1943 and then had stints with the outfits of Tommy Dorsey (1944), Georgie Auld (1945), Gene Krupa, Woody Herman's First Herd (1946), Stan Kenton (1947–48), Chubby Jackson (1949), and Herman's Second and Third Herds (1949–50).

Due to his range and attractive sound, Porcino became a studio musician. He also played jazz along the way with Pete Rugolo, Count Basie (1951), Elliot Lawrence, Charlie Barnet, and once again Herman (1954) and Kenton (1954–55). Porcino, who recorded with Charlie Parker in 1951 (taking a solo on "Lover"), in 1957 moved to Los Angeles, where he became quite busy in the studios. He found time to co-lead the Jazz Wave Orchestra with Med Flory, worked with the Terry Gibbs Dream Band (1959–62), and in the 1960s went on many tours backing singers. Porcino continued playing with big bands, including those of Buddy Rich (1968), Thad Jones-Mel Lewis (1969–70 and 1975–76), and Herman (for at least a fourth time in 1972). He also led a big band during the early 1970s, backing Mel Torme on a record date.

Al Porcino moved to Munich, Germany, in 1977, where he has worked with radio orchestras and led a European big band (recording with Al Cohn) up to the present time. Although he rarely soloed through the years, his sound, phrasing, and impressive range added excitement to many ensembles.

LPs to Search For: with Chubby Jackson: *The New York Scene in the '40s* (CBS 65392)

GERARD PRESENCER

b. Sept. 12, 1972, London, England

Gerald Presencer is considered one of the top "Young Lions" of British jazz. He started playing trumpet when he was ten and within a year was performing with the National Youth Orchestra. Since the late 1980s, Presencer has played with the Charlie Watts Quintet (1991–92), Clark Tracey, Bob Wilber's big band, John Dankworth, Pete King, Gail Thompson's Gail Force, Stan Tracey, and Don Weller, and with such Americans passing through the country as Bill Watrous, Shorty Rogers, Bill Holman, Teddy Edwards, Harold Land, Herb Geller, and Louie Bellson.

Recommended CDs: *Platypus (Linn 79)*, with Charlie Watts: *Tribute to Charlie Parker with Strings* (Continuum 19201)

The unofficial founder of Retro Swing and a humorous personality,
Louis Prima's episodic career was at its height during the 1950s.

LOUIS PRIMA

* * * * * * * * * * *

b. Dec. 7, 1911, New Orleans, LA, d. Aug. 24, 1978, New Orleans, LA

Louis Prima had a rather interesting career, with several very different periods. His older brother, Leon Prima, also played trumpet in their native New Orleans. The younger Prima had violin lessons from the time he was seven but taught himself trumpet in 1925, when he was 13. He played locally in New Orleans until 1932, when he moved to New York, briefly joining Red Nichols. By 1934, Prima was leading an increasingly popular combo at the Famous Door on 52nd Street (Pee Wee Russell was his clarinetist during 1935–36) and initiating an extensive series of New Orleans-flavored jazz recordings. Prima, who was proud of his Italian ancestry but never shy to joke about it, was a Louis Armstrong-inspired trumpeter and a good-humored vocalist not all that different in the early days from Wingy Manone.

Prima, who composed "Sing Sing Sing" (Benny Goodman's big hit in 1937), led a short-lived big band in 1936 and then a more successful one starting in 1939. Although not thought of as one of the stars of the swing era, Prima had hits in "Angelina" and "Robin Hood," working steadily throughout the 1940s. However, by the early 1950s, he was definitely at a crossroads musically. His music was being dominated by corny novelties and he was thought of as passé.

The trumpeter had discovered a talented teenage singer in the late '40s, Keely Smith, whom he married in 1952. In 1954 he ran across the fiery R&B tenor saxophonist Sam Butera in New Orleans and quickly signed up Butera and his group, which he named The Witnesses. Prima combined all of his favorite styles of music, and the result was a new and unusual formula, one that over four decades later would be the basis for the retro swing movement: Prima's Dixieland-oriented trumpet combined with Keely Smith's middle-of-the-road pop vocalizing, Butera's heated R&B band, swing standards, accessible comedy, a constant shuffle beat, an early rock and roll sensibility, and some show biz trappings along with lots of energy. The result was a very entertaining show that cut across many musical boundaries. Prima became a hit with his new and often-wild show in Las Vegas, and during the second half of the 1950s he was a major attraction, recording regularly for Capitol, including classic versions of "That Old Black Magic" and a pair of medleys: "Just a Gigolo/I Ain't Got Nobody" and "When You're Smiling/The Sheik of Araby." At the height of their fame, Louis Prima and Keely Smith starred in the very entertaining 1959 film *Hey Boy! Hey Girl!*

It all began to end when Prima and Smith were divorced in 1961, although the trumpeter-singer worked steadily through the 1960s, using Butera's band. The last real high point to his career took place in 1967, when he supplied the voice for a character in the Walt Disney cartoon *The Jungle Book*. Prima continued working with gradually decreasing success until he suffered a major stroke in 1975, falling into a coma and dying three years later. Little did Louis Prima know in his later years that two decades later his music of the 1950s would be emulated by scores of retro swing bands and vocalists.

Recommended CDs: *1934–1935* (Classics 1048), *Plays Pretty for the People* (Savoy 4420), *Capitol Collectors Series* (Capitol 94072)

Box Set: *The Capitol Recordings* (8 CDs; Bear Family 15 776)

LPs to Search For: *1935–1936* (The Old Masters 38), *1936* (The Old Masters 39), *1937–1938* (The Old Masters 62), *The Wildest* (Capitol 755), *The Call of the Wildest* (Capitol 836)

Film Appearances: *Rhythm on the Range* (1936), *You Can't Have Everything* (1937), *Start Cheering* (1937), *Manhattan Merry-Go-Round* (1937), *Rose of Washington Square* (1939), *Senior Prom* (1958), *Hey Boy! Hey Girl!* (1959), *Twist All Night* (1961), *La Donna di Notte* (1962), and *Rafferty and the Gold Dust Twins* (1975). In addition, Louis Prima provided the voice for King Louie of the Apes in *The Jungle Book* (1967).

TONY PRINGLE

* * * * * * * * * * * * * *

b. Liverpool, England

Tony Pringle, whose cornet style is most influenced by Bunk Johnson and, to a lesser extent, by Mutt Carey and Kid Thomas Valentine, has been the leader of the New Black Eagle Jazz Band since it was formed in 1970. He originally played in trad bands in England, preferring revivalist New Orleans groups over Dixieland. In 1967 he moved to the United States, settling in Massachusetts the following year. He freelanced in the New England area, eventually landing a day job as a computer engineer. Pringle and clarinetist Tommy Sancton cofounded the

New Black Eagle Jazz Band, and the band solidified with its success at the New Orleans Jazz Festival in April 1971. Tony Pringle's group, which is now 30 years old, has recorded steadily through the decades for such companies as GHB, Dirty Shame, Fat Cat Jazz, Philips, Stomp Off, and its own Black Eagle label.

Recommended CDs: with the New Black Eagle Jazz Band: *New Black Eagle Jazz Band* (GHB 59), *Old-Fashioned Swing* (Stomp Off 1346)

LPs to Search For: with the New Black Eagle Jazz Band: *1981* (Stomp Off 1048), *At Symphony Hall* (Philo 1086), *Tight Like This* (Stomp Off 1054), *Dreaming the Hours Away* (Stomp Off 1065), *Don't Monkey With It* (Stomp Off 1147)

MARCUS PRINTUP

b. Jan. 24, 1967, Conyers, GA

An excellent hard bop trumpeter, Marcus Printup has plenty of potential. He started playing trumpet when he was nine and worked in funk bands as a teenager. Printup attended the University of North Florida, playing in a tentet called Soul Reason for the Blues. Another Marcus, pianist Marcus Roberts, discovered him in 1991 and added him to his band for tours the following year, but primarily as road manager! However, Printup learned a lot about the music business, and he had an opportunity during Robert's solo tours to play a few duets with him near the end of the concerts.

Since then, Marcus Printup has worked with the Lincoln Center Jazz Orchestra, performed with Betty Carter, recorded with Carl Allen, toured with Wynton Marsalis (when he was performing "Blood on the Fields"), and recorded regularly as a leader for Blue Note, including a tribute to Freddie Hubbard that cofeatures Tim Hagans (*Hubsongs*).

Recommended CDs: *Song for the Beautiful Woman* (Blue Note 30970), *Unveiled* (Blue Note 37302), *Nocturnal Traces* (Blue Note 59367), *Hubsongs* (Blue Note 59509), with Marcus Roberts: *Blues for the New Millennium* (Columbia 68637)

Film Appearances: Marcus Printup appears briefly in the Sean Connery film *Dancing About Architecture* (1998).

BERNIE PRIVIN

b. Feb. 12, 1919, Brooklyn, NY, d. Oct. 9, 1999, Westchester, NY

Bernie Privin was a superior first trumpeter who could solo whenever he was given the chance. "I started playing the mellophone at the age of seven at a orphan home. When I heard Louis Armstrong at the age of 13, I begged my father to buy me a trumpet, and the next day, after much pleading, I had a $16 Carl Fischer trumpet. I joined the New York School of Music at 50 cents a lesson. Next time I'll find a professional teacher!" Within two years, Privin was playing professionally.

Privin started off working with Harry Reser (1937), and he had the opportunity to play with quite a few of the major swing-era big bands, including Bunny Berigan, Tommy Dorsey, Artie Shaw (1938–39), Charlie Barnet (1940–41), and Benny Goodman (1941–42), in addition to Mal Hallett and Jerry Wald. While in the military, Privin was a soloist with Glenn Miller's Army Air Force Band during 1943–46. He was back with Benny Goodman during 1946–48. After freelancing in the studios, he became a member of the staff of CBS (1952–76), although he occasionally toured with Goodman. Privin, who considered his favorite trumpeters and main influences to be Armstrong, Bobby Hackett, Roy Eldridge, and Billy Butterfield, played in the 1970s with Pee Wee Erwin, the Tommy Dorsey Orchestra, and the New York Jazz Repertory Company. Bernie Privin was active into the 1990s and considered his favorite personal record to be his hard-to-find 1956 Regent album *Dancin' and Dreamin'*.

Recommended CDs: *Glenn Miller's Army Air Force Band 1943–44* (Bluebird 6360)

LPs to Search For: *Dancin' and Dreamin'* (Regent 6027)

JACK PURVIS

• • • • • • • • • • • •

b. Dec. 11, 1906, Kokomo, IN, d. Mar. 30, 1962, San Francisco, CA

Of all the trumpeters in this book, the one with the most bizarre life was Jack Purvis, a fascinating personality whose complete story will probably never be found out. Purvis was involved in so many odd adventures and escapades in his life that it is almost as if there were three of him!

First his musical career: Purvis' mother died when he was a child, and he spent several years in a training school, where he learned trumpet and trombone. He played in high school orchestras and dance bands in Kokomo as early as 1921 and gigged in Indiana in 1923 as a teenager. Purvis spent a period in Lexington, Kentucky, with the Original Kentucky Night Hawks and in 1926 toured New England with Bud Rice's band. Next up was a stint with Whitey Kaufman's Original Pennsylvanians (1926–27). After a short period playing trombone with Hal Kemp, in July 1928 Purvis visited France with George Carhart's Band. Back in the United States, in 1929 he rejoined Hal Kemp's orchestra, this time on trumpet.

Purvis appeared on records with Kemp, Smith Ballew, the California Ramblers, the Carolina Club Orchestra, Roy Wilson's Georgia Crackers, Ted Wallace, and Rube Bloom during 1929–30. Most significant were two numbers cut on December 17, 1929, with the Hal Kemp rhythm section (the intriguing "Copyin' Louis" and "Mental Strain at Dawn") and a pair of interracial sessions that he led in 1930. The latter utilized such sidemen as trombonist J.C. Higginbotham, tenor saxophonist Coleman Hawkins, and bass saxophonist Adrian Rollini. Purvis' playing is full of fiery bursts, unrealized potential, and some crazy chance taking, just like his life was. Although the Louis Armstrong influence was unashamedly part of his style (few white trumpeters sounded as much like Satch at that point in time), Purvis also sounds quite original in spots. If he had continued in this direction, he might have been one of the top trumpeters in jazz.

Purvis left Kemp in early 1930, played a bit with the California Ramblers and several radio orchestras, recorded with the Dorsey Brothers, occasionally sat in as fourth trumpeter with Fletcher Henderson (spontaneously improvising his ensemble parts), and was mostly with Fred Waring during 1931–32. Purvis traveled through the South with Charlie Barnet in 1933. In Los Angeles he did some writing for the George Stoll Orchestra and some studio arranging for Warner Bros., including composing "Legends of Haiti" for a 110-piece orchestra! After being off the scene, in 1935 he returned to New York, led a quartet, made his final recordings (with Frank Froeba), toured for a couple of weeks with Joe Haymes' Orchestra, and then dropped out of sight.

But that is only a small part of the Jack Purvis Story. John Chilton in his *Who's Who of Jazz* and Dick Sudhalter in *Lost Chords* (both books are highly recommended) have pieced together some but not all of the details of Purvis' unique life. In 1925, Purvis took time off from his playing with the Original Kentucky Night Hawks to learn how to pilot a plane. A few years later, when someone bet Purvis that he could not fly under all of New York City's bridges, he reportedly rented a plane and proved him wrong!

In 1928, when Purvis was hired for the George Carhart band, he played with the orchestra on the first night of their transatlantic voyage to France. He then ran across a couple of famous aviators, talked them into letting him share their first-class cabin, and was not seen by the other musicians for the rest of the trip, choosing instead to play with the Ted Lewis band, which was entertaining the first-class passengers. After rejoining Carhart's group in Paris, a couple of weeks later he was spotted by his roommates making a rather quick exit from their hotel room via the roof while being chased by French policemen. He had apparently conned an American tourist out of his traveler's checks!

At one point in the late 1920s, Jack Purvis ran the short-lived School of Grecian Dancing in Miami. Because he was soon wanted by the local police due to moral charges with the ill-fated school, he had to quit Hal Kemp's band in January 1930, when a Florida tour was planned. By then he had earned the reputation of setting his hotel rooms on fire and not paying his bills.

Purvis' Southern trip with Charlie Barnet was full of colorful incidents. Passing through Louisiana, Purvis managed to talk himself into an appearance with the New Orleans Symphony playing *The Carnival of Venice*. He deserted Barnet for a time in El Paso, Texas, when he decided to work as a pilot flying cargo (probably illegal goods) between Mexico and the United States. And during his Los Angeles stay, he was arrested at one point for standing in the middle of a busy road tunnel and playing his horn; he told the police that he loved the acoustics! After his period with Warner Bros. ended, Purvis worked for a time as a chef in San Francisco. There have also been rumors that he worked as a mercenary in South America and as a chef in Bali, but those are unconfirmed!

In 1937 Purvis walked into a club in San Pedro, California, carrying a horn and calling himself Jack Jackson (the name of a British trumpeter). He told the bandleader (Johnny Catron) that he had been a ship's cook on a freighter and that police were after him about a murder investigation. A few months later he was working as a cook in Texas, but that job was cut short when he was sent to prison in June for being involved in a robbery in El Paso. In jail, Purvis directed and played piano with a prison band, the Rhythmic Swingsters, broadcasting on radio station WBAP regularly in 1938. Purvis received a conditional pardon in August 1940 but soon violated it and spent six more years in prison until being released on September 30, 1946. Jack Purvis' later jobs (he never returned to music) included flying planes in Florida, working as a carpenter, and being a radio repairman in San Francisco. He committed suicide in 1962, maybe.

Quite consistent with his bizarre and mysterious life is the fact that a man who looked like Jack Purvis and was about the right age showed up at a gig by cornetist Jim Goodwin, and they had long discussions about his life on two occasions. It was 1968!

LPs to Search For: *Satchmo Style* (Swing 8451)

Recommended Reading: *Lost Chords* by Richard M. Sudhalter (Oxford University Press, 1999)

CHELSEA QUEALEY
. . . .
b. 1905, Hartford, CT, d. May 6, 1950, Las Vegas, NV

Chelsea Quealey was a versatile trumpeter who was on many record dates in the late 1920s and '30s as a sideman. He started off playing saxophone before switching to trumpet. Quealey worked with Jan Garber (1925) and the California Ramblers (1926–27), also recording with the Goofus Five and the Little Ramblers (small groups taken out of the California Ramblers). He sailed to England in December 1927, recording with Fred Elizalde and working steadily for a couple of years. When he became temporarily ill, Quealey returned to the United States in June 1929. He played with Don Voorhees, the California Ramblers a second time, briefly with Paul Whiteman, and Ben Pollack.

Quealey recorded with Mezz Mezzrow (1934) and worked with Isham Jones (1935–36), Joe Marsala, Frankie Trumbauer (1937), and Bob Zurke's big band (1939–40). Chelsea Quealey (who never led his own record date) played Dixieland at Nick's and other New York clubs in the 1940s before spending his last four years working in California and Las Vegas. He passed away from heart trouble at the age of 44 or 45.

Recommended CDs: *The Goofus Five* (Timeless 017), *The Little Ramblers* (Timeless 062)

DON RADER
. . . .
b. Oct. 21, 1935, Rochester, PA

A solid bebop trumpeter, Don Rader was started on trumpet when he was five by his father, who was a professional trombonist. He studied at Sam Houston State Teachers College and the U.S. Naval School of Music (1954–55). Rader became known for his work with big bands, including those of Woody Herman (1959–61), Maynard Ferguson (1961–63), Count Basie (1963–64), Terry Gibbs, Louie Bellson, Harry James, Stan Kenton, and Les Brown (off and on during 1967–72 and 1986–90). He also contributed arrangements to many of these ensembles and was often used by Henry Mancini for his recordings

In 1972 Rader settled in the Los Angeles area and formed a quintet, often working with altoist Lanny Morgan and the Toshiko Akiyoshi/Lew Tabackin big band. He also became a busy jazz educator. Rader spent much of the 1982–90 period in Europe (often working with Peter Herbolzheimer's orchestra) and lived during most of the 1990s in Australia, although he occasionally visited the United States. As a leader, Don Rader (who is still in prime form these days) has recorded for such labels as DRM (1973), PRB (1976), Discovery (1978), Jet Danger (1980), Bellaphon (1994), and Tall Poppies (1998).

Recommended CDs: *Foreign Affair* (Bellaphon 45034), *Off the Beaten Track* (Tall Poppies 130)

LPs to Search For: *Polluted Tears* (DRM 3236), *Wallflower* (Discovery 796), *Anemone* (Jet Danger 5310), with Woody Herman: *Woody's Winners* (Columbia 2436), with Lanny Morgan: *It's About Time* (Palo Alto 8007)

HUGH RAGIN

• • • • • • • • • • • •

An inventive avant-gardist who can also play powerful bebop (as shown on his brilliant *An Afternoon in Harlem* CD), Hugh Ragin worked with Roscoe Mitchell, the David Murray Octet, John Lindberg, and, for four years, Anthony Braxton, in addition to leading his own groups. He has an appealing and flexible tone, along with a very open style. Hugh Ragin has thus far recorded as a leader for Cecma, CIMP, and (most recently) Justin Time.

Recommended CDs: *Gallery* (CIMP 177), *An Afternoon in Harlem* (Justin Time 127), *Fanfare & Fiesta* (Justin Time 152), with John Lindberg: *Trilogy of Works for Eleven Instruments* (Black Saint 0082), with Roscoe Mitchell: *Nine to Get Ready* (ECM 1651), with David Murray: *Hope Scope* (Black Saint 120139)

LPs to Search For: *Metaphysical Question* (Cecma 1007)

FREDDY RANDALL

• • • • • • • • • • • • • • •

b. May 6, 1921, London, England, d. May 18, 1999, Devon, England

Freddy Randall was plagued by bad health in the later part of his career but is still considered to have been one of Great Britain's finest mainstream swing/Dixieland trumpeters. "At the age of about 15, I went to a shop with the intention of buying a guitar (being a keen Django Reinhardt fan) but, as the cheapest instrument in the window was a trumpet, changed my mind. I never quite knew that I was going to be a professional musician. It simply crept up on me."

Randall, who was self-taught, played with the St. Louis Four in 1939. After serving in the Army (1940–42), he played with John Dankworth and Freddy Mirfield's Garbage Men (a comedy band) but otherwise mostly led his own groups when not performing as a guest soloist with other English orchestras. Randall made many Dixieland records during 1948–57 and played with such visiting Americans as Wild Bill Davison, Bud Freeman, Pee Wee Russell, and Sidney Bechet. He visited the United States in 1956 in a cultural exchange program that gave Louis Armstrong a chance to play in England.

Unfortunately a serious lung ailment forced Randall to retire in 1958 when he was 37, and he missed the height of the trad jazz boom in England. Randall was able to return for a time as a part-time player during 1963–65 before largely retiring again. In the early 1970s he was persuaded to play with what was billed as "Britain's Greatest Jazz Band." After some tours and personnel changes, he co-led the Freddy Randall-Dave Shepherd Jazz All-Stars with clarinetist Shepherd for a few years, including a recorded performance at the 1973 Montreux Jazz Festival. Freddy Randall, who also played with Teddy Wilson when the pianist visited England, became semiretired after the mid-'70s, playing only now and then, although he still made rare appearances until quitting permanently in 1993.

LPs to Search For: *His Great Sixteen* (Dormouse 5), *Freddy Randall-Dave Shepherd Jazz All-Stars* (Black Lion 194), *Live at Montreux* (Black Lion 214), with Benny Waters: *Benny Waters-Freddy Randall Jazz* (Jazzology 124)

IRVING "MOUSE" RANDOLPH

• •

b. June 22, 1909, St. Louis, MO, d. Dec. 10, 1997, New York, NY

A solid swing player with an unfortunate nickname, Irving "Mouse" Randolph stayed busy during the peak years of his career before spending decades in obscurity. He played early on with Fate Marable on riverboats and worked with the territory bands of Walt Farrington (1923–24), Willie Austin (1925–26), Art Sims-Norman Mason (1926), Floyd Campbell (1927–28), Alphonso Trent (1928), and J. Frank Terry (1929–30). Randolph spent the 1931–33 period working in Kansas City with Andy Kirk's Twelve Clouds of Joy. After he moved to New York, Randolph played with Fletcher Henderson (1934), Benny Carter, and Luis Russell before working for four years with Cab Calloway (1935–39), receiving occasional solo space.

Randolph finished off the swing era with the big bands of Ella Fitzgerald (really the Chick Webb ghost band) during 1939–42 and Don Redman (1943). He gained some recognition and solo space while with clarinetist Edmond Hall's sextet (1944–47), but his career never went beyond that point. Randolph worked with many low-profile swing, Latin, and R&B bands during the next decade, and he had a long stint with the Chick Morrison Orchestra (from 1958 into the early 1970s). But, other than a session with Harry Dial's Bluesicians in 1961, Irving Randolph made no significant recordings after 1947, and he never had the opportunity to lead his own record date. It is a pity that the mid-1950s revival of mainstream swing missed him completely.

Recommended CDs: *Chu Berry 1937–1941* (Classics 784), with Cab Calloway: *1937–1938* (Classics 568), *1938–1939* (Classics 576), with Edmond Hall: *1944–1945* (Classics 872)

ENRICO RAVA

b. Aug. 20, 1939, Trieste, Italy

Enrico Rava is one of the most respected trumpeters from Italy, a lyrical free jazz player with a mellow tone. Rava actually started on trombone when he was 16 (originally playing Dixieland) before switching to trumpet and modern jazz after seeing Miles Davis play. Rava began to gain some recognition when he performed with Gato Barbieri (1964), Steve Lacy (on and off during 1965–69, including a period in South America), Mal Waldron, and Lee Konitz.

Spending time in New York starting in 1969, Rava often played with Roswell Rudd (on and off during 1969–78), the Jazz Composers Orchestra, Charlie Haden's Liberation Music Orchestra, Don Cherry, Abdullah Ibrahim, and Bill Dixon. He made his first recording as a leader back in 1960 (three songs), cut records for several labels during 1972–74, and in 1975 started recording regularly for ECM. Since then, Rava has played with the who's who of free jazz and the avant-garde, including the Globe Unity Orchestra, Gil Evans (1982), Cecil Taylor (1984 and 1988), and Archie Shepp (1985) plus many of the top European players. In 1985 Enrico Rava returned to Italy, where he mostly leads a variety of groups (including an occasional big band), appearing at festivals and clubs all over Europe.

Recommended CDs: *The Pilgrim and the Stars* (ECM 1063), *Enrico Rava Quartet* (ECM 1122), *Rava String Band* (Soul Note 1114), *Electric Five* (Soul Note 1214) *Italian Ballads* (Music Masters 65166), *Live at Birdland Neuburg* (Challenge 71011), *Duo en Noir* (Between the Lines 004), with Steve Lacy: *The Forest and the Zoo* (ESP 1060)

MICHAEL RAY

b. Dec. 24, 1962, Trenton, NJ

Michael Ray, one of Sun Ra's best musicians of the 1980s, sees himself as the keeper of the Sun Ra flame, even though the posthumous Ra band is actually led by altoist Marshall Allen. Early on, Ray worked with R&B acts, including Patti LaBelle, the Delfonics, and the Stylistics, and he loves to mix jazz with funk. Ray was a member of Ra's Arkestra off and on during 1978–93, recording over two dozen albums with Ra, who called him his "Intergalactic Research Tone Scientist." During the same period (1979–90), the trumpeter played regularly with the R&B group Kool and the Gang.

Ray, who has lived in New Orleans since 1989, put together his Cosmic Krewe in 1991, two years before Ra's death. Since then it has become one of the most popular bands in the city, combining Ra's show-biz science fiction trappings with funk à la Kool. Michael Ray, an excellent trumpeter who also sings occasionally, has recorded with his band for Evidence and Monkey Hill.

Recommended CDs: *Michael Ray and the Cosmic Krewe* (Evidence 22084), *Funk If I Know* (Monkey Hill 8142), with Sun Ra: *Mayan Temples* (Black Saint 120121), *Salute to Walt Disney* (Leo 230)

DIZZY REECE

· · · · · · · · · · · ·

b. Jan. 5, 1931, Kingston, Jamaica

Alphonso "Dizzy" Reece is one of the great hard bop trumpeters but, despite a few gems, he has not been documented enough throughout his career. Reece played baritone horn for a few years before switching to trumpet when he was 14. He worked in his native Jamaica with Jack Brown's swing band in 1947, moved to Europe the following year, played with Don Byas during 1949–50, and worked throughout the continent with various bebop groups. In 1954 Reece moved to London, where he played with Kathy Stobart, Terry Shannon, Kenny Graham's Afro-Cubists, and Tony Crombie's big band. The trumpeter recorded as a leader for Tempo, spent periods of time living in Paris, Portugal, and London, and worked with some of Europe's top bop musicians, including Martial Solal and Victor Feldman. He recorded *Blues in Trinity* with the visiting Donald Byrd in 1958.

In October 1959 Reece moved to the United States. He received an initial outburst of publicity, recording two strong albums for Blue Note during 1959–60 and an additional set for New Jazz in 1962. But he never really caught on, and eventually he returned to Europe. Dizzy Reece toured Europe with Dizzy Gillespie's big band in 1968, was part of the Paris Reunion band (1985), played with the Clifford Jordan big band in the early 1990s, and is still active today, though generally overlooked.

Recommended CDs: *Blues in Trinity* (Blue Note 32093), *Asia Minor* (Original Jazz Classics 1806)

LPs to Search For: *Soundin' Off* (Blue Note 4033), *Manhattan Project* (Bee Hive 7001), *Blowin' Away* (Interplay 7716)

WAYMON REED

· · · · · · · · · · · ·

b. Jan. 10, 1940, Fayetteville, NC, d. Nov. 25, 1983, Nashville, TN

Waymon Reed was an excellent trumpet soloist whose style fell between swing and bop, but he could never adapt to being thought of as Mr. Sarah Vaughan! He grew up in Nashville, studied at the Eastman School of Music, and played with Ira Sullivan in Florida.

Reed toured with James Brown (1965–69) and was a member of the Count Basie Orchestra on two occasions (1969–73 and 1977–78), getting occasional solos. He also had opportunities to work with Frank Foster and the Thad Jones-Mel Lewis Orchestra. After marrying Sarah Vaughan (who was 16 years his senior) in the late 1970s, Reed left Basie. During 1978–80 he led his wife's backup band, but that did not work too well. Shortly after they were divorced, Waymon Reed was stricken with cancer, and he died at the age of 43.

Recommended CDs: with Sarah Vaughan: *The Duke Ellington Song Book, One* (Pablo 2312-111)

LPs to Search For: *46th & 8th* (Artists House 10)

REUBEN "RIVER" REEVES

b. Oct. 25, 1905, Evansville, IN, d. Sept. 1975, New York, NY

With the success of Louis Armstrong's Hot Five and Seven recordings for Okeh during 1925–28, some of the other record labels in 1929 did what they could to build up trumpet stars of their own. While Brunswick obtained the services of Jabbo Smith and Victor promoted Henry "Red" Allen, Vocalion signed up Reuben "River" Reeves, an erratic but exciting player who was always colorful. The 15 selections that he cut that year for Vocalion are the trumpeter's main recorded legacy. Unfortunately, like Jabbo Smith, Reeves would sink into complete obscurity soon afterwards, unknown even to most record collectors.

Reuben Reeves started out playing piano as a child at the insistence of his mother (herself a pianist), but in high school he switched to trumpet so he could play with his school band. In the summer of 1923, Reeves toured with a group led by Bill Smith. Although he moved to New York in February 1924 to study dentistry, Reeves soon chose to freelance around the city as a trumpeter. Moving to Chicago, during 1925–28 Reeves was a regular with Erskine Tate's orchestra. During that period he also studied at the American Conservatory in Chicago and gained a master's degree. Reeves was a member of Dave Peyton's band in 1928, taught music at a high school during the day, and later in the year formed a band that appeared at the Regal Theatre. Mayo Williams, an important record producer, was quite impressed by Reeves and gave him what must have seemed like a big break, signing him to record regularly for Vocalion.

With the exception of two obscure titles cut with Fess Williams' Joy Boys in April 1928, the 15 selections made by Reuben Reeves' River Boys in 1929 were his debut on record. With such impressive sidemen as clarinetist Omer Simeon, Darnell Howard on alto and clarinet, the versatile pianist Jimmy Prince, singer Blanche Calloway, and Reuben's older brother, trombonist Gerald Reeves, these performances are quite rewarding and often wild. Reuben Reeves sometimes shows off the influence of Louis Armstrong (his "River Blues" is a near copy of Armstrong's "West End Blues") but also includes the reckless chance taking of Jabbo Smith along with Reeves' own exuberant shouts, shakes, and growls. "Parson Blues" finds Reeves nearly laughing through his horn, while on "Moanin' Low" his tonal distortions sometimes sound close to Bubber Miley (although with less subtlety). In ways, Reeves sounds like a young Roy Eldridge: combative, competitive, and colorful, even when he misses. He shows off a great deal of potential and is consistently fiery.

However, the remainder of Reuben Reeves' career was anticlimactic. Because he was not a singer or an innovator, the rise of the Depression resulted in his losing his chance for stardom. Reeves played with pianist Jerome Carrington's group in early 1931, was a member of Cab Calloway's orchestra during 1931–32 (appearing on all of Cab's recordings of that era), and in 1933 reorganized the River Boys as a 12-piece swing orchestra. Their one recording date contains surprisingly little playing from its leader. By 1936 Reeves was back in New York, and a few years later he joined the National Guard, playing trumpet with the 369th Infantry Band and serving in the Pacific during World War II. Upon his discharge in 1946, he began an association with Harry Dial's Blusicians that lasted until 1955 but was often on a part-time basis. A 1946 radio broadcast with Dial's quartet (released on an IAJRC LP titled

Benny Moten/Harry Dial) shows that the trumpeter had advanced a bit through the years, hinting at Hot Lips Page and Harry James while still retaining his characteristic shakes. However, Reeves did not participate in the Dixieland revival, only played jazz part-time during his last decade, and spent his last three years working as a bank guard. An RST CD has all of Reuben Reeves' recordings as a leader and reminds listeners of the great talent that somehow got away.

Recommended CD: *Reuben Reeves and Omer Simeon* (RST 1516)

KID RENA
• • • • • • • • •

b. Aug. 30, 1898, New Orleans, LA, d. Apr. 25, 1949, New Orleans, LA

It was Henry "Kid" Rena's misfortune that his one opportunity to record found him sounding ill and out of tune. Rena was actually highly thought of in New Orleans, noted for his wide range and strong tone. He was a student at the Colored Waifs' Home during the same period as Louis Armstrong, and he replaced Armstrong in Kid Ory's band in 1919 when Satch left to play on riverboats with Fate Marable.

Unlike Armstrong, Rena chose to stay in New Orleans, just visiting Chicago a few brief times in the 1920s. He headed popular groups during the 1920s, was with the Tuxedo Brass Band for many years, led a big band (the Pacific Brass Band) in the '30s, and often used George Lewis on clarinet along with his brother Joseph Rena on drums. Unfortunately he was under the weather when he had his only opportunity to record in 1940, a date that also included clarinetist Alphonse Picou and trombonist Jim Robinson (it has been reissued by American Music). Rena sounds 82 rather than 42, and, in addition, the recording quality is pretty poor. Kid Rena, who was active until bad health forced his retirement in 1947, never had a second chance to show future listeners if his strong reputation was deserved.

HERB ROBERTSON
• • • • • • • • • • • • • • • •

b. Feb. 21, 1951, Plainfield, NJ

Herb Robertson, whose tonal distortions once led to his being dubbed by *Cadence* magazine as "the Cootie Williams of the '80s," is an utterly unpredictable player, well aware of past styles but quite original. He attended Berklee during 1969–72 and then became involved in avant-garde jazz, playing and recording with Tim Berne, Rashied Ali, Paul Motian, Ray Anderson, Dewey Redman, Mark Helias, Bobby Previte, Joe Fonda, Lou Grassi, and even David Sanborn (on one of the R&B altoist's few creative jazz dates).

Among Herb Robertson's recordings (for the JMT, CIMP, and Cadence labels) is an unusual tribute to the compositions of Bud Powell.

Recommended CDs: *Certified* (JMT 849 150), *Little Motor People* (JMT 514 005), *Sound Implosion* (CIMP 110), *Falling in Flat Space* (Cadence 1065)

LPs to Search For: *Transparency* (JMT 85002), *Shades of Bud Powell* (JMT 834 420)

CLAUDIO RODITI

. . . .

b. May 28, 1946, Rio de Janeiro, Brazil

One of the finest jazz trumpeters to emerge from Brazil, Claudio Roditi is equally skilled at bebop, Brazilian music, and Afro-Cuban jazz. His father played guitar and violin.

When I was six years old, my mother had me studying piano with a cousin of hers. After that I started trying to play bongos; percussion instruments have always had a big influence on me. When I was nine I heard a school marching band rehearsing behind our house. I walked to the band room, and when I spotted a trumpet, I fell in love with the instrument and asked my father to buy me one. By the time I was 15, I was very involved with music and jazz in particular, so I had a feeling I was going to go into music professionally."

Roditi attended Escola Nacional de Musica and Conservatorio Nacional de Musica in Rio de Janeiro. He worked as a studio musician in Brazil and came to the United States to study at Berklee (1970–71). Based in the Boston area for a few years, Roditi freelanced, playing with Alan Dawson and in a quintet led by Brazilian guitarist Amaury Tristao that also included Charlie Rouse.

Since moving to New York City in 1976, Roditi has worked in many situations. His mellow sound, flexibility, and mastery of bop and Brazilian music have made him quite valuable. Among his key associations have been Bob Mover, Herbie Mann (1978–80), Dizzy Gillespie's United Nation Orchestra during 1988–92 ("playing with Dizzy Gillespie was a highlight in my career"), Slide Hampton's Jazz Masters, and especially Paquito D'Rivera (starting in 1983). Claudio Roditi, who took occasional vocals in his earlier days, has recorded as a sideman with many top artists (including Dave Valentin, Jimmy Heath, Ricky Ford, Gary Bartz, Mark Murphy, Jeannie Bryson, Jim Hall, Horace Silver, and McCoy Tyner among others) and led his own dates for Greene Street, Milestone, Uptown, Candid, Mons, RTE, and Reservoir. "My music is a combination of Brazilian music and American jazz. Hopefully I have succeeded in blending the two styles, which have a lot in common."

Recommended CDs: *Two of Swords* (Candid 79504), *Milestones* (Candid 79515), *Free Wheelin'— The Music of Lee Morgan* (Reservoir 136), *Samba Manhattan Style* (Reservoir 139), with Paquito D'Rivera: *Who's Smokin'* (Candid 79523)

LPs to Search For: *Claudio* (Uptown 27.27)

RED RODNEY

. . . .

b. Sept. 27, 1927, Philadelphia, PA, d. May 27, 1994, Boynton Beach, FL

Red Rodney's life was about taking advantage of a rare second chance after having nearly thrown everything away the first time around. Born Robert Chudnick, he first played in a bugle and drum choir, receiving a trumpet as a Bar Mitzvah gift when he was 13. Rodney developed very quickly, attended the Mastbaum Vocational School, and within two years was a member of Jerry Wald's orchestra, despite being only 15. Because the World War II draft was taking away many of the top sidemen, talented teenagers were able to get lucrative jobs with name bands during that period. Rodney had short-term associations with the orchestras of Jimmy Dorsey, Elliot Lawrence, Georgie Auld, Benny Goodman, and Les Brown. His first idol was Harry James (that influence can be heard on a Jimmy Dorsey V-disc recording from 1944 of "Oh What a Beautiful Morning"), but by the following year Rodney was listening closely to Dizzy Gillespie and learning how to play bebop.

Rodney gained some attention for his solos with Gene Krupa's bop-oriented big band in 1946 and also worked with Buddy Rich, Claude Thornhill, and Woody Herman's Second Herd (1948–49). In 1949 he replaced Kenny Dorham in the Charlie Parker Quintet, where for the next two years he played regularly with Bird; Rodney is outstanding on their performance at a Christmas Eve Carnegie Hall concert in 1949 (reissued by Jass). Unfortunately, it was during this period that Rodney became a heroin addict, which greatly disturbed Parker.

In 1951 Rodney was busted, and he spent most of the 1950s going in and out of prison. He did lead five record dates during the decade (including a couple in which he was joined by Ira Sullivan on second trumpet, tenor, and alto), but he had largely blown his opportunity for stardom.

Eventually Rodney was able to give up drugs totally, but a long period spent playing for Las Vegas shows (most of the 1960s) was nearly as destructive, making his jazz chops quite rusty. Against the odds, in 1972 he moved to New York and began a long and gradual comeback. He recorded for Muse regularly during 1973–81, not only regaining his old form within a few years but exceeding it. However, Rodney was in danger of being stuck playing bebop standards for the rest of his life despite being only 53 in 1980.

The year 1980 would be the turning point, for that is when he formed a quintet with Ira Sullivan. Because Sullivan was always very forward looking and had no desire just to play the older tunes, and because Rodney was looking for fresh inspiration, the group became a postbop band, one influenced by the innovations of Ornette Coleman and featuring new, advanced tunes by its pianist, Garry Dial. Its recordings for Muse and Elektra Musician rank with Rodney's finest work of his career. Even after Sullivan returned to Florida in the mid-1980s, Rodney continued playing modern acoustic music, featuring at first James Morrison and then the young tenor saxophonist Chris Potter. The filming of Clint Eastwood's *Bird*, which portrayed Rodney sympathetically and featured him ghosting his own solos, gave him plenty of publicity, and Red Rodney was voted to the Downbeat Hall of Fame shortly before his death in 1994 at the age of 66.

"I have been very lucky in as much as I have played my very best from the age of 50 on. Life experiences have made me a better person as well as musician, and my history shows that I am truly a human triumph because of my virtual disappearance from jazz, only to return and become more successful than ever."

Recommended CDs: *The Red Rodney Quintets* (Fantasy 24758, *Live at the Village Vanguard* (32 Jazz 32167), with Charlie Parker: *Charlie Parker and Stars of Modern Jazz at Carnegie Hall* (Jass 16)

LPs to Search For: *Modern Music from Chicago* (Original Jazz Classics 048), *The Red Arrow* (Onyx 204), *Superbop* (Muse 5046), *The 3 R's* (Muse 5290), *Alive in New York* (Muse 5307),

Hi Jinx at the Vanguard (Muse 5267), *Live at the Village Vanguard* (Muse 5209), *Night and Day* (Muse 5274), *Sprint* (Elektra Musician 60261)

Recommended Books: *Talking Jazz* by Ben Sidran (Pomegranate Artbooks, 1992)

Film Appearances: *Beat the Band* (1947) with Gene Krupa's orchestra.

Videos to Get: *Birdmen and Birdsongs, Vol. 1* (1990; Storyville 6048), ghosting the trumpet solos for his own character in *Bird* (1992; Warner Home Video 11820)

BOBBY RODRIGUEZ

. . . .

b. East Los Angeles, CA

Bobby Rodriguez is most significant as an inspiring jazz educator, an exciting conductor of college stage bands, and the director of jazz studies at the Los Angeles County High School of the Arts. He is also a fine trumpeter who is influenced by Lee Morgan, Freddie Hubbard, and Latin music. Rodriguez knew that he wanted to be a trumpeter when as a nine-year-old he saw Harry James playing on TV. The next year he started playing trumpet, and by the time he was 14 he was playing gigs. He was such an impressive player from an early age that Rodriguez was set to sign a contract with Pacific Jazz as a teenager; unfortunately that opportunity disappeared when he was drafted into the Army.

After his discharge, Rodriguez studied at Rio Hondo College and Cal State University, Long Beach, worked as a disc jockey at Los Angeles' jazz radio station KBCA (1969), and toured with the R&B group the Brothers Johnson. Since then he has become an educator in the Los Angeles area and worked with many performers, including Lalo Schifrin, Ray Charles, Herbie Hancock, Gerald Wilson's big band, Don Ellis, Louie Bellson, Willie Bobo, Poncho Sanchez, and (most recently) the Clayton-Hamilton Jazz Orchestra.

Bobby Rodriguez, who has a Latin jazz combo and sometimes leads a big band formerly headed by the late trumpeter Bobby Bryant, has recorded as a leader for Sea Breeze, JVC/JMI, and his Latin Jazz Productions label.

Recommended CDs: *Latin Jazz Explosion* (Latin Jazz 124), *A Latin Jazz Christmas* (JMI 7504), *Latin Jazz Romance* (Latin Jazz 125)

SHORTY ROGERS

. . . .

b. Apr. 14, 1924, Great Barrington, MA, d. Nov. 7, 1994, Van Nuys, CA

An excellent trumpeter and flugelhornist whose quiet sound and middle-register playing defined "cool jazz," Shorty Rogers was most important as an arranger (both in jazz and for the movies) and as an organizer of sessions. Born Milton Michael Rajonsky, he remembered in 1990: "I played bugle since the age of five in various drum and bugle corps in Lee, Massachusetts, and in New York City, where the family moved when I was nine. At the age of 13, my father asked me what I wanted for a present for my bar mitzvah. He got me a used trumpet in a pawn shop for $15. When I was 14, I got a job playing in the Borscht belt at a hotel: $5 a week, food, and a shared room, for the whole band!"

Rogers studied at the High School of Music and Art during 1939–42, and a week after his graduation he was already working with Will Bradley's orchestra. Next Rogers moved to Red Norvo's group (with whom he recorded) until mid-1943, when he was drafted into the Army. Rogers played with the 379th A.S.F. Band. After being discharged in September 1945, he became an important part of Woody Herman's First Herd, for whom he wrote some of his first arrangements, in addition to playing in a mighty trumpet section with Sonny Berman, Pete Candoli, Marky Markowitz, and Conrad Gozzo.

After Herman broke up the band in late 1946, Rogers worked with Charlie Barnet and Butch Stone before joining Herman's Second Herd (1947–49). Rogers, who by then had a major name, wrote such pieces as "Keen and Peachy" (based on the chords of "Fine and Dandy"), "That's Right," "Keeper of the Flame," "More Moon" (a feature for Gene Ammons), and "Lemon Drop" for Herman. Shorty followed that up by becoming a significant contributor to Stan Kenton's Innovations Orchestra (1950–51), providing a few of the only swinging charts in Kenton's book at the time. Among his originals were "Jolly Rogers," "Round Robin," and "Viva Prado." Rogers was always quite proud of his piece "Art Pepper," and he thoroughly enjoyed writing notes for Maynard Ferguson that were much higher than any he would have thought of attempting to play himself!

Settling in Los Angeles, Rogers played with Howard Rumsey's Lighthouse All-Stars during 1951–53 before breaking away to lead Shorty Rogers and the Giants starting in 1953. As with so many of the other, more talented Herman and Kenton sidemen, Rogers (who in the early 1950s became one of jazz's first flugelhornists) became both a busy studio musician and an important figure in West Coast cool jazz. Shorty led a series of impressive and influential dates for Capitol (1951), Victor, Atlantic, and MGM. He was even more important than most of his contemporaries, for not only did he play trumpet and write, but he hired musicians for studio and film work, helping to get jazz into films (including most notably 1953's *The Wild One* and 1955's *The Man with the Golden Arm*).

Rogers became so busy in the studios that he largely stopped playing after 1962 for 20 years, sticking to writing for television and films. In 1982 he got out his horns again (sticking mostly to flugelhorn) and became more active in jazz, frequently teaming up with altoist Bud Shank. In 1989 they co-led a new version of the Lighthouse All Stars (which included Conte Candoli). Although Shorty Rogers' own playing was not quite as strong as it had been previously, he was a very welcome force on the jazz scene during his last years when he was recognized as a West Coast jazz legend.

Recommended CDs: *Swings* (Bluebird 3012), *Yesterday, Today and Forever* (Concord Jazz 223), *America the Beautiful* (Candid 79510), with Woody Herman: *The Thundering Herds 1945–1947* (Columbia 44108), with Stan Kenton: *The Innovations Orchestra* (Capitol 59965), with Lighthouse All-Stars: *Sunday Jazz à la Lighthouse* (Original Jazz Classics 151)

Box Sets: *The Complete Atlantic and EMI Jazz Recordings* (6 CDs; Mosaic 6-125)

LPs to Search For: *Short Stops* (Bluebird 5917)

Film Appearances: with Woody Herman: *Hit Parade of 1947* (1947), with Jack Teagarden: *The Glass Wall* (1953), The Man with the Golden Arm (1955)

Videos to Get: *Shelly Manne/Shorty Rogers-Jazz Scene USA* (1962; Shanachie 6012)

WALLACE RONEY

· · · · · · · · · · · · · ·

b. May 25, 1960, Philadelphia, PA

F orever in Miles Davis' shadow, Wallace Roney sounds very close to his idol (particularly from Davis' late 1960s period), even when he is playing newer originals. Roney, whose father loved Miles and Lee Morgan, had a trumpet around the house that the youth (who took piano lessons starting when he was five) was soon playing. Roney developed fast and was playing professionally by the time he was 13. He appeared on an obscure record with poet Haki Madhubuti in 1974, when he was just 14.

Roney studied for a year apiece at Howard University and Berklee, and played with the big bands of Abdullah Ibrahim (1979) and Art Blakey (1980). When Wynton Marsalis left the Jazz Messengers for six months to tour with Herbie Hancock's V.S.O.P. in 1981–82, Roney was his substitute. He worked with Chico Freeman and Ricky Ford, freelanced, and during 1986–89 managed to be a member of both the Jazz Messengers and the Tony Williams Sextet, finally choosing the latter. Roney played with Williams through 1996 but also had his own projects along the way. He toured Europe with the George Gruntz Concert Jazz Band in 1991, which led him to play (and get some solo space) with Miles Davis at that year's Montreux Jazz Festival when Davis revisited Gil Evans' classic arrangements. The connection between the two was reinforced when Roney filled the trumpet spot after Davis' death in a Miles tribute band (which also included Wayne Shorter, Herbie Hancock, Ron Carter, and Tony Williams) and played Davis' role with Gerry Mulligan's Rebirth of the Cool Nonet.

Roney, whose younger brother is tenor and soprano saxophonist Antoine Roney and whose wife is pianist Geri Allen, has mostly led groups in recent years, other than touring with Chick Corea's Tribute to Bud Powell band in 1996. In addition to his many records as a leader for Muse and Warner Brothers, he has appeared as a sideman on many CDs, including with Marvin "Smitty" Smith, Christopher Hollyday, Kenny Barron, Randy Weston, Kenny Garrett, James Spaulding, and Vincent Herring.

Whether Wallace Roney (who is now in his early forties) will eventually develop his own musical identity apart from Miles Davis is not known yet.

Recommended CDs: *The Standard Bearer* (Muse 5372), *Seth Air* (Muse 5441), *Crunchin'* (Muse 5518), *Misterioso* (Warner Bros. 45641), *The Wallace Roney Quintet* (Warner Bros. 45914), *Village* (Warner Bros. 46649), with Art Blakey: *Feeling Good* (Delos 4007), with Chick Corea: *Remembering Bud Powell* (Stretch 9012), with Gerry Mulligan: *Rebirth of the Cool* (GRP 9679), with Tony Williams: *Angel Street* (Blue Note 48494), *Native Heart* (Blue Note 93170), *The Story of Neptune* (Blue Note 98169), *Tokyo Live* (Blue Note 99031)

LPs to Search For: with Art Blakey: *Killer Joe* (Storyville 4100)

Recommended Reading: *Jazz Profiles* by Reginald Carver and Lenny Bernstein (Billboard Books, 1998)

ADI ROSNER

· · · · · · · · · · ·

b. May 26, 1910, Berlin, Germany, d. Aug. 8, 1976, Berlin, Germany

Adi (also known as Eddy) Rosner had a strange and somewhat tragic life, greatly affected by events beyond his control and guilty of nothing but his desire to play jazz. Of Polish descent, he was born Rosner Adolph Ignatievich, studied music at the Berlin Hochschule fur Musik, and began playing jazz in 1928. He picked up experience working with Willi Rose-Petosy (1929) and the Weintraub Syncopators (1930–33). Due to the rise of the Nazis, who banned jazz, Rosner worked in the Netherlands (1933) and Belgium (1934–35) before settling in Poland, where he led a band. He recorded four songs for French Columbia with his swing orchestra in Paris in 1938.

When Poland was invaded by Nazi Germany in 1939, Rosner fled to the Soviet Union. Although jazz had been pushed underground by the Communist regime in the 1930s, swing was considered a worthwhile way to spread propaganda during the war years. Rosner therefore worked steadily during the first half of the 1940s, entertaining Russian troops and being used by Stalin as an example of the Soviet Union's "enlightened" society. However, after World War II ended and the Cold War with the United States got under way, jazz was outlawed again and Rosner was sent to a labor camp, where he spent nine years (1946–55). After his eventual release, Adi Rosner had to abandon jazz. So he formed a symphony orchestra and primarily played classical music during his last two decades, moving back to Berlin in 1973, three years before his death.

Recommended Reading: *Red and Hot: The Fate of Jazz in the Soviet Union* by S. Frederick Starr (Limelight Editions, 1985)

JIM ROTONDI

· · · · · · · · · · ·

b. Aug. 28, 1962, Butte, MT

A top-notch trumpeter, Jim Rotondi is a perfect example of the type of artist who producer Gerry Teekins regularly records for his Dutch Criss Cross label: American, hard bop oriented, swinging, and underrated.

Rotondi started playing piano when he was eight, switching to trumpet four years later. After graduating from North Texas State University in 1985, he freelanced, playing on cruise ships and for shows. Since being a part of the Ray Charles Orchestra during 1991–92, Rotondi has performed with many straightahead musicians, including Junior Cook, Cecil Payne, Lionel Hampton (1995), the George Coleman Octet, the Michael Weiss sextet, Lou Donaldson, Curtis Fuller (1997), and his own One for All sextet. In addition to his sessions as a leader for Criss Cross, Jim Rotondi has recorded with Eric Alexander, Charles Earland, Giacomo Gates, Steve Davis, David Hazeltine, Randy Johnston, and John Pizzarelli among many others. He is a valuable player to have around!

Recommended CDs: *Introducing Jim Rotondi* (Criss Cross 1128), *Jim's Bop* (Criss Cross 1156), *Excursions* (Criss Cross 1184), with Eric Alexander: *Alexander the Great* (Highnote 7013), *Mode for Mabes* (Delmark 500), with One for All: *Optimism* (Sharp Nine 1010), *Upward and Onward* (Criss Cross 1172), *Long Haul* (Criss Cross 1193)

STACY ROWLES

• • • • • • • • • • • • •

b. Sept. 11, 1955, Los Angeles, CA

The daughter of pianist Jimmy Rowles, Stacy Rowles is a talented cool-toned flugelhorn player and vocalist who often emphasizes ballads and little-known standards. "When I was 12, I found my Dad's army trumpet in his dresser. I stole it, honked on it, then asked Dad how you play it!" She played piano from age four and drums at seven but trumpet (and later flugelhorn) became her main instrument after her first experience with the horn.

Based in the Los Angeles area throughout her career, Rowles played with Clark Terry early on (1975), made her recording debut in 1984, and worked with her late father, Maiden Voyage, and the Jazz Birds in addition to currently leading local groups. "I was blessed to be born into a family of very talented people. I would like to carry on the blessing, in my own way, and do the best I can to play the music our family loves."

Recommended CDs: *Me and the Moon* (American Jazz Symposium 1001), with Jimmy Rowles: *Looking Back* (Delos 4009)

LPs to Search For: *Tell It Like It Is* (Concord Jazz 249), with Jimmy Rowles: *With the Red Mitchell Trio* (Contemporary 14016)

ERNIE ROYAL

• • • • • • • • • • • •

b. June 2, 1921, Los Angeles, CA, d. Mar. 16, 1983, New York, NY

The brother of altoist Marshall Royal (who was nine years older), Ernie Royal was primarily a first trumpeter who could belt out high notes in big bands and studio orchestras, but he was also a capable (if underused) soloist. He started playing trumpet when he was ten and was a professional five years later. Royal worked in Los Angeles with Les Hite (1937–38) and Cee Pee Johnson (1939). Both of the Royal brothers were with Lionel Hampton's orchestra (1940–42), and Ernie hit the famous screaming high notes on the hit recording of "Flying Home."

After serving in the military during 1942–45 (where he played with a Navy band), Royal worked in San Francisco with Vernon Alley and in Los Angeles with Phil Moore. He was part of the Count Basie Orchestra in 1946 and was a member of Woody Herman's Second Herd (1947–49), being lead trumpeter with both bands. Royal also played with Charlie Barnet and briefly with Duke Ellington in 1950 before spending two years in Paris, where he worked with Jacques Helian's orchestra and recorded eight selections (six reissued on a Xanadu LP) as a leader.

After returning to the United States, Royal played with Wardell Gray (1952) and had two stints with the Stan Kenton Orchestra (1953 and 1955), recording his only full album as a leader for Urania in 1954. After that, Ernie Royal was primarily a studio musician, becoming a member of the staff at ABC (1957–72) and uplifting many orchestras with his anonymous but brilliant ensemble playing.

LPs to Search For: *Accent on Trumpet* (Urania 1203), with Coleman Hawkins: *Accent on Tenor Sax* (Urania 1201)

Film Appearances: *The Secret Fury* (1950)

KERMIT RUFFINS
. . . .

b. 1964, New Orleans, LA

A 'n intriguing trumpeter-vocalist who is never shy to create a party atmosphere, Kermit Ruffins is a very popular figure in New Orleans. He originally gained fame as the leader of the Rebirth Brass Band, an R&B-oriented parade and party group that was inspired by the innovative Dirty Dozen Brass Band. Since leaving Rebirth in the early 1990s, Ruffins has had a successful career as a bandleader. His repertoire includes New Orleans jazz standards, more modern jazz tunes, and his own originals, most of it played with a healthy dose of funk added in. Kermit Ruffins, who has recorded joyous albums for Justice and Basin Street, is also a notable cook.

Recommended CDs: *World on a String* (Justice 1101), *The Big Butter and Egg Man* (Justice 1102), *Hold on Tight* (Justice 1103), *Swing This* (Basin Street 0102)

JORGEN RYG
. . . .

b. Aug. 11, 1927, Denmark

J orgen Ryg is a truly obscure European jazz trumpeter. He was already nearly 18 before he started playing music. After spending time in the Army, he freelanced in Denmark. During 1954–55, Ryg recorded his only album as a leader, an excellent quartet date for Emarcy that finds him sounding very influenced by Chet Baker. His activities and whereabouts since then are difficult to trace, so Jorgen Ryg's place in this project is symbolic of all of the fine European trumpeters who are virtually unknown in the United States and who have been left out of jazz history books due to their geography.

LPs to Search For: *Jorgen Ryg Quartet* (Emarcy 36099)

CHASE SANBORN
. . . .

R ight before the manuscript for this book was completed, I ran across one additional trumpeter who had to be included despite the lack of available information. Chase Sanborn's debut as a leader features him playing standards with a quartet/quintet that is sometimes augmented by fellow trumpeter Guido Basso. His warm tone and swing-to-bop style on his highly enjoyable Canadian session, along with his ability to swing at every tempo, makes Chase Sanborn one to watch for in the future.

Recommended CD: *Good to the Last Bop* (Brass Tactics 1)

JORDAN SANDKE

b. Feb. 20, 1946, Chicago, IL

The career of Jordan Sandke, the older brother of Randy Sandke, started off strong, but Sandke has maintained a low profile in recent years. He started on drums when he was 11. "When I was 13, I was playing drums in a small combo with some of my school friends, one of whom had a cornet. One day at a rehearsal I picked it up and got a pretty good sound right off. My first influences were Louis Armstrong and Bix Beiderbecke. Later came Charlie Parker, Clifford Brown, Roy Eldridge, and Coleman Hawkins."

Sandke earned degrees in ancient history and classical languages at Chicago University (1962–68) but then decided to become a professional musician. He played at first with blues and R&B bands, including Mighty Joe Young (1969–70), Junior Parker (1970–71), and Howlin' Wolf, recording with the last (1970), and Johnny Ross and the Soul Explosion (1968). Sandke studied at the New England Conservatory of Music (1974–77) and worked in Boston during 1977–78. After moving to New York in 1978, the talented swing-based trumpeter played with the Widespread Depression Orchestra (throughout the 1980s), Vince Giordano's Nighthawks, Jaki Byard's Apollo Stompers (1985–87), the Buck Clayton big band (1988–91), Panama Francis, and Walt Levinsky's Great American Swing Band (1987–89).

Jordan Sandke, who led a band at Roseland during 1991–92 and recorded an album for Stash, said in 1991 that one of his main goals was to make a recording playing the music of Coleman Hawkins and Roy Eldridge. Unfortunately he has not appeared on records since that era.

Recommended CDs: *The Sandke Brothers* (Stash 575)

RANDY SANDKE

b. May 23, 1949, Chicago, IL

An important trumpeter best known for his work with prebop bands but actually interested in all eras of music, Randy Sandke overcame an early illness to develop into a major player. "I was introduced to jazz originally through my older brother, Jordan. When I was about ten, we started collecting jazz records. Around that time my brother began playing the trumpet, and shortly after I began as well. My mother was an amateur pianist and both my brother and I also played piano." After extensive music instruction in high school, Sandke attended Indiana University (1966–69), and in 1968 he formed a rock band with tenor saxophonist Michael Brecker. "His dedication and musical discipline were almost frightening but it had a big influence on me." Sandke was offered a chance to join Janis Joplin's band, but he developed a hernia in his throat. An operation was successful but Sandke lost his confidence and gave up the trumpet for most of a decade. "I made a living accompanying dance classes on piano at Bennington College (Vermont) from 1970–73, and while there I also began playing the guitar. When I moved to New York in 1973, I continued to work on both instruments until I started playing trumpet again in 1979."

This time Sandke quickly surpassed his earlier form. He became one of the most technically skilled trumpeters in trad jazz, playing with Vince Giordano's Nighthawks for five years, Bob Wilber (1983–85), the Benny Goodman Orchestra during 1985–86 ("I was impressed by the almost brutally detailed way he rehearsed a band and the way he would always surprise the band with something new every time he played"), the Newport All-Stars, and the Buck Clayton big band (1986–91) in addition to appearing at many classic jazz parties and festivals with fellow all-stars. Sandke, who has visited Europe over 20 times, very effectively played the roles of both Louis Armstrong and Bix Beiderbecke on long-lost vintage material for his *Re-Discovered Louis and Bix* recording.

Randy Sandke, who has led albums for Stash (including one that he shared with brother Jordan), Jazzology, Concord Jazz, and Nagel-Heyer, is also quite capable of playing more modern styles of jazz and classical music.

"I am most proud that, after some severe setbacks, I managed to end up standing on my own two feet. Some people have called me a jazz revivalist, but I consider myself a jazz survivalist."

Recommended CDs: *Stampede* (Jazzology 2211), *I Hear Music* (Concord Jazz 4566), *Get Happy* (Concord Jazz 4598), *The Chase* (Concord Jazz 4642), *Calling All Cats* (Concord 4717), *Awakening* (Concord Concerto 42049), *Re-Discovered Louis and Bix* (Nagel-Heyer 058), with the New York All Stars: *Plays More Music of Louis Armstrong* (Nagel Heyer 046)

Videos to Get: *Flip Phillips' 80th Birthday Party* (1995; Arbors ARVHS2)

ARTURO SANDOVAL
●●●●●●●●●●●●●●●●●●●●

b. Nov. 6, 1949, Artemisa, Havana, Cuba

One of the most remarkable trumpeter virtuosos in jazz history, Arturo Sandoval can apparently play anything on his horn, whether it be stratospheric high notes, warm ballads in his lower register (he has a fat tone), or very rapid runs of notes over complex chord changes. He may not yet have accomplished as much as his tremendous potential would allow, but he is currently at the peak of his powers. Sandoval is also a heated scat singer (reminiscent of Dizzy Gillespie), a talented pianist, and an enthusiastic timbales player.

The son of an auto mechanic in Cuba, Sandoval started off with extensive classical trumpet lessons, attending the Cuban National School of the Arts (from which he graduated in 1967) as a teenager. He was one of the founding members of the Orquesta Cubana de Musica Moderna, which was considered Cuba's elite band. Wanting to play more adventurous music (jazz by a different name), in 1973 Sandoval, altoist Paquito D'Rivera, and pianist Chucho Valdes were three of the key players who broke away to form Irakere; Valdes became its leader.

Sandoval met his idol, Dizzy Gillespie, on May 17, 1977, when Dizzy was part of a group of top American musicians (including Stan Getz, Earl Hines, Ry Cooder, and Daniel Amram) who were visiting Cuba. Sandoval, who only spoke Spanish at the time, volunteered to drive Gillespie and Ray Mantilla around Havana. The next day Dizzy was amazed to hear his "chauffeur" playing blazing solos with Irakere!

As long as he toed the government line, Sandoval was occasionally able to travel abroad and appear at international jazz festivals. He left Irakere in 1981 to form his own group, and the following year he recorded an album in Finland with Gillespie. However, Sandoval felt quite restricted under Fidel Castro's communist system, wanting the freedom to play whatever music he desired. In July 1990 Sandoval was on tour with Dizzy Gillespie's United Nation Orchestra (a band that included D'Rivera, who had left Cuba a decade earlier) when he defected with his family in Rome.

Sandoval soon settled in Florida. His first American concert took place at the Village Gate on August 20, 1990, with the orchestras of Tito Puente and Mario Bauza. The trumpeter signed with GRP (where his first CD was logically titled *Flight to Freedom*), formed a high-powered group, and immediately became a popular attraction. Most of Sandoval's GRP releases are quite rewarding and some are quite wondrous. He played with the United Nation Orchestra during Gillespie's final year, appeared with the GRP All-Star Big Band, James Moody, and T.S. Monk, and was featured on soundtracks by Dave Grusin. Sandoval has toured constantly with his exciting Afro-Cuban combo, worked as an educator in Florida, and during 1998–99 occasionally led a Cuban big band, Hot House.

Since he had been registered as a member of the Communist Party in Cuba (because, ironically, it made it easier for him to tour and defect), Sandoval was initially denied U.S. citizenship, even though he played regularly at benefits for the Democratic Party and spoke out constantly against Castro. After a long behind-the-scenes battle and a public outcry, in 1999 he finally became an American citizen. An HBO movie, *The Arturo Sandoval Story*, was released in 2000. Starring Andy Garcia as Sandoval (with the trumpeter ghosting the solos for his own character), the story fairly accurately depicts the remarkable trumpeter's years in Cuba and his successful flight to freedom.

Recommended CDs: *Straight Ahead* (Ronnie Scott's Jazz House 008), *Flight to Freedom* (GRP 9634), *I Remember Clifford* (GRP 9668), *And The Latin Train* (GRP 9701), *Swingin'* (GRP 9846)

Videos to Get: *GRP All-Star Big Band* (1992; GRP 9672)

CARL SAUNDERS

● ● ● ● ● ● ● ● ● ● ● ● ● ●

b. Aug. 2, 1942, Indianapolis, IN

Carl Saunders is a rare double, being both an in-demand first trumpeter (most notably with Bill Holman's orchestra) and a major (if greatly underrated) soloist. Only a select few in jazz history have managed to excel at both roles during the same period of time.

My uncle Bobby Sherwood had a big band in the swing era. My mother Gail sang with his band, and during my first five years I was on the road with them. Bobby's other sister, Aunt

Caroline, married Dave Pell, who was playing tenor sax in the band at the time. When Dave started his octet, I used to listen to the records at home. What stuck out most to me was the trumpet playing of Don Fagerquist.

Saunders, who considers his main influences to be Sherwood, Fagerquist, and Kenny Dorham, began playing trumpet when he was 11, in junior high school. "My Mom was Stan Kenton's first singer at Balboa Ballroom when he started his band. So when Stan came to Las Vegas in 1961, where we lived, she talked to him and got me in the band when I was 18." Saunders actually played mostly mellophonium while with Kenton (1961–62) and from then on worked with many big bands, including those of Bobby Sherwood (1962–63), Si Zentner, Perez Prado, Harry James (1966), Maynard Ferguson, Charlie Barnet, Buddy Rich, and Benny Goodman (1967). "I had a bad reputation for opening my mouth on gigs, standing up for the guys against leader abuse. Buddy Rich fired me three times!" Saunders played in many show bands backing commercial acts through the years, particularly in Las Vegas during 1972–84.

After moving to Los Angeles in 1984, he joined Bill Holman's orchestra (as a nonsoloing first trumpeter), and has since worked with Supersax, the Dave Pell Octet, Bob Florence's Limited Edition, Gerald Wilson's big band, and the Phil Norman Tentet in addition to countless combos. It was not until 1995 that Carl Saunders had an opportunity to lead his own record date (the brilliant *Out of the Blue*), and that has been followed up by another worthy gem, *Eclecticism*, both for the tiny SNL label.

Recommended CDs: *Out of the Blue* (SNL 1), *Eclecticism* (SNL 2), with Bob Florence: *Earth* (MAMA 1016), with the Phil Norman Tentet: *Yesterday's Gardenias* (Sea Breeze 3029), *Live at the Lighthouse* (Sea Breeze 3044)

Recommended Videos: Carl Saunders takes a mellophonium solo during *Stan Kenton: Music of the '60s* (1962; Vintage Jazz Classics 2007)

TOMMY SAUNDERS
• • • • • • • • • • • • • • • •

b. Detroit, MI

Although he was inspired by Wild Bill Davison and sometimes leads a Wild Bill legacy band, Tommy Saunders is a strong trad cornetist with his own sense of humor. He began on cornet when he was seven and at nine was already playing in his older brother's band. Saunders led bands in junior high and high school (always concentrating on freewheeling Chicago jazz) and served in the Navy, attending the U.S. Naval School of Music. After his discharge, he worked a day job at first. In the early 1960s Saunders played in the Midwest with trombonist Pee Wee Hunt. After that stint ended, he formed the Surf Side Six in Detroit, a band that lasted 20 years. The group got its name because for its first three years it played regularly at the Surfside Lounge. That engagement was followed by playing six nights a week for 11 years at the Presidential Inn, so the band was rarely out of work!

The Surf Side Six recorded with its guest Wild Bill Davison and on its own for the Bountiful, Jim Taylor Presents, and Lorelei labels. Since the mid-1980s, Tommy Saunders has continued leading bands in the Detroit area, recorded for Parkwood, Arbors, and Nagel-Heyer, and appeared at many classic jazz festivals throughout the United States and Europe. He is one of the unheralded greats of today's Dixieland scene.

Recommended CDs: *Detroit Jazz All Stars* (Parkwood 115), *Call of the Wild* (Arbors 19146), *Exactly Like You* (Nagel-Heyer 023), with Wild Bill Davison: *Surfside Jazz* (Jazzology 25)

BOB SCHULZ

• • • • • • • • • • •

b. July 1, 1938, Reedsburg, WI

A powerful Dixieland cornetist and a strong singer who is reminiscent of Clancy Hayes, Bob Schulz considers his idol to be Bob Scobey. He started on trumpet in grade school and played in his high school marching band but did not discover jazz until college, loving trad jazz. In 1961 Schulz helped found the Riverboat Ramblers, a band he played with regularly in Madison, Wisconsin, for 18 years. He also worked with Jim Beebe and James Dapogny's Chicago Jazz Band.

After being heard by Turk Murphy at the St. Louis Ragtime Festival in 1979, he was hired by the trombonist and relocated to the San Francisco Bay area. He was a member of Murphy's last band (1979–87). Since then he has played with the Delta Jazz Band, the Golden Gate Rhythm Machine, Jimmy Diamond's Nob Hill Gang, the San Francisco Starlight Orchestra, the Jelly Roll Jazz Band, the Royal Society Jazz Orchestra, the Minstrels of Annie Street, the Frisco Syncopators, and the two-cornet Down Home Jazz Band (with Chris Tyle) in addition to his own ensembles (usually called the Frisco Jazz Band). Bob Schulz has recorded as a leader for Jazzology and Stomp Off.

Recommended CDs: *Bob Schulz and His Frisco Jazz Band* (Jazzology 206), *Thanks Turk!* (Stomp Off 1288), *Travelin' Shoes* (Stomp Off 1315), with Turk Murphy: *Concert in the Park* (Merry Makers 12)

LPs to Search For: with the Down Home Jazz Band: *Hambone Kelly's Favorites* (Stomp Off 1171), *Yerba Buena Style* (Stomp Off 1190), with Turk Murphy: *San Francisco Jazz* (Merry Makers 114)

MANFRED SCHOOF

• • • • • • • • • • • • • • •

b. Apr. 6, 1936, Magdeburg, Germany

Manfred Schoof is an important avant-garde trumpeter from Germany. After extensive musical study, Schoof played with Gunter Hampel's quartet (1963–65). He led one of the first European free jazz groups (1965–68), a combo with pianist Alex Schlippenbach. Schoof was also with Schlippenbach's Globe Unity Orchestra from 1966 into the 1980s; his "Ode" was recorded by the groundbreaking ensemble in 1970.

Manfred Schoof, whose style is both colorful and adventurous, has worked with George Russell (1969–71), the Francy Boland-Kenny Clarke big band (1968–72), his New Jazz Trio (1969–73), Michel Pilz (1974–79), Mal Waldron (1974–80), Albert Mangelsdorff, and George

Gruntz's Concert Jazz Band. He has also led various ensembles (including a big band in the 1980s), and composed and arranged for other orchestras.

Recommended CDs: with George Gruntz: *Happening Now!* (Hat Art 6008), *First Prize* (Enja 6004)

LPs to Search For: *Voices* (L&R 41005), *The Early Quintet* (FMP 0540), *European Echoes* (FMP 0010), *Distant Thunder* (Enja 2066), with the Globe Unity Orchestra: *Live in Wuppertal* (FMP 160), *Hamburg 1974* (FMP 650)

BOB SCOBEY

· · · · · · · · · · · · ·

b. Dec. 9, 1916, Tucumcari, NM, d. June 12, 1963, Montreal, Quebec, Canada

Bob Scobey was a top-notch Dixieland player and one of the leaders of the San Francisco trad jazz revival. He was raised in Stockton, California, and started on cornet when he was nine, switching to trumpet five years later. Scobey played with dance bands during the second half of the 1930s. Meeting Lu Watters in 1938 was a major turning point, helping to greatly increase his interest in 1920s jazz.

Scobey was a key member of Lu Watters' Yerba Buena Jazz Band during 1940–42 and 1946–49, serving in the Army during 1942–46. His close interplay with Watters in the two-trumpet group was at times reminiscent of King Oliver and Louis Armstrong in the 1923 Creole Jazz Band, although the Yerba Buena Jazz Band developed its own sound and did not directly copy its predecessors.

Scobey led his first recording sessions for Trilon in 1947, and in 1949 he went out on his own, forming his Frisco Jazz Band. The three-horn Dixieland-oriented septet recorded extensively for Good Time Jazz, Verve, and Victor, often featuring vocals by banjoist Clancy Hayes. Scobey, who also recorded with Sidney Bechet (1953) and Bing Crosby (1957), in 1959 relocated to Chicago, where he played regularly at his Club Bourbon Street for a time.

Bob Scobey also worked in Las Vegas, New York, and San Francisco but died from cancer at the age of 46 in 1963. His widow, Jan Scobey, later came out with an impressive book documenting his life.

Recommended CDs: *The Scobey Story, Vol. 1* (Good Time Jazz 12032), *The Scobey Story, Vol. 2* (Good Time Jazz 12033), *Bob Scobey's Frisco Band* (Good Time Jazz 12006), *Scobey and Clancy* (Good Time Jazz 12009), *Frisco Band Favorites* (Good Time 60-010), *Bob Scobey, Vols. 1 and 2* (Jazzology 275 and 285)

Box Set: with Lu Watters: *The Complete Good Time Jazz Recordings* (4 CDs; Good Time Jazz 4409)

Recommended Reading: *He Rambled! 'Til Cancer Cut Him Down* by Jan Scobey (Pal Publishing, 1976)

ANDY SECREST

• • • • • • • • • • • • •

b. Aug. 2, 1907, Muncie, IN, d. 1977, Los Angeles, CA

Imagine being hired by the top dance orchestra in the world to imitate someone else! It was Andy Secrest's fate always to be associated with Bix Beiderbecke. The similarity of Secrest's tone to Beiderbecke's led him to join Paul Whiteman's prestigious orchestra as a fill-in for Bix.

Andy Secrest was a promising cornetist as a teenager growing up in Indiana. He picked up early experience with Freda Sanker's orchestra in Cincinnati and also worked with Ted Weems and Ray Miller. His first important job was with Jean Goldkette's orchestra, playing with a slightly later version of the band than the famous edition with Beiderbecke. Secrest's first recording, "One Night in Havana," was made with Hoagy Carmichael and His Pals on October 28, 1927, but it was a Goldkette selection from six weeks later, "Here Comes the Showboat," that reportedly caught Whiteman's ear. It is not obvious what attracted Whiteman's attention since Secrest merely takes a two-bar break in a brief tradeoff with fellow cornetists Nat Natoli and Sterling Bose; all three sound like Bix!

In January 1929, bandleader Paul Whiteman found himself in a jam. His star cornetist, Bix Beiderbecke, was on a downward slide and had just suffered a mental breakdown, caused to a large extent by his alcoholism. Many of the orchestra's hotter arrangements had feature spots for Bix and would suffer without his presence. Whiteman was impressed by Secrest, a 21-year-old who read well and could simulate the sound and style of Bix, although he did not possess his genius. Secrest was hired to take Beiderbecke's place and, even upon Bix's surprise return the following month, he remained. As Beiderbecke continued to decline, Secrest gradually took over his solo work, both with Whiteman and on the recording dates of Frankie Trumbauer. His nearly identical tone would lead record collectors decades later to argue over whether it was Secrest or Bix who took solos on certain records from the era. Trumbauer's "Baby, Won't You Please Come Home" was particularly confusing, for Secrest has a break right before Bix takes the actual solo chorus. Other Andy Secrest appearances on records that were sometimes mistaken for Beiderbecke (who left Whiteman in the fall of 1929) were "What a Day" and "Alabamy Snow" with the Mason/Dixon Orchestra, "Nobody's Sweetheart," "Happy Feet," and "After You're Gone" with Whiteman, Eddie Lang's version of "March of the Hoodlums," and such numbers with Frankie Trumbauer as "Nobody but You," "Shivery Stomp," and "Manhattan Rag."

Perhaps it was unfair for the youngster always to be thought of as a Bix Beiderbecke imitator, but he was unable to outgrow the stereotype. After leaving Whiteman in 1932 when he was 25 (a year after Bix's death), Secrest played with Ted Weems (1933–34) and moved to Hollywood, where he worked steadily in the secure but anonymous role of a studio musician, often as part of Victor Young's orchestra. In 1938 he emerged to play for a few months with Ben Pollack's orchestra, sounding fairly individual on Pollack's recordings of "Looking at the World Through Rose-Colored Glasses" and "After You've Gone." But Secrest did not choose to pursue a career in jazz, being content to stay in the studios. Starting in 1949 he played at a few Dixieland festivals and appeared on some obscure recordings, but by the late 1950s Andy Secrest had left music altogether to work in real estate.

Recommended CDs: with Frankie Trumbauer: *Vols. 1 and 2* (The Old Masters 107 and 108)

LPs to Search For: *Ben Pollack Big Band* (Golden Era 15067)

Recommended Reading: *Bix-Man and Legend* by Richard Sudhalter and Philip Evans with William Dean Myatt (Schirmer Books, 1974)

CHARLIE SEPULVEDA

b. July 15, 1962, Bronx, NY

Charlie Sepulveda is a fiery hard bop trumpeter often featured in Afro-Cuban jazz settings. Born in the Bronx, in 1970 (when he was eight) his family moved to Puerto Rico. Sepulveda studied music extensively and became a professional while a teenager, playing locally with Willie Rosario, Ralphy Levit (1978), Julio Castro (1978–79), Bobby Valentin (1980–83), and El Cano Estramera (1983–84).

Sepulveda had an increasingly greater profile working with Eddie Palmieri, Ray Barretto (1985–86), Hector La Voe (1985–87), Tito Puente, Celia Cruz, Johnny Pacheco, Dr. John, the Fania All-Stars (1990–91), and Dizzy Gillespie's United Nation Orchestra (1991). Charlie Sepulveda has headed groups since 1989, led CDs for Antilles and Tropijazz, and recorded as a sideman with most of the foregoing stars plus Hilton Ruiz, Dave Valentin, the Tropijazz All-Stars, Manny Oquendo's Libre, and Steve Turre.

Recommended CDs: *The New Arrival* (Antilles 314 510 056), *Algo Nuestro* (Antilles 314 512 768)

DOC SEVERINSEN

b. July 7, 1927, Arlington, OR

A technically skilled high-note trumpeter, Carl "Doc" Severinsen found fame as the bandleader and sidekick on Johnny Carson's *Tonight Show* rather than as a creative jazz musician. In fact, Severinsen (whose early hero was Bunny Berigan) has always been essentially a swing player and, although he has admired more modern trumpeters, he has never felt compelled to create new music himself.

Severinsen started his career playing with Ted Fio Rita's band in 1945. He worked with the Charlie Barnet Orchestra during 1947–49, at one point being one of three "screamers" in the band, along with Maynard Ferguson and Ray Wetzel. Severinsen played with the Tommy Dorsey big band during 1949–51 and then became a busy studio musician, occasionally appearing in jazz settings (including a few dates with Benny Goodman) but mostly functioning as an ensemble player.

In 1962 Severinsen joined the Tonight Show Orchestra, and in 1967 he succeeded Skitch Henderson as its leader, staying for 25 years, until Carson retired in 1992. Doc became better known for his outlandish wardrobe than for his musicianship, although fellow trumpeters often raved about him. Severinsen recorded eight swing-oriented records for the Command label during 1960–67, but those were often as notable for demonstrating the possibilities of stereo than for any creative playing. The Tonight Show Orchestra did not record until 1986 but did eventually cut three fine records for Amherst. Doc Severinsen also played fusion with his group Xebron and performed classical, pop music, and swing with pops orchestras. He still occasionally tours with the *Tonight Show* alumni. But it is surprising that he has never felt motivated to lead a small-group straightahead recording and show the jazz world what he can really do.

Recommended CDs: Tonight Show Band (Amherst 3311), *Vol. 2* (Amherst 3312), *Once More with Feeling!* (Amherst 94405)

Recommended Videos: Jazz Festival, *Vol. 2* (1962, with Mike Bryan's group; Storyville 60740)

CHARLIE SHAVERS
• • • • • • • • • • • • • • • •

b. Aug. 3, 1917, New York, NY, d. July 8, 1971, New York, NY

One of the greatest jazz trumpeters of all time, Charlie Shavers' wide range, impish sense of humor, beautiful sound, and creative swing style are difficult to match. He could seemingly play anything on his horn, yet Shavers never became famous.

He started on piano and banjo before switching to trumpet as a youth. Shavers freelanced as a teenager, and in 1935 he worked with Frankie Fairfax's band in Philadelphia. After playing in New York with Tiny Bradshaw and Lucky Millinder, Shavers became a member of the John Kirby Sextet. As a key member of Kirby's popular group during 1937–44, Shavers proved to be quite flexible, contributing many arrangements and writing the standard "Undecided." Although an extroverted player, Shavers usually utilized a mute in this atmospheric band, blending in with the unusual ensemble sound and giving the group (which also included clarinetist Buster Bailey and altoist Russell Procope) a lot of its personality.

Shavers, who also recorded with Jimmie Noone, Johnny Dodds, and Sidney Bechet during the era, left Kirby when work started becoming slow in 1944, joining Raymond Scott's CBS Orchestra for a few months. He had a longtime association with Tommy Dorsey's orchestra (off and on during 1945–56) that probably hurt the development of his career. Shavers was well featured and constantly praised by Dorsey, but he was somewhat stuck in an orchestra that was emphasizing nostalgic swing. Shavers did occasionally break away, recording with the Esquire All-Stars, going on tours with Jazz at the Philharmonic (where he successfully engaged in trumpet battles with Roy Eldridge), and working with Benny Goodman a bit in 1954. It is a pity that during this period, when Shavers often recorded as a sideman, that producer Norman Granz never thought of having the trumpeter lead his own record dates for his high-profile labels.

Shavers was primarily with Tommy Dorsey until the trombonist's sudden death. After Dorsey's demise in 1956, Shavers often had a quartet (trying unsuccessfully to capitalize on Jonah Jones' fame), toured now and then with the Tommy Dorsey ghost orchestra, led record dates for Everest, and visited Europe, where in 1970 (with saxophonist Budd Johnson) he made his final recordings. Even in death Charlie Shavers was overshadowed, for he died two days after Louis Armstrong!

Recommended CDs: 1944–1945 (Classics 944), *Shavers Shivers* (Soundies 4117), with John

A virtuoso with a strong sense of humor and a mildly reckless style, Charlie Shavers should have been a big star.

Kirby: *1938–1939* (Classics 750), *1939–1941* (Classics 770), *1941–1943* (Classics 792)

LPs to Search For: *Like Charlie* (Everest 1127), *Live at the London House* (Hep 23), *Live from Chicago* (Spotlite 154)

Film Appearances: *Sepia Cinderella* (1947) with the John Kirby Sextet

Videos to Get: Shavers trades off with Buck Clayton on "This Can't Be Love" on *Trumpet Kings* (1958; Video Artists International 69076)

BRYAN SHAW

• • • • • • • • • • •

b. 1955, CA

I t is always a happy occasion when a new talent suddenly appears out of nowhere. In the case of Bryan Shaw, he was virtually unknown in 2000 when his debut CD as a leader, *Night Owl*, was released. What was unusual is that he was already in his mid-forties.

An early associate of trombonist Dan Barrett (they went to the same high school and would end up as brothers-in-law when Barrett married Shaw's sister), Shaw was originally given a cornet by his father to help him overcome asthma. Unlike Barrett, Shaw preferred staying home, and he managed to avoid gaining much recognition through the years. He did studio work, worked at Disneyland with the Pearly Band, played in such trad bands as South Frisco Jazz Band and the High Sierra, toured with Helen Forrest, and performed with local classical music groups. But finally, with the guidance of Barrett (the musical director of the Arbors label), Bryan Shaw made a guest appearance on Moon Song and recorded his impressive *Night Owl*, showing that he is one of the top mainstream swing trumpeters around today.

Recommended CD: *Night Owl* (Arbors 19159), with Dan Barrett: *Moon Song* (Arbors 19158), with South Frisco Jazz Band: *Emperor Norton's Hunch* (Stomp Off 1342)

CLARENCE SHAW

* * * * * * * * * * * *

b. June 16, 1926, Detroit, MI

Clarence Shaw made a small but memorable impact on jazz history in his recordings with Charles Mingus. Shaw first played piano when he was four and added trombone two years later. He served in the military, was wounded, and, while in an Army hospital in Detroit, heard Dizzy Gillespie's playing on "Hot House." That record inspired Shaw to start playing trumpet. Within a few weeks he was a strong enough player to be performing at a Detroit club.

Shaw worked with Lester Young, Wardell Gray, and Lucky Thompson plus other top players in the 1950s. He made a strong impression in 1957 when he worked with Charles Mingus, recorded three albums, including *East Coasting* and *Tijuana Moods*, displaying a haunting and memorable tone that appealed to the bassist. After leaving Mingus, he was based in Chicago and (under the name of Gene Shaw) recorded three albums as a leader for Argo during 1962–64. But since that time Clarence/Gene Shaw has dropped out of sight.

Recommended CDs: with Charles Mingus: *East Coasting* (Bethlehem 302), *Modern Jazz Symposium of Music* (Bethlehem 4009), *New Tijuana Moods* (RCA 68591)

LPs to Search For: *Breakthrough* (Argo 726)

WOODY SHAW

* * * * * * * * * * * *

b. Dec. 24, 1944, Laurinburg, NC, d. May 10, 1989, New York, NY

One of the most important trumpeters to be active in the 1970s, Woody Shaw took the sound of Freddie Hubbard and the innovations of hard bop and John Coltrane and moved them forward toward modal music and freer areas of jazz. His father (Woody Shaw Sr.) was a member of the gospel group the Diamond Jubilee Singers. The younger Shaw grew up in Newark, New Jersey, began playing trumpet when he was ten, and worked early on with local R&B bands. He played with Rufus Jones, Willie Bobo's band in 1963 (a unit that included Chick Corea and Joe Farrell), Larry Young, Tyrone Washington, and Eric Dolphy (1963). Shaw made his recording debut on Dolphy's *Iron Man* and traveled to Eu-

Woody Shaw combined the sound of Freddie Hubbard with the innovations of John Coltrane to create his own original style.

rope to join the multireedist. Unfortunately, by the time the 19-year-old trumpeter arrived, Dolphy had died. He stayed overseas for a year anyway, playing with Kenny Clarke, Bud Powell, Johnny Griffin, and Nathan Davis.

Shaw returned to the United States in 1965 and was soon recognized as one of the top up-

and-coming trumpeters. He worked with the Horace Silver Quintet (1965–66), Chick Corea, Jackie McLean (1967), McCoy Tyner, Andrew Hill, and Max Roach (1968–69). Shaw's ability to play both inside (hard bop) and outside (free) was very valuable, along with his rather original improvising style, which was influenced by Dolphy and Coltrane. Shaw had a quintet with Joe Henderson (1970), worked with Gil Evans, and was a member of Art Blakey's Jazz Messengers during 1971–73. He recorded as a leader for Contemporary and Muse, although his most lasting statements were made for Columbia during 1977–81.

The 1970s, however, were a difficult time for acoustic jazz musicians, and Shaw was never prosperous. He was a sideman with the Junior Cook-Louis Hayes Quintet in 1975, becoming a co-leader after Cook left. The band in 1976 served as the Dexter Gordon Quintet when the great tenor made his triumphant return to the United States.

Shaw led groups on and off during 1977–86. But despite steady recordings (for Enja, Musician, Red, Muse, and Timeless, in addition to Columbia), he never became a household name except among his fellow musicians. Perhaps if Shaw could have lasted a little longer, he might have had a more lucrative career, but failing eyesight (he was nearly blind near the end), drugs, and a growing weariness plagued him during his last years. Woody Shaw's life ended quite tragically. In February 1989 he fell down a flight of subway stairs, was hit by a train, and lost an arm; he died three months later.

In addition to his recordings as a leader, Woody Shaw appeared on quite a few dates as a sideman, including with Eric Dolphy, Horace Silver, Art Blakey, Dexter Gordon, Woody Herman, Lionel Hampton, Larry Young, Bobby Hutcherson, Hank Mobley, Joe Henderson, Jackie McLean, Roy Brooks, Nathan Davis, Kenny Garrett, Benny Golson, and Mal Waldron. His influence continues to grow each year.

Recommended CDs: *Song of Songs* (Original Jazz Classics 1893), *The Moontrane* (Muse 5472), *Little Red's Fantasy* (32 Jazz 32126), *Last of the Line* (32 Jazz 32024), *Time Is Right* (Red 123168), *Live, Volume One* (Highnote 7051)

Box Set: *The Complete CBS Studio Recordings of Woody Shaw* (3 CDs; Mosaic 3-142)

Videos to Get: *Paris Reunion Band* (1988; Proscenium Entertainment 10004)

JACK SHELDON

. . . .

b. Nov. 30, 1931, Jacksonville, FL

Jack Sheldon has always been more than just a trumpeter, for he is a hilarious and rather spontaneous (if somewhat tasteless) comedian and an underrated singer. As a trumpet player, Sheldon's style is boppish while tied to the swing tradition, and he has long had his own sound, particularly when he reaches for a high note (which sometimes sounds like a cry).

Sheldon started playing trumpet when he was 12 and was gigging in public within a year. He moved to Los Angeles in 1947, went to Los Angeles City College, served in the Air Force (playing in military bands), and, starting in 1952, worked regularly in the L.A. area. Sheldon played with the who's who of modern jazz around town, including Jimmy Giuffre, Wardell Gray, Jack Montrose, Dexter Gordon, Chet Baker (a close friend), Art Pepper, the Dave Pell

Octet, and Herb Geller. Sheldon worked and recorded as a member of bassist Curtis Counce's quintet and played with the Stan Kenton Orchestra (1958) and Benny Goodman (1959).

Sheldon has also worked on an occasional basis as an actor. He starred in the 1964–65 television series *Run Buddy Run*, was a longtime member of the *Merv Griffin Show* orchestra (where he was a wisecracker), and appeared in the Bette Midler movie *For the Boys*. Sheldon had occasional reunions with Benny Goodman (including playing at Goodman's 40th anniversary Carnegie Hall concert in 1978), was with the Bill Berry big band in 1976, and has led swinging combos, often teaming up with pianist Ross Tompkins.

Since the early 1990s, the Jack Sheldon Orchestra (which plays mostly Tom Kubis arrangements) has gained a strong following, performing swing standards that showcase its leader's exuberant vocals and set backgrounds for his colorful trumpet solos. Still, many listeners often wait impatiently for each song to end so they can hear what Sheldon will say next!

Recommended CDs: *Hollywood Heroes* (Concord Jazz 4339), *On My Own* (Concord Jazz 4529), with Curtis Counce: *You Get More Bounce with Curtis Counce* (Original Jazz Classics 159), *Carl's Blues* (Original Jazz Classics 423), *Landslide* (Original Jazz Classics 606)

LPs to Search For: *Stand By for Jack Sheldon* (Concord Jazz 229)

Film Appearances: *Freaky Friday* (1976), *For the Boys* (1990)

Videos to Get: *Stan Kenton: Music of the '60s* (1962; Vintage Jazz Classics 2007), *Jack Sheldon in New Orleans* (1989; Leisure Video), *Flip Phillips' 80th Birthday Party* (1995; Arbors ARVHS2)

SHORTY SHEROCK

b. Nov. 17, 1915, Minneapolis, MN, d. Jan. 26, 1980, Northridge, CA

Clarence "Shorty" Sherock was an excellent swing trumpeter who could also play Dixieland and bop. Sherock worked locally in Gary, Indiana, while still in high school, and he attended the Illinois Military Academy. Sherock worked with many big bands during the swing era, starting with Charlie Pierce, Dell Coon, Ben Pollack (1936), Frankie Masters, Jacques Renard, Jack Pettis, Seger Ellis, and Santo Pecoro's combo. Influenced by Roy Eldridge, Sherock was a prominent soloist with Jimmy Dorsey (1937–39). He worked with Bob Crosby (1939–40) and was one of Gene Krupa's stars during 1940–41 before the arrival of Eldridge. Sherock also played with Tommy Dorsey (1941), Raymond Scott, Bud Freeman, Bob Strong, Alvino Rey, and Horace Heidt (1942–45).

One of Sherock's most prominent performances was as the trumpet soloist at the very first Jazz at the Philharmonic concert (1944), taking solos that fell between swing and Dixieland. He led a big band (1945–48), worked with Jimmy Dorsey again during 1949–50, and then became a studio musician. In later years Sherock recorded Dixieland with Matty Matlock (1958) and swing with Benny Carter (1962), staying active in the studios until 1979. Sonny Sherock's only dates as a leader were four septet numbers in 1946 and six selections with his 1947 big band, so he can accurately be thought of as primarily a valuable sideman.

Recommended CDs: with Benny Carter: *Opening Blues* (Prestige 2513), with Jazz at the Philharmonic: *The First Concert* (Verve 314 521 646), with Gene Krupa: *Drum Boogie* (Columbia/Legacy 53425)

BOBBY SHERWOOD
• • • • • • • • • • • • • • • • •

b. May 30, 1914, Indianapolis, IN, d. Jan. 23, 1981, Auburn, MS

Bobby Sherwood was very talented in a variety of areas but never quite hit it big. He was a strong swing trumpeter, played rhythm guitar, wrote arrangements, and even sang decently. Sherwood was born to parents who performed in vaudeville, and he traveled with them from an early age. He played banjo when he was seven, later switching to guitar and adding trumpet. Sherwood became a professional musician in the late 1920s, and in 1933, when he was 19, he replaced Eddie Lang (who had unexpectedly died) as Bing Crosby's guitar accompanist. He worked with Crosby for three years.

Sherwood spent the prime years of the swing era (1936–42) as a studio musician in Los Angeles, appearing on jazz records now and then, including strumming his guitar on Artie Shaw's hit version of "Frenesi." In 1942 he was persuaded by Johnny Mercer to form a big band of his own and was quickly signed to Mercer's label, Capitol. Sherwood's plan was to have a studio orchestra and continue working in Los Angeles. However, his first recording date resulted in a surprise hit in "The Elk's Parade," and he was forced to form a real big band and tour the country.

Sherwood mostly played trumpet with his orchestra, in addition to writing most of the arrangements and taking some vocals. The big band (which along the way had such sidemen as Stan Getz, Zoot Sims, Dave Pell, Flip Phillips, Serge Chaloff, and Carl Fontana) lasted for seven years. But even with a second hit in 1946's "Sherwood Forest," it was a constant struggle. In 1949 he gave up, returned to the studios, and began working occasionally as an actor. In 1954 Bobby Sherwood recorded four songs for Coral as an overdubbed one-man band (playing trumpets, mellophone, trombone, vibes, piano, guitar, bass, and drums in addition to being a vocal quartet!), and in 1957 he recorded an obscure big band album of tunes from *Pal Joey*. Otherwise, he was lost to jazz during his final 30 years.

Recommended CDs: *The Issued Recordings 1942–1947* (Jazz Band 2143)

LPs to Search For: *Out of Sherwood's Forest* (IAJRC 35), *Pal Joey* (Jubilee 1061)

Film Appearances: *Campus Sleuth* (1948)

BOBBY SHEW
• • • • • • • • • • • •

b. Mar. 4, 1941, Albuquerque, NM

Bobby Shew is a very versatile bop-oriented trumpeter, equally at home with big bands and small combos, as first trumpeter and as featured soloist. Shew (who was born Robert Joratz) played guitar when he was eight, switching instruments at age ten when his stepfather, during spring cleaning, ran across a trumpet he had forgotten about. Shew played with a variety of local bands as a teenager. Although he would become an important jazz educator, he was actually mostly self-taught!

Shew attended the University of New Mexico (1959–60), played with the NORAD band while in the military, and worked with the Tommy Dorsey ghost orchestra (1964–65) and the big bands of Woody Herman (1965) and Buddy Rich (1966–67), both as a lead player and as an occasional soloist. He spent nine years working in show bands in Las Vegas, which built up his endurance if not his name. Shew moved to Los Angeles in the mid-1970s, became a studio musician, and worked with the Toshiko Akiyoshi-Lew Tabackin Orchestra for eight years, gaining some recognition for his solos. Along the way he also worked with Benny Goodman, the Horace Silver Quintet, Terry Gibbs, the Juggernaut, Maynard Ferguson, Louie Bellson, Art Pepper, Bud Shank, and Teddy Edwards, among others.

An important jazz educator who has conducted countless clinics and inspired many young trumpeters, Bobby Shew has led record sessions for Jazz Hounds, Inner City, Sutra, Atlas, Delos, Pausa, Mopro, Mons, Double Time, and MAMA.

Recommended CDs: *Trumpets No End* (Delos 4003), *Playing with Fire* (MAMA 1017), *Tribute to the Masters* (Double-Time 101), *Heavyweights* (MAMA 1013)

LPs to Search For: *Telepathy* (Jazz Hounds 30003), *Outstanding in His Field* (Inner City 1077), *Breakfast Wine* (Pausa 7171), *'Round Midnight* (Mopro 111)

BOB SHOFFNER

. . . .

b. Apr. 30, 1900, Bessie, TN, d. Mar. 5, 1983, Chicago, IL

Due to his relatively few recordings and low-profile career as a sideman, Bob Shoffner is rather obscure. But, as shown on his one session with Luis Russell in 1926, he combined elements of both his idol, King Oliver, and his contemporary Louis Armstrong in impressive fashion.

Shoffner grew up in St. Louis, and when he was nine he started playing drums and bugle. He switched to trumpet in 1911, also doubling on piano. After two years in the Army during World War I, in 1919 Shoffner worked in St. Louis and on riverboats with Charlie Creath. The trumpeter spent time in the Midwest playing with territory bands (including Everett Robbins' Jazz Screamers) before settling in Chicago in 1922. Shoffner worked with Honore Dutrey at the Lincoln Gardens, spent a brief period in 1924 with King Oliver's Creole Jazz Band (as Louis Armstrong's first replacement), had short stints with Dave Peyton and Lottie Hightower's Nighthawks, and then rejoined Oliver, staying from May 1925 to February 1927. He was on King Oliver's records of 1926 but had little to do, since the leader took all the solos. However, Shoffner is heard more prominently on a date with Lovie Austin's Blues Serenaders (1925), in the backup groups accompanying Ida Cox and Ozie McPherson, and most notably on ten songs with clarinetist Jimmy O'Bryant.

Best of all for Shoffner was his November 17, 1926, session with Luis Russell that uses the nucleus of King Oliver's band. The four selections find Shoffner receiving a lot of solo space, sounding a bit like Oliver, but also playing phrases closer to Louis Armstrong's on his early Hot Five records. Unfortunately Shoffner had some trouble with his lip the following year, causing him to leave Oliver and have an operation in St. Louis. By the end of 1927, he was back in action, but his career never really took off. Shoffner worked with Charles Elgar (1928), Erskine Tate, Jerome Carrington, and McKinney's Cotton Pickers (summer 1931), with his only other recordings during the era after the Russell date being little-known sessions with Alex Hill (1929), Half Pint Jaxon (1933), and Jesse Stone (1937). He worked in Chicago with Jaxon, subbed with Earl Hines' band, played briefly with Fess Williams and Fletcher Henderson in New York, was with Hot Lips Page's orchestra for part of 1938, and in 1940 organized his own short-lived big band. By the end of the year, Shoffner had gotten a day job with the government. He played music on a part-time basis for a few years (recording four titles with Richard M. Jones in 1944 that showed he was becoming familiar with Red Allen) but eventually retired completely from music.

In 1957, tenor saxophonist Franz Jackson organized his Original Jass All-Stars, a group filled with veteran Chicagoans, and Bob Shoffner was persuaded to come out of retirement. Jackson's band recorded five albums (three for Pinnacle, one for Phillips, and one for Riverside that has been reissued on CD), playing rough but colorful renditions of trad jazz and blues. Bob Shoffner (who in his early sixties displayed a crisp style reminiscent of latter-day Rex Stewart) was a regular member of the group until illness forced him to retire in 1965.

Recommended CDs: with Franz Jackson: *Chicago—The Living Legends* (Original Jazz Classics 1824), with Richard M. Jones: *1927–1944* (Classics 853), with Luis Russell: *1926–1929* (Classics 588)

DON SICKLER

• • • • • • • • • • • •

b. Jan. 6, 1944, Spokane, WA

An excellent straightahead trumpeter and arranger, Don Sickler has actually become best known for his work as a record producer and for his ability to transcribe songs and solos from hard bop records. He studied piano with his mother from age four and began playing trumpet when he was ten. Sickler formed a Dixieland band when he was 12, which a year later was playing at dances. After graduating from Gonzaga University in 1967, he moved to New York, studied at the Manhattan School of Music, and played in Broadway show bands. Sickler freelanced as a trumpeter while becoming important behind the scenes through his work in music publishing.

Sickler worked with Philly Joe Jones in the late 1970s and was the music director and one of the trumpeters in the Tadd Dameron tribute band Dameronia during 1982–85. He arranged for Art Blakey's big band in 1989 and played with Superblue, the Clifford Jordan Big Band, Candido, James Williams, Jaki Byard, Panama Francis, and the Joe Henderson Orchestra. In addition to being a record producer at Blue Note and working as a jazz educator (associate music director at Columbia University), Don Sickler's greatest playing exposure was as trumpeter and arranger for the T.S. Monk Sextet during 1991–98.

Recommended CDs: *The Music of Kenny Dorham* (Reservoir 111), *Superblue* (Blue Note 92997), with Dameronia: *Live at the Theatre Boulogne* (Soul Note 121202), with T.S. Monk: *Take One* (Blue Note 99614), *Changing of the Guard* (Blue Note 89050), *The Charm* (Blue Note 89575)

LPs to Search For: with Dameronia: *To Tadd with Love* (Uptown 27.11), *Look, Stop and Listen* (Uptown 27.15)

CARL "TATTI" SMITH

· · · · · · · · · · · · · · · · · ·

b. 1908, Marshall, TX

Carl "Tatti" Smith is known primarily for his playing on one recording session, filling in for an absent Buck Clayton on the Jones-Smith, Inc. date from October 9, 1936, that was Lester Young's debut recording. Smith plays so brilliantly and tastefully throughout the four titles ("Lady Be Good," "Evenin'," "Boogie Woogie," and "Shoe Shine Boy") that it is quite surprising that he never went any further with his career.

Smith early on worked with territory bands in the Midwest, including Terence Holder (1931) and Gene Coy (1931–34). He moved to Kansas City and joined Basie in 1936 but was let go (along with several other musicians, including violinist-guitarist Claude Williams) when producer John Hammond persuaded Count to make some changes after the band reached New York in 1937. Smith did play and record with Skeets Tolbert's Gentleman of Swing (1938–40), and he had short stints with the Hot Lips Page big band, Leon Abbey, Benny Carter, and Chris Columbus (1944). But after World War II, he moved to South America, playing music for a time in Argentina and Brazil. Carl "Tatti" Smith has not been heard from since the 1950s.

Recommended CDs: with Count Basie: *1936–1938* (Classics 503), with Skeets Tolbert: *1931–1940* (Classics 978), *1940–1942* (Classics 993)

JABBO SMITH

· · · · · · · · · · · · ·

b. Dec. 24, 1908, Pembroke, GA, d. Jan. 16, 1991, New York, NY

Jabbo Smith was one of the most exciting trumpeters of all time. In 1929, Jabbo's only competition as the top trumpet star in jazz was Louis Armstrong. Smith was just 20 at the time, but his colorful style foreshadowed the later innovations of Roy Eldridge and challenged Armstrong's supremacy. And yet within two years, Smith was completely forgotten, never to fulfill his potential.

Born Cladys Smith (a cousin's name was Gladys), he gained the nickname of Jabbo while a teenager. Smith's father died when he was four, and at six his mother, who found it very difficult to work as well as raise her son, left Jabbo at the famed Jenkins' Orphanage in Charleston, South Carolina. While there, he learned both the trumpet and the trombone, touring with the notable orphanage band from the time he turned ten. "They taught everyone in the same room," Smith told me in 1981. "They really taught us a bit of each of the instruments. Trombone was my favorite. But since there were already several trombonists, they handed me a trumpet. I was always trying to get out of there. I ran away every time I got the chance. Once

I ran away and played in a band with Eagle Eye Shields in Jacksonville; I was 12 or 13. I played with that group for a few months, until they caught me."

In 1925, when he was 16, Jabbo Smith left the orphanage permanently. "I snuck myself out. I went to Philadelphia, where my sister lived, and joined Harry Marsh's band. Later I went to Atlantic City and joined the band led by my classmate Gus Aiken, and soon afterward I bumped into Charlie Johnson." Jabbo Smith became one of the many star soloists featured with Charlie Johnson's Paradise Ten, staying with the highly rated unit from the autumn of 1925 into early 1928. Of the six titles recorded with Johnson during this period, Smith takes exciting (and typically death-defying) solos on "Charleston Is the Best Dance After All," "Paradise Wobble," and "You Ain't the One." He also appeared on record with singer Eva Taylor, Perry Bradford's Georgia Strutters, and even Duke Ellington, subbing for Bubber Miley on November 3, 1927. His solos on the two takes of "Black and Tan Fantasy" impressed Ellington enough to offer the 19-year-old a job with his orchestra. But in a major error of judgment (one of several he would make), Jabbo turned Duke down, feeling that he would be underpaid!

As it turned out, Jabbo Smith was soon fired from Charlie Johnson's band due to his constant tardiness and excessive drinking. He joined the pit orchestra of the show *Keep Shuf-flin'* and, with pianist James P. Johnson, Fats Waller (on organ), and Garvin Bushell's reeds, recorded four titles on March 27, 1928, as the Louisiana Sugar Babes, that are most notable for their restraint and lyricism. After the show folded in Chicago in November 1928, Smith worked with many local bands, including those of Carroll Dickerson, Sammy Stewart, Earl Hines, Erskine Tate, Charles Elgar, and Tiny Parham. He also engaged in a few legendary trumpet battles with Louis Armstrong, always losing but gaining some points for his bravado and advanced ideas.

After Jabbo dominated a pair of records with banjoist Ikey Robinson's quintet in January 1929 ("Ready Hokum" and "Got Butter on It"), he began to record for Brunswick as the leader of the Rhythm Aces; it was hoped that his record sales would compete favorably with Louis Armstrong's. Nineteen selections were recorded by Jabbo, and the music was quite passionate and advanced for the time. "I used pretty much the same band that Ikey did: Omer Simeon on reeds, Lawson Buford on tuba, Cassino Simpson on piano, and Ikey himself on banjo. The trouble now is that many years later I can hear each of my mistakes and can always think of ways I could have played my solos better!"

Jabbo Smith at 20 was an erratic but very exciting trumpeter, overreaching at times and often on the edge of losing control, but far ahead of most of his contemporaries in terms of range, speed, and complexity of ideas. He was also a superior vocalist (whether scatting or singing the words of "Till Times Get Better") and takes a fine trombone solo on "Lina Blues." His most memorable trumpet playing takes place on "Till Times Get Better," the explosive "Jazz Battle," "Band Box Stomp," "Sweet and Low Blues" (Smith's very fast double-time runs behind Simeon's reading of the melody sound boppish), and "Decatur Street Tutti."

But instead of 1929 being one of Jabbo Smith's best early years, it would prove to be the peak of his career. The records did not sell well, and the advent of the Depression halted his recording career. In addition, a preoccupation with hard drinking coupled with the desire to stay in the Midwest led to Smith's anonymity and quick decline. In 1930 he started moving back and forth between Chicago and Milwaukee. "Milwaukee was a fine place. I played up there, got a steady gig, liked the city, and just chose to stay. I got married in 1932 and settled there for a long time." Although he was with Claude Hopkins' big band during 1936–38 (appearing on two disappointing record sessions) and recorded four selections at his own obscure date in 1938 (routine numbers with an octet), Jabbo Smith had missed his chance for stardom. He should have moved in 1930 to New York, where his impressive sight-reading abilities and exciting solo style might have led to fame or at least steady work. Instead, after appearing at the 1939 New York World's Fair with Sidney Bechet, he spent several years playing at a low-profile job in Newark, New Jersey. In 1944 Jabbo moved back to Milwaukee, where he led local groups on a part-time basis and worked at a day job with Avis Rent-a-Car for 13 years.

In 1961 Roy Eldridge and pianist Sammy Price made a bet as to whether or not Jabbo Smith was still alive; Price lost. That same year, guitarist Marty Grosz and some amateur musicians persuaded Jabbo (then 52) to rehearse with them. In 1984, two LPs put out by Jazz Art Productions (*Hidden Treasure, Vols. 1 and 2*) consist of material from those sessions. The streaky records show that if Jabbo had had the desire and the discipline, it still might not have been impossible for him to make a comeback. Unfortunately, it came to nothing. Ten years later Smith appeared at a traditional jazz festival in Holland, playing trombone, and in the mid-1970s he toured and recorded with European bands, but it was much too late. His trumpet playing sounded feeble and weak. Jabbo sang and played in the musical show *One Mo' Time* during 1979–82 but gave up playing trumpet after 1983. He continued singing on an irregular basis (including a week with the Mel Lewis Orchestra at the Village Vanguard and at a few festivals in 1986–87 with Don Cherry's quintet), until strokes made him inactive.

Instead of being recognized as one of jazz's all-time greats, Jabbo Smith is a forgotten legend today. But he was great when he was 20!

Recommended CDs: *1929–1938* (Challenge 79013)

Recommended Reading: *American Musicians II* by Whitney Balliett (Oxford University Press, 1996), *Voices of the Jazz Age* by Chip Deffaa (University of Illinois Press, 1990)

JOE SMITH
● ● ● ● ● ● ● ● ● ●

b. June 28, 1902, Ripley, Ohio, d. Dec. 2, 1937, New York, NY

During an era when jazz trumpeters were often evaluated by how "hot" they played, Joe Smith could be said to have been one of the first "cool" brassmen. He started a mini-movement that would include Arthur Whetsol and Harold "Shorty" Baker (with Duke Ellington), Bobby Hackett, Miles Davis, Chet Baker, and even Rick Braun (although it is doubtful that the last has ever heard of Joe Smith!). Smith's lyrical playing was very highly rated, as was his mellow tone, and he was Bessie Smith's favorite trumpeter, partly because he complemented her voice rather than competing with her. Smith also had a very different sound on the plunger than most trumpeters, playing it in a sweet and introverted fashion.

Smith's father led a brass band in Cincinnati, and all six of Joe's brothers played trumpet; most famous was Russell Smith, who worked for years playing lead with Fletcher Henderson. Joe Smith was taught trumpet by his father, played locally, and visited New York for the first time in 1920. After working a bit in Pittsburgh, in January 1922 he went to Chicago to join the Black Swan Jazz Masters, a combo led by Fletcher Henderson that was accompanying Ethel Waters. In July he left the show, touring with Mamie Smith (1922–23), playing with Billy Paige's Broadway Syncopators, and becoming a greatly in-demand sideman for recordings, particularly for blues singers. In the 1920s (mostly 1922–27), Smith accompanied such blues-oriented performers as Andrew Copeland, Ida Cox, Ethel Finnie, Rosa Henderson, Alberta Hunter, Maggie Jones, Ozie McPherson, Hazel Meyers, Josie Miles, Julia Moody, Ma Rainey (an eight-song session in 1926), Clara Smith, Mamie Smith, Trixie Smith, Mary Straine, Evelyn Thompson, and Ethel Waters (21 selections). Smith gained his greatest fame in this context for the 19 songs that he recorded with Bessie Smith during 1924–27, including such classics as "Cake Walkin' Babies from Home," "The Yellow Dog Blues," "At the Christmas Ball," "Young Woman's Blues," "Muddy Water," and "Send Me to the 'Lectric Chair."

After spending much of 1924 working with the Noble Sissle/Eubie Blake show *The Chocolate Dandies*, Smith became a regular member of Fletcher Henderson's orchestra in April 1925. He had recorded with Henderson as early as 1921 and was on most of the sessions of 1923 into early '24. When he first officially joined Henderson in 1925, Smith offered an alternate, cooler solo style to that of Louis Armstrong. He received his share of solo space during the next few years, despite the presence of Tommy Ladnier and Bobby Stark, and he was a fixture with the orchestra (other than during brief periods off) until October 1928.

After leaving Henderson, Smith worked with violinist Allie Ross, spent over a year with McKinney's Cotton Pickers (summer 1929 until November 1930), rejoined Henderson for a couple of months, played with Kaiser Marshall's band, and then had a second stint with McKinney's Cotton Pickers (1931–32). Unfortunately, his health began to fail in 1932. Smith moved to Kansas City, worked a little with Bennie Moten and Clarence Love, and in 1933 tried to play a job with Fletcher Henderson in Detroit but became seriously ill and had to stop. Joe Smith, the unofficial founder of "cool jazz," spent his last few years in a sanatorium in New York, where he died in 1937 from paresis at the age of 35.

Recommended CDs: with Fletcher Henderson: *1925–1926* (Classics 610), *1926–27* (Classics 597), *1927* (Classics 580), with Bessie Smith: *The Complete Recordings, Vol. 3* (Columbia/Legacy 47474)

KEITH SMITH
• • • • • • • • • • • •

b. Mar. 19, 1940, London, England

Nicknamed "Mr. Hefty Jazz," Keith Smith is a solid Dixieland player with strong technical skills and a real feeling for the music. He became a professional in 1957, playing with the Powder Mill Lane Stompers, the San Jacinto Jazz Band, Mickey Ashman, and Bobby Micklebrugh's Confederates. Smith founded the Climax Jazz Band, with whom he first recorded in 1963. In 1964 he visited the United States for the initial time, performing in New Orleans with George Lewis, in California with Barney Bigard, in Chicago with Lil Harden Armstrong, and in New York with Eddie Condon, Tony Parenti, Kenny Davern, and Dick Wellstood. Smith topped off that productive trip by recording with Capt. John Handy.

Having made a lot of friends, Smith had many opportunities to play with New Orleans jazz veterans whenever they visited Europe, including Alvin Alcorn, Jimmy Archey, Darnell Howard, and Pops Foster. He toured Europe in 1966 with the New Orleans All-Stars and worked with Papa Bue's Viking Jazz Band during 1972–75, visiting the Far East.

In 1975 Smith formed the band Hefty Jazz and started a record label with the same name. In 1981 he fronted the Louis Armstrong All-Stars (using five of the former All-Stars) for 100 concerts in Europe, and in 1984 he produced *Stardust Road*, which celebrated Hoagy Carmichael's music and starred Georgie Fame. A flexible player in the New Orleans idiom, Keith Smith has recorded through the years for '77,' GHB, Philips, Flutegroove, Jazzology, and his Hefty Jazz label.

Recommended CDs: *Keith Smith/Jimmy Archey* (GHB 217)

LPs to Search For: *Minstreal Man* ('77' 12/9), *Toronto '66* ('77' 12/30), *Ball of Fire* (Hefty Jazz 103), *Keith Smith's Hefty Jazz* (Jazzology 145), with Dick Wellstood: *Some Hefty Cats* (Hefty Jazz 100)

LOUIS SMITH
• • • • • • • • • • • •

b. May 20, 1931, Memphis, TN

I n 1958, Louis Smith was one of the most promising trumpeters in jazz, but he chose to be an educator rather than risk living the jazz life. Smith had studied music at Tennessee State University, toured with the Tennessee State Collegians, and played in an Army band (1954–55). He became a teacher at Booker T. Washington high school in Atlanta, playing in clubs in his spare time. Smith recorded with Kenny Burrell in 1956 (*Swingin'*). In 1958 the trumpeter led two albums (including one in which altoist Cannonball Adderley used the pseudonym of "Buckshot la Fonque") and appeared on Burrell's Blue Lights. He also toured with the Horace Silver Quintet for three months.

However, the 27-year-old turned his back on active performing, teaching at the University of Michigan and later in the Ann Arbor public school system. Other than a 1960 album with the Young Men from Memphis, he did not appear on records again until 1978. Smith (then 47) hooked up with the Steeplechase label, recording two albums during 1978–79. Ten more years passed before he appeared as a sideman on an album by pianist Mickey Tucker (*Sweet Lotus Lips*). He once again signed up with Steeplechase, and in the 1990s Smith (who was still in his musical prime) led at least six albums for the Danish company. It is a pity that Louis Smith was not active in the 1960s, when he might have made his biggest impact. But since he is still around (unlike some of his contemporaries), perhaps he made the right decision after all!

Recommended CDs: *Here Comes Louis Smith* (Blue Note 52438), *Just Friends* (Steeplechase

333196), *Ballads for Lulu* (Steeplechase 31268), *The Bopsmith* (Steeplechase 51489), with Kenny Burrell: *Blue Lights, Vols. 1 and 2* (Blue Note 57184)

LPs to Search For: *Smithville* (Blue Note 1594)

WADADA LEO SMITH

b. Dec. 18, 1941, Leland, MS

One of the most intriguing of all the avant-garde trumpeters, Wadada Leo Smith is expert at contrasting silence with sound in dramatic fashion. Where Don Cherry, Lester Bowie, and Bobby Bradford at times had elements of their style that were fairly accessible, Smith's dry, introverted playing has generally been more forbidding.

After brief periods playing drums, mellophone, and French horn, Smith settled on the trumpet. He worked early on with blues and R&B bands, served in the military, and in 1967 moved to Chicago, where he became a member of the Association for the Advancement of Creative Musicians (AACM). By then Smith was already a very advanced improviser with original ideas of his own. He worked with Roscoe Mitchell and the Creative Construction Co. (a unique trio with multireedist Anthony Braxton and violinist Leroy Jenkins). Smith made a documentary film (*See the Music*) with altoist Marion Brown in 1970, toured Europe with Henry Threadgill, and started the Cabell label in 1971 after moving to New Haven, Connecticut. His first release for Cabell (*Creative Music*) featured him as the only performer, playing trumpet, flugelhorn, wooden flute, harmonica, bells, and zither.

Smith formed his band New Dalta Ahkri around that era, using that name for his future groups. Among his collaborators during the next 20 years were Anthony Braxton (1976), Anthony Davis, Oliver Lake, Derek Bailey (when he visited England in 1977), Bobby Naughton, Dwight Andrews, Wes Brown, Vinny Golia, and other top avant-garde players, including the Bill Smith Trio (with whom he recorded when he visited Canada in 1983).

After becoming a Rastafarian in the 1980s, he changed his name to Wadada Leo Smith. He moved to the Los Angeles area in 1993 to become a full-time educator at Cal Arts but still plays uncompromising music. During his career thus far, Wadada Leo Smith has recorded as a leader for Freedom, Kabell, Moers, ECM, Nessa, FMP, Black Saint, Nessa, Sackville, Tzadik, 9 Winds, and Wobbly Rail.

Recommended CDs: *Rastafari* (Sackville 3030), *Go in Numbers* (Black Saint 120053), *Prataksis* (9 Winds 199), with Anthony Braxton: *Three Compositions of New Jazz* (Delmark 415), with Henry Kaiser: *Yo, Miles!* (Shanachie 5046), with John Lindberg: *A Tree Frog Tonality* (Between the Lines 008)

LPs to Search For: *Creative Music* (Kabell 1), *The Mass on the World* (Moers 1060), *Divine Love* (ECM 1143), *Spirit Catcher* (Nessa 19)

PAUL SMOKER

. . . .

b. 1941, Muncie, IN

An adventurous improviser, Paul Smoker has had some diverse musical experiences throughout his career. He grew up in Davenport, Iowa (Bix Beiderbecke's home town), started on piano when he was six, and switched to trumpet at ten, with Harry James as his early inspiration. He worked with the legendary pianist Dodo Marmarosa in the early 1960s, took lessons from Doc Severinsen in 1964, and studied at the University of Iowa. Smoker taught at the University of Wisconsin, Oshkosh (1968–71), the University of Northern Iowa (1975–76), and Coe College (1976–90). As a musician, he started becoming interested in avant-garde jazz by the late 1970s. Smoker's first record as a leader (1984's *QB*) used Anthony Braxton in his quartet. He has worked with Braxton off and on since then and has been a member of both Joint Venture and Phil Haynes' 4 Horns & What? Along the way, Smoker also played with Art Pepper, Frank Rosolino, and Dave Liebman in addition to performing modern classical music.

In 1990 Paul Smoker moved to Rochester, New York, and finally became a full-time musician. He has thus far led albums for Alvas, Sound Aspects, Hat Art, 9 Winds, and most recently CIMP.

Recommended CDs: *Genuine Fables* (Hat Art 6126), *Halloween '96* (CIMP 129), *Standard Deviation* (CIMP 186), with Fonda-Stevens Group: *Live at the Bunker* (Leo 301)

LPs to Search For: *QB* (Alvas 101), *Mississippi River Rat* (Sound Aspects 006), *Alone* (Sound Aspects 018), *Come Rain or Come Shine* (Sound Aspects 024)

VALAIDA SNOW

. . . .

b. June 2, 1900, Chattanooga, TN, d. May 30, 1956, New York, NY

Valaida Snow had a unique life, one that was almost idyllic (particularly for a black woman during the era), until tragedy struck. She was a superior trumpeter (certainly the finest female player of the swing era), an excellent singer, a skilled arranger, and an important entertainer. Valaida (her sisters were named Lavaida and Alvaida!) learned music from her mother, who was a music teacher. At 15 she started playing trumpet in public, and by the early 1920s Snow was appearing in shows, often as the star, due to her appeal as a singer, dancer, and trumpeter. In 1924 she was featured in the Noble Sissle/Eubie Blake musical *In Bamville* (which later became known as *The Chocolate Dandies*).

Valaida first ventured overseas in 1926, when she worked with Jack Carter's band in Shanghai. Two years later she was the headliner at Chicago's Sunset Café during a period when Louis Armstrong and Earl Hines also performed at the venue. In 1929 she traveled abroad again, performing in the Soviet Union, the Middle East, and Europe.

In the early 1930s Valaida starred in the Sissle/Blake revue *Rhapsody in Black*. She recorded with the Washboard Rhythm Kings in 1932, worked in the Grand Terrace Revue in

Glamorous and multi-talented, Valaida Snow was a big hit overseas in the 1930s.

Chicago with Earl Hines the following year, appeared in the Blackbirds of 1934 in England, recorded with Noble Sissle (1935), and then spent most of the rest of the 1930s overseas, recording as a leader in London (1935–37), Stockholm, and Copenhagen (1939–40). Up to that point, it had been quite a life.

Valaida was quite popular in Europe, and, with the outbreak of World War II, she was foolish enough to think that she was safe. But she was arrested in Denmark in 1941 and spent two horrifying years in a concentration camp before being released on a prisoner exchange. On returning to the United States, both her physical state and her spirit were quite weak. She partly recovered (at least physically) and resumed her career, recording 14 songs during 1945–46. Valaida Snow worked into the mid-1950s (although recording only six additional numbers: four in 1950 and two in 1953) but did not regain her former popularity. She died in 1956, two days shy of her 56th birthday, suffering a massive cerebral hemorrhage after playing at the Palace Theater in New York.

Recommended CDs: *Queen of Trumpet and Song* (DRG 8455)

LPs to Search For: *Hot Snow* (Rosetta 1305)

Film Appearances: *L'alibi* (1936), *Pieges* (1939)

LEW SOLOFF

• • • • • • • • • • •

b. Feb. 20, 1944, New York, NY

A powerful high-note trumpeter, Lew Soloff is also a superb soloist. Soloff grew up in Lakewood, New Jersey, played piano for eight years (starting when he was five), and began on the trumpet at the age of ten. He started his career playing with show bands in the Catskills during 1958–65, and attended the Eastman School of Music during 1961–65. Soloff has been associated with many top musicians throughout his productive career. He was a member of the Gil Evans Orchestra from 1966 until Evans' death in 1988, played with Blood, Sweat and Tears during its prime years (1968–73), and worked with the big bands of Thad Jones/Mel Lewis, Carla Bley, and George Gruntz. Among his many other gigs are those with Machito, Tito Puente, the Joe Henderson/Kenny Dorham big band, Clark Terry, Slide Hampton, the Manhattan Jazz Quintet (in the 1980s), Ray Anderson's Pocket Brass Band, and at various times both the Lincoln Center Jazz Orchestra and the Carnegie Hall Jazz Band. This does not count his recordings with the likes of Sonny Stitt, Stanley Turrentine, George Russell, Clark Terry, Mongo Santamaria, Hilton Ruiz, Jimmy Heath, and nearly all of the names that have been mentioned.

Despite his prominence in the jazz world, Lew Soloff (who had led earlier dates in Japan reissued on *Evidence*) did not get to record his first American CD as a leader until *With a Song in My Heart* in 1999.

Recommended CDs: *But Beautiful* (Evidence 22005), *Trumpet Legacy* (Milestone 9286), *With a Song in My Heart* (Milestone 9290), with Ray Anderson: *Don't Mow Your Lawn* (Enja 8070), *Where Home Is* (Enja 9366), with Gil Evans: *There Comes a Time* (Bluebird 5783), *Plays the Music of Jimi Hendrix* (Bluebird 8401), *Bud and Bird* (Projazz 671), *Farewell* (Projazz 680), with the Manhattan Jazz Quintet: *Manteca* (Evidence 22111), *My Favorite Things* (Projazz 648), *Reunion* (Sweet Basil 7301)

Videos to Get: *Gil Evans and His Orchestra* (1987; View Video)

HERBIE SPANIER

b. Dec. 25, 1928, Cupar, Saskatchewan, Canada

Herbie Spanier has long been a top bop-oriented trumpeter from Canada. Mostly self-taught, Herbie Spanier began his career leading the Boptet in 1948. He spent time playing in Chicago (1949–50), Toronto (1950–54), New York City (1954), Montreal (1956–58), Los Angeles (1958–59), and back in Montreal, eventually settling in Toronto. Spanier played with Paul Bley (1954–55 and 1958–59), the Claude Thornhill Orchestra, and Hal McIntyre. In Canada, Herbie Spanier has worked with dance bands, the CBC orchestras, Nimmons 'n Nine Plus Six (1971–80), and his own groups.

Recommended CDs: *Anthology 1962–93* (Justin Time 55-2), *Anthology Vol. 2 1969–94* (Justin Time 61-2)

Recommended Reading: *Jazz in Canada: Fourteen Lives* by Mark Miller (Nightwood Editions, 1988)

MUGGSY SPANIER

b. Nov. 9, 1906, Chicago, IL, d. Feb. 12, 1967, Sausalito, CA

Predictable but always enthusiastic, Francis "Muggsy" Spanier was a popular Dixieland player for many years. His first instrument was drums, before he switched permanently to the cornet at 13. Within two years, Spanier was a professional. In the 1920s he played in Chicago with Elmer Schoebel (1921), Sig Meyers (1922–24), Charlie Straight, Charles Pierce, Floyd Town (1925–28), and Ray Miller. Influenced primarily by King Oliver (along with touches of Louis Armstrong), Spanier had his own sound by the time he made his earliest recordings with the Bucktown Five in 1924.

Spanier spent seven years (1929–36) giving some credibility (along with trombonist George Brunies) to the cornball music of singer-clarinetist Ted Lewis. But whatever the merits of the job, it saw Muggsy through the worst years of the Depression. Spanier was next a featured soloist with Ben Pollack's big band (1936–38) but then became seriously ill in January 1938. After he recovered, he thanked the doctors at the Touro Hospital by naming a blues after them ("Relaxin' at the Touro"). In 1939, Spanier formed his Ragtimers, a four-horn, eight-piece Dixieland band that recorded 16 selections (dubbed later on "The Great 16"), which would inspire the Dixieland revival movement a few years later, including classic versions of "Big Butter and Egg Man," "I Wish I Could Shimmy Like My Sister Kate," and "Mandy, Make Up Your Mind." As it turned out, the group was formed a little too early (swing was still very much king at the time), and Spanier could not find enough work for the Ragtimers to survive.

The cornetist joined Bob Crosby's orchestra (1940–41) and then led a similar big band during 1941–43, recording eight titles before breaking up. By 1944, Dixieland was becoming quite popular. Spanier was heard in freewheeling combos for the next 20 years, usually as a leader, except when guesting with Eddie Condon, during a few months in 1944–45 when he was working with Miff Mole, and for a period in the 1950s when he was playing in San Francisco with Earl Hines. Muggsy Spanier, whose final record as a leader was a 1962 set that found him temporarily back with a big band, saw no reason to change his personal style, and he played hard-charging Dixieland until bad health in 1964 forced his retirement.

Recommended CDs: *1939–1942* (Classics 709), *Manhattan Masters 1945* (Storyville 6051)

LPs to Search For: *Muggsy Spanier 1924–1928* (Retrieval 108), *Relaxin' at the Touro* (Jazzology 115), *Rare Custom 45's* (IAJRC 42), *Columbia, the Gem of the Ocean* (Mobile Fidelity 857)

Recommended Reading: *The Lonesome Road* by Bert Whyatt (Jazzology Press, 1995)

Film Appearances: with Ted Lewis: *Is Everybody Happy?* (1929) and *Here Comes the Band* (1935), with Bob Crosby: *Sis Hopkins* (1941)

CHARLIE SPIVAK

• • • • • • • • • • • • • • • •

b. Feb. 17, 1907, Kiev, Ukraine, d. Mar. 1, 1982, Greenville, SC

Charlie Spivak was not really a jazz soloist, but he was admired for his pretty tone, which uplifted ensembles and was particularly memorable on ballads. Born in the Ukraine, Spivak moved with his family to the United States as a child, growing up in New Haven, Connecticut, and starting on the trumpet when he was ten. He was a member of Paul Specht's dance orchestra during 1924–31 and kept quite busy during the Depression, working with the big bands of Ben Pollack (1931–34), the Dorsey Brothers (1934–35), and Ray Noble (1935). During 1936–37 Spivak worked in the studios and became the highest-paid studio musician in New York. During 1937–39 he was back with big bands, those of Bob Crosby, Tommy Dorsey, and Jack Teagarden. Rarely ever taking solos, Spivak was greatly valued for his professionalism and the lift that he gave trumpet sections.

In November 1939 Glenn Miller financed Charlie Spivak's first orchestra. That particular band did not catch on, but a year later he had much greater success with a new ensemble. Emphasizing ballads and his tone (he was billed as "the sweetest horn in the world"), the Charlie Spivak Orchestra sometimes was quite capable of playing credible swing, particularly in the mid-1940s, when its personnel included altoist Willie Smith. Among Spivak's better recordings were "Autumn Nocturne," "Star Dreams," and his theme, "Let's Go Home."

Spivak's big band lasted long after the end of the swing era, until 1959. Charlie Spivak continued leading big bands on a part-time basis in Florida, Las Vegas, and finally at Ye Olde Fireplace in Greenville, South Carolina, for many years, recording as late as 1981.

Recommended CDs: *For Sentimental Reasons* (Vintage Jazz Classics 1041), *Live Broadcast Air-Checks* (Jazz Hour 1054)

LPs to Search For: *1943–1946* (Hindsight 105)

GREGG STAFFORD

b. 1954, New Orleans, LA

An impressive trad trumpeter, Gregg Stafford is one of the few African Americans from his generation who is helping to keep the older New Orleans style alive. A professional since he started playing with local brass bands as a teenager, Gregg Stafford has thus far led four CDs, including a set that features a reunion by Big Bill Bissonnette's Easy Riders Jazz Band.

Recommended CDs: *That Man from New Orleans* (Jazz Crusade 3033/4), *And the Easy Riders Jazz Band* (Jazz Crusade 3048), *Streets of the City* (Jazz Crusade 3053), *Dance at the Dew Drop* (GHB 401)

TERELL STAFFORD

b. Nov. 25, 1966, Miami, FL

An excellent hard bop trumpeter, Terell Stafford has been increasingly in demand for straightahead sessions during the past decade. Stafford played viola when he was 11, guitar at 12, and trumpet the following year. His first inspiration was Chuck Mangione (who was very popular at that time) before he became influenced by Clifford Brown and Lee Morgan. Stafford, who grew up in Chicago and Silver Springs, Maryland, gained a degree in music education from the University of Maryland in 1988 and studied at Rutgers during 1988–91.

Associated with the Young Lions movement that became prominent after Wynton Marsalis rose to fame, the trumpeter gained some recognition for his playing and recording with Bobby Watson's Horizon (1991–95). Since then, Stafford has worked with Victor Lewis, Kenny Barron, McCoy Tyner's Latin All-Stars, the Carnegie Hall Jazz Band, Cedar Walton, Sadao Watanabe, Herbie Mann, Billy Taylor, the Lincoln Center Jazz Orchestra, the Mingus Big Band, the Vanguard Jazz Orchestra, and the Clayton Brothers, among others. Terell Stafford, who teaches at Temple University and is scheduled in the fall of 2001 to teach at Juilliard, has led sessions for Candid and Nagel-Heyer.

Recommended CDs: *Terrell Stafford* (Candid 79702), *Centripetal Force* (Candid 79718), *Fields of Gold* (Nagel-Heyer 2005), with the Clayton Brothers: *Siblingity* (Qwest/Warner Bros. 47813), with Bobby Watson: *Present Tense* (Columbia 32400)

MARVIN STAMM

b. May 23, 1939, Memphis, TN

A valuable sideman for decades, Marvin Stamm is underrated by the jazz public but well respected by his fellow jazz musicians. He started playing trumpet when he was 12 (initially attracted to the instrument when he heard Clyde McCoy's recording of "Sugar Blues") and graduated from North Texas State University in 1961. Stamm has worked with

Terrell Stafford helps keep the hard bop tradition alive in the 21st century.

quite a few major big bands in his career, including Stan Kenton (1961–62), Woody Herman (1965–66), Thad Jones/Mel Lewis (1966–72), Duke Pearson (1968–72), Bob Mintzer (1984), the American Jazz Orchestra, and the George Gruntz Concert Jazz Band (starting in 1987). Stamm also worked with Benny Goodman (1974–75) but has actually spent most of his career since 1966 as a top New York studio musician.

Although Marvin Stamm has been a strong asset on many record dates, he is heard at his best on his own sessions, recording as a leader for Verve (1968), Palo Alto (1983), and more recently Music Masters.

Recommended CDs: *Bop Boy* (Music Masters 65065), *Mystery Man* (Music Masters 65085)

LPs to Search For: *Machinations* (Verve 8759)

Videos to Get: *Frank Rosolino Quartet/Stan Kenton* (1962; Shanachie 6311)

TOMASZ STANKO

. . . .

b. July 11, 1942, Rzeszow, Poland

A lyrical and moody soloist who explores avant-garde jazz, Tomasz Stanko has never been shy to take chances. He studied violin and piano before switching to trumpet when he was 16. Stanko formed the Jazz Darings (which included pianist Adam Makowicz) in 1962, and it ranks as one of the first European jazz groups influenced by Ornette Coleman. Stanko was associated with pianist-composer Krzystof Komeda during 1963–67 and led a quintet that featured the legendary if short-lived Zbigniew Seifert on alto and violin (1968–73).

Stanko co-led a quartet with drummer Edward Vesala, performed with the Global Unity Orchestra (1970), and worked with violinist Michal Urbaniak. In the 1980s he started performing in the West fairly often, including with such adventurous Americans as Chico Freeman, Jack DeJohnette, Rufus Reid, Lester Bowie, and David Murray. Tomasz Stanko, who played with Cecil Taylor's big band in 1984, has continued playing fresh and vital music (usually with his own groups) up to the current time, recording for ECM.

Recommended CDs: *The Montreux Performance* (ITM 1423), *Twet* (Power Bros. 33860), *Matka Joanna* (ECM 1544), *Music of Krzystof Komeda* (ECM 1636), *From the Green Hill* (ECM 1680), with Gary Peacock: *Voice from the Past* (ECM 1210), with Cecil Taylor: *Segments II Winged Serpent* (Black Saint 121089)

LPs to Search For: *Music for K* (Muza 607), *Purple Sun* (Calig 30610), *Balladyna* (ECM 1071)

BILL STAPLETON

. . . .

b. May 4, 1945, Blue Island, IL, d. 1984

B ill Stapleton was a fine hard bop trumpeter. He studied at North Texas State University (1963–67 and 1971) and became best known for his playing and arranging with Woody Herman (1972–74). He arranged five of the pieces on Herman's *Giant Steps* album and took solos on several of Herman's big band records during the period. Bill Stapleton also worked with Bill Holman in Los Angeles (1974–75) and performed with Woody Herman at the 1981 Concord Jazz Festival.

Recommended CDs: with Woody Herman: *The Raven Speaks* (Original Jazz Classics 663), *Giant Steps* (Original Jazz Classics 344)

LPs to Search For: with Alan Broadbent: *Palette* (Granite 7901)

BOBBY STARK

. . . .

b. Jan. 6, 1906, New York, NY, d. Dec. 29, 1945, New York, NY

B obby Stark was one of the greatest trumpeters that no one has ever heard of. His playing on Fletcher Henderson's 1928 version of "King Porter Stomp" (and its remakes in 1932 and 1933) topped the classic Bunny Berigan improvisation with Benny Goodman in 1935 that became so famous, but few listeners in the swing era even knew about Henderson's earlier recordings. And, although Stark was well featured with Henderson, he was underutilized and largely overshadowed while with Chick Webb's orchestra.

Stark began playing the alto horn when he was 15 and studied piano and reed instruments before switching to trumpet. He was a professional by late 1925 and had short associations with many bands, including those led by Edgar Dowell, Leon Abbey, Duncan Mayers, Bobbie Brown, Bobby Lee, Billy Butler, and Charlie Turner, plus the early McKinney's Cotton Pickers and Chick Webb's first group (1926–27). Stark's most important association was with Fletcher Henderson's orchestra, where he was a featured soloist from November 1927 into mid-1934 (other than for a short period with Elmer Snowden in 1932). Stark replaced Tommy Ladnier in Henderson's band and sat in the trumpet section next to Russell Smith, Rex Stewart, and later on Henry "Red" Allen. Although a slight Louis Armstrong influence can be heard, Stark basically had his own crisp sound and an inventive improvising style, being featured for solo choruses on many of Henderson's dates, holding his own with Coleman Hawkins and Benny Carter. Stark can also be heard on sessions by the Chocolate Dandies (1930) and Horace Henderson (1933).

Stark never became a big name despite his consistent and heated solos. After leaving Henderson, he was with Chick Webb's orchestra during 1934–39. But Taft Jordan (who had a similar style) was the main trumpet soloist, and Stark was barely heard from. He stayed with Webb until the drummer's death and was part of the orchestra for a year (1939–40) when it was fronted by Ella Fitzgerald. After a period freelancing, Stark was in the Army during 1942–43, gigged with Garvin Bushell and Benny Morton in 1944, and recorded with Helen Humes before dying prematurely at the age of 39. Perhaps if he had had the business sense to try to form his own band in 1934 rather than joining Webb, Bobby Stark would be a household name in jazz today. He certainly had the talent.

Recommended CDs: with Fletcher Henderson: *1927* (Classics 580), *1927–1931* (Classics 572), *1931* (Classics 555), *1931–1932* (Classics 546), *1932–1934* (Classics 535)

TOMMY STEVENSON

. . . .

b. 1914, d. Oct. 1944, New York, NY

Tommy Stevenson was one of the first important high-note trumpeters. His playing with Jimmie Lunceford during 1933–35 is the reason he is included in this book. Little is known about his early life or even where he was born. While with Lunceford, Stevenson hit notes that were higher than any played on record previously; check him out at the conclusion of "Rhythm Is Our Business." For unknown reasons, he left Lunceford in March 1935. Although he played and recorded with the big bands of Blanche Calloway (1935–36), Don Redman (1939–40), Coleman Hawkins, and Lucky Millinder (in addition to working with Slim Gaillard), Stevenson did not receive any real solo space, mostly playing lead. Tommy Stevenson died suddenly of lobar pneumonia at the age of 30 while working with the Cootie Williams big band.

Recommended CDs: with Jimmie Lunceford: *Vol. 1 1927–1934* (Masters of Jazz 12), *1934* (Masters of Jazz 18)

MICHAEL "PATCHES" STEWART

b. July 31, 1955, New Orleans, LA

Michael "Patches" Stewart always considered Miles Davis to be one of his main influences ("He was always reinventing himself"), and thus far he is best known for filling in the role of Davis with Marcus Miller's band, a group based closely on Miles' last band.

"Growing up in New Orleans, there was jazz everywhere, in the streets, on the radio, TV. When I was ten, the junior high school band came to our school to perform for us, and one of the songs was 'Bugler's Holiday,' which featured three trumpeters. When I heard that music, something clicked inside of me and I knew I wanted to do that." In junior high Stewart signed up to play trumpet but, because the music department was out of trumpets, he started on French horn for a year before switching. "I made a youthful decision to turn down scholarships I was offered to Berklee and other local universities in favor of 'real world' experience." Stewart, who made his recording debut at 16 on Patti LaBelle's hit record of "Lady Marmalade," gained experience in studio and session work with R&B and pop groups, including the Brothers Johnson (1979–80), Quincy Jones (1981–82), David Sanborn, Lenny White, George Duke, and Rickie Lee Jones, among others. He was a member of Al Jarreau's band for nearly eight years (1983–90).

When in his earlier days he wore a pair of bell bottom pants with patches all over them, Stewart gained the nickname of "Patches," a name he has happily kept ever since. He first joined Marcus Miller's group in 1989, a band that became an unofficial Miles Davis memorial group after Davis' death in 1991. Michael "Patches" Stewart has thus far led two CDs for Hip Bop: the acoustic *Blue Patches* and the electric *Penetration*. "I love jazz, and keeping it alive is the best contribution I can make. I'm proud to be associated with jazz."

Recommended CDs: *Blue Patches* (Hip Bop 8016) *Penetration* (Hip Bop 8018), with Marcus Miller: *Sun Don't Lie* (GRP 8908), *Tales* (PRA 60501), *When Summer Comes* (PRA 60201)

REX STEWART

b. Feb. 22, 1907, Philadelphia, PA, d. Sept. 7, 1967, Los Angeles, CA

Rex Stewart was a colorful and explosive cornetist, one whose half-valve technique was featured and celebrated by Duke Ellington on "Boy Meets Horn."

Stewart grew up near Washington, D.C., and originally played piano, violin, and alto horn before settling on cornet. He was a professional by the time he was 14, working on riverboats and touring with Ollie Blackwell's Jazz Clowns (1921). Stewart moved to New York by 1923, freelancing before playing regularly with Elmer Snowden (1925–26). He became a member of the Fletcher Henderson Orchestra in 1926. Although he sounds excellent on recordings, the 19-year-old did not feel up to sitting in a chair that two years earlier had been Louis Armstrong's. After a couple of months he departed, playing with Horace Henderson's Collegians and other lesser-known bands.

By 1928, Stewart felt more confident and he returned to Fletcher Henderson's big band, becoming one of the main soloists during 1928–30 and 1932–33, playing with Alex Jackson and McKinney's Cotton Pickers between those two Henderson stints. Stewart led a big band during 1933–34 and worked with Luis Russell (he stars on Russell's recording of "Old Man River"). In December 1934 he joined Duke Ellington's orchestra, staying for 11 years (other than for a few months in 1943). Stewart became famous during this period, appearing on countless records with Ellington (sharing the trumpet/cornet solo space with Cootie Williams and later Ray Nance) and also leading small-group sessions of his own (usually under Duke's supervision).

In December 1945, Stewart left Ellington. He put together a combo called the Rextet, went with them to Europe in October 1947, and stayed overseas until spring 1950, also working and recording in Australia along the way. Back in the United States, Stewart was frequently heard in Dixieland settings in the 1950s, along with some mainstream swing dates. He organized and recorded with the Fletcher Henderson Reunion Band in 1957–58 and was seen in prime form on the television special *The Sound of Jazz* (playing with Red Allen, Pee Wee Russell, and Coleman Hawkins). Stewart was featured at Eddie Condon's club during 1958–59, became a disc jockey, and wrote about jazz history. His articles appeared in magazines, his book *Jazz Masters of the Thirties* is a classic, and his autobiography, *Boy Meets Horn* (written with Claire Gordon and covering his life up until 1948), is also worth getting. Rex Stewart's trumpet chops declined during the 1960s, but he still played occasional concerts as late as 1966 and never lost his enthusiastic style.

Recommended CDs: *Rex Stewart and the Ellingtonians* (Original Jazz Classics 1710), *Trumpet Jive!* (Prestige 24119), *Late Date* (Simitar 56132), with Duke Ellington: *The Duke's Men, Vol. 1* (Columbia/Legacy 46905), *The Duke's Men, Vol. 2* (Columbia/Legacy 48835), *Great Ellington Units* (Bluebird 6751), with Fletcher Henderson: *1927* (Classics 580), *1927–31* (Classics 572), *1931* (Classics 555), *1931–32* (Classics 546)

LPs to Search For: *The Irrepressible Rex Stewart* (Jazzology 36)

Recommended Reading: *Jazz Masters of the Thirties* by Rex Stewart (Da Capo Press, 1972)

Film Appearances: *Rendez-Vous de Julliet* (1949)

Videos to Get: *The Sound of Jazz* (1957; Vintage Jazz Classics 2001)

DANNY STILES

* * * * * * * * * * * * *

d. Jan. 1, 1998, Orlando, FL

Danny Stiles is best remembered for his association with trombonist Bill Watrous. In the 1960s Stiles (an inventive straightahead trumpeter) was the contractor for Milt Lindsay (Merv Griffin's musical director) and was involved in a lot of studio work. When Watrous formed his Manhattan Refuge Orchestra in the early 1970s, Stiles was his main trumpet soloist (along with Dean Pratt), being featured on "Dichotomy," "Fourth Floor Walk-Up," "Dirty Dan," and "The Tiger of San Pedro." He also led three albums (with a quintet that costarred Watrous) for the Famous Door label. By the mid-1980s, Danny Stiles was becoming discouraged with his career and largely dropped out of sight. He eventually moved to Orlando, Florida, where on New Year's Day 1998 he committed suicide.

LPs to Search For: *In Tandem* (Famous Door 103), *One More Time* (Famous Door 112), *In Tandem into the '80s* (Famous Door 126), with Bill Watrous: *Manhattan Wildlife Refuge* (Columbia 33090), *The Tiger of San Pedro* (Columbia 33701)

IRV STOKES
• • • • • • • • • • •

b. Nov. 11, 1926, Greensboro, NC

Although he began playing in the late 1940s, it took nearly 50 years before Irv Stokes started gaining recognition as a fine swing trumpeter, and it was just in the nick of time.

He began private lessons on the trumpet when he was 12. After attending A&T College in his hometown of Greensboro, NC (1943–47), Stokes moved to New York, where he worked with the Mercer Ellington Orchestra (1948–49) and had a stint with Duke Ellington (1949–50). Stokes spent the next three decades playing steadily but without any fame, working with (among many others) Erskine Hawkins, Tiny Bradshaw, the Jimmie Lunceford ghost band, Andy Kirk (1953–56), Buddy Johnson's orchestra (1956–58), and the house band at the Apollo Theater and in the pit bands of Broadway shows.

Stokes was with the Thad Jones-Mel Lewis Orchestra (1978–79) and had solo space with Panama Francis' Savoy Sultans, Oliver Jackson (off and on during 1982–89), the Illinois Jacquet big band (1988–89, including their one recording), and the Count Basie Orchestra (1990). He also had bit parts in films and commercials. After working with the Statesmen of Jazz (1997–98), including touring Japan, Irv Stokes made an excellent CD for Arbors, only his second album as a leader. Unfortunately he suffered a serious stroke in August 1999 and has not played since.

Recommended CDs: *Just Friends* (Arbors 19199), with Lou Donaldson: *Man with a Horn* (Blue Note 21436), with Chuck Folds: *Remembering Doc Cheatham* (Arbors 19208), with Bobby Watson: *Year of the Rabbit* (New Note 1008)

LPs to Search For: *Broadway* (Black & Blue 33151), with Panama Francis: *The Savoy Sultans* (Classic Jazz 149), *Vol. II* (Classics Jazz 150)

FRED STONE
• • • • • • • • • • •

b. Sept. 9, 1935, Toronto, Ontario, Canada, d. Dec. 10, 1986, Toronto, Ontario, Canada

Fred Stone was a Canadian flugelhornist who impressed Duke Ellington. He started on trumpet at 12 and four years later was playing with his father's orchestra. Stone worked with the CBC Symphony Orchestra and was with Phil Nimmons' bands (1965–70) and the Rob McConnell Boss Brass (1968–70). He was a member of the Ron Collier Orchestra in 1967 when they recorded with Duke Ellington (*North of the Border*). Three years later, in 1970, Stone joined the Duke Ellington Orchestra in time to record *New Orleans Suite*; he can be heard soloing on "Aristocracy à la Jean Lafitte." After leaving Ellington, Fred Stone settled back in Toronto, where he led bands and worked in the studios and on television. He led only one record date in his life, an obscure sextet set in 1972 for the Canadian CBC label.

LPs to Search For: with Duke Ellington: *New Orleans Suite* (Atlantic 1580)

Recommended Reading: Boogie, Pete and the Senator by Mark Miller (Nightwood Editions, 1987)

RON STOUT

A versatile utility player, Ron Stout has been a fixture on the Los Angeles jazz scene during the past 15 years. Although he is sometimes buried in big bands without much feature space, he is actually a talented hard bop soloist. Ron Stout's most significant associations thus far have been with Woody Herman (1986–87), Horace Silver (1992–93), the Bill Holman Orchestra, and the Phil Norman Tentet. He has not yet had an opportunity to lead his own record date.

Recommended CDs: with Phil Norman: *Yesterday's Gardenias* (Sea Breeze 3029), *Live at the Lighthouse* (Sea Breeze 3040), with Horace Silver: *It's Got to Be Funky* (Columbia 53812), *Pencil Packin' Papa* (Columbia 64210)

BENNY STRICKLER

b. Jan. 9, 1917, Fayetteville, AK, d. Dec. 8, 1946, Fayetteville, AK

Benny Strickler is a lost legend in jazz history, a trad player who was just barely documented during his brief life. After playing locally in Arkansas, he moved to California in 1936. During the next few years he played with Ben Pollack, Joe Venuti, the Seger Ellis Brass Choir (with whom he made his recording debut), Vido Musso, and Wingy Manone's short-lived big band but made a major mistake by turning down a job with Artie Shaw. Strickler did get to tour with Bob Wills' Texas Playboys (1941–42) during the period that the Western swing violinist added a jazz horn section; Strickler helped get Danny Alguire in the band too.

When Bob Wills disbanded in August 1942, Strickler was offered a job with the wartime Yerba Buena Jazz Band; Lu Watters, Bob Scobey, Turk Murphy, and Wally Rose were all in the military at the time. Strickler appeared on a few radio broadcasts, and six titles were later issued. That is fortunate, because within a few weeks he was diagnosed with tuberculosis and had to stop playing altogether. Benny Strickler returned to Fayetteville, entered a sanatorium, and, although he had plans to make a comeback, died before his 30th birthday.

Box Set: with the Yerba Buena Jazz Band: *The Complete Good Time Jazz Recordings* (6 selections on the 4 CDs; Good Time Jazz 4409)

BYRON STRIPLING

b. Aug. 20, 1961, Atlanta, GA

A brilliant trumpeter who can play just like Louis Armstrong but is also quite credible performing hard bop, Byron Stripling has strong technical skills and a wide range. He studied at the Eastman School of Music (1979–83) and worked with the big bands of Clark Terry (1981), Lionel Hampton (1984), and Woody Herman (1985) before traveling the world with the Count Basie Orchestra (when it was directed by Thad Jones and Frank Foster) on and off during 1985–89. Stripling also played with the big bands of Buck Clayton and Dizzy Gillespie (1988), in the studios, and in classical settings. In 1987, after a worldwide search, he won the starring role of Louis Armstrong in the musical *Satchmo: America's Musical Legend.*

Stripling has appeared on many records as a lead trumpeter, but in the late 1990s he was finally being recognized as a potentially major soloist. He played with the GRP All-Star Big Band, the Lincoln Center Jazz Orchestra, and the Carnegie Hall Jazz Band, recording as a leader for Nagel-Heyer. Although Byron Stripling (who can also sound like Clifford Brown) does not want to be typecast as a Louis Armstrong-influenced New Orleans player, there are few things more exciting than hearing him perform "Ain't Misbehavin'" or "Struttin' with Some Barbecue" in Satch's style.

Recommended CDs: *Stripling Now!* (Nagel-Heyer 2002), *Trumpetblowingly Yours* (Nagel-Heyer 1010), with the New York All-Stars: *We Love You, Louis!* (Nagel-Heyer 029), *Play More Music of Louis Armstrong* (Nagel-Heyer 046)

DICK SUDHALTAR

b. Dec. 28, 1938, Boston, MA

E qually talented as a trumpeter/cornetist and as a jazz journalist, Dick Sudhaltar has certainly had a productive and multifaceted career. "My father was a jazz saxophonist who owned quite a few jazz records. Between the records, his playing, and the periodic visits to our homes of jazz stars (such as Bobby Hackett and Phil Napoleon), it would have been remarkable if I hadn't become interested in jazz." Sudhaltar had piano lessons as a child, and when he was 12 he heard Paul Whiteman's recordings of "San" and "When," which featured Bix Beiderbecke cornet solos. "Then and there I decided that I wanted to make a sound like that. With some persuasion, my parents consented to let me rent a cornet from Carl Fischer Music for three months."

Sudhalter had opportunities in the late 1950s to sit in with Pee Wee Russell, Bud Freeman, and Jimmy McPartland. After graduating from Oberlin College in 1960, he moved to Germany, where he played with the Riverboat Seven (1960–66). A professional journalist, he was the European correspondent for UPI during 1964–72. Sudhalter always played music on at least a part-time basis, performing in England with the Anglo-American Alliance (1966–68) and Sandy Brown (1972–74). In 1974 he formed the New Paul Whiteman Orchestra, taking the Bix Beiderbecke solos himself. After returning to the United States, he played with many trad and mainstream groups, including the New California Ramblers (1976–78), the New York Jazz Repertory Company (1976–79), the Loren Schoenberg Orchestra (starting in 1981), the Classic Jazz Quartet (with pianist Dick Wellstood) in 1984–87, and Mister Tram Associates (1987–88). Sudhalter has played on the soundtracks of several Woody Allen films and led record dates for Audiophile, Stomp Off, and Challenge.

Dick Sudhalter has also been a jazz educator and a jazz reviewer for the *New York Post* (1978–84), written many liner notes, and authored two remarkable books, *Bix-Man and Legend* (1974) and *Lost Chords* (1999), along with an upcoming biography of Hoagy Carmichael. "I'd like to do what I do as well as possible, and create music with dignity and beauty in the company of kindred spirits. I've always regarded the making of music as a great gift, a responsibility. I would like to leave behind me evidence that I was here."

Recommended CDs: *Anglo American Alliance* (Jazzology 274), *Get Out and Get Under the Moon* (Stomp Off 1207), *After a While* (Challenge 70014), *With Pleasure* (Audiophile 159), *And Connie Jones* (Challenge 70054), *Melodies Heard, Melodies Sweet* (Challenge 70055), with Loren Schoenberg: *Time Waits for No One* (Music Masters 5032)

Recommended Reading: *Traditionalists and Revivalists in Jazz* by Chip Deffaa (Scarecrow Press, 1997)

IDREES SULIEMAN

. . . .

b. Aug. 27, 1923, St. Petersburg, FL

A talented trumpeter, Idrees Sulieman (born Leonard Graham) never gained much fame, but his playing was always a strong asset to bop dates. He studied at Boston Conservatory and picked up early experience working with the Carolina Cotton Pickers and the Earl Hines Orchestra (1943–44), the latter during the period when Charlie Parker and Dizzy Gillespie were with Hines. Sulieman worked during the second half of the 1940s with Mary Lou Williams, Thelonious Monk (1947), the Cab Calloway Orchestra, the Count Basie Big Band, Dizzy Gillespie, Illinois Jacquet's jump combo, and Lionel Hampton.

Sulieman was prominent on a Coleman Hawkins recording in 1957, particularly on one song, where he demonstrated circular breathing by holding a single note for several choruses. Sulieman worked with Randy Weston (1958–59) and, after touring Europe with Oscar Dennard in 1961, decided to settle in Stockholm, becoming a longtime expatriate. Sulieman, who doubled for a time on alto sax, moved in 1964 to Copenhagen, where he worked with radio orchestras and the Kenny Clarke-Francy Boland Big Band. He recorded as a leader for Swedish Columbia (1964) and Steeplechase (1976 and 1985).

Idrees Sulieman, who appeared on records as a sideman through the years with quite a few major players (including Monk, Hawkins, Weston, the Clarke-Boland Orchestra, Gene Ammons, John Coltrane, Tommy Flanagan, Donald Byrd, Max Roach, Mal Waldron, Don Byas/Bud Powell, Eric Dolphy, Dexter Gordon, Horace Parlan, and Thad Jones), moved back to the United States in the mid-1990s, settling in Florida, where he still occasionally plays.

Recommended CDs: *Now Is the Time* (Steeplechase 31052), *Bird's Grass* (Steeplechase 31202), *Groovin'* (SteepleChase 31218), with Gene Ammons: *Jammin' in Hi Fi* (Original Jazz Classics 129), *Blue Gene* (Original Jazz Classics 192), with Eric Dolphy: *Stockholm Sessions* (Enja 3055), with Coleman Hawkins: *The Hawk Flies High* (Original Jazz Classics 027), with Bud Powell: *Tribute to Cannonball* (Columbia/Legacy 65186)

CHARLES SULLIVAN

b. Nov. 8, 1944, New York, NY

A fine post-bop trumpeter with a flexible style, Charles Sullivan is respected by his fellow musicians (and has the resume to prove it), although he has not recorded all that much through the years. After playing locally and studying at the Manhattan School of Music, he worked with Lionel Hampton (1968), Roy Haynes' Hip Ensemble (1969), Count Basie (as lead trumpeter in 1970), Lonnie Liston Smith, Sy Oliver, Norman Connors, Abdullah Ibrahim, the Thad Jones-Mel Lewis Orchestra (1974), Sonny Fortune, Carlos Garnett, Bennie Maupin, Ricky Ford, Eddie Jefferson, and Woody Shaw, among others.

Sullivan led the Black Legacy Big Band (1975–80), toured with the George Gruntz Concert Jazz Band (1980–82), and worked with the Mercer Ellington Orchestra (1981) and the McCoy Tyner Big Band (1985–92). The trumpeter, who changed his name in recent times to Kamau Muata Adilifu, has led dates for Strata-East, the Japanese Trio label, and Arabesque. Until the Arabesque CD came out, he had maintained a fairly low profile for some time.

Recommended CDs: *Kamau* (Arabesque 0121)

LPs to Search For: *Genesis* (Strata-East 7413), with Ricky Ford: *Loxodonta Africana* (New World 204)

IRA SULLIVAN

b. May 1, 1931, Washington, DC

A very talented multi-instrumentalist who came out of bebop but has always stretched beyond it, Ira Sullivan is equally skilled on trumpet, flugelhorn, tenor, alto, soprano, and flute. Sullivan came from an extremely musical family, studying trumpet with his father (starting when he was four) and saxophone with his mother. He played on the radio (imitating Clyde McCoy on "Sugar Blues") when he was just six and had his first gig the following year. A major part of the Chicago scene starting in 1949, Sullivan was a member of the house band at the Bee Hive club (1952–55), where he had the opportunity to play with Charlie Parker, Lester Young, Roy Eldridge, and Sonny Stitt, among others.

Sullivan was with Art Blakey's Jazz Messengers in 1956 but quit after a few months because he preferred to stay in Chicago. In 1962 he moved permanently to Miami, where he became very involved in the school system, eventually teaching at the University of Miami (electric bassist Jaco Pastorius was one of his students), leading bands locally. Other than a few occasions when he recorded elsewhere, Sullivan stayed put until his old friend Red Rodney talked him into co-leading a quintet in 1980. He agreed to record and travel with Rodney on the condition that the band would be performing new music rather than merely recreating past bebop glories. The result was one of the most consistently inventive jazz groups of the early 1980s.

Since then, Sullivan has remained home in Florida, recording all too infrequently, and not in recent times; in the past he led sessions for ABC-Paramount, Delmark, Atlantic, Horizon, Flying Fish, Galaxy, Stash, Muse, and his Strings-Attached label. Ira Sullivan remains a legendary figure.

Recommended CDs: *Nicky's Tune* (Delmark 422), *Blue Stroll* (Delmark 402), *Bird Lives!* (Vee Jay 2-950)

LPs to Search For: *The Incredible Ira Sullivan* (Stash 208), *Ira Sullivan…Does It All* (Muse 5242), *Strings Attached* (Strings-Attached 7140), with Red Rodney: *Hi Jinx at the Vanguard* (Muse 5267), *Night and Day* (Muse 5274), *Alive in New York* (Muse 5307), *Spirit Within* (Elektra Musician 60020), *Sprint* (Elektra Musician 60261)

BOB SUMMERS

b. Aug. 21, 1944, Turlock, CA

Bob Summers has long been an excellent hard bop trumpeter based in the Los Angeles area. He received a bugle for a Christmas present when he was seven and at eight began taking cornet lessons, eventually switching to trumpet. Summers attended the Naval School of Music starting in 1963 and Berklee during 1967–71. After his graduation from Berklee, he worked with the big bands of Woody Herman (1971–72), Maynard Ferguson (1973–75), Bill Holman (1978–79), and, what he considers the high point of his career, Count Basie (1980–85). Settling in Los Angeles, Bob Summers rejoined the Bill Holman Orchestra (with whom he recorded) and led two fine (but long-out-of-print) albums for the Discovery label in 1984 and 1987.

Recommended CDs: with Count Basie: *Me and You* (Original Jazz Classics 906)

LPs to Search For: *Inside Out* (Discovery 897), *Joy Spring* (Discovery 946)

JOHN SWANA

b. Apr. 26, 1962, Norristown, PA

A creative hard bop trumpeter, John Swana has thus far been documented mostly by the Criss Cross label. He started playing trumpet when he was 11 and studied at Temple University, graduating in 1987. Swana worked in Philadelphia with Don Patterson, Shirley Scott, Mickey Roker, Cecil Payne, and the Joe Sudler Swing Machine.

His recordings as a leader for Criss Cross (including *Philly:New York Junction*, which teams him with Joe Magnarelli) have given Swana more visibility, as have his gigs in New York along the way. John Swana co-led a group with Johnny Coles (1996–97), played with drummer Gerry Gibbs (1996–98), and has worked with Charles Fambrough. He is one of the finest straightahead trumpeters on the scene today.

Recommended CDs: *Introducing John Swana* (Criss Cross 1045), *And Friends* (Criss Cross 1055), *Feeling's Mutual* (Criss Cross 1090), *In the Moment* (Criss Cross 1119), *Philly:New York Junction* (Criss Cross 1150), with Eric Alexander: *New York Calling* (Criss Cross 1077), with Benny Golson: *Remembering Clifford* (Milestone 9278), with Chris Potter: *Presenting Chris Potter* (Criss Cross 1067)

CHARLIE TEAGARDEN

b. July 19, 1913, Vernon, TX, d. Dec. 10, 1984, Las Vegas, NV

The younger brother of the great trombonist Jack Teagarden (1905–64), Charlie Teagarden was always in Jack's shadow, although he was a strong talent himself. His sister, Norma (two years older), was a fine pianist, his brother, Cub, (two years younger) played drums, and their mother, Helen, was a ragtime pianist.

Charlie played early on with Herb Brooks' Oklahoma Joy Boys and Frank Williams' Oklahomans. In 1929 he moved to New York, where he worked alongside Jack in Ben Pollack's orchestra (1929–30), with whom he made his recording debut. Teagarden played with Red Nichols (1930–31), Roger Wolfe Kahn (1932), and, for a long period (1933–40), Paul Whiteman. During the Whiteman years, Charlie and Jack Teagarden teamed up with C-melody saxophonist Frankie Trumbauer in 1936 to form the Three T's. Recordings resulted but no real commercial success.

Teagarden worked with brother Jack's big band and freelanced in the early 1940s before serving in the Army (1942–45). After his discharge he was briefly with Harry James in 1946, assisted his brother with his struggling big band for a few months, and then had a rewarding association with Jimmy Dorsey (1948–50) that included recordings with Dorsey's Original Dorseyland Jazz Band, a Dixieland combo. He would play primarily Dixieland for the remainder of his career, including with Ben Pollack's Pick-a-Rib Boys (1950–51), in a trio with pianist Jess Stacy and drummer Ray Bauduc (1951–52), and with Bob Crosby (off and on during 1954–58) and clarinetist Pete Fountain. Teagarden was based in Las Vegas after 1959. He had a last reunion with Jack Teagarden at the 1963 Monterey Jazz Festival (which also included Norma and his mother, Helen), gigged with Lionel Hampton and Pete Fountain, and was semiretired in the 1970s. Considering his ability, it is surprising that Charlie Teagarden led only one record date in his entire career, a long-out-of-print LP for Coral in 1962, *The Big Horn of Little T*.

Recommended CDs: with Jimmy Dorsey: *Original Dorseyland Jazz Band* (Jazz Crusade 3035), with Jack Teagarden: *The Indispensable* (RCA 66606), *100 Years from Today* (Grudge Music 4523)

LPs to Search For: *The Big Horn of Little T* (Coral 57410)

Film Appearances: The Jimmy Dorsey short *Catalina Interlude* (1948)

CLARK TERRY

. . . .

b. Dec. 14, 1920, St. Louis, MO

Clark Terry has the happiest sound in jazz. His flugelhorn solos are full of the joy he feels at playing music, and Terry is instantly recognizable within two or three notes. It is impossible not to love his playing and his personality.

Terry was an important link in the St. Louis trumpet tradition between Dewey Jackson (an uncle played tuba in Jackson's Musical Ambassadors) and Miles Davis (a lifelong friend who was inspired by Terry's playing). Clark Terry worked in St. Louis in the early 1940s (including with George Hudson), served in the Navy (where he played with a dance band), and was featured with the orchestras of Lionel Hampton (1945), George Hudson, Charlie Barnet (a fairly modern outfit during 1947–48), and Count Basie (1948–49). Terry remained with Basie at first when the pianist was forced to cut his group back to a septet. However, Duke Ellington noticed Terry's playing, and in 1951 he hired the trumpeter.

During his eight years with Ellington, Terry developed from a Dizzy Gillespie-influenced bebopper into an uncategorizable soloist with his own distinctive sound. He was one of Duke's many soloists, getting feature spots (particularly on "Perdido") and also leading sessions along the way for Emarcy, Riverside, and Argo, including a date in which Thelonious Monk was his pianist in a quartet.

Terry began to double on flugelhorn around 1957, and by the early 1960s that was his main instrument. He left Ellington in 1959 to tour Europe with the Quincy Jones Orchestra (1959–60) as part of Harold Arlen's show *The Free and Easy*. Shortly after the show closed, Terry returned to the United States to become one of the first full-time black studio players, joining the staff of NBC.

Unlike many other studio musicians, Clark Terry always played jazz in clubs. He was a member of the Gerry Mulligan Concert Jazz Band (their recording of "Blueport" has a very humorous tradeoff between Terry and baritonist Mulligan), co-led a quintet with valve trombonist Bob Brookmeyer, and made a classic recording with the Oscar Peterson Trio. On this last, he spontaneously sang "Mumbles," a purposely incoherent vocal that poked fun at the more primitive blues singers. That number became so popular that Terry has included nonsensical scat singing as a regular part of his performances ever since.

Terry, who was part of the Tonight Show Band when it was based in New York, has worked steadily up to the present time at countless clubs and jazz festivals. He has also unselfishly given hundreds (possibly thousands) of clinics to young students and spread the joy of jazz around the world, simply by being himself. Among his projects during the past 30 years were a big band in the 1970s, recordings for the Pablo label in all-star settings, duets with bassist Red Mitchell, and reunions with fellow Ellington alumni. In addition to the labels already mentioned, he has recorded as a leader for quite a few other companies, including Candid, Moodsville, Verve, Cameo, Impulse, Mainstream, Polydor, MPS (including his personal favorite album, *Clark After Dark*), Vanguard, Enja, Chiaroscuro, and Chesky.

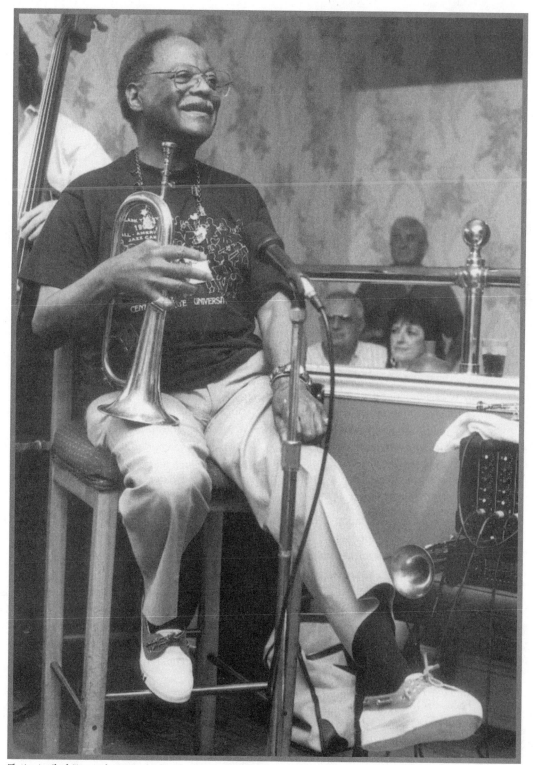

The joy in Clark Terry's playing makes his music impossible to resist.

PROFILES OF THE TRUMPET KINGS 363

Clark Terry, who began to show his age in his playing only in the late 1990s, when he was nearing 80 and having some health problems, remains quite youthful, enthusiastic, and swinging, symbolizing the very best in jazz.

Recommended CDs: *Serenade to a Bus Seat* (Original Jazz Classics 066), *Duke with a Difference* (Original Jazz Classics 229), *In Orbit* (Original Jazz Classics 302), *Color Changes* (Candid 9009), *Yes, the Blues* (Original Jazz Classics 856), *Squeeze Me* (Chiaroscuro 309), *The Clark Terry Spacemen* (Chiaroscuro 309), *What a Wonderful World* (Red Baron 53750), *One on One* (Chesky 198), with Duke Ellington: *Uptown* (Columbia 40836), with Oscar Peterson: *Oscar Peterson Trio Plus One* (Verve 818 840)

LPs to Search For: *Tread Ye Lightly* (Cameo 1071), *The Power of Positive Swinging* (Mainstream 56054), *Clark After Dark* (MPS 68194), *To Duke and Basie* (Enja 5011)

Recommended Reading: *Jazz Spoken Here* by Wayne Enstice and Paul Rubin (Louisiana State University Press, 1992), *The World of Duke Ellington* by Stanley Dance (Charles Scribner's Sons, 1970)

Videos to Get: *Flip Phillips' 80th Birthday Party* (1995; Arbors ARVHS2)

JAY THOMAS

• • • • • • • • • • • •

b. Oct. 27, 1949, Seattle WA

Jay Thomas, like Benny Carter, Ira Sullivan, and Glenn Zottola, is equally skilled on trumpet, saxophones (in his case alto, tenor, soprano) and flutes. A fine bop-based player, Thomas can also play swing quite credibly. The son of a trumpeter, Thomas started out on that instrument. Later, when he added tenor and alto, he reportedly learned those axes so quickly that he was gigging on them within a month. He attended Berklee (where he took up the flute), played with Machito in New York during one summer, and recorded with James Moody. Thomas spent 1974–78 in San Francisco but eventually chose to be based in Seattle.

Among his associations through the years have been Slim Gaillard (with whom he recorded and toured England in the early 1980s), John Stowell, Herb Ellis (making a couple of memorable appearances on the guitarist's *Roll Call* CD), and pianist Jessica Williams. Jay Thomas has appeared on over 50 CDs, including six as a leader (for Discovery, Stash, Hep, Jazz Focus, and his McVouty label), in addition to recording with Gaillard, Ellis, Jessica Williams, the James Knapp Orchestra, the Ramsay/Kleeb Orchestra, Dave Friesen, Elvin Jones, and his wife, singer Becca Duran.

Recommended CDs: *Easy Does It* (Discovery 956), *360 Degrees* (Hep 2060), *Blues for McVouty* (Stash 562), *Rapture* (Jazz Focus 013), *Live at Tula's* (McVouty 109), *12th and Jackson Blues* (McVouty 62399), with Herb Ellis: *Roll Call* (Justice 013), with Jessica Williams: *Joy* (Jazz Focus 014), *Jessica's Blues* (Jazz Focus 018)

JOE THOMAS

b. July 24, 1909, Groves, MO, d. Aug. 6, 1984, New York, NY

The swing trumpeter Joe Thomas was no relation to any of the many other jazz Joe Thomases, including the tenor saxophone soloist with Jimmie Lunceford. Thomas started playing professionally with Cecil Scott in 1928 and with such territory bands in the Midwest during the 1929–34 period as Darrell Harris, Eli Rice, Shuffle Abernathy, and Harold Flood. In 1934 Thomas moved to New York, working with Charlie Turner's Arcadians (1934), the Fletcher Henderson Orchestra (1934), Fats Waller, Baron Lee (1934–35), Henderson again (replacing Roy Eldridge during 1936–37), Willie Bryant (1937), Claude Hopkins (1938–39), and Benny Carter's big band (1939–40).

The trumpeter, who always considered Louis Armstrong to be his main influence, spent the 1940s performing in small groups, including with James P. Johnson, Joe Sullivan, Teddy Wilson (1942–43), Barney Bigard (1944–45), Cozy Cole (1948), and Bud Freeman (1949). He led a session apiece for HRS and Keynote in 1946 and along the way was on combo sessions by Cozy Cole, Red Norvo, Lil Armstrong, Don Byas, Benny Carter, Art Tatum, and Fats Waller, among others.

Thomas recorded frequently during the early to mid-1940s. But with the change of modern jazz from swing to bop, he slipped into obscurity. He freelanced around New York, sometimes leading groups and playing Dixieland. Of his later associations, most notable was his playing with the 1957 Fletcher Henderson reunion band, Eddie Condon (1964), and Claude Hopkins (1966). Still, by the time Joe Thomas had retired in the 1970s, he was forgotten by all but the most dedicated record collectors, a victim of jazz's rapid evolution.

Recommended CDs: *Mainstream* (Koch 8511), with Claude Hopkins: *Swing Time* (Prestige 24215)

MALACHI THOMPSON

b. Aug. 21, 1949, Princeton, KY

An underrated avant-garde trumpeter, Malachi Thompson grew up in Chicago and has returned to be an important force in its modern music scene during the past decade. Thompson started on piano at five. But after hearing Count Basie's orchestra at a concert, he persuaded his parents to get him a trumpet when he was 11. In 1966 he was with Troy Robinson's Jazz Workshop Ensemble, and he joined the AACM the following year. Thompson worked with some of the most advanced improvisers in jazz during the next seven years, including Muhal Richard Abrams, Henry Threadgill, Leroy Jenkins, John Stubblefield, Kalaparusha Maurice McIntyre, and Lester Bowie.

He graduated from Governor's State University and in 1974 moved to New York, where he was soon performing with many of that city's top musicians. Thompson was a member of the Collective Black Artists Orchestra and worked with the Sam Rivers big band, Joe Henderson, Jackie McLean, Roland Alexander (1975–79), David Murray, Ken McIntyre, and the short-lived Sam Wooding Orchestra (1976). In addition, Thompson was associated with Archie Shepp off and on during 1979–88 and was part of Lester Bowie's various brass bands, including the Sho-Nuff Orchestra (1979), the NY Hot Trumpet Repertory Co. (1982–84), and Brass Fantasy (1984–88).

Thompson was out of action completely during 1989–90 due to lymphoma, but he made a full comeback in the 1990s when he moved back to Chicago. He formed Africa Brass in 1991, currently leads the Freebop Band, and has also worked as a music educator. Malachi Thompson, who led albums for the Ra label (1972 and 1981) and has recorded several CDs for Delmark since the mid-1990s, has continued playing adventurous music up to the present time.

Recommended CDs: *The Jaz Life* (Delmark 453), *Lift Every Voice* (Delmark 463), *New Standards* (Delmark 473), *Buddy Bolden's Rag* (Delmark 481), *47th Street* (Delmark 497)

LPs to Search For: *The Seventh Son* (Ra 102), *Spirit* (Delmark 442)

CLIFFORD THORNTON

b. Sept. 6, 1936, Philadelphia, PA

Clifford Thornton is a fine free jazz cornetist who doubles on valve trombone. He attended Temple University (1956–56), played with tuba player Ray Draper (1956–57), and served in the military, touring Korea and Japan with an Army band (1958–61). After his discharge, Thornton settled in New York, where he worked with Sun Ra, Pharoah Sanders (1963–67), Marzette Watts, John Tchicai, and other members of the free jazz movement. He led the New Arts Ensemble during 1967–68, making his recording debut as a leader for the tiny Third World label.

During the late 1960s, many avant-garde jazz players spent time in Europe. Thornton was overseas during 1969–70, playing with Archie Shepp, Dave Burrell, and Sunny Murray. After returning to the United States, he settled down as a member of the faculty at Wesleyan University.

LPs to Search For: *Freedom and Unity* (Third World 6936), *The Panther and the Lash* (America 6113), *Communications Network* (Third World 12272), *The Gardens of Harlem* (JCOA 1008)

CHARLES TOLLIVER

b. Mar. 6, 1942, Jacksonville, FL

One of the great trumpeters to emerge during the second half of the 1960s, Charles Tolliver seemed headed for stardom. Self-taught on the trumpet, Tolliver grew up in New York. After attending Howard University, he played with Jackie McLean and Joe Henderson

(1963–65) and was a member of Art Blakey's Jazz Messengers in 1965. Tolliver spent a year in Los Angeles (1966–67), working with Willie Bobo and the Gerald Wilson Orchestra.

Back in New York, Tolliver was a member of both Max Roach's band and the Horace Silver Quintet during 1967–69. His fat tone, powerful sound, and flexible style (which fell between hard bop and the avant-garde) made Tolliver an asset in many musical situations, including with McCoy Tyner, Booker Ervin, Andrew Hill, Gary Bartz, Roy Ayers, and Oliver Nelson. In 1969 he formed a quartet with pianist Stanley Cowell called Music Inc., and the two cofounded Strata-East Records in 1971. Tolliver also used the name Music Inc. for an occasional big band that he led in the mid-1970s.

Maybe the time was not right for an important new player (although the 1970s had a serious shortage of significant new trumpeters). In any case, Tolliver slipped away from the limelight after 1975 (when he was still just 33), becoming a teacher. Charles Tolliver had led record dates for Freedom, Strata-East, Enja, and Black Lion during 1968–75, but since then he has been heard on only two Strata-East releases, one apiece from 1977 and 1988. It is not too late yet for a major comeback!

Recommended CDs: *Grand Max* (Black Lion 760145), *Live at Slugs* (Strata East 14), *Live in Tokyo* (Strata East 16), *Compassion* (Strata East 7)

LPs to Search For: *Paper Man* (Black Lion 30017), *The Ringer* (Freedom 1017), *Impact* (Enja 2016), with Andrew Hill: *Dance With Death* (Blue Note 1030), with Jackie McLean: *It's Time* (Blue Note 4179), *Action* (Blue Note 4218), with Horace Silver: *Serenade to a Soul Sister* (Blue Note 4277)

GOSTA TORNER

. . . .

b. Oct. 27, 1912, Stockholm, Sweden, d. Nov. 11, 1982, Stockholm, Sweden

One of Sweden's top swing trumpeters, Gosta Torner began playing professionally in the late 1920s. He was a major part of the Swedish jazz scene of the 1930s and '40s, working with Sune Lundwall (1933–35), the Sonora Swing Singers (1936–38), Arne Hulphers (1937–40), Sven Fors (1940–42), and fellow trumpeter Thore Ehrling (1941–50). Gosta Torner, who made a strong impression at the 1949 Paris Jazz Festival with the Swedish Jazz All Stars (playing opposite Charlie Parker, Miles Davis, and Sidney Bechet), stuck to mainstream swing and Dixieland throughout his career. He led groups starting in 1943 and recorded as a leader in 1940, 1943–44, 1948–49, 1951, and 1953, with a full album in 1964.

Recommended CDs: *Trumpet Player* (Phontastic 9301), with Thore Ehrling: *Jazz Highlights, 1939–55* (Dragon 236), *Flash* (Phontastic 9318), with the Swedish Jazz All Stars: *Parisorkestern 1949* (Dragon 349)

LPs to Search For: *Living Legend* (Phontastic 7607)

CY TOUFF

• • • • • • • • • •

b. Mar. 4, 1927, Chicago, IL

Since there will probably not be a survey on jazz bass trumpeters in the future, Cy Touff (along with Marshall Brown) logically fits into this book!

Touff began playing piano when he was six and spent time playing C-melody sax, xylophone, and trumpet. He started his professional career on trombone, playing in an Army band during 1944–46. After his discharge, Touff studied with Lennie Tristano and worked with many bop-oriented groups, including the combos of Charlie Ventura and Shorty Sherock, and the big bands of Ray McKinley and Boyd Raeburn.

In the late 1940s, Touff heard Johnny Mandel play bass trumpet and liked the sound so much that he decided to permanently switch instruments. He worked with the Woody Herman Orchestra during 1953–56 and recorded a gem as a leader for Pacific Jazz in 1955. Since leaving Herman, Cy Touff has freelanced in Chicago, playing in styles ranging from Dixieland to hard bop, leading an album and a half for Argo during 1956–58, working in the studios, and recording in the 1980s with Clifford Jordan and Von Freeman. He has been semiretired during the past decade.

Recommended CDs: *Cy Touff, His Octet and Quintet* (Pacific Jazz 93162)

LPs to Search For: *Touff Assignment* (Argo 641)

NICK TRAVIS

• • • • • • • • • • • •

b. Nov. 16, 1925, Philadelphia, PA, d. Oct. 7, 1964, New York, NY

A technically skilled trumpeter with an appealing tone, Nick Travis (who was born Nicholas Travascio) was considered a valuable player during his short life. He was a professional by the time he was 15. After studying at the Mastbaum School of Music, Travis played with Johnny McGhee, Mitchell Ayres, Vido Musso, and Woody Herman (1942–44) before he was drafted. After his discharge in 1946, Travis worked with the big bands of Ray McKinley (on and off during 1946–49), Benny Goodman (the bebop orchestra of 1948–49), Jerry Wald, Gene Krupa, Ina Ray Hutton, Tommy Dorsey, Tex Beneke, Woody Herman again (1950–51), Jerry Gray, Bob Chester, Elliot Lawrence, and Jimmy Dorsey (1952).

Since there were few full-time big bands left by the early 1950s, Travis became a studio musician in New York. He did catch on as one of the star soloists with the Sauter-Finegan Orchestra (1953–56), later working with the Gerry Mulligan Concert Jazz Band (1960–62) and playing lead trumpet at Thelonious Monk's famous Lincoln Center concert of 1963. Travis's death at age 38 from ulcers was unexpected. Although he led only one album in his career (an obscure quintet date from 1954), Nick Travis recorded as a sideman with such notables as Al Cohn, Zoot Sims, Billy Byers, Tony Aless, Manny Albam, Bill Holman, Coleman Hawkins, Maynard Ferguson, Joe Morello, Tom Talbert, Stan Getz, and Gerry Mulligan, plus many of the big bands already listed. He seemed to have a bright future.

Recommended CDs: with Zoot Sims: *Zoot* (Original Jazz Classics 228)

LPs to Search For: *The Panic Is On* (Victor 1010), with Al Cohn: *The Progressive Al Cohn* (Savoy 1126)

NAPPY TROTTIER

b. Norway, MI, d. Sept. 21, 1997, Appleton, WI

A solid Dixieland trumpeter based in Chicago, Nappy Trottier gained most of his recognition for his late 1960s work with Art Hodes, which included recordings as a sideman for Delmark and an appearance (recently released on videotape) on Hodes' local television show. Earlier, Trottier worked with Frank Gillis' Dixie 5 in Detroit and briefly with Jack Teagarden before settling in Chicago to play at Jazz Ltd. in a group with Miff Mole. He also played trad jazz with Don Ewell (including a 1959 album), Darnell Howard, George Brunies, and Clancy Hayes, recording with the Al Capone Memorial Jazz Band in 1973. Nappy Trottier made his living in real estate, but his playing was always an asset in Dixieland settings.

Recommended CDs: with Barney Bigard: *Bucket's Got a Hole in It* (Delmark 211), with Art Hodes: *Up in Volly's Room* (Delmark 217)

LPs to Search For: with Don Ewell: *Yellow Dog Blues* (Audiophile 66)

Recommended Videos: *Art Hodes' Jazz Alley, Vol. 2* (1968; Storyville 6065)

TOMMY TURRENTINE

b. Apr. 22, 1928, Pittsburgh, PA, d. May 13, 1997, New York, NY

Tommy Turrentine (who was six years older than his brother, tenor saxophonist Stanley Turrentine) had the potential to be one of the greats of hard bop, but bad health forced his early retirement. Turrentine began on violin, switching to the trumpet when he was 11. He started his career playing with the orchestras of Snookum Russell (1945–46), Benny Carter (1946), and George Hudson (1947–49) before serving in the Army. Turrentine was with the new Count Basie Orchestra for a short time (1951–52), gigged with Gay Crosse in Cleveland (1952), and was a member of Earl Bostic's backup band (1952–53). He freelanced for the next few years, playing with Charles Mingus during part of 1956.

Turrentine's most significant period began in 1959 when he and his brother Stanley joined Max Roach's band (1959–60). Turrentine led his only record date in 1960 and fared quite well as a sideman, recording with Horace Parlan, Paul Chambers, Abbey Lincoln, Booker Ervin, Jackie McLean, Sonny Clark, Dexter Gordon, Lou Donaldson, Big John Patton, and his brother. Unfortunately, after the mid-1960s he was rarely heard from and became a forgotten legend, a subject of "whatever became of" questions from jazz collectors. Every once in a while Turrentine would briefly reappear, recording with his brother in an anonymous background role in the mid-1970s, playing with Clarence "C" Sharpe and Barry Harris in the early 1980s, and with Sun Ra in 1988. But Tommy Turrentine's health never recovered enough for him to make a comeback.

Recommended CDs: *Tommy Turrentine* (Bainbridge 1047), with Sonny Clark: *Leapin' and Lopin'* (Blue Note 84091), with Jackie McLean: *Fickle Sonance* (Blue Note 25444), with Stanley Turrentine: *Jubilee Shout* (Blue Note 84122)

Box Sets: with Horace Parlan: *The Complete Blue Note Sessions* (5 CDs; Mosaic 5-197), with Max Roach: *The Complete Max Roach Plus Four Sessions* (7 CDs; Mosaic 7–201)

LPs to Search For: with Paul Chambers: *1st Bassman* (Vee Jay 3012), with Dexter Gordon: *Landslide* (Blue Note 1051)

CHRIS TYLE

• • • • • • • • • • •

b. 1955, Vancouver, WA

A regular in the trad jazz scene of New Orleans since 1989, Chris Tyle grew up in Portland. He played with Don Kinch's Conductors Ragtime Band, worked with Turk Murphy in 1979, and led a swing band, Wholly Cats. Since moving to New Orleans, Tyle has played with Hal Smith (with whom he co-led the Frisco Syncopators), Steve Pistorius' Mahogany Hall Stompers, Jacques Gauthe's Creole Rice Jazz Band, and John Gills' Crescent City Rhythm Kings, in addition to leading the Silver Leaf Jazz Band. An expert on early jazz, Chris Tyle has recorded full-length tributes to Benny Strickler, Jelly Roll Morton, the 1944 Bunk Johnson band, King Oliver, Freddie Keppard, the city of New Orleans in general, and the often-overlooked composers of New Orleans jazz. He has also recorded with the Down Home Five, Jacques Gauthe, John Gill, and Duke Heitger.

Recommended CDs: *A Tribute to Benny Strickler* (Stomp Off 1235), *The Smiler* (Stomp Off 1258), *Sugar Blues* (Stomp Off 1298), *Here Comes the Hot Tamale Man* (Stomp Off 1311), with the Silver Leaf Jazz Band: *Streets and Scenes of New Orleans* (Good Time Jazz 15001), *Jelly's Best Jam* (Good Time Jazz 15002), *Great Composers of New Orleans* (Good Time Jazz 15005)

WARREN VACHE

• • • • • • • • • • • • •

b. Feb. 21, 1951, Rahway, NJ

A lthough the Young Lions movement is often attributed to the rise of Wynton Marsalis in 1980, Warren Vache and tenor saxophonist Scott Hamilton actually preceded Marsalis by five years. They were among the first world-class younger players of the era who chose to play acoustic jazz (in their case mainstream swing) rather than fusion or post-bop.

Vache's father, Warren Vache, Sr., is a fine bassist and jazz journalist, while his brother, Allan Vache, plays clarinet. He started on piano when he was five. "When I was nine and the instrumental music program at school started, my dad chose the trumpet for me because, as a bassist, he thought I would get more work on that instrument." At 15, Vache (who would later switch to cornet) had his first job playing in a dance band. He took lessons from Pee Wee Erwin and attended Montclair State College in New Jersey (1970–75). One of his first important jobs was working with Benny Goodman (occasionally during 1975–85, including the

Warren Vache sparked the Mainstream Swing movement of the mid-1970s and remains a major trumpeter today.

40th anniversary celebration of Goodman's Carnegie Hall concert). Vache often gigged at Eddie Condon's club (1976–79) and early on played with Dick Hyman and Vic Dickenson.

A swing stylist with a pretty tone, and flexible enough to play both heated Dixieland and bop, Vache teamed up regularly with Scott Hamilton during 1976–85. They often appeared on each other's records, with Rosemary Clooney, and with various all-star groups for the Concord label. The cornetist switched to the Muse label in the early 1990s and has also recorded as a leader for Nagel-Heyer and Zephyr. Warren Vache, who did quite well as an actor in the 1985 film *The Gig*, has remained a busy freelancer, appearing constantly at clubs, classic jazz festivals, and jazz parties. As for the future, in 1990 he said, "My goal is simply to swing and play good changes, also to continue to grow emotionally, improve musically through performance and composition, and keep my family fed at the same time!"

Recommended CDs: *Midtown Jazz* (Concord Jazz 4203), *Easy Going* (Concord Jazz 4323), *Horn of Plenty* (Muse 5524), with Scott Hamilton: *With Scott's Band in New York City* (Concord Jazz 4070)

LPs to Search For: *First Time Out* (Audiophile 196), *Blues Walk* (Dreamstreet 101), *Polished Brass* (Concord Jazz 98), *Iridescence* (Concord Jazz 153)

Recommended Reading: *Swing Legacy* by Chip Deffaa (Scarecrow Press, 1989)

Film Appearances: *The Gig* (1985)

OSCAR VALDAMBRINI

b. May 11, 1924, Turin, Italy, d. Dec. 26, 1997, Rome, Italy

A top-notch Italian bop player, Oscar Valdambrini was best known for his work with tenor saxophonist Gianni Basso in the 1950s. The son of a top violinist, Valdambrini studied violin himself at the Turin Conservatory. However, he soon switched away from classical music and the violin, choosing to play jazz trumpet instead. Valdambrini played locally, gigged with Rex Stewart when the cornetist was visiting Italy in 1948, and co-led a quintet with Basso on and off from 1952 to 1974. The Basso-Valdambrini Quintet backed such visiting Americans as Gerry Mulligan, Chet Baker, Stan Getz, and Miles Davis during 1955–60, performed with Lars Gullin, and recorded (under Basso's name) for the Italian Columbia, Music, Jolly, RCA, Ricordi, Fonit, GTA, and Verve labels.

Valdambrini also worked with the Armando Trovajoli big band (1957–58) and visited New York in 1962. He was associated with the Gil Cuppin Orchestra (1964–71), played with Giorgio Gaslini (1968–69), and joined such American bands when they played overseas as Duke Ellington (1968–69), Maynard Ferguson (1970–71), and Lionel Hampton. He co-led a sextet with Basso during 1972–74, and, after Basso's departure in 1974, he kept it as his main group into the 1980s. Later in life, Oscar Valdambrini (who led only one record date under his own name) played with Dusko Goykovich and Kai Winding, visiting New York for a final time in 1993.

KID THOMAS VALENTINE

b. Feb. 3, 1896, Reserve, LA, d. June 16, 1987, New Orleans, LA

A very primitive trumpeter who often played staccato notes and slid between notes, Kid Thomas Valentine became a hero in the 1960s to fans of New Orleans revival jazz. He started on trumpet when he was ten and was with the Pickwick Brass Band (1910) when he was 14. In 1914 Valentine played with clarinetist Edmond Hall in the Hall Brothers family band. He moved to New Orleans in 1922 and often led bands during the next couple of decades, performing locally. Valentine first recorded in 1951 (when he was already 55), he performed often at Preservation Hall after it opened in 1961, and he played in New Orleans until he was 90. Valentine, who sometimes teamed up with altoist Capt. John Handy, made a lot of records along the way for such labels as AM Music, Center, Mono, '77,' NOJS, Jazzology, Riverside, Jazz Crusade, GHB, La Croix, Storyville, Shalom, Sonet, Smoky Mary, and Maison Bourbon. Kid Thomas Valentine, whose groups were often called the Algiers Stompers, had a wide vibrato and a very unusual tone, used mutes a lot, was often purposely humorous, and certainly was a very expressive player.

Recommended CDs: *The Living Legends* (Original Jazz Classics 1833), *The Living Legends* (Original Jazz Classics 1845), *Live in Denmark, Vols. 1–4* (Storyville 6026, 6027, 6028, and 6029), with Capt. John Handy: *All Aboard, Vol. 1* (GHB 41)

LPs to Search For: *Kid Thomas with Raymond Burke* (Jazzology 30), *Kid Thomas and the New Black Eagle Jazz Band* (GHB 145)

Recommended Reading: *The Jazz Crusade* by Big Bill Bissonnette (Special Request Books, 1992)

MIKE VAX

• • • • • • • • •

b. 1944

Like the late Al Hirt, Mike Vax tends to be a bit overqualified for the occasional Dixieland dates that he performs, being essentially a boppish big band trumpeter. He led a campus band at the College of the Pacific and played lead in the U.S. Navy Show Band while in the military. Vax was a member of the Stan Kenton Orchestra from May 1970 until September 1972. In 1973 he organized the first of many big bands, one that recorded with altoist Art Pepper for that year's *Evil Eyes* release. Since then, Vax has worked with the Dukes of Dixieland, become a jazz educator, recorded an exciting (but out-of-print) set in 1985 with the four-trumpet octet Trpts., and worked in a variety of settings in Northern California, including at the head of the New Oakland Jazz Orchestra.

Recommended CDs: *Alternate Route* (Sea Breeze 2102), *I Remember You* (Master Communications 801), *Creepin' With Clark* (Summit 273)

LPs to Search For: *Evil Eyes* (Arto 117945), *And His Southern Comfort All-Stars* (Sacramento Jazz 21), with Trpts.: *Transforming Traditions* (Black-Hawk 51701)

RAY VEGA

• • • • • • • • •

b. Apr. 3, 1961, New York, NY

A superior Afro-Cuban jazz player, Ray Vega has worked with the who's who of Latin jazz. Originally Vega wanted to play alto in junior high school, but since the only instruments he had to choose from were trumpet and trombone, he began on trumpet, inspired by Freddie Hubbard. Vega studied at New York City's High School of Music and Art and the Johnny Colon School of Music (where his teacher was Jerry Gonzalez).

Vega has worked with James Spaulding, Wessell Anderson, Louie Ramirez (1985), the Luis "Perico" Ortiz Orchestra, Hector Lavoe (1987), Mongo Santamaria (1987–92), Johnny Pacheco, Eddie Palmieri, Ray Barretto's New World Spirit (1990–94), the Joe Henderson big band, Pete Rodriguez (1991–92), Mario Bauza's big band, Tito Puente (1994–99), Chico O'Farrill, and the Lincoln Center Jazz Orchestra. Ray Vega's bright sound and ability to play both lead trumpet and heated solos keeps him in great demand.

Recommended CDs: *Ray Vega* (Concord Picante 4735), *Boperation* (Concord Picante 4867), with Ray Barretto: *Taboo* (Concord Picante 601), *Contact!* (Blue Note 56974), with Tito Puente: *Mambo Birdland* (RMM 84047), with Mongo Santamaria: *Live at Jazz Alley* (Concord Picante 4427)

AL VIZZUTTI

. . . .

b. 1952, Missoula, MT

A brilliant technician with an impressive range, Al Vizzutti gained some recognition in the jazz world for his work with Chick Corea. Vizzutti started on trumpet when he was nine (taking his first lessons from his father, who also played trumpet) and developed so quickly that in high school he was asked to perform with the University of Montana Band. In 1967 he met Doc Severinsen, and since then he has often played with Doc, including with the Tonight Show Orchestra many times in the 1970s and '80s. Vizzutti studied at the East-man School of Music (performing with the professional faculty brass quintet while still a freshman) and worked with the Rochester Philharmonic Orchestra. While at school, he had opportunities to play concerts with Stan Getz, Gerry Mulligan, Dizzy Gillespie, Toots Thiele-mans, Dave Brubeck, Bill Watrous, Thad Jones, and others, usually as lead trumpeter. After graduating from Eastman, Vizzutti worked with Woody Herman's orchestra (1978–79).

Vizzutti spent a couple of years touring with Chick Corea, appearing on his *Secret Agent, Tap Step,* and *Touch Stone* albums. He recorded a few albums as a leader in the early 1980s (for Headfirst, Four Leaf Clover, and Bainbridge) and recently for Summit, but Al Vizzutti (who is greatly respected for his technical skills by his fellow trumpeters) chose to become a studio musician rather than a solo jazz artist, conducting clinics and adding high notes anonymously to studio sessions.

Recommended CDs: *Skyrocket* (Summit 179), with Chick Corea: *Tap Step* (Stretch 9006)

LPs to Search For: *A. V.* (Headfirst 9700), *Rainbow* (Four Leaf Clover 5054), with Chick Corea: *Secret Agent* (Polydor 6176)

CUONG VU

. . . .

b. 1969, Vietnam

C ertainly one of the top jazz trumpeters ever born in Vietnam, Cuong Vu is an explorative player with a very fertile musical curiosity. His mother was a Vietnamese pop singer, and his father played several instruments. When he was six, he emigrated to the United States with his mother, growing up in Seattle. Vu started on the trumpet when he was 11. After high school, he studied at the New England Conservatory of Music (saxophonist Joe Maneri was one of his teachers), and his mind opened up to avant-garde jazz. He moved to New York in 1994 after graduating, and he has worked with such players as Dave Douglas, saxophonists Chris Speed and Andy Laster, pianist Myra Melford, bassist Mark Helias, and drummers Gerry Hemingway and Bobby Previte, among others.

Cuong Vu, a member of Orange Then Blue in the early 1990s and Jeff Song's Lowbrow, has led unusual bands (Scratcher and Vu-Tet) and impressed many listeners and musicians with his unpredictable and highly original style.

Recommended CDs: *Bound* (Omnitone 12002), *Pure* (Knitting Factory Works 286), with Chris Speed: *Yeah No* (Songlines 1517), *Deviantics* (Songlines 1524), *Emit* (Songlines 1532)

JACK WALRATH

• • • • • • • • • • • • • •

b. May 5, 1946, Stuart, FL

A versatile trumpeter with an open mind, Jack Walrath is famous for his work with Charles Mingus but has actually had a wide-ranging career. He grew up in Montana. "When I was nine, my mother told me that I should take music lessons and asked me what I wanted to play. I was familiar with Clyde McCoy's 'Sugar Blues' and I said that I wanted to play that thing that goes 'wah-wah.' The next year she took me to hear Louis Armstrong, and that was my first experience with live music." Walrath attended Berklee (1964–68) and spent time in Los Angeles playing with R&B groups, Change (a band with bassist Gary Peacock), and the avant-garde Revival (1969–71). After touring with Ray Charles (1971), he moved to New York.

Walrath played with the Paul Jeffrey Octet, then spent four years playing with Charles Mingus' last groups (1974–78), where his flexible inside/outside playing worked quite well. He also contributed arrangements, including for Mingus' *Me, Myself An Eye* record. Since then, Walrath has worked with Charli Persip's Superband (1978–90), Danny Richmond (1979–81), Sam Rivers (1979–84), Carlos Ward, Muhal Richard Abrams (1988–91), Mingus Epitaph (1989–91), George Gruntz's Concert Jazz Band (1991), and the Jazz Tribe. He led Mingus Dynasty for a couple of years (starting in 1989) and has recorded with the Mingus Big Band. But mostly in recent times Jack Walrath has been leading his own bands. Through the years he has recorded as a leader for Gatemouth, Stash, Steeplechase, Red, Muse, Spotlite, Blue Note, Evidence, Jazz Alliance, TCB, ACT, and Mapleshade.

"I went from traditional jazz directly to avant-garde and went back through bebop and hard bop. I love the unpredictable, the new, and the eclectic. I have been influenced by unlikely and world music sources, and I have come to believe in 'free music.'"

Recommended CDs: *In Montana* (The Jazz Alliance 10030), *Master of Suspense* (Blue Note 46905), *Neohippus* (Blue Note 91101), with the Jazz Tribe: *The Next Step* (Red 123285), with Charles Mingus: *Changes One* (Rhino/Atlantic 71403), *Changes Two* (Rhino/Atlantic 71404)

LPs to Search For: *Revenge of the Fat People* (Stash 221), *A Plea for Sanity* (Stash 223), *Wholly Trinity* (Muse 5362)

LU WATTERS

• • • • • • • • • • • • •

b. Dec. 19, 1911, Santa Cruz, CA, d. Nov. 5, 1989, Santa Rosa, CA

In 1939, when swing was king and New Orleans jazz had long been pushed underground by the big bands, Lu Watters emerged to help lead the New Orleans revival movement. Watters had attended St. Joseph's Military Academy, formed his first jazz band back in 1925, and worked in swing and dance bands in the 1930s. His late-'30s swing band (based in San Francisco) was influenced by Bob Crosby's. In 1939 Watters formed the Yerba Buena Jazz Band, a two-trumpet octet that looked back toward King Oliver's Creole Jazz Band for inspiration but soon developed its own sound, featuring Bob Scobey, trombonist Turk Murphy, and pianist Wally Rose.

The Yerba Buena Jazz Band played regularly at the Dawn Club starting in December 1939 and recorded for Jazzman Records. Soon the exciting group had built up a large following and was creating a stir. In 1942 Watters, Scobey, Murphy, and Rose were in the military, but a wartime version of the Yerba Buenas (which briefly featured the ill-fated Benny Strickler) carried on. Watters spent 1942–45 in the Navy, part of the time leading a 20-piece big band in Hawaii.

In 1946, the band regrouped at the Dawn Club on Annie Street, playing at that location until they switched their home base to Hambone Kelly's in June 1947. Their freewheeling music (which included such Watters originals as "Big Bear Stomp," "Sage Hen Strut," and "Emperor Norton's Hunch") was so popular that the Yerba Buena Jazz Band (credited with playing "San Francisco style") became an influential force in the trad jazz movement. In 1949, after Scobey and Murphy departed to form their own important bands, Watters continued as the group's only trumpeter, with banjoist Clancy Hayes taking vocals. But after business fell off a lot during 1950, Watters broke up the band and retired from music to cultivate other interests, including being a cook and studying geology. He said later that he could see the eventual commercialization of Dixieland coming and he did not want to be a part of it.

Watters did not pick up his horn again until 1963, when a utility company in Northern California announced plans to build a nuclear power plant on an earthquake fault. Watters played at a couple of protest rallies with Turk Murphy's band (sounding as strong as ever) and recorded one final record before permanently retiring. Fortunately, the power plant was never built.

Lu Watters did not play in public again during his final 25 years. Today, over 60 years since the formation of the Yerba Buena Jazz Band, there are countless trad bands patterned after the two-beat Watters group, which, like its role model (King Oliver's Creole Jazz Band), is now considered classic.

Recommended CDs: *Vol. 1 1937–1943* (San Francisco Traditional Jazz Foundation 105), *At Hambone Kelly's 1949–50* (Merry Makers 10), *Together Again* (Merry Makers 8), *Blues over Bodega* (Good Time Jazz 12066)

Box Set: *The Complete Good Time Jazz Recordings* (4 CDs; Good Time Jazz 4409)

Recommended Reading: *Emperor Norton's Hunch* by John Buchanan (Humbleda Productions, 1996)

FREDDY WEBSTER

. . . .

b. 1917, Cleveland, OH, d. Apr. 1, 1947, Chicago, IL

Dizzy Gillespie said that Freddy Webster had the greatest tone he ever heard on the trumpet, and Miles Davis called him an important early inspiration. Yet because he recorded relatively little (never leading his own record date) and died young, Freddy Webster is one of the mystery figures of jazz history.

Webster picked up a lot of experience playing with big bands, but rarely soloing, including with Earl Hines (1938), Erskine Tate, Benny Carter, Eddie Durham, Lucky Millinder, Jimmie Lunceford (1942–43), Sabby Lewis, and Cab Calloway. His best solos on record date from

1945–46 on sessions led by Miss Rhapsody, Frankie Socolow, and Sarah Vaughan. Although his spot on "If You Could See Me Now" with Vaughan has been greatly praised, he is actually barely heard on that record (just eight bars); "You're Not the Kind" with Sassy is a better showcase.

Freddie Webster had short stints with the John Kirby Sextet and the Dizzy Gillespie big band that went unrecorded. One of many bebop musicians who had a drug problem, Webster died from a fatal heroin overdose that was rumored to have been meant for Sonny Stitt; he was just 30.

Recommended CDs: with Sarah Vaughan: *1944–1946* (Classics 958)

LPs to Search For: *Bebop Revisited, Vol. 6* (Xanadu 208)

PAUL WEBSTER
• • • • • • • • • • • • • •

b. Aug. 24, 1909, Kansas City, MO, d. May 6, 1966, New York, NY

Paul Webster was Jimmie Lunceford's high-note trumpeter (succeeding Tommy Stevenson). His flights into the stratosphere inadvertently had a major influence on Stan Kenton's musical thinking, since Kenton grew to love the sound of Lunceford's brass section. Webster attended Fisk University and first worked as an embalmer (!) before deciding to become a professional musician. He played in Kansas City with George E. Lee (1927), Bennie Moten (1927–28), Tommy Douglas, and Eli Rice before joining Lunceford, briefly in 1931 and then more significantly during 1935–44.

After the Lunceford years ended, Webster was lead trumpeter with Cab Calloway (on several occasions during 1944–52), Charlie Barnet (1946–47 and 1952–53), Sy Oliver (1947), Ed Wilcox (1948–49), and Count Basie (1950). Paul Webster, who never led his own record date, played on only a part-time basis after 1953 but occasionally guested with Sy Oliver's orchestra into the 1960s.

Recommended CDs: with Jimmie Lunceford: *Stomp It Off* (GRP/Decca 608), *For Dancer's Only* (GRP/Decca 645)

ALEX WELSH
• • • • • • • • • • • •

b. July 9, 1929, Edinburgh, Scotland, d. June 25, 1982, Middlesex, England

An exciting Dixieland cornetist, Alex Welsh is one of the unsung giants of England's trad movement. Welsh originally played accordion in high school and worked at a day job. He was nearly 20 before he started playing cornet, but by 1951 he was strong enough to be performing with Archie Semple. After working with the Nova Scotia Jazz Band and Sandy Brown's Blue Five, he moved to London in May 1954. Within a month he had his own band, playing at clubs, concerts, and festivals. In 1957 Welsh turned down an offer to join Jack Teagarden's group since he preferred to stay in England.

When American trad and swing players visited Great Britain, Welsh's band was often hired to accompany the stars, including Red Allen, Rex Stewart, Ruby Braff, Wild Bill Davison, Bud

Freeman, Pee Wee Russell, Earl Hines, Dicky Wells, Ben Webster, and Eddie "Lockjaw" Davis. Welsh recorded with both Davison and Braff, and his band made a rare United States appearance at the 1968 Newport Jazz Festival. Although his health started to decline in the late 1970s, Alex Welsh (who recorded for Lake, Decca, Dormouse, Columbia, Strike, Polydor, and Black Lion), continued playing until his final gig, two weeks before his death.

Recommended CDs: *BBC Jazz Club, Vol. 4* (Upbeat Jazz 122), with Ruby Braff: *Hear Me Talkin'* (Black Lion 760161)

LPs to Search For: *Music of the Mauve Decade* (Columbia 1219), *It's Right Here for You* (Columbia 1322), *At Home With Alex Welsh* (Dormouse 16), *If I Had a Talking Picture of You* (Black Lion 2460150)

SCOTT WENDHOLT

b. *July 21, 1965, Patuxant River, MD*

A solid hard bop trumpeter, Scott Wendholt has thus far had a wide variety of experience and displayed great potential. Wendholt grew up in Denver and attended Indiana University (1983–87). After playing locally in the Midwest, he moved to New York in 1990. Since then, Wendholt has played with the Carnegie Hall Jazz Band, the Vanguard Jazz Orchestra, the Mingus Big Band, and the orchestras of Maria Schneider, Toshiko Akiyoshi, Louie Bellson, Bob Mintzer, Woody Herman, and Joe Roccisano, in addition to working with Fred Hersch, Vincent Herring, Don Braden, Bruce Barth, Kevin Hays, Daryl Grant, Roberta Piket, Bobby McFerrin, and Joanne Brackeen, among many others. Scott Wendholt has recorded as a leader for Criss Cross and Double-Time.

Recommended CDs: *The Scheme of Things* (Criss Cross 1076), *Through the Shadows* (Criss Cross 1101), *From Now On* (Criss Cross 1123), *Beyond Thursday* (Double-Time 128), *What Goes Unsaid* (Double-Time 164)

RAY WETZEL

b. *1924, Parkersburg, WV, d. Aug. 17, 1951, Sedgwick, CO*

O ne of the great high-note trumpeters, Ray Wetzel might have had a career on Maynard Ferguson's level were it not for his premature death. As a teenager, Wetzel played with the Woody Herman orchestra during 1943–45, although he did not have an opportunity to solo. While with Stan Kenton during 1945–48, Wetzel both led the ensembles and was heard in some short solo spots.

Wetzel, who also recorded with the Metronome All-Stars (as part of Kenton's orchestra), Vido Musso, Eddie Safranski, and Neal Hefti, was a member of Charlie Barnet's remarkable trumpet section (along with Maynard Ferguson, Doc Severinsen, and Rolf Ericson) in 1949; he was featured on "Over the Rainbow." He married bassist Bonnie Addleman that year and worked with Henry Jerome (1950), back with Kenton (1951), and finally Tommy Dorsey. Ray Wetzel died in an automobile accident at the age of 27.

Recommended CDs: with Charlie Barnet: *Capitol Big Band Sessions* (Capitol 21258), with Stan Kenton: *From Coast to Coast* (Jazz Unlimited 2051)

Box Set: with Stan Kenton: *The Complete Capitol Studio Recordings 1943–1947* (7 CDs; Mosaic 7-163)

Film Appearances: with the Woody Herman Orchestra in *Earl Carroll Vanities* (1945)

KENNY WHEELER

• • • • • • • • • • • • • • •

b. Jan. 14, 1930, Toronto, Ontario, Canada

One of the major jazz trumpeters of the 1980s and '90s, Kenny Wheeler can play both inside and outside, has a wide range, and is an underrated composer. Wheeler started on trumpet (originally cornet) when he was 13. He worked locally in Ontario and attended the Toronto Conservatory of Music during 1946–47. In 1952, when he could not get a visa to live in the United States, Wheeler moved to England instead, balancing dance band jobs with modern jazz gigs. He freelanced, working with Roy Fox, Buddy Featherstone (1955–57), Vic Lewis, Woody Herman's Anglo-American Herd (1959), and the Johnny Dankworth Orchestras (1959–65).

Wheeler gained a strong reputation while with Dankworth, being one of the big band's main soloists. Dankworth even recorded a set of his compositions (*Windmill Tilter*), an album that also featured the young guitarist John McLaughlin. In the mid-'60s, Wheeler became

Kenny Wheeler's adaptability to any musical situation has made him a valuable trumpeter for 35 years.

quite interested in the freer sounds being played by some of the younger players, and he gradually switched from bop-based music to the avant-garde while not being shy to show off his roots. He worked with Tubby Hayes, Joe Harriott, Ronnie Scott, Mike Gibbs, John Stevens' Spontaneous Music Ensemble (1966–70), Tony Oxley (1969–72), and the Globe Unity Orchestra (starting in 1972).

As a member of the Anthony Braxton Quartet (1972–76) and Azimuth (a trio with pianist John Taylor and singer Norma Winstone), Wheeler became well known in American jazz circles. His long string of recordings for ECM (1975's *Gnu High* matched him with Keith Jarrett, Dave Holland, and Jack DeJohnette) gave him an international reputation. Wheeler, who performed with Bill Bruford (1977), the United Jazz and Rock Ensemble (starting in 1978), and the Dave Holland Quintet (1983–87), has also worked along the way with Ronnie Scott, the Kenny Clarke-Francy Boland orchestra, Stan Getz, Lee Konitz, Evan Parker, and Derek Bailey in addition to his own groups.

Kenny Wheeler at 71 is currently one of the most vital trumpeters of the 21st century.

Recommended CDs: *Gnu High* (ECM 825 691), *Deer Wan* (ECM 829 385), *Around 6* (ECM 1156), *Double, Double You* (ECM 1262), *Flutter By, Butterfly* (Soul Note 121146), *Music for Large and Small Ensembles* (ECM 843 152), *The Widow in the Window* (ECM 843 196), with Anthony Braxton: *Live* (Bluebird 6626), with Dave Holland: *Jumpin' In* (ECM 1269), *Seeds of Time* (ECM 1292), *The Razor's Edge* (ECM 1353)

LPs to Search For: with Johnny Dankworth: *Windmill Tilter* (Fontana 5494)

Recommended Reading: *Boogie, Pete and the Senator* by Mark Miller (Nightwood Editions, 1987)

Videos to Get: *Dave Holland Quintet: Vortex* (1995; View Video)

ARTHUR WHETSOL
• • • • • • • • • • • • • • • • • •

b. 1905, Punta Gorda, FL, d. Jan. 5, 1940, New York, NY

Arthur Whetsol was famous for his lyricism and his haunting tone, which combined to form an atmospheric style that worked perfectly with Duke Ellington's early orchestra. Born Arthur Schiefe, he took his mother's maiden name, Whetsol. Growing up in Washington, D.C., Whetsol was a childhood friend of Duke Ellington's, and he played with Duke as early as 1920. He also worked in Washington, D.C., with Claude Hopkins and the White Brothers Orchestra. When Ellington went up to New York in late 1923 (his second trip to the Big Apple), Whetsol took a chance and went with him as an original member of the Washingtonians, a group that was led at the time by banjoist Elmer Snowden. After a few months, during which he made a strong impression (his quiet trumpet matched well with the alto of Otto Hardwicke), Whetsol returned to Washington to study medicine at Howard University. His replacement was the much more extroverted Bubber Miley.

By March 1928 Arthur Whetsol had completed his studies and he rejoined Ellington. Where before, Duke was merely a sideman with Snowden's struggling orchestra, by 1928 his group was starring nightly at the Cotton Club. But rather than Whetsol's not fitting in with

Ellington's "jungle band," his lyrical and sweet sound was a perfect contrast to the flamboyant plunger mute styles of Bubber Miley and his successor, Cootie Williams. Ellington loved having highly individual voices in his ensemble, and he made his old friend an important part of the orchestra's sound. Whetsol tended to be featured as first trumpeter on slower numbers, and his playing in the ensembles of pieces such as "Mood Indigo" and "Black Beauty," although seemingly effortless, caused other trumpeters (who tried to duplicate his expertise) trouble for decades. Whetsol can be seen quite prominently playing "Black and Tan Fantasy" in the early part of the 1929 Ellington short film *Black and Tan*.

Whetsol was with Duke Ellington's orchestra until the summer of 1936, when his health started to become troublesome and he had to stop playing. Although he tried to come back a couple of times, Whetsol was suffering from a brain disease that killed him in 1940 before he turned 35. All of his recordings (with the exception of two numbers cut with singer Roy Evans in 1928) were made within the world of Ellington. Arthur Whetsol's sound remained a vital part of Duke's music even after his death, in the playing of Harold "Shorty" Baker and other lyrical and soft-spoken trumpeters.

Recommended CDs: with Duke Ellington: *The Okeh Ellington* (Columbia 46177)

Box Set: with Duke Ellington: *Early Ellington* (3 CDs; GRP/Decca 3-640)

Film Appearances: *Black and Tan* (1929), a film short with Duke Ellington

JOHNNY WIGGS

• • • • • • • • • • • • • •

b. July 25, 1899, New Orleans, LA, d. Oct. 9, 1977, New Orleans, LA

A New Orleans player with a gentle sound, Johnny Wiggs really had two careers as a trumpeter, with a long period in between. Born John Wigginton Hyman (becoming known as Johnny Wiggs in the 1930s), he originally played mandolin and violin but was inspired to switch to cornet after he heard King Oliver. Wiggs studied music at Loyola University and was a professional by 1920. He played in the South with the New Orleans Owls, Norman Brownlee (1924–25), Happy Schilling, Peck Kelly, Ellis Strakato's Hotel Jung Roof Band, and Earl Crumb's Suburban Gardens Band. Wiggs (as John Hyman) recorded in 1927 with his Bayou Stompers and the following year with clarinetist Tony Parenti.

With the onset of the Depression, Wiggs became a part-time player, working mostly as a teacher. However, the success of the New Orleans revival convinced him to return to music. By 1948 he was leading his own band, playing steadily until 1974. Johnny Wiggs (who made records with George Lewis and Lizzie Miles) recorded often as a leader during 1948–57 (for New Orleans, Commodore, Southland, Steiner-Davis, Golden Crest, Paramount, and Jazzology), with some additional sessions during 1968–73 (for Fat Cat Jazz and Pearl).

Recommended CDs: *Sounds of New Orleans, Vol. 2* (Storyville 6009), 3 songs on *Recorded in New Orleans, Vol. 2* (Good Time Jazz 12020), with Tom Brown: *And His New Orleans Jazz Band* (GHB 3)

LPs to Search For: *Congo Square* (New Orleans Records 7206), *Johnny Wiggs at Preservation Hall* (Pearl 5)

JOE WILDER

b. Feb. 22, 1922, Colwyn, PA

Trumpeter Joe Wilder's pretty tone, lyrical style, strong technical skills, and professionalism made him both an ideal studio musician and a fine swing-based jazz improviser. Wilder studied at the Mastbaum School of Music in Philadelphia and performed with the big bands of Les Hite (1941) and Lionel Hampton (1942–43). While in the Marines, he co-led a band, returning to Hampton after his discharge. Wilder worked with the orchestras of Jimmie Lunceford (1946–47), Lucky Millinder, Sam Donahue, and Herbie Fields before becoming a studio musician. Although he was with Count Basie's big band for six months in 1954 and toured the USSR with Benny Goodman in 1962, Wilder mostly was content to play behind the scenes, whether in the pit orchestras for Broadway musicals or as a member of the staff for ABC-TV (1957–73).

Joe Wilder, whose haunting solos are always subtle and memorable, has never thought of himself as just a jazz player (in the early 1960s he recorded an album of classical trumpet pieces), which unfortunately has led him to be a bit underrepresented on records. However, he did lead albums for Savoy (1956) and Columbia (two in 1959), co-led a set with Joe Newman for Concord, and in the 1990s recorded two CDs for Evening Star; he also appeared on records during the past decade with Benny Carter, the Tom Talbert Orchestra, and the Statesmen of Jazz.

Recommended CDs: Wilder 'n Wilder (Savoy 1191), *Hangin' Out* (Concord Jazz 4262), *Alone with Just My Dreams* (Evening Star 101), *No Greater Love* (Evening Star 103)

LPs to Search For: The Pretty Sound (Columbia 1372), *Jazz from Peter Gunn* Columbia 8121)

Recommended Reading: American Musicians II by Whitney Balliett (Oxford University Press, 1996), *In the Mainstream* by Chip Deffaa (Scarecrow Press, 1992)

Videos to Get: The Sound of Jazz (1957; Vintage Jazz Classics 2001), *Flip Phillips' 80th Birthday Party* (1995; Arbors ARVHS2)

COOTIE WILLIAMS

b. July 24, 1910, Mobile, AL, d. Sept. 15, 1985, New York, NY

One of the top trumpeters of the 1930s, Charles Melvin "Cootie" Williams had a colorful and eventful career. Williams early on played trombone, tuba, and drums in a school band. He was mostly self-taught on the trumpet, gigging in Alabama as a teenager. When he was 14, Williams toured for the summer with the Young Family Band, a group that included Lester and Lee Young. He also played in Florida with Eagle Eye Shields and with Alonzo Ross' De Luxe Syncopators (1926–28).

Moving to New York in 1928, Cootie Williams recorded with James P. Johnson, worked with Chick Webb and Fletcher Henderson, and in February 1929 joined Duke Ellington's orchestra as the replacement for the alcoholic Bubber Miley. Miley was famous for his mastery with mutes and for creating a wide variety of unusual sounds, blending in perfectly with trombonist Tricky Sam Nanton. Williams played open horn for his first couple of weeks with Duke, until it finally dawned on him that he was in Miley's spot. He learned fast (assisted by Nanton) and eventually surpassed his predecessor.

Williams was one of Ellington's main stars in the 1930s, taking both open and muted solos; "Concerto for Cootie" was just one of his many features. He also led eight small-group sessions during 1937–40, using other Ellington sidemen and Duke himself on piano. It was therefore a major surprise when, in November 1940, he left Ellington's band to accept a more lucrative offer from Benny Goodman, who offered him a one-year contract. Bandleader Raymond Scott saluted the occasion by writing and recording the song "When Cootie Left the Duke." With Goodman, Williams had plenty of solo space, both with the big band and a version of the Benny Goodman Sextet (actually septet) that included tenor saxophonist Georgie Auld and guitarist Charlie Christian.

After the Goodman period ended, in October 1941 Williams asked Ellington for his old job back. However, Duke, who by then had Ray Nance in Cootie's spot, suggested that he form his own big band instead. Williams followed the advice, and he soon had an orchestra that was playing regularly at the Savoy Ballroom. The Cootie Williams Big Band was the first to record a pair of Thelonious Monk tunes ("Epistrophy" and "'Round Midnight"), featured the advanced trumpeter Joe Guy (as a contrast to the leader) in 1942, and during 1944–45 had such interesting soloists as pianist Bud Powell, altoist-singer Eddie "Cleanhead" Vinson, and tenor saxophonist Eddie "Lockjaw" Davis.

The big band broke up in 1948, but Williams continued at the Savoy with a smaller group, having an R&B hit with a showcase for the honking tenor of Willis Jackson called "Gator." Williams worked steadily in the 1950s but mostly in obscurity, not recording at all during 1951–56 (other than four vocal titles). Since he was still identified with Duke Ellington after all this time, it was only right that in the fall of 1962 he rejoined Ellington, after a 22-year "vacation." Although he was now older and played in a much sparser style than earlier, he was still a powerful trumpeter, making every expressive growl count. Cootie Williams quickly became again one of Ellington's main stars, and he remained with the big band until Duke's death in 1974. Cootie Williams recorded one final album with Mercer Ellington in 1975 and retired in the late '70s, secure in his position as one of jazz's great swing trumpet stars.

Recommended CDs: *1941–1944* (Classics 827), *1945–1946* (Classics 981), with Charlie Christian: *The Genius of the Electric Guitar* (Columbia 40846), with Duke Ellington: *Jubilee Stomp* (Bluebird 66038), *The Okeh Ellington* (Columbia/Legacy 46177), *The Duke's Men, Vol. 1* (Columbia/Legacy 46905), *The Duke's Men, Vol. 2* (Columbia/Legacy 48835), *70th Birthday Concert* (Blue Note 32746), with Benny Goodman: *Featuring Charlie Christian* (Columbia 45144)

Box Set: with Duke Ellington: *Early Ellington* (3 CDs; GRP/Decca 3-640)

LPs to Search For: *Typhoon* (Swingtime 1003), *The Big Challenge* (Fresh Sound 720)

Recommended Reading: *The World of Duke Ellington* by Stanley Dance (Charles Scribner's Sons, 1970)

Videos to Get: *Duke Ellington: Memories of Duke* (1984, filmed mostly in 1968; A*Vision 50187)

FRANC WILLIAMS

b. Oct. 20, 1910, Mills, PA, d. Oct. 2, 1983, Houston, PA

A fine section player who occasionally soloed, Franc Williams had a pretty tone and a swing-oriented style. In the 1930s and '40s he worked with Frank Terry's Chicago Nightingales, Fats Waller's big band, Claude Hopkins, Edgar Hayes, Ella Fitzgerald, Sabby Lewis, and Machito (1944). Williams gained his greatest recognition while with Duke Ellington during 1945–49, but because he was the lead trumpeter, solo space was quite rare. He was back with Ellington briefly in 1951 but otherwise mostly freelanced with Latin bands (including Tito Puente) for the next two decades. Ironically it was in the 1970s, when he was already in his sixties, that Franc Williams finally gained some exposure: with the Harlem Blues and Jazz Band, his Swing Four (1975–76), and especially as a member of Panama Francis' Savoy Sultans.

LPs to Search For: with Panama Francis: *And the Savoy Sultans* (Classic Jazz 149), *Vol. II* (Classic Jazz 150)

RICHARD WILLIAMS

b. May 4, 1931, Galveston, TX, d. Nov. 5, 1985, New York, NY

R ichard Williams was a strong soloist with a big sound and a wide range, so it seems odd that his career did not go much further, particularly since he played with many top musicians along the way. Williams actually started on tenor sax, gigging with local bands in Texas. But after he attended Wiley College and spent four years in the Air Force (1952–56), he emerged as a trumpeter. Williams played with Lionel Hampton in 1956–57, attended the Manhattan School of Music, and during 1959–64 worked on and off with Charles Mingus, his most famous association. Williams also played with Gigi Gryce (1959–62), Oliver Nelson, Yusef Lateef, Quincy Jones, Lou Donaldson, Slide Hampton, Eric Dolphy, Orchestra USA, Rahsaan Roland Kirk, Randy Weston, and Booker Ervin during the era. He seemed poised for stardom when he recorded his one album as a leader, an exciting quintet set for Candid in 1960, but there were no encores.

The trumpeter worked primarily as a sideman throughout his career, recording with Duke Ellington in 1965 and 1971 and playing with the Thad Jones-Mel Lewis Orchestra (1966–70), Gil Evans (1972–73), the Clark Terry Big Band, Mingus Dynasty (the early 1980s), and pit bands for Broadway musicals. Yet when Richard Williams passed away in 1985 at the age of 54, he was still little known, even to jazz listeners.

Recommended CD: *New Horn in Town* (Candid 79003), with Yusef Lateef: *Live at Pep's* (GRP/Impulse 134), with Charles Mingus: *Mingus Dynasty* (Columbia/Legacy 52922)

TOM WILLIAMS

b. Apr. 12, 1962, Baltimore, MD

Tom Williams is an excellent hard bop trumpeter who is heard at his best on his two Criss Cross CDs. The son of a music teacher, Williams began playing trumpet when he was five. He switched to drums for a time before settling on trumpet in junior high school. Williams considers his main influence to be Kenny Dorham. He attended Towson State University, worked in the show band for Sophisticated Ladies, and spent three years with the Mercer Ellington Orchestra. In the early to mid-1980s Williams worked with Ray Charles, Bill Hardman, Larry Willis, Charlie Rouse, Dizzy Gillespie, Jackie McLean, Hank Jones, and other straight-ahead artists. Looking for a more secure lifestyle, he joined the U.S. Army Field Band's Jazz Ambassadors in 1987, three years later switching to their Washington, D.C., band, Pershing's Own.

Despite being in the service, Tom Williams has occasionally been able to travel to New York for recordings, including dates with Jimmy Heath, Antonio Hart, Steve Wilson, Donald Brown, Ron Holloway, and Larry Willis.

Recommended CDs: *Introducing Tom Williams* (Criss Cross 1064), *Straight Street* (Criss Cross 1091), with Steve Wilson: *New York Summit* (Criss Cross 1062)

STU WILLIAMSON

b. May 14, 1933, Brattleboro, VT, d. Oct. 1, 1991, Studio City, CA

The younger brother of pianist Claude Williamson, Stu Williamson was a valuable trumpeter and valve trombonist in the 1950s before drugs completely ruined his life. Williamson moved to Los Angeles in 1949 and played with the Stan Kenton Orchestra (1951 and 1954–55), Woody Herman's big band (1952–53), the Lighthouse All-Stars (1954–55), Shelly Manne (1955–58), and the who's who of West Coast Jazz. Williamson, who began doubling on valve trombone in 1954, also worked steadily in the studios, where his mellow tone and fluent style were major assets. As a leader he recorded two albums for Bethlehem during 1955–56 (reissued by Fresh Sound), and he appeared on many records as a sideman, including with the just-mentioned groups, Zoot Sims, Elmo Hope, Clifford Brown, Art Pepper, Benny Carter, Mel Torme, Terry Gibbs, Lennie Niehaus, and quite a few others.

After such a promising start, Stu Williamson became less active after 1962 and stopped playing music altogether in 1968 (when he was 35), dropping completely out of the music scene and becoming a hopeless drug addict, a sad waste of talent.

Recommended CDs: *Stu Williamson Plays* (Fresh Sound 2011), *Pee Jay* (Fresh Sound 2003), with the Lighthouse All-Stars: *In the Solo Spotlight* (Original Jazz Classics 451), *Volume 6* (Original Jazz Classics 386), with Shelly Manne: *Vol. 4 Swinging Sounds* (Original Jazz Classics 267), *More Swinging Sounds* (Original Jazz Classics 320)

CLIVE WILSON

. . . .

b. Aug. 19, 1942, London, England

Clive Wilson is a solid New Orleans revival cornetist. He played piano as a child and when he was 16 bought his first cornet, inspired after hearing George Lewis' band during their British tour. Wilson earned a degree in physics at Newcastle University but decided to become a musician instead, moving to New Orleans in 1964.

He was a member of the Young Tuxedo Brass Band (1966–68 and 1970–73), recorded with Capn. John Handy, subbed with the Olympia Brass Band, and worked with Freddie Kohlman, Dave "Fat Man" Williams, and Papa French's Original Tuxedo Jazz Band (1974–77). Wilson toured with Bob Greene's *World of Jelly Roll Morton* (1979–82) and played in Europe with clarinetist Herb Hall. Clive Wilson is best known today for leading the Original Camellia Jazz Band, a group that he formed back in 1979; drummer Trevor Richards became co-leader in 1982.

Recommended CDs: *Original Camellia Jazz Band* (GHB 304), *That's My Home* (Jazzology 249), *Jazzology All Stars 50th Anniversary Jazz Bash* (Jazzology 350)

LPs to Search For: with Barry Martyn: *On Tour 1969* (Swift 4)

JOHNNY WINDHURST

. . . .

b. Nov. 5, 1926, Bronx, NY, d. Oct. 21, 1981, Poughkeepsie, NY

A talented Dixieland player with a warm sound who peaked rather early in his career, Johnny Windhurst was done in by alcohol, trying in vain to keep up with the hard drinkers who populated the Eddie Condon gang.

Self-taught (he never learned to read music), Windhurst started playing professionally in 1944. At 19 he was tapped as Bunk Johnson's replacement with Sidney Bechet's short-lived band in 1945, acquitting himself very well, as can be heard on surviving broadcasts from their residency at Boston's Savoy Café. Windhurst was based in Boston for a time, worked with Nappy Lamare (1947–48) in Los Angeles, led the Riverboat Five, and during 1952–53 played at Eddie Condon's. He recorded with Eddie Condon in 1950, was with the groups of George Wettling (1953) and Jack Teagarden (1954), and led Dixieland bands, often in the Midwest. Windhurst recorded with Barbara Lea (1955–57), Jack Teagarden (1955), Walt Gifford's New Yorkers, Lee Wiley, and his quartet in 1956 (his only set as a leader).

Unfortunately the excessive alcohol intake (which never seemed to bother such diehards as Wild Bill Davison and Jimmy McPartland) took its toll. After working at Condon's during 1959–60, Windhurst largely dropped out of music. In later years he occasionally played at a local club in Poughkeepsie, New York, called Frivolous Sal's Last Chance Saloon, and for him it was his final chance. Johnny Windhurst died in 1981 of a heart attack at the age of 54, having largely wasted his final 20 years after such a strong start.

Recommended CDs: with Eddie Condon: *Dr. Jazz Series, Vol. 1* (Storyville 6041), *Dr. Jazz Series, Vol. 8* (Storyville 6048), with Barbara Lea: *Barbara Lea* (Original Jazz Classics 1713), *Lea in Love* (Original Jazz Classics 1743)

LPs to Search For: *The Imaginative Johnny Windhurst* (Jazzology 3), with Sidney Bechet: *Jazz Nocturne Vols. 4–6* (Fat Cat's Jazz 004, 005, and 006), *Jazz Nocturne, Vols. 10–12* (Fat Cat's Jazz 010, 011, and 012)

LAMMAR WRIGHT

• • • • • • • • • • • • • • •

b. June 20, 1907, Texarkana, TX, d. Apr. 13, 1973, New York, NY

Lammar Wright was a talented if underutilized soloist who had two longtime associations. As a 16-year-old he joined Bennie Moten's orchestra in 1923, staying for five years. He left in 1928 to join the Missourians, and his timing was perfect. He shared the trumpet solos with R.Q. Dickerson during the band's three recording sessions of 1929–30 and stayed with the orchestra when it was taken over by Cab Calloway. Wright was with Calloway for most of the glory years, staying until 1942, although his solo space (particularly in later years) was quite limited.

After the Calloway period, Wright played first trumpet in the big bands of Don Redman (1943), Cootie Williams (1944), Claude Hopkins (1944–46), and Lucky Millinder (a few times during 1946–52). With the end of the big band era, Wright became a studio musician and a music teacher, recording in later years with Arnett Cobb, Count Basie, and the Sauter-Finegan Orchestra. Lammar Wright was the father of Lammar Wright Jr. and Elmon Wright, both of whom played trumpet with Dizzy Gillespie's big band in the 1940s.

Recommended CDs: with Cab Calloway: *Cab Calloway and the Missourians 1929–30* (JSP 328), with Bennie Moten: *1923–1927* (Classics 549)

SNOOKY YOUNG

• • • • • • • • • • • • • • •

b. Feb. 3, 1919, Dayton, OH

One of the more beloved trumpeters in jazz, Eugene "Snooky" Young has been both a well-respected first trumpeter and a solid swing soloist who is particularly effective using mutes. Young began his career playing with Eddie Heywood Sr., pianist Graham Jackson, the Wilberforce Collegians, and Clarence "Chic" Carter (1937–39). When he was 20, in 1939, Young joined Jimmie Lunceford's orchestra and made a strong impression, taking swinging solos (his spot on "Uptown Blues" is considered a classic) and uplifting the ensembles.

In 1942 Young left Lunceford's band, had short stints with Count Basie (1942) and Lionel Hampton, and then moved to California. He worked in the Los Angeles area with Les Hite, Benny Carter, Gerald Wilson's early bebop orchestra, and Hampton again before spending a second period with Basie's big band (1945–47). At that point, Snooky's career took an unexpected detour. He returned home to Dayton and played locally for a decade.

In 1957 Young re-emerged, rejoining Count Basie's orchestra, playing first trumpet for five years and really contributing to the band's sound with his perfectly in-tune upper-register notes. In 1962 he became a full-time studio musician (at first in New York before settling permanently in Los Angeles). Young worked with the Tonight Show Band (1972–92), Jaco Pastorius' Word of Mouth Orchestra, and the big bands of Benny Goodman and Thad Jones/Mel Lewis. In the 1990s, Snooky Young was still in close-to-prime form, popping out high notes while playing with Gerald Wilson and the Clayton-Hamilton Jazz Orchestra.

Recommended CDs: *Snooky and Marshall's Album* (Concord Jazz 4055), with the Clayton-Hamilton Jazz Orchestra: *Groove Shop* (Capri 74021), with Jimmie Lunceford: *1939–1940* (Classics 565), *1940–1941* (Classics 622)

LPs to Search For: *The Boys from Dayton* (Master Jazz 8130), *Horn of Plenty* (Concord Jazz 91)

Recommended Reading: *The World of Count Basie* by Stanley Dance (Charles Scribner's Sons, 1980)

Film Appearances: Snooky Young ghosts the trumpet solos for Jack Carson in *Blues in the Night* (1941)

ZEKE ZARCHY
. . . .

b. June 12, 1915, New York, NY

A fine swing and Dixieland player, Zeke Zarchy is one of the last significant musicians left from the original Glenn Miller Orchestra.

My brother was three years older than me and played banjo. I trailed along with him to rehearsals and loved the music. When I was 11, I visited a second cousin's home when he had a four-piece band rehearsal and was fascinated with his trumpet playing. My brother bought me my first horn. My idol, as well as the idol of everyone else I knew, was Louis Armstrong. I knew I wanted to be a musician after my first job. I was 14 years old and played my first gig, four hours, for $1!

When Zarchy was 20, he joined Joe Haymes' Orchestra (1935–36). He spent some time with most of the top white swing bands, including Benny Goodman, Artie Shaw, Bob Crosby (twice during 1937–39), Red Norvo, and Tommy Dorsey (1939–40), usually playing first trumpet and not getting many solos. He spent part of 1940 with Glenn Miller's orchestra before joining the staff of NBC for two years. While in the military (1942–45), Zarchy had the opportunity during 1944–45 to play with Miller's Army Air Force Band.

After his discharge, Zarchy became a studio musician in Los Angeles, working with Paul Weston and many orchestras. Zarchy, who recorded with Boyd Raeburn (1945), Benny Goodman (1947), Woody Herman (1947), and Bob Crosby (1950–51) among many others, has been featured with many swing reunion bands through the years, including quite a few gatherings of Glenn Miller alumni. Zeke Zarchy finally had some opportunities to solo in the 1980s and '90s, playing Dixieland at classic jazz festivals with the Great Pacific Jazz Band, paying tribute to Louis Armstrong with his rendition of "Potato Head Blues."

LPs to Search For: with the Great Pacific Jazz Band: *Plays the Music of Louis Armstrong* (Sacramento 531)

JAMES ZOLLAR
• • • • • • • • • • • • •

b. July 24, 1959, Kansas City, MO

Although thought of as a post-bop player, James Zollar has a remarkably wide-ranging resume, attesting to his versatility and flexibility. Zollar started on trumpet when he was 12, growing up in San Francisco (where he studied with Woody Shaw) and San Diego. Early in his career he played swing, blues, and bebop with Jay McShann, Eddie Vinson, the Cheathams, Big Joe Turner, and Roger Neumann's Rather Large Band. In 1985 Zollar worked with the Mercer Ellington big band and recorded with swing violinist Claude Williams. Since then he has performed everything from swing and hard bop to Afro-Cuban and avant-garde jazz with the likes of Panama Francis, Lester Bowie, Sunny Murray, Craig Harris, Charli Persip's big band, Bob Stewart, Steve Coleman's Five Elements, Mongo Santamaria, Hamiet Bluiett, Henry Threadgill, Hilton Ruiz, the Sam Rivers big band, Don Byron, and David Murray, among many others. James Zollar (who has led a CD for Naxos) is definitely a difficult trumpeter to typecast!

Recommended CDs: *Soaring with Bird* (Naxos 86008), with David Murray: *Dark Star* (Astor Place 4002), with Bob Stewart: *Goin' Home* (JMT 834 427)

GLENN ZOTTOLA
• • • • • • • • • • • • •

b. Apr. 28, 1947, Port Chester, NY

Glenn Zottola, a versatile mainstream swing player, has the unusual double of trumpet and alto sax. Zottola first started playing trumpet when he was three and he performed in public at age 13 in his family's jazz club. Among his more notable associations through the years have been Lionel Hampton (1970), Mel Torme, Tex Beneke, the Benny Goodman Sextet (1977–79), Bobby Hackett, Bob Wilber's Bechet Legacy, Butch Miles, Maxine Sullivan, John Clayton, and Peanuts Hucko (with whom he toured Europe in 1991). Although he has not become as famous as he should be, Glenn Zottola (whose dates as a leader for the defunct Dreamstreet and Famous Door labels have yet to be reissued on CD) is certainly an impressive player.

Recommended CDs: with Steve Allen: *Plays Jazz Tonight* (Concord Jazz 4548), with Bob Wilber: *Bechet Legacy* (GHB 201), *Ode to Bechet* (Jazzology 142)

LPs to Search For: *Live at Eddie Condon's* (Dreamstreet 105), *Steamin' Mainstream* (Dreamstreet 107), *Secret Love* (Famous Door 141), *Stardust* (Famous Door 149), *Christmas in Jazztime* (Dreamstreet 110)

They Also Played Trumpet

I n addition to the 479 Trumpet Kings, I thought it would be interesting to have a section devoted to musicians who were famous at other things but also somewhere along the way played trumpet. The recordings that are recommended feature these musicians on trumpet at least part of the time. Though it was tempting to put Clint Eastwood (who played trumpet in his youth) in this section, he unfortunately has never recorded on trumpet!

The 29 individuals documented here would never consider themselves to be trumpeters first, although several were/are talented enough to have had a full-time career in that area if they had not been sidetracked into more lucrative fields.

MOSE ALLISON
• • • • • • • • • • • • •

b. Nov. 11, 1927, Tippo, MS

M ose Allison has been famous since the late 1950s as a witty and insightful lyricist, a unique singer, and an eccentric pianist whose colorful down-home improvisations give the impression of driving around in a pickup truck and having adventures along the way.

Mose Allison as a trumpeter? In high school in the early 1940s, the self-taught Allison started playing trumpet for the fun of it, although he does not seem to have played any serious gigs on the instrument. On November 18, 1957, on his second record as a leader, he plays a very effective three-minute muted solo on "Trouble in Mind," hinting at both Harry "Sweets" Edison and (oddly enough) King Oliver. In fact, Mose Allison plays well enough that it is surprising that he never recorded on trumpet again.

Recommended CDs: *Local Color* (Original Jazz Classics 457)

DAN BARRETT

• • • • • • • • • • • •

b. Dec. 14, 1955, Pasadena, CA

Dan Barrett is one of the finest trombonists in the current classic jazz scene, being able to emulate anyone from Jack Teagarden to Tricky Sam Nanton while playing primarily in his own swing/trad style. His background (including stints with the South Frisco Jazz Band and the Golden Eagle Jazz Band) is in 1920s jazz and Dixieland, but Barrett has also played more swing-oriented music with guitarist Howard Alden, Benny Goodman, and singer Rebecca Kilgore. Since the early 1990s, he has been the musical director for the Arbors label.

Although he will always be best known as a trombonist, Barrett is also a very effective cornetist, with an appealing tone and a solid range. Surprisingly little has been made of his doubling, but his cornet solos are of such a high quality that it does not sound like it is being played on his second-best instrument!

A versatile swing trombonist, Dan Barrett plays the coronet so strong that it certainly does not sound like his second instrument.

JOE BUSHKIN
• • • • • • • • • • • •

b. Nov. 2, 1916, New York, NY

A fine swing pianist, a charming vocalist, a songwriter (his main hit was "Oh Look at Me Now"), and one of the last survivors from the swing era, the still-active Joe Bushkin worked with (among others) Billie Holiday, Bunny Berigan, Eddie Condon, Muggsy Spanier, the Tommy Dorsey Orchestra (1940–42), Benny Goodman, Louis Armstrong, and Bing Crosby.

Never a serious trumpeter, Bushkin nevertheless played a little bit of trumpet (for atmosphere) on the odd comedy number "Private Jives" (with Bud Freeman and Minerva Pious cast as characters) in 1938. His few "encores" were on "Something in Your Smile" in the mid-1960s (from an album of *Doctor Doolittle* themes) and two flugelhorn solos on his 1977 record *100 Years of Recorded Sound*, sounding a bit like Ruby Braff during "I've Grown Accustomed to Her Face."

JOHNNY CARISI
• • • • • • • • • • • •

b. Feb. 23, 1922, Hasbrouck Heights, NJ, d. Oct. 3, 1992, New York, NY

Johnny Carisi's main fame is for having composed "Israel," a complex blues that was recorded by the Miles Davis Birth of the Cool Nonet. His most significant work throughout his career was as an arranger for jazz orchestras (including those of Ray McKinley, Charlie Barnet, and Claude Thornhill), for the studios, and in classical music.

Self-taught on trumpet, Carisi played primarily with obscure big bands during 1938–43, served with Glenn Miller's Army Air Force Band, and was a member of the Claude Thornhill Orchestra (1949–50). He played trumpet on only an infrequent basis during his last 40 years, though he did work with Gil Evans, Brew Moore (1969–70), and Loren Schoenberg. A trumpeter who fell between cool jazz and swing, Johnny Carisi can be heard playing at his best on the session included in the Bluebird reissue listed next (which includes versions of his compositions "Israel," "Lesterian Mode," and "Springsville").

Recommended CDs: *The RCA Victor Jazz Workshop* (Bluebird 6471)

HOAGY CARMICHAEL
• • • • • • • • • • • • • • •

b. Nov. 11, 1899, Bloomington, IN, d. Dec. 27, 1981, Palm Springs, CA

One of America's finest songwriters, Hoagy Carmichael was responsible for such songs as "Stardust," "Georgia on My Mind," "The Nearness of You," "Skylark," and "Up the Lazy River," to name just five. He was a decent pianist and a personable singer, appearing in many Hollywood movies, playing a world-weary but wise pianist and confidant.

Carmichael always loved jazz of the 1920s (he wrote the trad standard "Riverboat Shuffle"), and one of his idols and good friends was Bix Beiderbecke. In fact, his great affection for the music led him to play cornet now and then during that decade, generally with more enthusiasm than talent. Hoagy can be heard happily jamming along with the ensembles on his recordings of "Friday Night" and "Walkin' the Dog" from 1927–28. But by 1929 he was concentrating on other areas of music, and his cornet playing was forgotten.

LPs to Search For: *Curtis Hitch and Hoagy Carmichael* (Fountain 109)

BENNY CARTER

* * * * * * * * * * * * * *

b. Aug. 8, 1907, New York, NY

Benny Carter has had a remarkably long and productive career. One of the great alto saxophonists of the late 1920s (and the early 1990s!), Carter has had a distinctive voice on the instrument for over 70 years. In addition, he has long been a major arranger, an underrated composer, a significant bandleader, and along the way also played effective clarinet (in the 1930s) and even tenor and piano.

Although trumpet was never Benny Carter's main instrument, it was his first horn and his favorite ax throughout his long career, even though he never played it on a full-time basis. His mother gave him piano lessons back in 1917, and he bought his first cornet in 1921. However, Carter grew impatient at not being able to master the horn in a few hours (!) and he soon traded it in for a C-melody sax. A cousin, trumpeter Cuban Bennett (who unfortunately never recorded), was an early influence on his jazz style and, ultimately, his trumpet playing when he took it up again a few years later.

A professional musician by 1924, by 1927 Carter was playing alto sax and arranging for Charlie Johnson's orchestra. In 1928 he led the Wilberforce Collegians and started doubling on trumpet. He did not play trumpet during his periods with Fletcher Henderson (1928–31) and McKinney's Cotton Pickers (which he led during 1931–32). But when he began heading his big band in 1932, he brought back the trumpet, displaying a thoughtful improvising style and a warm tone. Carter's talents were too plentiful for him to restrict himself to one horn, although in 1935 he did work for three months as a trumpeter with Willie Bryant's orchestra. He spent the 1935–38 period overseas, where he was kept quite busy and played as much trumpet as he ever did in his life.

Carter picked up the trumpet now and then after returning to the United States in 1938, including for an excellent session with Lionel Hampton and as a double with his big bands of 1939–46, although he was always best known as an altoist. He appeared in the film *Stormy Weather* playing "Honeysuckle Rose" on trumpet with a group led by Fats Waller, took a few solos during a 1958 album with Earl Hines (*Swingin' the Twenties*), and recorded on the horn as late as 1989 for a set with Phil Woods.

Benny Carter always said that, although he loved the trumpet, he never felt as if he had enough time to practice it. However, his relatively few recordings on the instrument show that he really was a masterful swing stylist.

Recommended CDs: *1933–1936* (Classics 530), *1937–1939* (Classics 552), *Swingin' the Twenties* (Original Jazz Classics 339), *My Man Benny, My Man Phil* (Musicmasters 5036)

Film Appearances: *Stormy Weather* (1943) with Fats Waller

DICK CARY

* * * * * * * * * *

b. July 10, 1916, Hartford, CT, d. Apr. 6, 1994, Glendale, CA

Dick Cary had so many talents, as a pianist, an arranger, and even a peck horn player, that his trumpet playing tends to be overlooked. He actually started out as a violinist but made his initial mark on piano, playing with Joe Marsalis (1942), working at Nick's (1942–43), having a stint with the Casa Loma Orchestra, and, after the Army, being an original member of the Louis Armstrong All-Stars (1947). He was associated with Eddie Condon's groups in the 1950s (as an arranger, on peck horn, and occasionally on trumpet), worked with Bobby Hackett and Pee Wee Russell, and was an active participant in the trad jazz scene until his death, although his writing for his rehearsal bands in his later years was often quite adventurous.

As an occasional trumpeter, Cary had a cool tone (he could have fit well into 1950s West Coast jazz) and a subtle style. His hard-to-find recordings as a leader are generally the best spots to hear his trumpet playing.

LPs to Search For: *Hot and Cool* (Stereocraft 106), *The Amazing Dick Cary* (Circle 18)

JOHN CHILTON

* * * * * * * * * * * * *

b. July 16, 1932, London, England

The author of several major jazz books, John Chilton is much better known as a writer than as a musician. Among his works have been *Who's Who in Jazz* (a very valuable book tracing the lives of jazz musicians born before 1920) and biographies of Billie Holiday (*Billie's Blues*), Sidney Bechet (*The Wizard of Jazz*), and Coleman Hawkins (*The Song of the Hawk*), among others.

John Chilton has actually played trumpet in trad bands in his native England for decades. Among his associations have been Bruce Turner's Jump Band (1958–63), Alex Welsh, Mike Daniels, the Swiss King (1966–68), and the Feetwarmers (in the 1970s and '80s). The last group often backed singer George Melly.

LPs to Search For: with George Melly: *At It Again* (Reprise 4084), *Let's Do It* (Pye 131), *Makin' Whoopee* (Pye 147), *The Many Moods of Melly* (Pye 6550).

LARRY CLINTON

b. Aug. 17, 1909, New York, NY, d. May 2, 1985, Tucson, AZ

Larry Clinton was one of the more highly respected arrangers of the swing era. After writing arrangements for the big bands of Isham Jones, Claude Hopkins, the Dorsey Brothers, Jimmy Dorsey, Tommy Dorsey (the hit "The Dipsy Doodle"), and the Casa Loma Orchestra, he led some studio sides in 1937. Because those records sold quite well, in 1938 he reluctantly left the studios to tour with a big band, featuring the vocals of Bea Wain and having a hit of his own with his adaptation of "My Reverie."

Although Clinton (who was a self-taught musician) had had earlier stints on trumpet with other bands and played trumpet for the first year or so with his orchestra, like trombonist Glenn Miller, he never really soloed. By mid-1938 he held his trumpet more than he played it. He occasionally played in the ensembles through the years but was not really heard, posing with a trumpet as late as 1958 for the cover photo of his album *My Million Sellers*.

ORNETTE COLEMAN

b. Mar. 9, 1930, Fort Worth, TX

Ornette Coleman is one of the major jazz innovators of the past 45 years. His alto playing caused a bit of an uproar when his quartet with Don Cherry debuted at New York's Five Spot Café in 1959. Coleman and his musicians improvised without using chord structures, basing their solos on the mood of the piece and their intuitive interplay. Coleman's tone was very speechlike (purposely going in and out of tune). And although Ornette's flights tended to be full of spontaneous melodies, listeners debated for years not only whether what he was playing was good jazz, but whether it was music at all!

Over time, nearly all of Coleman's detractors have grudgingly acknowledged his importance in free jazz, and he has long been a very influential force in avant-garde music. His work with his quartet, his writing for classical ensembles, and (starting in the early 1970s) his free funk explorations with the electric Prime Time have all been quite original.

As if he were not controversial enough, in 1965, when Coleman emerged from a nearly three-year period off the scene, he started playing trumpet and violin in public, as occasional contrasts with his alto. While Coleman's alto playing had improved and become even more fluent than before, he seemed to play the violin as if it were drums. On trumpet, Coleman's volume was much more impressive than his sound or his limited technique, and the more conservative listeners regarded his trumpet blasts as more of an annoyance or a joke than something to be taken seriously.

Most of the time Coleman used his trumpet only briefly on records, perhaps for part of one or two songs, since the alto remained his main voice. There was one unfortunate exception: In 1967 when he recorded *New and Old Gospel* with altoist Jackie McLean, instead of its being a summit meeting of altos (which might have resulted in a classic), Coleman played trumpet throughout the entire program, making the music much more erratic. Fans of Ornette Coleman's trumpet playing will find this workout (his most extensive trumpet solos on record) quite intriguing, but otherwise it is definitely for specialized tastes!

Recommended CDs: with Jackie McLean: *New and Old Gospel* (Blue Note 53356)

JOEY DEFRANCESCO

· · · · · · · · · · · · · · · · · ·

b. Apr. 10, 1971, Springfield, PA

When Joey DeFrancesco arrived on the scene in the late 1980s, the popularity of the Hammond B-3 organ had been in retreat for 15 years, as the instrument was replaced by the electric piano and synthesizer. However, DeFrancesco's enthusiasm, talent at emulating Jimmy Smith, and high energy literally brought the organ back from the dead and made it easier for veterans of the instrument to make comebacks.

Joey DeFrancesco, a high-energy organist, plays occasional trumpet in a lyrical style touched by Miles Davis.

In addition to his organ workouts, DeFrancesco has been an excellent if part-time trumpeter for some time, sounding a bit like Miles Davis (with whom he had played keyboards in 1988). He takes four fine trumpet solos on 1992's *Reboppin'* and plays primarily trumpet on two CDs led by his father, organist Papa John DeFrancesco.

Recommended CDs: *Reboppin'* (Columbia 48624); with Papa John DeFrancesco: *Doodlin'* (Muse 5501), *Comin' Home* (Muse 5531)

JIMMY DORSEY
. . . .

b. Feb. 29, 1904, Shenandoah, PA, d. June 12, 1957, New York, NY

Jimmy Dorsey was a major alto saxophonist and clarinetist as early as 1925, appearing on many records during the next decade, often with his brother, trombonist Tommy Dorsey. After an argument led the siblings to break up the Dorsey Brothers Orchestra of 1934–35, Dorsey struggled with his big band for six years until having hit records featuring the vocals of Helen O'Connell and Bob Eberle. Dorsey's jazz playing took a back seat during the swing era, but he remained a fine musician and enjoyed playing Dixieland, including with his 1949 Original Dorseyland Jazz Band (a combo taken out of his big band). In 1953 Jimmy and Tommy formed a new Dorsey Brothers Orchestra, a nostalgia band that stayed active and had a regular television show until the co-leaders' deaths during 1956–57.

The Dorseys' father was a musician and a music teacher who taught his sons several instruments early on. Jimmy Dorsey's first instrument was actually the cornet, which he played when he was practically an infant. He was featured on cornet in his father's band from the time he was seven until he switched to alto sax when he was 11. Once in a great while in the 1920s and early '30s, he would pick up a trumpet and play a few notes on it. For the February 28 and May 8, 1933, sessions by the Joe Venuti-Eddie Lang Blue Five, Jimmy alternates between alto, clarinet, and trumpet on six numbers, not sounding bad on the last . Unfortunately he seems never to have played trumpet seriously again during his remaining 24 years.

LPs to Search For: *Joe Venuti and Eddie Lang 1930–1933* (Swaggie 819)

TOMMY DORSEY
. . . .

b. Nov. 19, 1905, Shenandoah, PA, d. Nov. 26, 1956, Greenwich, CT

The "sentimental gentleman of swing" was world renowned for his beautiful tone on trombone. He played with his older brother Jimmy on and off during 1925–35 in many settings, ranging from Dixielandish jazz to commercial studio orchestras. After he left the Dorsey Brothers big band in 1935, Tommy Dorsey formed a successful orchestra of his own that, after Bunny Berigan uplifted his hit records of "Marie" and "Song of India" in 1937, was one of the major big bands of the swing era. Dorsey remained a household name up until his death in 1956.

Few of Tommy Dorsey's fans probably realize that he played trumpet in the 1920s. Unlike Jimmy, who picked up the horn only as a novelty, Tommy was an intriguing player whose dirty tone and bluish style was a major contrast to his smooth trombone; he sounded like a completely different musician. He recorded fairly frequently on trumpet during 1927–29, including four numbers in which he was the only horn in a quartet/quintet; perfect for blindfold tests! Tommy Dorsey played trumpet on an occasional basis into 1935 but almost never again after he started leading his big band.

LPs to Search For: *Trumpets and Trombones, Vol. 1* (Broadway 112), with Joe Venuti: *Stringing the Blues* (Columbia JC2L 24)

BILLY ECKSTINE

* * * * * * * * * * * * * * *

b. July 8, 1914, Pittsburgh, PA, d. Mar. 8, 1993, Pittsburgh, PA

The main importance to jazz of Billy Eckstine, who was an influential and popular baritone singer, is that during 1944–47 he led one of the first bebop big bands. Despite lucrative offers to become a single, he kept the orchestra (which featured most of the top younger modernists at one time or another) together as long as possible.

While touring with the big band, Eckstine learned how to play valve trombone and trumpet, occasionally recording on the former in the 1940s. He became such a successful middle-of-the-road pop singer in the 1950s that his jazz background was often forgotten by fans of his hit records. However, in 1960, for a live vocal set in Las Vegas (*No Cover, No Minimum*), Billy Eckstine, for the only time in his career, took a few surprisingly effective solos on trumpet.

Recommended CDs: *No Cover, No Minimum* (Roulette 98583)

MERCER ELLINGTON

* * * * * * * * * * * * * * * *

b. Mar. 11, 1919, Washington, DC, d. Feb. 8, 1996, Copenhagen, Denmark

The son of Duke Ellington and forever stuck in his father's shadow, Mercer Ellington had several careers, leading bands (1939, 1946–49, and 1959), being the road manager for the Cootie Williams Orchestra, serving as singer Della Reese's musical director, and working as a salesman, a record company executive, and a disc jockey. During the ASCAP strike of the early 1940s, he helped out his father by composing several important songs, including "Things Ain't What They Used to Be," "Blue Serge," "Moon Mist," and "Jumpin' Punkins."

Mercer Ellington played trumpet from an early age but must not have been that impressive. Other than four numbers in 1946 in which he played behind trumpeter-singer Jacques Butler, he did not even appear on his own records! He was a member of his father's trumpet section off and on during 1965–74 but never soloed and was more important as Duke's road manager. And once he took over the Duke Ellington Orchestra upon his father's death, his trumpet was put away forever.

BENNY GOODMAN

b. May 30, 1909, Chicago, IL, d. June 13, 1986, New York, NY

Benny Goodman was one of the greatest clarinet players ever, the King of Swing, the leader of the most popular big band of 1935–37, and one whose success helped more than anything else to launch the swing era. Benny Goodman began playing clarinet when he was 11, and he rarely let the instrument out of his sight after that, practicing constantly, no matter how famous and skilled he became. At 16, he was a soloist with Ben Pollack's orchestra, during 1929–33 he was a busy studio musician, and he led his first big band in 1934. After a year of struggle, on August 21, 1935, his orchestra caused a sensation at Los Angeles' Palomar Ballroom that was felt nationwide. Even after the swing era ended and his music was considered out of style, Goodman remained a household name, working as often as he wanted to up until his death in 1986.

So what is he doing in a trumpet book? During his studio days, Goodman (whose brothers Freddy Goodman and Irving Goodman were section trumpeters during the swing era) sometimes was assigned anonymous solos on alto and baritone sax. And on one occasion, his second recording date as a leader (June 4, 1928), he took the second cornet solo (following Jimmy McPartland) on "Jungle Blues." It was the only time in his career that the King can be heard on a brass instrument, and he fares pretty well.

W.C. HANDY

b. Nov. 16, 1873, Florence, AL, d. Mar. 28, 1958, New York, NY

In a word association game, the name W.C. Handy would probably generate the response "St. Louis Blues." Sometimes thought of as the father of the blues (although in reality he often gathered together and published the work of others), Handy's main significance is as a pioneer composer who published such songs as "Memphis Blues," "Beale Street Blues," "Careless Love," "Aunt Hagar's Blues," "Ole Miss," and "Yellow Dog Blues," plus the immortal "St. Louis Blues."

William Christopher Handy was also a musician, performing at least as early as 1896 as a cornetist. He led bands in the South and in 1917 relocated his Memphis Orchestra to New York, making recordings during 1917, 1919, and 1922–23. Unfortunately Handy was not a jazz player or even a particularly good cornetist, playing very straight and with a weak and inflexible tone. After 1923 he played only on an infrequent basis. In 1939 he recorded four numbers with an all-star sextet taken from the Luis Russell band (which at the time was Louis Armstrong's backup group), but W.C. Handy still sounds very straight (having apparently never learned to swing) and quite out of place even while playing his own tunes.

Recommended CDs: *W.C. Handy's Memphis Blues Band* (Memphis Archives 7006)

EDDIE HARRIS

• • • • • • • • • • • •

b. Oct. 20, 1934, Chicago, IL, d. Nov. 5, 1996, Los Angeles, CA

An innovator with the electric saxophone, Eddie Harris always had his own sound on tenor sax. After serving in the military, his first record in 1961 resulted in a hit version of "Exodus." At that early stage, Harris could already hit very high notes on tenor perfectly in tune, had a cool but warm sound, and displayed a healthy sense of humor. His career would include such highlights as composing the standard "Freedom Jazz Dance," performing a historic set at the 1969 Montreux Jazz Festival with pianist-singer Les McCann, recording comedy albums, and showing that the electric sax could be played creatively, in settings ranging from hard bop to funky soul jazz.

One of Harris' innovations was introducing the reed trumpet to jazz. He can be heard doubling on the reed trumpet in 1969's *Free Speech* and getting quite heated on *Instant Death* two years later. But it never replaced the tenor as Eddie Harris' main instrument. And other than for Rahsaan Roland Kirk (who played it only briefly), it never caught on. Still, it seems like a potentially exciting double for saxophonists!

Recommended CDs: *Steps Up* (Steeplechase 31151), *Eddie Who?* (MCA/Impulse 33104)

LPs to Search For: *Free Speech* (Atlantic 1573), *Instant Death* (Atlantic 1611)

NEAL HEFTI

• • • • • • • • • • •

b. Oct. 29, 1922, Hastings, NE

The success of Count Basie's second orchestra (formed in 1952) was partly due to Neal Hefti's swinging arrangements. Hefti (who composed "Cute," "Whirly Bird," "Little Pony," and "Lil' Darlin'") has been a very famous arranger ever since, writing countless scores for motion pictures, television, and record dates.

However, Hefti began his career as a trumpeter. "My older brother, John, was a record collector and had every Ellington record; that was my introduction to jazz. At ten, I received a used trumpet for Christmas. We were a poverty-stricken family and my parents believed that music was my only way out of the Depression and the Dust Bowl." Hefti, who also played tuba, French horn, and bass in high school orchestras, performed on trumpet with the Omaha Symphony (1940–41) and worked with the big bands of Charlie Barnet and Charlie Spivak. He was part of Woody Herman's orchestra (1942–46) during the period when it became the Herd, marrying Herman's singer, Francis Wayne. While with Herman, Hefti arranged such tunes as an updated "Woodchopper's Ball," "Blowin' Up a Storm," "The Good Earth," and "Wild Root," composing the latter two. Originally a swing trumpeter, he was able to adapt his style to bop and is heard at his best on four songs recorded with Lucky Thompson in 1946 including a humorous number called "From Dixieland To Bop."

In 1990 Neal Hefti said: "From 1946 through 1960, my playing time as a trumpeter became more and more sporadic as I was concentrating on composing. I haven't seriously touched the trumpet since 1960 and don't even own one, having given my last one to an orphanage years ago. But I miss it. I would like to become a 'born again' trumpet player someday." Despite that hope, his last recording on trumpet is the 1956 sextet album *Left and Right*.

Recommended CDs: with Lucky Thompson: *1944–1947* (Classics 1113)

LPs to Search For: *Left and Right* (Columbia 8316)

QUINCY JONES
• • • • • • • • • • • • • •

b. Mar. 14, 1933, Chicago, IL

A world-famous producer and arranger, Quincy Jones has had many accomplishments in different fields of music. In the 1950s he was a talented arranger for boppish big bands, writing for Lionel Hampton, Dizzy Gillespie, and his own orchestra (1959–61). In the '60s he continued writing (including for Count Basie, Frank Sinatra, and many different singers), led occasional record dates, and became an important record company executive. After the early 1970s he permanently left jazz for pop music, although since then he has had some jazz groups record for his Qwest label, persuaded Miles Davis to perform Gil Evans arrangements at the 1991 Montreux Jazz Festival, and recently co-led a Basie-oriented big band CD with Sammy Nestico.

Before he had fully developed as a writer, Quincy Jones was a trumpeter, playing in Seattle, where he grew up. His period with Lionel Hampton (1951–53) found him, in his last year, sitting in a trumpet section next to Clifford Brown and Art Farmer; maybe that is why he gave up playing! Other than recording on flugelhorn in 1957 with "The Jones Boys" (a sextet consisting of the unrelated Thad, Reunald, Jimmy, Eddie, and Jo Jones), Quincy Jones pretty much put away his horn by 1954 and probably never recorded a trumpet solo.

RAHSAAN ROLAND KIRK
• •

b. Aug. 7, 1936, Columbus, OH, d. Dec. 5, 1977, Bloomington, IN

A truly remarkable musician, Rahsaan Roland Kirk was so talented in so many unusual ways that contemporaries had difficulty assessing him. Kirk, who was blind, could play three saxophones at once (tenor, stritch, and manzello), often constructing two completely independent lines by splitting his mouth in two. He mastered circular breathing and routinely took 20-minute one-breath solos full of an endless assortment of ideas. He could play the flute and the nose flute simultaneously, was able to sound like a traditional New Orleans player on clarinet, and on tenor (where he was influenced most by Johnny Griffin) he could play expertly in any style, from R&B, swing, and bebop to completely outside.

In 1975, Kirk added the reed trumpet to his arsenal of instruments. On the album *The Case of the 3-Sided Dream in Audio Color*, he plays a version of "Bye Bye Blackbird" (unfortunately divided into two parts) that finds him sounding exactly like a muted Miles Davis on reed trumpet, and then following it up with a close impression of John Coltrane on tenor. Kirk also played reed trumpet on a version of "That's All" from the following year's *Other Folks' Music*, but did not live long enough (felled by a stroke) to further explore that now nearly extinct instrument. It is a pity that Rahsaan Roland Kirk and Eddie Harris never got together for a reed trumpet tradeoff!

LPs to Search For: The Case of the 3-Sided Dream in Audio Color (Atlantic 1674), *Other Folks' Music* (Atlantic 1686)

JOHNNY MANDEL

b. Nov. 23, 1925, New York, NY

A major composer and songwriter, Johnny Mandel has written many film scores through the years and such standards as "The Shadow of Your Smile," "Emily," "Close Enough for Love," and "A Time for Love."

Mandel, who wrote arrangements as early as age 13, first made his living performing trombone and trumpet in big bands of the 1940s. His trumpet playing was largely restricted to section work with the orchestras of Joe Venuti (1943) and Billie Rogers. Mandel mostly played trombone with the big bands of Boyd Raeburn, Jimmy Dorsey, Buddy Rich, Georgie Auld, Alvino Rey, and Woody Herman (his Second Herd in 1948). He also doubled on bass trumpet in the late 1940s, inspiring Cy Touff to switch instruments. But after working with Chubby Jackson, Elliot Lawrence, and Count Basie (1953) and gigging with Zoot Sims, Johnny Mandel (who probably never soloed on records) became a full-time arranger-composer.

CAL MASSEY

b. Jan. 11, 1927, Philadelphia, PA, d. Oct. 25, 1972, New York, NY

Cal Massey was best known in jazz as a composer, although none of his songs really became standards. His originals included "Bakai" (recorded by John Coltrane), "Message from Trane," and "Cry of My People," and among those top musicians who recorded his songs were Freddie Hubbard, Jackie McLean, Lee Morgan, and Archie Shepp.

Massey also worked as a trumpeter now and then. He studied trumpet with Freddie Webster in the mid-1940s and played in groups headed by Jay McShann, Jimmy Heath, and Billie Holiday. By the mid-1950s he was mostly concentrating on writing, and Cal Massey's only recording as a trumpeter was a fine 1961 album for Candid that unfortunately went unreleased (other than for one song) for decades.

Recommended CDs: Blues to Coltrane (Candid 79029)

BILLY MAY

b. Nov. 10, 1916, Pittsburgh, PA

Billy May has been an important arranger since the late 1930s. During 1951–54 he led a popular big band that was notable for its sliding reeds and melodic swing. May's many arrangements for Frank Sinatra gave him fame, and he has done extensive writing for films and television.

For the first decade or so of his working career, May was a trumpeter. "I started on tuba at 14, changed to trombone at 17, and started doubling on trumpet, which I played primarily by the time I was 22. I am self-taught both as an instrumentalist and as an arranger/composer." May was a member of Charlie Barnet's orchestra during 1938–40 and wrote the classic arrangement of "Cherokee." Unfortunately he took almost no solos, since Bobby Burnet was Barnet's main jazz trumpeter, but he did take a comic vocal on the hilarious recording of "The Wrong Idea." May worked with the Glenn Miller Orchestra during 1940–42 and briefly with Les Brown before becoming an arranger for the studios. "I stopped playing the trumpet altogether in 1945 and never considered myself to be an outstanding trumpet player; most of the high points in my career have been as the result of my arranging." Billy May did mention in the questionnaire that he was proud of the 1959 Capitol album *Billy May's Big Fat Brass*, since it featured top playing from trumpeters Conrad Gozzo, Pete Candoli, and Uan Rasey.

RALPH PETERSON

b. May 20, 1962, Pleasantville, NJ

A hard-swinging drummer, Ralph Peterson (who leads the Fo'tet) has the potential to be a bandleader on the level of an Art Blakey. Since four of his uncles and a grandfather played drums, percussion was definitely in his background. Peterson, who started playing drums when he was three, worked with Out of the Blue, David Murray, and the Terence Blanchard-Donald Harrison Quintet before putting together bands of his own. His recordings for Blue Note and Evidence are consistently inventive straightahead dates.

So why is Ralph Peterson in this book? On the 1990 Blue Note CD *Ornettology*, he concludes the quartet set with a brief cornet solo on "There Is No Greater Love," sounding quite credible and making listeners wonder when he will be playing an encore!

EDDIE SAUTER

b. Dec. 2, 1914, New York, NY, d. Apr. 21, 1981, Nyack, NY

One of the most adventurous arrangers to emerge from the swing era, Eddie Sauter's charts for Red Norvo (1936–39), Benny Goodman (1940–41), and Artie Shaw were quite unpredictable, dissonant in odd spots, and generally exciting. Other notable high points in the writer's career included his work for the Sauter-Finegan Orchestra in the 1950s and for Stan Getz's *Focus* album in 1961.

During 1936–37, Sauter frequently played trumpet and mellophone with Norvo's orchestra. However, because he was considered more talented as a writer than as a player, he soon gave up his horns, having apparently taken no solos on records.

JACK TEAGARDEN

b. Aug. 29, 1905, Vernon, TX, d. Jan. 15, 1964, New Orleans, LA

One of the most influential trombonists in jazz history, Jack Teagarden in the late 1920s played with such relaxed virtuosity that the trombone no longer sounded like a bulky percussive instrument. His style was much more advanced than anyone else's on trombone at the time, and by the mid-'30s there were scores of instrumentalists who were playing in a similar way. A talented blues and swing singer too, Teagarden made many joyful records through the years. His big band (1939–47) was a major struggle. But after a period with the Louis Armstrong All-Stars (1947–51), he was solvent again, spending his last dozen years leading a solid Dixieland band.

Just like Benny Goodman, Jack Teagarden recorded once on trumpet. On June 6, 1929, with the Whoopee Makers, Teagarden takes a two-chorus trumpet solo on "It's So Good," playing notes that listeners could easily imagine his performing on trombone.

Imagine a trumpet section made up of Benny Goodman, Jimmy Dorsey, Tommy Dorsey, and Jack Teagarden!

RALPH TOWNER

b. Mar. 1, 1940, Chehalis, WA

One of the founders of Oregon and a master of the acoustic guitar, Ralph Towner has a unique style that stretches between folk, post-bop jazz, and world music. He is renowned for his work with Oregon and for his solo records for ECM.

Although it is known that he doubles on piano, Towner also played trumpet in his early days. He started with piano at the age of three and began playing trumpet two years later. His main focus shifted after he studied classical guitar in Vienna in the mid-1960s. Towner worked with Paul Winter during 1970–71, meeting up with Collin Walcott, Glen Moore, and Paul McCandless. The quartet broke away to form Oregon in 1971. In addition to his guitar and piano playing, during the 1971–75 period and on 1978's *Out of the Woods*, Towner occasionally played trumpet, flugelhorn, and mellophone, using those brass instruments as additional colors rather than as alternative solo voices.

Recommended CDs: *Distant Hills* (Vanguard 79341), *Winter Light* (Vanguard 79350), *Out of the Woods* (Discovery 71004)

GERALD WILSON

· · · · · · · · · · · · · ·

b. Sept. 4, 1918, Shelby, MS

A colorful arranger for decades, Gerald Wilson came to fame in the 1960s, when he recorded a series of exciting big band albums for Pacific Jazz and World Pacific, all of which have been reissued on a limited-edition Mosaic box set. Wilson, who is proud of being one of the first writers to utilize five-part harmonies in his arrangements, has been a fixture in the Los Angeles area since the early 1940s, and he has led orchestras on at least a part-time basis since 1960, never slowing down.

Wilson was originally a trumpeter. He grew up in Memphis and Detroit, played with the Plantation Music Orchestra, and then had what he considers his most important musical association, playing with Jimmie Lunceford's orchestra during 1939–42. He took occasional solos with Lunceford and contributed arrangements to "Hi Spook" and "Yard Dog Mazurka," soloing on the latter and a few other numbers, although Snooky Young was the main trumpet star.

After leaving Lunceford and settling in Los Angeles, Wilson worked with the big bands of Les Hite, Benny Carter, and Willie Smith before leading a bop-oriented orchestra during 1944–47. By then he was de-emphasizing his playing in favor of developing as a writer. Wilson both played and wrote for the Count Basie and Dizzy Gillespie big bands and freelanced (mostly in Los Angeles) during the 1950s, including recording on trumpet for small-group dates with Curtis Counce and Leroy Vinnegar, among others. By 1960, when he put together his new big band, Gerald Wilson restricted his trumpet playing to ensemble work, and a few years later he stopped playing altogether, carving out an important career for himself as an arranger-composer.

Recommended CDs: with Curtis Counce: *Carl's Blues* (Original Jazz Classics 423), with Jimmie Lunceford: *1940–1941* (Classics 622), with Leroy Vinnegar: *Leroy Walks* (Original Jazz Classics 454)

Important Jazz Reference Books

All Music Guide to Jazz, 3rd edition, edited by Scott Yanow, Michael Erlewine, Vladimir Bogdanov, and Chris Woodstra (Miller Freeman, 1998)

The Biographical Encyclopedia of Jazz by Leonard Feather and Ira Gitler (Oxford University Press, 1999)

Jazz in the Movies by David Meeker (Da Capo Press, 1981)

Jazz—The Rough Guide by Ian Carr, Digby Fairweather, and Brian Priestley (Penguin Books, 1995)

The New Grove Dictionary of Jazz, edited by Barry Kernfeld (St. Martin's Press, 1988)

Who's Who of British Jazz by John Chilton (Casell, 1998)

Who's Who of Jazz by John Chilton (Chilton Publishing Co., 1978)

Photo Credits

About the Author

Scott Yanow has been a self-described jazz fanatic since 1970 and a jazz journalist since 1975. Jazz editor of *Record Review* (1976-84), he has written for *Downbeat, JazzTimes, Jazziz, Jazz Forum, Coda, Jazz News, Jazz Now,* and *Strictly Jazz* magazines. Yanow currently is a regular contributor to *Cadence, the L.A. Jazz Scene, Mississippi Rag, Jazz Improv, Jazz Report,* and *Planet Jazz.* He has penned over 250 album liner notes and is estimated to have written more jazz record reviews than anyone in history. Editor of the *All Music Guide to Jazz* and author of *Duke Ellington,* Yanow also wrote *Swing, Bebop,* and *Afro-Cuban Jazz* for the *Third Ear— The Essential Listening Companion* series, and is proud of having written five full-length reference books in 22 months. It is his goal to collect every good jazz record ever made and to have time to listen to them!

Index

DeFrancesco, Joey, 397–398
DeFrancesco, Papa John, 398
Deparis, Sidney, 128–129
DeParis, Wilbur, 128
Desvignes, Sidney, 11
Detroit Jazz scene, 192
Deuchar, Jimmy, 129
Dickerson, Carroll, 26, 132
Dickerson, Roger ("R.Q."), 130
Dillard, Bill, 130–131
Dirty Dozen Brass Band, 115–116, 320
Dixie Syncopators, 287
Dixieland jazz, 3, 109
Dixon, Bill, 3, 131–132
Doc Wheeler's Sunset Orchestra, 21
Dodds, Baby, 26, 133
Dodds, Johnny, 25, 132, 133
Dolphy, Eric, 66, 331–332
Dominique, Natty, 132–133
Don Byron's klezmer band, 135
Donald, Barbara, 133
Dorham, Kenny, 3, 133–134
Dorsey Brothers Orchestra, 50, 91, 398
Dorsey, Jimmy, 233, 334, 398
Dorsey, Tommy, 45, 91, 229, 288, 398–399
Dougherty, Red, 151
Douglas, Billy, 11
Douglas, Dave, 4, 134–136, 235
Dr. Stoll's Medicine Show, 163
Drakes, Jesse, 136
Drewes, Billy, 136
Drewes, Glenn, 136–137
D'Rivera, Paquito, 23
Duke Ellington Orchestra, 54, 399
Dukes of Dixieland, 29
Dunham, Sonny, 137–138
Dunn, Johnny, 2, 138–139, 259
Durante, Jimmy, 62
Dutrey, Honore, 25

E

Eagle Brass Band, 12, 57, 238
Eardley, Jon, 139
Earl Hines Orchestra, 163, 166
Eastwood, Clint, 391
Easy Riders Jazz Band, 349
Eckert, John, 140
Ecklund, Peter, 140

Eckstine, Billy, 399
Eddie Heywood Sextet, 95
Edison, Harry "Sweets," 55, 141–142
Ehrling, Thore, 142–143
Eldridge, Roy, 165, 166, 169
Eldridge, Roy "Little Jazz," 2, 16, 55, 123, 143–145
electronic valve instrument (E.V.I.), 257
Elias, Elaine, 71
Ellington, Duke, 2
    Arthur Whetsol and, 380
    Barry Lee Hall and, 183
    Bubber Miley and, 259–260
    Cat Anderson and, 21
    Clark Terry and, 362
    Cootie Williams and, 382–383
    Fred Stone and, 355–356
    Freddie Jenkins and, 205–206
    Louis Metcalf and, 255, 256
    Mercer Ellington and, 399
    Money Johnson and, 210
    Ray Nance and, 273–274
    Rex Stewart and, 354
    Shorty Baker and, 36
    Taft Jordan and, 216
    Willie Cook and, 108
Ellington, Mercer, 108, 183, 399
Elliott, Don, 145–146
Ellis, Don, 15, 146–148
Ellis, Herb, 29
Elman, Ziggy, 148–149, 176
Elysian Fields Orchestra, 88
Ericson, Rolf, 149
Erskin Tate's Vendome Orchestra, 26
Erskine Hawkins Orchestra, 41, 189
Erwin, George "Pee Wee," 150
Eubanks, Duane, 151
Eubanks, Kevin, 151
Eubanks, Robin, 151
Eureka Brass Band, 12
Eurojazz Orchestra, 269
Evans, Gil, 121, 152, 284
Evans, Miles, 152
Evans, Paul "Doc," 151
E.V.I. (electronic valve instrument), 257

F

Fabulous Dixielanders, 209
Faddis, Jon, 4, 20, 152–153, 165

THE TRUMPET KINGS